MANAGING
MEDIA ORGANIZATIONS

Longman Series in Public Communication

Series Editor: Ray Eldon Hiebert

MANAGING MEDIA ORGANIZATIONS

Effective Leadership of the Media

John M. Lavine • Daniel B. Wackman
University of Minnesota

Longman
New York & London

Managing Media Organizations: Effective Leadership of the Media

Longman Inc., 95 Church Street, White Plains, N. Y. 10601

Associated companies:
Longman Group Ltd., London
Longman Cheshire Pty., Melbourne
Longman Paul Pty., Auckland
Copp Clark Pitman, Toronto
Pitman Publishing Inc., New York

Executive editor: Gordon T. R. Anderson
Production editor: Elsa van Bergen
Text design: Angela Foote
Cover design: Joseph DePinho
Production supervisor: Judith Stern

Library of Congress Cataloging-in-Publication Data

Lavine, John M.
Managing media organizations.

(Longman series in public communication)
Bibliography: p.
Includes index.
1. Mass media—Management. I. Wackman, Daniel B.
II. Title. III. Series.
P96.M34L38 1987 659 87-4044
ISBN 0-582-28634-4

Compositor: r/tsi typographic company, inc.
Printer: The Alpine Press, Inc.

8 7 88 89 90 9 8 7 6 5 4 3 2 1

Contents

ACKNOWLEDGMENTS ix

MANAGING MEDIA ORGANIZATIONS: An Introduction 1

Whom Is This Book For? 2
Why Media Management? 4
Outline of This Book 5

PART ONE AN OVERVIEW OF MEDIA MANAGEMENT AND MEDIA ORGANIZATIONS

Chapter 1 What Is a Media Organization? 9

Media Companies as Manufacturers 9
The Unique Characteristics of Media Companies 14

Chapter 2 Media Industries and Media Firms 22

The Development of Various Media Industries 22
Revenue Patterns of the Media 24
The Structure of Media Industries 32
Media Audiences 38
Media Credibility 43
Media Companies 44
Major Development Patterns in the Media 60

Chapter 3 Responsibilities of Media Companies 62

The Media Company's Mission and Goals 63
Management's Decisions: The Key Factor in Implementing Goals 65

PART TWO THE FUNCTIONS OF MEDIA MANAGERS

Chapter 4 What Do Managers Do? **75**

Major Approaches to Managerial Functions 75
Classical Management Theories 76
Primary Functions of Managers 85
How Media Managers Spend Their Time 86

Chapter 5 Planning and Decision Making **90**

An Overview of the Planning Process 90
Mission and Goal Setting 94
Backgrounding 100
Creating a Strategy 105
Putting Together an Action Plan 108
Principles and Tips for Planning 110
Planning in Action: Starting a Medical Journal 117

Chapter 6 Organizing Media Companies **127**

Organizing Workflow to Establish Structure 127
Major Elements and Functions of Organizing 136
Basic Forms of Organization 145
Developing a Major Organization Innovation in a Media Firm 150

Chapter 7 Financial Management **159**

Describing Media Firm Operations Financially 160
The Budget Process 170
Financial Concepts 173

Chapter 8 Working with People **182**

Balancing Production and People 182
Motivation 187
The Supervision Cycle 194
The People Development Cycle 204

Chapter 9 Leading Media Organizations **216**

Leaders as Individuals 217
Leadership Styles 220
Contingency Approaches to Leadership 222
The Competencies of Leadership 223
Our Conception of Leadership in the Media 225
The Organizational Challenge: Developing Leaders 229

Chapter 10 A Case Study for Part Two, KZZZ-FM 232

Background: KZZZ-FM's—Urban/Contemporary Radio 233
Problem 1. Planning KZZZ-FM Strategy. Do This in Conjunction with Chapter 5 236
Problem 2. Organizing to Implement the Strategy. Do This in Conjunction with Chapter 6 238
Problem 3. Budgeting to Implement the Strategy. Do This in Conjunction with Chapter 7 241
Problem 4. Staffing to Implement the Strategy. Do This in Conjunction with Chapter 8 244
Legal and Ethical Issues in the KZZZ-FM Case 247

PART THREE AREAS OF MEDIA MANAGEMENT ACTIVITY

Chapter 11 A Marketing Perspective for the Media 251

Media Managers' Activities 251
Media as a Bridge Between Advertisers and Audiences 254
The Marketing Mix 255
Product Life Cycle 257
Applying the Marketing Perspective to Media Managers' Activities 260

Chapter 12 Market Analysis and Product Planning 262

Market Analysis 262
Using Consumer Research in Developing Product Strategies 275
Other Considerations in Developing Product Strategies 282
Product Planning for the Advertiser Market 287

Chapter 13 Promotion and Sales of Media Products 290

A Framework for Thinking About Promotion 290
Developing Promotion Strategies 293
Promotional Tools for Attracting Audiences 297
Promotional Strategies in Action 301
Promotion and Sales to Advertisers 308

Chapter 14 Distribution, Production, and Pricing of Media Products 315

Perspectives for Viewing Distribution, Production, and Pricing 316
Distribution 319

Production 325
Pricing 330

Chapter 15 The New Gazette A Case Study for Part Three 334

The Situation 334
Background 335
Tentative Conclusions and Goals 341
Basic Strategy 341
Your Task 342

PART FOUR A MANAGEMENT PERSPECTIVE ON LEGAL AND SOCIAL RESPONSIBILITY ISSUES

Chapter 16 Media Managers and the Legal Issues That Confront Media Companies 351

Preventing Legal Problems 354
Dealing with Legal Problems That Arise 355
Major Areas of the Law 358

Chapter 17 The Media's Social Responsibilities 372
Major Trends Influencing the Media 372
A Long-Term Managerial Perspective 380
Business Objectives and Social Responsibilities 382
Some Lessons for Media Managers 389
A Closing Note 391

REFERENCES **393**

BIBLIOGRAPHY OF MEDIA MANAGEMENT AND ECONOMICS **397**

INDEX **437**

Acknowledgments

This book is dedicated to Max H. Lavine and Ralph B. Wackman. Their wisdom and skill as media managers are the text's inspiration. It is also in loving memory of our friend and colleague F. Gerald Kline. His vision and encouragement was instrumental to making the development of media management a reality in the journalism and mass communication curriculum.

In the writing of every text some persons are crucial to making the final product a reality. In this instance they include:

> Jean Olson, our wise and hard-working graduate assistant who helped bring the book together and who added substantive ideas, as well as a real feel for the language.
>
> Lesley and Bob Richardson, Kathy Donouhue, Rita du Charme, Leslie Hefler, and Arlene Carpenter. Their hours were long, but they were always available and willing when we needed them.
>
> Next there is Professor John Brandl, an economist at the Hubert Humphrey Institute; James Shaffer the Vice President/Chief Financial Officer for *The L. A. Times* and an adjunct professor of media management at the University of Southern California; Joan Grassel, a former student and now an advertising representative at *The Orange County Register;* and last, but first in importance, our editors, Gordon T.R. Anderson and Elsa van Bergen. Each of them gave patient review to various drafts of this work. Their wisdom added greatly to the final text.
>
> We also wish to thank the scores of students and professionals who tried out this material in classes and on the job in a variety of newspapers, magazines, broadcast stations, and advertising and public relations agencies. Their candid reactions were very helpful.

We are also deeply appreciative for support we received from Gerald Sass and the Gannett Foundation and from John Cowles, Jr., and the late John and Elizabeth Bates Cowles. Their confidence in us—not only in support of writing this book, but also in the importance of developing the study of media management as a vital part of journalism education—has been and continues to be very important to us.

Finally a personal note from each of us:

John Lavine: I am thankful to the people noted in the preceding not only for their herculean efforts, but also for their friendship and support. They made what otherwise could have been drudgery an exciting undertaking.

Then, there is Meryl, my wife and best friend. For her thanks are inadequate, not just for the support and love I received during the long months when I was working on this project, but for making each day we've been together richer, fuller, and more meaningful than I ever thought was possible.

I am also indebted to Meryl and to my son and daughter, Marc and Mimi, for being understanding about the time I took for writing when we could have been together and for tolerating my occasional feisty moods when work on the book fell behind.

Dan Wackman: I too am deeply grateful to the members of our team for their extraordinary effort in putting this book together. The way we worked truly illustrated teamwork at its finest.

My thanks to my family are profoundly felt. As the months of seven-day work weeks continued, their love and concern supported me in ways they cannot know:

To Kathy, my wife and friend, our relationship is the greatest joy in my life; your acceptance of the burden of a five-child family during this period made my effort on this book possible.

To my five children, your patience, understanding, and love during these months sustained me through a very difficult time. I thank all of you—Hillary, John, Wilie, Tim, and Gabrielle—for your support. I could not have done this book without it.

Special thanks to our one-year-old (at the time) Gabrielle. Our daily time together yanked me from my work, and thrust me into a little world shared just by the two of us, a world of wonderment and delight, a world that refreshed me daily so I could return to the world of the book renewed and ready to write.

Managing Media Organizations: An Introduction

Imagine that you are about to give the go-ahead to:

- develop a new direction for a floundering specialty magazine that has just hired you as its editor;
- launch a controversial, but creative, national advertising campaign on teenage pregnancy for an advertising agency for which you are creative director;
- lay off half the production employees of a daily newspaper where you are the superintendent because technological advances have eliminated their jobs and reassignment is impossible;
- commit millions of dollars to build a new use for videotex for a multimedia conglomerate of which you are the chief operating officer (COO), even though other, giant information companies have failed at just such efforts in the past;
- decide not to renegotiate the contract of the somewhat popular, but difficult to control, evening news anchor of a floundering television station of which you are news director. The station is tied for second place in a very competitive metro market, but its ratings are slipping.

These sorts of tasks typify the demanding, exciting world of media management.

As the United States moves from an industrial to an information society, the media represent one of the more dramatically changing growth sectors. Indeed, it is the speed of this change coupled with the unique nature of the media that makes managing information firms so challenging.

Another aspect of the media's uniqueness is their constitutionally and legally protected role. With that protection comes additional, heavy responsibilities; implementing those responsibilities is another duty of the media's leaders.

The media have other distinctive characteristics. One is that most media require their employees to function with a high degree of creativity and speed. Another characteristic, which is universal and often overlooked, is that with each production cycle the content of the media's messages must be fresh, new, and compelling. In most other industries the same product is produced over and over.

Today's media firms also face profound challenges from new forms of competition, startling advances in technology, and heretofore unheard-of media products and means of information distribution.

To effectively deal with all these factors requires managers who can do more than just "get the job done." It calls for effective leaders, which is why we subtitled this book *Effective Leadership of the Media*. Leadership in modern media firms is a theme we emphasize.

Before we get too far into our subject, however, let's stop and consider for whom this book is written, and what it will and will not do.

WHOM IS THIS BOOK FOR?

This text is intended for students and professionals who are interested in the media and for media employees who are about to move into management ranks. We realize that many information company employees and students have no desire to become information company executives. Yet, even for these people, there are reasons to investigate media management.

One reason is understanding where the media are going. What more appropriate way to start than to learn about the men and women who are making the decisions that determine the media's direction?

Another reason to understand media management is career advancement. Most information company employees begin as solo workers who want to sell or create advertising, report the news, take pictures, broadcast, or work in public relations. When hired they may have no thoughts about entering management. During the first two to ten years of their careers, however, a high percentage of these people will become supervisors of two or more colleagues.

Even among those who shun management roles entirely, there is a buildup of informal working relationships with "sources" or clients. Although these networks are less structured, they often require as much management skill as do formal ones within the organization.

Another force that has major impact on media organization employees and employers is the dramatic shift in the fundamental definition of what many media companies do. Increasingly, these firms and their staffs take on new markets, products, competition, technology, and jobs, all resulting from decisions made by media managers. This is another reason it is important to understand how and why media leaders act as they do.

What Will This Book Do?

This book is intended to help you learn:

- concepts and principles of media management;
- how media companies function today, and how they can position themselves for tomorrow;
- the changing nature of information companies' production, distribution, and promotion;
- how effective media executives lead and use their companies' resources. (Note: The simplistic, traditional definition of resources emphasizes the amount of money and other assets that media firms possess. We prefer a broader, more sophisticated formula of resources in the media: people, money, information, services, time, and technology.)

As a student or a media employee, why is an understanding of these things important for you? One reason is that a wide gulf exists between those staffers who sell or otherwise directly raise money for the media and those who produce the content: news, advertising campaigns, movies/videos, publicity releases, records, books, or entertainment. In advertising or public relations agencies this distinction usually arises between the creative workers and the account executives. In newspapers, magazines, and broadcast stations a similar division exists between employees involved in developing the news and those who sell advertising (and, in print companies, those involved with circulation). In most moviemaking, book publishing, and record companies, the writers, directors, and composers are usually separate from the investors, producers, marketing staff, and studio executives.

We recognize and support the importance of maintaining appropriate separation between news and sales departments; however, it makes no sense for staffers in one area to be ignorant about the work of their colleagues in other parts of the same organization. Having an understanding of what others do does not mean a newsperson will give in to an advertiser's pressure; it means just that: "understanding," not usurpation.

Another purpose of this book is to give you knowledge about the women and men who lead media companies. If you have an understanding of why those executives feel, think, and act as they do, it will improve your ability to garner more resources from your present or future bosses. That is important if you are a media employee; it is also valuable if you enter the organizational hierarchy and want to be a manager. You can learn management fundamentals here.

Finally, beyond discussing the essentials of media management, this book highlights some fresh, new ways for you to think about the future of the media organizations.

What This Book Will Not *Do*

Although this text will teach you the fundamentals of media management, it will not teach you how to be a media manager. No book can do that. To be an effective media company leader you need to know not only what you will find here, but you also need first-hand experience as an employee and as a manager. Except in the most unusual cases, there are few viable substitutes for those experiences.

Also, the text will not explain how the economy works or provide an in-depth analysis of management theories. It is important for you to learn about those subjects, but the most effective and efficient way to obtain that information is to take survey courses in economics, management, and business. Or, if that is not possible, you can read independently on those topics. An excellent book on economics is Paul Samuelson's classic text, *Economics*. Others are: *Macroeconomics* by Robert J. Barro, *Economics: Principles and Policy: Macroeconomics* (3rd edition) by William J. Baumal and Alan S. Blinder, *Microeconomics: Theory/Application* (5th edition) by Edwin Mansfield, and *Managerial Economics*, by Lawrence Southwick, Jr. If you would like a general background in management, our current favorite work is James F. Stoner's *Management*. We are also impressed with *Fundamentals of Management* by Donnelly, Gibson, and Ivancevich, and *Management* by Griffin. These and similar texts will help you develop a basic vocabulary and an understanding of economic, management, and business concepts.

WHY MEDIA MANAGEMENT?

The lines between traditional types of media are blurring. Many companies operate varying combinations of newspapers, broadcast stations, magazines, data bases, direct mail firms, shoppers, book publishers, billboard organizations, or combined advertising and public relations agencies. Their management has to have specialized knowledge about each of those industries, to be sure, but increasingly they will need general media management knowledge that will enable them to span and connect diverse operations.

That interconnection is becoming more important as new ways of delivering information create opportunities that transcend the boundaries of a single medium. Actually, even in firms that run only one media property, executives cannot afford to think of their firm as, for example, only a newspaper, broadcast station, advertising agency, or public relations firm. In each medium changes in technology, combined with the blurring of lines among the traditional media, make viewing the firm as it is or was in the past an anachronism.

These changes are the backdrop against which the essence of the media manager's job is cast; that essence is to deliver information or programming that people want or need in the most effective manner possible, irrespective of traditional media boundaries. Understanding the full implications of that charge requires shedding traditional viewpoints. It also frees information executives to think in terms of many new options for serving their audiences.

The management concepts and principles utilized in leading different types of media organizations are far more similar than different. Managers in all well-run information organizations plan, organize, budget, and work with people. They also engage in market analysis, product planning, promotion, production, and distribution.

Despite the cross-media understanding required of effective media managers, most of today's information professionals have worked in only one type of media. Similarly, the education offered in most schools of journalism and mass communication usually concentrates on a single media industry or occupation, print journalism, broadcast journalism, photo journalism, advertising, or public relations. Yet, for the reasons just noted, in the years to come that narrow view will change in keeping with the shifts in the media themselves and with the companies that own them.

This book is intended to teach you about media management in the context of the executive of tomorrow, not yesterday. One of our major goals, therefore, is to help you shed the view that a medium should be the same in the future as it is today. As a first step in that direction we emphasize the similarities across media, rather than their differences. We hope you will use that vantage point to free your thinking from too narrow and historic a view of what the media are.

After you've gained that broad view it is important that you learn as much as possible about the medium you are employed by or wish to work for. Reading books that focus on management of specific media such as newspapers, broadcast stations, agencies, and film companies, will increase your understanding. You will find an extensive list of such books in the Bibliography at the end of this text.

OUTLINE OF THIS BOOK

Managing Media Organizations is divided into four parts.

Part One describes what media companies do, presents comparative information about various types of media industries and firms, and discusses their responsibilities and goals. The first three chapters stress the similarity of media, while also pointing out some important differences.

Part Two includes Chapters 4 through 10. They discuss the idea of management, then detail the key functions of media leaders and managers: planning, organizing, budgeting, working with people, and leading. Chapter 10 is a case study using the concepts developed in each of Part Two's chapters.

Part Three is made up of Chapters 11 through 15, which identify the major areas of management within media organizations: marketing and market analysis; promotion and sales; product development, production, and distribution; and a case study to reinforce an understanding of the job of advertising manager. In this section, particular attention is given to the impact of changing technology, new forms of competition, and how media management is altered by shifts in the definition of media markets.

Part Four consists of two chapters that emphasize a management perspective toward legal and social responsibility issues. Chapter 16 discusses various laws and regulations that affect media managers and ways information executives should handle these concerns, as well as the lawyers who advise media leaders. Chapter 17 highlights media trends, their implications for information executives and society, and the special role that the media's social responsibility plays in determining an information leader's long-term effectiveness.

The book closes with a list of references, an extensive bibliography of sources for the subjects discussed, and an index.

How to Read This Book

The emphasis of this book is on managing today's and tomorrow's information organizations. We suggest that as you read you stop frequently to figure out how an important point made about one medium could be applied to another. For example, as you learn how a media manager goes about marketing a new program format for a radio station, ponder how a print media editor might develop a new section for a newspaper or visualize a new special interest magazine. Taking the time to ask and answer such questions will substantially increase your appreciation of how the concepts and principles in the book apply with equal validity across the media horizon.

We have tried to help you avoid a single medium bias. Throughout the text we use examples from all the media as well as real-life vignettes illustrating the major ideas in each chapter. Also at the end of Part Two and Part Three are case studies that enable you to put into practice the ideas you have learned.

A final note: Even if you are an experienced media manager, we suggest that you skim through Part One; although you will find in it some information you already know, few media employees or managers have the fully developed cross-media perspective emphasized in that section.

PART ONE

An Overview of Media Management and Media Organizations

CHAPTER 1
What Is a Media Organization?

Most media firms develop, produce, and distribute messages that inform, entertain, and/or persuade. At their most basic level, information firms are like other manufacturers: they produce and distribute a product (messages) and then, in order to sell that product, they select an audience and develop marketing, promotion, and sales strategies to reach the audience.

In the United States there is an ever-growing diversity of media, which we list in Exhibit 1.1. In this book we discuss most media, as well as relationships among many of them. At the same time, we concentrate on newspapers, magazines, radio and television, advertising agencies, and public firms. That emphasis is based on our best estimate of their impact on society, on their size as industries, and on their linkages to journalism and mass communication education.

We also detail how many organizations, which used to see their missions as involved with a single medium, now use their staffs and/or resources to simultaneously develop messages for several media.

In the next chapter we show comparisons of the dollars, people, and functions of different media industries and firms.

MEDIA COMPANIES AS MANUFACTURERS

Like all organizations that create a product, the media have basic steps in their manufacturing and distribution processes including a promotional and sales effort necessary to sell the product to relevant markets, which for media are advertisers, clients, subscribers, viewers, and listeners. A diagram to illustrate the process is shown in Exhibit 1.2.

EXHIBIT 1.1. TYPES OF MEDIA

Print
- Newspapers
- Magazines
- Shoppers
- Direct mail
- Catalogues
- Directories
- Books
- Specialty publications
- Outdoor advertising

Electronic
- Television
- Radio
- Networks
- Cable
- Videotex
- Satellite
- Data bases/banks (Dow Jones, Dialogue, Nexis, Lexis)
- Telemarketing
- Movies
- Home movies (VCR)
- Records and compact discs
- Low-power television

Agencies/Creative services
- Advertising agencies
- Public relations firms
- TV production companies
- Sound recording companies
- In-house advertising and public relations

EXHIBIT 1.2. STEPS IN MANUFACTURING AND SELLING MEDIA PRODUCTS

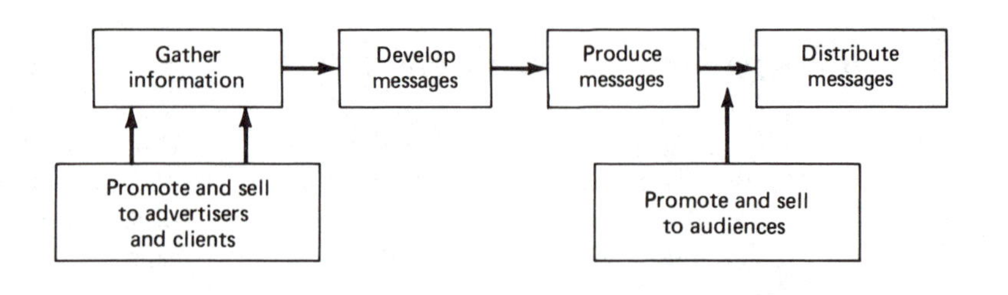

Major Steps in Manufacturing a Message

Each step in the process involves a variety of activities. Although specific facets of the activities differ across media, overall they are highly similar from one kind of information organization to another.

Gathering Information and Developing Messages. Gathering information for stories in a newspaper involves creating a list of ideas to be investigated and then sending reporters to check sources, public records, and, sometimes, electronic data bases. After developing the raw material the reporters and editors complete the stories together; that may entail pulling together several forms of information: words, photography, and graphics.

In advertising the message is persuasive, but information is gathered in the same pattern as for news. The client tells the agency about a product, its market, sales history, and positioning. These facts are combined with additional information about consumers' characteristics and desires. Then, creative personnel in the agency (copywriters, art directors) develop the creative strategy, specific words, photography, or graphics for the advertisement or commercial.

Producing Finished Copies of Messages. When print and broadcast media shift from gathering and developing messages to actually producing the finished product, there are technical differences between the two. In print the production stage involves typesetting, platemaking, and press runs versus film or video editing, splicing, sound dubbing, and color coordination for television or film. Nevertheless, for both media the same underlying process is involved.

Distributing the Message. The last stage, distribution, entails transporting the message. Newspapers distribute via trucks to delivery persons who take the papers to newsstands or homes, or they distribute electronically via a data base. Magazines use the same process; they also use the U.S. mails as a final distributor. (Newspapers use the mails when their readers are hard to reach.)

Broadcasters send their programs through the air from their transmitter and tower directly to the listener/viewer.

Cable companies gather signals from satellites and over-the-air or microwave transmission. They then deliver those signals via heavy coaxial wires (cables) to subscribers.

Motion pictures go from the producers to a network of distributors who sell them to movie theaters, cable companies, and video stores.

Advertising agencies simply send copies of the advertisements or commercials they produce to the specific media vehicles selected to disseminate the advertisement to a target audience. The media vehicles are the newspapers, magazines, broadcast stations, and direct mail agencies that carry out the distribution.

Changes in the Manufacturing and Distribution Process

In the past, production and distribution processes involved clear, definitive steps. Different people were involved in each stage of the process, with messages prepared and distributed in a sequential order. That still happens, but it is changing. As an example, consider how a newspaper used to be produced and distributed and how it is manufactured today.

A few years ago, the newspaper was divided into departments that corresponded to different steps in the manufacturing process. A reporter gathered information and phoned it in to a rewrite person, who wrote the first draft of a story and passed it on to a copy editor. One or two sets of editors polished the language, checked the content, decided where the story would appear on the printed page, and wrote a headline for it.

Next the message (now a news story) was sent to three other departments. In the first, compositors typeset the story. Next, stereotypers made a heavy cardboard impression of the type and then cast a plate impression of that cardboard by pouring molten lead against the impression and allowing it to cool. Finally, men in the press department put plates on the press and printed the day's newspaper. (There were, and still are, few female employees in the press rooms of daily newspapers or large magazines in the United States. For decades there have been a few women printers, however; and with the advent of computer and photographic technology, now not only are many composition departments managed by women, but also a majority of their staffs are female.)

After the paper was printed, people called mailers oversaw the stuffing of one section into another. They also made up bundles of newspapers for carriers and for the mail.

Changes in technology blended these steps and speeded the process. For example, today reporters not only gather information but also write their stories using computers, either portable ones or computers at the office. That eliminates the need for compositors to set type, for the reporters have done the keystroking and the story already exists in electronic form.

A copy editor may look at the story, but even that step is undergoing change. Now, before they give their stories to their editors, many reporters run their stories through computers that check spelling and grammar. Increasingly, editors construct the newspaper's pages on a computer, further reducing the need for compositors.

Stereotypers, who made hot metal plates, are also phantoms of the past. Soon no employee will be involved between the editor's terminal and the plate that goes on the press because newspaper and magazine layouts will be transmitted directly from the editor's computer to a laser that automatically cuts an alloy plate to put on the press. Moreover, technology already exists that allows the editor to direct nozzles on the press to spray ink on the paper in the form of words and pictures. That means that plate making, too, will soon be eliminated.

Automation has invaded the mailroom also. People are still necessary, but far fewer of them. Equipment exists to mechanically stuff the sections of a newspaper together and to count, address, bundle, tie, and prepare for mailing stacks of each issue.

Those are only some of the substantial changes in the methods of distribution; many more are on the way. For instance, while most Americans receive their daily newspaper through the mail, from a vendor or through private delivery systems, some papers, such as the *Wall Street Journal*, can be dialed up electronically from a home computer on Dow Jones News Retrieval. In some markets a subscriber can connect his or her computer to a two-way, interactive, videotex information service.

In the electronic media, the broadcast of fast-breaking news or sports events has undergone the same compression. Layers of people and hours of lead time to shoot, transport, and edit film are no longer required. Stories are beamed live from locations hundreds of miles from the station. Other messages are also distributed by various electronic means: cable, low-power TV, microwave, satellite, film, videotape, and compact disk, to name but a few.

Thus, in most media, the detailed, sequential nature of the production process has either vanished or is undergoing dramatic compression. Later we will look in more depth at the positive and negative results of those changes. In the meantime, it is enough to note that the advances in technology have had three effects:

1. While the changes have eliminated whole categories of skilled workers, they have provided those who gather and develop messages with increased control over their work.
2. The changes have created new categories of highly trained employees, such as computer programmers and technicians.
3. The technological developments have expanded the possibilities for less skilled or less heavily financed people to start their own media ventures in videotape, computer, or table-top publishing.

Promoting and Selling the Product

Media companies not only develop and produce information products, they also sell them. That necessitates making choices about the markets to serve and about promotion, sales, and, for many media, advertising strategies. The choice of market(s) profoundly affects the type of message that is produced and the strategies that are developed for promoting and distributing it.

Most media companies serve two markets. The first we call the *audience market*. If a media company is to be successful, it must gather an audience. This requires developing a product that is attractive to a particular audience segment, and then telling those people about the product.

For the audience there are always costs involved in utilizing media, even those information sources that purport to be free. For some it is money for a subscription, a monthly fee for a cable service, or the price paid for a book, movie ticket, or record. For so-called free distribution media, such as commercial television, radio, or giveaway newspapers or shoppers, the costs include one-time outlays to purchase a television or radio receiver and the cost to consumers of time spent with a medium. That is ongoing and represents a precious commodity.

The second market, the *advertiser market*, is of concern for many information organizations. Usually the advertiser market can be approached only after the media develop an audience of some size or, at least, after the information company convinces advertisers that an appropriate audience can be delivered.

Day to day, those two markets are seldom considered separately. When media managers begin to think about an audience segment they consider who would be interested in receiving their particular media product (message) and, simultaneously, which advertisers might be interested in that audience. As part of such an analysis, media executives do market research on both markets.

THE UNIQUE CHARACTERISTICS OF MEDIA COMPANIES

As businesses that manufacture products, information companies are similar in many ways to other U.S. industries. There are, however, five factors, shown in Exhibit 1.3, which differentiate the media from most manufacturing concerns.

Let's look at how each of those factors contributes to making the media unique.

Nature of the Product

Most media companies produce a perishable commodity—information, in the form of news, entertainment, or persuasive messages. That is less true of books and film than it is of newspapers and broadcast programs, but, in varying degrees, it applies to all media products. Once a message reaches its audience it loses much of its value. If it is not produced and distributed in a timely and effective

EXHIBIT 1.3. FACTORS DISTINGUISHING MEDIA FROM OTHER MANUFACTURERS

Nature of the product
Types of employees
Special organizational factors in media companies
Media's unique role in society
Blurring of lines between traditional media

manner, it also loses value. Effectiveness, timeliness, and perishability are closely intertwined, and collectively they have several important implications.

As we mentioned in the Introduction, one of the chief implications is that media companies must produce a new product during every production cycle: a new issue of the newspaper or magazine; a new episode of a television program or newscast; a new advertisement, book, record, or movie. By contrast, in other industries, any changes between cycles are usually made in the packaging of the product, not in the content. In the media the reverse is true; the packaging remains the same, but the content of the product must be developed from scratch.

This fundamental distinction between the media and most other industries is the factor that gives information organizations and their managers major challenges. It creates enormous deadline pressure, which demands a highly coordinated workflow. At the same time it requires constant creativity and innovation on the part of media workers. That means trying new things and, to some degree, bucking regimentation.

To understand this very important point, picture in your mind two groups of workers, one on an assembly line in an auto plant and the other putting together the evening news at a television station. In the auto plant, a great deal of creativity is required to produce the first car, but from there on every Ford should look just like every other one of the same model. What's more, although workers are expected to be quality conscious, they are forbidden to head off on their own to produce the 493rd Ford different from the 492nd one. Contrast that scene with the TV station where, if the content of the 493rd news show is anything like the 492nd, the station might as well go off the air. Reporters who do not show some enterprise in going off and finding new stories are soon looking for other employment.

Types of Employees

The nature of an information product demands that the staff who produce it be educated, professional, extremely hard working, and, in many cases, very creative. Although the new technologies which regularly impact on the media are important, an information organization's workers are its most valuable asset. Sophisticated equipment comes and goes, but when a new message must be created with each cycle, what endures is the abilities of the staff who use the equipment to form the message.

Media managers face another unique and particularly demanding challenge, one that is different from those faced by most other executives. Because information is most often gathered and sold away from the workplace, media executives cannot look out their office windows and observe their employees working. In fact, many of their youngest, least experienced colleagues are not even in the building; they are out, unsupervised, acting on behalf of the firm. Further, because message development is not a repetitive process, experienced professionals cannot teach new workers exactly how to write a story or create an advertisement or television show. Moreover, they are often unable to ensure that younger employees do not get the organization in trouble with laws of libel, slander, or antitrust.

On top of that, many media employees view themselves as members of a profession, not as workers for their employer. Many reporters, editors, producers, directors, writers, art directors, and performers feel a primary allegiance to the standards of journalism or advertising, for example, and a secondary allegiance to the company that provides their pay check. Moreover, when organizational and professional standards clash, those staff members are more likely to side with the profession than with the firm.

For example, there was a great hullabaloo when Rupert Murdoch purchased the *Chicago Sun Times* in the mid-1980s. Believing that Murdoch pandered to the baser tastes of his readers and ran newspapers of questionable journalistic integrity, many *Sun Times* staffers jumped ship. They were led by the most noted columnist in the *Sun Times'* stable, Mike Royko.

Here, then, was a clear demonstration of the culture and values of the media conflicting with what the employees perceived to be the standard of the *Sun Times'* new owner. Can you imagine the employees at a Chrysler plant quitting rather than working for Ford if the plant were sold? Unlikely, no matter what they thought about Ford cars.

Other examples of the importance of professional standards abound. Do you recall that in the early 1980s the broadcast news staffers of *National Public Radio (NPR)* said they would quit when their funding was threatened by President Reagan's budget cuts? The broadcasters claimed that reduced resources would result in a product of less than the minimum standards of professionalism they believed appropriate. In Hollywood and on Madison Avenue, there are legendary reports of screen directors or advertising agency copywriters stalking off a set or out of a campaign presentation when changes threatened to drag their movie or advertising campaign in a direction they found objectionable.

Those are not the only forces which compound information leaders' personnel problems. Many media organizations are small; they have only one or two levels between the top executive and workers at the lowest level of the firm. In such settings opportunities for workers to increase their salary or responsibility by incremental steps up the organizational ladder are limited or nonexistent. That means that to advance in their careers, employees must frequently move from one employer to another. That pattern of job mobility reinforces the employee's orientation to the profession rather than to a company.

Special Organizational Factors in Media Companies

Given the fast-paced, constantly changing nature of the media, you might guess that the best structure for an information company would be one which is stable and very organized, one where work moves in a predictable, timely fashion. How else can deadlines be met day after day after day?

Until recently that was the dominant structure of media organizations in the United States. Modern management thinking suggests, however, that the best format to accomplish the goals of a progressive media organization should not be quite so formal. A flexible, horizontal structure may be better than the traditional, rigid, vertical hierarchy preferred in most industrial corporations.

Media managers and leaders have to deal with a structure that must accomplish two somewhat contradictory objectives: (1) producing media products in an orderly fashion so crucial production deadlines can be met, and (2) producing media products containing fresh, innovative, informative, high-quality messages. Achieving the latter goal requires that employees have some freedom from rigid work schedules. We will have much more to say about how media executives deal with this challenge in later chapters.

Societal Role of the Media

As the watchdogs and interpreters of public issues and events, the media have a special role in American society. That is why they are the only business specifically protected by the Constitution's First Amendment. Additionally, there are many statutes directed at the media: copyright, libel, slander, defamation, shield, and privacy.

Other laws, although not designed specifically for the media, have substantial impact on them. In the arena of antitrust, a small group of U.S. daily newspapers, which would otherwise die because of competitive pressures, have been allowed to share all of their operations except news under an arrangement called a Joint Operating Agreement (JOA).

There are also economic and franchise protections of the media:

broadcasters are granted franchises, called channels or frequencies, from the Federal Communications Commission. Many print media use second class mail at lower postal rates that were established to foster regular news publications. Others use so-called book rates, which were established for the same reason.

Because of their unique role, information companies are far more visible than most businesses. Whether it's the report of the TV ratings race, a story about an advertising agency losing a major client, or something as commonplace as a magazine noting its circulation, the business side of the media is more regularly reported than is similar information of most other enterprises.

Equally obvious, but still uncharacteristic for any other business, is the attention given to the mistakes of the media. When a manager in a steel plant makes any but a crisis-level error, few people outside the plant ever hear about it. When a major columnist, newspaper, or network makes an error, that fact is headline news.

Even the media's noncreative, production employees are affected by the environment that grants their organization a powerful and unique role in this society. For example, if such noncreative, production workers say, "I'm at KMMM-TV. . .," or "I work for the *Daily Planet*. . .," or "I'm with the advertising agency that produced those zingy computer commercials you saw on prime time TV last week. . .," responses from others usually afford more status to the media employee than to those who do the same type of work at a routine industrial firm.

Like it or not, in our information-based society the media have a disproportionate, particularly visible, and often influential role. With that role comes the public's expectation that media will be credible and trustworthy. One attempt by information executives to foster that credibility and to enhance public trust is the development of codes of ethics for journalists and other media practitioners. Indeed, few other professions have such extensive codes directed toward conflict of interest, honesty, truthfulness, fairness, and access. And few professions disclose their mistakes or debate their shortcomings (real or imagined) as publicly as the media.

Although many media have adopted codes of ethics and standards for gathering and verifying information, they sometimes fail to adhere to those codes and standards. Even giant companies like CBS and *Time* magazine compromise themselves, as a recent book by Renata Adler (1986) documented, resulting in a loss of credibility for all media.

Further, journalistic codes of ethics are not legally enforceable, though they may be binding as work rules by information executives. That is a reality that media managers take into account as they lead their organizations. For instance, a precedent-setting labor relations case occurred in Madison, Wisconsin, when the *Capitol Times* introduced a work rule requiring reporters to follow a code of ethics. The code was based on a similar one adopted nationally by the Society of Professional Journalists, but members of the Newspaper Guild said that imposing the code as a work rule violated their union contract. It took years to litigate the matter through the National Labor Relations Board (NLRB), though eventually the newspaper won.

We delve deeper into the legal and societal roles of the media in Chapters 16 and 17, respectively.

The Blurring of Lines among Traditional Media

Another emerging and significant characteristic of media companies is one we mentioned in the Introduction: the blurring of the lines between traditional types of media. Previously, media executives thought of themselves as running a television station, a newspaper, a magazine, a radio station, a cable company, an advertising agency, or a public relations firm. With the increased demand for more and higher quality information, and with the flood of new technologies providing the ability to fulfill that demand, many of the traditional distinctions among the media no longer apply. Moreover, they will continue to diminish in the years to come.

Print. We are not suggesting that newspaper executives' primary role is other than to run their newspapers, for that is their first responsibility. However, most newspapers, even the smallest weeklies, write their stories on electronic word processors. As a result—and whether they know it or not—those publishers are now capable of delivering part of their content electronically. It is simply the choice of one button versus another that decides whether a story is sent to the press room for printing or to a computer for electronic delivery to a subscriber's home computer. The latter option is the first step in print media companies' exploration of a dazzling array of electronic, two-way (videotex) information delivery systems; some of them operate via cable, others by low-power TV or satellite.

Broadcast. A variety of specialized radio stations and cable TV channels exist. Many cut into markets that used to be the domain of specialty magazines and newspapers. For instance, religious broadcasters have largely displaced the religious press that was the prime pipeline to worshipers during the first half of this century.

Cable companies and TV stations are also taking business away from advertising agencies and public relations organizations by using their production facilities to produce low-cost, professional-quality commercials for advertisers. And some broadcasters are directly challenging the print media via videotex or by programming cable channels that appeal to persons with narrow interests, e.g., putting real estate ads with words and pictures on cable to compete with newspapers' classified advertisements. (As noted, print companies are also experimenting with delivering part of their information via data bases, such as Dow Jones News Retrieval or interactive cable. That thrusts them into roles that previously were the domain of the electronic media.)

Agencies. Other boundaries are also blurring. The trade press regularly carries reports of advertising agencies establishing public relations departments or P.R. subsidiaries. Some advertising firms have crossed the line between ad agencies and broadcasters by regularly purchasing, packaging, and reselling blocks of broadcast time. The agency sells the station's time to the agency's clients, thereby assuming the traditional role of the broadcaster.

Similarly, a number of progressive public relations firms have moved into synergistic ventures. Those with clients who also advertise reach out via public relations to establish their own advertising production facilities or companies. Others, which regularly sent messengers across town with news releases, have launched delivery services adding other people's packages to the firm's own deliveries. Still other P.R. companies have developed electronic newswire networks for the news releases of many public relations organizations.

Video. Recently you may have rented a movie from a video store and found advertisements before the movie. Whether the video rental firm or the motion picture distributor sell the advertisements, both companies changed the definition of how movies are viewed by the public. The video rental stores are also competing with TV stations and motion picture theaters.

In summary, while executives in every industry must contend with many constraints, media managers face some that are unique. They include:

- public policies as well as societal, legal, regulatory, and ethical limits that are different, more visible, and often more restrictive than those facing managers in nonmedia industries;
- the production of a product with content that is brand new each time it reaches the audience market or advertiser market;
- managing a work force whose most important employees are often headstrong and creative, possessing their own ideas about quality—employees who often have more allegiance to their profession than to their employers;
- making decisions in industries where traditional lines of demarcation are rapidly disappearing.

Within these constraints, media managers must balance their corporate and societal responsibilities in ways that will effectively serve the public, their employees, their bosses and, where appropriate, their organizations' shareholders. It is the very complexity of these constraints and responsibilities that creates the prime challenge for the management of media organizations. That challenge requires leadership, vision, and drive.

CHAPTER 2

Media Industries and Media Firms

This chapter traces the development of the various media industries. It reviews their historical patterns in revenues, ownership, structure, and audiences.* Those patterns have important management implications that are one focus of this chapter. They also define a significant part of the media's social responsibility, which is the topic of Chapter 17.

In the second part of this chapter we show how to compare management functions across information firms by detailing three specific media companies: an advertising agency, radio station, and daily newspaper. For each there is information about revenues and expenses, organizational structure, and employees.

THE DEVELOPMENT OF VARIOUS MEDIA INDUSTRIES

Every innovation, including each new medium, goes through a similar process of development, which is best described by the diffusion curve shown in Exhibit 2.1. At the beginning of that process (and the curve) no one utilizes the medium. Then, a few people use it. With time, the medium becomes viable as more and more people try it, which results in the curve going up at a much more rapid rate. Finally, when the great mass of all people who will ever use the innovation are doing so, the curve begins to level off. In effect, then, the diffusion pattern is a kind of S-curve.

If you compare the diffusion of media in the United States shown in

* Facts and figures reported in this chapter come from a wide variety of government, industry, and other publications.

EXHIBIT 2.1. DIFFUSION CURVE OF A NEW MEDIUM

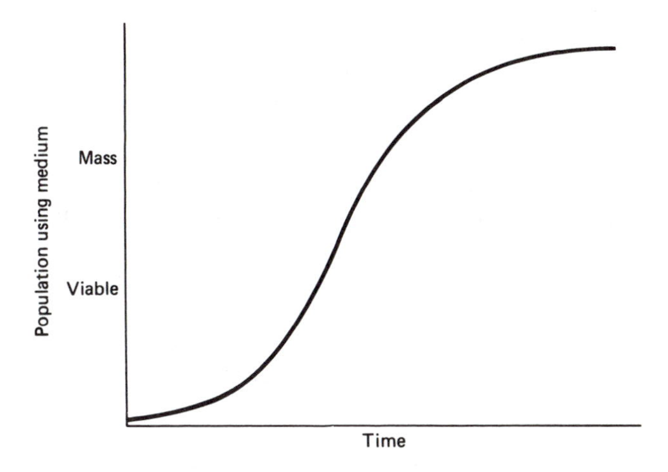

Exhibit 2.2, you will see that different media took various lengths of time to become true "mass media." For example, from the country's first newspaper in 1672 until papers became a mass medium in the 1830s, 160 years passed. By contrast, the diffusion period for magazines was 110 years; for radio, it was only 30 years; and for television, it was only 10 to 12 years.

Three basic reasons for the accelerated diffusion of electronic media are:

First, as the twentieth century progressed, U.S. society became more and more consumer oriented. Workers spent less time on their jobs. They also earned better wages, which resulted in their having more leisure time and more discretionary dollars to spend on leisure-related activities. Since broadcasting and electronics are entertainment-

EXHIBIT 2.2. DIFFUSION OF MEDIA IN U.S.

	Newspaper	*Magazines*	*Radio*	*Television*
Beginning	1672	1741	1906	post–WWII
Viable	1720s	early 1800s	late 1920s	late 1940s
Mass	1830s	1850s	1930s	mid-1950s

oriented, leisure activities, those two media rode the crest of the consumer society.

Second, broadcast media require lower user skill when compared to the print media of newspapers, magazines, and books. People must be literate to read, but only the most common language skills are necessary to enjoy broadcasts. An exception to this rule is the "new media" of electronic data bases and videotex; most often they utilize computers for the delivery of their information. Because the computer user must be able to read and type, the diffusion of new media has been slower than television's. That may change, however, when computers can be driven by voice commands or by pressing keys to activate pictures.

A third reason for the accelerated diffusion of the media is the rapid advance of technological developments that make new media possible. Changes in typesetting and printing technology moved slowly in the early days of newspapers and magazines. In contrast, new methods of production and dissemination of broadcast products were rapid. Today the rate of technological change for all media is faster than ever before.

Implications for Media Managers

What does all of this mean for media managers? There are two ways to respond to that question.

One response is that today many more alternative media are available than in the early part of the twentieth century or even at midcentury. That has dramatically increased the competition for both reader/listener/viewer audiences and for advertisers; therefore, media managers must think competitively. If they are to be effective they must focus their attention on what the competition within their industry and in other media is doing to win audiences and advertisers.

The second response is that the pace of overall change in the media is escalating at an extraordinary rate. If they are to lead their organizations effectively, media managers must constantly think change. No longer can stability of audiences, technology, or employees be assumed. Rather, executives should concentrate their attention on the kinds of changes that are and will be occurring, especially in the audience and advertiser markets, but also in technology, organization, and employees.

REVENUE PATTERNS OF THE MEDIA

The rapid diffusion of broadcast media resulted in a major shift in spending patterns among audiences and advertisers, but it did not increase the total percentage that American citizens and businesses spend on information, entertainment, and advertising. Total spending for media, including subscriptions, purchase of radio and television sets, and advertising resulted in a relatively stable annual figure of around 4 percent of U.S. gross national product (GNP) for the past 50 years. Recently, some fans of the new media have argued that those electronic advances will lead Americans to increase that percentage. Yet, if history is any guide, that is unlikely. What is more probable is simply a shift of dollars from present media to the new medium.

Trends in Advertising Revenues

The principal source of revenue for major media is advertising. In print, advertising accounts for about 75 percent of the revenue in newspapers and about 60 percent of magazine revenue, although there is wide variation across different types of print information products. Advertising accounts for virtually all of the revenue in commercial radio and television.

Advertising expenditures increased from about $2 billion in 1940 to more than $90 billion in 1985. Although that appears to be a staggering rise, it actually only kept pace with the growth in the GNP. In fact, the percentage of GNP devoted to advertising was relatively stable throughout this entire period, at 2.0 to 2.1 percent.*

The biggest change has been in the slice of the pie captured by different media. Exhibit 2.3 shows the proportions of advertising expenditures for print, broadcast, and other media in the 45-year period from the start of World War II in 1940 to 1985. Other media expenditures are for direct mail, catalogues, yellow pages and other directories, outdoor and transit, and specialty advertising. As Exhibit 2.3 indicates, spending for other media remained relatively steady at about 35 percent throughout this period. On the other hand, print media declined from 52 percent of total advertising revenues in 1940 to 35 percent in 1985, while broadcast advertising revenues increased from approximately 10 percent in 1940 to nearly 30 percent in 1985.

Total Advertising Revenues. Exhibit 2.4 shows the percentages of advertising for five major media—newspapers, television, radio, magazines, and business/farm publications—over the 45 years from 1940 to 1985. The most dramatic change occurred in the 1950–1955 period, when television became a true mass medium. Television had an immediate downward impact on the advertising revenues of newspapers and radio.

Since 1955, TV has steadily increased its share of media advertising revenues and newspapers steadily declined. In 1955 three advertising dollars were spent in newspapers for each dollar spent in television. Today, the ratio has narrowed to five dollars in newspapers for every

---

* Figures on advertising revenues are based on data compiled by Robert Coen, vice president of McCann-Erickson Advertising, Inc., and published in *Advertising Age,* Crain Communication, Inc.

EXHIBIT 2.3. TOTAL ADVERTISING EXPENDITURES FOR PRINT, BROADCAST, AND OTHER MEDIA: 1940–1985

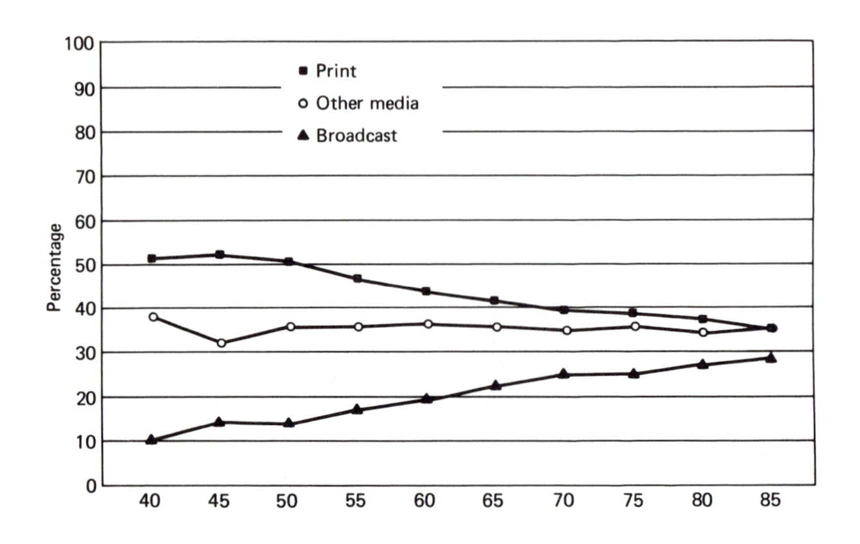

four dollars in television. After its initial decline from 1945 to 1955, radio stabilized its share at about 10 percent by repositioning itself as a local advertising medium. Magazines and business/farm publications, on the other hand, have shown a slow but steady decline to the point that together they now capture only 13 percent of total media revenues.

The pattern for total advertising expenditures might appear to suggest that newspapers and television are in head-to-head competition, but to a significant degree that is not the case. Rather, there are two advertiser markets, one national and one local. The competition is different in each and, thus far, those two media divide on which one dominates each market.

National Advertising Revenues. National advertisers are usually manufacturing and service companies that sell their wares across America. At the local level they typically sell through retail outlets, such as grocery and department stores, auto dealers, insurance agents, stock brokers, and a variety of specialty shops. At the present time, approximately $50 billion is spent annually by national advertisers. Of this amount, about 55 percent is spent on newspapers, magazines, business and farm publications, television, and radio. Among these five media

EXHIBIT 2.4. TOTAL ADVERTISING EXPENDITURES FOR FIVE MEDIA: 1940–1985

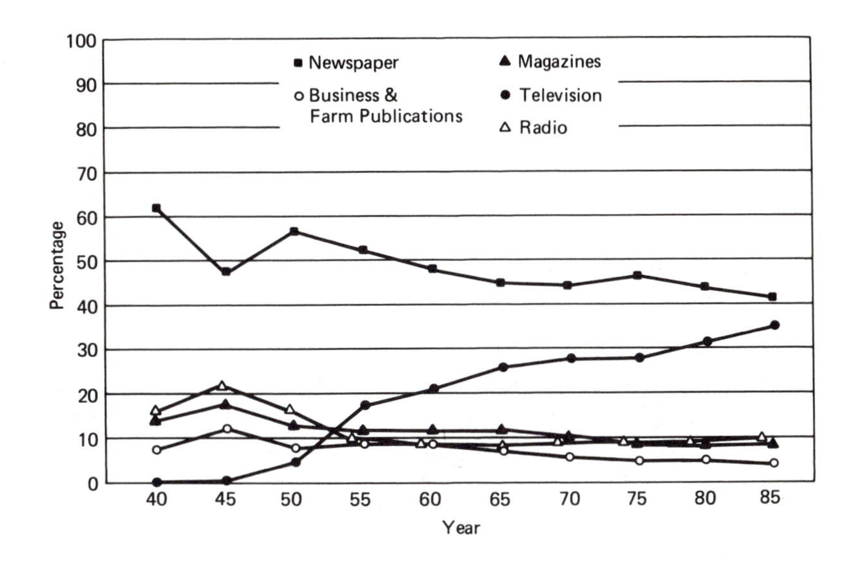

the pattern of national media advertising expenditures changed dramatically during the past four and one half decades. The other 45 percent is spent on such things as direct mail, catalogues, directories, outdoor, etc. The percentage of national advertising captured by this latter group has been highly stable throughout the 45-year period.

Exhibit 2.5 shows national media expenditures for five media during the 1940–1985 period. In 1940 and for the 10 years thereafter, magazines, newspapers, and radio had about equal shares of national advertising revenues. Business/farm publications also captured a large share. Then, when television burst on the scene, those patterns shifted. After 1955 television showed a steady growth to the point that it now captures over 55 percent of the national advertising placed in the major media. The declines for newspapers, magazines, and business/farm publications were steady throughout this period. Radio's share began to drop even earlier. It fell sharply from 1945 to 1955 and has remained small ever since.

Television is the dominant mass medium for national advertisers, though in recent years the revenues for network television flattened and in some cases declined. Still, even the large national expenditures for media, such as direct mail, and for magazine advertising are used only to reach carefully targeted markets, not the mass market of television.

EXHIBIT 2.5. NATIONAL ADVERTISING EXPENDITURES FOR FIVE MEDIA: 1940–1985

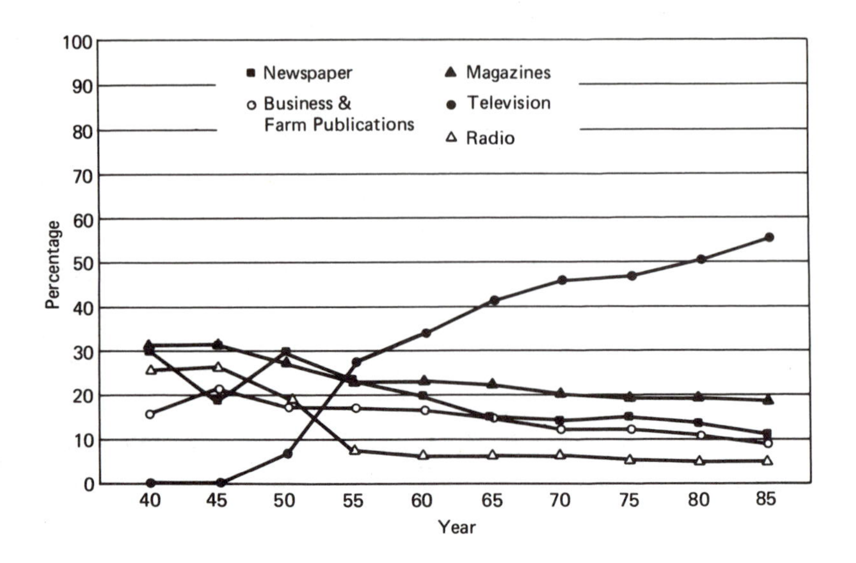

When these advertising sources are used to deliver information to mass audiences it is generally as a supplement to large TV campaigns.

Local Advertising Revenues. Typically, local advertisers are retailers, such as grocery, department, furniture, and drug stores; eating and drinking establishments; and a wide variety of specialty shops that sell everything from hardware or jewelry to clothing or children's toys. Local advertisers also include organizations like financial institutions and hospitals that do image advertising.

Exhibit 2.6 shows that the pattern of media expenditures among local advertisers is quite different than it is for national advertisers. Newspapers dominate local advertising, although this domination has declined during the 45-years since 1940. In 1940 newspapers accounted for over 90 percent of local print and broadcast advertising revenues, but this dropped to approximately 69 percent in 1985. Radio's share has been relatively stable since 1945. Meanwhile, television advertising slowly rose to its current level of 17 percent. Another force in local advertising is such media as directories, outdoor and transit. Group 2 media's share of local advertising was stable at about 22 percent throughout the 45-year period. (Those data are not shown in Exhibit 2.6.)

In summary, newspapers are the primary means for local advertisers

EXHIBIT 2.6. LOCAL ADVERTISING EXPENDITURES FOR THREE MEDIA: 1940–1985

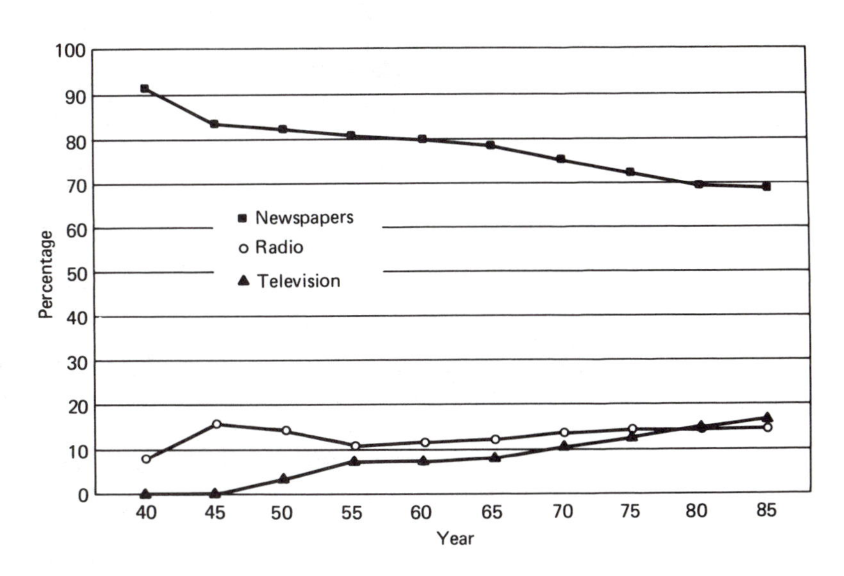

to reach mass audiences, although television is also active locally. The steady decrease in newspapers' share of those local dollars indicates the increased competition that exists today and is likely to grow in the future. Radio is a highly fragmented medium because of the large number of stations that reach any given region. Television has the dominant position in national advertising, but the networks have seen this role level off recently. Meanwhile, magazine and direct mail advertising are utilized to reach specific target audiences.

Implications for Media Managers

What are the implications of these advertising shifts among the media and of the emergence of different media for the media managers?

The arrival of a new medium creates competition with existing information organizations for advertising customers. For example, television's development and diffusion after World War II had a major impact on radio, magazines, and newspapers. Today, new alternatives in print, such as direct mailers and newspaper supplements, put formidable pressure on run-of-paper (ROP) advertising which heretofore was carried in the news columns of newspapers. Additionally, weeklies and shoppers have substantially increased their share of newspaper advertising revenue from about 7 percent of local advertising in 1967 to over 13 percent in 1985. Cable TV is becoming a viable advertising medium too, with revenues in the $1 billion range for the first time in 1986.

Simultaneously, the linkage of census data and zip codes increases the attractiveness of direct mail for both local and national advertisers. That, in turn, puts major pressure on specialized, targeted media like magazines and radio. It could also increase competition on local newspapers and television as advertisers seek cost efficiencies in reaching target markets.

The bottom line for media managers is that every medium faces more intense competition for advertising revenues now than ever before. Media managers must think competitively as they position their product and develop promotion plans to attract and sell their audiences to advertisers.

Another implication of the shifts in advertising for print media managers is a search for new income streams. Consumer magazines increased subscription and newsstand prices to regain revenues lost as advertising shifted from print to other media. During the past 15 years, the advertising/subscription revenue ratio for consumer magazines moved from 60 percent of total revenues received from advertising and 40 percent from subscriptions to 48 percent earned from advertising and 52 percent from subscriptions. In business magazines this ratio changed from 80 percent received from advertising and 20 percent from subscriptions to 65 percent earned from advertising and 35 percent from subscriptions.

In newspapers, the opposite trend is occurring. According to the Constant Dollar Study, advertising revenues were about 74 percent of the typical 20,000 circulation newspaper's revenues in 1959 compared to 26 percent from circulation, but by 1980 advertising rose to 79.5 percent and circulation fell to 20.5 percent (Wright & Lavine, 1982). Since 1980, newspapers have become more aggressive in subscription and newsstand pricing to counter this trend and maintain circulation as a major income stream.

However, increases in subscription prices often result in cancellations by low-income readers or they prevent nonsubscribers from becoming subscribers. That is especially true among low-income consumers, who are very sensitive to price increases. In their pricing decisions, then, newspaper managers must choose whether they truly wish to continue as a mass medium or whether they intend to become a class medium, purchased and used primarily by middle-income and upper-income segments of society.

The same issue confronts broadcasters as the spread of cable and low-power television increases the fragmentation of local broadcast markets. Network-affiliated TV stations are becoming less a "mass medium" as viewers spread their television watching over numerous channels. This increased fragmentation could leave newspapers as the only medium that has the potential to reach all segments of the audience. Such a possibility should have substantial impact on newspaper executives' decisions about whether to be a mass or class medium. That subject is not the point of this chapter, however; it is the focus of Chapter 17, which discusses the media's social responsibility from a managerial vantage point.

No matter what the outcome of these decisions, you can see the complexity of the trade-offs that media managers must make between audience-based and advertiser-based revenue. At the very least that complexity means all media managers must pay close attention to both direct and indirect competitors in positioning their products for the advertiser and audience markets.

As is true for the traditional media, a key question for managers of new media is how much audiences will pay for different types of information and entertainment or for the same information that is delivered in new ways. For example, how much will subscribers pay for extra cable services: HBO, Disney, Cinemax, or other new services, such as home-monitoring systems and shopping by cable? Has the availability of movies via rental video cassettes affected subscribers' willingness to pay for channels that deliver only movies? Will computer "bulletin boards" that can be accessed by home computers and appeal to individuals with particular interests hurt advertising sales on specialized cable channels or the sales of special-interest magazines?

Of course, some new media require a high initial price for hardware, software, and a phone modem, which is the device that allows the computer to exchange data with a distant electronic media source. A consequence of that level of expenditure was the failure of Knight-Ridder's Viewtron videotex system. Part of the reason Viewtron lost money was an unwillingness on the part of potential users to invest the money to purchase equipment to receive the service. Price was not the only issue, however; the lack of user friendliness of Viewtron was also a significant issue.

When a new medium requires both considerable time to learn and substantial knowledge and cost to access, the potential audience is severely diminished. In turn, the potential audience of computer-based media, such as data bases that are more difficult to operate than Viewtron, will be restricted until a much larger percentage of the nation's citizens become comfortable with computers or computers become far more user-friendly. It is true that there is accelerated movement in that direction, but media managers may have to wait until the present generation of grade school children become adults for computer literacy to permeate the society.

A significant, related question for new media is whether the audience they capture will be attractive enough to advertisers so that those with products or services to sell will pay to reach the audiences the new media provide. Another way to look at this is to question whether two income streams exist for the new media or whether audience-based revenue will have to carry the whole burden. Although some media are primarily or exclusively supported by audience revenues (books, recordings, movies), even these companies attempt to generate other income streams. They try to sell serializations, syndication, and television rights; they also bring out various editions and they repackage their messages whenever possible. Each variation is an effort to provide a stronger base of financial support.

THE STRUCTURE OF MEDIA INDUSTRIES

Despite the well-known giants, most media companies are small organizations, and there are many of them. That is because information organizations are usually designed to operate in specific locations, such as major metropolitan areas, small cities, or rural areas. This geographic focus is true for all the primary media except television networks, wire services, national magazines and newspapers, and some advertising and public relations agencies.

Numbers of Companies in the Various Industries

See Exhibit 2.7 for a summary of media outlets. The number of newspapers has been relatively stable for the past 40 years.* Since World War II, about 1,700 daily newspapers have existed in the United States. Although the failure of some notable newspapers has attracted much attention, the past decade has seen only a modest decline in the number of daily newspapers. In 1984 there were 1,688 daily papers;

EXHIBIT 2.7. OUTLETS IN MEDIA INDUSTRIES: 1985

Medium	*Number*
Daily newspapers	1,688*
Weekly newspapers	7,704
Magazine titles	10,809*
Commercial radio stations	8,792
Commercial television stations	982

* 1984 figures

* Figures on the number of newspapers and other media organizations in this section are compiled from a variety of sources, including *Editor and Publisher International Yearbooks, Broadcast Yearbook,* and Sterling and Haight (1978).

that number is down from 1,750 four decades earlier. Weekly newspapers underwent a decline also, dropping from around 8,100 in 1960 to around 7,704 in the 1980s.

The number of magazines, on the other hand, has shown a big increase since World War II. The 2,100 magazine companies in 1950 grew to over 2,800 by 1980. In addition to the 33 percent increase in the number of companies during those three decades, the number of magazine titles increased over 50 percent, growing from 6,960 in 1950 to 10,809 in 1984. And magazines continue to increase at a rate of about 250 new titles per year.

Both of the broadcast media also grew tremendously in the post–World War II period. The 2,800 commercial and educational radio stations in 1950 increased to 10,500 in 1985. AM radio stations showed a big growth spurt in both the 1950s and 1960s, with a doubling in the number of stations during those periods. FM radio stations had their major growth spurt in the 1960s and 1970s; they increased by more than 500 percent and continue that rapid rise into the 1980s.

A series of factors fostered radio's growth:

- FCC regulatory policies provided a stimulus to FM programming.
- Widespread diffusion of radio receivers with both FM and AM capabilities helped, as did superior stereophonic sound that can be broadcast and received only on FM.
- Licensing of additional radio stations by the FCC during that time also spurred the growth, as did the general deregulation of broadcasting in the late 1970s and early 1980s.

Growth in television after World War II halted for four years when the FCC ceased granting new station licenses. The lifting of the FCC freeze in 1952 resulted in a tremendous increase in stations during the next eight years so that by 1960 the number of TV stations rose by 500 percent. Congressional action requiring television manufacturers to provide UHF reception spurred further growth during the 1960s and the 1970s. It resulted in another 60 percent increase in the number of stations by 1980, the year in which the total reached 831. With the deregulatory emphasis during the presidencies of Jimmy Carter and Ronald Reagan, over 600 new stations were licensed, so that by the mid-1980s nearly 1,500 commercial and educational TV stations were in operation.

In summary, then, there is a pattern in the post–World War II period of large increases in the number of companies in all the primary media except newspapers. This resulted in a major increase in the number of media options available to audiences and advertisers.

Concentration of Ownership

Do not think that ownership has become more concentrated only in the cases of the few large media sales you may have read about during the past couple of years. Of course, Gannett, Thompson, Newhouse, Knight Ridder, and Rupert Murdoch added properties, and there were mega sales among a few advertising agencies, but these are not the exceptions, they are the norm. In almost every information industry and at every size level, the past 40 years has seen a sharp rise in ownership concentration. In this the media are not unique; they mirror the concentration patterns in much of American business, although the media lag behind other U.S. industries in their degree of concentration.

What drives this trend toward concentration? The basic reason is that media firms are very profitable. Pretax profits for publicly held companies in various media industries showed these rates in 1984: newspapers, 18 percent; broadcast, 18.5 percent; consumer magazines, 11.5 percent; business magazines, 14.5 percent; advertising agencies, 10.2 percent (Veronis, Suhler, and Associates, 1986). In all segments of the media industry during the 1980s, pretax profits substantially exceeded those of many large industries.

There are at least four other factors that lead to keen interest in purchasing the media. The first is that corporations, which make such purchases, become more profitable in the process of buying new media outlets because the purchased outlets add to cash flow and because media often out-perform the stock market's economic averages. The second is that larger, usually professionally managed, media corporations believe the management expertise they bring to smaller firms will result in even larger profits for the acquired companies. The third is ego and glamour; both are more gratified by owning a visible information company than from the ownership of most other companies.

A fourth factor may be the most powerful of all: scarcity. The purchase of independent information firms is attractive because newspapers and broadcast stations are relatively scarce commodities. Few cities have competing newspapers, and start-up costs for developing new ones are immense. As we noted, the number of broadcast stations has grown, but even liberalized licensing restrictions create an absolute ceiling. Similarly, the start-up costs for developing a new magazine are also quite high, and many fail. As a result, media conglomerates often find it easier to purchase an existing magazine than to develop a new one. There is also a limit on the number of talented people to build effective advertising or public relations agencies, just as there is a limited number of clients willing to pay for those services. Hence, people who want to own an agency are also drawn to consider buying an existing one rather than trying to build their own.

But why are independent firms willing to sell if they are so profitable? For at least three principal reasons. First, the offers they receive are often overwhelmingly generous. For example, in 1986, Ingersoll Publications Co. paid $200 million for the *Journal-Courier* and *New Haven Register*, two New Haven, Connecticut, papers that had respective circulations at the time of 37,829 and 90,618 daily and 139,000 combined on Sunday. According to the *Wall Street Journal* (May 22, 1986), "The price for the papers—about four times annual revenue—stunned Wall Street." Other similar examples abound. The owners of these companies can become instant millionaires by selling their firms, and they stand to make more money than they could ever expect to earn by running the company.

Second, the U.S. tax structure, including both inheritance and capital gains taxes, is a strong motivator for owners to sell. Under the existing tax system, independent, family-owned media firms often must be sold for the family to have enough cash to pay inheritance taxes. For many privately held or family-owned media firms, selling before that sort of tax situation develops and reaping enormous profits in the process is a very strong motivator.

Third is the matter of family ownership. Most media ventures were created by individuals or families, which find that by the second, third, or fourth generation some of the heirs are active in the business while others own shares, but have no involvement. These family members not only read about the lush prices paid for comparable properties but, given the large amounts of cash that constant modernization of the media requires, usually find themselves holding stock that yields only a modest return. Thus, they are "asset rich," but "cash poor," i.e., their stock is worth a lot if the company is sold, but it yields little cash in the meantime. Since they do not work at the company and are often generations away from attachment to family members who founded it, all they see is the opportunity to receive a lot of money if the family sells out. Those feelings create dissatisfactions, arguments, and, eventually, pressures to sell. (That was the case in the mid-1980s sales of the Louisville and the Des Moines newspapers, for example.)

What is the pattern of ownership concentration in American media in the twentieth century?* Chain ownership of newspapers began in the early 1900s. In 1910, 13 companies, owning an average of 4.7 newspapers each, controlled 2 percent of all daily newspapers. By 1930, 55 newspaper groups, owning an average of 5.6 papers each, controlled ownership of 16 percent of all dailies. More significant, however, was that the papers owned by these chains accounted for 43 percent of total newspaper circulation in the U.S.

Ownership patterns were stable through World War II, but began to change again in the postwar period. In the 1950s and 1960s the number of chains doubled, though their average size remained stable at about five newspapers per group. By 1970, newspaper groups owned 50 per-

* Figures on ownership concentration are based on data presented in Compaine et al., (1982).

cent of the total number of newspapers and controlled 63 percent of the total newspaper circulation.

In the 1970s the number of groups remained stable, but existing groups purchased more papers, resulting in an increase in the average number of newspapers each group owned to 7.4 papers per group in 1980. Groups now own two-thirds of all American newspapers and control 73 percent of circulation. You should take careful note of the fact that the pattern of newspaper concentration is not as simple as this summary implies. In Chapter 17 we draw some interesting distinctions between large and small, and public, private, and family-owned groups. That will give you a more subtle understanding of this discussion.

Ownership concentration in magazines has not changed as dramatically since World War II. In fact there was a slight decrease in concentration during that period. For example, in 1947 the four largest magazine companies accounted for 34 percent of magazine revenues; by 1977, this decreased to only 22 percent. Sales of the 20 largest magazine companies increased from 50 percent in 1947 to 59 percent of the total magazines sold in 1963. Since then they have fallen back to only 52 percent of total magazine sales. This contrasts with a current average of 76 percent of sales controlled by the 20 largest companies in a variety of American manufacturing industries.

Concentration in radio slowly increased after World War II, but by 1967 only 31 percent of the radio stations were owned by groups; essentially the same level of concentration existed in 1985, 33 percent. In television, there has been a continuous pattern of increasing concentration since the mid-1950s when 60 groups owned 39 percent of all TV stations. By 1982, 158 groups owned 73 percent of those stations, and since that time the numbers have risen slightly to 75 percent in 1985. Of course, ownership concentration of broadcast media is limited by FCC rules restricting the number of stations that can be owned by the same person or company. The limit used to be seven AM, seven FM, and five television stations. However, with deregulation the FCC allowed a doubling of the number of radio stations and an increase to seven in the number of TV stations; that caused a sharp rise in concentration in broadcasting, especially in the size of the audiences of stations owned by the larger groups.

In the advertising business, a recent spate of mergers has driven the industry toward more concentration with great force. As a result the largest agencies in history were formed during 1986, when some mega-mergers took place. These agencies claimed that the international nature of their business allowed them to provide distinct advantages to firms that do business in many countries. Whether that is true or not remains to be seen. As this text is completed, a number of multinational firms have merged to become mega-agencies. At the same time some very visible, major advertisers left the large agencies' client lists for smaller firms where the client believed it could receive more attention and exert more influence. Although these large agency mergers captured the headlines, keep in mind that the great majority of advertising agencies still operate as small, independent firms.

Cross-media ownership is another aspect of concentration that is noteworthy. In 1982, Benjamin Compaine analyzed the leading firms in six media industries: newspapers, broadcasting, cable TV, magazines, books, and movies. Of the 64 corporations included on his list, 5 were leaders in at least three industries and 13 others were leaders in two. Even more significant is that 26 percent of these corporations had holdings in at least three industries and another 33 percent in two. Thus, nearly three-fifths were multimedia firms. We have not continued Compaine's numbers to the present, but it does not take an updating to know that this trend is increasing; the headlines about acquisitions regularly reinforce that point.

In summary, most media firms are still small. Increasingly, however, these firms are being purchased by large companies, resulting in significant ownership concentration, often as multimedia conglomerates.

Implications for Media Managers

These trends toward concentration carry three implications for media executives.

First of all, small media firms that stay independent typically have a horizontal organizational structure; opportunities for advancement are limited because there are few levels between the employee or middle manager and top management. Thus, a key issue for media managers in small firms is how to develop job rotation and career advancement programs that retain the best employees. This is a difficult task. Tremendous creativity is required to devise meaningful ways to motivate top employees to continue to grow, develop, and remain with the firm when, because of its size and structure, advancement is nearly precluded.

In very small media companies—weekly newspapers, small circulation dailies, modest-size radio and TV stations, or small advertising or public relations agencies—it is often impossible to keep the best employees. For executives in these firms the question is not how to hold the staff, but how to maintain an orderly inflow of good people to replace those who go on to "bigger and better" positions.

Second, for companies that own several operating units the issues are different, though related. They can provide broader career opportunities for their best employees by shifting them from one of their outlets to another. To do this effectively requires ingenuity on the part of the company, as well as an ongoing commitment to the career development of their employees.

Management's challenge is to develop individual career plans that nurture the growth of both the firm and its best employees. That is difficult since a policy of regular transfers may fulfill the career aspirations of individuals, but have a negative impact on the organization. For example, shifting top-level editors or news directors from city to city may allow those employees to advance, but it is at the price of reducing the company's ability to best serve the communities in which it owns newspapers or broadcast stations. In-depth understanding of a community takes years to develop, and too rapid transfer of top news executives prevents them from developing that understanding. Employee-versus-corporation conflict is a typical example of why media managers need to find creative ways to develop job rotation policies that respond to individual career aspirations and still ensure that the media serve their audiences.

A final issue relates to the tendency of media corporations to set profit targets for their operating units. Overly ambitious profit targets may undermine a unit's ability to respond effectively to problems in its region. For example, local newspapers and broadcast stations' revenues are dependent on the state of the local economy. As a result, economic problems at the local level may prevent the operating unit from achieving its prescribed targets. That often forces a severe reduction in local budgets in order to meet the profit goals. An important question for corporate media managers is how to ensure adequate decision-making authority at the local level in a way that motivates the local operating unit's executives to consider broad corporate goals, yet creates incentives to provide a high-quality product for the viewers, listeners, or readers.

MEDIA AUDIENCES

At the turn of the century only three print media were available in the United States: newspapers, magazines, and books. Today, the media horizon has expanded. Television, radio, movies, recordings, data bases, free media, and direct mail compete for the public's attention. Further, with the advent of cable, home videocassette recorders and a variety of new sound systems, an increasing number of methods exist for using media products. These alternatives provide many options for individuals, and research shows that media use dominates people's leisure time. In a study by Robinson (1977), the average adult in the U.S. had about 37 hours per week available for leisure activities. Over half of that time, 19 hours per week, was spent using the media. That is another indication of the dominant role the media play in American society.

Media Usage Patterns

Most adults use a number of different media every day.* But usage patterns are quite varied, as you will see as we consider the media one at a time. See Exhibit 2.8 for a summary.

Newspapers. Newspaper circulation has declined substantially since World War II. From a high point of 487 copies per 1,000 adults in 1950, circulation dropped to only 360 papers per 1,000 adults in 1980. Readership also declined during that period. In the 1950s and 1960s nearly 80 percent of American adults read a paper every day. The turning point occurred in 1970, when readership began to decline so that in 1983, only 56 percent of American adults were habitual newspaper readers. On any single day, however, 69 percent read a newspaper. Readership also fell in every age group, though most dramatically among those under 40 years old. Fully 25 percent fewer under-40 adults are habitual readers today compared with 1967.

Magazines. Circulation per 1,000 adults has remained stable throughout the period since 1970. Because magazines have become more specialized, however, only four consumer magazines have circulations of over 10 million, the point at which they are considered mass media periodicals. More than 40 percent of consumer magazines have circulations of less than 150,000 and hundreds of professional and scholarly publications have very small circulations. Nevertheless, 94 percent of adult Americans report reading at least one magazine monthly, and most are exposed to between 5 and 10 magazines per month. In a typical day 28 percent of all adults read a magazine.

Radio. Two-thirds of American adults listen to the radio daily. Early morning and late afternoon "drive times" garner the highest attention;

EXHIBIT 2.8. REGULAR DAILY MEDIA USE BY ADULTS (U.S.): MID-1980s

Medium	*Adult Usage (%)*
Newspapers	69
Magazines	28
Radio	66
Television	85

* Figures on media usage patterns are taken from a number of sources, including Compaine et al. (1982), Dominick (1983), Jeffres (1986), and Meyer (1985).

radio listening falls off dramatically at night, when it is replaced by television. The biggest change in radio usage in the recent past was the shift from AM to FM. In 1973 only 28 percent of the listeners tuned to FM stations; by 1978 half of the listeners used FM and today nearly 70 percent of the radio audience listens to FM.

Television. Television is the most-used medium. In an average day, 85 percent of adult Americans watch some television. The highest viewing period is in "prime time," from 7 to 11 PM, when half of American households have sets on. That compares to early afternoons, when only one-third of the households are tuned in. The 33 percent figure increases throughout the afternoon to about 40 percent by dinner time.

At the same time, the spread of cable TV has decreased the networks' hold on the viewing audience. In 1985, network share of prime-time viewers was 77 percent, down 5 percent from four years earlier and 10 percent from 1975. Since these figures do not include time devoted to watching movies on VCRs, the networks' share of the television audience may be even lower than 77 percent.

Movies. Television had a greater impact on movie attendance than on any other medium. Moviegoing has declined dramatically from its heyday in the 1930s, when weekly attendance was over 90 million, which was nearly equal to the total population in the country at that time. Today weekly movie attendance is only 20 million although the population is more than 240 million. Three-fourths of moviegoers are under the age of 30.

Audience Characteristics for Various Media

Television is used quite heavily by all age and income groups. From a low point among teenagers and those in their early 20s, television viewing increases with age. Television viewing is substantial in all income and education groups, though it is lower among the better-educated, higher-income segments of the population.

Newspapers are the second most used mass medium, and they attract a large audience among those 30 years and older. Higher-income and better-educated people, whose numbers decline for television viewing, are more likely to be regular newspaper readers.

The other media have targeted, rather than mass, appeal. They attract small, narrowly defined audiences that result in high fragmentation of the whole. Three of the media—radio, movies, and records—have highest usage among teenagers and people in their twenties. This similar audience base creates a great opportunity for developing media tie-ins, i.e., information products that can be distributed in several media at the same time. Popular movies and record albums, such as *Saturday Night Fever, Flashdance*, and *Footloose*, were among the first to capitalize on this so-called audience synergism to market the same product in a number of channels, thereby increasing the income streams available for the same message.

Magazines and books also have highly fragmented audiences. Targeting of those publications is typically based on interest patterns. The audience for both of these print media is primarily adults 30 years old and older who are somewhat better educated and have moderate to high levels of income.

The Audience for News. Unlike general media usage, in which television leads, more Americans receive their news from newspapers than from television or radio, as is shown in Exhibit 2.9. On any given day, newspapers are read by 69 percent of American adults, TV news programs are watched by 67 percent, and radio news is heard by 48 percent (Gollin & Bloom, 1983). Of course, each day the specific composition of these three audiences changes. Nonetheless, on any given day, 91 percent of American adults claim to have paid attention to the news in at least one medium. Within that total, 25 percent use all three media, 40 percent utilize two, and another 26 percent get their news from only one.

In the past 25 years, audience preferences for news have changed considerably. In 1959, 57 percent of the adult population indicated a preference for getting their news from newspapers; by 1980 that number had declined to 44 percent (Roper Organization, 1981). Television increased from a 51 percent preference in 1959 to 64 percent in 1980. Radio declined from 43 percent in 1959 to 18 percent in 1980. (These figures exceed 100 percent in any year because respondents in the survey were allowed to give multiple preferences.) The pattern indicates a major shift in preference to television news and a decrease for both newspapers and radio.

Evaluation of the believability of different media shows a similar

EXHIBIT 2.9. AVERAGE DAILY NEWS CONSUMPTION BY ADULTS (U.S.)

Medium	*Usage (%)*
Newspapers	69
Television news	67
Radio news	48

pattern. When respondents in a survey were asked which medium they would believe if they got conflicting reports of the same news story, television showed a dramatic increase in the period from 1959 to 1980; it went from 29 percent to 51 percent (Roper Organization, 1981). Newspapers declined from 32 percent in 1959 to 22 percent in 1980. Radio and magazines showed a slight decline during this same period, going from a combined figure of 22 percent in 1959 to 17 percent in 1980.

The data on preferences and believability would suggest a move toward television domination of the news audience. However, it is more appropriate to view the media as complementary. Nearly half of adult Americans use both newspapers and TV for news in any given day (Gollin & Bloom, 1983). Further, 53 percent say they do not get enough news from TV coverage of big stories and want the added details that newspapers provide (Bogart, 1984).

Demographic patterns for news in the various media are similar to the more general demographic patterns for media use noted previously. For example, college graduates rely more heavily on newspapers for news, whereas persons with less education rely more on TV news.

Implications for Media Managers

1. Competition for audiences, including the audience for news, is great. As a result, much audience research is conducted to identify audience interests and preferences before specific media products are developed. This assists media managers in reducing risks in developing information products; that is important because such large investments are involved in both the production and the marketing of new print, broadcast, or electronic messages.
2. Audience fragmentation means that media managers must target their products to narrower and narrower audiences, especially for the more specialized media such as radio and magazines.
3. A challenge to newspapers is to win a greater share of younger and lower-income segments of the population, those who currently have relatively low readership rates. If readers among these segments do not increase, newspapers may become a "class medium," rather than the mass medium they have always been. Maintaining a mass audience is necessary for newspapers to continue to serve their social function. It also may be necessary for newspapers to win the younger audience if these people are to become subscribers when they reach their middle and older years.
4. Audience synergism among several media challenges information executives to determine how to best utilize multiple channel opportunities to capitalize on the same target market. For the teenagers and young adults, how can products simultaneously utilize television, movies, radio, and records? For the somewhat older and more affluent adult audiences, what book and television tie-ins can be developed to reach this audience segment effectively? Mini-series based on bestselling books are examples of this type of media tie-in.

MEDIA CREDIBILITY

Public confidence in the media has also come into question; in the trade publications it is referred to as the credibility crisis. The decline in the public's confidence in the media is part of a larger pattern that began in the mid-1960s, involving decreased public trust in all of society's institutions. During the Watergate period of the early 1970s, television news and the press did experience some increase in public confidence, but since then both have declined. In a 1984 Harris survey, only 28 percent of the American public expressed a great deal of confidence in the leaders of TV news, and only 18 percent had the same high level of confidence in the leaders of the press. Although these figures are not the lowest among the 14 institutions evaluated, they indicate some public dissatisfaction with the major news organizations.

Another survey presents ratings on a variety of aspects of credibility. In a 1984 Gallup poll conducted for *Newsweek*, both local and national news media were given high ratings for accuracy, fairness, and for reporting the news intelligently. They were given low rankings, however, for being politically biased, invading privacy, and sensationalizing the news; over half the American public agreed that the media are guilty of each of those actions. The media showed moderate rankings on two other aspects of credibility: negativism and arrogance. On all of these measures, local newspapers, local TV news, and radio were ranked more positively than nationally influential newspapers, TV network news, or national news magazines.

Recent studies by the Times Mirror Company (1986) and the Gannett Center for Media Studies (Whitney, 1985) show general patterns of findings similar to the Gallup *Newsweek* poll. In the Times Mirror study, however, national and local media were seen as equally believable, and overall favorability ratings of both national and local media were very high.

Although these data suggest that *crisis* is too strong a word for the current situation, the pattern of public perceptions indicates cause for concern about the media's credibility. Public support is crucial for the media to succeed as business organizations as well as to fulfill their responsibilities to inform society. If that special role is to be preserved for the media's economic sake and for the vital role they play in a free society, then information organization leaders must heed these trends and take steps to increase public confidence in their organizations.

Implications for Media Managers

While realizing that some tension over these matters is inevitable and appropriate, the pattern of public concern suggests that media managers must produce news products which do a better job of inspiring public trust. The public is concerned about how the electronic and print press treat the people they cover. For example, a majority feel that the media, especially the national news reporters, invade citizens' privacy. Media executives should enforce reporting strategies that get the story, but also show more respect for citizens' right to privacy. Similar actions should be taken to address the public's concern that too often the news is sensationalized.

Media managers should also increase their efforts to educate the public about the role and responsibilities of the press. A variety of surveys indicate that the public is relatively uninformed about the press' role in society and what the media's constitutional protection means. Educational efforts will help the average citizen understand why some tension and seeming invasion of privacy is in everyone's best interest. Improving that level of understanding will protect the information organizations' franchise and strengthen them as both social and business institutions.

MEDIA COMPANIES

In this section of the chapter we describe the operation of three typical media organizations: an advertising agency, a radio station, and a daily newspaper. We talk about the market each one serves and the functions each performs in terms of the message development, production, and distribution processes. We also provide an organizational structure and discuss the jobs in the firm. Then we present a simplified income statement showing the firm's major sources of income and expense.*

The Williams Advertising Agency

The Williams Advertising Agency is one of the top 10 firms in its market, with billings of $24 million last year. In its city 20 agencies had billings of $10 million or more; another 50 had smaller billings, most of them $1 million or less. Typically, the small agencies are one- or two-person shops. Williams Advertising has 25 clients with billings ranging from $4.5 million to $300,000. The agency serves 12 services accounts (restaurants, insurance, and other services), 8 business-to-business advertisers, and 5 packaged goods clients. Because of the nature of its clients, Williams does much more television advertising than a typical organization its size.

Organizations like Williams Advertising gather information about the market and consumers from their clients, then develop an advertising

---

* The three organizations described are actual media companies, although the names of the firms have been changed. Information was gathered through interviews with company executives and staff members.

campaign to achieve the client's objectives. A campaign involves creating an advertising strategy and advertising executions, i.e., specific advertisements and commercials. Williams next determines which media will be used to distribute the message to the target market, then contacts these media to buy specific time or space to carry out the media schedule. (Usually, advertising agencies participate in the steps in the message production process up to the point of producing a final version of the advertisement or commercials. That is done by other media, which actually print and/or distribute the message to the target audience.)

Williams's 47 employees are divided into five different departments, as shown in Exhibit 2.10.

Account Services Department. Account service personnel work with the client to gather information about the client's product or service, markets, and consumers. Account supervisors and account executives

EXHIBIT 2.10. ORGANIZATION CHART OF WILLIAMS ADVERTISING AGENCY

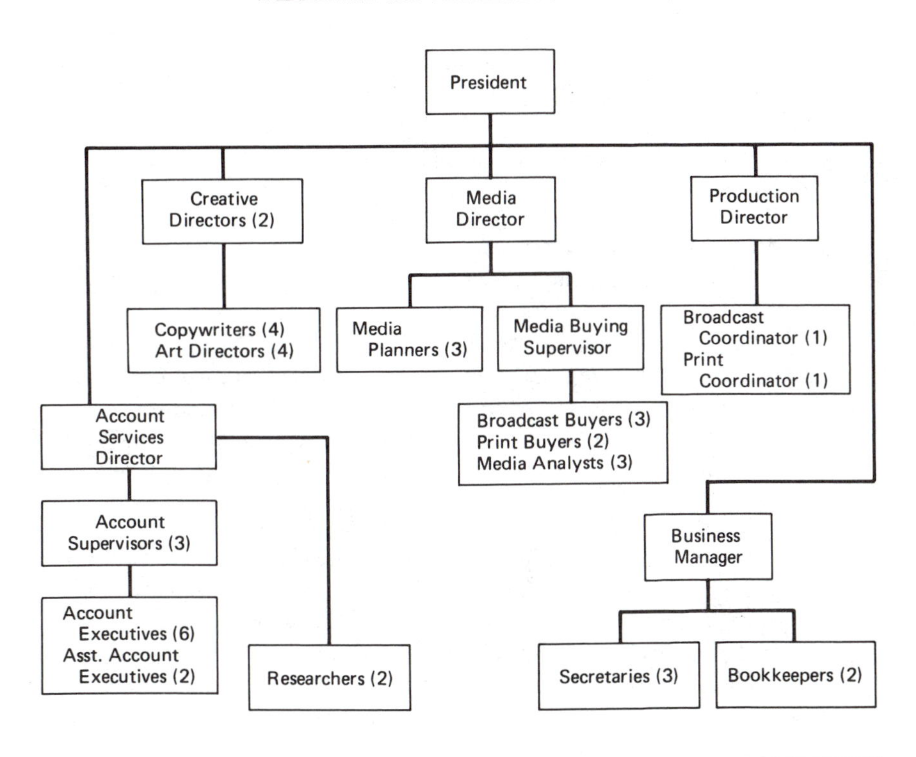

develop ideas about positioning the product and about the advertising strategy that will be followed. In the account services department, two researchers play a staff support role, conducting research on consumers.

(A "staff" function is one that is available to the personnel of the agency who develop the actual advertising; it is available, but there is no requirement that it be used. Thus, staff researchers represent a resource group that has no direct responsibility for getting out the product or service. They may be used or not used by the "line employees," those who do have direct responsibility to get out the product or service.)

Creative Department. This department includes copywriters and art directors who typically work as a team in developing the creative strategy and ideas for specific advertising executions. They write copy, plan the visual elements of specific ads, then hire outside suppliers (TV and radio production firms, typesetters, and printers) to produce final versions of the advertisements.

At Williams Advertising, copywriters and art directors work on varying numbers of accounts. One copywriter/art director team spends all of its time on the agency's largest client. Another copywriter handles 11 different accounts, pairing up with three different art directors in the process.

Production Department. The production department coordinates final copy with the creative department. It keeps track of where ads and commercials are in the production process and coordinates with the media department to send copies of the final version of advertisements to specific media.

Media Department. Media planners work with account executives to plan a media schedule that will effectively reach the client's target audience. Media buyers then purchase space and time in specific media, negotiating the best possible price. Since there is greater opportunity to negotiate price in broadcast, more experienced buyers are assigned to it than to print, where most prices are fixed. Because Williams uses television extensively, three media buyers work specifically on TV. They are supported by two media analysts.

Business Department. The business department handles secretarial and financial aspects of the agency. Secretaries fulfill all of their traditional functions of typing correspondence, reports, and contracts; bookkeepers track collections and expense payments and maintain the agency's accounting records. The business manager is both the chief financial officer and the office manager in the agency, although a senior secretary performs part of the office manager function for day-to-day concerns.

Financial Information. The income statement in Exhibit 2.11 shows the major sources of revenue and expenses of Williams Advertising. Several points are worth noting. First, service and packaged goods accounts generate more income on the average than do business accounts. That is true because consumer marketers typically spend a greater proportion of their marketing budgets on advertising than do business-to-business marketers.

Second, payroll is the dominant expense of the agency; it requires 58 percent of the total income Williams takes in. Salaries in the account services and creative departments are considerably higher than in other areas. The average accounts service salary is $35,000 and the average

EXHIBIT 2.11. INCOME STATEMENT OF WILLIAMS ADVERTISING AGENCY

Income		
Services accounts (12)	$1,250,000	
Packaged goods accounts (5)	770,000	
Business accounts (8)	590,000	
Total income		$2,610,000
Expense		
Salaries and wages		
Administration	$ 190,000	
Account services	486,000	
Creative	370,000	
Media	256,000	
Production	66,000	
Business	142,000	
Total payroll	$1,510,000	
Other operating expenses		
Office rent	$ 230,000	
Office supplies and services	157,000	
Memberships, dues, travel	86,000	
Payroll taxes and employee benefits	120,000	
Promotion, entertainment, new business	65,000	
Accounting and bank expenses	26,000	
Insurance	86,000	
Total other operating expenses	$ 770,00	
Total operating expenses		$2,340,000
Operating Profit		$ 330,000
Nonoperating expenses		
Depreciation	$ 102,000	
Interest	30,000	
Total nonoperating expenses	$ 132,000	
Profit before taxes (7.6 percent)		$ 198,000
Taxes	$ 46,000	
Profit after taxes (5.8 percent)		$ 152,000

salary for creative personnel is $37,000. In the media, production, and business departments, average salaries are around $22,000. This salary structure reflects both the responsibilities of different personnel and the level of experience. At Williams, account service and creative personnel are considerably more experienced than are the media and production staff members. A similar pattern holds in many agencies of Williams's size.

Promotion, entertainment, and new business expenses are very low, only 2.5 percent of total income. That reflects the kind of marketing Williams Advertising uses to secure clients. Although there are many competing agencies in almost every advertising market of size, agencies typically do not aggressively promote and sell themselves. Rather, they await an invitation from a client to make a sales presentation. Since clients typically retain the same agency for three to seven years or even longer, competition for clients is not cutthroat.

Finally, depreciation and interest expenses are only five percent of total budget, reflecting the fact that advertising agencies are not equipment intensive. Because most production is handled by outside suppliers, the agency typically does not need expensive equipment for TV, sound, or print production.

Williams' profit of $198,000 is 7.6 percent of sales. This profit figure is below average for the industry as a whole, but it is typical for agencies of this size. Furthermore, because agencies do not have to reinvest profit in major equipment, the agency owner will often take a percentage of the profit as extra salary or a bonus, thereby reducing the profit figure and minimizing the agency's tax liability. Williams Advertising's owner did not do so in this case, so 7.6 percent profit represents a good estimate of the agency's actual profitability.

KZZZ-FM Radio

KZZZ-FM is an "urban contemporary" music station located in one of the country's 10 largest metropolitan centers. It is one of 12 stations owned by a broadcasting corporation, City Media, Inc. KZZZ-FM's market is excellent, showing substantial population and retail sales growth during the past decade. Projections indicate the growth rate will continue to increase over the next 10 years. Radio revenues also increased at a substantial rate and are expected to grow even faster.

KZZZ-FM is one of 29 stations in the market. With that much competition, audience fragmentation occurs as audience segments are drawn to differing radio formats. In this market, the top 12 stations utilize eight different formats and capture about 70 percent of the audience. The remaining 17 stations account for about 30 percent of the total audience.

KZZZ-FM directly competes with one other station with a similar format. The urban contemporary format is designed to appeal to the black population, which is sizable in the region. KZZZ-FM is the second-ranking station with the black audience, its target market, and ranks 11th overall among adults. Although the station's signal covers a radius of 100 miles, the actual audience is concentrated within 25 miles. KZZZ-FM charges a unit price of about $125 per 30- or 60-second commercial. The station has 1,015 advertising accounts, three-fourths of which have been active in the last six months. Local advertisers comprise 725 accounts and 290 accounts are national advertisers.

Like most radio stations, KZZZ-FM promotes itself heavily to attract an audience. Its primary promotions are of two kinds: contests and concerts. The station gives away major prizes—such as trips, stereos, and an automobile—to contest winners three times a year, and for continuous promotion it gives away three record albums daily. The station also sponsors a concert series of prominent black recording artists, with KZZZ-FM paying most of the expenses so that concert ticket prices are kept low—only $4 to $5 per ticket. Also, the station advertises on a regular basis, making heavy use of billboards and bus advertising in areas of the city where the black population is concentrated.

KZZZ-FM does almost no information gathering to create its programming. Rather, as is the case with most radio stations, it simply collects prepackaged messages (records and wireservice news) and puts them together in a package for distribution to the audience. In addition, of course, it has major promotional and sales efforts to reach its listener and advertiser markets. Essentially the station is a distribution and sales organization, not really a message development medium like advertising agencies.

KZZZ-FM has 32 staff members organized into five departments as shown in Exhibit 2.12.

Programming. The largest department is programming. It includes six full-time and two part-time announcers (disk jockeys). Since the station carries news only during the daytime portion of its programming there is only one news director who compiles both wireservice news and weather information for the announcers to read once an hour.

Sales. The second largest department is sales. Six local sales representatives and two national sales representatives call on KZZZ's more than 1,000 accounts. Each representative handles about 120 accounts, although the most experienced sales staffers deal with larger accounts and, as a result, have fewer customers. The sales manager works with the staff and goes along with them on some presentations to major advertisers or advertising agencies.

Promotion. The promotion director plans both the promotional efforts and advertising campaigns of the station. Promotion assistants carry out the details involved in conducting the promotional campaigns.

EXHIBIT 2.12. ORGANIZATION CHART OF KZZZ-FM

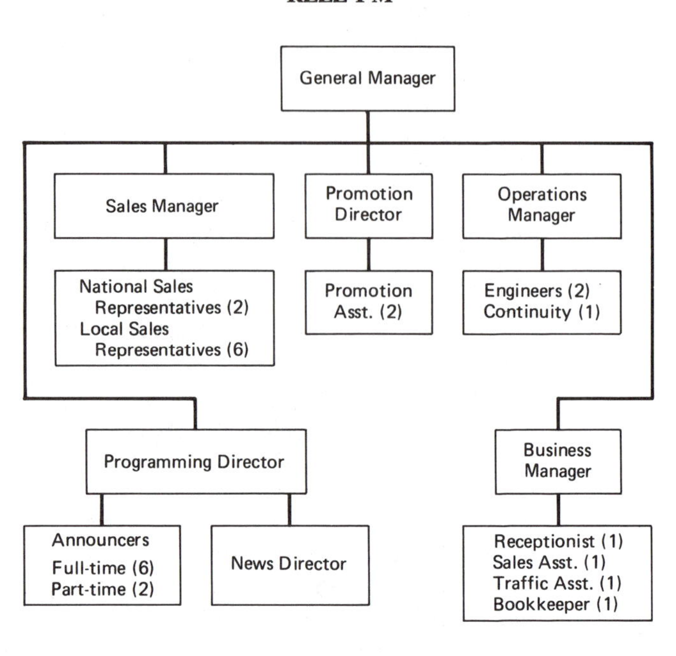

Operations. The operations manager oversees transmission and the equipment of the station. Two engineers perform the actual task of monitoring and maintaining broadcast equipment. A continuity person works with the programmers and engineers to assist in maintaining program flow. The continuity staff member also writes some of the commercials.

Business Department. The business department includes four positions: (1) receptionist; (2) sales assistant; (3) traffic assistant, who makes sure that recordings of commercials have arrived and are passed on to the engineers for transfer onto master tapes for the announcers; (4) bookkeeper, who handles all billing, collections, payments, and day-to-day accounting of the station. (The books are spot audited by an outside, independent accounting firm each month and they are formally audited annually.)

Financial Information. A simplified income statement for KZZZ-FM is shown in Exhibit 2.13. Note that the primary income is from local

EXHIBIT 2.13. INCOME STATEMENT OF KZZZ-FM

Income		
Local advertising	$2,434,000	
National advertising	1,051,000	
Total income		$3,485,000
Expenses		
Operating expenses		
Program	$ 316,000	
News	42,000	
Direct	524,000	
Technical	105,000	
Advertising sales	251,000	
Promotion	464,000	
Traffic	47,000	
Business and administration	359,000	
Total operating expenses	$2,108,000	
Total operating profit		$1,477,000
Nonoperating expenses		
Depreciation	$ 330,000	
Management fee	91,000	
Interest payment on debt	87,000	
Total nonoperating expenses	$ 508,000	
Profit before taxes (24.9 percent)		$ 869,000
Taxes	$ 403,000	
Profit after taxes (13.4 percent)		$ 466,000

advertisers, who account for 70 percent of sales. The 30 percent from national advertisers comes from national manufacturing companies that wish to reach the sizable black population in this market.

Promotional expenses to attract audiences and sales expenses to sell advertisers are substantial. The promotional and sales expenses total $715,000, which is 20 percent of total income. Contrast that to the 2.5 percent for promotional and sales expenses for Williams Advertising.

Although it is not shown in the figures, the total payroll for KZZZ-FM is $932,000. That represents 27 percent of the station's total income and is only about half the payroll expense, as a percentage, of an advertising agency. That is because radio stations are less labor intensive than advertising agencies, and stations that buy computerized programming from outside suppliers have even fewer employees in their announcing ranks.

The management fee of $91,000 is the amount paid to City Media, Inc., KZZZ-FM's owner. The corporation charges a fee to each of its stations in proportion to their revenues and profits.

In its income statement, KZZZ-FM shows a profit for the year of

$869,000, or 24.9 percent of sales. That figure is well above the average for a radio station and even though it is correct, it is not representative of KZZZ's usual operations. That is because the interest payment for this year is $87,000, which is the final interest paid on a debt incurred five years ago when the station purchased new transmission equipment. By contrast, last year the station's interest expense was $394,000. If this year's income statement were adjusted to add a more typical amount of interest expense, say $300,000, profit before taxes would be only 16.3 percent of sales, which is still a fine showing. It is also a more accurate picture of the likely profitability of an urban station, for operations like KZZZ-FM constantly face major investments in building and new technology. In such an environment higher interest expenses are typical and if that happens, the nearly 25 percent profit level would decrease substantially.

The New Gazette, *a Daily Newspaper*

The New Gazette is published in a region with a population of 115,000. It serves its metropolitan area, its home county, and parts of six other counties. *The New Gazette* has an average circulation of 27,500, is owned by a newspaper chain, and publishes six days a week, Monday through Saturday. A typical issue of the paper is 32 to 44 pages with approximately 45 percent news and editorial content and 55 percent advertising. That results in 17 pages of editorial and 21 pages of advertising on a typical day. *The New Gazette* is a broadsheet (that is, full-sized) publication.

Paid circulation has been stable for the past five years and is 17 percent over the paper's circulation in 1975 (23,000), when the chain purchased the newspaper. Advertising is currently zoned into two areas of very different size. Zone 1 encompasses a 12-mile radius around the city; circulation in this region is 24,100 out of approximately 35,000 households in the zone, for a penetration rate of 70 percent. Zone 2 extends from 12 to 38 miles west of the city; circulation in that territory is 3,400 out of 12,000 households, for a 30 percent penetration rate.

The New Gazette has 1,200 regular advertisers. About 800 of them run display ads and the remaining 400 purchase classified ads. Many other advertisers also purchase space in the paper on an irregular basis. The *Gazette* accepts preprint sections from major national and regional retailers.

As is true of the vast majority of daily newspapers, *The New Gazette* carries out all of the functions in the message development/production/distribution process. Its news/editorial and advertising staffs gather information and develop messages.

Locally prepared stories and ads make up the bulk of the paper's content, although wire services, syndicated material (columns, comics, and features), and advertisements from advertising agencies also are part of *The New Gazette's* "package." The production staff prepares the final copy and prints the paper and the circulation department distributes the paper through a street-carrier system in the city and motorized carriers and the U.S. mail in outlying areas. There are also some newsstand sales throughout the *Gazette's* region, but they represent a very small percentage of the total circulation.

The New Gazette has 121 full-time employees; 46 part-time employees each work about half-time, resulting in an equivalent of 144 full-time staffers. They are organized into the five departments shown in Exhibit 2.14.

News/Editorial. This department has 32 full-time and five part-time employees. Their job is to cover the news and prepare opinion and analysis pieces for the editorial page. Staff members (reporters and photographers) receive their assignments from subeditors who head areas of coverage, called desks.

Exhibit 2.15 presents a more detailed picture of the news/editorial department. It has seven desks, each with three to eight staff reporters, copy editors, or photographers. At *The New Gazette,* the desks are labeled sports, city news and politics, family life and living, the environment and out of doors, agriculture, and photo. (Across the country, coverage areas vary from newspaper to newspaper depending on the goals the editor sets.)

Once stories are written they are reviewed and edited by copy editors. In the case of important stories, the assigning editor or chief editor may also be involved in the editing process. Then the copy editors or page editors design the newspaper's pages, calculating space for local and wireservice stories and pictures. The total news/editorial space available is usually a function of the amount of advertising the *Gazette* receives daily, weekly, or monthly. Story and picture position are based on the subjects they report and on their importance in the judgment of the paper's news executives.

Advertising. This area, which is divided into four subdepartments, has 25 full-time and four part-time employees. The department is managed by an advertising director with middle managers who direct classified and display advertising sales, dispatch, and art.

Advertising representatives personally call on accounts and report to either the classified or display managers. The classified manager also oversees a telephone solicitation operation that is staffed by one full-time person and several part-timers.

The art department, which has only two employees, uses purchased art services and some locally designed graphics to produce advertisements for special "theme" sections or on "speculation" for sales representatives to show to clients or to respond to the needs of the

EXHIBIT 2.14. ORGANIZATION CHART OF *THE NEW GAZETTE*

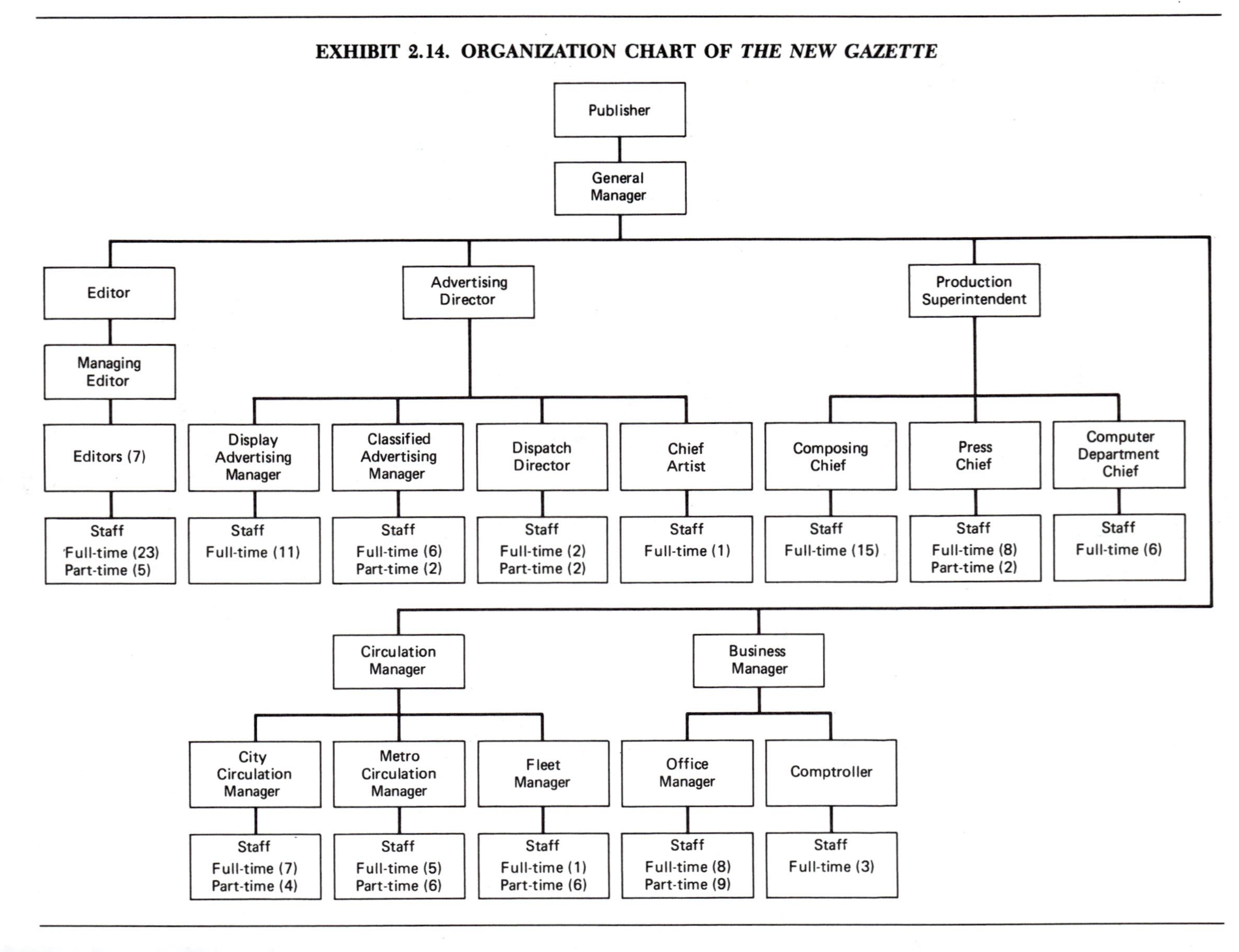

EXHIBIT 2.15. NEWSROOM ORGANIZATION CHART OF *THE NEW GAZETTE*

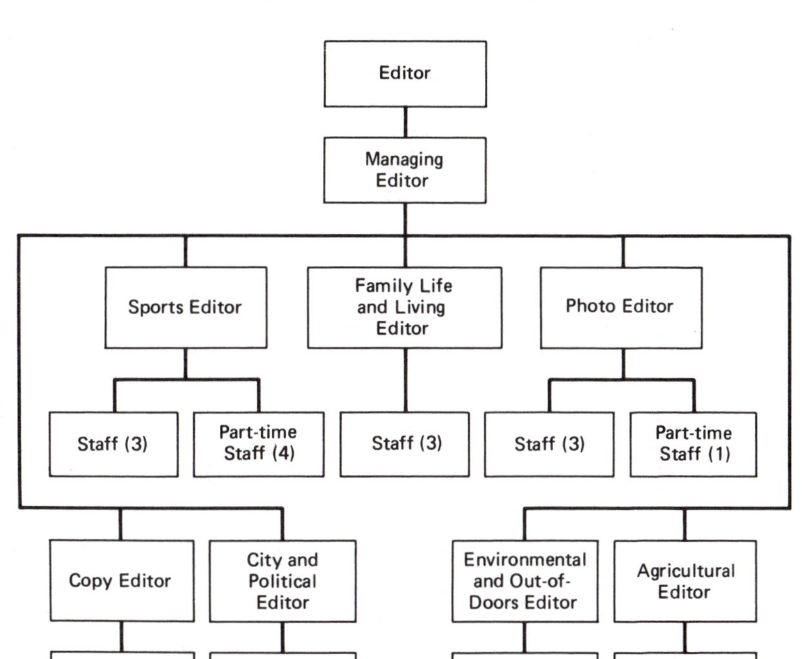

newspaper's advertising accounts. Of course, many retailers who advertise with the *Gazette* are chain owned; they often provide the newspaper with finished advertisements that are supplied to the local stores by their corporate owner. The dispatch department, as its name implies, delivers advertising proofs to accounts for final approval and makes sure that the ads reach the production department in a timely fashion.

Production. This department has three divisions: composition and camera, platemaking and press, and computer. Each of these areas has a manager who reports to the production superintendent. In all there are 34 full-time and two part-time employees in production.

While there are many jobs in these areas, a major one is paste-up. Personnel use photographically set type, created by the *Gazette's* advertising or news staffs or submitted by advertisers, and paste it on make-up pages. Other composition staff members photograph those pages and provide negatives to the plate and press departments. When negatives arrive in the press department, staff members make plates that are passed to pressmen who actually print the newspaper. All of this happens in lockstep order with tremendous time pressure. More and more, technology is collapsing these steps and controlling them by computers; as a result the computer department is becoming increasingly important in facilitating the entire process.

Circulation and Distribution. This department has 17 full-time staff members and the highest number of part-time employees, 26. Many of these staffers spend little time in the office; they supervise *Gazette* carriers and/or deliver newspapers across the newspaper's territory. They also spend time recruiting carriers and training them about sales and service, and they deal with customers' complaints. (The most frequent reason that subscribers give for canceling their subscriptions is poor delivery service.)

Business and Administration. This area includes everyone from clerks handling billings to top executives, i.e., the publisher, general manager, and business manager. There are 13 full-time and nine part-time employees here. The publisher and general manager are responsible for the overall direction of the *Gazette* and the hiring and firing of department heads. The business manager oversees a broad range of activities from cash management to accounting, and is assisted by clerical and computer personnel whose duties range from billing and collections to payroll and general accounting.

The New Gazette's staff is three times the size of Williams Advertising and four times as large as KZZZ-FM. As a consequence of its size the newspaper has more levels of management: five compared to three in KZZZ-FM and four in the Williams Agency. (To see this compare Exhibits 2.10, 2.12, and 2.14.) Nevertheless, most subdepartment managers supervise from eight to twelve staff members and therefore the newspaper has a relatively horizontal organization structure. This is typical of newspapers, even larger ones.

Financial Information. The income statement for *The New Gazette*, shown in Exhibit 2.16, provides a picture of last year's financial performance.

The New Gazette has three separate income streams. Circulation accounts for 22 percent of revenue, run-of-press (ROP) advertising accounts for 69 percent, and distribution of preprints makes up 9 percent of total income. Williams Advertising and KZZZ-FM each has only one income stream although both serve more than one market. (Williams has clients in three different sectors and KZZZ-FM has both national and local advertising accounts.)

Note the item on the *Gazette* income statement that refers to raw

EXHIBIT 2.16. INCOME STATEMENT OF *THE NEW GAZETTE*

Income		
Circulation	$1,560,000	
Advertising	4,890,000	
Preprint	620,000	
Total income		$7,070,000
Raw materials expense (newsprint and ink)	$1,234,000	
Gross margin		$5,836,000
Operating expenses		
News/editorial	$ 804,000	
Advertising	488,000	
Production	905,000	
Circulation	746,000	
Business and general administration	$1,410,000	
Total operating expenses	$4,353,000	
Total operating profit		$1,483,000
Nonoperating expenses		
Building depreciation	$ 38,000	
Equipment depreciation	184,000	
Total nonoperating expenses	$ 222,000	
Profit before tax (17.9 percent)		$1,261,000
Taxes	$ 517,000	
Profit after tax		$ 744,000

materials. Newsprint expense equals 14.5 percent of each revenue dollar of the paper. This high raw material expense is similar to what we find in other manufacturing companies, and is different from ad agencies and radio stations, which have little or no raw materials expense because they do not actually manufacture a product. (It should also be noted that whereas newsprint expense is a comparatively large figure for this 27,500 circulation daily, it is a far bigger percentage for larger newspapers. For a 250,000 circulation paper, for instance, it rises to 27 percent of each revenue dollar.)

There is no separate expense item for promotion. Instead, promotion expenses are part of circulation expenses and are comparatively small, about $50,000. When promotion expenses are added to the advertising department's promotion expenses, which reflect expenses necessary to attract advertisers, only 7.6 percent is spent for the newspaper's promotion and sales efforts. This is about one-third of the money spent by the radio station to promote itself to its audience and to sell advertising.

That comparison reflects the major difference in competition that radio and newspaper face. KZZZ-FM is one of 29 stations in its market and has to promote heavily to attract its audience. *The New Gazette* is the only daily newspaper in the city and nearby region. The paper does face competition from a metropolitan paper published about 80 miles away, but that is minor. Also, recall that Williams Advertising, which operates in a different type of competitive environment, spends only 2.5 percent for promotion and sales to new clients.

Depreciation is only 3.1 percent of *The New Gazette*'s income. This represents a long-term depreciation write-off schedule for the building and printing presses that the newspaper owns. Depreciation expenses for the Williams Agency are 3.9 percent, reflecting a much more rapid depreciation schedule for the agency's computer equipment. The comparable figure for KZZZ-FM is a 9.5 percent depreciation expense, which again reflects a more rapid write-off schedule for radio equipment.

Additionally, the radio station has major interest expenses in conjunction with the borrowing it did to finance its new equipment. *The New Gazette* has paid for all its equipment, so it shows no interest expenses. However, the impact of depreciation and interest expense will change dramatically in the future when the newspaper purchases sophisticated color press units and cameras. Given the size of those purchases, as well as the likelihood that a new building or addition to the present newspaper plant may be necessary to house them, the newspaper's ongoing expense in both of these areas far exceeds that of a typical advertising agency and will equal or surpass the radio station's.

Payroll expenses of *The New Gazette* (not shown in the income statement) are $2,361,000, or 33 percent of income. These figures suggest that newspapers and radio stations are relatively equal in terms of labor intensity, for payroll was 27 percent of the income of the radio station. That is probably misleading, however. Salary schedules in the small city are considerably less than in the metropolitan area where KZZZ-FM and Williams Advertising are located. Furthermore, the labor intensity of a company can be measured by three other, more sensitive, indicators.

The first is income per employee, which is calculated by dividing the total income of the firm by the number of employees. The income per employee figure for *The New Gazette* is $49,000, compared to $58,000 for Williams Advertising and $109,000 for KZZZ-FM. By this measure the newspaper and advertising agency are about equally labor intensive and the radio station is much less so.

The second measure is payroll as a percent of operating expenses. *The New Gazette*'s payroll is 54 percent of operating expenses compared to only 44 percent for KZZZ-FM and 65 percent for the Williams Agency. By this measure the newspaper is midway between the ad agency, which is highly labor intensive, and the radio station, which is moderately labor intensive.

Finally, the newspaper would in all likelihood be even higher on the labor intensity measures if it had to pay metropolitan wages to its staff as do KZZZ-FM and Williams.

Whatever measure is used, however, it is clear that both the ad agency and the newspaper are more labor intensive than radio. That is expected because key personnel for the agency and newspaper spend all their time gathering information and developing messages. In contrast, radio programming personnel pick and choose from records and news gathered by others, as most radio stations do not have their own newsgathering staffs. The packaging of information is much less people intensive than is the creation of messages in the form of news stories and advertisements. Nevertheless, radio is far more labor intensive than most nonmanufacturing companies because the packaging of news and entertainment information itself takes considerable time.

Implications for Media Managers

1. A key asset of every media company is its customers, both members of the audience and, where appropriate, advertisers. The firm's ability to gain audience attention is what makes newspapers, magazines, and broadcast stations attractive to advertisers. Given the increasing competition for audiences, a key issue facing executives of these firms is how to protect their existing audience base and add to it. A related question concerns the firm's advertiser base: how can they maintain current customers and win new ones?

   Answers to both these questions have implications for media executives' product, promotion, and distribution strategies. Only when successful strategies are developed can an information organization maintain profitability and protect its franchise in the market.
2. Another key asset of media firms is the skill and experience of its employees. As we just noted, media firms are labor intensive due to the time it takes to develop a new product with every production cycle. Employing a staff of increasingly professional knowledge workers creates a challenge for media executives. Part of that challenge is based on the fact that for many of these employees, their reward is intrinsic—the opportunity to exhibit their creativity and skills; those opportunities are not easy to identify or to provide consistently. Thus, an important personnel issue is how to structure the organization to nurture the abilities of creative, message-development staff while still meeting the firm's need to produce its information product on time and in a manner that is responsive to the market's needs and wants.
3. Always demanding, selling advertising is becoming increasingly competitive. All media are in fierce competition. That fact, combined with increases in professional selling efforts by other business-to-business organizations, creates a tough challenge for the sales representatives of information firms.

   In the past, many advertising sales personnel were inadequately trained. They could service accounts, but not sell or educate the accounts about the most effective way to advertise or about the benefits of using the sales representative's medium to reach a desired audience. If that pattern continues, media firms will suffer. Thus, a major issue for both sales managers and management above them is how to better prepare their sales staffs to function as knowledgeable professionals. As a first step, information companies have to provide continuous sales training. Part of that includes the development of sophisticated selling materials to support the sales staff. Too few organizations currently provide this level of support.

MAJOR DEVELOPMENT PATTERNS IN THE MEDIA

This brief review of changes in the media industries since World War II and of three specific media firms presents a picture of dynamic, fast-changing industries. Within the picture we have painted of that dynamism, five developments are of particular interest and importance for media managers.

1. Competition for both audiences and advertisers is increasing. That competition has impact on the financial performance of media companies by putting increased pressure on their profitability. Media firms must continually seek new ways to earn more money (income streams) and new ways to improve efficiency if they are to maintain high profit levels.
2. Audience fragmentation is rising. More radio stations, more magazines, and more distribution channels for video programming (cable and VCRs) result in narrower targeting of audience segments. This creates an increased emphasis on marketing; it results in more research on audience preferences and interests as well as increased effort to develop products and promotion strategies that attract specific target audiences.
3. Media firms are people-intensive businesses. They always have been, of course, because of the need to produce a new product with every production cycle. A major shift has occurred in staffing patterns, however, with a reduction in the significance of skilled workers (typesetters and printers) and an increase in the importance of professional knowledge workers and persons with computer skills. This shift creates major issues for media managers in organizing their firms and dealing with a host of related personnel issues.
4. Technology is a driving force behind changes in the media. Technological changes have created new media industries, new ways of developing and producing messages, new ways of distributing information, and new ways of promoting and selling media products. Some of the technologies require dramatic increases in a media firm's capital investments; others reduce those needs substantially. As never before, however, technology has the potential for increasing competitive advantages for media companies. At the same time, the rapid pace of technological change makes any competitive advantage only temporary. Media managers must continuously monitor and adopt new technologies to keep their firms competitive.
5. Ownership concentration in the media is increasing. This adds a new layer of management in many media firms; it reduces the independence of operating units; and it calls into question some of the basic social responsibilities of the media. Ownership concentration also creates new possibilities: improved career opportunities for employees, increased management and financial resources for individual media outlets, and the capacity to conceive and mount media on a scale that could not have been imagined a few years ago.

Taken together, all of these forces lead to a blurring of lines between traditional media. That is evident in competition among the media, audience fragmentation, and increased emphasis on marketing. All these factors focus attention on creating media products that utilize several channels to reach the same target audiences. Another facet of that blurring is the rise of knowledge workers and the increasing ease with which they move between media firms and types of media, often within the same information conglomerate. Further, technological advances have created new alternatives for distributing information in either print or electronic form. Ownership concentration has also increased the opportunity for activities that create media products involving cross-media tie-ins.

To operate effectively in such an environment, media leaders can ill afford to think of themselves as newspaper people, broadcasters, or advertisers. Instead, they must broaden their view to capitalize on the opportunities offered by the blurring of lines among the traditional media, a phenomenon we continue to explore in following chapters.

CHAPTER 3
Responsibilities of Media Companies

As leaders of businesses in a free enterprise economy, media managers are responsible to a variety of constituencies. Owners want a profit and a solid return on investment (ROI). To stay with the firm over time, quality employees require a fair wage, good fringe benefits and job security, and the opportunity to develop their individual talents.

The public also has expectations. The media are expected to play the role of the public's watchdog; that surveillance function is absolutely essential in a democratic republic like the United States. The public also expects the media to inform them about significant occurrences and trends, to interpret those happenings, and to act as a sounding board against which a broad cross section of citizens' opinions can be heard.

Gathering audiences for delivering information about various companies' products and services is another task of those media that carry advertising. Being an information bridge for commerce is a central role for many information firms in a consumer-oriented economy such as the United States. In the same vein, media that deliver entertainment and information are purveyors of the society's values and culture.

Because the media have major social and economic impacts and responsibilities, the concerns of insightful media managers extend beyond those of executives in other industries. Stated another way, as important as automobiles are to the United States, General Motors executives do not worry about their industry preserving basic freedoms or passing on the culture of the nation. On a day-to-day basis, GM managers do not have the degree of visible, interactive relationship with the public that is typical of media.

Information executives lead firms that are the primary source of information for the nation's citizens. As a result, their concerns go beyond whether their firms are profitable; they also worry about whether their organizations are doing an adequate job of providing quality messages: facts, analysis, entertainment, or advertising.

Further, the best media managers possess a sensitivity to ethical standards. They recognize that in the long run it is good business to demand the highest level of ethics from themselves and their staffs. They know that information companies gain credibility if they are trusted by the public, which enables them to better perform not only their social but also their economic roles.

THE MEDIA COMPANY'S MISSION AND GOALS

The interaction of these market, societal, and ethical forces is best observed in a media organization's mission and goals. While few media leaders actually take time to formally develop a mission for their firms, most could articulate an implicit mission if they were pressed to do so. We will go through that exercise thoroughly to give you a feel for what it involves and what it might mean to a company you could work for or someday lead.

One way to begin is to answer the straightforward question: What should be the mission of a hypothetical media company? Here are three alternative answers that could serve a real information firm:

1. The mission of a media/information organization is to constructively serve the company's stockholders, employees, and customers.
2. The mission of a media/information organization is to constructively serve the company's employees, stockholders, and customers.
3. The mission of a media/information organization is to constructively serve the company's customers, employees, and stockholders.

Because they contain the same elements, the three responses are similar. The difference in word order, however, is crucial.

Stockholders come before employees or customers in the first answer. That's a traditional approach, with the prime focus of a company's efforts on the owners' profit, return on investment, and asset appreciation.

In the second response, the employees come first. Such a response represents a shift in emphasis that took place between the 1950s and 1970s. It was then that managers recognized that if they treat their employees well, the result is a better "bottom line" (the profit or loss performance of their organization).

The third version represents today's management theory and practice. We believe the third alternative makes the most sense, for the media have little chance for success if the information they provide does not serve the needs and wants of their customers. A focus on customers as the top priority is expressed in today's business world as "the market perspective."

A word of caution: Do not interpret the market perspective too narrowly; it is not just finding out what customers want and giving it to them. The sophisticated market perspective focuses both on the long-term viability and credibility of the media and on the short-term desires of its audience and advertisers. That perspective entails developing messages that balance the desires of both constituencies with the media's responsibility to deliver information that citizens need to be well informed.

As we noted in Chapter 2, an information company's employees are its primary asset, more so than in many businesses. They form a team that is difficult to replace and vital if the firm is to provide the creative force necessary to discern, produce, and deliver the best possible information. Because of this, employees come second in the third answer.

To some it may seem odd to put the owners (stockholders) last. Yet, if the media's customers are well served and its employees are effective and enthusiastic, the company is most likely to produce solid financial results for its stockholders. It will also be a vibrant organization, well positioned for the future. On the other hand, if the audience or advertisers are unhappy or if employees are disgruntled, there is little chance that the owners will see a solid return on investment (ROI) or strong profits over the long term.

Translating the Mission into Goals

Having established a hypothetical media company's mission, how would a media manager work out the firm's goals? Because we are not doing this exercise for a particular medium or market we cannot be specific, but the process should begin with a list of likely goals, such as to:

- protect the company's franchise;
- produce a quality product or service;
- position the organization to prosper in the future;
- increase and/or maintain profits;
- know and serve its market;
- attract, train, challenge, promote, and keep the best possible employees.

What do you think is the most appropriate order for these items?

Following the same reasoning as for the mission statement, we believe the priority ranking that makes the most sense for an information company is the listing in Exhibit 3.1.

Why should a media firm make its mission and goals explicit? So that managers and employees will not simply react to events, but, using the goals and the plans that are constructed to implement them, will be able to make things happen. For most missions and goals to be reached, the staff must be proactive. That will occur only if employees understand what top management wants done. To develop such an understanding, the staff—both line workers and middle managers—must be

EXHIBIT 3.1. PRIORITIZED GOALS FOR AN INFORMATION COMPANY

1. Know and serve its market.
2. Produce a quality product and/or service.
3. Attract, train, challenge, promote, and keep the best possible employees.
4. Increase and/or maintain profits.
5. Position the organization to prosper in the future.
6. Protect the company's franchise.

aware of the firm's written mission as well as prioritized goals and plans to implement that mission. With such understanding there will be no confusion when competing demands arise, as they always do.

As we discuss in detail in Chapter 5, this process of developing explicit goals and plans and then setting priorities among them is one of every media manager's prime tasks. At either the top management or departmental level it establishes a sense of direction; it helps both managers and employees focus their attention and energy; it charts the course for the future.

MANAGEMENT'S DECISIONS: THE KEY FACTOR IN IMPLEMENTING GOALS

The mission and goals of a media company are implemented primarily by the decisions that media leaders make. In order for you to understand how this happens, we will describe how a group of real American daily newspaper executives shaped the direction of their companies in the 1960s and 1970s. At that time they faced enormous changes in technology and sharply increased competition.

The technological changes included (1) the shift to offset printing and (2) the increased utilization of computers in the composition (typesetting) process.

The cumulative effect of these two changes was enormous, especially during the latter 1970s and early 1980s. A Constant Dollar Study done of a cross section of U.S. daily newspapers by B.W. Wright and John M. Lavine (1982) found the following about a typical 20,000-circulation daily newspaper from 1959 to 1980. There was a reduction in payroll in the mechanical department of over 50 percent. Also, the number of mechanical department employees decreased from 41 to 24.5 and their salaries decreased by 17.6 percent, partly because of the reduced skill levels required to operate the newer equipment.

Each of the percentages are based on constant dollars. That means that the financial results from 1959 through 1980 were deflated by the government's Cost of Living Index back to 1959 dollars. Insofar as possible, that technique removes the impact of inflation, enabling us to see what the newspaper's management did, not what happened because inflation drove up revenues, prices, or expenses. Inflation is, after all, beyond the control of any media executive.

Technological changes at the prototypical 20,000-circulation newspaper produced a savings of some $400,000 per year. However, to achieve those savings, approximately one-half of the $400,000 was invested in the new technology. That meant that approximately $200,000 was left for management to count as profit or to use for other purposes.

Translating Goals into Decisions

To further your understanding of the impact of management decisions on a media company's goals, plans, and directions, put yourself in the place of the publisher of the hypothetical newspaper we have been discussing. What would you do as publisher if you had an additional $200,000 for the year? The principal options you have are listed below. Let's look at each option in more detail.

1. You could increase your news/editorial staff. That would enable you to produce more news and a larger and probably better news/editorial product. In turn, that expanded and higher quality product might make it possible to charge a higher price and/or attract more readers, which would offset some of the money you spent on product improvement. If you achieved either major increases in subscribers or advertisers, then, because of your paper's increased circulation base, you would add extra income to the paper's revenues.
2. You could increase your advertising staff. Having more sales people to contact potential advertisers might result in more advertising, thereby increasing ad revenue. Of course not every extra dollar would be profit, as the additional staff, labor, and newsprint devoted to additional advertising would have to be paid for.
3. You could increase your employees' wages, either across the board or on a merit basis.
4. You could invest in new technology to further increase productivity.
5. You could increase your marketing effort to strengthen the newspaper's circulation and/or advertising base. For example, you might expand into new regions to enhance total circulation or you could strive to increase household penetration in the upper-income neighborhoods, both of which would help your advertisers.
6. You might develop a total market coverage (TMC) product to diminish or stave off competition from shoppers and direct mail. Or you might develop a nonduplicating coverage (NDC) product to go to every nonsubscriber's home. Either would not only defend against shopper competition, but could be a boon to your advertisers and, in turn, increase what they're spending with the newspaper.
7. You could put the money into the paper's savings or pocket it as a salary

increase for yourself, or you could pay a dividend to the stockholders of the company.

The option or combination of options you select is a classic and very important management decision. Each choice has implications for the goals of the newspaper. To get a better feel for the impact of such decisions and the power of goals, let's carry your new-found role as publisher a step further and assume that your firm's goals are the ones discussed earlier and shown again in Exhibit 3.2.

How would such prioritization affect what you decide for the newspaper? Look at the goals; they have substantial impact on what you can do with the money.

For instance, consider option 1—to increase the news/editorial staff with the hope of producing more and better news. It highlights the first two goals, serving the newspaper's readers and improving the product.

Option 2: increasing the advertising staff to increase sales stresses the goal of making a bigger profit.

Option 3: increasing employees' wages emphasizes the goal of creating a more attractive work environment for your employees.

Option 4: investing in new technology could have implications for all of the goals, though most directly for increasing profits.

Option 5: increasing the marketing efforts to strengthen circulation and advertising might boost short-term profits via more circulation and advertising revenue. It would also position the newspaper to prosper in the future.

Option 6: developing a TMC or NDC highlights the goal of protecting the newspaper's franchise and it might mean more profits.

Option 7: pocketing the money or paying increased dividends to the stockholders responds to the end of serving yourself and/or the shareholders.

Any decision will directly or indirectly affect several of the firm's goals. More important for this discussion is that when you, as the newspaper's leader, make a choice about how to deploy the firm's resources, you either advance or thwart the goals of the organization. That is why it is particularly important to set goals thoughtfully. If goals are

---

EXHIBIT 3.2. PRIORITIZED GOALS FOR A DAILY NEWSPAPER

1. Know and serve your market.
2. Produce a quality product.
3. Attract, train, challenge, promote, and keep the best possible employees.
4. Increase and/or maintain profits.
5. Position your organization to prosper in the future.
6. Protect your company's franchise.

---

in place they will provide direction for the decisions of management and staff. If they are absent the odds are high that the actions taken will support a scattered set of objectives, ones that are reactive instead of proactive.

Decisions of U.S. Newspapers in the 1970s

What decisions were in fact made by the typical, 20,000-circulation U.S. daily newspaper during the 1970s? Different papers, of course, handled these issues differently, but looking at data from the Constant Dollar Study, the following pattern emerges:

The first option—increasing the news/editorial staff—was chosen. The news/editorial staff increased about 40 percent from 17 to 24. The news "hole," the percentage of space devoted to news as opposed to advertising, was also enlarged by 47.6 percent over the 21-year period.

Acting on the second option the typical 20,000-circulation newspaper enlarged its advertising staff by 50 percent, from approximately 12 to 18 people. In turn there was a 35.8 percent increase in the number of advertising pages.

In line with the third option—and expressed in constant dollars—salaries of news/editorial staff rose 14.2 percent; advertising salaries remained unchanged; and salaries of less skilled workers (primarily mechanical, circulation, and distribution staff) fell between 16 percent and 20 percent. The overall result was a decrease in salaries of approximately 12.5 percent from 1959 to 1980. Payroll as a percentage of revenue decreased from 48.2 percent to 36.9 percent, which meant that newspapers became less labor intensive.

Individual newspapers, and to some degree the industry as a whole, also acted on the other options:

- Increased marketing efforts strengthened circulation and improved advertising sales.
- Development of total market coverage or nonduplicating products staved off or met competition from shoppers and direct mail services. They also gave newspapers new ways to compete with broadcasting's claim that radio and television reach more of the market than does print. With that as a base, those new products also increased advertising revenues.
- A number of media companies increased salaries to managers and owners, as well as paying larger dividends to their stockholders.
- Increasing investment in new technology led to the introduction of microcomputers. That reduced the price of so-called front-end (single purpose) typesetting systems. Reporters and editors write and edit on computers that capture their keystrokes as they type, thereby saving the cost of having a printer rekeystroke the same words. The low cost of these systems puts them within reach of the smallest newspaper.

The money saved by investing in this new technology also dramatically reduced mechanical department expenses, from $200,000 in 1959 to a high of nearly $230,000 in 1971 to less than $150,000 in 1980. Since that savings represents a significant percentage of the constant dollar total revenue of $1.15 million for the typical 20,000-circulation newspaper in 1980, one might expect a similar increase in the paper's profits; a profit margin in 1980 of 18 percent compared to 13 percent profit in 1959. In fact, however, profit margins (operating profit as a percent of total revenue) moved from 13 percent in 1959 to a high of 16.6 percent in 1978, and fell to 13.9 percent in 1980. (Note: The actual revenue of a 20,000-circulation daily in 1980 is not $1.15 million. Rather, $1.15 million represents the revenue of that size newspaper deflated to 1959 dollars. The real revenue was nearly $4 million.)

Can you guess why this happened?

The Impact of External Factors on Management Decisions

It was partly the result of management decisions; the rest was caused by outside price increases that the media managers could not control and by changes in competition. That is, there were sharp increases in the cost per ton of newsprint in the 1970s. For the 20,000-circulation paper, in constant dollar terms, newsprint cost per ton fell from the late 1950s until 1973. After that it rose sharply and then leveled into a gentle decline in the 1980s. In 1959, 13.3 percent of each revenue dollar was spent on newsprint by the 20,000-circulation newspaper. By 1971 that figure had declined to 11.1 percent, but by 1980 it had increased to 14.5 percent.

Additionally, circulation and distribution costs increased 66 percent during these 21 years, reflecting major increases in fuel prices, increased wages of truckers, and steep hikes in postal rates.

If the newspaper's management had acted differently, it is possible that those rising outside costs could have been offset by more aggressive increases in what the newspaper charged for advertising and subscriptions. Both increased, but not enough to keep up with the rise in outside costs or inflation. For example, although the number of advertising pages rose by 32.9 percent during the 21 years from 1959 to 1980, advertising revenue rose only 14.3 percent. Thus, in constant dollars, the average page of advertising brought in less revenue in 1980 than it did 21 years earlier.

Why was this? Why didn't managers increase advertising rates enough to stay ahead of inflation or to offset steep hikes in what it cost them to buy newsprint and deliver their papers to their customers? The reason is that the competitive environment changed substantially during the period.

In 1980, there was far more competition for advertisers than in the 1960s or 1970s. There were more free distribution advertising sheets (shoppers), more radio stations, and a greater utilization of direct mail marketing to reach specifically targeted audiences. With all of those new or more aggressive competitors, prudent newspaper publishers did not automatically pass inflationary increases on to their advertisers. Instead, after assessing the competition they decided to price their advertising rates very carefully. On a strategic basis some went up a little, others remained the same, a few were reduced. This conservative approach, which also resulted from a downturn in the economy during the 1978–1980 period, saw profits fall from 16.6 percent in 1978 to 13.9 percent in 1980.

Overall, there was a decade-long decrease in the real cost of buying newspaper space, leading to a decline in advertising revenue. This occurred because of the management decisions made to meet the competitive environment. Those decisions had formidable impact; if advertising rates kept up with inflation, profit margins would have been 19 percent for the typical 20,000-circulation newspaper in 1982 instead of 13.6 percent.

An increase in the size of news/editorial staffs led to substantial increases in the space devoted to news and, presumably, more complete coverage of the communities that U.S. daily newspapers served. Did those changes translate into increased circulation revenues? No, they did not. In part, at least, that was the result of a management decision not to increase the price of subscriptions in line with inflation.

Why was such a decision made? There is a host of possible explanations, but an important one is that a smaller proportion of people were reading daily newspapers in the latter part of the 21 years from 1959 to 1980; the penetration rate of newspapers declined. Because one of the reasons people have for canceling their subscription is an increase in the price of the product, newspapers were careful to determine both how much to raise prices and when to put a rate increase into effect. In the 1970s, circulation was responsive to price. That was in direct contrast to the 1960s, when real circulation revenue increased 11 percent above inflation.

As we noted at the outset of this discussion, the point in describing what happened to the typical 20,000-circulation daily newspaper in the 1960s and 1970s is that pricing decisions are management decisions. They are choices made by media executives in response to a competitive environment that includes both competition for advertising dollars and competition for the attention of the reading public. To a large extent, competitive forces are beyond the media manager's control, but they must be considered when decisions are made. And when information organization managers do decide to lead their organizations in one direction or another, those choices have a major impact on everyone who works for them. They also affect the quality of their products, their revenues and expenses, and whether their company becomes stronger or more vulnerable.

Management decisions implement the goals of the organization. The responsibility of media executives is to formulate and clearly articulate those goals, as well as to communicate them widely so that decisions throughout the firm are guided by them. Developing goals and plans that undergird day-to-day decisions is one of the prime challenges confronting effective media leaders.

PART TWO

The Functions of Media Managers

CHAPTER 4

What Do Managers Do?

The question of what media managers do has two answers. The first focuses on the functions these executives perform. The second examines the activities they manage. Both of these areas of responsibility are examined in this text.

The functions are discussed here. We divide them into planning, organizing, financial management, and working with people. The activities an information executive manages are dealt with in Part Three, Chapters 11 through 15. They are marketing, promoting, producing, and distributing the messages that media companies create.

MAJOR APPROACHES TO MANAGERIAL FUNCTIONS

During the past 125 years, a number of theories about the functions of business and industrial management were developed. A brief review of the professional and academic literature reveals that it is easy for media managers to adapt and apply those theories to information organizations.

As we review the history of management theory, you will see how its prime thinkers tried to answer key questions about managerial functions. Questions such as:

- How should planning be conducted to better prepare companies for the future?
- What should be done to motivate employees and improve their performance?
- How should work be organized and structured to increase effectiveness and efficiency?
- What should be done to effectively manage company finances?

These inquiries were raised as manufacturing underwent a revolution in the latter part of the nineteenth century. Prior to that time, most production was done by small firms and was based on the notion of a craft guild or family performing the work. In that earlier era, workers were skilled craftsmen who produced a limited quantity of products such as jewelry and furniture. The print media was organized on a similar basis. Skilled printers set words into type and produced only a few copies of pamphlets, magazines, and books. Because the printing process was slow, it wasn't until the industrial and technological advances of the late nineteenth and the twentieth century that true "mass media" came into existence.

Today such mass media are commonplace, and the skill and time required to actually produce a printed message has dramatically declined. Yet, in some comparative configurations, the craft nature of the media continues. For instance, trade unions in major metropolitan daily newspapers are organized on a craft basis, with eight or more unions at some papers. They include traditional associations such as The Newspaper Guild, the International Typographical Union, the Graphic Communications International Union, as well as some relative newcomers, such as the Teamsters, the International Association of Machinists and Aerospace Workers, the International Brotherhood of Electrical Workers, and the Office and Professional Employees International Union.

Newspapers are not the only media that have unions. A major player in broadcasting is the Communications Workers of America, and the unions of Hollywood also are involved.

Another vestige of the craft organization of print media also exists in a few weekly newspapers. Some of them are still published by people who began as skilled printers or pressmen. Usually they started their careers as commercial printers who got into the business of publishing a weekly newspaper not as a journalistic endeavor, but as a way to utilize their idle composition and press capacity. Thus, it is appropriate to characterize these people as craft printers who publish a newspaper, instead of the other way around. For them the newspaper is only a part of their overall printing enterprise.

It is true that many younger weekly publishers do some commercial printing to supplement the revenues of their newspaper; however, they should not be confused with the craft printers. The difference is that most of this new generation of publishers do not own their own presses; their products are printed in a central printing plant. They are also not highly skilled compositors; they set type with user-friendly computers. For them the priorities are reversed. They are journalists first and printers second.

Classical Management Theories

Systematic research and theorizing about management began in the late nineteenth century, when the Industrial Revolution made possible the mass reproduction of products as well as the advent of the mass media. With mass production a new challenge arose for the owners of information firms: how could they more effectively organize their work to ensure quality and increase efficiency?

It was in response to challenges of just that type that classical management theory came into being. In this chapter we detail not only classical management theory, but others that followed it. Then we show how each theory applies to the media and to the functions of a media manager.

One of the earliest students of these problems was Charles Babbage, a professor of mathematics, who studied the efficiency of workers even before the Industrial Revolution (1792–1871). He analyzed each task performed in a factory, trying to isolate the various skills involved as well as the time it took to perform each function. From his analysis grew the principle of the division of labor. That is, Babbage suggested that each task be broken down into its simplest segments and that workers be taught just a few skills, ones that were easily learned and done on a repetitive basis. Those simplified jobs could then be organized in sequential fashion, the precursor of the Industrial Revolution's assembly line.

The idea of the division of labor saved money in several ways. It reduced the amount of worker training required. That meant lower pay, because less skill was required for each task. Further, since employees needed only a limited set of skills, their bosses could expect increased worker accountability.

Babbage's work was extended by Frederick W. Taylor (1911) in the United States. He was the father of "scientific management," the result of his careful, systematic study of production in steel mills. Taylor analyzed each job and designed the quickest and best methods for its performance. Then he established performance quotas for each worker's function based on his time studies and the equipment and materials available.

Taylor's analysis also led to the introduction of incentive pay. At first this was controversial. Workers were afraid to increase their productivity because they feared if they finished early, they would receive less compensation. Taylor met this fear with a differential pay scale, rewarding those employees who produced the most. He argued that such a system was scientifically justified because it was best for the company and for the worker.

The primary contribution of Babbage, Taylor, and their successors, Henry Gantt, and the husband-wife team of Frank and Lillian Gilbreth, was to create awareness that the tools and physical movements involved in a task could be made more efficient and rational. Also, the time and motion studies of these early management experts focused on improving work design and encouraging executives to seek the best way to get a job done. They also stressed identifying workers' abilities and rewarding them with money for improved productivity.

Just as the scientific management theorists' ideas advanced management's thinking, it also had some shortcomings. A major deficiency of these approaches was its too simplistic view of employees' motivations. The scientific management advocates relied too heavily on an "economic man" view, i.e., that people were motivated primarily by a desire for material gain.

Henri Fayol built upon scientific management by developing what he called classical organization theory. Where others focused on work to be performed, Fayol focused on the broader arrangement of people in the organization. He developed a comprehensive approach to many aspects of organizing, and his thoughts are noteworthy because he was the first to carefully articulate the primary functions of a manager.

Fayol defined managing in terms of five functions, ones that are quite similar to the classification we utilize for media managers. His were planning, organizing, commanding, coordinating, and controlling.

Fayol also listed 14 principles of management, shown in Exhibit 4.1. He chose the term "principle" to emphasize that "there is nothing rigid or absolute in administrative affairs; it is all a question of proportion. Seldom do we have to apply the same principle twice in identical conditions; allowance must be made for different and changing circumstances, for men just as different and changing, and for many other variable elements" (1949, p.19).

Classical management theory made two major contributions. It emphasized the importance of careful analysis of work and workflow, which resulted in developing many principles related to the management functions that relate to organizing (the topic of Chapter 6). It also emphasized that management is a series of functions that can be identified and learned by managers. That led to the development of management training in universities, companies, and industry training centers.

EXHIBIT 4.1. HENRI FAYOL'S 14 PRINCIPLES OF MANAGEMENT

1. division of labor
2. authority
3. discipline
4. unity of command
5. unity of direction
6. subordination of individual interest to the common good
7. remuneration
8. centralization
9. hierarchy
10. order
11. equity
12. stability of staff
13. initiative
14. esprit de corps

Despite the very personal style of the early media managers and their resistance to "professional management," executives slowly came to dividing media jobs into their basic functions: an assembly-line format for printing of newspapers and magazines, and later for production of broadcasting. They also added incentive pay for some employees. All these moves followed classical management theory quite closely. Classical management theory is outlined in Exhibit 4.2.

Some owners of print shops of the craft era did time and motion studies, then offered their employees incentive pay tied to the number of lines of type they produced. Eventually this incentive was refined and linked to the setting of correct, error-free, lines of type. The pay for sales people was also redefined to include a commission for each sale. Thus, even in the turn-of-the-century media, the initially controversial incentive pay concept of Frederick Taylor came to differentiate some of the best workers from the average.

Media owners also picked up Gantt's incentive pay for supervisors. If

---

EXHIBIT 4.2. CLASSICAL MANAGEMENT THEORY APPROACHES

Summary	Classical management theory had two primary thrusts: scientific management focused on employees within organizations and on ways to improve their productivity.
People	Noted pioneers of scientific management included Charles Babbage, Frederick Taylor, Frank and Lillian Gilbreth, and Henry Gantt. Classical organization theory focused on the total organization and on ways to make it more efficient and effective. Prominent classical organization theorists were Henri Fayol, Chester Barnard, and Mary Parker Follett.
Period of major interest	1895–mid-1930s; renewed interest in recent years as a means of cutting costs, increasing productivity, and other efficiencies.
Contributions	Laid the foundation for later developments in management theory. Identified management processes, functions, and skills that are still recognized as key today. Focused attention on organizing as key managerial function.
Limits	More appropriate for stable and simple organizations than for today's dynamic and complex organizations. Often prescribed universal procedures that are not really appropriate in some settings. Although a few writers were concerned with the human element, many viewed employees as tools rather than resources.

a shop foreman's team produced a specified amount of work on time, the supervisor received a bonus.

While movement in this direction was irrefutable, it was and remains problematic. We say that because establishing a media firm's departments to correspond to functional tasks created barriers between departments. That was somewhat of a barrier at the turn of the century, but today such divisions may be even more counterproductive, as the lines between the traditional media blur because of advances in technology, markets, and people's needs for information.

Behavioral Management Theories

Other management experts also affected the thinking of media managers. For instance, Mary Parker Follett (1918) and Chester I. Barnard (1938) built upon the work of the classical theorists and their work served as a bridge to current behavioral management theories. Both of them rejected the "economic man" view that was held by the classical theorists. Instead, they advanced a more sophisticated perspective of human psychology.

Barnard saw people coming together to achieve things they could not do alone. He postulated that as employees work for a common goal, they must satisfy their own needs. In turn, the wise company tries to meet its staffs' individual goals as well as the firm's. To that end, Barnard suggested that if meeting individual employee goals means limiting some of the company goals, to do so was best for the firm in terms of long-range worker productivity and stability.

Follett emphasized the significance of the group versus the individual, asserting that workers could develop fully in an organization only as members of a group. She argued that management and labor share a common purpose, but they can achieve it only by removing artificial distinctions between supervisors and subordinates. Follett believed leadership should be based not on the power of formal authority, as was traditional in classical theory, but on a manager's greater knowledge and expertise. For her, organization power was earned rather than assigned. This is a theme that was to become prominent in much current management theorizing.

The behavioral school is most closely associated with Hugo Munsterberg (1930) and Elton Mayo (1953). With backgrounds in psychology and sociology, they emphasized the social nature of man. This view asserts that people are motivated by social needs and desires that are rewarded by their relationships on the job. Munsterberg and Mayo saw employees as more responsive to work group pressures than to management control.

Mayo's research led to a phenomenon that has come to be known as the Hawthorne effect because of experiments he conducted at the

Hawthorne plant of Western Electric from 1927 to 1932. In those explorations, Mayo changed a number of features of the work setting, including changes that should have had negative impact. For example, he reduced the illumination in the workroom so employees had difficulty seeing what they were doing. Yet, their performance improved.

After introducing a series of positive and negative changes, Mayo and his colleagues realized that what remained constant with the experimental groups was the special attention that was paid to the workers in the groups. That increased attention is what caused their productivity to rise despite the negative conditions that were imposed on them in terms of pay, physical setting, or lengthy hours. From this experimentation Mayo proposed the Hawthorne Effect Principle; it is that paying special attention to individuals frequently causes them to increase their efforts and productivity even if that attention worsens working conditions.

The major advance of the behavioral theorists was to highlight the complexity of human psychology. They proved that the simplistic, economic-man notion was inadequate as an explanation of what motivates employees. Instead, a more sophisticated conception was needed, one that emphasized workers as social beings. The behavioral school theorists also suggested principles that would enable managers to integrate the theorists' ideas. In particular, the management experts highlighted the importance of executives' style; that led to a revolution in management training by emphasizing people-management skills, not expertise on getting things mechanically done.

See Exhibit 4.3 for an overview of the contributions of the behavioral theorists.

The shift from classical management thinking to that of the behaviorists is also clearly illustrated by the way it played out in the media. Managers who followed classical thinking saw their staffs as responding primarily to money; they paid little heed to job satisfaction. In the media, that led newspaper managers to provide few rewards other than occasional incentive pay, and that was given only to sales people and the best typesetters. People in news departments received lower base pay and, usually, no incentives. In fact, as a rationalization of this inequitable treatment, the classically oriented newspaper managers told themselves that news reporters so enjoyed the glory of their work that they wanted no incentives and were happy with wages that were far below those of other skilled workers employed by the newspaper. Finally, faced with the rise of behaviorist thinking from craft unions that were made up of better-educated print and broadcast employees, the more progressive media managers moved somewhat away from their outdated views and turned to the more sophisticated managerial approaches of today.

EXHIBIT 4.3. BEHAVIORAL MANAGEMENT THEORY

Summary	Behavioral management theory focuses on employee behavior in an organizational context. Stimulated by the birth of industrial psychology, the human relations movement supplanted scientific management as the dominant approach to management in the 1930s and 1940s.
People	Prominent contributors to this movement were Hugo Munsterberg, Elton Mayo, Abraham Maslow, and Douglas McGregor. Organizational behavior, the contemporary perspective on behavioral management theory, draws from an interdisciplinary base and recognizes the complexities of human behavior in organizational settings.
Period of major interest	Human relations enjoyed its peak of acceptance from 1931 to the late 1940s. Organizational behavior emerged in the late 1950s and is presently of great interest to researchers and managers.
Contributions	Provided important insights into motivation, group dynamics, and other interpersonal processes in organizations. Focused attention on working with people as key management function. Challenged the view that employees are tools and furthered the belief that employees are valuable resources.
Limits	The complexity of individual behavior makes prediction of that behavior difficult. Many behavioral concepts have not yet been put to use because some managers are reluctant to adopt them. Contemporary research findings by behavioral scientists are often not communicated to practicing managers in an understandable form.

With the constant prodding of their employees and the advances of new technology, these executives slowly transformed the workplace. They promoted workers based on ability rather than seniority. They began to look at how to better train their employees and how to improve work environments. They renovated the dingy, crowded, uncomfortable newsrooms and production areas that existed from 1900 to 1950 into the well-lit, air-conditioned, carpeted workplaces of today.

Another helpful impetus for these changes was brought about by the advent of new technology. Printing used to be done with letters cast in molten lead; thus, heat, soot, ink, and dirt were required to produce a magazine or newspaper. Conditions weren't much better in broadcast or movie production where short-lived, cumbersome vacuum tubes, hot lights, and huge equipment crowded in on every side. As technology became smaller, more reliable, and more humane in the 1960s and 1970s, information executives flocked to it. They did so not only to achieve productivity improvements but also because they realized the importance of improving their employees' physical and psychological well-being. They also looked sociologically at what could be done to improve worker relations, training, and interaction.

Indeed, because of the behaviorists' concentration on people and the use of psychology and sociology to explain employees' behavior, many modern media executives now put a great deal of thought and effort into their staffs and staff development. They send them to seminars, provide extensive on-the-job training, and offer feedback through job reviews and job analysis. All of these activities reflect an increasing, but compared to other industries late, concern by management for its employees.

These changes in attitude on the part of some media managers do not mean that the classical view of media workers has vanished nor that all present-day information executives balance the needs of their employees with the needs of the firm. In comparison with many U.S. industries, the media has only made a modest beginning toward development of modern personnel departments and awareness about the needs of staff members. Moreover, some of the hell-bent-for-profit firms use and discard their employees as if they were disposable parts in a throw away machine.

Still, the behavioral theories have much to offer media managers because information organizations are so people intensive and their staffs are better educated and more creative than are employees in many industries. What's more, the work of the behavioral theorists is used by the better media firms, and it forms the core of the key management function discussed in Chapter 8, Working with People.

Operations Research and Management Science

The operations research approach is the newest school of management thinking. It originated in World War II when Great Britain brought together mathematicians, physicists, and others to work on common problems in what were called operational research teams.

After the war, operational research procedures were adopted in many industries in Europe and in the United States. The core of the procedure, now called the management science approach, is to convene a mixed team of specialists to analyze a particular problem and propose a course of action. (See Exhibit 4.4.) Typically, the team constructs a mathematical model to simulate the situation. Then all the relevant factors bearing on the problem are entered into a computer and relationships among the variables are specified. By changing the values of the variables, the model can determine what the effects of each change would be if, for example, there was an increase in the cost of raw materials or a reduction in labor costs (Wagner, 1970).

Mathematical models are good for dealing with "what if" questions about concrete matters, such as capital budgeting, cash flow management, production scheduling, development of product strategies, and planning for manpower development programs. But they have not yet reached the stage where they can effectively deal with the people side of an information firm. Thus, mathematical models are of limited value to the media. That is not to say that information executives do not deal with physical problems, but the central part of their work focuses on staff who work in sales, in print or broadcast newsrooms, or at creative activities in advertising agencies, motion picture studios, or public relations firms. Management science theory makes its strongest contribution in relation to the managerial functions that deal with planning and financial management. They are addressed in Chapters 5 and 7.

EXHIBIT 4.4. MANAGEMENT SCIENCE THEORY

Summary	Management science theory focuses on applying mathematical models and processes to management situations. More specifically, it deals with the development of mathematical models to aid in decision making and problem solving. Management information systems are systems developed to provide information to managers.
Period of major interest	1940s to present
Contributions	The development of sophisticated quantitative techniques to assist in decision making. Application of models has increased understanding of complex organizational processes and situations. Focused attention on planning and financial management as key managerial functions.
Limits	Cannot fully explain or predict the behavior of people in organizations. Mathematical sophistication may come at the expense of other important skills. Models may require unrealistic or unfounded assumptions.

PRIMARY FUNCTIONS OF MANAGERS

This brief review of major approaches to management theory is the background for understanding the five major functions media managers perform. The classical approach speaks most directly to the organizing function (Chapter 6). The behaviorist approach addresses the challenges of working with people (Chapters 8 and 9). The management science approach focuses on planning and financial management (Chapters 5 and 7). In this section we discuss these managerial functions in detail. As you read the balance of Part Two, it is also important for you to bear in mind that even though we focus on each of the managerial functions separately so that you can learn about them, in an information organization they are interrelated and form the core of the media manager's role, as outlined in Exhibit 4.5.

You should also note that Chapter 5's discussion of the first managerial function, planning, is more than just a recitation of how a media executive draws up a blueprint of what a firm intends to do over time. A successful plan starts with the mission and goals of the information organization. After they are developed, media managers work out specific objectives and strategies for achieving those goals. Thus, it is one thing to set a goal of a magazine being committed to reporting "the news." It is quite another if that same magazine's editors decide to cover certain types of news. That latter goal requires detailed decisions about the priority coverage of specific subjects, as well as decisions on how the news will be reported, edited, packaged, and delivered.

Next, to have an effective plan, media managers must develop strategies for dealing with both the problems they confront and the opportunities available to them. A strategy may be broad or limited; often there are several strategies occurring at the same time. Strategies set the direction for reaching an organization's goals. After they are formulated, strategies are followed up by what we call action plans, which specify the work to be performed, who is to do it, how much it will cost, what

EXHIBIT 4.5. PRIMARY FUNCTIONS OF MANAGERS

Planning
Organizing work and technology
Financial management
Working with people
Leadership

resources are necessary, and the timetable for the completion of each activity. Developing action plans is the part of the planning process in which the managerial functions of organizing, financial management, and personnel management come into play.

That is why organizing work and technology (Chapter 6) is the second managerial function; it follows planning. Managers organize a media company's or department's work when they develop job descriptions, identify required skills, and determine the technology and resources that must be marshalled to accomplish their firm's plan.

The third function of media executives is financial management (Chapter 7). This includes analysis, budgeting, and decision making about finances. Each of these occur in conjunction with the planning process, particularly as action plans are developed. In the chapter we discuss finances from a managerial rather than an accounting or narrowly financial perspective.

Working with people (Chapter 8) is also linked to the planning process. As the most important asset of a media firm is its staff, working with people receives attention throughout this text, but Chapter 8 is devoted exclusively to it. There we focus on a variety of aspects of working with people, including supervision, motivation, recruiting, hiring, teaching, coaching, and firing. All of these are essential parts of a media manager's personnel function.

A final aspect of the media manager's role is leadership (Chapter 9). In our perspective, leadership provides a vision of where a media firm should be going and it moves the organization in that direction. Leadership is more than management; it is more than simply administering competently and efficiently. Being a media leader means making a difference, having an impact, "doing the right thing, not just doing things right" (Warren Bennis, 1984). In Chapter 9 we discuss how media managers can truly lead as they perform their other management functions.

HOW MEDIA MANAGERS SPEND THEIR TIME

Finally, as we conclude this introduction to Part Two, we devote a few paragraphs to "how" and "where" media managers spend their time. We do so to give you a broad perspective on what these executives do, before you study the details of the succeeding chapters.

Let's begin with the "where." Media managers occupy positions at various levels in their information organizations. The levels typically correspond to the scope of their responsibilities.

The responsibilities of top media executives, such as a general manager of a television station or the president of an advertising agency, relate to the organization as a whole. Middle managers are usually responsible for a department. They have such titles as editor, creative director, sales manager, production supervisor, and business manager. Many of these department head titles are presented in the organization charts you saw in Chapter 2. Lower-level managers are often called supervisors. They are responsible for specific work within a department. A sports editor, classified advertising manager, assistant producer, or office manager are examples of lower-level management positions.

Usually, middle- and lower-level managers have responsibilities only within a department or a subdivision of a department. Yet, in a few of the more unconventionally structured, flexible media firms, these people have responsibilities that cross department lines. For example, in *The New Gazette* (Chapter 2), the computer department manager is located in the production department on the organization chart, but has responsibilities for every computer in each department of the newspaper. That includes the system that serves the newsroom and production, another in the business office, and a third used in circulation.

Wherever media managers are located, they spend their time performing the functions listed above. How do they divide up that time? In one study examining time management in a number of manufacturing operations, the estimates presented in Exhibit 4.6 were made, (Mahoney, Jerdee, & Carroll, 1965). Although these figures do not correspond exactly to the functions we identify for media managers, they provide a sense of how all executives spend their time.

EXHIBIT 4.6. HOW TYPICAL MANAGERS SPEND THEIR TIME

Task	*Time (%)*
Planning	19.5
Investigating	12.6
Coordinating	15
Negotiating	6
Evaluating	12.7
Staffing	4.1
Supervising	28.4
Representing	1.8

For the media, how executive time is spent varies with the manager's position. Usually those in the lower levels of an information organization spend more time working with people, i.e., staffing, supervising, and evaluating. Managers near the top of the firm spend more time planning, coordinating, and negotiating.

The most typical figure that we've encountered for the time any media manager spends in true leadership and change is 15 to 20 percent. Even if the time spent in planning is near the top of that range, you can see that planning represents a minority, not a majority, of a media manager's time. Does that surprise you? It should, for it is at great variance with the popular stereotype that pictures executives spending most of their day in remote policy posts making decisions.

Actually, as the preceding list shows, the balance of a manager's time is divided among a host of activities. Exhibit 4.7 is a list of how managers spend their time in a group of newspapers published by one of the authors. Compare it with the generic time-distribution list in Exhibit 4.6.

The skills needed by managers at various levels correspond to the amount of time they spend on different functions (Katz, 1974). Top managers need stronger analytical abilities and people-management skills. Managers at lower levels also require people skills, but they are usually applied across a narrower spectrum of employees, say those within a department. At the same time, if they are to function effectively in their jobs, lower-level supervisors must possess more technical skills than top executives. That is true because the lower-level supervisors are more likely to be "working managers" who not only coach and teach, but still spend some of their time doing nearly the same kind of

EXHIBIT 4.7. HOW NEWSPAPER MANAGERS SPEND THEIR TIME

Task	*Time (%)*
Public relations	1.5–2
Staffing	4–4.5
Negotiating	6–7
Investigating	11–13
Evaluating	10–14
Coordinating	15–18
Planning	15–25
Supervising	20–30

work as those who work for them. At the very least, these managers will be regularly asked to answer very narrow, task-specific, technical questions by their staff. Such questions are not the day-to-day fare of executives on the top of a company.

CHAPTER 5

Planning and Decision Making

The planning process is a central function of media managers. This chapter provides an overview of that process and details its stages. Then it describes the types of decisions media executives make as they develop a plan, and illustrates the process by recounting how a plan was developed for a real, new, specialty magazine.

AN OVERVIEW OF THE PLANNING PROCESS

Why do media managers take time from an already crowded schedule to plan?

There are many answers to that question, but the fundamental one is that the planning process, and the plans it produces, are media executives' prime means to implement their vision of what the firm or department should be doing. A plan is an outline of how to move towards a media organization's goal. If it is effective, a plan provides the staff with clear information about that direction as well as specific actions that will be helpful to move toward the goal.

In its simplest form, looking at a plan is analogous to looking at a road map, first from a distance and then up close. From arm's length a map gives the "big picture" of an area. At close range, it provides a detailed view of the highways and byways one might take to move through the terrain.

Another metaphor for a plan follows.

Imagine a group of people hiking in a forest. The plan tells them the direction to travel; it makes suggestions about how to make the journey; and it includes a compass. While the group will use all those aids, their most valuable tool is still their own resourcefulness in figuring out what to do to arrive at their destination. The plan is helpful, but it is only an aide; it does not think for them.

Now reread the prior paragraph about the trip through the forest and replace the word "people" with the managers and staff of a media organization. For executives and employees in the media, the forest metaphor is similar to the one about the map, but introduces the idea of uncertainty and flexibility. Instead of being limited by the fixed schema of a chart, the forest scene envisions a journey into the unknown. The journey itself involves a series of interactive responses between the plan and the media staff's own actions and initiatives.

In a similar sense, the planning process provides direction by ensuring that employees interact through the plan with the ideas of their managers. Following it enables media staff members to better coordinate their thinking and their work. Having developed a plan also allows managers and staff to avoid making too many decisions in a crisis, for an essential part of planning includes anticipating problems and devising solutions for them before they occur.

Effective plans do not function from the top down. They should not be decrees issued by the boss. Approaches of that sort can be avoided by ensuring that the planning process involves not just executives but also employees from across the organization and, where appropriate, outside experts. Honest, open involvement of staff and knowledgeable outsiders introduces new points of view, which provides more options for planners. It also increases the likelihood that there will be understanding, if not consensus, when the plan is finally adopted.

Let us be clear about terms. The planning process is an ongoing system of interactions and decisions. The plan of a media organization is the result of that process, not the process itself.

The Planning Process

The planning process includes four steps shown in Exhibit 5.1.

Note the lines in Exhibit 5.1 from later steps back to earlier ones. They are important because what is learned at any point often provides information for modifying or even dropping earlier decisions. Thus, information gleaned during backgrounding usually leads to a revision of the initial goals. The wise media executive selects tentative goals so as to test the best ideas that are put forth first, then to have hypotheses about which goals are worth gathering background information on. The answers to those background questions, however, often cause change or elimination of some initial goals.

Mission and Goal Setting. Planning begins with establishing the media company's mission and then its goals. Without them organizations stagnate. Rather than being proactive, they react to situations; events move the media firm instead of vice versa.

EXHIBIT 5.1. MAJOR STEPS IN THE PLANNING PROCESS

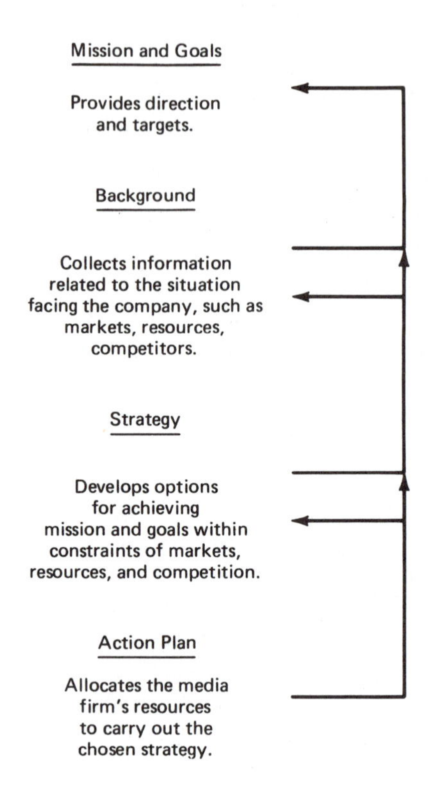

An effective way to write a mission statement was described in Chapter 3. Once such a mission has been agreed upon, the media manager can begin to outline the firm's goals. Because it is part intuitive and part rational, developing goals is time consuming and difficult; that is true at the firm or department level. Deciding on a future direction (setting goals) is, however, the first, mandatory step in the planning process.

Backgrounding. As the term implies, backgrounding entails gathering all of the information that might affect the media firm's ability to reach its goals. Done right, backgrounding is thorough and nonjudgmental. It should welcome conflicting or competing facts, trends, or ideas.

In this phase, media managers make an honest assessment of the organization's strengths and weaknesses. They do a complete analysis of their target market(s) for readers, viewers, listeners, and/or advertisers. They also carefully identify current and possible competitors and assess the strengths and weaknesses of such adversaries. In short, backgrounding entails amassing all available, relevant information.

Creating Strategies. The third step in the planning process is to develop strategies to attain the organization's goal(s). Developing them requires choosing broad means to move the firm or departments within it. Choosing strategies provides direction, but it also eliminates options. Both of these aspects of strategic decision making are important.

Having strategies to implement goals is crucial in the complex, fast-changing world of information. Strategies focus attention and help establish a coordinated, concentrated effort. They transform the desirable into the do-able.

Note that we use the plural of strategy, not the singular. That is because the planning process and running an information firm occur in real, dynamic time. No one strategy will work in every situation. The interaction within a company of employees and resources, as well as advances by competitors and technology, mandate that media workers have numerous strategies. At any given time, the staff will use the best one or combination of strategies to meet the situation.

In modern management, many executives believe that the key aspect of strategic planning is the emphasis we just gave it: flexible and dynamic to create a competitive advantage. Management experts talk about strategic planning as giving executives a sustainable advantage over the competition, as a way of increasing their firm's strengths relative to its competitors.

Developing An Action Plan. Action plans transform strategies into concrete form by:

- describing specific steps to be taken and indicating who should carry them out;
- identifying needed resources, such as people, money, information, services, time, and technology;
- clarifying the organizational structure that is necessary for effective coordination and control;
- finally, and this is too often overlooked, laying out a timetable for implementing a strategy and detailing ongoing, concrete ways to monitor progress.

Action plans also assume that circumstances will change in unforeseen ways. Hence, a key part of these plans is to encourage innovation, welcome resourcefulness, and yet keep the firm moving in an agreed-upon direction with good communication among everyone involved.

An action plan also utilizes the other major functions of media managers that are beyond planning. They are: (1) organizing work, jobs, and technology; (2) doing financial analysis, budgeting, and management; (3) recruiting, selecting, and working with staff; and (4) providing leadership.

Now, with this overview of the process in mind, we will detail each phase of planning using illustrations from a variety of real-life media situations. Throughout the discussion we will focus on the planning process itself, rather than on what a specific plan looks like for a specific media company or department. That's because the process applies to all media, all levels of the company, and all areas of management. Using the planning process, media managers can set missions and goals, background, choose strategies, and develop action plans to suit their needs and desires. That is what planning is all about.

MISSION AND GOAL SETTING

When executives talk about the mission and goals of a media company, they refer to different though related things.

Where do missions and goals come from? They do not magically appear from the ether. They are based on knowledge of what the market(s) want and need and on an analysis of the strengths of the information organization. In varying ways, both the mission and goals of a company determine the business(es) it will be in and the direction(s) it will follow.

To determine the appropriate course, media leaders should review all that they know or can discover about their industry and related ones. They should look for trends that are developing, markets to be served, and strengths of their organization and its competitors.

Yet, even when the results of that review are in hand, an executive is not able to add it up and find a sum that equals the firm's ideal goal. Beyond all the background information, mission and goals are best formulated when media executives add their best judgment about the information they have gathered and the hunches, based on experience, that they have developed in the process of determining what is happening. And even then the establishment of a mission, and particularly goals, should be tentative. They should not be fixed; both should be subjected to further review after the backgrounding and subsequent processes are complete.

Thus, the answer to where the initial goals and mission ultimately come from is that they are the judgment of top management. They are a risk, an educated guess about the right direction. We call that type of decision the *management factor*. Beyond all of the facts, trends, and analyses, the management factor is that final, essential judgment that is at the heart of any leader's decisions about what the organization should be doing and where it should be headed.

A Mission Statement

What is a mission statement? It is a statement of the organization's broad purpose. Mission statements are often semi-philosophical; they provide an overall vision for the firm. As is true of all such pronouncements, the mission statement should be periodically reviewed—though the intervening time for such review should be relatively long, between five and ten years. Despite that lengthy timeline, mission statements are not trivial. They are important because they provide a broad vision of the company's purpose. For example, contrast the alternatives statements considered by a media firm we worked with:

We are a newspaper company.	— or —	We are an information company.

The strategies and actions implied by each statement are very different. Under the one on the left, the organization sees itself as only putting out newspapers. Such a mission requires that the firm concentrate on improving the way it develops, produces, and distributes newspapers, but nothing else. In the right-hand statement the company broadens its focus to consider other sorts of information and other ways of delivering it. The firm could operate under that mission even if the company added other media businesses to its prime business, newspapers.

An alternative pair of contrasting mission statements about news coverage might be:

We cover the news that is important for our readers to know.	— or —	We cover the news that we can afford to cover.

The strategies and actions that flow from those statements are poles apart. The high-quality news product put out under the mission on the left would differ substantially from the limited product implicit under the one on the right. There would also be a significant difference between the organization of the staff of a company that followed the left-hand approach from one that adopted the one of the right. It is also likely that there would be equally large differences in the financial profiles of the newspaper that followed the left-hand statement from the one that adopted the one on the right.

Goals

Goals follow from a company's mission; they come after a fundamental statement of how the company sees itself. With its mission established, goals provide broad direction for fulfilling the mission.

Goals flow from three perspectives: (1) the wants of the top authority in the company: a CEO, board of directors, the owner, or a combination of those leaders; (2) the needs and wants of the customers; (3) a penetrating assessment of the strengths and weaknesses of the firm. In actual fact, goals are seldom chosen from only one perspective. Ideally they combine the best elements from each perspective. For our part, we believe media are best served if their goals are primarily based on the needs and wants of their customers, but with a healthy, hard look at ways to build on the firm's strengths. (This is a viewpoint we noted in Part One of this text. We will return to it at the beginning of Part Three when we discuss the market perspective.) Finally, goals should be reviewed by top managers with an eye to adding to them their own judgment (the management factor) to fine tune the organization's direction.

We put considerable emphasis on building on strengths, especially the talents of the firm's staff, because those strong points are a unique resource. Other firms can purchase new technology or prepackaged materials, but only the leaders of a media company possess the blend of talents in their staff. Those strengths allow the leaders to mobilize the staff to move in a new direction. If the executives' movements are wise and strategic, they will provide the organization or department with an advantage for a time. Eventually, competitors will figure out the direction of movement and the strengths; then they regroup to catch up. But by the time that happens, the media managers will be busy building up new strengths and forging ahead in another direction for another advantage.

Long-term Goals. Goals can be divided into two groups; long term and short term. Long-term goals usually cover a three- to five-year period. Given that comparatively lengthy time span, they are often stated in qualitative rather than quantitative terms. As a result, long-term goals have an intentional degree of vagueness. That is necessary if they are to be flexible enough to allow for the unexpected.

Short-term Goals. Short-term goals are for one year. They are far more specific and rigorous and are most often stated in quantifiable, measurable terms. To avoid confusion between long- and short-term goals, we will talk about the short-term ones as a media organization's objectives.

While short-term objectives should be as concrete as possible, media managers must see them for what they are: essential ingredients in a dynamic planning process. Objectives can play such a pivotal role if they build on a firm's strengths and if they are seen as dynamic, able to be changed as circumstances require. (If objectives are altered, however, the modifications must fit with the mission and long-term goals of the firm.)

Multiple Levels of Goals. The mission and goals of a media company actually exist at several levels, as shown in Exhibit 5.2.

Note that the goals of the company are forged with input from members of the staff. Company goals follow from the firm's mission statement, then they are translated into departmental and subdepartmental objectives by the staff.

Typically, specific objectives are established by middle managers and/or supervisors with a report back to the department head. That approach pushes formulation of concrete plans as close to where the action takes place as possible. In progressive firms that use a management-by-objectives (MBO) system, individual objectives often reflect departmental and firm goals as well as employee's personal aspirations and needs.

An example of the goals of a media company is shown in Exhibit 5.3. There the mission, company goals, departmental goals, and specific objectives are listed for two departments in a newspaper—news/editorial and promotion/circulation. Note how the goals become more specific and concrete further down the chart. From one level to the next they build upon and relate to each other.

In addition to departmental goals that link with the firm's, managers often develop separate goals for their departments. For instance, the news department often establishes goals based on the editor's and staff's analyses of their individual or group strengths, weaknesses, and oppor-

EXHIBIT 5.2. LEVELS OF GOALS IN MEDIA COMPANIES

Level of Goals	Ultimate Responsibility
Company Mission	Owner/CEO/top management
Company Goals	CEO and top management (but with input from a wide cross section of staff and experts)
Department Goals	Department heads (again with input from a cross section of departmental staff and, perhaps, experts)
Specific Departmental Objectives	Middle department managers (and selected staff at each level below the manager)

EXHIBIT 5.3. GOALS FOR A DAILY NEWSPAPER IN A CITY OF 350,000

Mission

Responsibly cover the news that the community wants and needs to know. (There is more to this mission, but this is the heart of the section that deals with news.)

Company Goals

1. News: Improve breadth of news report
2. News: Improve coverage of business
3. News: Strengthen minority group coverage
4. Circulation: Increase household penetration in low income and minority neighborhoods

Department Goals

News/editorial

1. Add coverage of small business
2. Improve coverage of businesses's dealings with government: cooperative linkages, conflicts, regulation
3. Develop regular reporting on the three most important minority groups in city and cover their political, economic, cultural involvements

Promotion/circulation

1. Recruit minority personnel for promotion/circulation
2. Develop inner-city distribution system
3. Launch an inner-city promotion

Specific Departmental Objectives

News/editorial

1. Create small-business beat
2. Develop business/government reporting teams
3. Hire minority reporters and establish three minority beats

Promotion/circulation

1. Hire four minority circulation supervisors
2. Recruit adult inner-city carriers and set up special incentive system for new routes there
3. Develop billboards and direct mail for a promotion

tunities. The editor, or even some individual reporters, might identify a writing problem, such as reporters turning out lengthy, ponderous leads for their stories. Improvement in this area could become a departmental or small-group objective.

In smaller media organizations, the process of setting goals is often more informal, though it contains the same elements. Most small information firms do not have an explicit mission statement, although the owner or top manager may possess a quite well-defined mental notion of the substance of such a statement. Even if a written mission does not exist, many smaller information companies develop company and/or departmental goals. And even if they are not written, the manager's implicit day-to-day reference to them may serve the same function. Of course, it is always best to have them written down, because when goals are not made explicit, the chances increase that managers and employees will pull in different directions. Thus, even for small companies, explicitly identifying goals is a prudent first step in effective planning.

Goals can and should be developed for every management activity: marketing, product development, promotion, production, and distribution. They can also help focus efforts with the primary management functions: planning, organizing, financial management, personnel, and leadership. Exhibit 5.4 gives examples of typical goals for each of those activities and functions.

Two final, extremely important points should be made about the

---

EXHIBIT 5.4. DEPARTMENTAL AND FUNCTIONAL GOALS

Departmental Goals	
Marketing	Increase circulation by 5% in next year Raise minority household penetration by 15%
Product	(See News/editorial in Exhibit 5.3)
Promotion	Investigate and launch a game or contest to improve readership and circulation
Distribution	(See Promotion/circulation in Exhibit 5.3)
Production	Add first phase of improved color reproduction capacity within six months and second phase within 18 months
Functional Goals	
Planning	Bring in an expert in planning to review the procedures not in place
Organizing	Develop mechanisms for improving interdepartmental communication
Financial	Develop a midmonth financial report that gives early warning on budget versus actual operations
Personnel	Provide career development counseling for all employees Work out a plan to reduce staff turnover rates by 15%
Leadership	Send assistant managers for public speaking classes and arrange for some speeches in the community to polish the new skills

sample goals in Exhibit 5.4 and about goals and objectives in general.

First, they should be few in number and prioritized. If an organization has too many goals, it will squander its energy. In such a case, goals only confuse; rather than pull everyone in the same direction, a helter-skelter effort will ensue. To provide clear focus and direction, managers and employees should consider only a few goals. And even among those few, everyone must know which ones are most important. Setting priorities ensures that a staff does understand, without having to ask, which goal or objective to select when they have limited time or resources.

Second, managers should set goals and objectives that are realistic. Raising expectations beyond that which can ever be attained guarantees failure. For example, in Exhibit 5.3 and Exhibit 5.4 there are two major goals for the promotion department: (1) develop billboards and a promotion for the inner-city; (2) launch a game or contest to improve circulation and readership. Both can be accomplished, but probably not at the same time. Priorities must be established; otherwise, the promotion department may try to do both projects at the same time and end up doing neither successfully.

BACKGROUNDING

Backgrounding develops information that bears on the organization's goals. The specific questions media managers ask depend on the types of goals that are at issue. Let's look at two examples that require very different kinds of information.

A Product Change

Linda Remy is the general manager of radio station KZZZ-FM. Her goal is to increase her station's market share and, as a consequence, its profit margin. Remy believes that KZZZ-FM's current format places a substantial limitation both on its share of the total audience and advertising revenues.

What kinds of information should she collect to provide a solid background for deciding on a new format? To begin with, she would want to know about the audience, advertisers, competitors, organization, and broader environment. To that end, she might ask:

Audience.

- Who are KZZZ-FM's current listeners?
- What are their demographic characteristics: their age, sex, income, education levels?
- How frequently do they listen to the station?

- How frequently do they listen to the competition?
- When do they listen?
- What are they looking for when they listen?

Advertisers.

- What kind of products are they advertising?
- What audiences are they seeking?
- What objectives do they have in using radio?
- What kinds of budgets do these companies have for advertising?
- Where else do they place their advertising dollars?

Competitors. Besides looking at her current customers (both listeners and advertisers) Remy is interested in developing information about the market as a whole and, specifically, about KZZZ-FM's competitors. To get that information, she wants to know:

- Who are the primary competitors for the audience segment the station has targeted?
- What is their market share compared to KZZZ's?
- Which competitors have increased their market share and which have lost it?
- What are the reasons for this movement?
- What is the advertiser profile for our competitors?
- Are they competing directly with this station for advertisers or are they appealing to different advertisers?

Organizational Information. Another set of information the station manager seeks includes organizational and technological data on KZZZ-FM and its competitors:

- What are the comparative technological advantages of different stations in the market?
- What are the primary strengths and weaknesses of KZZZ's staff and the staff of competitors?
- What are different stations' financial capabilities for making changes that require substantial input of capital for purchasing new technology or for carrying out a major promotional campaign?

Information about the Environment. Remy also seeks information about the broader environment in which she is operating:

- In this market, are retail sales growing at a fast pace, a relatively slow pace, or are they declining?
- Have advertisers changed the ways in which they spend their media budgets? What is the impact of new media vehicles, such as shoppers or cable systems, on advertising expenditures?

- What are some of the consequences of the major shift in listeners from AM to FM radio stations? How is this affecting our market?
- What does the deregulatory climate now confronting broadcasters mean for this station? What opportunities does deregulation present? What problems will it create?
- With the increased conglomeration of broadcast ownership, what changes occurred or are likely to occur in our market in terms of new, larger information competitors buying into the scene?
- How about changes in the interest rate structure linked to trends in the national economy? Will they increase or decrease our ability to finance changes that we might wish to make?

To answer these latter questions, Remy needs a very broad information search that relies heavily on information sources and experts outside KZZZ-FM.

A Departmental Reorganization

The preceding illustrates the type of information that an information executive would seek if the goal were to change a radio station's format. Linda Remy would want a quite different sort of information if she discovered that KZZZ-FM's lackluster performance was due not to the format but to poor performance in the advertising sales department. If the station is to achieve its goal of improving profits, the advertising department must improve.

In that instance, what kinds of knowledge does Remy need to modify that department in order to increase its effectiveness? Answering the following will give the station manager the information she needs to begin wrestling with that problem:

- In the advertising department, what specific tasks are being done well, poorly, or not at all?
- How effective is the coordination between the sales and the support staff? What are the barriers to adequate coordination?
- Would it be useful to redefine, add, eliminate, or consolidate any jobs in sales?
- Would it be helpful to change the station's or department's supervision structure?
- Is it necessary to change or promote any of the personnel? Should new people be hired? Should some staff members be reassigned to capitalize on their strengths and motivations?
- What can be done to improve the staff's capabilities to perform effectively? Is increased training needed? How strong is morale? What is the department's allegiance to their manager?

In this example, manager Remy would conduct a narrower information search, with much of the information she needs coming from sources inside the station.

Information Sources for Backgrounding

The preceding should provide you with a feel for the kinds of questions a radio station manager might ask when confronted with the need for a new format or to shore up poor financial or advertising performance. One approach called for going to primarily external sources for data; the other used internal facts and feelings. In both, the basic principle is to use a variety of sources to collect as much diverse, pertinent information as possible, bearing in mind the limitations of time, energy, and expense.

Customer, market, and financial information is based on data gathered by the station manager. She used internal sales figures and listener surveys. She also used external sources, such as Arbitron Ratings, to get a better handle on who listens to KZZZ-FM and its competitors.

Information about broader industry trends and performance came from external sources: trade publications, government documents, and news stories. (See Exhibit 5.5.) It also came from experts, e.g., lawyers specializing in deregulation, experts on technology, and consultants on marketing and sales.

Beyond the input from focus groups and ratings, judgments about strengths and weaknesses of the station's product and promotion were made by Remy. Collecting that sort of information involved a series of discussions with her management team and a cross section of the staff who were selected for their insightful and independent thinking. While Remy usually lead those discussions, there were times when she used a management consultant or facilitator to help in gathering and analyzing what is going on among the staff.

EXHIBIT 5.5. INFORMATION SOURCES FOR BACKGROUNDING

External
- Trade publications
- Government documents and records
- News stories
- Data services (Simmons Market Research Bureau, Mediamark, Nielsen, Arbitron, etc.)
- Experts and consultants
- Media managers in noncompetitive markets

Internal
- Company operational records (sales, expenses, personnel, production, etc.)
- Research conducted by media company
- Department managers
- Staff members

However such data gathering is organized, it is crucial that the staff be encouraged and reinforced with the notion that putting forth constructive criticism is seen by Remy as particularly desirable. That is the only way that non-managerial staff—who, after all, are closest to the day-to-day operations of the station—will really share what is happening and what might be improved.

Media managers should not assume that they are the fountain of all wisdom. For example, judgments on how well a new radio format might work and on problems associated with implementing it should include reactions by the staff as well as queries to other stations who are already using the format. As long as they are not competitors, the managers of other operations are likely to be willing to provide a blunt evaluation about the pitfalls and strengths of the format.

During the backgrounding process, managers often identify examples of possible strategies for achieving the station's goal. These might include:

- better ways to do what KZZZ-FM is now doing;
- new or expanded products that could be developed;
- new market segments or ways of defining potential customers;
- better or new approaches to marketing and selling;
- better or new approaches to distribution;
- better or new approaches to structuring the organization to more effectively manage the people in it;
- better or new approaches to financing.

Note that in the preceding list we use the phrase "better or new. . . ." That is because it is important to emphasize that not all planning changes should be seen as throwing out the old and starting over again. The best starting point is usually to focus on present strengths or activities since everyone is familiar with them and can more quickly see where they can be improved. When that route has been exhausted, then one might look for large changes. In the meantime, short-term, incremental change is easier to achieve than dramatic, totally new breakthroughs.

Moreover, incremental changes that build on a firm's peculiar strengths are, at least for a time, more difficult for a competitor to emulate because the competitor does not have the same strengths. Thus, the opponent not only has to figure out what Remy's station is doing that is new, but even after that is done the competitor would then have to gear up and acquire the strengths the Remy already has. Doing that is far slower for a competitor than if Remy had purchased a dramatic, new, fully computerized format. For if KZZZ-FM can purchase a new sound from a syndicate, chances are that her competitors can go out and buy a similar package. On the other hand, if Remy builds her version of a new format based on the personalities that are already on her staff and known to the listeners, then her opponents will take longer to develop a similar package. For her competitors will not only have to figure out what the new format is but they will have to wait months until, if they are lucky, their staffs build up credibility with the audience that is akin to what KZZZ-FM's staff already possess.

The "big fix" can be a seductive road, but for the reasons just noted it is also a hard one to drive. In some instances it can be fatal, because finding a dramatic new solution may be impossible, whereas bringing about more modest incremental change is almost always possible.

One other suggestion about backgrounding may be useful. In a number of areas of media management, models have been developed to help describe how things work. For example, there are models that depict how readers actually use a newspaper, what they read, and what impact it has on their decision to subscribe. Other models describe marketing and distribution frameworks to reach different market segments. Models of that sort can help in formulating questions that are prudent to ask when backgrounding. They are particularly helpful when a media leader must collect new, unfamiliar information.

CREATING A STRATEGY

Strategy is a very "in" term in management circles. The professional and academic management literature emphasizes "strategic thinking" as the key to American companies' response to each other and to foreign competitors. Indeed, one of the more popular treatments of this subject is *The Mind of the Strategist* by Kenichi Ohmae.

But what is a strategy? What are its key elements? As we reviewed the literature and talked with media managers, we found a number of different meanings of the word:

1. "A strategy is really no more than a plan of action for maximizing one's strengths against the forces at work in the business environment" (Kenichi Ohmae, 1983, p. 248).
2. "Strategy is the broad program for achieving an organization's objectives and thus implementing its mission" (James A.F. Stoner, 1982, p. 101).
3. "A strategy is a statement of an organization's investment priorities, the management thrust, and the ways it will use its strengths and correct its limitations to pursue the opportunities and avoid the threats facing it" (William E. Rothschild, 1976, p.10).

Thus, a strategy is a broad program, a statement of priorities, a plan of action.

Levels of Strategies

Media strategies come in various shapes and sizes. Bigger ones apply to media firms as a whole. Others are smaller, perhaps covering only how departments or individuals should carry out their work. In some management writings you will find the term *strategy* contrasted with *tactics*. The former refers to a broad set of actions; the latter to specific ones. For our part, we find it more descriptive to avoid talking about tactics. Instead, when strategies are actualized we refer to them as the fourth step in the planning process—the action plan.

Big Strategies. Under the leadership of its chairman, Allen Neuharth, the Gannett Company set as one of its goals in the early 1980s the development and sale of a national newspaper, *USA Today*. Once that goal was established, Gannett executives did an extraordinary quantity of background research and data collection to test the idea.

USA Today initially appeared as the entire strategy involved with developing a national information product to sell to advertisers who wanted to reach a national audience. In reality, as this text is being written, the new newspaper appears to be only a significant part of an even larger Gannett plan aimed at building a multimedia, combined national advertising "buy." Beyond the newspaper, the other pieces of that plan include the purchase of the nationwide Sunday newspaper insert, *Family Weekly* (renamed *USA Week-End*); the development of a color network of newspapers, including all of Gannett's and others that meet the information giant's standards for color reproduction; Gannett Outdoor, the largest billboard advertising company in North America; Gannett's broadcast properties; and the development of a sales organization to sell this national package.

Even as the larger strategy was being tried in the mid-1980s, many analysts concentrated only on the "wisdom" or "folly" of Gannett launching a national newspaper. Although interesting, that discussion missed much of what was happening. For beyond *USA Today*, Neuharth and his team were making a series of moves to position Gannett to present national advertisers with the "opportunity" to put their message not just before *USA Today* readers, but to deliver it to any American who came in contact with any of the parts of Gannett's multimedia offering.

In short, with strategic acquisitions and the *USA Today* launch, Neuharth developed a broad strategy for growth. All of the purchases, including the company's purchase of larger newspapers, such as those in Des Moines, Detroit, and Louisville, were components (substrategies) that fit together to achieve the broader one. Whether such a package will work is unknown at this time.

Similar large strategies are found in other media. A number of television stations, for example, are moving into video production, which used to be the domain of advertising agencies and movie production houses. The broadcasters produce commercials and documentaries for use by merchants and others not on their stations, but in stand-alone settings.

Also motion picture studios are spending billions purchasing theaters. Until recently, such moves were prohibited by the courts as violating antitrust laws, but the advent of other outlets for movies, such as cable and video stores, has removed antitrust concerns.

In the meantime, press lord Rupert Murdoch was willing to sell many of his U.S. newspapers so as to buy big television stations and a major Hollywood studio. He wants to create a new television network.

Advertising agencies played their role in this scene. Not only did the middle 1980s see mergers of big agencies into giant ones, but many of them started their own public relations firms, just as some of the big P.R. organizations purchased or began their own advertising agencies.

Little Strategies. Let us return to Gannett and *USA Today* for an example of a "little" strategy: pricing. When the newspaper was introduced, its newsstand price was 25 cents a copy. Gannett increased that to 50 cents per copy about a year after introduction, but when the company began to push carrier service, it offered subscribers a substantial discount to have the paper delivered to their home. This provided an incentive for people to accept carrier delivery, since the newspaper cost less delivered than purchased from a machine on the street. In turn, carrier service helped Gannett ensure five-day-a-week service, not the less than five-day-a-week newsstand pick-up used by most of the paper's readers. This helped *USA Today's* advertising sales, as it provided greater circulation stability.

Another example of a little strategy is a decision by television stations to recycle their product. Some sell weather information to competitors, such as cable systems; others sell a rerun of their 10 o'clock news segment for later showing by those same cable companies.

Evaluating Your Strategy

Developing a strategy really means choosing from among various options. Typically, media managers have several choices available for meeting each of the company's or department's goals. How do they decide which one to choose? That is a difficult question that is best answered by posing questions such as these:

- How do they fit with the information company's mission, goals, and values?
- What are the risks?
- What are the key constraints that will affect the plan, and how well do the strategies work within the constraints?

- Is the project too big or too small for the particular information company or department?
- Does the organization have adequate resources to implement the strategies?
- Does the plan fit with the major changes occurring in the market and industry?
- Is the timing right?
- How will competitors respond to the strategies?

The last two questions are crucial, for the key aspect of choosing a strategy is to gain a competitive advantage. Too many media managers focus only on their own organizations, on their own resources, or on things they know. They do not put enough energy into thinking about their competition or the marketplace. The astute executive develops strategies to respond to opportunities occurring in a dynamic environment, but most managers ignore crucial factors that create opportunities, i.e., changes in the behavior of readers, viewers, listeners, advertisers, and competitors. Even though the cliché "timing is everything" may be an overstatement, the timing of a strategy is very important. The best plan will fail if it is too early or too late.

Think how hard it would be to launch a national business newspaper, with the *Wall Street Journal* all but owning that niche. How difficult would it be to start a newspaper or television station against the best one where you live? Even if you feel the present outlet is weak, because it is established it has a substantial advantage over any you might launch. Many people have tried to start new media firms in direct competition with existing ones. If one follows the historical path, there is a high probability of two outcomes. First, the newcomer will fail or, at least, will not unseat the incumbent. Second, even if the project dies, the challenger may serve one positive purpose; it may cause the original media to improve so as to survive.

Another way to understand the importance of this point is to bear in mind that media provide information; they report the news, entertain, or sell something. Each of those messages is extremely dependent on the public's perception of the source that delivers the message. Think about your own reaction if you were to see a movie with a particular theme. Thereafter all similar offerings, even if they are well done, would seem like copies. You would say, "Oh, I've seen one like that before."

PUTTING TOGETHER AN ACTION PLAN

An action plan translates strategy into concrete terms. It is the phase in which the planning process expands into the other major managerial functions: organizing work and technology, financial management, and hiring and working with staff, and leading them. Action plans are developed by asking and then answering:

1. Questions about organizing:
   What specific actions must be taken to implement the strategy; what tasks need to be performed; in what order; with what amount of coordination?
   How much time will each task require? How are the tasks linked together and to jobs?
   How will the jobs interface to facilitate coordination?
   Where should responsibility be lodged?
2. Questions related to financial analysis and budgeting:
   What are the dollar costs involved for the media firm's resources of people, information, services, time, technology?
   How will the project be financed; from internal sources, with outside borrowing, other?
3. Questions relating to working with people:
   Who will be assigned to different jobs? What is the fit of their strengths with the skills and talents required by the jobs?
   What training or other job preparation may be necessary?
4. Questions about leadership:
   Does the organization or department have executives with the necessary leadership depth to motivate the employees to try the plan and to see and take the risks necessary to compensate for the unexpected?
   Given the strengths of the staff, what is the best role for the manager to play? Is it time to be a play maker or a coach on the sidelines? What is the best metaphor to motivate and teach the staff what is expected?

Example of an Action Plan

Think back to the radio station reorganization. Suppose Linda Remy discovered that her sales staff spends 25 percent of its time on paperwork. After a careful review, she concludes that the paperwork is useful, but secretaries could do half of it.

Remy also learns that only two of the nine sales people have had sales training and that it consisted of only brief, one-on-one coaching by the sales manager. As station manager, Linda decides on two strategies: (1) provide additional administrative support for the sales staff; (2) provide systematic sales training by experts in radio sales. Her action plan to carry out these strategies is shown in Exhibit 5.6.

Looking at the exhibit just cited, we see that effective implementation of a media manager's strategies requires staff commitment, energy, time, and often financial resources. This suggests consideration of another important set of issues:

- What are the key steps in preparing groundwork in a media organization for change?
- Who needs to be sold on the strategy and plan?

EXHIBIT 5.6. ACTION PLAN TO IMPLEMENT STRATEGIES WITHIN A RADIO STATION'S ADVERTISING DEPARTMENT

What	*Who*	*When*	*Resources*
Hire two people to support sales staff	Sales manager	Within 30 days	$30,000 salary $ 2,000 equipment
Conduct in-house sales training	Consultant	Within 30 days	$ 2,000 salary $ 1,000 for workshop arrangements, materials
Add half-hour sales training to bi-weekly sales meeting	Sales manager	Immediately after workshop	None

- What kinds of information and what types of input does the staff need to become committed to the action plan?
- What kind of start-up supports, such as material and people's time, are required?
- What initial results are needed to move the project along in the organization?

In summary, developing an action plan to carry out a media organization's strategy involves two distinct steps. The first is outlining the strategy and developing estimates of the resources and people required to execute it. The second entails preparing a concrete action plan for moving the strategy from the idea stage to implementation. Both are necessary because plans never sell themselves; the persistence, support, and hard work of media leaders at all levels of the firm is what sells them. Without a major commitment by a determined executive, a plan seldom gains the necessary organizational support, development, or power required to make it a reality. Further, providing staff members with a clear idea of the direction (goals and strategies) the company is following and giving them a rough outline (action plan) of how to get there are both crucial ingredients in winning staff support.

PRINCIPLES AND TIPS FOR PLANNING

Planning is hard work. This section discusses some key principles and tips to follow for improving the chances that the planning process will be effective. Exhibit 5.7 summarizes key points.

EXHIBIT 5.7. PRINCIPLES AND TIPS FOR PLANNING

Planning is a continuous, dynamic process.

Build on strengths.

Develop plans in small, manageable steps.

Establish benchmarks to evaluate progress.

Create "what-if" scenarios to deal with anticipated problems.

Involve staff in planning to increase commitment.

Do plans before the budgets to avoid being driven by financial considerations.

Both rational and intuitive decision making occurs in planning.

Planning Is Dynamic

To appreciate those principles and tips, step back in your thinking for a moment. Until now, planning has been described as if it were a neat, sequential, always successful process. That description was necessary to explain the planning process, but a description of that sort does not reflect reality. Even if media managers follow the outline of this chapter to the letter, their efforts will not run in such a smooth, step-by-step fashion; they never do.

For instance, once established, goals represent an ideal. In most cases the information discovered during backgrounding necessitates a modification of the original goals. (Recall that Exhibit 5.1 showed that each step of the planning process may be modified by later information.) Thus, when she gathers background information, Linda Remy might discover that another station is about to announce that it has hired the son of the owner of the town's largest department store to sell for it. That store is KZZZ-FM's biggest advertiser, and it will pull all its ads off Remy's station in two months, when its contract with KZZZ-FM runs out. If Remy's goal of doubling retail revenues during the next year included the advertising of the big department store, then the revelation would force her to modify her goal, lower her target or, perhaps, change the entire focus of her plan.

Things like that often happen. When media managers gather background information they often learn that strategic options that appeared promising are useless because others have adopted them already (the timing is off). Another possibility could be that in a call to a station in another part of the country, Remy finds that the seemingly strong new format she was going to adopt did not work as well as predicted.

Even if strategies do initially appear viable, when action plans are developed, unexpected problems with the strategies may surface. In turn, these road blocks may require a significant overhaul of the plan. For example, what if changing the format of Linda's station turns out to be impossible not because the new one is weak, but because the source of the programming has an exclusive contract with a competitor in the market?

Planning is a dynamic process in areas other than backgrounding. As actual implementation of the plan begins, some parts will unexpectedly fail while others may work better than expected. When that happens, facile executives swiftly review and modify the plan; they do not wait for the beginning of the next planning cycle to make adjustments. We've encountered too many media organizations in which local managers say annual planning cycles cannot be changed in midstream because "our firm does not do planning at this time of year. . . ."

Such an attitude demonstrates a near fatal flaw in a media leader as well as a gross misunderstanding of the role of the process. If it is to fulfill its potential, the planning process must be ongoing, not static. Even though plans contain a great wealth of specific information about what will be done, by whom, and when, the media manager should recognize when circumstances change, as they always do, then the action plan, the strategy, and even the goals may need to be modified. The smart executive thinks of planning as an open-ended, continuous, dynamic process. It should not be scrapped just because one thing goes awry, but it also must never be viewed as a set of rigid rules that cannot be changed.

Build on Strengths

An important guiding principle in developing a plan is to build upon the strengths of the firm, department, and staff rather than on their shortcomings. That is not to say that media managers should ignore weaknesses, but, rather, that most progress comes from utilizing strengths and skills.

As an example, an advertising agency we know was viewed by other agencies and clients as a terrific planning organization. The agency, which we will give the pseudonym of Mischa Advertising (MA) built on its clients' marketing efforts and it effectively transformed them into solid advertising campaigns. As strong as Mischa was in planning, however, its creative execution was average or even below average. These two aspects of the agency's reputation resulted in three years of lackluster growth.

Recognizing the problem, Mischa's managers tried to promote growth through emphasizing what they felt the market wanted: a strong creative effort. Luck was on their side, or so it seemed, for several of the agency's next campaigns included powerful ads that worked. While the agency was not quite sure what made those campaigns successful, Mischa Advertising executives developed a promotional campaign emphasizing their firm's creative abilities. The campaign also worked, though in the long run it was unfortunate that it did because MA had not really developed a staff capable of offering a strong creative product on a consistent basis.

The promotion campaign brought in business, and Mischa signed several new clients who switched their advertising because of the creative promise. Initially there was exhilaration at MA, but in less than two years those clients were gone and they took others with them by badmouthing MA's veracity. Only the clients who appreciated Mischa's excellent planning remained.

In retrospect, Mischa Advertising's top management realized they made a serious mistake by not building upon their strength in planning and then using it to attract new clients until MA's creative department was up to delivering on the promise of consistent creativity.

Develop a Plan in Small Increments

Whenever possible, a plan should include an opportunity to test new ideas in small, manageable increments. Although that may be difficult in some instances; for example, when deciding whether to change the format of a radio station, a test of a less than all-encompassing magnitude can provide assurance that the plan seems prudent before significant amounts of resources are committed to it.

Media executives can test a plan in many ways. For instance, a newspaper or magazine could produce a prototype and measure audience reactions to it. In 1985 and 1986 Time Incorporated did this in a formidable way. It spent more than $15 million testing various versions of *Picture Week* in select U.S. markets. Then, late in 1986, when most of the wrinkles appeared to be ironed out of the proposed national picture weekly, the nation's largest media company announced that it was dropping the idea. Executives at Time Incorporated said that their extensive testing proved that launching the magazine on a national basis would cost $100 million and that the new product would not succeed. Certainly, $15 million is a lot to lose on a magazine that will never be, but it is far less than the $100 million a less cautious company might have spent if they had skipped the test market inquiries and begun with a national launch.

Proposed television series are often produced on the basis of a few episodes or pilot shows. Then they are aired for a focus group. If the reaction is favorable, the shows may be further tested by being aired to a nationwide audience before the network commits to a full 26-week series.

Of course, advertising campaigns are routinely tested on focus groups and in limited, trial markets. So are movies, stage plays, as well as small runs of books.

Benchmarks and What If's

Plans should almost always contain benchmarks, agreed-upon points at which progress will be concretely assessed. Establishing benchmarks before an action plan begins helps the media manager decide what should be measured and what results are expected. Failure to meet benchmarks provides choice points for going to a back-up plan, changing course, or dropping the idea entirely. Thus, if Linda Remy's KZZZ-FM changed its format and conducted a major promotional campaign to introduce the new sound, the next ratings period would provide an opportunity to determine the station's short-term success. Although the four months between ratings are usually not sufficient to reach a final judgment, ratings are an important, objective test. With the results from that third of a year, Remy and her colleagues could determine whether their audience share was moving in the right direction.

Remy might even be able to specify an interim ratings target on the way to the final goal. Then, if the station did not reach the interim objective, she should study the ratings book to see what her direct and not-so-direct competitors were doing. Using several "what if" scenarios that she should have developed as part of her plan, station manager Remy could then do the following:

- If the data indicated an impact of the new format on the audience share of Remy's direct competitors, then promotional efforts within the target market should be strengthened in an attempt to continue to win away more listeners.
- If, on the other hand, data showed no effect on her prime competitors' audience share, but an impact on the audiences of her indirect competitors, then she might decide to broaden the definition of the potential audience she intended KZZZ-FM to reach. In turn, that would entail a modification of the format and a broader promotional effort to a wider segment of listeners.

In either situation, if she engaged in careful analysis in the early stages of the planning process, Remy would be able to far more effectively respond to those several anticipated, but unwanted, outcomes.

Employee Involvement

Who should be involved in the planning process? Should it be just the top management and/or department heads or should line employees be included?

Many management experts make a strong case for limiting the number. They say that if the group is too large the process will be slow to respond and cumbersome, which can be harmful because time is often of the essence in the media and clarity when dealing with an idea (a message) is vital for setting strategy.

There are other planning mavins who say that the more employees involved in developing a plan, the greater will be the staff's commitment to it. Such an approach calls for including as many workers as possible. Especially in the media, where people all across the firm have expertise and work with the messages that are developed, it is a waste of mental resources not to tap each employees' best input. Yet, unless they are asked to contribute, staff members seldom volunteer. And if they do not get involved their commitment may be lacking. That could result in a death knell for turning an idea into successful reality, which is fatal in a media firm.

As we have seen it operate in numerous media companies, the more important question is not who should be involved in the planning process, but when. That is a difficult decision because premature or excessively late involvement can be just as disfunctional as none at all. Only experience and "political savvy" will teach media executives when to bring middle managers and general staff members into planning.

One effective way that often avoids problems in this area is to choose a small task force or ad hoc committee of employees from all levels of the firm to work on a plan. That way top management receives constant input from people who are closest to the problems. Moreover, after the process is over, the task force is available to help educate others at their own levels about the plan. Further, the early presence in the planning process by staff members from every level of the firm provides other employees with the confidence that the plan is not being handed down from the top, but has been developed with "wisdom" from their peers.

There is an interesting twist in all of this. It is that just as one cross section of managers and line employees should be involved in planning, a similar group should be isolated from it. That latter group should be told that they are being kept away because they have been chosen to critique the plan. That is important because a major difficulty for most media leaders is getting good evaluations. Many employees might see criticism of the bosses' ideas as threatening. The only way to reduce the perceived risk of being a critic is if those who are being negative do so because top management asked them to perform that function. With that invitation they are protected. Indeed, in some instances it is also worthwhile to supplement this internal group of critics with external evaluators.

Do the Plan before the Budget

A plan should be developed before the company's budget process begins. Developing it then frees the thinking of media managers from prior control by their accounting or finance department. If that freedom is not built in, there is always the fear that managers will make what we call accounting, not management, decisions. Unfortunately, once the budget process begins, too many media managers become bound up in questions about last year's numbers, staffing, and limits. Starting from a vantage point that contains all of those constraints increases the probability that this year's plan will include and repeat last year's mistakes.

Of course, saying that planning should start before budgeting, does not mean that the two should remain separate. They must be integrated, but that fusion should happen only after some fresh thinking and new financial considerations.

Rational and Intuitive Decisions

Rational decision making serves planning, because its process uses factual information, analyzes those facts, weighs the pluses against the minuses, and chooses the best alternative. Much decision making in media companies is rational. However, many managerial decisions are not wholly rational, and they do not fit that neatly into a plan. They are based on facts and a media leader's experience, intuition, feelings, and emotions. Each of those latter ingredients are every bit as important to the astute executive as is rational analysis. Often, after all of the facts are gathered, sifted, and winnowed, feelings and intuition are the most appropriate final barometer for making a decision.

For instance, it would be counterproductive if the editorial page editor of a daily newspaper made his or her decisions based only on logic. The editorials of the paper would be passionless, reflecting little of the fire that only genuine emotion can elicit.

There are other good reasons why intuitive decisions are important and should be respected. Also, creative leaps are moves that bring together a wide variety of information in ways that are initially difficult to appreciate. They are vital to the media, and they are crucial for developing new strategies. The process by which these new ideas are developed is similar to the process a talented copywriter goes through in creating a new advertising strategy. The essence of that process is based on intuition.

Intuition and emotion should be respected also because much of the media's most important information is not quantifiable. It is, therefore, not susceptible to the concrete analysis that is necessary in the manipulation of numbers; that sort of rationality simply does not apply to assessing an outstanding movie, a fine book, or a great newspaper. It also does not apply to one of a media manager's more important functions, making decisions about people. There are few situations in which factual analysis will provide the best judgment about which employee is the best person for a particular job when the choice is between two of nearly equal ability and experience. And no summing up of facts is a sure predictor of how a staff will respond to an opportunity, incentive, or crisis. There simply is no set of facts that leads to the best plan or strategy.

Experience and intuition are crucial also when it comes to making decisions about values. When information executives have to deal with the values of employees, clients, or audiences, it is useless to do so only on a rational basis. We recall the following story told to us by a daily newspaper publisher:

"In the early 1960s, my composing room and press room were all male. I believed that we ought to hire more women and minorities because it was the right thing to do and because we would get better employees. My foreman disagreed. He gave me a list of 'facts' such as: men were needed because the metal fonts for the line casters were too heavy for women to lift, etc. After a number of lengthy discussions where he added to his arguments, I told him that I appreciated his arsenal of facts, but from then on the only staff he could hire were women or nonwhites.

"After the smoke caused by my declaration cleared and a couple of years passed, we had a new problem. The same foreman wouldn't hire any white males! He'd found a superior, untapped reservoir of excellent employees. He said he didn't intend to spend time on 'second-rate white males who, as a group, do not have comparable skills, willingness to work, or ability to learn as do the women and minorities who welcomed the chance to have our comparatively high paying jobs.' "

The point we are making is not that intuitive decisions are better or worse than rational ones. Of course not. It is that the most effective managerial decisions involve a combination of a media executive's rationality, intuition, emotions, and ethics. If all of these are not tapped, the decisions will be less than they could be or should be.

PLANNING IN ACTION: STARTING A MEDICAL JOURNAL

The rest of this chapter is an example of the planning process. It describes how one of the authors used planning to develop a new scientific journal for a very complex medical subspecialty, pediatric neurology.

(In this vignette, proprietary information has been protected. Despite those changes, its factual essence has been retained.)

John Lavine is the head of an information company, the primary thrust of which is the publication of daily and weekly newspapers. They account for 65 to 70 percent of the firm's revenues. Commercial printing of newspaperlike products comprises the remainder of the company's income.

When it began years ago, that "outside" printing provided a solid new revenue stream. Lavine installed the first web offset printing press in his region in the mid-1960s. Then he was able to charge a price that resulted in gross profit margins of 35 to 50 percent. Over the years, however, those margins declined to between 20 and 30 percent because of the willingness of new competitors to work for less and less.

Setting Goals for the Company

That decline in profit margin, coupled with the gypsy nature of doing work for others, led the publisher to two conclusions. First, it would be more profitable to concentrate company resources on developing the products the company owned. Second, the introduction of microcomputers heralded the beginning of a revolution: a move to personal computers and table-top publishing. That change could, however, further erode profits because those computers were increasingly user friendly and affordable. At the same time, the new technology opened a way to assist Lavine's company in its move toward the development of new publications.

As a result, the publisher decided to expand his firm's mission: the publishing or printing of newspapers owned by Lavine or others. He would develop new, wholly-owned publications that built on the strengths of his organization and that focused on bringing high-quality information to new market niches where few, if any, competitors exist. Note how Lavine sought incremental growth based on his staff's strengths to expand the mission.

Now the question was how could Lavine develop new products that would fulfill that revised mission? Historically, most media companies have answered that question by starting with a new product idea. Lavine decided, however, to approach the problem by seeking out audiences, not products. The audiences should have two characteristics: a desire for specific information to be used in their work, and the presence of advertisers who want to reach the audience. If Lavine could identify such an audience, he was confident he could put together the right product to fill the void. In short, the information company head made a fundamental shift in the starting point for growth. Instead of focusing on a product he zeroed in on the marketplace and its wants and needs.

With that mind-set sharpening his thinking, an opportunity soon presented itself. One day, literally in the course of an afternoon walk, Dr. Kenneth Swaiman, a close physician friend, told Lavine that although he had helped found the Child Neurology Society nearly a decade ago, the doctor's one sorrow was that pediatric neurologists did not have "their own refereed medical journal."

"Why don't they?" Lavine asked.

The answer was succinct. When the Child Neurology Society began, there were 50 to 100 pediatric neurologists in the United States. Now, there are more than 600 in this country and significant numbers in Europe, Japan, and elsewhere. Moreover, the total is growing.

"There is another reason we do not have our own journal," Swaiman added thoughtfully. "When we began, the Child Neurology Society was offered a share of the adult neurology society's journal. We accepted that offer, but now it's hurting us. Although the society receives 25 percent of the adult journal's profits, far less than that percentage of articles in the adult magazine are devoted to the problems of children. Moreover, the substantial revenues that the CNS used to receive from the profits of the adult journal are falling.

"All of this is taking place at a time when the number of pediatric neurologists is dramatically increasing. Further, since a high percentage of pediatric neurologists are academic doctors doing both clinical and basic research, their output of new information is formidable. Yet, its propagation is being dramatically short-changed by the small number of research articles published in the existing adult neurology journal."

During the next few months, Lavine and the physician discussed the idea of a new medical journal in earnest. Dr. Swaiman explained that he had investigated this possibility earlier, but the prices he received from printers were prohibitive. He showed his publisher friend a file of price quotes. With a practiced eye, Lavine saw that the big publishing houses who put out journals for the adult medical specialties had included in their pricing sizeable overhead costs and generous profit margins. If he could figure out a way to dramatically reduce those prices, Lavine could get into a new business that fit the goals that he had established from his expanded mission statement:

- produce your own product;
- use the skills of your newspaper colleagues and much of the newspaper's infrastructure;
- test the new technology of microcomputer table-top publishing to determine if that form of publishing could be beneficial to the rest of your company's efforts or to building a specialty journal publishing company;
- find a market niche to fill with a high-quality product and advertisers who want to reach the people in that niche.

Backgrounding

The next step was straightforward. Lavine developed the necessary background information and did a market analysis. His questions came rapid fire:

1. Who is the audience?

   Dr. Swaiman provided the answer: pediatric neurologists, neurologists who take care of both adults and children, developmental pediatricians, neurosurgeons, some family practice doctors, and neuropsychologists.
2. Are there advertisers who want to reach this audience?

   Again the answer was positive. A number of drugs are specially directed towards children with neurologic difficulties. Also, a few companies make equipment for these doctors, and several publishers print journals and books that deal with child neurology.

3. What about the potential size of the markets?

   The potential number of subscribers is limited. Therefore, until advertisers realize that they are getting their message delivered to precisely the audience they want, it is unlikely that advertisers will spend as much for a small-circulation pediatric neurology journal as they regularly spend for a large-circulation adult neurology journal insertion. Further, Lavine can expect fewer potential advertisers than in the adult publications because only a subset of all neurology drugs are appropriate for children. The two men conclude that this means a new journal must plan to receive most of its revenue from subscribers.

4. Geographically, demographically, and economically, what are the key characteristics of the subscribers?

   Although Dr. Swaiman knows the number of child neurologists across the globe, he suggests the only ones they count on to subscribe to the journal are U.S. pediatric neurologists and a subset of those in Japan and Europe. Of course, some other specialists in America will also subscribe, as will a significant percentage of the overseas pediatric neurologists, but Lavine believes it is best to plan for the minimal response as a standard against which to test whether the journal concept is a viable venture.

Armed with this initial information, Lavine and Dr. Swaiman gathered other market data. They determined how frequently potential advertisers run their current ads in adult journals and how much they pay for these ads. They also studied the adult journals' circulation patterns in terms of types of subscriber, and amount paid for different classes of subscription. Then the two conducted separate interviews with a sample of pediatric neurologists to further test the need for such a journal.

In short, they did everything that was possible and economic to learn about the key characteristics of the audience and advertising markets, both as a whole and segmented. They laid out the audience and advertisers demographically and added information they unearthed about the independent, commission-paid advertising representatives who specialize in calling on the agency people who represent drug companies. They learned what these representatives do, how much they charge, and what results they can expect. This was necessary because one small journal could not afford to build and pay an advertising staff of its own and because there was not enough work for a full-time staff.

Throughout Lavine's search, the characteristics he paid the most attention to were the benefits sought by the audience. He and Dr. Swaiman concentrated on what the audience market wanted and needed to know. That inquiry was significantly aided by an extensive set of focus group interviews both the physician and the publisher held with pediatric neurologists.

Exhibit 5.8 lists the considerations dealt with in the backgrounding process for a new publication.

One other interesting piece of information emerged during back-

EXHIBIT 5.8. KEY BACKGROUND INFORMATION FOR NEW MEDICAL JOURNAL

Audience: primary	Pediatric neurologists (600 in U.S. and other sizeable groups in Europe and Japan)
Audience: secondary	Neurologists who treat adults Developmental pediatricians Neurosurgeons Neuropsychologists
Advertisers	Drug companies that manufacture relevant drugs Certain equipment manufacturers Publishers
Other possible income streams	Author page fees Reprint sales
Competitors	No direct competitors; adult neurology journals are indirect competitors

grounding. As Lavine looked at other journals to gauge the competition in the marketplace, two additional income possibilities became apparent. In newer scientific publications it is common for authors (physicians, scientists, and other health professionals) to pay a modest amount for each page in the journal that their article uses. That fee does not buy them entry into the journal; it is charged only if their article is accepted by a panel of experts. The fee's purpose is to help the journal offset the cost of publication.

Another tradition is for authors to buy reprints of their articles from the journal to send to other scientists who inquire about the authors' research findings. The publication does not handle requests for such reprints, but it makes a modest profit on selling reprints to the authors.

Developing Your Product Strategy

With the exploration completed, it was time to develop the product strategy to fill the market niche (Exhibit 5.9). While Lavine's inclination as a newspaper publisher was to print the journal on newsprint so he could increase the use of his presses and hold costs down, the production of a prototype issue on high-grade white newsprint proved that such a move was unsound. When the prototype was shown to Dr. Swaiman and a few other physicians, they unanimously said it would kill the project because it looked "cheap" when compared to other journals that were printed on glossy paper.

EXHIBIT 5.9. KEY ELEMENTS OF PRODUCT STRATEGY

Product features
- Quarterly publication
- 64 pages per issue
- 50 pages of referred articles on pediatric neurology only
- Print on high-quality paper
- High-prestige editorial board

Strengths for implementing strategy
- Dr. Swaiman's international reputation
- Editorial expertise and skills
- No direct competitor
- Technological advantages to increase production efficiency
- Organizational capability for primary production and business function

They reasoned that physicians are a conservative group. As such, the doctors would believe that a journal that did not look high quality could not have outstanding content, even if it did. Selected advertisers who saw the prototype on newsprint expressed a similar reaction. Once again Lavine was reminded of the importance of public perception about the media.

The universal reaction left the publisher with no choice but to print the journal on glossy magazine stock. Since that is a form of printing that Lavine could not do on his newspaper presses, costs would increase. The additional expense for going to an outside printer was not that great, however, and Lavine's newspaper staff could still provide the new venture with functions ranging from typesetting through circulation and supervision of the magazine's advertising representatives. The only step the newspaper team would not provide was the actual printing; it would be contracted to an outside vendor. Thus, the new magazine appeared to be viable, even though circumstances (backgrounding and testing) produced some changes in the original concept. The magazine did not meet all of Lavine's initial goals, but it met most of them.

Next, as the publisher and Dr. Swaiman developed their strategy and then an action plan, they did a product analysis, listing their strengths and weaknesses and those of the competition. The key strengths they identified were:

- expertise and editorial skills, as well as Dr. Swaiman's international recognition in his field;
- no direct competitor in the market;
- technological advantages in understanding the emerging table-top publishing

microcomputer technology and the ways to merge it with professional typesetting;
- organizational strengths in handling circulation, production, advertising sales, and publication bookkeeping.

Based on that analysis, the two friends concluded that it was worthwhile to take the risk and go ahead with the publication of a journal that they named *Pediatric Neurology*. What they had to offer was strong. For subscribers, their journal offered more than the adult neurology journals because it would give the reader more pages of content devoted to the neurologic problems of children. *Pediatric Neurology* would be targeted only to professionals who have an interest in the field of pediatric neurology, therefore promotion would be simplified by the fact that the names of these people are readily available on the membership lists of professional organizations.

The only area that they could not settle initially was pricing, because Lavine had not precisely calculated the cost of producing a journal such as the one the partners envisioned. While he worked on that he also dealt with some other outstanding issues.

One of these was to come up with a specific product strategy. They had already chosen the market and figured out the "essence" of the product in relation to the competition. To complete that task they tried to determine how much balance they could create among the three major forces consumers respond to:

- high quality and creativity;
- excellent service;
- low price.

Lavine knew that a perfect balance of these forces is rarely achieved; one of them usually overshadows the others. But *Pediatric Neurology* might be an exception. After all, Dr. Swaiman was not only extremely skilled as an editor, but his international reputation would bring to the journal's editorial board physicians and scientists with a breadth and depth that was unparalleled. The board members would "referee" the research articles submitted to the magazine, guaranteeing high-quality information from researchers who wanted to be associated with peers of such distinction.

The journal would fulfill Lavine's goal of serving an audience in depth. He and Dr. Swaiman decided it should aim at 60 to 64 pages per issue, with about 50 of them devoted to articles about the neurologic problems of children. The balance would go to advertisers.

Thus, all that remained was the third consideration: price. Here Lavine's years in newspapering came into play. Beyond being an early user of offset printing, he had pioneered a way to make a microcomputer communicate over a phone line with his firm's typesetting mainframe computer. (Remember this was in the early 1980s, before table-top publishing and telecommunications were a viable alternative for a venture of this sort.) This meant that if Dr. Swaiman or any scientists wrote their research articles on a computer, no one would ever again have to capture those keystrokes. It also meant that all the editorial work done in Swaiman's office, which was 100 miles from Lavine's newspaper, could be captured and transmitted over phone lines. That could greatly reduce production costs. To transfer those advances to the magazine required only standardizing on what was then the most widely accepted technological base in the microcomputing world, an IBM personal computer, a word processing software called WordStar®, and telecommunications via a Hayes modem.

When the publisher did a spreadsheet analysis that utilized conservative sales and revenue figures and liberal cost projections, the total cost for production of the journal was far below any of the quotes Dr. Swaiman received from other publishing firms. This meant the partners could charge a low subscription price for *Pediatric Neurology.*

Building an Action Plan

The next step was to develop specific organizational and financial plans, as outlined in Exhibit 5.10. After conversations with their accountants, Lavine and Swaiman agreed on an appropriate structure for their new venture, one that would maximize their strengths and minimize problems. They would be partners in an independent company; that eliminated any risk for Lavine's other partners or management team at the newspaper. It also allowed Dr. Swaiman to share in the building of assets if the journal was successful. Because partnerships are delicate arrangements among business colleagues—and they are even more delicate among close friends like Lavine and Swaiman—the two worked out not only the duties of each partner but also a buy/sell agreement in case one of them wanted to leave or became disgruntled with the performance of the other.

They also outlined jobs that needed to be filled and identified who on their respective staffs could help with the project. And they described the types of people they might need to hire and what functions would be contracted out to others (printing and advertising sales).

A careful review of the market data and pricing of the *Pediatric Neurology* competition convinced Lavine that the initial subscription price should be 55 to 60 percent of the price of the adult neurology journals. That should keep it low enough to attract readers and, if it went well, they could always raise the percentage after a strong base was established. The pricing strategy was adopted to provide quick penetration of the market; in such an approach it is important that price not be a barrier.

EXHIBIT 5.10. KEY FEATURES OF THE ACTION PLAN

Organizational features:

Lavine–Swaiman partnership for new journal

Internal functions
- Editorial management
- Preparation of journal for printing
- Promotion
- Circulation
- Financial management

External services utilized
- Editorial review
- Printing
- Advertising sales

Pricing	subscription priced at 55–60% of adult neurology journal (indirect competitor)
Projections	conservative sales figures (e.g., 500 after first year; 1,000 after third year; 2,000 after five years); modest author and reprint sales; no ad sales (average expense figures)
Promotional strategy	early direct-mail call for articles combined with solicitation of subscriptions; this created "escape hatch" if circulation projections were highly inaccurate

The partners further projected a conservative economic picture by figuring on revenue from only 500 subscribers in the first year, 1,000 at the end of the third year, and 2,000 in five years. Further, while they knew they would have some advertising, their revenue projections contained income only from circulation, reprints, and page charges to authors. All net advertising income, which is total advertising revenue minus agency and sales representatives' commissions, was treated as extra, unanticipated income.

Expense projections included costs for telephones, typesetting, printing, promotion via direct mail, postage for mailing the journal to subscribers, and salaries.

When he ran the expenses against the revenues Lavine determined the project would come close to breaking even if the journal met its projections. If they received any appreciable advertising or a larger than anticipated circulation response, there would be positive cash flow. However, a first-year operating profit was unlikely, since the start-up costs for incorporation and buying computers would more than offset any profit.

Two other points should be made. One is that while the case described in the preceding actually happened, it is not typical. Seldom are media products launched with a very small investment and the likelihood of a rapid turnaround. In fact, the medical journal partners thought they would have to put some money into the venture so they secured a $25,000 line of credit at a local bank. Fortunately they did not have to use it, although each partner did put in $5,000 for working capital.

Further, since both men were fully employed, neither of them had to earn a salary from *Pediatric Neurology*. Thus, the small "black ink" operating profit that the journal actually achieved was misleading. If the partners had been paid for their time, the journal would have incurred substantial losses, which is typical of start-up ventures.

For their part, Lavine and Dr. Swaiman thought that if they could make the publication operational with a minimal investment and if it at least had a positive cash flow by the end of the first year, *Pediatric Neurology* should be considered a success because it proved the merit of the concept.

Last, but equally important, as part of their action plan the partners devised an escape hatch to protect against disaster. They began soliciting subscriptions for the journal in April, with the first copy scheduled to go to subscribers the following January. (That much lead time was required if articles were to be subjected to a referee and revision process.) The call for scientific papers to be published in *Pediatric Neurology* included the initial solicitation of subscriptions. Because it went out so far in advance of publication, Lavine and Dr. Swaiman realized that by autumn they would know by the response to the subscription announcement if the journal was a success. In actual fact, when August arrived they already had 550 paid subscribers. The new medical journal was a success four months before the first issue rolled off the press.

Postscript: Two years after *Pediatric Neurology*'s first issue and as this text was being finished, the journal was still strong. However, two other journals had been launched against it. Although their copying of Lavine and Dr. Swaiman's publication represents some verification of the partners' wisdom in seeing an information market that needed and wanted information, the small niche that the journal fills cannot profitably maintain three competitors. *Pediatric Neurology* has two advantages in the market, however; it was the first publication, and it has by far the more distinguished editorial board and quality of editorial content, as well as number of paid subscribers. Whether that is enough to ensure survival and prosperity is uncertain, however, though the partners remain optimistic.

CHAPTER 6

Organizing Media Companies

One of a media manager's principal functions is to organize the firm's staff. That means establishing a structure in which employees in different positions can most effectively do their own work and coordinate their activities with others.

The basic concepts underlying organizational structure are division of labor and job specialization. As we noted in Part One, every medium has to gather information and then create, produce, promote, and distribute its messages. In a one-person advertising or public relations agency, the owner performs all these tasks. As the organization grows, a division of labor occurs; when that happens, organizing begins with an analysis of the workflow.

ORGANIZING WORKFLOW TO ESTABLISH STRUCTURE

The Sequence of Organizing

Five major steps occur in setting up an organizational structure in a media company:

- identifying the tasks to be performed;
- arranging the tasks in sequential order;
- assigning the tasks to positions (jobs);
- determining how to coordinate and control the flow of work;
- putting all the parts together in an overall structure.

The first three items describe decisions that are usually made by managers of departments involved with the specific activities of a media company, activities such as production, marketing, distribution, and promotion. The fourth requires input from department heads working with top management. The final item is the responsibility of the company's leaders.

To illustrate how this process works, we will follow it through the news department of a newspaper.

Identify Tasks to Perform. What are the various tasks that need to be performed in gathering information and developing messages for the newspaper? Exhibit 6.1 sets out some, though by no means all, of the duties:

Arrange Tasks in Workflow Sequence. Most of the tasks identified in Exhibit 6.2 fall into three major clusters: gathering information, writing the story, and editing the story. That sequence is usual for a newspaper.

Note that within each of the groupings we listed tasks in the order in which they are most often performed as information is gathered, stories are written, and copy editing is completed. (Some of the tasks in the longer list in Exhibit 6.1 are not included in Exhibit 6.2, but are included later in this analysis.)

Assign Tasks to Jobs. The three clusters could be used to describe three specific jobs: information gatherer, writer, copy editor. In the past, many stories, especially for the larger daily newspapers, developed in just that sequence. The information gatherers (reporters) out in the field collected the facts and phoned them into the paper's office, where a writer actually wrote the story and passed it on to a copy editor.

EXHIBIT 6.1. TASKS IN A NEWSPAPER NEWS DEPARTMENT

Interview people
Determine angle for stories
Read news clips and news releases
Read newspapers and books
Read others' reports, magazine articles
Write stories
Write headlines
Edit copy
Use libraries and government documents
Identify and assign future story ideas
Determine position of the story in the paper
Evaluate the quality of stories
Tighten language in copy

EXHIBIT 6.2. WORKFLOW IN CREATING NEWS STORIES

Gather Information →	Write Story →	Copy Edit Story
Read news clips, read papers and books, read news releases, read reports and magazine articles, interview sources, use libraries and government documents	Determine angle of story, write story	Edit story, tighten up language, lay out pages and write headlines

That three-step process took place when transportation was difficult and reporters worked a long way from the office. Today those three jobs often collapse into two. Reporters often gather the information and write the story. Editors then check it, tighten the language, and write a headline for it.

Whether they are national, or regional, or local newspapers, most of these publications cover a wide variety of events. To ensure that major topics of interest are reported, the newspaper's editors establish "beats" (specific subject areas which a given reporter regularly follows). Beats for a paper might include government, education, business, information processing, or lifestyles. Because many stories do not fall into these categories, however, newspapers also employ general assignment reporters who, as their title implies, report on a wide range of topics. Additionally, for reporting on major or complex events, many large papers use teams that include a number of reporters with varied expertise. On occasion a newspaper will also add outside experts to the team.

Coordination and Control of the Workflow. In the original list of tasks associated with news gathering (Exhibit 6.1), three were identified but not included in the clusters in Exhibit 6.2. They are assigning, evaluating, and positioning stories; all are considered control tasks. That is, *assigning* ensures that specific reporters cover designated stories the editors want in the week's edition. *Evaluating* protects the quality standards of the paper. *Positioning* determines on what page and in what spot a story will appear; it allows the editors to control the "play" of the story.

Because reporters are frequently away from the office collecting information and writing stories, coordination of their activities is necessary. Coordinating ensures that the staff covers events on a priority basis and without duplicating efforts, that the newspaper's resources are utilized effectively, and that the greatest depth of coverage results. In the newsroom this translates into three major jobs: editing, reporting, and copy editing. Exhibit 6.3 presents these jobs with the supervisory functions (coordination and control) included in the chart.

Establishing Overall Organizational Structure

Up to now this workflow analysis focused on how a single story comes together. It showed the division among information gathering, writing, editing, and supervision. Although that is a helpful description of the processing of a single story, in practice editors, reporters, and copy editors work simultaneously on a myriad of stories. In actuality a news department is structured to ensure that all stories in process come in at a certain level of quality and timeliness. Many departments achieve the goals of quality and timeliness by organizing the news operation into subdepartments, each one responsible for a specific kind of information. That results in a layering of management, with subdepartment editors reporting to the editor-in-chief, who is responsible for the entire operation. A typical newsroom organization chart is shown in Exhibit 6.4.

So far we have looked only at the news department. A newspaper's top manager, the publisher, works with every department head to conduct a similar analysis, which results in detailed organization charts for each departmental area. An overall chart for the organization might look like Exhibit 6.5.

Note that on the organizational chart departments are arranged from left to right, in the order in which they contribute to the manufacturing process. The news/editorial and advertising departments create messages, production produces the message, and circulation/promotion distributes and sells the paper to readers. The business department collects the money and handles all the accounting functions of the

EXHIBIT 6.3. WORKFLOW WITH SUPERVISORY FUNCTION

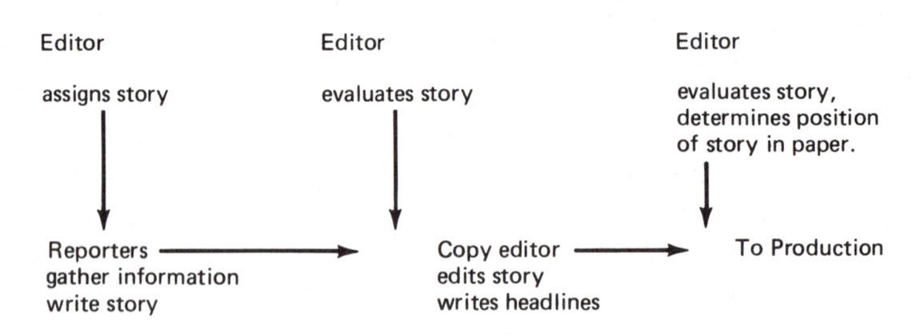

EXHIBIT 6.4. NEWS/EDITORIAL DEPARTMENT ORGANIZATION CHART

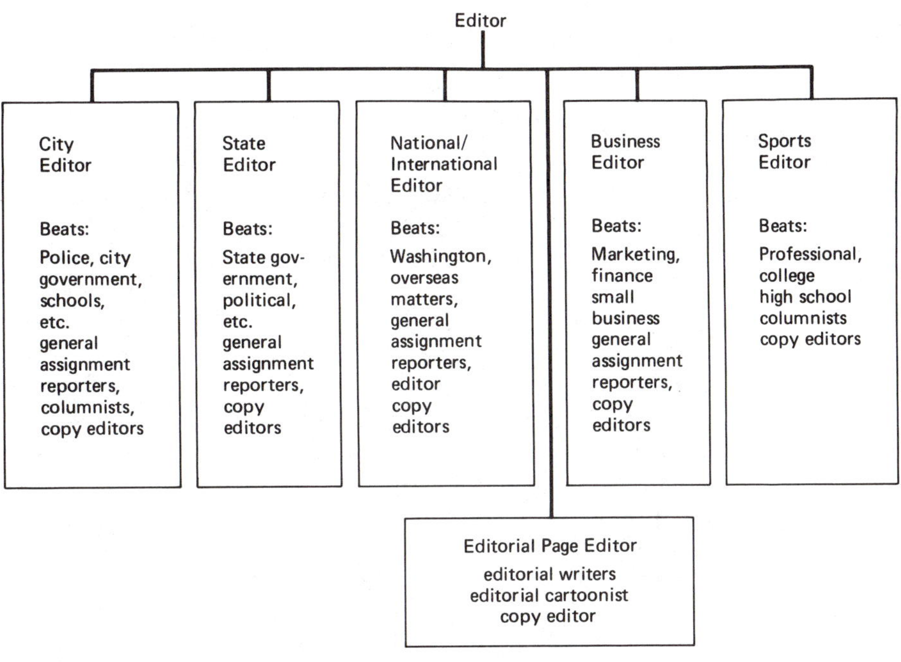

organization as well as other broad managerial functions, such as personnel. The heads of all of these areas report to the publisher, who is responsible for coordinating the organization as a whole.

This is a simplified newspaper organization chart. Most real publica-

EXHIBIT 6.5. SIMPLIFIED NEWSPAPER ORGANIZATION CHART

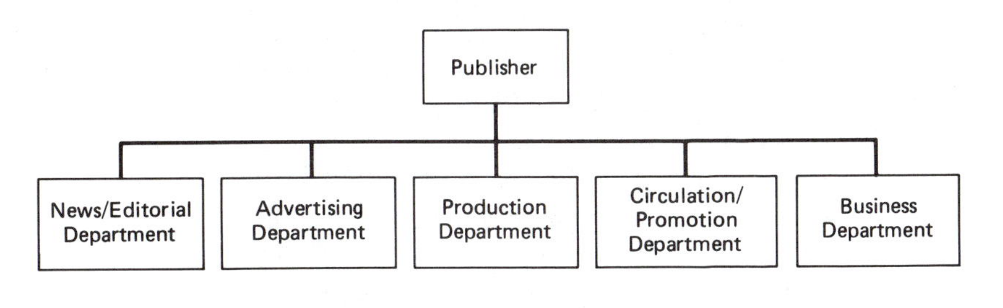

tions have more departments, such as a computer department, marketing, etc. Some of those fit under the departments found in Exhibit 6.5 (e.g., computers might be under production), while others stand alone. As the number of departments and employees increases the paper adds additional layers, such as a general manager who supervises some of the departments on behalf of the publisher.

The Goals of Organizing

A media company has three prime goals when it organizes to carry out its mission and plans: predictability, effectiveness, and efficiency. Predictability establishes a series of routines to guarantee that necessary tasks will be performed in a timely fashion. Effectiveness means doing work in a manner that produces a high-quality product or service. Efficiency focuses on completing the work at a reasonable cost.

As is true in many areas of media management, there is a trade-off among these three objectives. For example, if an information organization concentrates too much on increasing efficiency, its capacity to be effective, particularly in terms of developing new and innovative messages, may be limited. Media managers must decide how best to balance these objectives.

Different media companies require a different balancing of the three goals. One factor influencing that balance is a tight timetable which leaves few breaks between production cycles. Thus, daily newspapers must adhere to tight deadlines if each edition is to reach the subscribers on time. Contrast that with an advertising agency, which usually has several weeks or even months to produce a single ad or a full-blown campaign, or a book publisher, which produces books by the month or season. Predictability is important for each of these firms, but it is more urgent for newspapers than for ad agencies or book publishers.

A second factor in determining the appropriate balance between predictability, effectiveness, and efficiency is the amount of competition for audiences and the resulting profit margins that exist in a particular industry. On a comparative basis, newspapers are usually in a low-competitive situation, at least so far as their news product goes. But they face increasing (moderate) competition for advertising dollars.

By contrast, a radio station with a number of direct competitors (up to 30 in major markets) faces intense competition both for audience and advertising dollars. That tough competitive environment puts great pressure on the station's profit margins and forces more emphasis on efficiency than is true for a newspaper.

A third crucial factor affecting the balancing of objectives is the media's need to innovate. Newspapers must develop new coverage patterns to meet changes in audience interests and events. The pressure on newspapers to be innovative in their presentation of the news, however, is not nearly as great as it is for advertising agencies, book authors, and movie makers. These media firms must continually develop new, powerful and creative ideas to satisfy their clients and audiences. They can be expected to put greater emphasis on effectiveness than do newspapers.

The examples just cited demonstrate how organizational demands are based on an analysis of the need for predictability, effectiveness, and efficiency, and how the balance between those three goals varies substantially from one medium to another. (It also varies among firms within the same medium.) In either instance, the balance between the three results in a variety of organizational structures found in today's media companies. Several of them are described in some detail later in the chapter.

Determinants of Structure

Four key factors influence the organizational structure of an information organization: (1) mission and strategy; (2) technology; (3) skill level of its managers and staff; (4) size and resource base.

Mission and Strategy. The mission and strategy of a media firm are the principal determinates of its organizational structure. Management theorist Alfred Chandler (1962) emphasizes that point with the summary phrase, "Structure follows strategy" (p. 14). In a classic study Chandler showed convincingly that changes in corporate strategy preceded and then led to a variety of specific changes in the organization's design.

For example, if a newsmagazine defines its mission as providing very broad news coverage of its region, the editor will probably establish a large number of beats. Subsequently, if that mission is redirected to providing more intensive analysis of only the business news in the area, the editor will establish teams of specialized reporters to develop more in-depth reports.

If a TV news operation defines its mission as providing eye-witness coverage, it will purchase technology and organize its staff to provide a great deal of live, remote reporting. If the station subsequently switches its mission and redirects it to be an independent broadcaster specializing in showing old movies, the station's management might sell off the news equipment, eliminate the news staff, and instead invest in a large movie library with either a purchased news service, such as Cable News Network (CNN), or with no news at all.

Technology. Advances in technology have a major influence on the way media companies organize. As we noted in Chapter 1, in daily newspapers, jobs, such as compositor, and even whole departments, such as stereotyping, disappeared because of advances in technology. At the same time computers had two significant effects. They gave reporters and editors unprecedented control over the production of the final printed page and, in the process, they reshaped the paper's organization.

Similar changes have occurred in each of the media. In TV, broadcasting satellite technology and helicopters broadened the geographic area for live coverage of fast-breaking stories. In turn, this influenced how news directors organized their television reporting staffs. Those advances also spawned new, highly specialized jobs: computer and telecommunications specialists who oversee satellite transmissions. In advertising agencies, artists were added who are expert in computer-aided design. And in Hollywood, who would have thought that computer programing experts would be essential for making movies, but from Lukas Film to Walt Disney they are now commonplace. Think of the role they played in offerings such as *Tron*, *Star Wars*, and *Startrek*.

People. People, particularly those with expertise and highly developed skills, are the third factor influencing a media company's organization. The abilities and attitudes of the firm's workers and managers, coupled with their need to work with each other, must be seriously considered for an effective structure to be put in place.

Increased education has created more sophisticated media employees. As a result more reporters and editors have specialized training to handle more complex stories, and they want to do so. In both print and broadcast news this has resulted in the establishment of new reporting beats, such as health, technology, economics, science, and senior citizens. Advertising agency personnel know far more about marketing and, increasingly, about research, as do many of the more sophisticated public relations firms. And production workers in most media know a great deal about computers and telecommunications.

Keeping these highly trained employees motivated presents a special challenge. To keep being enthusiastic a talented staff need broad latitude in which to exercise their creative abilities. In many media companies that comes with job redefinition, increased responsibility, or expanded decision-making authority. Job enrichment approaches are also used to keep key media staffers performing at peak levels.

To gain new understanding of how to make all this happen, department heads and top executives in information firms are aggressively studying new management techniques.

Size and Resources. The last essential factor in shaping organizational structure is the size and resource base of the media firm. Historically, most media companies were small, but with the increasing concentration of ownership during the past 20 to 30 years, that is no longer the case. What this will mean to the dominant structures of information organizations is still unclear, though some facets of the changes to come are already visible.

One is that ownership concentration has changed some aspects of the organizational structure of every print, broadcast, and agency outlet that functions as an operating unit of a larger company. Unlike the small, independent organizations of the past, these firms have a new layer of reporting, with heads of operating units (publishers, station managers, etc.) accountable to central corporate management. That multilayered structure changes the decision-making patterns of individual units: newspapers, broadcast stations, and advertising and P.R. agencies.

Another impact is the dramatic change in the resource base of individual firms owned by very large media conglomerates, such as The New York Times Company, Time Incorporated, Knight-Ridder, Times-Mirror, or CBS. Those giant companies have enormous financial and personnel resources to carry out big projects; Dow Jones, national distributors of the *Wall Street Journal*, or Knight-Ridder's videotex projects are but a few of the notable examples. Being owned by a company that undertakes projects of that size is bound to impose a different view of organizational structure and processes on those who lead the parent firm as well as on those who direct its local operating units.

As you might guess, the consequences of increased size are not always positive. Many publishers of local Gannett properties told us, for example, that their corporate bosses were so focused on *USA Today* that the local operating units were forced to act more as satellites to the new project than as local publishing companies. To a significant degree they were precluded from acting as autonomous units focused on their own communities and regions. The differences in focus were manifestations of the differing position in the structure of the various management levels, and the consequences of those structural differences were formidable.

Increased size and greater resources have other outcomes. Chief among them are job specialization and more organizational complexity. Typically, new layers of management are introduced to cope with an expanded need for coordination and control in producing media products. At some point in a media firm's growth, a major restructuring also takes place; old patterns, often based on interpersonal relationships, are replaced by a structure based more on power and formal management principles. In most instances these changes are simply a response to the organizational demands of increased numbers of people and more resources. (Remember, resources mean more than money; they also include people, services, information, time, and technology. In a modern media company such an expanded definition always applies, but it is particularly applicable when one looks at what a big media conglomerate brings to the situation.)

MAJOR ELEMENTS AND FUNCTIONS OF ORGANIZING

Thus far you have learned that organizing (building a structure) is done for two primary purposes: to coordinate work flow and to establish effective control. We will now expand the discussion of how media managers accomplish these objectives.

Job Definition and Analysis

The starting point for media managers in developing an organizational structure is the nature of the work to be performed. To produce and sell messages, each medium requires the performance of numerous tasks. The beginning of organizing is usually to divide those tasks into a series of related tasks (jobs), as we showed earlier in the analysis of editors, reporters, and copy editors.

When executives analyze key characteristics of media jobs, they consider the factors shown in Exhibit 6.6.

In other words, the manager must determine a job's depth and scope. Job depth refers to how much control employees exert over their work. When rigid standards are set and work is organized in great detail, job depth is low. If only general guidelines are developed and employees are free to decide how to accomplish their goals, then depth is high. Job scope refers to the number of different operations a particular job requires and the frequency with which a work cycle is repeated. The fewer the operations and the greater their repetition, the lower the job scope.

Now, assume you are publisher of a trade magazine, such as the leading one in TV and radio called *Broadcasting*. Let's see how you would apply these concepts to your organization. From that analysis it will be easy to discern the substantial differences in the job depth and scope of various media jobs.

A classified advertising sales staff person who sells advertisements over the telephone and is required to follow specific guidelines has low

---

EXHIBIT 6.6. KEY CHARACTERISTICS OF MEDIA JOBS

Breadth of knowledge, skill, talent, and experience required
Large portion of the total work completed by one person
Job is important for others inside and outside the organization
Autonomy and responsibility for determining what will be done and how it will be done
Feedback about job performance forthcoming

---

job depth and job scope. A reporter covering a beat has high job depth, though perhaps relatively low job scope. Administrative assistants in *Broadcasting*'s personnel department may perform a wide variety of tasks, indicating high job scope, but their work may also be closely directed by the personnel manager, indicating low job depth. Editors, advertising department managers, and other department heads have high job depth and high job scope.

These concepts are useful when thinking about organizing work because there is substantial evidence that job satisfaction and productivity are tied to both of these aspects of an employee's work (Hackman, 1977). In particular, job simplification (low depth, low scope) has serious consequences for individual satisfaction and motivation. That is why job "enlargement" and "enrichment" programs, as well as alternative work schedules, were developed. They all increase media employees' feelings of control over their work.

Coordination

Coordination involves integrating objectives and activities of separate jobs or different units of a media firm to effectively and efficiently achieve organizational goals. Job and unit activities differ in the degree to which they need to be integrated. That difference depends on the nature and communication requirements of the task and on the overall level of interdependence among the units. When a task requires high information flow from others, then extensive coordination is necessary.

Basic Mechanisms for Achieving Coordination. Five management mechanisms are used to achieve coordination. They are:

- overall structure and chain of command;
- plans and goals;
- rules and procedures;
- increasing potential for coordination;
- reducing need for coordination.

Chain of Command. A media firm's chain of command, typically expressed in its organization chart, establishes the working and reporting relationships among subunits and the staff in those units. It outlines a media company's flow of information. It also performs the function of clarifying accountability, which helps to resolve conflicts by indicating who is responsible for making particular decisions.

Goals and Plans. A media organization's goals and plans assist coordination by helping to point each department and employee in the same direction. That is particularly useful when a production process is complex and requires substantial delegation of authority to various subunits.

Think about the coverage of a political convention by a TV network. That is a large, complicated, distant story requiring many reporters and camera crews, as well as transmission from the convention back across the country to network headquarters and then out to member stations. To handle the task effectively, it is absolutely essential that the network have formal goals and detailed plans. Too much is going on at too fast a pace with too many people involved in different locations for such a project to be undertaken unless all the structural components are integrated. Plans that include clear delegation of authority are necessary to handle both the routine and the unexpected.

Rules and Procedures. A helpful way to think about rules and procedures is to view them as managerial decisions made to handle routine events before the events occur. When a media firm's rules and procedures are understood and used regularly, employees do not have to communicate with managers about routine matters. As a result, staff members can act more rapidly; also managers have time to deal with the unexpected or major situations.

When the three basic coordinating mechanisms are not adequate for the needs of a media company, additional mechanisms may be desirable. Actually, there are two primary ways to deal with that situation. The media manager can look for ways to increase the *potential* for coordination or for means to reduce the *need* for coordination.

Increasing Potential for Coordination. A media firm can increase potential for coordination in two directions: vertically or horizontally. In a vertical mode, the manager creates an information system to transmit data and information up and down the levels of the firm. Management information systems (MIS) operate both formally and informally in each medium; they track activities such as finance, production, and marketing. By checking budgets, production information, or sales data, executives and staff members are better able to plan and coordinate their activities with people in other departments. If, however, editors spend too much time analyzing problems in departments other than their own, for example, in production, time will be wasted and coordination is likely to be replaced by information overload about an area with which the editors are only tangentially involved. Then, the editors' own productivity will fall.

Horizontal coordination, which cuts across the chain of command, almost always develops informally through contact between individuals in different departments. Increasingly, media executives are finding horizontal linkages very helpful for both coordination and innovation. In many firms top managers are establishing them on a formal basis.

An informal example of horizontal coordination would be the ties an individual public relations account executive develops with a photographer in the P.R. firm's in-house photographic department. Those ties can smooth out potential problems about the timetable for preparing proofs of pictures that the executive promised to deliver to clients. That sounds like a constructive linkage, and it may be. Yet, sometimes those informal ties clash with formal ones. For instance, suppose the general manager of the agency and the head of the photo department work out horizontal coordination plans. If the account executive and an individual photographer have a separate and different arrangement, then, even though that informal plan might facilitate the AE's work, the arrangement could be counterproductive to what is best for the agency as a whole.

Liaison roles may facilitate coordination. A way around such a situation is to assign liaison roles to individuals, charging them with maintaining bridges between units. Liaison personnel have the formal power to cut across department lines and take care of problems before they explode into major conflicts.

In Exhibit 6.7, the assistant advertising manager of a magazine that does its own production holds a liaison role. Part of the formal job description gives the assistant advertising manager the responsibility and authority to smooth operations between the advertising and production departments.

Task forces or committees can also deal with problems involving a variety of organizational units. Committees usually exist on a continuing basis, whereas task forces are formed as needed to deal with special issues or problems, and they disband when the matter is resolved. Both groups fulfill a liaison function.

Exhibit 6.8 outlines a task force for putting out a magazine's Tenth Anniversary edition. The primary work in this project involves only the advertising and news departments; note, however, that all relevant executives are on the task force, to insure coordination. Moreover, the publisher chairs the group. That means there is someone with ultimate authority who is present to settle disagreements between the department leaders should any arise. (Of course, the publisher's presence also signals the importance of the project to the company.)

EXHIBIT 6.7. LIAISON ROLE

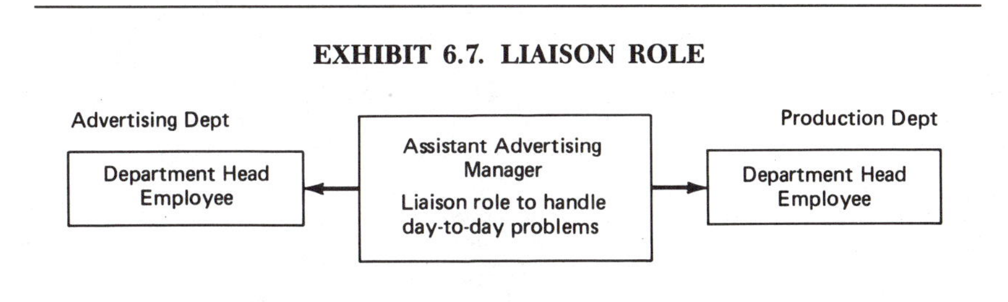

EXHIBIT 6.8. TASK FORCE MEMBERS

Tenth Anniversary Edition Task Force
Publisher
Advertising Department Head
News/Editorial Department Head
Marketing Department Head
Production Department Head

A broad integrating role, often carrying the title project manager, is another approach to deal with a specific product, service, or project that requires a high degree of coordination. As shown in Exhibit 6.9, the project manager is responsible for all aspects of the magazine's Tenth Anniversary edition project and has formal authority to coordinate and guide activities associated with the project.

Reducing the Need for Coordination. Sometimes, even when additional mechanisms are developed for increasing coordination potential, they are not adequate. On those occasions an alternative approach is to change conditions so as to reduce the need for tight coordination.

One way for a media leader to do that is to create what has been called "slack resources." A department is given extra workers, materials, or time in order to perform especially burdensome tasks. That way, when a work peak is reached the department has sufficient resources to respond. The need for excess coordination is eliminated.

Does such an approach sound wasteful? Maybe. But if the problem

EXHIBIT 6.9. PROJECT MANAGER'S ROLE

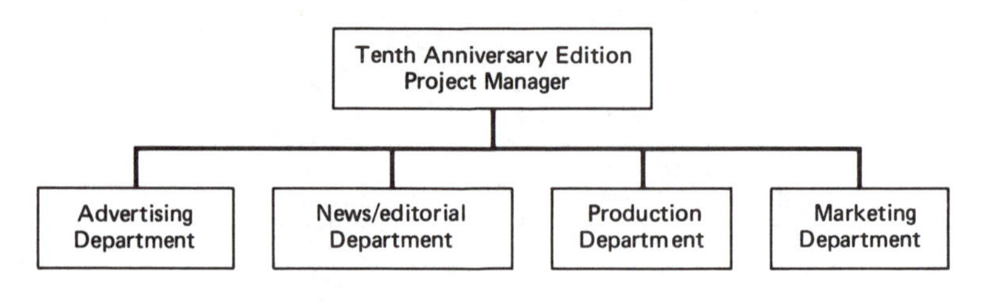

being dealt with is important enough to the medium, it may be more than worthwhile. For example, an average news organization may need only 30 reporters in its news department or six photographers in its photo department. Yet, when a big story breaks, having four extra reporters and one extra photographer translates into someone from each department who can respond instantly. If those extra people were not present there would be a severe loss of time to coordinate who will be pulled off other assignments to cover the major event.

A second approach is to change the character of an organizational unit and move to a "self-contained" structure. A self-contained unit has responsibility for all aspects of a particular product. Such a unit could be established to design, manufacture, distribute, and market the magazine's Tenth Anniversary edition. The new group would contain all the specialists that it needs and thereby require no coordination with other departments.

Gannett provides a number of examples of this approach. When it began *USA Today*, the media company pulled staff members from each of its newspapers across the country. On loan to the new venture, they put out the national newspaper until a permanent staff was developed. Initially the staff was a temporary task force; the permanent staff is a free-standing unit.

Even after *USA Today* was in place, Gannett did not put permanent employees of the new paper in every part of the country to handle production or circulation. Those functions are handled by each local Gannett newspaper. Thus, the circulation and production managers for the *St. Cloud Daily Times* in central Minnesota have had those responsibilities added to their job descriptions. In that part of their jobs they report to national circulation and production managers for *USA Today*, as well as to their local publisher. In the terms we've been using, the national managers are project managers, coordinating employees from different operating units (local newspapers) for the *USA* project. Those national executives worry about the newspaper going from the St. Cloud plant to the Twin Cities, Minneapolis and St. Paul, but they pay no attention to whether the *Daily Times* reaches its customers or not.

A similar structural form has been used for a long time in companies with a brand management or divisional systems. In either format, a separate division is set up to handle all aspects of business related to one brand or product. (To find out more about this form of organization, read the management literature on brand management at Proctor & Gamble, Pillsbury, General Mills, and other package goods companies.)

The primary consideration in selecting the best approach for coordination is matching an organization's capacity for linking activities with its needs. To do that a media manager asks the following questions:

- How much information is needed to perform the required work?

- How much information can the company process?
- If the need is larger than the firm's capacity, can the organization either increase coordination potential or reduce the need for it?
- Is the expense of creating, using, and maintaining information-handling capabilities justified by the organization's needs?

Those questions are important because failure to bring coordination capability in line with needs produces either ineffectiveness or inefficiency.

Control

Control is an important aspect of media organizations and their structure. Although the word *control* conjures up some unpleasant connotations, particularly the one of threatening personal freedom and autonomy, it is a helpful management tool, and it need not be negative. Control is necessary if employees and employers are to know that what takes place conforms to what was planned. Unless control mechanisms are in place to monitor organizational activity, no one in an information company really knows whether the organization is heading in the direction management intended.

Robert Mockler (1972) views control as a four-step process, as shown in Exhibit 6.10.

Note that in this perspective there is little or no threat to personal freedom or autonomy. What is described is a process that can include meaningful employee participation. For example, in many media firms

EXHIBIT 6.10. CONTROL AS A FOUR-STEP PROCESS

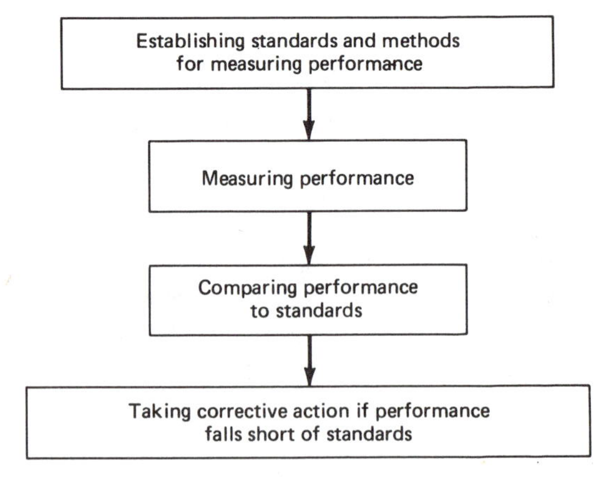

employees participate in the setting of standards. Similarly, both media employees and their supervisors often contribute to performance assessment and they share the feedback. Under that sort of participatory system, control is neutral with no implication of any reduction of employees' authority to make decisions or freedom. In fact, that system substantially expands the usual bounds of employee authority.

Organizations exert control in two principal ways. One is through a variety of nonfinancial incentives; the second is through financial means.

Nonfinancial Methods. Nonfinancial control is accomplished by setting standards for work produced or for sales, standards which vary with the medium and the situation. For instance, advertising sales employees of a highly specialized magazine and those from a television station are likely to be judged by far different criteria. After all, the specialty publication has a limited number of advertisers who pay a comparatively high rate for the magazine's narrow, high-interest audience. That is just the opposite of the TV station in a major metropolitan market, which has numerous competitors and hundreds of potential customers. The standards for the specialty magazine and the television station diverge on the number of sales calls made, the type of leads generated, the kind and number of new customers developed, and the definition of a successful advertising representative.

Sales staff are not the only ones with nonfinancial standards. Media production people have quotas for such things as the amount of film to be shot, number of copies to be run during a certain time period, number of allowable errors, or percentage of allowable waste. Setting standards for such concrete items as sales calls or production materials used is relatively easy. It is far more difficult to set them for the quality of message developed.

Think how easy it is to set a simple, fixed "number of stories produced" versus the difficulty in establishing a standard for "improvement in the depth or readability" of stories. The latter is achievable because competent writers know when language is fresh or boring or if a story explains why an event took place instead of just reporting that it happened; yet, those are subtle, challenging measurements to establish. Similarly, advertisements can be judged by their effectiveness for the client, not just the number produced. Whether dealing with effective advertisements, better stories, or more artistic films, we are describing quality standards. They can be established to effectively measure the quality of media employee's work, but both managers and employees should recognize that they are not easy to set up.

Two other approaches to control particularly relevant to assessing performance are measuring key results areas and management by objectives (MBO). Key results areas are those aspects of a medium that must function effectively in order for the entire organization to succeed (Stokes, 1968). Book publishers have to sign up authors and produce their books or the firm will cease to exist. Other key results areas for book publishing include marketing, financial transactions, manager-subordinate relationships, and many of the aspects of the manufacturing process. Typically, broad controls are established by upper-level managers for these key results areas. Then lower-level managers develop more detailed control standards to monitor results for their work unit as a whole or for individual employees.

Management by objectives involves setting goals for individual employees' performance and then following a plan of periodic performance reviews to assess how well an employee is meeting the objectives (Drucker, 1954). To be most effective, objectives should be set and reviewed jointly by the manager and employee. (We will have more to say about MBO systems in Chapter 8, where we address many aspects of personnel management.)

Financial Methods. Financial incentives and limits are the most universal control mechanism. They are so important that we deal with them at some length in the next chapter. For now we only note that the key financial control mechanism affecting most media companies and staff is the budget. For revenue-generating units, such as advertising or subscriber sales, both revenue and expense budgets are important; for departments that cannot produce revenue, such as news or bookkeeping, only the expense budget applies.

Setting up local profit centers within the organization is another financial control mechanism that often has impact on a large number of employees. For instance, if a large media company's regional radio station in Pittsburgh is given a profit target, then reaching it becomes an important aspect of management control of the station by the parent concern. In advertising agencies specific accounts may be assigned profit levels with an account executive put in charge of maintaining financial control to reach that target.

Communication

John B. Winsor, president and chief executive officer of Winsor Communications, is a particularly effective media manager. Beginning in his early 20s, he built a multimedia organization that includes newspapers, shoppers, commercial printing, film making, and a firm that records audio-cassettes for libraries. Asked about this topic, Winsor said, "Management is simple. . . .It just takes the 3 Cs: control, control, and control." Then he smiled, erased the dogmatic-sounding formula, and defined his real 3 Cs: "control, coordination, and communication."

Communication is the means by which coordination and control occur; it is a bridge rather than an independent organizing function.

Media firms have to move many kinds of data and information among their employees, and that interaction must occur in a timely fashion, for information is often useless if it is late. Without effective communication neither coordination nor control are achievable.

BASIC FORMS OF ORGANIZATION

Media firms usually have one of two structures that are based on one of three operational modes. Both those terms, *structures* and *operational modes*, refer to the way the company is organized. In their simplest form, most media firm's structures are vertical or horizontal, whereas their operational modes are functional, market, or product based.

Vertical versus Horizontal Structures

What distinguishes a vertical from a horizontal media firm? Vertical structure entails a number of layers of management, whereas horizontally structured organizations have only a few. Vertical and horizontal structures are also very different in span of management or span of control (the number of subordinates who report directly to a given manager).

Vertical media firms have relatively few employees reporting to any manager, usually from four to six. Horizontal organizations have a larger number. Exhibits 6.11 and 6.12 show simplified organization charts for the same advertising agency, organized first horizontally and then vertically. The agency employs 62 people. Note that there are five layers of employees in the vertical organization chart compared to only three layers in the horizontal organization chart.

There is no rule which makes a vertical structure preferable to a horizontal one. To determine which is preferable, several factors must be considered: the degree of routinization of employees' tasks, the complexity of their jobs, the interdependence of jobs in the workflow, the amount of supervision required, and the interrelationships among people.

More media organizations are organized horizontally than vertically. That is because many of them are comparatively small, tasks are complex and nonroutine, and staff members must interact with different managers about different projects. Under those conditions, horizontal structures improve the potential for coordination.

A negative consequence of horizontal organization is that it provides fewer opportunities for advancement in authority and responsibility, which results in a chronic pattern of job movement as personnel shift from one firm to another to gain increases in pay and responsibility. That is true in small advertising agencies as well as in print and broadcast media. As a matter of fact, it is a problem for all information industries.

EXHIBIT 6.11. HORIZONTAL ORGANIZATION CHART OF AN ADVERTISING AGENCY

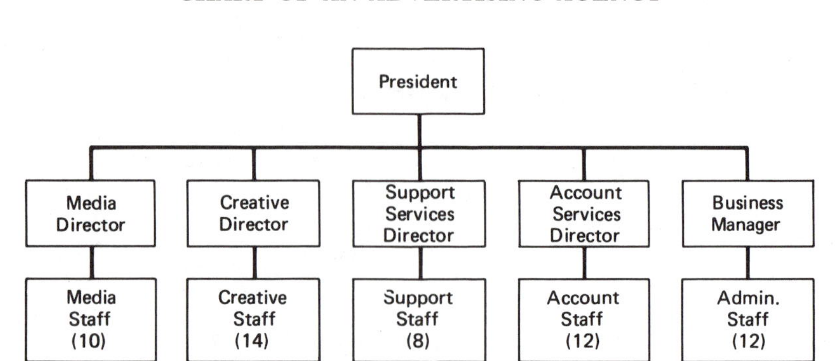

The only break in that picture is a little discussed but actually positive aspect of the rise of large media conglomerates. By necessity, the giant media corporations are vertically structured. In these companies, employees gain access to a clear career ladder that allows them to advance by moving from smaller units to larger ones. Moreover, moving them up the ladder is in the corporation's best interest. After all, the employee is already familiar with the company's way of doing business. The firm knows far more about the employee than can be learned about an outsider. The mere existence of the ladder is also a significant morale booster for employees; they know there is a strong opportunity for them to advance if they do a good job.

Functional, Market- , or Product-Based Operational Modes

Operational mode describes how media firms organize to distinguish between function, product, or market. Organization by function brings together all people engaged in one activity or several closely related activities. Magazines or newspapers are functionally organized if they have news/editorial, production, circulation, advertising, and business departments. Indeed, most media firms have a functional department structure.

Product- or market-based organizations often exist within larger media companies, where the firm has divisions that gather into one unit everyone involved in the production, marketing, and distribution of a single product message or related groups of product messages. A variation on that theme is a company organized on a single type of medium's customer or market. In that configuration a division is responsible for

EXHIBIT 6.12. VERTICAL ORGANIZATION CHART OF AN ADVERTISING AGENCY

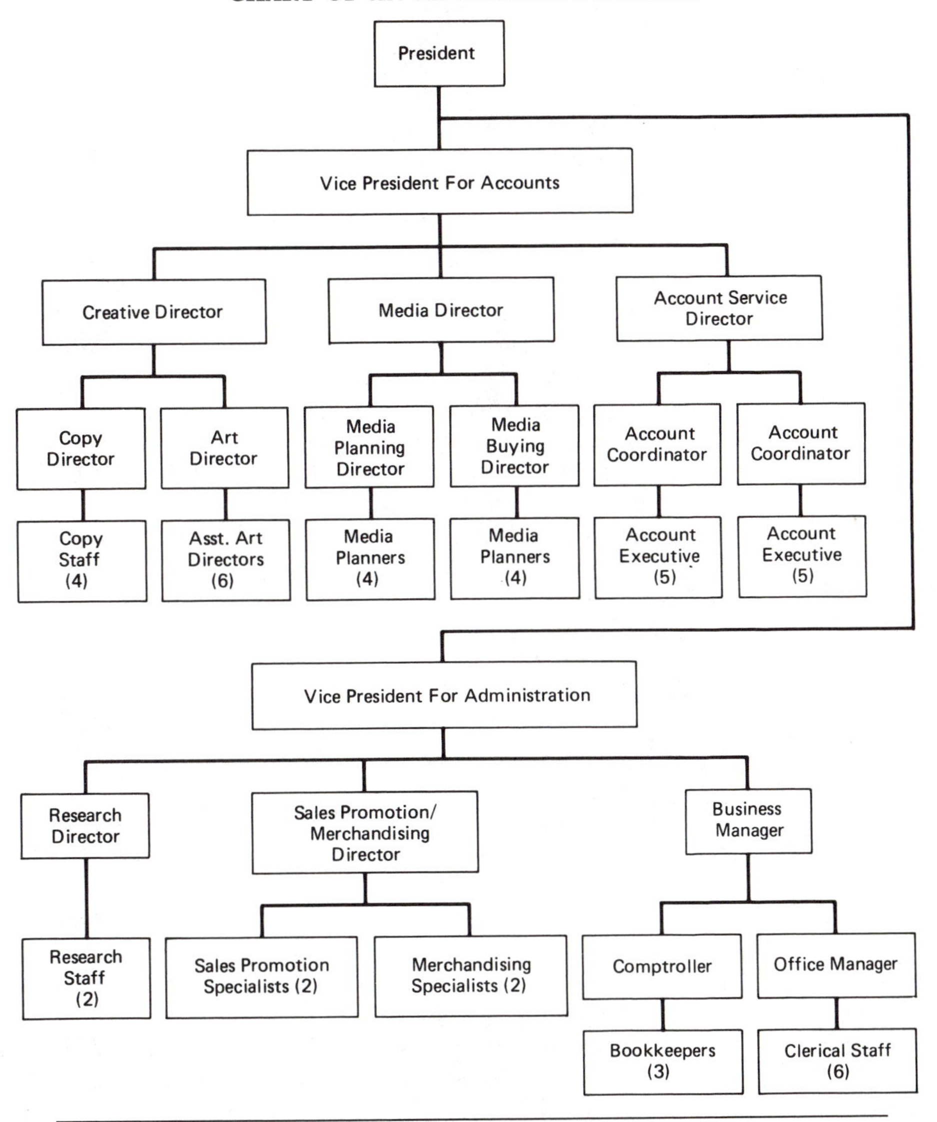

the production, sale, and distribution of a series of messages aimed at a particular group of customers. Krause Publications (KP), a very successful specialty publisher, uses this format. One KP division serves readers and advertisers who collect coins by publishing several numismatic newspapers and annual guides which give the value of the world's coins and paper money. A second division serves collectors of old cars by producing newspapers and magazines for antique auto buffs; another is directed at those who collect baseball cards, etc.

Many advertising agencies and public relations firms are organized along market lines with, for example, separate divisions for clients in consumer products, business products, or services.

Organizing for Innovation: Matrix Organization

For the media a newer, less used and more sophisticated organizational form is the matrix. It was developed to combine the strengths of both the structural forms and operational modes which were just discussed. In a matrix organization, permanent functional departments perform specific functions, but teams carry out projects which require departmental linkage. Members of a project team are drawn from the various departments and report to a project manager who is responsible for the outcome of the team's work. At the same time, team members continue to report to their departmental managers.

Matrix structure is the way Gannett organizes the circulation and printing of *USA Today*. Production and circulation managers at Gannett's local newspapers are responsible to their publisher for day-to-day activities, but they also report to regional and national production managers or circulation executives in conjunction with their activities for *USA Today*.

The matrix structure came into its own in the aerospace industry, where innovation is particularly important. It proved to be effective in creating an environment in which innovations occur at a rapid rate. Success there led to its adoption in many other industries, although it is used less frequently than the other two forms of organization: departmental and product/market.

One problem with the matrix format is that not everyone is comfortable with it, for a matrix spawns uncertainty and requires high levels of flexibility and cooperation among the people involved. It also necessitates open and direct lines of communication, both vertically and horizontally. Often, special training in new job skills and interpersonal relations is necessary for managers and subordinates to assure the effective functioning of a matrix.

For the media, overcoming those hurdles is usually worthwhile, for innovation is every information organization's lifeblood. If the media are to bring out an effective, needed, and desired new product with each cycle, then they must constantly improve and change what they do. The management literature is replete with information on innovation, but we particularly recommend Rosabeth Moss Kanter's (1983) *The Change Masters*. It presents a sharp contrast to the traditional perspective of most management texts. Other modern management analysts who utilize similar or new perspectives are Schon (1971), Galbraith (1982), Van de Ven (1980), March (1981), and Weick (1979).

Media Organizations as Political Systems

In Kanter's view (Exhibit 6.13), media organizations are primarily political systems, not the economic entities described by most management experts. As with all political systems, power is the key.

More specifically, Kanter argues (and we agree) that developing and utilizing power is absolutely essential for turning inventive ideas into innovations. Kanter identifies three major power tools: *information*: data, technical knowledge, expertise, and organizational information; *resources*: money, equipment, people, time, and space; and *support*: endorsements, approval, and legitimacy in the organization. Those three tools of power are the means by which ideas are transformed into innovations.

Three primary mechanisms exist for developing and circulating power in media companies:

1. Open communication enables leaders to locate and use information to shape a project.
2. Network forming arrangements assist leaders in building a coalition of supporters to form the political base necessary for developing an innovation.
3. Decentralization of resources allows leaders to gather the resources necessary to move an innovation from the idea stage to the implementation stage.

Viewing media companies as political systems focuses attention on the process of moving an innovation from a simple idea into action. For instance, in describing a prototypical innovation in a corporate environment, Kanter identifies three waves of activity:

1. Problem definition: acquiring and using information to shape a feasible, focused project with saleability
2. Coalition building: creating a network of backers who agree to provide resources and/or support
3. Mobilization: investing the acquired power tools (information, resources, and support) in the project to activate the project team to bring the innovation from idea to use

---

EXHIBIT 6.13. KEY ASPECTS OF POWER IN ORGANIZATIONS

Power tools
1. Information
2. Resources
3. Support

Mechanisms for developing and exercising power
1. Communication systems
2. Networking
3. Decentralization of resources

Another innovation process Kanter identifies is what she calls "energizing the grassroots." This process involves five overlapping stages:

1. initial education about the innovation and building of support;
2. gathering information and diagnosing needs;
3. forming teams and planning actions;
4. carrying out the actions to implement the innovation;
5. integrating and diffusing results of the innovation within the overall system.

Note in this analysis the clear emphasis on the processes occurring over time. That contrasts with an emphasis on organizational structure found in most discussions of management. And that very important shift flows from seeing the organization as political in nature; political movements happen over time.

In turn, a central management concept in this perspective is *empowerment*, the idea of developing more forms of power, utilized by more people, in more parts of the firm. Kanter's research identified corporate culture as a major factor influencing the kinds of processes and structures that occur in a company. She found that when the culture of an organization leads to a spirit of empowerment and involvement, innovation occurs on a continuous basis.

The concepts of organizational culture and empowerment have important implications for media leaders. As we emphasize repeatedly—in Part One, in Chapter 5 (planning), and in Chapter 9 (leadership)—the heads of media firms have special responsibility for creating a vision and culture that spawns innovation. A major mechanism for producing constant innovation and high-quality performance is empowerment, which means the expansion and dispersion of power within the firm. To reach that end a media firm's structure must be flexible, not the rigid, inflexible organization that characterizes too many media firms. To cement your understanding that organizing is a powerful change agent in the innovation process, read the following example.

DEVELOPING A MAJOR ORGANIZATION INNOVATION IN A MEDIA FIRM

This is the story of The Charles Advertising Agency (not its real name, though what follows is an account of an actual agency; only proprietary matters have been changed). Charles was very successful, one of the top agencies in its market. The agency was known as a highly creative shop which had strong growth for many years. During the past five years, however, the growth rate slowed substantially.

Also, the agency wasn't able to crack the $50 million barrier in billings. True, it gained some large clients, but it also lost them when the clients needed more services than Charles could provide. Part of the problem was understood by the agency's leadership; the firm served too many small clients. Management also knew that was a surface reason; the underlying cause of the stagnation baffled Charles's top executives.

Throughout its history, Charles Advertising's goal was to develop highly creative campaigns, and much of the agency's work succeeded in reaching that goal. The vexing thing was that neither the agency's owner, Robert Charles, nor his staff could explain why their advertising worked in one instance and failed in another. This lack of understanding created several serious problems.

The first problem was that doubt crept into the agency, eroding morale. Top management asked, more frequently than in the past: What if our agency's creative "feel" disappears; what if the agency's good people run out of ideas or their creative juices stop flowing? What will Charles do then?

The second barrier was even more ephemeral. Without either a clear notion of how good, creative ideas were arrived at or an extensive research base, the agency was not able to attract larger clients. Sometimes Charles also had trouble discovering the right strategy for a client, but a bigger problem was that the firm could not demonstrate through sophisticated consumer analysis why certain proposed strategies were best. Something had to be done.

Setting Goals

Charles's top management began the change process by reviewing their vision and goals. When the review was complete, their two principal goals—taking risks for themselves and their clients, and developing highly creative advertising—were retained. Management believed that acting on those principles was still the best way to build a top-notch advertising agency.

Charles's leadership did expand other areas of their vision, however. After careful review of everything they were doing and wanted to do, Robert Charles and his team laid out where they wanted the agency to go by summarizing in writing their primary mission: "The consistent production of blockbuster advertising; highly creative, focused advertisements that cut through the media clutter and work with extraordinary effectiveness for their clients." Such a summary may sound only like a copywriter's catchy summary, but it is far more than that. As you will see in the following, it is a powerful standard that formed the foundation of many key decisions that had to be made by the firm's executives.

Backgrounding

The next step was to apply that standard. Top managers examined the staff, structure, and client base to see whether Charles Advertising could achieve "blockbuster advertising" as the firm was then configured.

Initially, they examined each of these issues independently. Then they pooled their findings.

In looking at their staff, they asked, Do these people understand marketing? Do they understand the markets we are working in? Do they understand consumers? Is each of our staff members and each of our departments contributing to blockbuster advertising? Is everyone here accountable for achieving such a goal?

The answers to those seemingly simple questions were illuminating. For example, as talented as the creative staff was, management concluded that the creatives relied too heavily on instinct. Copywriters and art directors needed to learn more about consumer research and how to interpret that data to improve their creation of advertising campaigns.

By contrast the account service staff had a number of inexperienced people who did not understand modern, sophisticated marketing. Also, because of high turnover that department was often stretched too thin. That meant that although account executives were good at developing rapport with clients, their department lacked the depth to develop plans and strategies for the agency's accounts. Too often the account executives appeared to have a poor understanding of their clients' markets and of consumers.

In part this was true because the two-person research staff was not only small, but it made little difference on the type of advertising that Charles produced. The researchers were sometimes helpful in evaluating the likely effectiveness of the agency's ads, but on a continuing basis they did not contribute to a better understanding of the consumers for whom advertisements were developed. The researchers also had no direct responsibility or accountability in the development of ad campaigns; they were in a staff (support) position, not a line (direct responsibility) position. Hence, they were not expected to be an integral part of "blockbuster advertising."

Yes, there were staff weaknesses, but there were also some real strengths, particularly in the creative department. Even that proved to be a problem, however, for it was judged by Charles's management to constitute a talent imbalance. The creative staff's wealth of experience and expertise carried such authority in decision making that the creatives simply overpowered the account service people. What was needed, then, was a better balance among creative, marketing, and consumer-oriented staff members.

Besides the imbalance in decision making, a second structural problem was identified. Clients typically employed two or three people on their own staffs who were involved in the advertising planning process, but too often the only Charles person to bring the agency's point of view to the client was the account executive. Without supporting personnel from the agency to help develop strong data to back up Charles's recommendations, inexperienced account executives had trouble defending the agency's strategic suggestions. On many occasions they were bowled over by the views of the clients' staff. This led to dissatisfaction with the account executives' performance among Charles' creative personnel.

A final problem was related to Charles' present list of clients. A number of them were too small to benefit from the idea of blockbuster advertising. They simply didn't have adequate budgets for funding the work needed to create very strong, extremely well-researched campaigns. Moreover, the mix was uneven. Besides too many small accounts, the stability of the agency depended on a few very large clients; when one of them left the departure created havoc for a lengthy period of time.

Following a careful, brutally frank analysis, Charles' top management concluded that the process used in the agency to develop blockbuster advertising was poor. It was too hit or miss, and it relied too heavily on the innate talents of a strong creative staff. Loading up with creative talent was a wise strategy for developing a highly creative shop, which Charles had become, but the agency's leadership realized that such an approach produced an inadequate structure for creating true blockbuster advertising that would stimulate growth. Major restructuring was in order.

Charles's Strategy for Change

Top management began by elaborating what Charles Advertising's new vision and specific goals would be. What they arrived at is shown in Exhibit 6.14.

In short, what the new vision required was a different process for developing advertising and, perhaps, a new structure as well. To that end, Charles' leaders looked at a variety of new processes and forms used in different advertising agencies in the U.S. and abroad. After an extensive review they settled on one developed in Great Britain and adapted at that time by only a few major American firms.

Developing clearly focused blockbuster advertising was seen as possi-

---

EXHIBIT 6.14. CHARLES ADVERTISING AGENCY'S VISION AND GOALS

Vision
- Consistent production of blockbuster advertising

Goals
- Develop better teamwork to create the healthy dynamic tension necessary for producing blockbuster advertising campaigns
- Achieve a solid national reputation to increase client base of larger advertisers
- Regain double-digit financial growth

---

ble only when each Charles staffer had more knowledge and deeper understanding about consumers. The key to attaining that level of understanding was a new job in the agency, the account planner/researcher, which was shortened to "the account planner." This person would be responsible for studying the consumer and for bringing a deep understanding of the consumer into the development of the advertising campaign.

In the past the account executive, working with research personnel, was supposed to bring the consumer's perspective to the staff's discussions. Sometimes, however, even if it contradicted the consumers' wants or needs, account executives also had to represent the client's marketing perspective in agency discussions as well as build good relationships with the client. These multiple and often conflicting responsibilities resulted in inadequate attention to the consumer.

Robert Charles and his team took care of that by separating the function of representing the consumer from the account executive's role and giving it to the new person in the process, the account planner. Responsibility to thoroughly research consumers' characteristics, needs, and wants was a central part of this role. In the process, Charles made a dramatic and fundamental change in the way account teams were organized. The account planner was not only an extra person to help shoulder the work of the account teams in the development of a campaign but the planner also was expected to bring a sophisticated, research-based understanding of consumers to their discussions. The old and new structures are shown in Exhibit 6.15.

From now on Charles Advertising's campaigns would be developed through a team process with three sources of input: the account planner/researcher focusing clearly on the consumer, the account executive focusing on the client's marketing perspective and on client devel-

EXHIBIT 6.15. CHARLES ADVERTISING AGENCY'S ACCOUNT TEAMS BEFORE AND AFTER REORGANIZATION

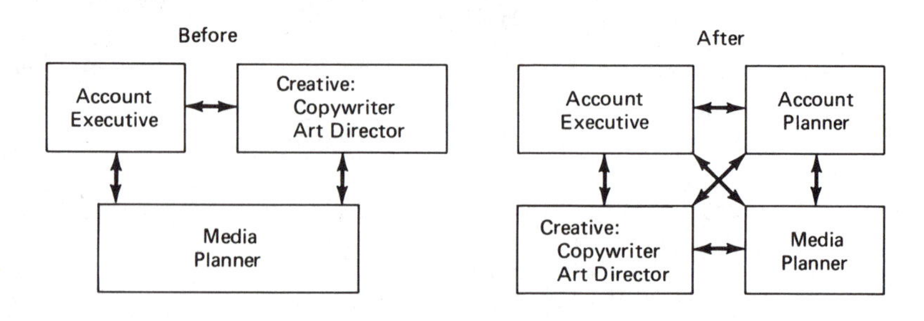

opment, and the creative staff (copywriters, art directors) presenting a creative message perspective. At the center of the process would be the account planner's data on what the consumer wants and needs. Additionally, the agency's media planner would continue to contribute expertise regarding strengths and weaknesses of various media vehicles (specific publications, TV shows, and radio stations).

This new view of the advertising campaign planning process required much higher levels of teamwork, for under it planning involved these three major phases:

1. In the research stage, the account team learns about the marketplace, the product, and the consumer. A wide variety of information is gathered and synthesized; everyone works together to create a far deeper understanding of the client's situation and consumer needs than advertising agencies normally possess.
2. Developing the advertising campaign strategy is done by a group. The account planner, account executive, creative staff, and media planner bring to the discussions their own perspectives, but they work together to develop a single-minded, one-directional (focused) advertising theme.

   This was very important in Charles's strategy, for the agency's leaders found that in the past the different perspectives would suggest different themes. Too often that resulted in a scattering of ideas. Although these were usually resolved by the creative group's dominance, that outcome frequently meant that insights about the consumer were ignored. In this new planning process, strategy was to be focused and yet consensual. It reflected solid input from all members of the team. Since developing that sort of consensus is often difficult, the new process was sure to take additional time.
3. In the monitoring stage the team evaluates the ideas that they produce, then tests and evaluates consumer reaction to them to determine whether the strategy is being executed effectively. This all occurs before the campaign theme and advertisements are presented to the client.

A key to the success of this approach is that the account planner plays an exceedingly active role in each step of the campaign's development. In the research phase the planner works most closely with the account executive. Together they develop extensive background information about the product, market, and consumer. In the strategy development phase, the group works together. Finally, in the monitoring phase, all participants again work together, although not necessarily simultaneously. The planner connects with creative staff and the media planner separately, attempting to maintain focus on the consumers to insure that their perspective is considered.

An Action Plan for Change

With this new organizational strategy, Charles Advertising believed it had both an effective process and an appropriate new structure for achieving blockbuster advertising. Not all of the agency's problems were solved, however.

One of the most vexing problems that remained was that the Charles staff included only one person qualified to fill the pivotal role of account planner. Thus, as soon as they adopted the new structure, the agency's executives moved to recruit two highly qualified people. Management believed it was important to hire experienced advertising staffers to provide a counterbalance to the high levels of expertise on Charles's creative staff. The two recruits were from account executive positions in other relatively large, recognized agencies.

Two more changes facilitated Charles's increased emphasis on the consumer and on research. The agency subscribed to two electronic data bases enabling account planners to access more sophisticated information on consumers. Then, all the employees attended day-long, bimonthly meetings during which outside experts came in to talk about changes in American consumers' values, lifestyles, motivations, and attitudes.

After one year in operation with this new structure, Charles's managers cite several costs and benefits:

1. Using the planning process lengthens the time line for producing an advertising campaign because the process demands the involvement of more staff and increased management time.
2. It is estimated that the new process costs clients an additional $30,000–$50,000 per year to adequately plan and conduct their campaigns. The new process, and its resulting cost increase, were phased in gradually with different clients during the two years. Despite the gradual nature of the change, it did result in the loss of several small clients. However, that loss is acceptable in light of the agency's goal to gain national recognition by attracting larger national clients.
3. The new system, which may not parallel the client's structure, can challenge the client's standard operating procedures in dealing with Charles. Initially there was an increase in tension between the agency and clients, but after the first campaign was launched and the improved results were seen, that problem disappeared.

Four major benefits were identified:

1. The change in Charles's culture meant that so-called gut instincts were put into perspective by what the research revealed about consumers. The insights about consumers' attitudes, values, and motivations, which grew out of the research, provides a springboard for creative strategies. It improves the chances of producing better ads and increases Charles's ability to show clients why the agency's strategy will work.
2. Although the research department was abolished, its function was actually heightened and dispersed throughout the agency, creating a much closer link between research information and every agency function. The account planner/researcher moved from a support role to a pivotal line position with direct responsibility for the ads that are produced, which is a far more powerful base.

3. Hiring experienced people for the planner role, to increase the "power" of the account and planning functions compared to the creative functions, resulted in a much more balanced structure inside the agency. The larger number of agency personnel involved in planning also counterbalanced the members from the client's staff.
4. With this strengthened organization, Charles Advertising was able to satisfy its larger clients' needs for more sophistication and service. It was also able to attract new clients who looked for an organization that could provide them with in-depth knowledge of the consumer and a focused, coordinated approach. Developing and nurturing these new, large clients was a natural outcome of the organizing strategy Charles adopted.

Putting Concepts into Action

Now let us review the more important management concepts that Charles Advertising utilized as it went about establishing a new organizational structure.

The managers at the agency clearly defined what their firm should accomplish, the mission and goals. That was a vital step in motivating and directing the changes that were eventually made.

Charles's leaders then evaluated their operations and determined that the agency's structure thwarted consistent, defensible development of focused, blockbuster advertising because they did not have documented, in-depth research about the consumer for whom the advertising was intended. Putting research experts in the powerful role of account planners, combined with a shift to team-orientation, was a major, essential step in achieving the agency's mission.

Each change at Charles Advertising was based on a blunt, searching analysis of job functions and workflow. That resulted in reducing the scope of the account executive's job with an important, but largely ignored, part of their work being shifted to account planners. The account planner's job was constructed by putting the consumer part of the account executive's previous role together with the research function. This move was buttressed by an ongoing, unequivocal commitment of Charles management to deepen the agency's understanding of the consumer.

The analysis by the agency's executives of Charles's workflow and work functions resulted in the clarification of jobs and a new organizational structure, which centralized around the account planner's role in the process and the creation of an account team. The development of that team concept represented a way of coordinating activities and bridging departmental barriers.

Previously the account service department, media department, and creative departments worked more individually than in unison. At some meetings all the points of view were brought together, but there was seldom a real sense of teamwork. By contrast, the new structure increased the lateral communication between departments, providing a coordination mechanisms to increase the probability of continually innovative, truly blockbuster advertising.

Recruiting experienced people provided an important counterbalance to the power of the creative people already at Charles. This showed clear recognition by top management that an agency is a "political" organization, with all of the attendant pressures and dynamics.

Further, legitimizing different perspectives in the agency was necessary if consensus decision making was to thrive. To borrow a term from Rosabeth Moss Kanter, account planner/researchers had to be "empowered" so they could bring increased consumer information into the agency's development of advertising campaigns. One of the keys to this change was that the account planner's role in the structure was undergirded by support from Charles's top management. (The fundamental importance of that leadership role is one we expand upon in Chapter 9.)

Finally, Charles Advertising's leaders consciously moved to change the agency's culture from simply being a creative shop, which relied heavily on the instincts of its creative staff, to a creative agency where insight and intuition were based on research and in-depth understanding of the consumer. That shift, combined with the enthusiastic participation, leadership, and unfailing support of top management, was critical to legitimize the new account management structure and process. Slowly, Charles's culture began to reflect the new direction. In turn, of course, this facilitated the true integration of the new structure into the culture of the organization.

As this chapter is written, Charles Advertising is once again experiencing double-digit growth with new and bigger clients buying its services. Some pockets of resistance are present, however, both within the staff and with certain clients, and a fairly high level of tension still remains. Thus, what was not yet clear was the impact of the account planners and the structural change they represented on the overall organization, its culture, and its clients. That long-range impact is the subject of study by Charles's top managers as this text goes to press.

CHAPTER 7

Financial Management

This chapter has two major themes.* First, what really counts in financial management is the action that media executives initiate after analyzing their company's financial performance. Accounting and budgeting are important tools in that analysis.

Second, financial analysis is a narrative in numbers that explains what a media company is doing, has done, or plans to do. It tells a story and provides media managers with information that is vital to their effective decision making. In the same way that words are descriptive tools, so are numbers. And just as writers make words spring to life, media executives give numbers vibrancy and force when they use them as the basis of their decisions.

To appreciate these two points, examine a television station general manager who is considering the purchase of a mobile transmitter that bounces signals from a dish on top of a van to a satellite and then back to the station. The unit enables a station to air live remote broadcasts from any location which can be reached by road.

One of the factors in the manager's decision is financial: the station must have the money to pay for such a unit. Thus, the executive has to determine if enough cash or credit is available to buy the new transmitter. Although such a unit is very costly, the primary ingredient in this decision is not financial; it is managerial. The general manager must decide if the unit can:

- add enough extra depth to the station's news broadcasts to draw more viewers;
- beat the competition by using the unit's high tech publicity appeal to attract some advertisers who want to be associated with "the cutting edge" of the media;

* The authors express particular thanks for advice on this chapter to David Ashton, comptroller of Lavine Media, Inc., and Edward Ahneman, partner, Wipfli, Ullrich & Co., certified public accountants of Wisconsin. They both deserve praise for this chapter's strengths and no blame for its weaknesses, which belong only to the authors.

- help the station's image because the competition already has a mobile transmitter and the station will seem old-fashioned and thus will lose business without it.

In summary, the manager must consider the station's:

- position in the market;
- public relations image;
- ability to attract a larger audience-market and advertiser-market;
- protection of its franchise against its competitors;
- financial (cost-benefit ratio) that would result from the purchase.

Note that all the preceding items, except the last one, are non-financial.

This chapter provides an overview of some of the basics of financial analysis, but that too is secondary to showing how managers use financial information and tools to lead a department or a company.

We define many terms throughout the chapter and in a special section on financial concepts at the end. Don't bother to turn to that section as you read, however, for we've found that most readers understand the terms when they see them in context. We urge everyone, however, even those who understand the terms or have a financial background, to read the financial concepts section because it is an integral part of this discussion. As you will see when you go through it, that section not only clarifies ideas in the chapter, but it elaborates on them and advances some new concepts that are not found elsewhere in Chapter 7.

DESCRIBING MEDIA FIRM OPERATIONS FINANCIALLY

In its simplest form, the money and assets of a media company follow a circular course. First, there is money, which a media firm spends to buy equipment, such as a mobile TV transmitter. Money is also used to pay employees and to purchase materials (e.g., raw materials, such as paper, ink, and videotape, or messages produced by others, such as scripts, syndicated materials, wire services, and art work). It is also used to create products: magazines, newspapers, television programs, advertising campaigns, and movies.

Next, the firm sells its inventory (products) to someone else, thereby creating accounts receivable, which are monies owed to the firm by advertisers, subscribers, or clients who purchase the media company's product or service. Finally, when the accounts receivable are collected, the firm has more money to start the cycle again. That cycle of activity can be seen in Exhibit 7.1.

While the cycle represents the way money works for a media organi-

EXHIBIT 7.1. WHEEL OF MONEY AND CURRENT ASSETS

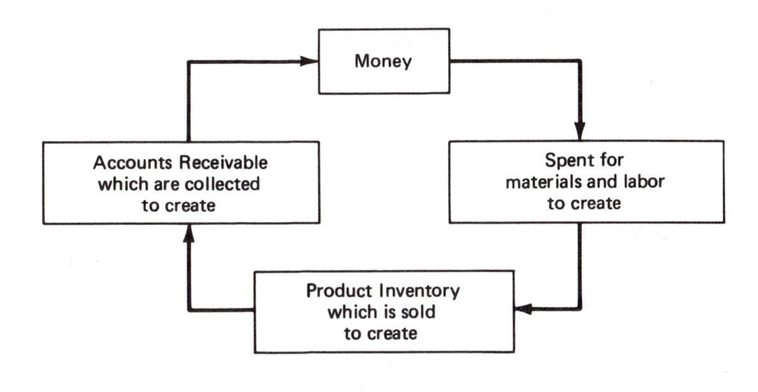

EXHIBIT 7.2. WHEEL OF MONEY AND PROFITS

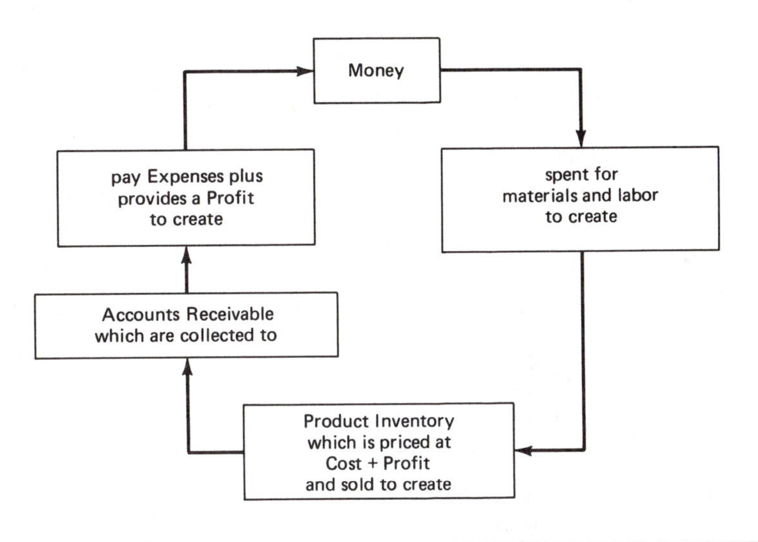

zation, it also demonstrates an important principle. That is, if a media manager can make the wheel turn more rapidly, increased profits will accrue to the firm. Why is this principle true? Because each time the wheel revolves, the firm collects enough money to pay for all the costs associated with creating, producing, and distributing a message, but it also adds value to the materials and effort of its employees. This added value is reflected in the price of the media product. Thus, when the firm sells the product and collects money, the total is more than the product's costs, yielding an additional amount, called profit. The profit cycle is pictured in Exhibit 7.2.

With each revolution the profits of the firm increase; the more revolutions the more profits are collected. It is true that many variables—particularly quality, market acceptance, and competition—can distort that outcome. Still, Exhibit 7.2 provides one standard by which to measure departmental or corporate performance.

The Income Statement

However, we're getting ahead of the story. Before we talk about performance standards, let's take that simple wheel model and apply it to a media firm's operation. In Exhibit 7.3 you will find some of the key ingredients arranged in vertical form in an income statement.*

An income statement focuses attention on the financial performance of the organization during some period of time, usually a monthly and annual basis. The income statement shows three major categories of entries:

1. Revenues: sources of income
2. Operating Expenses: expenses directly linked to the operations of the company (e.g., rent, wages, marketing and promotion, materials, supplies, etc.)
3. Nonoperating Expenses: expenses linked to the company's long-term investments (e.g., depreciation and interest) and to its relationship with a larger corporate entity (e.g., the management fee paid by a radio station to its corporate owner)

Operating expenses are under greater control by management than

EXHIBIT 7.3. INCOME STATEMENT

Total Revenues
− Total Operating Expenses
= Operating Profit (Loss)
− Total Nonoperating Expense
= Profit (Loss) Before Income Taxes
− Income Taxes
= Net Profit (Loss)

* Another type of important financial statement is the balance sheet, which is illustrated and explained in the financial concepts section.

are nonoperating expenses because nonoperating items are subject to control by outside forces, e.g., government regulations (depreciation), bank policies (interest), and corporate control (management fee).

Exhibit 7.4 is an example of an income statement, showing the past three years of radio station KZZZ-FM, which you first encountered in Chapter 2. (KZZZ-FM is also the subject of a case study found in Chapter 10. The case puts into practice the ideas and concepts of Chapters 5 through Chapter 9.)

If a media manager were to describe in words KZZZ-FM's fortunes for the past year, the executive would say: The station lost $234,000 on revenues of $3.1 million, compared to a before-tax profit of $869,000 in the previous year. Three factors brought this about:

EXHIBIT 7.4. INCOME STATEMENT FOR KZZZ-FM

	This Year	*Last Year*	*Two Years Ago*
Sales/Revenue			
Local	$2,487,259	$2,434,941	$2,194,550
National	653,302	1,051,010	1,041,470
Total revenue	$3,140,561	$3,485,951	$3,236,020
Expenses			
Operating expenses			
Program	$ 352,989	$ 316,426	$ 255,277
News	44,158	41,631	39,183
Direct	465,560	524,146	525,067
Technical	133,784	105,521	82,849
Sales	259,009	251,295	199,340
Promotion	519,791	464,063	408,598
Traffic	45,368	46,782	40,527
General and administrative	412,892	358,325	415,718
Total operating expenses	$2,233,551	$2,108,189	$1,966,559
Total operating profit	$ 907,010	$1,377,762	$1,269,461
Nonoperating expenses			
Depreciation	$ 356,905	$ 329,749	$ 326,156
Management fee	97,000	91,000	91,000
Interest	687,500	87,600	394,682
Total nonoperating expenses	$1,141,405	$ 508,349	$ 811,838
Profit (Loss) before taxes	$ (234,395)	$ 869,413	$ 457,623
Taxes	$ -0-	$ 400,000	$ 220,000
Net profit	$ (234,395)	$ 469,413	$ 257,623

1. Revenue decreased by about $345,000.
2. Operating expenses increased by about $125,000.
3. Due to major investments in a new transmitter facility late last year and a new 6,000-square-foot studio facility early this year, interest payments increased by about $600,000.

The result of these changes in revenues, operating expenses, and interest was a loss of about $234,000 for the year, compared to the prior year's profit.

There are many ways a radio station manager might change aspects of KZZZ-FM's operation and, in the process, change the station's profit performance.

For example, Exhibit 7.5 shows the same income statement with one pivotal change: the station introduced a talk show on personal investing

EXHIBIT 7.5. REVISED KZZZ-FM INCOME STATEMENT

	This Year	*Last Year*	*Two Years Ago*
Sales/Revenue			
Local	***$2,942,648***	$2,434,941	$2,194,550
National	***953,302***	1,051,010	1,041,470
Total revenue	$3,895,950	$3,485,951	$3,236,020
Expenses			
Operating expenses			
Program	***$ 490,900***	$ 316,426	$ 255,277
News	44,158	41,631	39,183
Direct	465,560	524,146	525,067
Technical	133,784	105,521	82,849
Sales	259,009	251,295	199,340
Promotion	519,791	464,063	408,598
Traffic	45,368	46,782	40,527
General and administrative	412,892	358,325	415,718
Total operating expenses	$2,371,462	$2,108,189	$1,966,559
Total operating profit	$1,524,488	$1,377,762	$1,269,461
Nonoperating expenses			
Depreciation	$ 356,905	$ 329,749	$ 326,156
Management fee	97,000	91,000	91,000
Interest	687,500	87,600	394,682
Total nonoperating expense	$1,141,405	$ 508,349	$ 811,838
Profit (Loss) before taxes	$ 383,083	$ 869,413	$ 457,623
Taxes	$ 150,000	$ 400,000	$ 220,000
Net profit	$ 233,083	$ 469,413	$ 257,623

that attracted the advertising of a host of stock brokerage and banking institutions. (Here and subsequently throughout the chapter, changes in a financial report are shown in italics and boldface type.) As a result, under Revenue you will find a substantial increase in sales: $455,389 in local advertising sales and $300,000 in national advertising for a total increase of $755,389. Under Operating Expenses you will see an increase of nearly $138,000 in program expenses. These changes result in a pretax profit of almost $393,000, compared to the $234,000 loss in Exhibit 7.4.

Now suppose that KZZZ-FM's manager decided to purchase some new equipment that allows reductions in the station's technical staff and,

EXHIBIT 7.6. REVISED KZZZ-FM INCOME STATEMENT AFTER ADDING NEW EQUIPMENT, A BEEPER SERVICE, AND CUTTING THE TECHNICAL STAFF

	This Year	*Last Year*	*Two Years Ago*
Sales/Revenue			
Beeper service	***$ 12,000***		
Local advertising	$2,942,648	$2,434,941	$2,194,550
National advertising	953,302	1,051,010	1,041,470
Total revenue	$3,907,950	$3,485,951	$3,236,020
Expenses			
Operating expenses			
Program	$490,900	$316,426	$255,277
News	44,158	41,631	39,183
Direct	465,560	524,146	525,067
Technical	***115,784***	105,521	82,849
Sales	259,009	251,295	199,340
Promotion	519,791	464,063	408,598
Traffic	45,368	46,782	40,527
General and administrative	412,892	358,325	415,718
Total operating expenses	$2,353,462	$2,108,189	$1,966,559
Total operating profit	***$1,554,488***	$1,377,762	$1,269,461
Nonoperating expenses			
Depreciation	***$ 365,905***	$ 329,749	$ 326,156
Management fee	97,000	91,000	91,000
Interest	687,500	87,600	394,682
Total nonoperating expenses	$1,150,405	$ 508,349	$ 811,838
Profit (Loss) before taxes	$ 404,083	$ 869,413	$ 457,623
Taxes	$ 160,000	$ 400,000	$ 220,000
Net profit	$ 244,083	$ 469,413	$ 257,623

at the same time, enables the company to start a paging/beeper service to be run off of KZZZ-FM's tower. Initially no new sales people will have to be hired to sell the beeper service. The current staff can introduce the paging system to local businesses when they make their regular advertising sales calls. In Exhibit 7.6, KZZZ-FM continues the additions due to the financial talk show, but also includes added revenue of $12,000 from the beeper service and a reduction of $18,000 in the technical staff.

Finally, look at the increase in depreciation of $9,000. That represents one-fifth of the $45,000 KZZZ-FM paid for the new equipment, reflecting a five-year straight-line depreciation schedule the station used.

If we add together savings in the technical staff salaries ($18,000) and the extra revenue from the beeper service ($12,000), the station's total return on investment for the change is $30,000 the first year. This is two-thirds of the equipment cost and represents a very rapid pay-back on the investment.

Budgeting and Budgets

Budgeting is a powerful management tool. (It could be called fiscal planning, for it enters the planning process during the Action Plan phase. However, the business/management world refers to it simply as "budgeting.")

The budgeting process is straightforward. It simply lays out expected revenues and expenses for the next year. Exhibit 7.7 shows the major categories in a media firm's budget.

The major components of a budget should appear familiar, because they correspond to items in KZZZ-FM's income statement. A budget is designed to organize those items.

When used effectively, budgets are of immense help to media managers. They pinpoint things that need to be changed or opportunities that exist. They are also effective in monitoring change.

For instance, as shown in Exhibit 7.8, KZZZ-FM's owner, City Media, Inc., projected a budget for the station to go from losses of nearly a quarter of a million dollars for this year to profits of about that much

EXHIBIT 7.7. COMPONENTS OF A BUDGET

Revenue Each source of revenue listed separately

Expenses Each expense category listed separately; they are divided into two categories:

Operating expenses
Nonoperating expenses

EXHIBIT 7.8. KZZZ-FM BUDGET

	This Year	*Next Year (Budget)*
Revenues		
Local	$2,487,259	$2,760,000
National	653,302	684,000
Total	$3,140,561	$3,444,000
Operating expenses		
Direct	465,560	485,000
Technical	133,784	135,000
Program	352,989	400,000
News	44,158	50,000
Sales	259,009	270,000
Promotion	519,791	540,000
Traffic	45,368	50,000
General and administrative	412,892	403,000
Total operating expenses	$2,233,551	$2,333,000
Operating profit	$ 907,010	$1,111,000
Nonoperating expenses		
Depreciation	$ 356,905	315,000
Management fee	97,000	50,000
Interest	687,500	495,000
Total nonoperating expenses	$1,141,405	$ 860,000
Profit (Loss) before taxes	$ (234,395)	$ 251,000

next year. How can KZZZ-FM achieve a nearly half million dollar turn around?

In a number of ways. First, in response to the station's new programing format, local sales rose about $273,000 and national sales increased about $30,000. The format change accounts for the comparatively large increases in programming and promotion expenses. At the same time, other operating expenses basically held the line.

Nonoperating expenses changed substantially for several reasons. Depreciation decreased about $40,000 because the equipment that KZZZ-FM had purchased was in the second year of its depreciation schedule. City Media, Inc., lowered the management fee it charged KZZZ-FM for corporate support because the conglomerate calculated the station's share as a base amount plus a percentage of the station's profit. The poor showing of KZZZ-FM eliminated the percentage part of the management fee. The $192,000 reduction in interest expense occurred because interest is tied to the prime interest rate, which has substantially declined.

Departmental Budgets

Departmental budgets are subunit microcosms of companywide budgets. These budgets provide useful information for expressing managers' decisions. For example, the budgets for KZZZ-FM's sales department, shown in Exhibits 7.9 and 7.10, express decisions made by the station's general manager and its sales manager. They show the role that the sales department is expected to play in KZZZ-FM's turnaround. Before you read further, study those figures and try to explain to yourself what happened.

Top-down Budgets. The answer is that the budget changes in Exhibit 7.9 reflect the plan of KZZZ-FM's general manager, Linda Remy, who was brought in from another station that is also owned by City Media. By paying an excellent salary, Remy planned to hire a top-notch sales manager. She also decided to restructure compensation for sales personnel by linking their wages more directly to sales. (Note the decreased salaries and greatly increased commissions.) Remy believed this would motivate stronger performance, generating the major sales increases projected for KZZZ-FM (shown previously in Exhibit 7.8).

The new sales manager was expected to drastically cut other expenses, such as the lavish entertaining and partying favored by the prior manager and the sales staff. The new executive was also expected to reduce phone charges and eliminate most club memberships. The total budget for the sales department for the upcoming year would then be $270,000, an increase of $11,000 from the current year. The extra money was expected to result in a 10 percent increase in sales.

Bottom-up Budgets. Remy did fire the incumbent manager, but in-

EXHIBIT 7.9. REMY'S TOP-DOWN SALES DEPARTMENT BUDGET

	This Year	*Next Year (Budget)*
Sales Department		
Salaries: Manager	$ 50,000	$ 75,000
Salaries: Staff	130,589	100,000
Commissions	13,119	67,982
Auto expenses	8,335	9,500
Entertainment	34,954	7,890
Telephone	21,112	9,238
Memberships	889	290
Miscellaneous	11	100
Total sales expenses	$259,009	$270,000

stead of going outside the station for a replacement, she promoted the best salesman in the department, Bob Dunn, to the manager's post. After careful analysis, Dunn proposed the budget shown in Exhibit 7.10. It stayed within the $270,000 total Remy imposed, but spent the money in a different way.

First, Dunn took the unusual step of setting a salary for himself that was $10,000 less than Remy budgeted for the new sales leader. Then, instead of adding the difference to the station's profit, Dunn proposed that $5,000 of this be added to commissions and the balance to other departmental expenses.

While it may appear unwise in the short run for Dunn to set his own salary lower than what was offered, that decision was smart in the long term, because part of his salary is based on a commission that is calculated on the income produced by the sales staff. Thus, if the $5,000 is seen by the staff as a meaningful incentive and if they work harder to earn it, Dunn's team will produce not only more sales for KZZZ-FM but also more commission for their new boss. Further, the new sales manager knew that this move would impress Remy with his commitment. Dunn was used to living on the salary he received, so he felt that a $15,000 raise was sufficient and he gambled that the extra $10,000 that he did not take was better used as a boost for the station and an investment in his future.

Next, Dunn budgeted $2,100 in miscellaneous expense to send several underachieving members of the sales staff to a training course. He also fired three people whom he knew were poor performers with no chance of improvement. Simultaneously, he convinced two young, very

EXHIBIT 7.10. DUNN'S BOTTOM-UP SALES DEPARTMENT BUDGET

	This Year	*Station Manager's Budget*	*Sales Manager's Budget*
Sales Department			
Salaries: Manager	$ 50,000	$ 75,000	$ 65,000
Salaries: Staff	130,589	100,000	100,000
Commissions	13,119	67,982	72,982
Auto expenses	8,335	9,500	9,500
Entertainment	34,954	7,890	10,490
Telephone	21,112	9,238	9,238
Memberships	889	290	690
Miscellaneous	11	100	2,100
Total sales expenses	$259,009	$270,000	$270,000

effective sales reps at competing stations to join KZZZ-FM. When those moves were complete, total sales department compensation showed a slight decline, but it rose on a per-person basis.

Finally, Dunn increased both the entertainment and memberships amounts proposed by Remy. He convinced his boss that a larger level of expenditure for these items was necessary if his sales force was to meet its goals.

General manager Remy developed the top-down budget based on her experience at other City Media, Inc., stations. From her position at the top of the station she produced a budget that was reasonable in its size as well as its general allocation of expenditures. The bottom-up budget was built by Bob Dunn. From his position down in the sales ranks close to the customers, Dunn was in a better position to know how to effectively spend money in KZZZ-FM's market.

Neither Remy's budget nor Dunn's is clearly superior; neither is right or wrong. They simply represent different orientations. Moreover, because the two proposals do not differ on the total amount to be spent, it was easy for Remy and Dunn to reach agreement.

For his part, Dunn's budget will build morale in his department because it allows him to offer more money for commissions. Also, the outside salespeople he brought in owe their loyalty to him; and by his firing the poor performers, the insiders know that their new leader will not stand for anything less than an all-out effort. Dunn also must feel good about Remy's confidence in him. She supported all of his changes.

What was the outcome of all of these changes? The real station that KZZZ-FM represents began to recover, partly as a result of changes in the sales department. As this text was completed, it is not yet strong and profitable, but it came within 3 percent of the budgets you have just worked with, and it came in only 1 percent under the total revenue projected in Exhibit 7.8.

THE BUDGET PROCESS

Now, having established a feel for the components of budgeting, let's look carefully at how the budget process works. Just as in nonfiscal planning, budgeting begins well in advance of the start of the operating year. Some media companies function on a calendar year; many use a fiscal year. (A fiscal year does not follow the calendar, but covers another 12-month period. Fiscal years are arbitrary; they are used only for accounting purposes.)

Zero-based Budgeting

Starting with a so-called zero-based budget is ideal. Just as in planning, media managers want to achieve certain financial goals without

EXHIBIT 7.11. MERGING THE PLANNING AND BUDGETING PROCESS

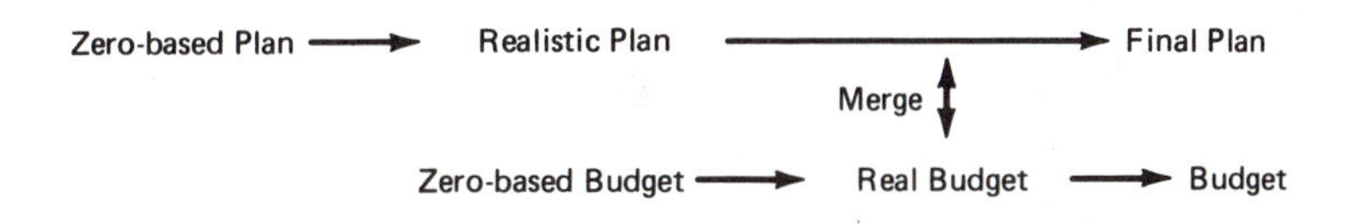

the restraints of the company's financial history. In zero-based budgeting, everything goes back to zero; the slate is wiped clean, and the manager builds an ideal budget without worrying about what happened in prior years. Developing a zero-based budget stretches an executive's thinking and often provides new insights. By contrast, if a manager begins with last year's budget, the new one is likely to include all of the prior year's wrong-headed premises. That is a poor basis for planning for the future.

Having started with a clean slate, media leaders should return to reality. Eventually, the zero-based budget must be fused with the prior record of performance. Not everything done in the past is bad; indeed, much of it might be excellent. In turn, the budgeting process moves planning and budget development from a zero-based ideal to brutal reality. The final budget for the new year reflects not only the firm's prioritized goals, strategies, and plans, but also its actual fiscal operations from previous years.

Exhibit 7.11 diagrams the planning and budgeting process. Note that zero-based budgeting does not begin until both the ideal and the realistic plans have been developed. That way the plan drives the budget, not vice versa. Also, the merger of the plan and budget begins when the plan is realistic, but the budget is still zero base. This approach allows some continued "blue sky" idealism and openness; it also provides encouragement for new ideas until the last possible moment.

Before we leave this process, try to think of ways that realistic budgets are built. We've given you some hints. One is the zero-based approach. Another is by basing what you want to happen in the future on the past year. A third is either from the top down or from the bottom up. In better managed media firms, elements of all of these are used in building budgets.

Involving Staff in the Budgeting Process

Whenever possible, employee involvement is also very important in the budgeting process, just as it is in the broader planning process discussed in Chapter 5. Involvement results in better information and higher commitment to the budget.

Even as a newcomer to KZZZ-FM, Linda Remy involved department heads and other crucial employees as she built her budget. She did that by talking to all the members of the sales department, picking one of them to lead the department and then letting him set the final sales department budget. Although Bob Dunn's budget proposal could be changed by the station manager, Remy took care to maintain Dunn's ideas. She knew that if department heads are allowed to construct and implement their own budgets, and if what they propose does not exceed her spending limits, then the following is likely to occur:

- The department will run more smoothly because its head usually knows far better than does the general manager what can and cannot be accomplished.
- The department head and staff have invested in the budget. They are more determined to make it work than if the spending plans were given to them.
- Following this approach also allows managers who run subunits and departments within the firm to have a significant hand in directing the priorities and actions of the staffers who report to them.
- If, in turn, department heads build their budgets with input from the staff who work for them or if they make sure that the budget accomplishes some goals the staff really wants, the budget can actually motivate personnel. (In Dunn's case that included restoring some funding for memberships, entertainment and, most important, the increase in staff commissions.)
- Similarly, if top management at KZZZ-FM involves department heads in establishing profitability as a major goal for the station as well as setting target figures to accomplish that goal, the department heads will feel committed to making the station profitable. They will push hard to achieve "their" goal.

Sophisticated Financial Management

Many departmental accounting statements are far more sophisticated than the one we showed you for KZZZ-FM's sales department. For example, a sales manager might want monthly data on the cost of each call the sales staff makes on an advertiser. It is calculated by dividing total department costs by the number of sales calls made during the month; similar figures can be developed for individual sales personnel. Costs can also be divided by the number of minutes sold or by the number of contracts signed. With that information, the sales manager can analyze each sales representative's performance over time and project the amount of income that is likely to be generated by each advertising account.

Such an analysis would allow KZZZ-FM's sales manager to advise his account representatives which clients should be contacted by telephone instead of in person or, in some cases, who should be dropped from KZZZ-FM's client list. The time gained from that culling could then be used by the sales representatives to concentrate on more profitable or higher-potential accounts.

Of course, none of these decisions should be based solely on a statistical analysis. Yet, financial statistics provide important information to shape a media manager's judgments. For further information about sophisticated approaches to financial management, review Matz and Usry (1980) *Cost Accounting: Planning and Control* and other books available on managerial accounting.

FINANCIAL CONCEPTS

As we noted at the beginning of this chapter, what follows is not a glossary but an explanation of the financial concepts we use. It contains working definitions and, more important, a description of how definitions are applied across the media and for KZZZ-FM. As you will see, these definitions are not formal; they are descriptive and designed for the layman or new manager.

Items Related to the Income Statement

Operating Revenue or Operating Income. All the revenue that a media company earns from any of its day-to-day operations is operating revenue. Contrast it with nonoperating income, which springs from occasional and uncontrollable sources, such as interest earned on a firm's spare cash.

Most of KZZZ-FM's operating revenue comes from selling advertising spots on the air, but some of it could come from related ventures, such as the pocket paging beeper service mentioned earlier. Both the advertising revenue and the pocket pager rentals provide operating revenue. Many media earn operating revenue through the sale of time or space to advertisers. Some media sell subscriptions, access to cable signals, or movies directly to audience members, while others sell services, such as advertising campaigns, and public relations efforts.

Operating Expenses. As the name implies, operating expenses are the other side of operating revenue. It is all the costs of running a station or media enterprise directly linked to the firm's operation: rent, wages, marketing and promotion, materials, supplies, and more.

Working Capital. Working capital is part of the station's financial underpinnings; it is the money used to operate KZZZ-FM day to day. It comes from investors and from cash flow. A more technical definition of working capital is current assets (cash, accounts receivable, inventory) minus current liabilities (accounts payable, accrued expenses payable). See the section, Balance Sheet, below, for an elaboration of these terms.

Cash Flow. Another way to look at money is as cash flow. It is the money available to operate the firm and it passes through the business over time.

To understand cash flow, let's return to the beeper paging business of KZZZ-FM. Earlier in this chapter we said the station's general manager, Linda Remy, might take on this new venture although estimates showed that it would not initially make a profit. The investment was made because within 18 months beeper sales, combined with reductions in the technical staff, would pay for the new venture.

Beeper sales would bring additional money (cash flow) to the station. That extra cash would enable Remy to hire one extra employee to oversee the beeper traffic. Equally important, the new employee could also act as KZZZ-FM's receptionist, a priority need for the station, but one that Remy couldn't afford until the additional cash from the beeper service was available.

Many media companies grow through using the cash flow gained from the purchase of other media firms. That is why many media executives look more closely at cash flow than at profits when they consider an acquisition. The heads of large information organizations believe that their expertise will eventually improve weak profits, even if it takes time to do so. For them, cash flow is one of the better indicators of a potential acquisition's viability. It also is important because it adds cash to the parent firm.

Expenses. Expenses are crucial to any manager since the old adage, a penny saved is a penny earned, is often true: money not spent (as expense) goes directly to the bottom line (to the firm's profits). Controlling expenses is one of the more challenging facets of running an information organization. It takes good judgment to know when not to spend money, but even better judgment to recognize when money should be risked to generate new revenue.

Profit and Loss. If revenues exceed expenses, there's a profit. If revenues are less than expenses, there's a loss. Profits are used in a variety of ways: as working capital to pay operating expenses; as investment capital to purchase equipment or to repay loans; as return on investment to stockholders via dividends.

Opportunities for Improving Profits. For the media manager there are numerous opportunities to improve profits. The two primary ways are through revenue generation and by holding down expenses. Other ways include purchasing labor-saving equipment to increase efficiency, investing working capital to earn the highest return on investment when the capital is not being used (cash management); taking full advantage of the legal allowances in the tax code to reduce taxes; and improving the productivity of members of the staff.

Return on Investment (ROI). ROI is fairly self-explanatory; it refers to making a profit on money spent on people, projects, equipment, or other investments. In its simplest form, it can be expressed by the formula:

$$\text{Return on Investment (ROI)} = \frac{\text{Profit}}{\text{Investment}}$$

In the case of KZZZ-FM, the station might, for example, invest excess revenues earned during a good quarter in short-term bonds at a high interest rate. The interest received would be a return on investment.

Managers use the term ROI more broadly than to refer just to money earned on investments, however. ROI often refers to the return on the money which the station makes by investing in either its own people or new capital equipment.

For example, suppose the new KZZZ-FM sales manager, Bob Dunn, goes to a meeting at a resort. The cost of the trip is $1,000, plus $1,000 for Dunn's time, but he returns with two new sales ideas that eventually bring in $15,000 in new advertising revenue. The station's $2,000 investment yielded $15,000 in sales. That gross $13,000 profit is a healthy return on a $2,000 investment. And, as a matter of fact, the return on that investment may well be greater than $13,000, for if the ideas work once they probably will work again, creating additional return on the investment.

A manager can view ROI for the company as a whole, a department, or a project. If the calculation is to be precise, an additional expense for the value of the money—what it could earn if it were simply invested in securities—should be deducted from the gross profit.

Payback. Payback is the amount of time it requires to pay off an investment. In general, the faster the payback, the greater the return on investment. Payback is calculated by dividing the initial investment by the financial benefits received for the year (increased revenue and decreased expenses). In the KZZZ-FM example, the equipment for a beeper system cost $45,000. It brought in increased revenue of $12,000 and expense reductions for technical staff of $18,000, which was a total financial benefit of $30,000. The payback period on this investment is $45,000/$30,000 = 1.5 years.

Capital Investments. This term refers to money invested either in plant or major equipment. Media firms' capital expenditures refer to money spent for new technology and, occasionally, a building.

The term capital is used to differentiate large, fixed, physical investments from operating or day to day expenditures for things. Media organizations must pay for electricity (an operating expense) on a monthly basis because it is used all the time. On the other hand, KZZZ-FM's purchase of a mobile transmitter or a building represents an occasional capital expense that lasts for many years. Capital expenditures become nonoperating expenses when they are depreciated.

Depreciation. The amount by which wear and tear from use reduces the value of a company's building and equipment each year is depreciation. How long it takes for these assets to lose their value as they wear out determines the percent of their cost that can be taken as a depreciation expense. Buildings and some equipment may last 20 years or more; they utilize a slow depreciation schedule, 15–30 years. Computers and most office equipment lose their value rapidly so they have fast depreciation schedules, 3–5 years.

Items Related to the Balance Sheet

Chapter 7 focuses on the ongoing operation of a company; that is, what it does day to day during a quarter or a year. By contrast, the balance sheet describes a company in financial terms at a specific point in time. The balance sheet for KZZZ-FM as of June 30, 1986, is shown in Exhibit 7.12, before the station made its major investments.

Current Assets. Cash, marketable securities, bank accounts, accounts receivable (money owed to the company by customers), and inventories of the company are all current assets. They are thought of as "current assets" because they can be turned into cash quite readily.

Fixed Assets. Such things as land, plant, and equipment less the accumulated depreciation are fixed assets. These are included in the Other assets category in the balance sheet.

Other examples of assets that fall here include the value of an FCC license and what is often termed good will, the value of the name of the company and its position in the marketplace. For many media concerns that is a comparatively large figure, for the land and equipment they own may have relatively low value, but the good will—the call letters of a radio station or the name of a newspaper or magazine—has substantial value. Think what it would mean to have the name the *New York Times* if you owned and were selling a newspaper in New York. Would you pay as much for the *New York Times* if it were called the *New York Globe*? No one would suggest that the *Globe's* good will is equal to that of the legendary *Times*.

All of the items listed above are on the asset side of a balance sheet

EXHIBIT 7.12. KZZZ-FM BALANCE SHEET, JUNE 30, 1986

Assets		
Current assets		
Cash	$ 10,300	
Accounts receivable	$ 625,400	
Total		$ 635,700
Other assets		
Property and equipment	$ 430,000	
FCC license	$6,360,000	
Total		$6,790,000
Total assets		$7,425,700
Liabilities and net worth		
Current liabilities		
Accounts payable	$ 125,000	
Accrued expenses	$ 74,300	
Income taxes payable	$ 45,000	
Total		$ 244,300
Long-term liabilities		
Note to City Media, Inc.	$5,335,000	
Note to bank	$ 325,000	
Total		$5,660,000
Total liabilities		$5,904,300
Retained earnings	$1,075,000	
Common stock at book value	$ 446,000	
Total net worth		$1,521,400
Total liabilities and net worth		$7,425,700

ledger. They are balanced by the *liabilities* and *net worth* side of a ledger.

Current Liabilities. Current liabilities include the bills to be paid and are called accounts payable, and accrued expenses payable. All items that have been purchased recently and for which total payment is due in a comparatively short time appear as current liabilities. This year's portion of long-term debt is also a current liability.

Long-term Liabilities. These are liabilities due over a long period of time. Mortgages and other long-term bank borrowing is included here, as are notes owed to other lenders; an example is KZZZ-FM's note payable to City Media, Inc., its corporate owner.

Current and long-term liabilities combine to make up total liabilities.

Net Worth. This is determined by adding the book value of the firm's stock to its *accumulated retained earnings* (i.e., the company's profit accumulated over a period of years) to establish net worth. Both of these items are owed to the firm's stockholders, at least in a theoretical sense.

Combining net worth with current and long-term liabilities produces a category called Total liabilities and net worth, which together must equal Total assets to balance the ledger.

Borrowing

Few information companies can generate the kind of revenue necessary to avoid outside borrowing. When a company borrows money it is reflected on the balance sheet, usually as a long-term liability. Borrowing is one of the subtle and often overlooked but very significant factors in determining profit and loss.

For example, when KZZZ-FM borrowed money in 1981 for new equipment, it projected that interest rates would rise no higher than 9.75 percent. That was a reasonable projection because the rate was 8.25 percent at the time, and interest rates had never risen above 9.5 percent. Thus, the company anticipated no problem in repaying the loan for those capital purchases. Their projections showed that even if interest rates rose to 10.80 percent, they could still afford to make the payments out of the station's profits.

Within a year, however, interest rates shot up to an unprecedented 18 to 21 percent. Retail business plummeted, and many accounts stopped advertising with the station. Others, who had always paid their bills in 30 days, stretched that period out to 45 to 180 days. The station couldn't cut off these late-paying accounts because business was so bad. Indeed, KZZZ-FM relied on them for what income it did receive. As you might expect, the economic downturn caused the station's profits to fall at exactly the time the cost of borrowed money was rising dramatically. KZZZ-FM had huge interest payments, which were a major factor in creating losses in 1982 and 1983.

Managerial Accounting

As its name implies, managerial accounting looks at a company's financial statement not just to gain a financial perspective, but to provide management with indicators of performance that will lead to actions to improve the company's operation.

Some categories of managerial accounting are obvious: revenue forecasting, major classifications of expenditures, budgets, capital investments, and ROI.

Managers also benefit by comparing their firm's performance to industrywide figures for similar firms. One method of making this comparison is regression analysis; it allows firms of dissimilar size to be compared, at least on a percentage basis. It is important to recognize some of the problems in making comparisons.

For example, in 1985 it was reported that Morton Zuckerman paid a princely sum for *U.S. News & World Report*. Zuckerman is a large real estate developer who said he would move the magazine into one of his real estate properties. In the process, one of the major expense items for the magazine would go from the new owner's right pocket to his left. That is, Zuckerman, the owner and publisher of *U.S. News & World Report*, would be paying rent to Zuckerman, the landlord. As a result, *U.S. News & World Report* could make somewhat less money and still satisfy its new boss. If other magazine operators compared their performance to *U.S. News*, their comparisons would be invalid because of the effects of Zuckerman's dual interests.

Another challenge for information companies is that they make investments in nonconcrete items, which are difficult to value. For example, it is hard for a motion picture company to assess the value of movies on the shelf. However, it is even more difficult for a radio or television station to assess the value of its format or its programs or for a newspaper to determine the worth of its circulation.

Financial Accounting and Ratio Analysis

This is the kind of accounting done by certified public accountants (CPAs) and bankers when they focus on the financial health of a company. They use the company's income statement and balance sheet to develop ratios that describe various aspects of a company's financial condition and performance: stability of a company, how well a company utilizes its assets, and the firm's profitability. We illustrate several of these ratios here, using information from KZZZ-FM's 1986 income statement and balance sheet.

Quick or "Acid Test" Ratio. The acid test ratio is a measure of the solvency of a company, i.e., how well a company has its current liabilities covered. It is computed by dividing liquid assets (those readily converted into cash) by current liabilities. For KZZZ-FM the quick ratio is:

$$\frac{\text{Cash + accounts receivables}}{\text{Current liabilities}} = \frac{\$\ 635{,}700}{\$\ 244{,}300} = 2.6$$

At the present time, KZZZ-FM has plenty of liquid assets to cover its short-term liabilities.

Accounts Receivable Turnover. How effectively a company uses its current assets, called the accounts receivable turnover, shows how many times the accounts receivable have "turned over" in a year. It is calculated by dividing sales by accounts receivable. For KZZZ-FM, this ratio is:

$$\frac{\text{Sales}}{\text{Accounts receivable}} = \frac{\$3{,}140{,}561}{\$\ 625{,}400} = 5.0$$

If this ratio is low, as it appears to be here, it may indicate the company is not collecting its accounts fast enough. In effect, KZZZ-FM is serving as a banker for its advertising customers by "lending" them money past the due date of their account. Even if KZZZ-FM charges interest on overdue accounts, however, KZZZ-FM's liquidity could suffer if that situation continues. Further, the station may have credit losses from customers who won't pay. Ratios like this one provide information on a company's effectiveness in cash management.

Return on Net Worth. This ratio shows the company's profitability from the point of view of the owners, i.e., the percentage of their net worth that the company makes as a profit. It is calculated by dividing net profit (loss) before taxes by net worth. Because KZZZ-FM had a loss this year, the ratio will show a negative figure:

$$\frac{\text{Net loss before taxes}}{\text{Net worth}} = \frac{\$(234{,}495)}{\$\ 1{,}521{,}000} = (15.4\%)$$

Profits increase a company's net worth, and losses reduce it. If a station continues to experience losses, it will not be long before the company's net worth would disappear entirely. At that point the stockholders no longer really "own" the company; rather, those who have loaned money to finance the station own it.

Ratios like these are most useful when seen in a comparative way. For example, calculating the ratios for a number of years can show a trend. Comparing the ratios to industry figures can reveal how a company is doing compared to competitors. Comparing ratios to those developed from a company's budgets can also show how well it is doing in meeting targets.

There are many other ratios that can be used to assess the liquidity and safety of a media company, its profitability, and its effectiveness in utilizing its assets. To elaborate on them would take us far afield. We suggest that you consult an accounting text or an accountant if you are deeply interested in this sort of analysis. Some common ratios for such financial analyses are listed below in Exhibit 7.13.

EXHIBIT 7.13. COMMON RATIOS FOR FINANCIAL ANALYSIS

Liquidity and Safety

1. Quick or "acid test" ratio $= \dfrac{\text{Cash + Accounts receivable}}{\text{Current liabilities}}$

2. Current ratio $= \dfrac{\text{Current assets}}{\text{Current liabilities}}$

3. Debt to worth ratio $= \dfrac{\text{Total liabilities}}{\text{Net worth}}$

Profitability

1. Net profit margin $= \dfrac{\text{Net profit before taxes}}{\text{Sales}}$

2. Return on net worth/equity $= \dfrac{\text{Net profit before taxes}}{\text{Net worth}}$

3. Return on assets $= \dfrac{\text{Net profit before taxes}}{\text{Total assets}}$

Asset Utilization

1. Accounts receivable turnover $= \dfrac{\text{Sales}}{\text{Accounts receivable}}$

2. Collection period $= \dfrac{360}{\text{Accounts receivable turnover}}$

CHAPTER 8

Working with People

Chapters 5 through 7 focused on three of the five functions media managers must master: planning, organizing work and technology, and fiscal management. Each is an integral facet of an information executive's effectiveness. None, however, is more important than the fourth and fifth functions: how media managers work with and lead the staff who report to them. Working with staff and leadership are the focus of this chapter and the next.

Working with people breaks down into two broad perspectives. The first is the balance between producing an effective product and nurturing each employee's aspirations. The second looks at two cycles supervisors participate in when they work with people: supervising the work cycle, which occurs continuously, and the personnel development cycle, which occurs intermittently throughout an employee's career. Both perspectives require managers to focus on employee motivation, but in some instances, motivating employees to do what is best for the firm may conflict with nurturing the aspirations of the employees for themselves.

BALANCING PRODUCTION AND PEOPLE

Media managers constantly wrestle with the issue of balancing a concern for production with a concern for the staff with whom they work. In any organization as time driven as the media, tasks need to be performed on time, at a high level of quality and effectiveness, and at a reasonable cost. That is why much of the organizing function we discussed in Chapter 6 concentrates on planning for efficient and effective workflow.

Despite the importance and demands of their jobs, information executives should not lose sight of the fact that their staffs, not the executives, do the bulk of the work. As a result, if media managers want to be effective over the long term, they need to be just as concerned with the well being of their employees as with meeting deadlines or making a profit.

In order to examine how executives act on that concern, we briefly review the fundamental approaches to personnel management that have been developed through experience and by experts. Then we focus on applying those approaches to working with media employees.

The Managerial Grid®

How can media managers take into account a dual concern for production and for staff? One way is illustrated by The Managerial Grid, shown in Exhibit 8.1. It was developed by management theorists Blake and Mouton (1985).

Note that the managerial grid has two dimensions: concern for production and concern for people. They are the different and, it is hoped, overlapping orientations media managers may have toward their employees. From their work, Blake and Mouton highlighted five basic managerial styles:

EXHIBIT 8.1. THE MANAGERIAL GRID®

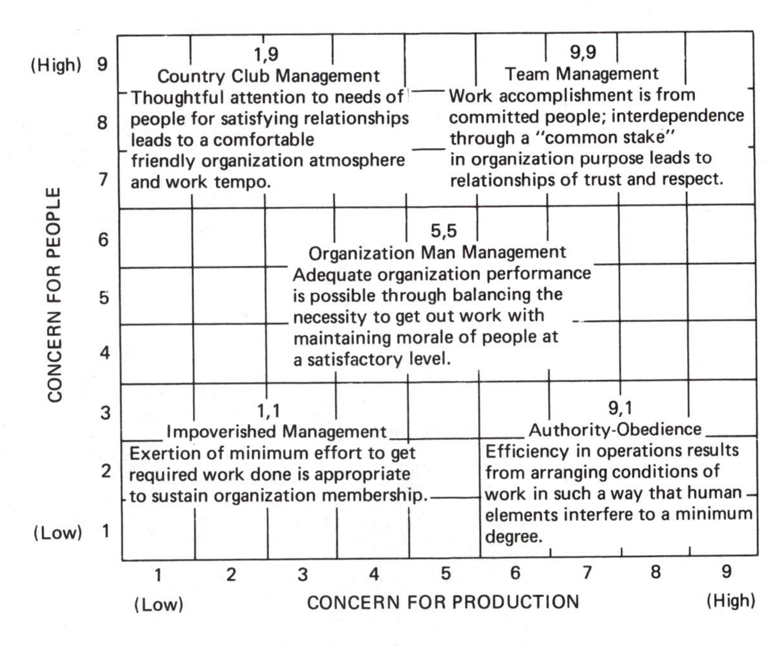

Source: Blake, Robert R., and Mouton, Jane Srygley. *The Managerial Grid III: The Key to Leadership Excellence.* Houston: Gulf Publishing Company, Copyright © 1985, page 12. Reproduced by permission.

- An "impoverished leader" (1, 1) exerts a minimum effort to get the work done or to sustain a sense of belonging to the work group and organization.
- An "authority-obedience" leader (9, 1) concentrates on task efficiency, but shows little interest in developing morale among subordinates.
- A "country club leader" (1, 9) focuses on being considerate and supportive of employees, but task efficiency is a low priority.
- A "middle-of-the-road leader" (5, 5) attempts to balance the necessity of getting out the work while maintaining a satisfactory level of morale among subordinates.
- A "team leader" (9, 9) attempts to facilitate both production and morale by coordinating and integrating work-related activities, developing commitment in people, and building a sense of interdependence by creating a common stake in the organization.

In Blake and Mouton's system, team leadership is the preferred style because it fully acknowledges the interdependence between the task and people dimensions. Actually, the 9, 9 orientation is a managerial strategy that can be adapted to various situations by modifying specific tactics.

For example, a television news director will maintain close contact with a new reporter throughout an assignment. They will discuss the purpose of the assignment thoroughly before the reporter begins (e.g. likely sources, projected length of the report, angle for the story) and talk frequently as the story develops. With an inexperienced reporter, the news director will use such tactics as maintaining a short-term perspective, focusing on small units of behavior, coaching, and providing immediate feedback.

The news director will use different tactics with a highly experienced reporter. For example, they will discuss the purpose of a series of stories the reporter will be doing instead of just a single story. The news director will offer suggestions and criticisms concerning the broad approach to the assignment taken by the reporter, rather than providing feedback on specific actions.

Situational Leadership

As its name implies, Paul Hersey's (1985) model of situational leadership builds on the same situations that were described at the television station: the need to adapt a leadership style to the situation. Research shows a key variable influencing the effectiveness of work performance is the relationship between the leader and the led. Matching executive style with employee needs results in a cooperative relationship and high performance. And a mismatch may have the opposite result.

For instance, reporters who view their editor as supportive of staff members' efforts to do high-quality, professional work are likely to write better stories than those who view their editors as simply interested in getting stories in on time. The first editor is sensitive to the reporters' need to maintain high professional standards. The second editor ignores those needs.

Hersey's emphasis on the relationship between manager and employee is highlighted by the concept of "employee readiness for task performance." For Hersey, the crux of effective management is adapting leadership style to the employee's readiness state.

In Hersey's view, employee readiness has two components: the staff member's ability: the knowledge, experience, and skill a person brings to a particular task; and the media worker's willingness: the confidence, commitment, and motivation to carry out the assignment.

Hersey identifies four states of readiness by combining levels of ability and willingness. These are shown in Exhibit 8.2.

Carrying his analysis further, Hersey notes that different leadership styles are appropriate for different readiness states. He defines leadership style in terms similar to the Blake and Mouton grid: concern for production involves directive behaviors, and concern for people involves supportive behaviors.

Hersey's full model of situational leadership is shown in Exhibit 8.3. The one-word descriptions in the figure—telling, selling, participating, and delegating—indicate the basic intent of the four leadership styles included in the situational model.

Leadership styles one and two are leader directed. Style one is most effective when an employee is in a low state of readiness. For example, a cub reporter may feel overwhelmed by a reporting assignment. An editor, observing the reporter's hesitancy, becomes directive by telling the reporter how to do the assignment: sources to contact, questions to probe, how to structure the story, etc. The editor provides substantial guidance, but must be careful not to provide too much support; that would make it appear as if the editor were rewarding low standards and taking away responsibility from the reporter.

Style two is most effective when an employee is eager to do a job, but may not have all the knowledge and skills needed to do it at a high quality level. That is how a competent new photographer who does not know the region or the photographic philosophy of the TV station might feel, or how an experienced general assignment reporter might feel

EXHIBIT 8.2. EMPLOYEE READINESS

High	R4	Able and willing/motivated
Moderate	R3	Able, but unwilling/insecure
Moderate	R2	Unable, but willing/motivated
Low	R1	Unable and unwilling/insecure

EXHIBIT 8.3. SITUATIONAL LEADERSHIP MODEL

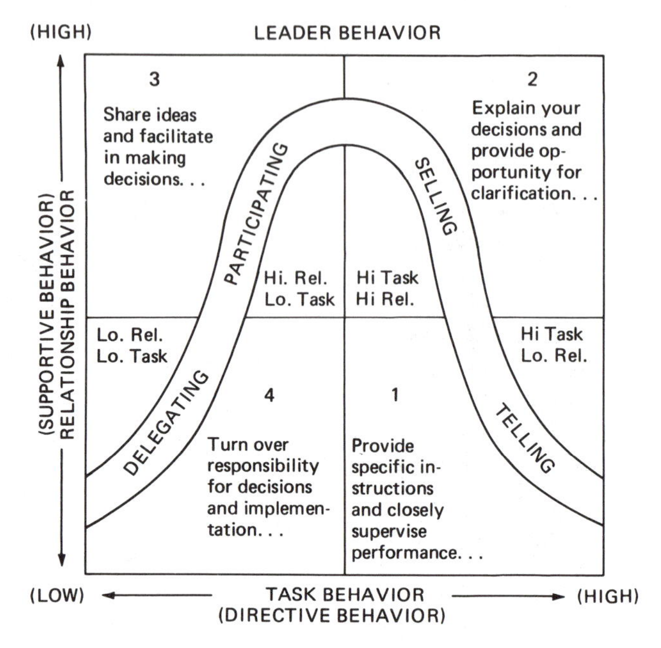

FOLLOWER READINESS

HIGH	MODERATE		LOW
R4	R3	R2	R1
Able & Willing or Motivated	Able but Unwilling or Insecure	Unable but Willing or Motivated	Unable & Unwilling or Insecure

Source: Copyrighted material from Leadership Studies, Inc. All rights reserved. Used by permission.

when doing the first few stories on a new beat. In that circumstance, the news director provides both direction and support. By explaining how a story should be covered, then providing an opportunity for clarification, the TV executive "sells" the reporter and photographer on their ability to do the job and gets them to psychologically buy into the assignment.

Styles three and four are less leader directed and more employee directed. Style three, involving high levels of supportive behavior and low levels of direction, works best when staff members are able to perform effectively, but for some reason are unwilling to do so or are insecure about their abilities. In that situation, a news director joins with the staffers in sharing the development of an assignment. The TV news manager "participates" with them in defining how the story will be covered. Major features of this leadership style include encouragement of input, involvement by the staff members, and reassurance that they can do the job as mirrored in their news director's confidence.

Style four is most appropriate when an employee is both eager and able. For example, when a top-notch reporter proposes to develop an important investigative story, a wise news director or executive producer steps out of the way, delegating responsibility to the reporter. The news executive will offer support and periodically check on how things are going, but primarily turns initiative for contacts over to the reporter.

One implication of this more complex model is that a key attribute of media managers is their diagnostic ability. Effective executives are able to diagnose two aspects of their employees: the staff members' abilities (knowledge, experience, and skills) and their employees' willingness to perform (confidence, commitment, motivation). Both can be difficult to judge, but ability is more obvious, because it is usually demonstrated in the employee's performance. Gauging an information worker's willingness or motivation to perform can be more difficult, subtle, and variable.

MOTIVATION

The way media managers view their staff's motivation and orientation to work is often linked to basic assumptions the executives make about people. Managers' beliefs about why human beings function as they do often determine what actions they take with their employees.

Stop for a minute and put yourself in the shoes of a media executive. How would you answer these questions:

- Why do people work for this information organization?
- What are my employees seeking to achieve from their work?
- How much supervision does my staff require?

Your answers tell a great deal about your assumptions concerning people. Now, as you read the following discussion, check to see how your views correspond to the perspectives presented.

Theories X, Y, and Z

In 1960, Douglas McGregor identified two perspectives on management possessed in varying degrees by most managers. They are called Theory X and Theory Y (Exhibit 8.4).

Theory X sees people as lazy, preferring to be told exactly what to do, avoiding responsibility, having little ambition, and above all wanting

EXHIBIT 8.4. THEORY X AND Y ASSUMPTIONS

Theory X assumptions
1. People do not like to work and try to avoid it.
2. People do not like work, so managers have to control, direct, coerce, and threaten employees to get them to work toward organizational goals.
3. People prefer to be directed, to avoid responsibility, to want security; they have little ambition.

Theory Y assumptions
1. People do not naturally dislike work; work is a natural part of their lives.
2. People are internally motivated to reach objectives to which they are committed.
3. People are committed to goals to the degree that they receive personal rewards when they reach their objectives.
4. People will both seek and accept responsibility under favorable conditions.
5. People have the capacity to be innovative in solving organizational problems.
6. People are bright, but under most organizational conditions their potentials are underutilized.

Source: The Human Side of Enterprise, Douglas McGregor. (New York: McGraw-Hill, 1960, pp. 33-34, 47-48.) Used with permission.

security. To the extent that media executives see their staff that way they will believe that to get work done employees must be controlled, coerced, threatened with discipline, and punished. Theory X is rooted in the "scientific management" approach developed by Frederick Taylor at the turn of this century (see Chapter 4). According to Taylor (1947), most people find work inherently unpleasant, and thus the money they earn is the prime motivation for their spending hours on the job.

Theory Y is different. It views mental and physical effort as a natural and important part of human activity. It assumes that people will exercise self-control and self-direction if they are committed to the objectives of their job. For information executives who operate under Theory Y, developing and maintaining a satisfactory work environment is essential for gaining high levels of staff performance.

Theory Y grew out of the work of Elton Mayo (1953) and his associates and is often termed "the human relations approach." (See Chapter 4.) This perspective emphasizes the role of social processes in the workplace. It assumes that employees want to feel useful and important, that belonging to a social group is significant, and that nonfinancial rewards are often more important than money in motivating employees over the long term.

Many reporters, advertising agency copywriters, or broadcasters reflect Theory Y. They talk about the excitement and challenge of their work, about the spirit they share with their colleagues (including their bosses), and about their own standards and desire to do a good job as the prime force that motivates them. They also note that winning a major award or getting a choice assignment often means more than a raise.

A third approach, proposed by William Ouchi (1981), came from observations about the differences between working in Japan and in the United States (see Exhibit 8.5). Theory Z proposes that security is especially important. In the Japanese management system, security is insured because most workers have lifetime employment in a single company. The Japanese-style organization is committed to that long-term relationship, with regular and clear-cut performance reviews providing the feedback that most employees require in order to function effectively.

Theory Z also emphasizes development of trust relationships between the leader and the led. That emphasis is based on the assumption that people's motivations are primarily internal, but that those feelings must be reinforced by a visible commitment to the employee by the employer. Theory Z sees collective decision making and group responsibility as providing the necessary social support for top-level performance. It does that by creating the security that enables employees to generate new ideas without fear of rejection or failure.

Do any of these theories reflect your views? Does one of them correspond closely with what you have experienced? Perhaps your views, like ours, represent a blend of these perspectives.

As we have worked with, supervised, and observed media staffers for more than 20 years, it is clear to us that information company employees vary widely in their reactions to, and attitudes about, work. It is also true that some of the more impersonal, bottom line media compan-

EXHIBIT 8.5. CHARACTERISTICS OF JAPANESE AND AMERICAN ORGANIZATIONS

Japanese Organizations	*American Organizations*
Lifetime employment	Short-term employment
Slow evaluation and promotion	Rapid evaluation and promotion
Nonspecialized career paths	Specialized career paths
Implicit control mechanisms	Explicit control mechanisms
Collective decision making	Individual decision making
Collective responsibility	Individual responsibility
Wholistic concern	Segmented concern

Source: William Ouchi, *Theory Z*, © 1981, Addison-Wesley Publishing Company, Inc., Reading, MA. p. 58. Reprinted with permission.

ies, such as Thompson Newspapers, appear to follow Theory X; they seem to see their employees as not very motivated or, at least, they try to rigidly control their staffs' behaviors.

By contrast, the wise media executive believes that the use of a single theory or approach is too simplistic and often counterproductive. The challenge for these media leaders is to learn more about their employees and to find out what is important to them. What does each staff member find stimulating and exciting? What do they expect from their work, and more broadly, from their life? If media managers can answer these questions, they can begin to improve their team's motivation.

Specific Approaches to Motivation

What is motivation? For media workers it is an internal state: the individual wishes, desires, and drives that move the information employee to action. Motivated staff members work hard, sustain a rigorous pace, and direct their behavior toward what they feel are important goals. Motivation is a process that begins with some unfulfilled needs. Such needs lead to goal-directed behavior which, if the behavior is successful, fulfills the needs. The key concepts here are needs, need fulfillment, and reward.

Maslow's Hierarchy of Needs. Needs are deficiencies within the individual that provide the spark for behavior. Maslow's (1970) "hierarchy of needs" identified five levels of drives within the individual: physiological, safety, social, esteem, and self-actualization. Maslow placed them in a hierarchy to emphasize that lower-level needs, such as physiological and safety, must be satisfied before higher-level ones can be achieved.

Work in information organizations is related to the fulfillment of these needs. For example, comfortable employment conditions and salary at an electronic data base firm, like Dow Jones News Retrieval, are related to the fulfillment of physiological needs. But security and social needs are fulfilled by linkages with, for example, other news executives or computer experts who understand the new technology of computer bulletin boards and videotex. Job security and company policies also fit in here.

Although there is some relationship between Maslow's hierarchy of needs and features of the work environment, utilizing this perspective is not particularly helpful for thinking about job motivation. Other theorists' viewpoints prove more useful.

Herzberg's Two-factor Theory. Herzberg (1966) identified two sets of conditions related to employee motivation (Exhibit 8.6). First, the absence of certain conditions on a job results in dissatisfied employees. Herzberg called these "maintenance" factors, because they are necessary to maintain a reasonable level of work satisfaction. They include

EXHIBIT 8.6. MAINTENANCE AND MOTIVATIONAL FACTORS

Maintenance Factors	*Motivational Factors*
Pay and security	Achievement
Working conditions	Recognition
Interpersonal relationships	Responsibility
Supervisors	The work itself
Company policy and administration	Advancement and growth

such elements as salary, job security, working conditions, status, and interpersonal relationships with supervisors, peers, and subordinates.

The second set of conditions has a different function. When they are present, high levels of motivation and job satisfaction often result. Their absence, however, does not produce dissatisfaction. Herzberg uses the term "motivational factors" to indicate that these items positively relate to employee attitudes. He identifies six such factors: achievement, recognition, advancement, responsibility, satisfaction with the work itself, and the possibility of personal growth.

Herzberg believed that unless employees' maintenance needs are fulfilled, the staff members will be dissatisfied. But fulfillment of these needs alone will not result in highly motivated, high-performing workers. What is needed to generate strongly motivated employees is fulfillment of their motivational needs, which correspond to the upper levels of Maslow's hierarchy.

Different Employees Have Different Needs. Research indicates that different types of employees vary considerably in the importance they place on different needs. For example, in one study (Hofstede, 1972), the following differences emerged:

- Workers with low skill levels listed the following as their top four needs: physical conditions of work, security, earnings, and benefits.
- Clerical workers emphasized social needs: cooperative environment, a manager who cares about them, friendly co-workers, and departmental efficiency.
- Research and development professionals focused on self-actualization needs: challenge, autonomy, and the chance to use their skills.
- Technical personnel showed a more mixed need profile: security, earnings, challenge, and a manager who cares about them.

Media managers can use these distinctions to identify differences in the needs of their employees. Thus, reporters, copywriters, art directors, and other professionals involved in message creation are likely to place high importance on self-actualization needs, similar to R&D professionals. Office staff may place more emphasis on social desires. Production staff, as well as unskilled employees, are likely to stress wages and security, and sales personnel may show a more mixed profile that tilts towards the challenge of the R&D professional, but contains a fair quotient of the technical personnel as well.

Rewards

How are needs fulfilled? In the motivational process, behavior is activated by an unfulfilled need. Then, if the behavior is successful, the need is fulfilled and the individual experiences a reward, either extrinsic or intrinsic.

Extrinsic Rewards. Extrinsic rewards occur outside the scope of one's job. Extrinsic rewards can be financial: additional benefits, profit-sharing, pay incentives, deferred compensation, or nonfinancial: professional recognition, promotions, or friendships. Most are related to Herzberg's maintenance factors, but note that some have clear implications for motivational needs as well, e.g., promotions and professional peer recognition. Extrinsic rewards arise from various sources within the organization, including formal management policies, informal groups, co-workers, and even from sources outside the organization.

Intrinsic Rewards. Intrinsic rewards are part of the job and arise from the work itself. They include autonomy, variety, significance, and identity. They relate very closely to the basic job characteristics described in Chapter 6. Intrinsic rewards are tied to the higher-level needs in Maslow's hierarchy, particularly the need for self-actualization, and to Herzberg's motivating factors.

It is interesting that the concepts of job enrichment and job enlargement that were discussed in Chapter 6 grew out of the analysis of motivating factors (Hackman, 1977). They capitalize on the intrinsically rewarding nature of certain aspects of work. By enriching or enlarging jobs, media organizations can heighten employees' motivation by fulfilling more of the staff members' needs.

For media companies, extrinsic rewards are clear-cut: money, promotions, travel, and commissions. Most media firms link extrinsic rewards directly to performance for sales people or department managers. Unfortunately, we see few organizations in any of the media where top management understands the merit in developing a list of monetary rewards for employees in nonrevenue-producing areas such as news, production, or business.

Many media jobs (reporter, copywriter, art director, TV production staff member) involve considerable intrinsic rewards. Yet, extrinsic rewards are no less significant for maintaining satisfaction of employees involved in those activities, just as those rewards are important for staffers who are in sales. What is discouraging is that at some level media executives know that; otherwise they would not hold so many competitions for best news story, best news picture, best advertisement or commercial, and best TV or radio coverage. These contests, which number in the hundreds, are sponsored by local, state, and national media associations.

Professional recognition is important, and it can be arranged with comparative ease inside a media firm. Think how satisfying it would be if you worked for a public relations agency or a radio station and your boss publicly recognized you for producing first-class work. Or wouldn't you find it fulfilling if your department head recognized your accomplishments before your friends and family at an annual in-house recognition dinner? In the same vein, wouldn't an editor be as excited and turned on by a cash bonus because her magazine made a profit as an advertising sales person in the same organization?

Given the changing nature of work within media firms, intrinsic rewards are not so obvious, but they are as powerful as extrinsic ones. A few of the more subtle intrinsic rewards include the chance to carry out a new project, attendance at a seminar, and other forms of job enrichment and job enlargement.

At least one media company, Knight-Ridder (KR) understands the importance of both intrinsic and extrinsic rewards for its employees. KR says it will provide support every year to further each staff member's own professional development. Such a commitment is time-consuming and expensive for the company, but it is a strong motivator for employees.

Media managers have many options for improving motivation, and they should think creatively to develop them. Even in departments like a newsroom, where productivity is difficult to measure, editors have numerous possibilities. What about dinners, trips, a chance to be an editor or to head up a team? What about further training or time to do a story that isn't on the schedule but which the staff member initiates? What about bringing in outside experts to help the news staff improve the quality of their work?

Another variation on that theme is illustrated by a media manager we observed. He is general manager of a 10,000-circulation daily newspaper. He bet his seven-person advertising sales staff a dinner at a fine restaurant that he could sell more new advertising contracts than they could during the slowest month of the year. As you might guess, the staff beat the executive. In fact, since the manager never revealed how many contracts he brought in, there is some question as to whether he actually sold more than the one he flaunted around the office on the second day of the wager.

What is important in this situation is the manager's wisdom in developing an incentive that challenged the staff. He knew them well enough to be sure that they would take the bet seriously and work hard to bring in new accounts so they would beat the boss. In the end the most important reward the staff received was neither the dinner nor the substantial amount of money they earned for each of the new contracts they signed or even the psychological satisfaction of winning. It was the understanding that during the most difficult time of the year, when departmental history indicated it was impossible to get new accounts, the sales representatives were able to generate more new contracts than they had in a number of the supposedly better months.

Before closing this discussion on motivation, we want to be sure you take special note of our heavy emphasis on rewards. Unlike Theory X, which focuses on control and perhaps punishment, most managers' more thoughtful discussions about motivating employees emanate from Theories Y and Z. An underlying principle of both of those theories is that desire for gain is a much stronger motivator than the fear of loss.

In the remainder of this chapter we apply the theories you have just reviewed and look directly at information executives' interaction with their staffs. Media company department heads (editors, news directors, advertising sales managers, creative directors, and business managers, to name a few) have two cycles of activity. The first is short-term; we call it the *supervision cycle*. The other is long-term; we label it the *people development cycle*.

THE SUPERVISION CYCLE*

The supervision cycle is a series of activities that occur on a regular, though cyclical, basis. The cycle usually takes place in a limited time, a day or two, although it can stretch over several weeks or longer.

Four major activities are involved in the cycle, shown in Exhibit 8.7.

EXHIBIT 8.7. THE SUPERVISION CYCLE

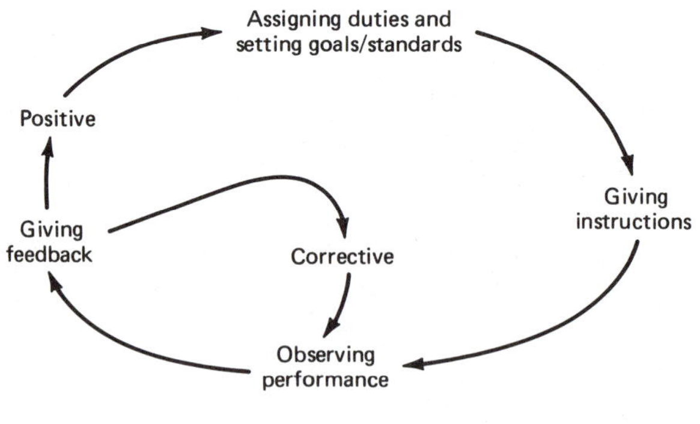

Assigning duties and setting goals/standards
Giving instructions
Observing performance
Giving feedback
Corrective
Positive

* The idea of the supervision cycle is articulated in *Working Together: Productive Communication on the Job*, by Sherod Miller and Daniel Wackman (Littleton, CO: Interpersonal Communication Programs, Inc., 1985).

Setting Goals and Standards or Assigning Duties

The first activity is assigning duties to an employee and setting performance standards for that work. Thus, when an advertising agency begins working with a new client, the account services director explains to the account executive the objectives that the agency is trying to achieve with the client and the actions needed to reach them. If the actions to be taken are clear-cut, then the account services director focuses on the standard of performance that is expected.

Even when the account services director's plan is fully developed, it is important to give the account executive an opportunity to comment on the stated goals and performance standards. That way, if the director's standards are either too high or too low, or if circumstances exist that may prevent attainment of the desired level of performance, the account services director can learn where changes should be made. That avoids frustration and lost time; it also allows account executives to know that their opinions are valued.

Input of that sort is important not only for employees' self-esteem but also because agendas from their managers influence staff members' work, and few employees are initially comfortable with change. Sensitivity to the reaction of staff to change is vital. Setting goals and performance standards with employees provides a key opportunity for media managers to cultivate the involvement and commitment of the people they supervise.

Take another instance. A *Newsweek* magazine editor gives one of her reporters a specific assignment. The editor already has a clear view of the scope of the story and how to approach it. Nonetheless, she solicits the reporter's suggestions on treatment, potential sources, roadblocks to getting information, and time required for information gathering and writing. Asking for the reporter's input clarifies the assignment, warns the editor about potential pitfalls, and strengthens the reporter's involvement in the project.

Giving Instructions

The second activity in the supervision cycle often blends into the first one. Media managers provide specific instructions to staff, including an explanation of the executives' priorities for the job. Setting priorities also allows executives to clear up rumors and provide specific instructions on new procedures. Finally, establishing priorities goes a long way towards ensuring that work will be finished on a timetable that satisfies top management and meets the information organization's complex, overlapping delivery demands.

When everyone from the top to the bottom of the firm or department is involved in developing a timetable, the attitude about producing the story is quite different than if the editor said the project should be completed "sometime." Too often that happens, and when the story is not done in four days—as the chief editor desired, but never articulated—the editor-in-chief is upset. In turn, the assigning (middle level) editor may have set her sights on completing the story in a week. In this situation she feels unfairly treated when her chief expresses irritation after four days. Further, the reporter, who heard no clear date for completion, may have a number of other stories to do and may not plan to work on the story for two weeks. He too will feel abused if he catches the assigning editor's wrath. In short, such a system is sure to anger and frustrate everyone involved in the news process, but all of that could be avoided if participation and clarity were the rules.

Observing Performance

The third phase in the supervision cycle is observing performance. Here's where the popular concept of "managing by wandering around" is most effective. Editors interact most effectively with their staff by getting out of their offices to see what's going on. Going into the staff's work space and asking how things are going provides a wealth of information about performance.

We recall our first visit with Charles Brumback, the publisher of *The Chicago Tribune*. The meeting took place in his palatial office in the Tribune Tower. When we commented on the magnificent view of the Chicago River and downtown loop, Brumback said that he couldn't wait to move into a far more modest, glass-enclosed office located in the middle of the *Tribune*'s work space on a lower floor. The publisher was far less interested in a fancy office than in working where he could see more of his staff, where they could see him, and where he could talk to them as he went about his daily duties.

Managers also monitor performance through reports on such essentials as productivity, number of errors, number of stories, quality improvement in stories or ads, production waste, and success rates in sales calls. Reports and personal observations are complementary; they provide supervisors with both objective data and subjective observations of how things are going.

One of the more important things for a media manager to watch when observing performance is the energy level and mood of employees. When things are going well staff members are attentive, their energy is high, and they're in a good mood. When things are going poorly disagreements between colleagues are more frequent and the sensitive leader feels the tension in the air. Those sorts of "vibrations" affect performance. The wise media manager watches for them, tries to figure out why they are present, and what can be done to lessen or eliminate them.

Giving Feedback

The fourth phase in the cycle involves giving feedback on performance. It seems axiomatic that the *Newsweek* chief editor and assigning editor should praise the reporter who writes a top-notch story. Yet, in the pressure of deadlines and work loads, too few media executives extend meaningful praise in a timely fashion. Of those who do say "job well done," some give praise so late that the impact is lost. Others do it so routinely and with so little enthusiasm that their staff correctly views it as a pro forma comment, not a sincere one. The bottom line, however, is that executives should look for things to compliment. As Ken Blanchard says in *The One Minute Manager*, "Catch them doing something right" (Blanchard & Spencer, 1982, p. 81).

Positive feedback is an extremely powerful motivator, yet some media managers seem reluctant to use it; they believe they must adopt the stereotype of the hard-boiled boss. That model ignores a great deal of research on learning which indicates that reward and praise are extremely important to most employees, even to those who brush off compliments with comments like: "I don't care who likes my (ad, story, movie, report); all that matters to me is that I like it." Of course it is important for the creator to like it, but it is also important to hear that peers and the boss are impressed.

Another type of feedback can be corrective. It is used when performance is not up to standard, when agreed upon procedures are not followed, or when a staff member needs assistance to get the job done. Corrective feedback does not have to be approached in a negative way, although many media managers do so. Instead, it can provide a positive opportunity to help improve performance. Moreover, employees will hear it that way, too, because few employees want to turn out bad work. Whether a staff member perceives corrective feedback as negative or supportive, however, depends largely on how media managers communicate it.

Strategies for Communicating with Your Staff

Communication is a key process in each phase of the supervision cycle, indeed in all aspects of media management. The skills and strategies involved in effective communication are among the more important aspects of effective leadership. Further, communication is the primary method managers have for influencing their staffs. Research indicates that managers (and people in general) typically use one of the three approaches to motivate others shown in Exhibit 8.8 (Kipnis & Schmidt, 1985).

Most experienced media executives tailor their use of different strategies, or combinations of strategies, to the particular situation. The strategy they choose often depends on four major situational factors:

Balance of Power. Research shows the most important factor in determining which strategy people use is the balance of power. The person who holds power in a situation is more likely to use a hard strategy. Typically, this begins with reasonable attempts to direct change, but if

EXHIBIT 8.8. THREE STRATEGIES FOR MOTIVATING OTHERS

Hard Strategy	Aggressive, demanding; often involves pressure tactics such as shouting, accusing, blaming;
Soft Strategy	Polite, pleasant; often includes flattery and placating behaviors;
Rational Strategy	Logical; often relies on facts, explanation, and bargaining.

there is any reluctance or resistance, it quickly shifts to aggressiveness. Soft strategy is often used when a person is in the underdog position with little or no power. If things go sour, sulking and complaining may result. Rational strategy is generally used when power is relatively equal and neither party has an edge.

Influencer's Objectives. Hard strategy is often used when the influencer, the manager or employee, wants to change someone else's behavior. Soft strategy is employed when the influencer's goal is to personally receive some benefit, such as time off or a better assignment. Rational strategy is typically used when the goal is to gain benefits for the organization or work group as a whole, not just for oneself.

Anticipation of Resistance. When no resistance is anticipated, people typically use a rational strategy. However, when resistance is expected, people will choose either hard or soft strategies, depending on their power position.

Manager's Self-Esteem. The fourth factor is really more a personal characteristic than a situational factor. People who have low self-esteem and who hold power in a situation are likely to use a hard strategy. They tend to believe that others will not comply with simple requests and won't pay attention unless they are treated roughly. The result is that they bark orders, make demands, and refuse to discuss the issues involved.

Each of the preceding strategies works when used with the right person at the right time. However, the long-term costs of hard and soft strategies can be considerable, even when they are successful in the short run. Hard strategy creates hostility and resistance; it damages rapport and trust. Soft strategy lessens the influencer's own self-esteem because using it may feel humiliating and it may result in a loss of respect from the person in charge.

People who rely on rational strategy frequently appear to be the most satisfied with themselves and with their results because they used logic, reason, and compromise. All of these are more positively valued in the present U.S. society than yelling (hard strategy) or pleading (soft strategy).

Media managers are in a position which often results in their use of hard strategies. The situation they face pushes them in that direction. They have the power, they want to change their employee's behavior, and they often confront enormous time and competitive pressures. Furthermore, their independent and often creative employees can be very resistant to new ideas. All these factors create a tilt toward hard strategies. The long-term cost of using that approach may be high, however, which is why effective interpersonal communication skills are valuable.

Attentive Listening: The Key Communication Skill

Communication is often thought of as talking effectively: persuading, explaining, advising, generating options. Certainly, much has been written about how executives' speaking ability is important, but this ability may not have as much impact as how well media managers listen. One way for managers to make sure they listen effectively is to use the "attentive listening process." It is quite simple: let other people tell their stories spontaneously. Don't direct them, just encourage them.

That may sound easy, but it isn't, especially for media personnel who are often very verbal. Just listening is not easy. Most people are tempted to jump in and offer an opinion, comment, or fact. This is particularly true in tough situations when information organization personnel face pressure, blame, or perhaps threats. In those instances it is human to want to explain what was meant or to defend one's self. Yet, those are just the times when it's particularly important for the manager to listen for a long, intent time and say very little. After all, when pressure builds and tension rises, it is hard for employees to hear what an executive has to say until staff members have told their stories.

Now some media managers will respond to this approach with: You must be kidding! I don't have time to listen to all those stories. Good managers don't have time to *not* listen. After all, if their team believes that something is wrong, the staff's performance will be affected until the problem is solved or, at least, fully listened to by the executive.

In actual fact, attentive listening takes less time and is more productive than other ways of connecting with employees or getting information from them. Surprised? Here's why: Most employees can freely tell their own story in two to four minutes. What lengthens the time is for them to phrase what they have to say in response to their supervisor's questions. Moreover, when media employees are given the freedom and courtesy to talk about an issue in their own way, the leader gets fresher, higher-quality information. Staff members will often say things they might not think to say if the conversation is limited by the boss' questions.

There is another advantage. When the full story is heard at the beginning, a media manager does not have to waste time going back for more information and can focus on just the items that need clarification. Letting people speak their piece also builds rapport, reduces fear, and generates trust. Quality listening time invested in one situation puts money in the "relationship bank" for resolving future issues earlier and more productively.

The secret of attentive listening is to go into the information employee's world and try to experience the situation from the speaker's vantage point. That does not come naturally; often emotions interfere when anyone tries to be a better listener. But even when their emotions are high, managers in information companies can open themselves to others by using the five skills listed in Exhibit 8.9 below:

Look and Listen. At its best, employee/employer communication is a series of feedback loops. Being alert to both what is said and how it is said is crucial. Most conversations in the media focus on facts, ideas, analyses, proposals, assignments, and calls to be made. If they were asked, staffers for a newspaper, magazine, ad agency, or broadcast station would say that such talk is "rational" and "manageable." Yet, feedback about the feelings of reporters, sales staff, and technical personnel and their needs are just as important in understanding them as the facts they recite. Smart media managers look for nonverbal cues and pay as much attention to staff members' tone, pace, and inflection as to their words.

Acknowledge Messages. Acknowledging employees' messages lets them know, both verbally and nonverbally, that the media manager is following what is being said. Acknowledgments range from a nod of the head or an "uh-huh" to brief interpretations like, "That sounds important," or "I can see you're really concerned," or "That must have been exciting." Sincere acknowledgment—and again, employees will quickly

---

EXHIBIT 8.9. FIVE SKILLS FOR ATTENTIVE LISTENING

Look and listen
Acknowledge messages
Invite more information
Check out/clarify information
Summarize to insure understanding

---

discern if it is not sincere—reassures them that the executive is trying to understand what is being communicated.

Invite More Information. Watch as an editor uses the first two skills in listening to one of his or her reporters tell his or her story:

REPORTER: "I've been having a lot of trouble with the zoning change story. (*Editor notices downcast eyes.*) I've done these stories before, but I just can't seem to get going on this one." (*Editor notices quick glance from reporter.*)

EDITOR: (*Nods head*) "Do you want to talk about it, Jack?"

REPORTER: "I'd like to, Susan. You know that I've always been willing to deal with difficult sources." (*Editor notices reporter look directly at her.*)

EDITOR: "Uh-huh."

REPORTER: "But the last four times I've talked with Councilman Williams, we've ended up arguing with each other, and the last time he really berated me." (*Reporter again looks directly at editor.*)

EDITOR: "That sounds like it's tough to take."

REPORTER: "You bet it is! (*Reporter nearly shouts this out.*) I didn't like it one bit, and I'll bet there were a dozen people watching. I was livid, but I didn't lose my cool. (*Reporter clenches teeth and continues.*) No way was I going to give Williams the satisfaction of losing my composure in front of him." (*Pauses*)

Notice how the editor watched and listened carefully and used the reporter's nonverbal cues to respond by acknowledging the difficulty of the situation. The editor's actions helped the reporter to talk comfortably, and she came out with a wealth of significant information. Sensitive media managers know that when members of their team tell their story, they often pause, looking for a response. Many people misconstrue the pause as an invitation to jump in and take charge of the conversation. Editors often do this by asking questions or giving advice, such as:

"Okay, here's how to handle the story. First, go see Councilman Williams and ask him for a copy of the bill and his reasons for supporting it. Next, go see Commissioner Bennett—you know she can't stand Williams—and ask her what the problems are with the bill. Then. . ."

Jumping in like this has two negative consequences. First, the editor has not allowed the reporter to relate all the pertinent information so her advice may not be appropriate for the situation. Second, and more important, the editor has demonstrated to the reporter that she does not really wish to hear the reporter's full explanation. Wise executives resist the temptation. Instead, they use the break to gather more information by inviting the employee to continue with phrases such as:

"That's interesting, tell me more."

"I'd like to hear more about what you're saying."

"What else can you tell me? What are the pro's or con's?"

"What else do you think I need to know?"

An invitation to continue is a very powerful message. It says two things to the reporter: What you are saying is important to me, and I have time to listen so keep talking.

Watch the difference in the editor-reporter vignette when the editor invites more information instead of jumping in with advice as she did above:

EDITOR: "That sounds like an unpleasant situation with Williams. What else do you want to tell me?"

REPORTER: "I'm willing to work on the story, but Williams is a central figure in it. The way I'm feeling now, I don't think I could do a fair story about the proposed zoning change. I think I'd let my feelings color the story."

The same approach is particularly effective when others challenge or attack a media manager. Instead of counterattacking, the effective leader can diffuse the attack by asking the antagonist to say more. An account executive or art director expects the boss to react. If the response is, instead, an invitation to "tell me more of your concerns," that may produce extra, valuable information. Indeed, such a response can be a turning point in a tough situation. It may also enable both the manager and employee to share important information without attacking or defending.

Check Out and Clarify Information. As the media manager listens to staffers tell their stories, most of the pieces will fall into place. Sometimes, however, despite listening carefully, acknowledging what's been said, and issuing an invitation to say more, the executive may still desire more detailed information. At that point it's time to ask specific, open-ended, and probing questions to help fill in missing information and clarify what happened both overtly and covertly:

"Who was there?"

"What was decided?"

"How did you feel after the meeting?"

"If you were in charge, how would you have handled it?"

The specific questions often start with that old reporter's litany: who, what, where, when, or how. They elicit further description and details. Often the most crucial missing information, however, relates to others' intentions, not just the facts. Asking staff members what they would have done in a situation or how they feel about it often clarifies their more "hidden" agendas.

In the editor-reporter vignette the reporter provided a great deal of information, but the editor isn't entirely clear about what the reporter wants. Here's where more direct questions come into play:

EDITOR: "What do you want to do about this situation, Jack?"

REPORTER: "Frankly, Susan, part of me wants off of this story. . .(*Reporter looks directly at Susan, the editor, who nods*). . . and part of me wants to continue with it. I think a really fine story could be written to bring together current information with information I developed in earlier stories. But, as I said, I'm concerned about slanting it too much because of my feelings about Williams. I'm really torn between doing the story and asking you to take me off it. What do you think?"

Notice how Jack, the reporter, ended with a question. That often signals that an employee is finished, that he has completed his story. As his supervisor, Susan can simply answer the question or use one other listening skill before replying.

Summarize to Insure Understanding. Summarizing involves two steps: (1) stopping for a moment and repeating back in the editor's own words what the executive just heard as the main points of Jack's story; and (2) asking the reporter for confirmation of the accuracy of the editor's understanding, or for clarification if a point was missed.

Summarizing serves two important functions in communication. First, it demonstrates understanding by showing staff members that the media manager understood what was said. If the executive's summary is accurate, staffers will know that the person in charge truly paid attention, which, in turn, will increase their confidence in the executive.

Further, summarizing punctuates the conversation. It signals that the first chapter of the story is finished and the manager is now ready to move on to chapter two. Stated another way, summarizing indicates that the supervisor just finished being a follower or an interested observer and now is beginning to lead. Watch how this works as we return to the editor-reporter vignette.

EDITOR: "Let me make sure I've got this straight before I tell you what I think, Jack. Councilman Williams treated you terribly. You're furious with him—so much so that you don't think you can do a balanced story where he's involved. That's why you'd like to be off the story. On the other hand, you think the story could be a good one, and you have a lot to contribute to it. So you're not sure what you want to do next. Is that about it?"

REPORTER: "Yes, but let me add one more thing. I really hesitated about telling you this because I'm not a quitter and I don't let sources intimidate me." (*Reporter looks squarely at Susan.*)

EDITOR: "I know that, Jack. I've seen you handle too many tough assignments to think of you as a quitter. You're plenty tough enough for me."

REPORTER: "Thanks, Susan. I appreciate that."

EDITOR: "All right." (*She pauses, smiles and gives him a supportive look.*

> *Then, she turns.*) "Now let's figure out what to do about the story. First, I want you to tell me what would make this a really first-rate story. . . ."

In difficult, pressured situations summarizing doesn't come easily, especially when things are tense and it seems like a summary is slowing down the business to be accomplished; however, taking the time to summarize is necessary to insure that understanding is achieved. Summarizing is especially important when misunderstandings could be costly, or when misunderstandings seem to be occurring.

The five attentive listening skills are particularly effective tools for media managers to create understanding and build strong relationships with their staffs. If managers listen effectively, their understanding of their employees grows, and as they demonstrate that understanding, rapport and trust improve. In turn, that paves the way for those who report to the executive to share more of themselves, which further strengthens the bonds. Creating positive cycles of listening, understanding, and trust ought to be a goal for every effective media manager.

At this point, a natural question to ask is: "What about talking, isn't it important too?" Of course it is. Effective speaking helps staff understand and appreciate managers. To really build a solid working relationship, each person needs to understand the other. The individual also needs to have the sense of being understood.

Speaking and listening are important for developing the mutual understanding upon which strong relationships are based. Unfortunately, most people's listening skills are not as well developed as their speaking ability; that is why we emphasize the listening.

For more information on speaking use any of the many books or other resources on the subject; they abound and will give you plenty of information. Of course there are books on listening too, although often that is an overlooked aspect of management. In a fast-paced arena like the media, which deals with constantly changing ideas and messages, we believe listening deserves more attention in the preparation of effective managers and employees. An excellent book on the subject is *Effective Listening* by Steil, Barker, and Watson (1983).

THE PEOPLE DEVELOPMENT CYCLE

Besides supervising employees, media managers work with their staff through another, longer-term process. We call it the people development cycle, and it involves the four phases pictured in Exhibit 8.10.

Hiring

Before media executives fill any post, they ought to carefully develop a job description. In the fast-moving world of information organizations,

EXHIBIT 8.10. THE PEOPLE DEVELOPMENT CYCLE

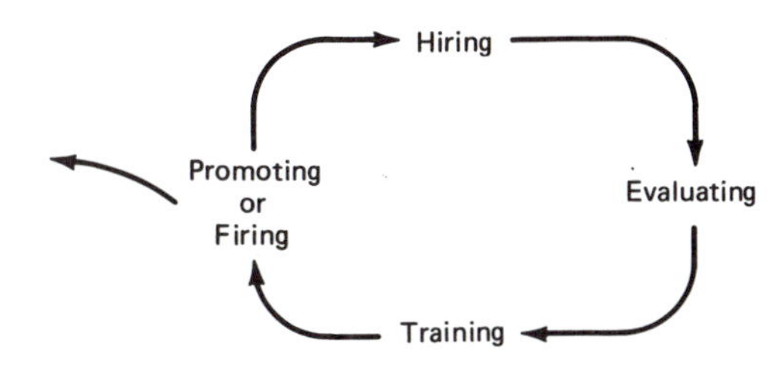

nearly every job has changed since the last time it was filled. Additionally, executives usually need to identify the skills and personal characteristics necessary for high-level job performance, since they were often only implied in traditional descriptions which focused on the minimal skills needed to fill the post.

When prospects are interviewed, media executives should consider how the applicant's strengths and weakness fit with the job. It is at that point when a list of skills and personal characteristics necessary to fill the position comes in handy. In an ideal situation, media managers will try to tailor the job to fit a person's strengths, at least to a substantial degree. That is done not only to promote employee happiness but also because it is more likely that a job can be changed than can an individual's traits. While fitting the job to the person is the ideal, it is also very difficult because media managers must consider the needs of the firm as well as the individual.

Another principle in hiring is to compare the prospective staff member's strengths and weaknesses with those of their colleagues and with the manager's own strengths and shortcomings. A smart strategy is to hire people with complementary skills in order to broaden the capabilities of the department or organization. At the same time, the manager should be wary about employing someone who does not share a common set of values. Disagreements about fundamental values, especially in something as ethically sensitive as the media, is guaranteed trouble.

Some Tips on Finding Good Employees. The first task is to conduct a diligent search, and we mean search in the broadest and deepest sense of the term. Even if the market is flooded with applicants or if the firm has no openings at the moment, smart managers never stop looking for prospects. These leaders consistently invest time in developing contacts and building a network so that, when they have an opening, they can turn to a stable of proven, well-researched achievers.

Spending time that way is a prudent investment. That is why the better media managers put as much energy into searching for good employees and selling them on the merits of their firm as they do in selecting the best applicant when they have an opening. When we talk to executives about this, they explain that if they develop a superior pool of candidates, whomever they choose is likely to be outstanding.

Why is it so vitally important to maintain a list of prospects?

Because choosing from an outstanding talent pool of potential hires ensures that even the third person on the list will be excellent. Every employer makes mistakes when it comes to hiring. The way to cut the odds of selecting someone who is weak is to put energy into making the quality of the applicant pool so high that the number three person is just as talented as the number one.

Media managers can use a variety of sources to build a strong prospect file. Many monitor award competitions and keep a file of those reporters, copywriters, art directors or other staffers who regularly do outstanding work. The winners who are employed by smaller media firms are apt to be particularly good candidates for job transfer because the size of the organizations that employ them often limits their advancement.

Many media employers also cultivate ties with journalism school faculty in their area or with faculty in schools that specialize in teaching subjects directed toward the activities of the employer. They are likely to be a rich source of references for top-quality students. Many faculty stay in touch with graduates; they can provide leads to experienced professionals interested in making a job change.

Friends and colleagues also hear about talented people; the wise manager gets to know the best employees who work elsewhere. That is especially true if the talented outsider is rumored to be interested in switching jobs.

Media managers in smaller organizations can form linkages with colleagues in larger firms; they can ask the executives at the large firm to send promising people for whom they do not have an opening to the smaller organization. Then they can work out an arrangement to provide experience and seasoning for young professionals, with the explicit understanding to send back first-rate staffers when they are ready to move up and the large organization has an opening.

Common Sense Guidelines When Interviewing and Hiring

1. Check references: never depend only on what is on an application or resume; talk to previous employers. Many former bosses will not write anything negative for fear of employee reprisal or legal action. But the media are populated by friendly managers who often respond candidly to direct questions about ex-employees. Questions that provide helpful information include:

- Would you rehire this person?
- Why did the individual leave your firm?
- Were you sorry to lose this employee?
- What did this person do effectively . . . and ineffectively?
- If the employee had stayed with your firm, would he/she have warranted a promotion in the near future?

2. Don't just interview prospects, if at all possible, provide a trial period. We've encountered a number of media executives who ask job finalists to take a couple days of vacation from their present post. Then, the prospective employer pays the candidate to work for those vacation days on a kind of pretrial basis. It's amazing what one can learn in a few days of working with a potential colleague that could never be discerned in an interview spanning just a few hours.
3. Consider using tests and other measures to check the instincts of the executive doing the hiring about a potential employee, but treat this information only as supplementary. Even in a company such as Knight-Ridder, which is famous for using batteries of tests, the results of such examinations only supplement KR executives' judgments. As Doug Harris, then KR vice-president for personnel, told a 1985 gathering of professionals and professors who teach media management, "Tests are never used as the sole or decisive basis for employment decisions. Executive judgments are always the deciding factor."
4. Ask probing questions. It is amazing how candidly most interviewees will answer them. For example, if an obviously interested executive says, "We simply will never have enough time to really get to know each other. Why don't you tell me your three prime strengths?", applicants will do so. If that response is followed by, "Now, would you tell me your three major weaknesses?", most applicants will also respond with equal frankness.

   Applicants will also respond frankly to questions such as: "What are your salary expectations one and five years from now?" Or, "Will you stay with us for at least three years? . . . If we train you, we would expect that as a return." (This latter question is not legally binding, but it sets a tone for the media manager's expectations.)
5. Focus on the candidate's strengths: Management guru Peter Drucker argues that employees should always be hired for what they can contribute. To the greatest degree possible, Drucker advises employers to forget about staff members' weaknesses. Though executives must pay attention to weaknesses that impinge on other employees or on the operations of the firm, most weaknesses are not of that sort. They are just present; it make no sense to dwell on them if they are not likely to substantially affect performance or if they cannot be changed. Remember, most ingrained traits do not change in adults.

Evaluation

Throughout employees' careers, evaluation is crucial to their development. The evaluation process should occur regularly. Done well, it provides a chance for meaningful feedback on many aspects of a staff member's performance. As part of an evaluation meeting, objectives, goals, or benchmarks for future evaluations should also be agreed upon between the employee and employer. Whenever possible, the objectives should be measurable and clearly stated at the beginning of the review period.

What we just outlined constitutes a formal performance appraisal conducted on a regular basis. Such appraisals usually occur annually, but sometimes they are done semiannually or even quarterly. Performance appraisals' four major functions are to:

- let employees know concretely how their current performance is rated;
- identify those employees who deserve merit pay increases;
- locate employees who require additional training;
- identify employees who are candidates for promotion.

A variety of performance appraisal approaches and systems have been developed. The best known of these is management by objectives (MBO).

Developed 30 years ago by Peter Drucker (1954), the MBO approach has the three key elements shown in Exhibit 8.11.

MBO is called by different names in various media companies. Whatever its title, the philosophy of MBO flows directly from Theory Y assumptions about staff members: people employed by the media derive a great deal of satisfaction from working effectively.

Do MBO systems help improve performance? Studies found MBOs generally have a positive impact. For example, evidence clearly indicates that individuals who determine their own goals show higher performance and tend to aim for an improvement over past performance. If they achieve their improvement, they again set higher goals for themselves (Meyer, Kay, & French, 1965).

There are problems if too many objectives are set or if objectives are impossible to accomplish. And it stands to reason that individuals tend to accept goals more readily when they are involved in setting them. Also, providing regular feedback about performance typically leads to more improvement on the job. In the same vein, a periodic review process leads to positive effects on employees' attitudes, confidence in

---

EXHIBIT 8.11. KEY ELEMENTS IN A MANAGEMENT-BY-OBJECTIVES (MBO) PROGRAM

1. Major areas of individual responsibility are defined in terms of objectives, i.e., measurable results.
2. Regular feedback on performance is given; often employees can monitor their own performance.
3. Employees participate with managers in both goal-setting and performance appraisals.

---

management, and ability to accept criticism if the review is future focused, concrete, participatory, and positive.

Clearly, MBO has major advantages to offer to both individual employees and the organization. For media staff members the main advantages are an increased sense of involvement and a better understanding of the organization's and supervisor's expectations. This helps staff members to focus their efforts where they are most needed, and where they are more likely to be rewarded. Further, under this system employees know they will be evaluated on how well they accomplish their objectives, not on the basis of their personal traits or their boss' biases.

Exhibit 8.12 presents six-month goals for an advertising manager at a television station.

In some instances, MBO systems have not worked well. For example, a study by Herbert H. Meyer and his colleagues found that employees who are formally criticized about their job performance once or twice a year tend to become defensive and resentful, and their performance may decline (Meyer, Kay, & French, 1965).

They suggest that the goal of an appraisal system be the improvement of future performance. Now that sounds fine, but it is difficult to achieve if managers simply act out the role of judge and jury as they conduct evaluations. To avoid this, the researchers recommend that executives and employees jointly set performance goals at the beginning of the review period. Then, at the end, they evaluate progress toward those goals together. Participatory appraisal leads to both greater satisfaction and higher job performance.

As the comments above imply, one problem with MBO systems is that some managers do not have the interpersonal skills and manage-

---

EXHIBIT 8.12. SIX-MONTH GOALS FOR AN ADVERTISING MANAGER IN A TELEVISION STATION

1. Produce local and retail and product revenue in first six months of 1987 as established in budget. (25 points)
2. Increase sales to restaurant/theatre/movie sector by 60 percent in first six months of 1987. (4 points)
3. Develop innovative promotion/sales packet for Class 2 retailers in first quarter of 1987 and test impact during second quarter. (6 points)
4. Increase sales of our in-house commercial production service by 40 percent in first six months of 1987. (5 points)
5. Stay within advertising expense budget in first six months of 1987. (2 points per quarter; 4 point total)
6. Maintain average actual rate at 85 percent of rate card figures in first six months of 1987. (2 points per quarter; 4 point total)

---

ment style necessary for communicating a sense of support. By contrast, MBO is likely to succeed when the staff sees it as a way of helping them to develop their careers and to put out a better product.

A potentially serious drawback for using MBO systems in media firms is the possibility of a conflict between creativity and the rigidity of the MBO system's concrete objectives. For instance, employees may fail to try something new and risky because it is not on their list of objectives. If that happens, opportunities for both the employee and the organization may be lost. One way to guard against that unfortunate situation is to set objectives that encompass qualitative aspects of performance, as we saw in Exhibit 8.12. For example, ask for creativity and innovation in the employee's performance and really reward those activities when they are attempted, even if they fail. There can be no guarantee that a new, adventurous effort will succeed. The reward should come for attempting the innovation.

Training

Some large media organizations, Knight-Ridder and Gannett, for example, have well-developed approaches to employee training and career development. But even in small media companies, staff members need and deserve opportunities to improve their skills. Moreover, in any size firm, employers who provide training opportunities on an ongoing basis will have better motivated, more productive employees.

(John B. Winsor of Winsor Communications, who was mentioned in Chapter 6, typifies a CEO of a small firm who provides excellent training for his staff members. Winsor mandated that a regular activity of his assistant would be to learn about effective training, and then institute it throughout his organization.)

Training comes in many forms. Large media organizations conduct in-house seminars on specialized topics. They also send their employees to seminars put on by such groups as the American Newspaper Publishers Association, the American Press Institute, The Poynter Institute, the 4-A's, the National Association of Broadcasters, and many state and local trade organizations.

The most important training, however, is that conducted by an in-house person on a day-to-day basis. Although sometimes held in groups, most training is done one on one. In such instances, managers serve as "coaches," helping their employees to improve their skills, develop better strategies, and increase confidence.

Training, in this sense, is a fundamental part of the effective media manager's personnel work. Suppose editors of a small magazine take time to improve their writers' skills. The next issue of the magazine may be a little late or the editors may put in longer hours to act as writing coaches, but over time the magazine's staff will turn out better stories. That pays off in the long run. It also demonstrates to the staff that the editors care about their professional development and, as a result, the writers will usually work harder.

Of course, there are risks in training staffers, especially if it is done by outsiders in professional seminars or courses. For example, the employee may make new contacts and leave; high staff turnover is commonplace in smaller media firms. Further, an insecure media manager could be threatened by an employee "full of new ideas." But these risks are worth taking to create a stronger, more productive, higher quality work force.

Firing

The reverse of hiring is firing, a particularly unpleasant, but important, part of the personnel process. For managers with any feeling and sensitivity, dismissing an employee remains one of their more painful assignments, no matter how many times the executive has done it.

When should a staff member be fired? No outsider can fully answer that question, but the wise manager should, at the very least, be able to answer yes to questions 1 and 2 and no to 3 and 4:

1. Has the manager done everything possible to make the employee successful?
2. Has the media executive been clear to the employee about his or her shortcomings and suggested concrete steps to take to correct those problems?
3. Is there any other place in the firm to put the employee that better suits his or her talents and allow the staffer to succeed?
4. Is there anything the media manager is doing to cause the problem or anything that can be changed without undermining the manager's own effectiveness?

Even if the answers to these questions justify letting an employee go, the executive may procrastinate. After all, firing someone is painful. If it is deserved, however, media managers must consider their responsibility to the firm to take decisive action when it is warranted. That, after all, is what the executive is paid for; managers are not doing their job if they avoid the appropriate, though unpleasant, action.

Effective employers also recognize that they are responsible for everyone who works for them. It is unfair to other employees to have to carry the extra load of one who is not performing. That hurts the firm and everyone in it. Equally important, it hurts the weak employee who, in the long run, would be better off in a job where success is possible.

Several other points about firing are noteworthy. If two or three employees are fired from the same job, something is probably wrong with how people are hired to fill the post, with the way the job is structured, with the boss, or with a combination of these factors.

Further, the personnel process is cumulative. Unless employees commit a flagrant wrong, they should not be let go on the basis of a single incident. Firing should be based on a pattern of ineffectiveness which has not been corrected even after fair warning is given and help is provided to change objectionable behavior.

Finally, when letting anyone go, media managers must comply with state and federal equal employment opportunity laws. (Most media are covered by federal laws because the information products from most media firms cross state lines.) Rather than just meet the minimal requirement of such statutes, however, we argue that those laws should be met in their fullest spirit because it is good business to do so. The media are so visible that running afoul of such legislation is sure to hurt an information company's image. Additionally, all employees will be more comfortable with the separation process if those who are fired are dismissed only for just cause and are treated fairly in the process. (Chapter 16 discusses laws affecting the media and the attitude media managers can adopt towards those laws. It provides an extended discussion of matters of this sort.)

A Special Challenge: Working with Creative Staff

A special challenge for media managers is to work with their "creative" staff, the people who gather information and develop messages or who sell. They are a vital asset of any media company. Without their effective performance, media products will become hackneyed, which may ultimately result in the failure of the firm, or in insufficient revenue.

One aspect that makes this a challenge for media managers is that people with high levels of creative reportorial writing, or copyediting skills, or outstanding sales talent are difficult to find. Thus, whatever the condition of the employment market, good people are always in high demand. Combined with the horizontal structure of most media companies, this creates the potential for constant raiding of a firm's best employees by executives in other companies. As we noted earlier, lateral movement between media firms is common as employees seek new challenges and new responsibilities. And good managers keep an ever-present eye on outstanding performers in other firms.

How can this situation be countered? The issue of fending off job transfers and raids is really the flip side of how to create a context in which a staff can use its skills to the fullest. Perhaps the best way to begin dealing with both of these issues is to recognize that the motivational needs of these staff members are likely to be Maslow's (1970) self-actualizing needs: desire for autonomy, a chance to practice their craft, and the opportunity to face a challenge.

As a starting point, smart media managers determine as completely as possible what each of their employees wants, both in the short term and in the long term. Then, together with their employees, they work to develop a career plan that responds to those wants. There are many ways to do this. For example, the executive can find out if employees are thinking about going into management and, if so, help them develop a plan so the staff members can begin to learn management skills. With others it may require creation of new personal challenges as the employees mature in their present posts. Or it may entail determining whether they wish to have increased variety in their work, and then thinking up ways to provide broader task responsibilities, such as assignment to major projects.

A management style emphasizing strong support, clear expectations, and low levels of monitoring and control is likely to work best with creative employees. The information executive should ask staff members what management can do to make work more fulfilling, and then act upon these suggestions if they appear to be at all reasonable. In short, management should try to build a challenging and supportive environment that will foster high levels of productivity among creative team members.

Recently we organized a conference, "Ways to Increase the Productivity of Creative Media Employees."* Managers and employees from daily newspapers, radio and TV stations, and advertising agencies analyzed this topic for two days. By the end of the conference, the group developed the prioritized list of methods to enhance creativity in media firms shown in Exhibit 8.13.

Postscript: Unions

There is another major aspect of some media managers' personnel work, the role of labor unions. We do not cover unions in this book because trade unions are not a factor in most media companies, but some comments on their role are in order.

A comparatively small percentage of all media organizations are unionized. Even in daily newspapers, where they exist in many metropolitan and some middle-size papers, they are absent from the great majority of U.S. daily and weekly newspapers. The same is true in broadcasting: unions exist in some metropolitan TV stations and a few middle-size markets, but they are not present in the vast majority of U.S. television or radio units. Unions hardly exist at all in advertising or public relations agencies or other types of print outlets, such as book publishing, small magazines, or direct mail. They do exist in the TV networks and major film studios, but not in most independent film and video operations.

---

* This conference was held May 4–6, 1986, in Minneapolis. It was sponsored by the Media Management and Economics Resource Center (MMERC) which is located in the School of Journalism and Mass Communication of the University of Minnesota, with support from the American Newspaper Publisher's Association (ANPA) Foundation and the Minnesota Journalism Center.

EXHIBIT 8.13. METHODS TO ENHANCE CREATIVITY IN MEDIA FIRMS

1. Reward creative success with greater challenges and recognition; use psychological and tangible incentives "bucks, bennies, and strokes"; use competitive compensation.
2. Allow the freedom to take chances and to see projects through to completion; encourage risk taking.
3. Set high standards for quality and performance; be specific about expectations.
4. Establish an environment that fosters ongoing, effective, two-way communication; develop a meaningful performance review system; use feedback.
5. Convey the big picture; convey a vision.
6. Have top management dedicated to creativity; management characteristics should include maturity, honesty, humility, imagination, vision.
7. Hire creative people who can work with each other; encourage networking among creative employees.
8. Involve workers in setting standards and, where possible, goals.
9. Have an appreciation for and knowledge of creative workers' jobs.
10. Play to strengths; match the employee and his or her interests to the job; design the job for the employee.
11. Teach time management and productivity skills.
12. Establish competition at all levels.
13. Provide training opportunities, both in-house and out-of-house.
14. Structure a forum for receiving and discussing ideas and implement the results whenever possible.
15. Use humor and have fun.

Some media managers are intent on driving unions out of their organizations. Others believe that unions serve a valuable function and they are able to work effectively with their union employees. These managers view unions as just one of many methods for employee/employer decision making; as having pluses and minuses, just as other arrangements do.

We subscribe to that latter view. What gives trade unions value in a particular media setting is whether they represent the best method of decision making. The answer to that question is affected by many factors, such as the number of employees involved, their level of autonomy, their location(s), the attitude of management, the role of both executives and employees.

A key issue in evaluating whether unions can work well in a specific media company is to determine how committed both management and labor are to making union negotiations function constructively.

If a media manager is involved in an organization or industry where unions are active, the subject of union activity should be studied carefully for there is great deal to learn about working with unions, from strategy and planning, to cost, training, and law.

We do not belittle nor minimize this subject; indeed, it is a fascinating one in which the authors have a special interest. For instance, just at the moment that unions are losing numbers in newspapers, their role in worker participation committees that bring union members and managers together to jointly decide noncontract issues is increasing. That is a change that may foreshadow new arrangements of employee/employer decision making in the future.

If you are interested in unions, we urge you to read some of the fine academic and professional books on unions and management. A good starting point is *What Do Unions Do?* by Richard B. Freeman and James L. Medoff (1984). It is the finest study of trade unions we've ever read.

CHAPTER 9
Leading Media Organizations

As the title of this book indicates, the best of media management is more than simply getting the station on the air, the news to the public, or an advertising or public relations campaign to the client. If we were to choose one word to define media management, it would be leadership. That is the reason for the subtitle of this book: *Effective Leadership of the Media.*

Near the end of this chapter we develop a more complete conception of what media leaders do and what leadership entails. In it we elaborate on the relationship and the distinction between leaders and leadership. For now we begin simply with:

1. Media leaders have a variety of personal characteristics and act in ways that communicate a vision that mobilizes others to move in a certain direction.
2. Media leaders have profound impact on the managerial functions you read about in Chapters 5 through 8 (planning, organizing, budgeting, personnel).
3. Media leaders not only see what's coming and influence their staffs and the management functions within their firms, but they are particularly effective in capitalizing on circumstances, even negative ones, that happen outside their company or industry.
4. Distinct from the leaders of information organizations, but of course intimately tied to them, is the concept of media leadership. This does not refer to the characteristics leaders possess, the actions they take, or the functions they carry out. Rather, it refers to the impacts leaders have on their organization; to the sense of direction, stability, and confidence they provide to the organization's staff and to the firm or department as a whole.

Leaders and leadership are complex and fascinating subjects that are central to media; yet they are anything but a new area of interest. Indeed, great thinkers have analyzed leadership and the qualities of leaders for thousands of years. The role of Moses as the person chosen to lead the Jews out of Egypt (and other prophets who led them in other situations) is a significant and repeated point of discussion in the Old Testament. Plato also zeroed in on leadership in his discussion of philosopher-kings in *The Republic*. Machiavelli set forth his view of leadership in *The Prince*. And today, in any modern library or bookstore, if you browse in the management section you will find shelves full of books on leadership. This quest for an understanding of leadership endures because it is central to comprehending the pivotal role people play in shaping not only the media and every business, but all of the institutions of society.

LEADERS AS INDIVIDUALS

Early accounts of leadership focused primarily on the individual and on the special traits that made a leader. Lists of characteristics were proposed, such as those below:

Intelligence
Charisma
Courage
Extrovertedness
Extraordinary communication ability
Dedication
Initiative
Decisiveness
People skills
Self-assurance

A classic example of one person who combined most of those traits is Winston Churchill. Credited with pulling England and eventually all of the Allies together during World War II, Churchill possessed most of the characteristics that casual observers associate with leadership. He was an extraordinary communicator who could rally those who listened to what he said or wrote. Brilliant, decisive, charismatic, he was "a man for his time."

Yet, Warren Bennis, a management expert who we will discuss later in this chapter, provides two other components for a conception of media leaders and leadership. The first applies to effective media leaders who may or may not possess Churchill's attributes. He also makes an extremely important distinction between leaders and managers. (We have added the word "media" to Bennis's idea to emphasize this point.): " . . . (Media) leaders are people who do the right thing; (media) managers are people who do things right. Both roles are crucial" (1984, p. 16).

Then, building on his definition of the leader, Bennis moves the discussion from the individual level to the broader organizational context: " . . . one of the key problems facing American (media) organizations . . . is that they are underled and overmanaged. They do not pay enough attention to doing the right thing, while they pay too much attention to doing things right" (1984, p. 16).

Before we focus on the media organization, let's begin with the individual.

Stereotypic Characteristics of Media Leaders

The media has had its share of legendary leaders. One thinks of William Paley, who had the vision to pioneer broadcasting with CBS, or autocratic, but brilliant Abe Rosenthal of *The New York Times*. Then there is the *Washington Post's* editor, Benjamin Bradley, and managing editor, Howard Simons, who had the courage to break open the Nixon-era Watergate case for publisher Katherine Graham. After her husband died, Mrs. Graham's own self-assurance and intelligence saw her assume the helm and, with no experience, build the newspaper to new levels of excellence as well as financial success.

There is Norman Cousins, whose drive and intellect built and for decades edited *The Saturday Review*, and Ted Turner, whose audacity built Cable News Network (CNN). Allen Neuharth is the newsman with no formal marketing training who became chairman of Gannett, and built it into one of the largest media empires in the land by his extraordinary marketing genius, as well as his financial savvy. There is also determined, insightful Kay Fanning, who dared to turn a daily newspaper around in chauvinistic Alaska, and then to refurbish the *Christian Science Monitor*. Other media leaders had the vision, persistence, charisma, and courage to break the rule that "it couldn't be done": Samuel Goldwyn built a film empire; Carly Byer developed a worldwide public relations firm; David Ogilvy and Leo Burnett both created nationally recognized advertising agencies, and the brothers Saatchi built the world's largest advertising firm. At the same time, Frances Preston, called by many musicians "our spiritual leader" and "a great businesswoman" (*Fortune*, January 5, 1987) had a profound impact on the record industry in the U.S. (and, in turn, on broadcasting and film making) as chief executive of one of the two major music-licensing organizations, Broadcast Music Inc.

Each of these women and men, as well as the far larger group that is less well known and just now moving into leadership ranks, are living examples of many of the leadership traits we listed.

Different Media Leaders Have Different Traits

Despite the strong traits commonly associated with leadership, it is interesting to note that researchers found no single set of characteristics that worked for every leader or in every situation. Indeed, just as Churchill was verbal and bombastic, Mahatma Gandhi was effective because of his ascetism and use of nonviolence.

There are other notables who delivered ideas (messages) or images to the public, yet are little known for their verbal prowess. Their impact, however, is no less profound. One thinks of artists Vincent Van Gogh, Georgia O'Keeffe, and Henry Moore. Unlike Picasso, who was very verbal and public, each of that former trio was comparatively quiet. It was their work, not their words, that shaped modern art.

Many professionals and critics believe that the best prose nonfiction writer in America today is John McPhee, the "writers' writer." Yet, McPhee is shy, warm, and so pleasant to talk with that people he interviews tell him far more than they plan. McPhee shuns interviews about himself and does not allow the use of his photo on his books. Still, his work is so outstanding that William Shawn, editor of *The New Yorker* until 1987, would devote virtually an entire issue to a McPhee essay or one of his new books.

And whereas many people know the volatile, public Allen Neuharth of Gannett, few have heard of James Batten, the president of Knight-Ridder Inc., or Eugene Roberts, the Knight-Ridder executive editor of *The Philadelphia Inquirer*. Yet, in 1986, Knight-Ridder won more Pulitzer Prizes in one year than any other major newspaper group has ever won. Batten is credited by many in his company with being the "soul" of that multibillion dollar corporation because he cares for and connects with each person he meets and because he motivated, protected, rewarded, and made quality news a prime value at KR. And Roberts, who is respectfully and lovingly called "the Buddha" for his silent, thoughtful manner by some of his colleagues, turned the *Inquirer* into one of the finest papers in the nation. Batten is courtly and low key in style. Roberts is often silent to the point that the less than observant think he is uninterested. In fact, both care passionately about quality and have built a firm and a newspaper that rival the best in the nation.

What we have seen in our encounters with leadership in many media companies is that many different kinds of people have the capacity to lead their organizations. Some have had charisma, charm, and people skills. Others were tyrants. Still others maintained very low profiles. Yet, even such a recluse as *The New Yorker* magazine's legendary editor, William Shawn, is acknowledged for his extraordinary effectiveness in working with some of the finest writers in the English language. Shawn may shun the limelight, but his ability to attract and work with literary giants like McPhee and E.B. White made *The New Yorker* one of the most enduring and successful literary magazines in the United States.

Research about Leadership Characteristics

Many researchers have attempted to identify a core set of traits that characterize leaders. But when they studied countless people and firms, management experts and psychologists who specialize in analyzing leadership observed what we've just described.

They began by trying to discover a core set of characteristics that were present in all leaders. They reasoned that if the traits of leaders could be identified, organizations could pick people with those skills and thus become far more sophisticated in choosing their next generation of management. Researchers used two approaches to search for these leadership traits. Some compared the traits of leaders with those of followers. Others compared the traits of effective leaders with those of ineffective ones. The studies in both categories were disappointing. While leaders were found to be somewhat brighter, more extroverted, and more self-confident than nonleaders, researchers found people with similar characteristics among both leaders and followers (Stogdill, 1948; Ghiselli, 1971; House & Baetz, 1979).

LEADERSHIP STYLES

The experts then decided that the search for traits was too simplistic. It was an approach based on the wrong assumption: that leaders are born, not made, and that leadership characteristics are inherent in some people and missing in others. Since the same traits were not common in all leaders, management experts and researchers shifted their attention to "leadership styles."

Styles of Media Leaders

Among today's media leaders there are sharp contrasts in style. Ted Turner is bold and bombastic, but Dow Jones's chairman, Warren Phillips, though equally courageous, is quieter; he is virtually unknown to the public at large. Yet, Phillips demonstrated amazing vision and courage when he risked hundreds of millions of dollars on developing the *Wall Street Journal* into the first national satellite-delivered newspaper, and followed it by building *Dow Jones News Retrieval*, one of the largest and more successful electronic information data bases.

Alvah Chapman, the chairman of Knight-Ridder Inc., pushed the use of videotex in the U.S. Although KR eventually folded its videotex operation, Chapman deserves praise for having the courage and self-assurance to try to develop the new technology. Moreover, Chapman's conservative, mannerly style enabled him to develop the base of support from KR's Board of Directors and from the investment community to allow KR to mount and push its *Viewtron* videotex project for as long as it did, with generally laudatory comments. (KR did not suffer a total loss on *Viewtron*. The company has used some of the knowledge it gained to bolster its electronic business information services.)

One of the more poignant cases that illustrates the impact of different leadership styles in the media is the reign of Abe Rosenthal as executive editor of *The New York Times* and then, beginning in 1986, of his successor, Max Frankel.

When Rosenthal took over the helm of the *Times* the paper had gone through a period of decentralization and, as a result, a loss of focus. A brilliant, mercurial autocrat, who ran the newsroom with fear and decisiveness, Rosenthal's style and intelligence are credited with giving the *Times* a sharp new focus. Under his direction, news coverage expanded into neighborhoods surrounding New York where it had never been; it also expanded the definition of "newspaper" with its coverage of such subjects as arts and life styles and a flood of special sections.

Yet the Rosenthal style had its limits. By 1986 the editor's halfhearted attempts at grooming a successor and the growing dissatisfaction with his autocratic manner created such bad morale in the newsroom that publisher Punch Sulzberger forced him into early retirement. According to a report in the *Washington Journalism Review*, Sulzberger moved to replace Rosenthal because the newsroom dissension was so widespread it reached the *Times* Board of Directors.

Who replaced Rosenthal? His nemesis, Max Frankel, the Pulitzer Prize-winning reporter, who for 10 years had been the head of the editorial page of the *Times*.

Few people offer more distinctly different management styles than Rosenthal and Frankel. There are stories that Frankel has a temper, and he admits that he constantly wrestles with his tendency to be impulsive. Yet, the hallmarks of the Frankel way of leading center on team building, on caring as much about the person as the institution, and on being solid, predictable, and open to younger staff members and people down in the ranks.

It will also be interesting to watch the differences in style between William Shawn the legendary, former editor of *The New Yorker* and its new editor, Robert Gottlieb, formerly president of one of book publishing's major houses, Alfred A. Knopf, Inc. Gottlieb had no prior *New Yorker* experience which irritated Mr. Shawn, who objected to Gottlieb's appointment because presumably, the new editor might not know the magazine's (and Shawn's) style—and revere it.

Research on Leadership Styles

The studies of researchers and management experts have a great deal to say about management and leadership styles. For example, Robert Bales (1951) examined how groups functioned. He found that effective groups have some form of shared leadership, with one person performing a task function and another performing a social/group-maintenance function. For example, one advertising copywriter might guide the group by forcefully presenting the ideas for the new ad campaign and by encouraging the other members of the account team to make decisions. A second member of the team, perhaps the account executive, might perform the group-maintenance function by responding to the ideas and feelings of other group members. Perhaps because of the rather different orientations those two functions require, Bales found they were handled separately in most groups. A person who could perform both roles successfully, however, would be an effective leader.

Other researchers focused on the style a manager may use in working with subordinates. Two leadership styles were identified, corresponding closely to Bales's leadership functions. Task-oriented managers direct and supervise subordinates closely to ensure that the task is performed to the bosses' satisfaction. Managers with particular responsibility for making sure messages are developed on time, such as assistant editors in print news operations and producers in television news, often approach their jobs in a very task-oriented fashion.

Elsewhere, employee-oriented managers try to motivate subordinates. They encourage group members' performance by allowing media staff to participate in decisions affecting them and by forming friendly, respectful, and trusting relationships with their employees.

Eventually, management theorists took these basic ideas and developed conceptions of management as leadership styles. In Chapter 8 you read about one of these, The Managerial Grid developed by Blake and Mouton (1978). Others who developed similar approaches include Victor Vroom (1976), and Rensis Likert (1961, 1967).

Each of these approaches assumes that leadership styles can be learned. That assumption, of course, explicitly rejects the bias of trait-oriented researchers who believe that leaders are born, not made.

CONTINGENCY APPROACHES TO LEADERSHIP

Returning to the description of Max Frankel's leadership style at *The New York Times*, some would argue that Frankel's style is effective because he is a master at adapting to the situation. For example, Frankel says that in working with staff members, he looks for what motivates them, what their interests are, and what is good in the situation. Then he chooses a response that he thinks will be effective with that particular person in that particular situation. Frankel's approach is what management experts call a contingency approach to leadership.

A number of contingency models of leadership were developed to try to identify factors that are most important in a given set of circumstances. The models tried to predict the leadership style that will be most effective in various situations. All of the contingency models are similar in two respects. They identify similar situational factors that executives should consider when they choose one leadership style or another, and they use the same general classification of managerial styles in their analysis; all are offshoots of The Managerial Grid.

For example, Fiedler (1965, 1971) identified three elements in work situations to monitor when choosing between a task-oriented or an employee-oriented leadership style:

- the quality of the leader-follower relationship;
- the task structure;
- the leader's power position.

In what they labeled the path/goal model, Martin Evans (1970) and Robert House (1971), focused on the ways managers influenced subordinates. In his initial work, Evans delineated how managers determine the availability of "goals" (rewards) and clarified the "paths" to be taken to reach them. House expanded the path/goal theory by suggesting contingency variables that help determine the most effective leadership style, particularly personal characteristics of subordinates, environmental pressures, and demands in the work place.

The path/goal leadership model may be particularly useful for media companies because of its emphasis on personal characteristics of subordinates, and on work place pressures and demands. As we noted before, key employees in media firms are often creative, headstrong, and highly motivated. Dealing effectively with them is likely to require a different leadership style than would be useful with other kinds of workers. Similarly, the media world is fraught with deadline pressure and high-performance demands. Path/goal theory may provide useful guidelines for leadership in this high-pressure environment.

A third major contingency model is Hersey's (1985) situational theory, described in Chapter 8. Its key contingency variable for selecting a leadership style is the follower's readiness. This theory is called a life-cycle approach because it assumes subordinates go through a cycle of first learning how to perform a task and then achieving motivation to do so. Leaders can nurture this development by adapting their behavior to the subordinate's level of maturity in learning and performing the task. This theory has created considerable excitement in management circles because it not only focuses on task performance, but also on personal development.

Its emphasis on the leader's role in developing staff makes the situational leadership approach particularly relevant for media firms. More than in most companies, the creative talents of its staff are the keys to the company's success in the marketplace. Only fresh, innovative material will continue to attract sizeable audiences. An approach highlighting people development is clearly of value to media firms.

THE COMPETENCIES OF LEADERSHIP

As you might guess, with such a keen interest in leadership, the quest for determining common elements that "worked" for all leaders continued.

Several researchers decided to identify people with recognized leadership to see if they had similar traits (Bennis, 1984; Kanter, 1983;

Zenger, 1985). They were looking for individuals who, to quote Warren Bennis, one of the researchers, "affect the culture, are the social architects of their organizations and create and maintain values" (Bennis, 1984, p. 16).

For example, Bennis identified 90 leaders; 60 corporate CEOs and 30 from the public sector. He interviewed them and observed them in action. There were dramatic differences in the specific personality characteristics and styles of the leaders that Bennis observed. Nevertheless, he discovered some important similarities.

Bennis called these commonalities "leadership competencies." They are not simply similar behavioral styles or responses in the same situation. Rather, they are broad leadership themes that are best viewed as tasks that must be performed if executives want to move beyond mere management to making a real impact on their department or organization. Bennis identified the leadership competencies listed below:

1. *Management of Attention.* By ideas, actions, personal hard work, and vision, leaders command people's time and attention. Leaders express a commitment that attracts others to the leaders' goals, direction, and purpose.
2. *Management of Meaning.* An essential ingredient of managing attention is being able to communicate a vision to others. Effective leaders make their vision tangible to others throughout the organization, even in the face of competing views from opponents and special interests.
3. *Management of Trust.* Trust is crucial for employees and firms, for only when media staff members have confidence in their leaders does the company really thrive. Media examples of this abound. NBC was revitalized in the mid-1980s by Grant Tinker, who managed attention and meaning effectively, but perhaps succeeded primarily because he was trusted by those who worked for and with him. Tinker didn't get their trust by default, however; it was earned by what he accomplished. In a study Bennis showed that staff members would much rather follow executives they can count on, even when they disagree with their viewpoint, than managers they agree with, but who shift positions frequently (Bennis, 1984, p. 18).
4. *Management of Self.* This competency is obvious in one respect, but subtle in another. It means that leaders must know their own abilities and weaknesses, and they must be able to effectively use, compensate for, or alter them to fit different situations. There is another, seemingly contradictory, aspect of management of self. Most successful leaders do not fully internalize the concept of failure. What others call failure, the true leader usually sees simply as "a mistake" or as another step in the journey to move people and their organizations.

Bennis's conception, as well as those of others adopting a similar point of view, shifts the focus of leadership analysis in a significant way (Kanter, 1984; Zenger, 1985). As we noted at the beginning of this chapter, the initial thinking and research on leadership concentrated on the individual. First, it focused on personality characteristics and traits, then on behavior styles and patterns, and finally on flexibility in using leadership styles. The more recent conceptions focus on the leader's position in the larger organization, and they emphasize the leadership tasks that must be performed in order to give direction and movement to the organization. Most significantly, the new conception explicitly recognizes that the essential problem of leadership is the marshaling of human resources and the motivation of people.

Effective leadership has impact throughout an organization. It results in the empowerment of media employees which, for Bennis, "is the collective effect of leadership" (1984, p. 19).

In fact, Bennis goes so far as to argue that effective leadership is *the* key to organizational performance. He says: "If I have learned anything from my research it is this: the factor that empowers the workforce and ultimately determines which organizations succeed or fail is the leadership of those organizations. When strategies, processes, or cultures change, the key to improvement remains leadership" (1984, p. 16).

OUR CONCEPTION OF LEADERSHIP IN THE MEDIA

The conception of leadership in media companies that we developed is based on the approaches to leadership described in the preceding. As we said at the beginning of this chapter, we see media leaders and media leadership as two separate sides of the same coin.

Media leaders are encompassed by:

- consideration of the qualities that leaders possess and exhibit;
- the functions that they perform in their roles as media managers;
- how they capitalize on circumstances beyond their control.

Media leadership, as distinct from the individual leadership, is the other major ingredient in this equation.

- Media leadership is the impact leaders have on an organization by carrying out those broad leadership tasks that provide direction, stability, and purpose to the organization.

Let's look at each one of those items in turn:

Qualities of Media Leaders

The key qualities we see in media leaders represent our own thinking as well as a blending of those identified by other researchers. Our definition includes 10 significant characteristics that enable media managers to exert leadership:

1. Possession of a vision of where their department or firm should go and, by a variety of means, the ability to convince other people to join them in moving in that direction.
2. The ability—by example, through speeches, and/or by their decisions—to be effective communicators who can describe their vision with words or pictures that colleagues and others can easily understand.
3. The ability to listen effectively and respect others' views, as well as to let their team know that what the staff members are doing is important and valuable to the media company.
4. A tough, realistic, and extremely perceptive insight when it comes to evaluating themselves and the people who work for them. Only by recognizing true strengths and weaknesses in themselves and others can positive qualities be developed and negative ones be overcome.
5. The ability to attract and select potentially able employees, teach them, motivate them, and, equally important, organize them into effective work groups.
6. A special skill at identifying and prioritizing important issues.
7. The capacity to mobilize the necessary resources (people, money, information, service, time, technology) to get the work done.
8. The courage and drive to champion new ideas and see them through to completion.
9. The insight to know that innovations can happen in every setting, from the largest to the smallest, from the most exciting to the most mundane. What they look for are new and better ways of doing things. Usually, these innovations are created from existing conditions. The test of the effectiveness of media leaders is their skill at taking circumstances that everyone else has accepted as immutable and figuring out a way to use them to accomplish something new.
10. A commitment to their employees, recognizing that when work is interesting and staff members feel fulfilled, the quality of their performance will be high.

Functions of Media Leaders

Effective leadership of media companies involves a second aspect as well: top-level performance in the role of manager. As John Zenger puts it, "Truly effective executives and managers—those who contribute most to their organizations—combine managerial and leadership skills" (1985, p. 44).

This facet of leadership is grounded in the leaders' performance of their primary management functions:

- planning,
- organizing work and technology,
- financial budgeting and analysis,
- working with people.

To be an effective leader, a media manager must play a vital role in each of those areas.

In the planning process, effective executives show their vision of where the firm should go. With that vision clearly in mind they then are highly skilled at involving people, both inside and outside the organization, in developing and buying into the plan.

Effective leaders also really listen to others' ideas and then use those thoughts more effectively than they have been used before. Leaders who are effective over the long run have less ego invested in implementing their own ideas and are committed to finding, defining, and implementing the best idea, whether it is theirs or someone else's.

Once direction and plans are agreed upon, media leaders play a key role in organizing work to accomplish the goals laid out in their plan. That may mean rethinking how things have been done in the past. In some situations it may even require setting up a new structure. It also means being flexible enough to reach across departments or outside the information organization.

Media leaders build budgets and marshal resources to accomplish the work that needs to be done. Particularly important in this phase is using their leadership qualities to mobilize the people, money, information, services, time, and technology needed to implement their vision. In carrying out this function, effective media leaders are just like skillful politicians involved in negotiating and building coalitions to gather the necessary support and resources.

Last, but really the most important, successful information company executives are extremely skilled at working with people. They are able to determine what sort of people are needed, then find and recruit or "grow" those sorts of individuals in the firm. They also have to be effective in communicating to staff members what needs to be done, capitalizing on staff strengths, and working with staff so the people who report to them are continually developing their talents.

In short, effective leaders perform their managerial role with zest and vitality. They apply their leadership qualities to their management functions because it is not enough to "do things right." They must see and "do the right things."

Capitalizing on Outside Circumstances

A third element in our conception of leadership involves circumstances or, more precisely, the ability to capitalize on circumstances. In the middle 1980s, for example, many small U.S. weekly newspapers (1,000 to 2,000 circulation and $100,000 to $250,000 in annual revenues) were very marginal operations; some were near collapse. The smart owners of these properties seized on the advent of table-top publishing with microcomputers and used it to make those papers profitable and strong again.

Circumstances usually involve factors that are outside media leaders' immediate control. Some of the more important ones are listed below:

Family connections	Abundant resources
Personal connections	Fortunate timing
Good staff	Favorable technological changes
Corporate culture	Favorable economic conditions
Easy competitors	Luck

Many major media figures became leaders by understanding and taking advantage of circumstances; that is, by being in the right place at the right time and seizing the opportunity. For example, some were born to their lofty posts or married into them: Arthur Ochs Sulzberger of *The New York Times*; Katherine Graham, and now her son, Donald, of *The Washington Post*; and Christy Hefner of *Playboy*. Once at the helm, each of them became active, strong executives in their own right.

Other current media leaders capitalized on different circumstantial factors. Allen Neuharth has been the prime force in building Gannett, but he would not have had the opportunity without the legacy others left and the support they gave him. Frank Gannett and then Paul Miller created a financially solid organization. Miller also fostered Neuharth's development and gave him the opportunity to run the company. Without that base of accumulated power, champions who supported him, and technological advances to facilitate his vision, the Gannett chairman would not have become a powerful media leader.

Another factor that is critical in leadership is timing. The first person who takes an action often becomes a leader simply by filling a void, by being first. Henry Luce saw a need for a national newsmagazine and started *Time*, the first magazine of its type. Today, however, another weekly newsmagazine, which would be fourth in a field that already appears strained to support *Time*, *Newsweek*, and *U.S. News*, would have little chance for survival.

Technological changes often pave the way for leaders. Among media leaders, Ted Turner could not have developed the CNN network, or Allen Neuharth *USA Today*, or Warren Phillips the national *Wall Street Journal*, unless the appropriate technology arose to make those advances possible.

Tim Giago, an American Indian editor and publisher, used the expertise he gained on his *Lakota Times* in South Dakota and the comparatively low-cost and easy-entry skills needed on microcomputers to launch Native American Publishing, Inc., in 1987. This company is dedicated to publishing a chain of weekly newspapers for Indian reservations in Minnesota, Michigan, Wisconsin, and Oklahoma.

In summary, media leaders do not operate in a vacuum. They must recognize that their effectiveness is shaped by all sorts of outside forces: the people to whom they report, the culture of the media firm that employs them, the strengths and weaknesses of their staff, the actions of their competition, the advances in technology, and the availability of a broad range of resources. They must capitalize on the opportunities that circumstances present to move their department or organization forward.

Leadership's Impact on the Organization

Media leaders, then, are people with a variety of qualities, who exercise managerial functions effectively and capitalize on circumstances. Yet the same thing can be said about many media managers who are not leaders. What makes leaders different than "mere" managers is that they move their organizations or departments.

Having an impact or making a difference is what leadership of media organizations is about. Leadership only occurs—and media managers only lead—in the context of an organization, which may be a small work group, a department, a company, or a large corporation.

Leadership provides direction for the organization by capturing people's attention and mobilizing their energy and support for a particular purpose, goal, or strategy. Leadership provides stability and strength for the organization by creating a sense of confidence, based on trust of the leader, among the staff. In short, leadership fulfills those broad organizational tasks described by Bennis, Kanter, and Zenger that move and shape organizations.

The organizational tasks these analysts identified, leadership tasks or competencies, provide the linkage between individual leaders and the organization. Individuals can best function as leaders if the organization provides a context in which people (employees) see a purpose and a direction and in which they feel trust and confidence in their bosses and in each other. In short, organizations have the need for leadership. Individuals fulfill this need when they combine qualities, functions, and circumstances to move their organization, whether it be work group, department, or company as a whole. When this happens, then media managers become media leaders in the fullest sense of the term.

THE ORGANIZATIONAL CHALLENGE: DEVELOPING LEADERS

If Bennis is correct when he says, " . . . the key to improvement is leadership," then media organizations cannot wait and hope that leaders will emerge to guide them into the future. Rather, they have the responsibility to systematically identify and develop people for positions of leadership, preparing them to act as leaders, not just as managers.

That is a major challenge. To meet it what is needed is for those who presently run the media to recognize the role that their organization's culture and reward system plays in fostering both the rise of leaders and the level of acceptance that staff members exhibit for them. That means changing many corporate media cultures, restructuring many firm's reward systems, and across the board making a long-term investment in achieving such a goal. Now, the question is, how to accomplish such a change. It's not easy, but it can be done, and perhaps more easily now than at any prior time in the history of media companies.

The prime reason is that executives in each medium associate with other managers who work for large media conglomerates, or the executives themselves are employed by a big company. Thus, today it takes little effort to get to know personnel specialists in one's own industry who train staff members with a view of management and leadership similar to our conception. Furthermore, discussion of leadership training is the focal point of many professional associations and meetings.

What this means is that the top executives of even the smallest media companies can see and adapt training materials for a firm the size of theirs. They can also learn about and fashion for their own purposes such things as management by objectives plans, which include significant rewards for allowing younger or newer firm members to take the initiative and try their ideas. If there are rewards for senior managers for allowing this latitude to young staff members, then everyone will realize that taking the initiative is valued in the ad agency, magazine, or radio station.

Of course there are many other tools for the organization to use to change its culture and make clear that leadership is not only rewarded, but should be welcomed by everyone. For instance, employees can be sent to short courses, formal school, or industry training sessions where they gain access to the excitement of new ideas. Departments that have "done things right," but not too often "done the right thing," could be combined with a department that is more proactive, for example, or a new department leader could be brought in from elsewhere in the firm or from another media organization. Of course, these are but a few of the many changes a firm may employ to make leadership development a high priority.

Perhaps the time is right for media organizations and others to transform leadership development by shifting its emphasis in a manner similar to the movement in planning that occurred in the last decade. Throughout the 1950s, 1960s, and into the 1970s, planning was seen as a lock-step process of setting goals and objectives, developing plans, and monitoring results, which led into another round of planning. As the 1980s approached, a new conception of planning developed; the notion of strategic planning as a continuously evolving process that focuses attention on the "bigger picture," i.e., the entire competitive situation within which the organization operates. Thus, the emphasis changed from simply fulfilling objectives to creating powerful competitive strategies that take into account the organization and its competitors. Nevertheless, many of the elements crucial to effective strategic planning had been identified and refined during the earlier period.

Similarly, leadership development may go through the same change. Throughout the 1950s, 1960s, and 1970s, the emphasis has been on training individuals in managerial and leadership styles and behavior patterns, and recognition of various important situational factors that influence how media leaders should behave. The new conception suggests a shift to a more sophisticated notion of leadership as the development of broad competencies in individuals. But leadership development also focuses on what the organization can do. It includes items such as selecting those who demonstrate leadership potential (not everyone is suited for, or wants to be, a leader), devising opportunities for development of these competencies within the organization, and creating training programs that go beyond styles, behaviors, and contingencies to provide systematic education in the ways of performing key leadership tasks.

Many of the pieces are in place for such a leadership development program within U.S. media. The challenge for media firms is to act on this perspective, using those pieces that are already in place (tools such as personnel selection, performance appraisal systems, and training programs) to systematically focus attention and resources on leadership development. Those aspects of selection, review, performance appraisal, and training that contribute nothing to leadership development or detract from it should be discarded. At the same time, additional elements will need to be created if American media are going to be able to systematically develop the leadership talent that they need in the future.

This is indeed a major challenge, but if Bennis is correct, if, as "strategies, processes, or cultures change, the key to improvement remains leadership," then media companies must act upon this challenge. In the final analysis their viability in the future depends on their ability to identify, nurture, and develop leadership within their own organization.

If you are particularly interested in leadership, one easy place to get a good basic reading list of what is available is *Stogdill's Handbook of Leadership*, edited by Bernard M. Bass (1981).

CHAPTER 10

Case Study for Part Two, KZZZ-FM

Chapters 5 through 9 told you about the functions media managers perform. Now it is time for you to put those functions to work. In the case that follows, we return to early 1987 and KZZZ-FM, a station you met first in Chapter 2 and then in Chapter 7.

The focal point of this case is for you to gain an understanding and appreciation for the *process* that media executives go through when they carry out the functions in Chapters 5–8: planning, organizing, financial management, and working with their staff. That is why we've divided the case into four problems which correspond to Chapters 5 through 8.

You will note that we don't devote a section of this case to the penultimate function of media management, leadership, which is the subject of Chapter 9. That seeming omission was intentional. We have not allocated a separate part of this case to leadership because we expect you to show your understanding of it in the same way that the best media managers do, by highlighting leadership as you wrestle with each of the other management functions.

Your challenge, then, is to try to solve each problem without looking ahead to the next one. (Information in later problems is not very helpful in analyzing earlier ones, anyway.) In the process, you should explicitly demonstrate how what you have learned about leadership permeates your response, just as it would the response of a media manager.

Finally, bear in mind that this case study has no right and wrong answers. What it has are opportunities and challenges. If you are to benefit from working the case, that learning experience will come from developing your own solutions to it, using the concepts and ideas presented in Part Two.

BACKGROUND: KZZZ-FM— URBAN/CONTEMPORARY RADIO

KZZZ-FM is an urban/contemporary music station located in one of America's larger metropolitan centers. The market is strong and during the past few decades it showed substantial population and retail sales growth. Moreover, projections indicate that growth will continue to increase over the next 10 years, though at a somewhat slower rate. Radio revenues also grew rapidly during the years gone by, and they are expected to continue to rise for at least the next 10 years.

Unfortunately, KZZZ-FM has not shared in that growth. During the past two years, its ratings were unstable, and in the year which just concluded (1986), they plummeted to new lows. Revenue followed the same pattern, resulting in a substantial loss for 1986. That was partly due to decreases in revenue and partly to major increases in expenses resulting from substantial new investments in late 1985 and early in 1986.

Now the primary objective for KZZZ-FM is to *regain profitability.*

A Brief Introduction to Radio

In contemporary American society, radio, much like magazines, is a highly segmented medium. For example, KZZZ-FM is one of 29 stations in its market competing for a share of the audience. The standard media managers use when they make a radio programming decision is to determine the audience segment they wish to target and then develop or purchase a "format" (programming that will attract that audience segment). Of course, they also use substantial promotion to tell the targeted audience about the unique and desirable characteristics of their station and its "sound" (format).

Radio audiences are typically segmented by age groups or by sex, though some are identified by race or ethnic background, such as those that broadcast in Spanish for a Hispanic audience. Because a significant share of the disposable income in the U.S. is found in the 18–49-year-old group, competition for that audience segment is fierce. Because music and other content preferences vary considerably within the large 18–49 age group, radio executives find it extremely difficult to develop a format that will attract significant numbers of people from each subsegment of that larger age category; some subsets are 18–24, 25–34, 35–44, male, female, Hispanic, black, white.

Most stations focus on a smaller target audience, choosing a broadcast format that has proven appeal to an audience segment. In KZZZ-FM's market, the top 12 stations utilize eight different formats. These stations attract over 70 percent of the audience, and 17 other stations divide the remaining 30 percent. The eight formats of the leaders with their corresponding target audiences are shown in Exhibit 10.1. (Note: When you study the figure, do not assume that target audiences in the right-hand column are all-inclusive; they are a long way from complete. What they are is a thumbnail summary of the group who listens most to a particular format in that market.)

Market

Total radio revenues in KZZZ-FM's market grew at an annual rate of 19 percent during the past five years. That put its metro area in the top group of growth markets in the country. What's more, radio revenues there are expected to reach nearly $110 million by next year. The market has a population of about 3.3 million. Although population growth is not as rapid now as it was, the increase is still strong and is expected to top 4 million in the 1990s. The two population groups growing most rapidly are blacks and those whites in the 30–45 "baby boom" age group.

Retail sales were over $22.9 billion in 1986, and they are expected to double by 1995. As detailed below in Exhibit 10.2, this market is rated an "A" in terms of projected population, retail sales, and radio sales growth. The $96.7 million radio revenue in 1986 represents 13.6 percent of the total media advertising revenues of $711 million, and it is 0.42 percent of total retail sales of $22.9 billion.

Competition

Reviewing 1986's performance, it is clear that KZZZ-FM slipped badly in the ratings compared to the prior year. Its average quarter-hour share decreased by nearly one third between spring of 1985 and spring of 1986, falling from 4.7 to 3.2. In the meantime, its top competitor for the black audience, KAAA-FM substantially increased its share. Exhibit 10.3 shows the three-year pattern of ratings for the top 12 stations in the market.

EXHIBIT 10.1. FORMATS AND AUDIENCES

Format	*Target Audience*
Top 40	15–24-year-olds
Album-oriented rock	males, 18–34
Adult contemporary	females, 18–34
Beautiful music	females, 25–49
Country and Western	25–64
News/talk	30–49, elderly
Nostalgia	35–65
Urban/contemporary	Blacks, 18–49

EXHIBIT 10.2. SUMMARY DEMOGRAPHICS AND SALES OF KZZZ-FM MARKET

	1984	*1985*	*1986*	*1987**	*1988**	*1989**
Total Population (in millions)	3.1	3.2	3.3	3.4	3.5	3.7
Black Population (in 100,000s)	488	512	542	560	579	605
Retail Sales (in billions)	18.6	20.3	22.9	25.4	28.4	31.9
Radio Revenues (in millions)	74.4	87.0	96.7	108.9	122.4	137.8

* Estimates and projections for the years 1987–1989

EXHIBIT 10.3. THREE-YEAR RATINGS FOR THE TOP 12 STATIONS IN THE KZZZ-FM MARKET

Station	*Format*	*Spring 1984*	*Spring 1985*	*Spring 1986*	*Average Estimated Rates: 1986*
KZZZ-FM	Urban/Contemporary	4.2	4.7	3.2	$125
KAAA-FM	Urban/Contemporary	6.9	6.4	9.1	145
KBBB-FM	Contemporary hit radio	5.3	7.7	10.7	198
KCCC-FM	Country	7.2	7.5	6.4	195
KDDD-FM	Beautiful music	7.5	6.7	8.4	205
KEEE-FM	Album-oriented Rock	7.3	5.6	7.4	175
KFFF-FM	Album-oriented Rock	4.9	4.9	5.8	135
KGGG-FM	Adult Contemporary	5.9	5.2	3.8	240
KHHH-FM	Nostalgia	5.4	3.8	3.5	95
KIII-AM	News/Talk	4.5	4.1	3.5	130
KJJJ-FM	Country	6.0	6.9	4.9	170
KLLL-FM	Adult Contemporary	4.9	4.0	4.7	170

Exhibit 10.4 shows KZZZ-FM's performance in spring 1986 ratings for various demographic groups. Note that the station ranks only fourth among blacks even though just two stations (KZZZ-FM and KAAA-FM) program specifically for the black audience.

EXHIBIT 10.4. KZZZ-FM DEMOGRAPHIC RANKINGS IN SPRING 1986

Demographic Group	*KZZZ-FM Rank*
Adults 18–34	7
Adults 25–49	10
Adults 18–49	11
Women 18–34	9
Women 25–49	12
Black	4

Financial Performance

In the year just ended, KZZZ-FM lost $234,000 on revenues of $3.1 million. Sales decreased by $345,000 and operating expenses increased by $125,000. Additionally, due to major investments in a new transmitter late in 1985 and a new 6,000-square-foot studio early in 1986, interest payments increased by approximately $600,000 for this year compared to $87,600 in 1985. Exhibit 10.5 shows KZZZ-FM's financial performance in the past three years.

KZZZ-FM is a moderate-sized station. In its market, three stations grossed in excess of $10 million for the year, while seven others had revenues between $5 and $10 million. KZZZ-FM ranked 12th in revenue, accounting for 3.2 percent of total radio sales in the area.

PROBLEM 1. PLANNING KZZZ-FM's STRATEGY
DO THIS IN CONJUNCTION WITH CHAPTER 5

The point of this problem is for you to learn about planning in general and about strategies and action plans in particular. The best way to gain insights in those areas is to pretend that you are Linda Remy, the station manager of KZZZ-FM. You met her in Chapter 7 when City Media, Inc., the owner of KZZZ-FM, sent Remy to the station with a specific objective: to regain profitability. In developing a strategy to reach that goal, consider the following:

1. Are there alternative audience segments that KZZZ-FM might target? How attractive are those segments to advertisers? How much competition is there for those segments?
2. If the answer to No. 1 is that there are no attractive alternative audiences, what are the advantages of the present KZZZ-FM audience? Are there alternative formats for increasing ratings in the present audience? Would it be possible to develop a new format, or a combination of formats, to more effectively reach the present audience?

EXHIBIT 10.5. INCOME STATEMENT FOR KZZZ-FM

	1984	*1985*	*1986*
Sales/Revenue			
Local	$2,194,550	$2,434,941	$2,487,259
National	1,041,470	1,051,010	653,302
Total revenue	$3,236,020	$3,485,951	$3,140,561
Expenses			
Operating expenses			
Program	$ 255,277	$ 316,426	$ 352,989
News	39,183	41,631	44,158
Direct	525,067	524,146	465,560
Technical	82,849	105,521	133,784
Sales	199,340	251,295	259,009
Promotion	408,598	464,063	519,791
Traffic	40,527	46,782	45,368
General and administrative	415,718	358,325	412,892
Total operating expenses	$1,880,907	$2,108,189	$2,233,551
Operating profit	$1,355,113	$1,377,762	$907,010
Nonoperating expenses			
Depreciation	$ 326,156	$ 329,749	$ 356,915
Management fee	91,000	91,000	97,000
Interest	394,682	87,600	687,500
Total nonoperating expenses	$ 811,838	$ 508,349	$1,141,515
(Loss) Profit before taxes	$ 543,275	$ 869,413	$ (234,395)
Taxes	$ 220,000	$ 400,000	$ -0-
Net profit	$ 323,275	$ 469,413	$ (234,395)

3. If the answer to No. 1 is that there are alternative target audiences, define a new target audience for KZZZ-FM. What formats could be used to reach the new target audience? Would it be possible to develop a new format or a combination of formats to more effectively reach that target audience?
4. Can any expenses be reduced to make significant savings possible at KZZZ-FM? If so, how?

After considering these questions, list several strategies you might use to enable KZZZ-FM to regain profitability. For each strategy, list reasons and/or data that support this strategy, and identify problems or barriers that may prevent the strategy from being successful.

Finally, choose the best strategy and summarize why you have selected it; cite relevant data and explain your reasoning. Also, acknowledge possible difficulties with the strategy and think about ways to deal with them.

(Note: The one option which you are not allowed to employ in your response to Problem 1 is to shift to a talk/news format. We reserve that for use with Problem 2 of this case. *Do not go on to Problem 2 until you have completed this one.*)

PROBLEM 2. ORGANIZING TO IMPLEMENT THE STRATEGY *DO THIS IN CONJUNCTION WITH CHAPTER 6*

Now, assume that the strategy developed for KZZZ-FM was to shift to a talk/news format that is aimed at the 30–49-year-old target market. That age group is large; it is the baby boom generation of post–WW II now reaching age 40. Thus, it is a potentially profitable market segment for KZZZ-FM if you can attract a decent share of it. (This change in format is, of course, a major departure for KZZZ-FM in terms of both target market and programming. We chose the 30–49 target market and a talk/news format because it is quite different from what we thought you would choose when you responded to Problem 1. As a result, you will be able to take a fresh look at the station, as if you were starting anew.)

Background Information on Talk Radio

Talk radio was developed in the late 1960s and became a relatively popular format in the 1970s. The number of talk outlets decreased somewhat in the 1980s, but most major markets have one or two, though they are usually AM stations. In KZZZ-FM's market, there are two talk/news stations, both AM. One, KIII is the 10th ranking station with a current share of 3.5, down from 4.1 in 1985 and 4.5 in 1984. KNNN is the 14th ranking station, with a current share of 2.9, down from 3.5 in 1984 and 3.8 in 1985.

Although the ratings decline of both talk/news stations may indicate weaknesses in the format, it made sense for you to convert KZZZ-FM to that format for several reasons:

1. Radio listeners listen predominantly to FM: in your market the 13 FM stations control 71 percent of the audience, and the 16 AM stations have only 29 percent. No other FM station has a talk/news format.
2. The talk show hosts and topics covered on the other two AM stations, KIII and KNNN, appeal to an older audience. Most callers sound older, and rating profiles indicate over half of their audiences are in the over-50 age range.
3. Research in a variety of cities indicates that talk radio fulfills many of the needs, wants, and desires of the audience who call in. Nearly one-third of the callers want to chat with the host. One-fourth use the station as a forum for their opinions, information they wish to share, or causes they wish to promote. Repeat callers are more likely to be seeking companionship; yet, approximately 40 percent of the callers during most time periods on talk

shows are new. Audience members become active participants in the show and, typically, become quite involved with the programming after initial participation; moreover, every day many new participants are added to the group of listeners. As a result, talk radio has high potential for creating substantial audience loyalty.

Organization of the Programming Department

In this problem, think of yourself as the station's programming director, Katie Pierce. In the present (nontalk) programming department you head a staff of six full-time disc jockeys and two part-timers who work weekend shifts. The full-time DJs work six 4-hour shifts from Monday through Friday, and one weekend day. Each DJ has his or her own time slot. On the weekend day, when a full-time DJ is not working a part-timer fills in; they often use canned material for major program segments. DJs punch all the buttons to put their records, tapes, compact disks, and advertisements on the air.

Programming also includes a news director who pulls wire copy from national and local AP wires, edits it into short news breaks, and fills it in with weather reports and scores of games of interest to KZZZ-FM's listeners. Emphasis on news has been small and news breaks are aired only during the day.

The programming department in most music stations is organized and staffed in the manner shown in Exhibit 10.6. Talk radio stations, however, do not mirror that setup (see Exhibit 10.7).

In one staffing pattern, each talk show segment involves three people: (1) the on-air host; (2) a producer/technician who handles the control panel, lines up guests and develops background information on upcoming topics, and monitors transmission; and (3) a person to screen calls. Screening may simply involve identifying name and topic for discussion, or it may be more intensive (e.g., asking callers what they are going to say).

EXHIBIT 10.6. CURRENT ORGANIZATION CHART OF THE KZZZ-FM PROGRAMMING DEPARTMENT

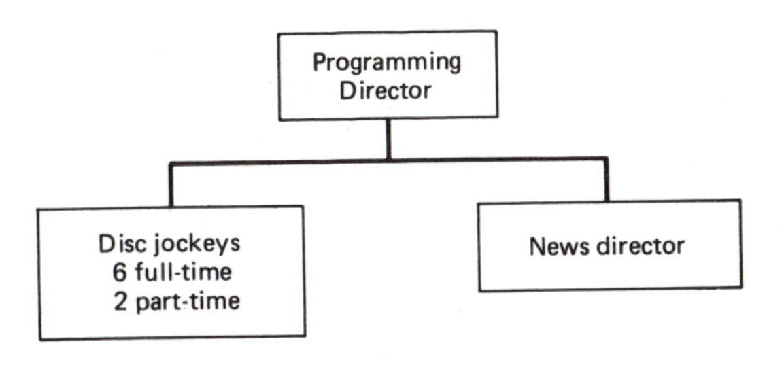

EXHIBIT 10.7. ALTERNATIVE STAFFING PATTERNS FOR TALK RADIO

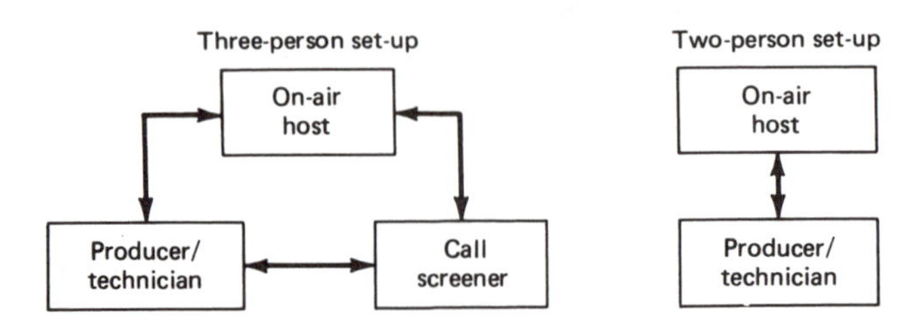

Another staffing pattern involves only two people, the on-air host and the producer/technician who handles the control panel. With that arrangement, there is no screening of callers. Some radio experts believe this arrangement is better because it maintains greater spontaneity. Moreover, with the four-to-seven-second electronic delay commonly used on talk radio, the host can maintain program control without screening, for the delay allows the host to delete profanity, abusive behavior, and promotions, or to cut off callers entirely.

Typically, one host will cover a two- or three-hour time slot. Producer/technicians and telephone screening personnel will work with two hosts. In addition to their duties during programming, the producers arrange for guests, identify topics of interest, and give background to the hosts about special discussion topics.

Additional personnel who may be involved in a station's programming include news, weather, and traffic personnel. Sometimes these people are members of the station's staff; sometimes they work for a programming service, which is coordinated by the producer/technician.

Some talk show segments may involve a nationally syndicated host. There are any number of choices that vary in personality, style, topic (sex with Dr. Ruth to general talk with Larry King), and time slots. Typical programming strategies involve blending different personality and conversational styles, e.g., comic, light conversation, passive listeners, rude, political philosophy (arch conservative, liberal, moderate), with topic variety, e.g., sports, counseling, economic advice, general.

Developing KZZZ-FM's Programming Strategy and Organizing the Programming Department

As Katie Pierce, the programming director, your job is to develop a strategy for talk radio and an organization plan to implement it. At this point, do not worry about budget. (We will cover that next.) It would be a good idea to review Chapter 6 on organizing, however. To develop your programming strategy, ponder the following questions:

- How much emphasis will you put on news as part of your overall format? How will the news component be delivered?
- What kind of balance of hosts, topics, guests, etc., will you utilize to try to attract your target audience (30–49 year olds)?
- Will you utilize any syndicated talk show segments as part of your overall programming strategy? If so, what kind of hosts and what topics will be the focus?
- How long will program segments be? Will length vary by host or topic?

Then, to develop your organization plan, think about the following:

- For each program segment, will you use screening or not? Why? Will your policy be the same or different from one program segment to another? Why?
- How many news people will be required to effectively implement your news emphasis? Can some of this news programming (e.g., weather, traffic reports, etc.) be done by outside programming services instead of hiring your own people?
- Will you need to add another layer of management in the programming department? If so, how might your department be organized into subdepartments, and how much time might be required for management purposes within the subdepartment?

When you have answered those question, lay out the program schedule for your station on a day-by-day basis. Indicate the topics you will cover in different time slots and whether you will use local or syndicated hosts for each time period. Make sure you clearly indicate where news segments fit into the time segments.

Next, develop an organization chart to show how you will structure your programming department. Indicate the job titles and the number of people needed in each category. Write a brief job description for each job. If you establish them, show the subdepartment structure.

For both the programming schedule and organization, be clear about the rationale for your decisions. The reasoning you use is more important than your specific solution, though both must be thorough.

Finally, but very important, *do not go to Problem 3 until you have finished this one.*

PROBLEM 3. BUDGETING TO IMPLEMENT THE STRATEGY
DO THIS IN CONJUNCTION WITH CHAPTER 7

KZZZ-FM had a sales increase of approximately 8 percent in 1984 and 1985. That compared to an increase of 17 percent for the industry as a whole in the station's market. Similarly, radio sales increased 13 percent from 1985 to 1986, but KZZZ-FM had a decrease of 10 percent for the same period.

KZZZ-FM had a profit on sales of about 17 percent in 1984, and an apparent profit of nearly 25 percent in 1985. This was inflated, however, because there were few debt-related expenses in 1985. In 1986, with two new facilities, interest payments increased by $600,000. The loss, as a percent of sales in 1986, was about 7 percent. To maintain a profit level of 9 percent would have required a sales increase in 1986 of nearly 10 percent. (Review Exhibit 10.5 for details of KZZZ-FM's financial performance.)

For 1987, which just began, KZZZ management projects a sales increase of 15 percent to $3.61 million. That is based on the expectation that Katie Pierce's new format will create a larger and more attractive audience for advertisers. Industry projections for the new year in the market indicate that a 13 percent sales increase is expected.

KZZZ-FM's management is using the same ratios for revenues and expenses as were achieved in 1985, when the station last made a profit. Of course, those figures were adjusted for increases in nonoperating expenses that resulted from the large investment. Operating expenses are set at 61 percent of revenues: $2.2 million. Depreciation, interest, and the management fee should be 30 percent of revenues: $1.08 million. The projected pretax profit is $330,000, 9 percent of revenues.

In 1985, programming expenses were about $520,000, divided among program ($316,000), news ($42,000), and direct expenses attributable to programming ($164,000). Direct expenses are music fees, other syndication fees, broadcast rights for certain programs, and other outside services. These costs represent about 25% of operating expenses. The programming budget for the new year will be $575,000.

Perhaps the easiest way to think about the 1987 programming budget is to put it on a weekly basis. The annual programming total of $575,000 will provide a weekly budget of $11,000. That means that Pierce needs to allocate that amount across three categories of content: local-origination talk, syndicated talk, news.

In talk/news radio, the great bulk of expenses are salary expenses and fees for syndicated programming. The salary pattern in 1987 for hosts in a market this size are:

Top notch (suitable for best audience times)	$40–60,000
Good (suitable for second best audience times)	$30–45,000
Okay (suitable for secondary audience times)	$20–30,000
Rookies (suitable for fringe times)	$15–20,000

Producer salaries range from $15–30,000, depending on demands of job, experience, etc. Producers typically work with two hosts.

Here is an example of a way to convert a salary figure into a weekly programming cost for a six-day two- or three-hour time slot:

Good host salary	$40,000
Producer (1/2 of salary)	$12,000
Total	$52,000/52 weeks = $1000 per week

Syndication arrangements are made in a variety of ways. One is that a syndicator purchases time from the station for a fee and takes all advertising revenue. In another the syndicator and station develop a barter relationship where the syndicator provides programming and the station provides promotion, then they split the results on a predetermined basis.

To simplify matters as you do this section of the problem, you should assume that KZZZ-FM will pay direct fees for all syndicated programming it uses. Weekly syndication fees for various levels of host are:

Top notch	$900–1300
Good	$700–1000
Okay	$500–800

News personnel receive relatively low salaries in radio. To hire a news director, you would pay $20–23,000. News staff members receive salaries ranging from $12–16,000. One news person can be expected to produce about 30 minutes of content per day.

In developing your budget for the programming department, assume that the average programming segment is 2.5 hours per day, or about 10 segments per day. News segments are interspersed with the talk segments, providing a break for the hosts. However, you may wish to develop some lengthier segments each day or on the weekend.

In fact, the overall weekend program schedule may be quite different than the regular weekday fare. Calculate your budget by taking one-sixth of a weekly cost figure for a one-day time slot on Saturday or Sunday, e.g., good syndicated host = $115–170 per day.

Here, then, is what you should do:

1. Based on your programming strategy and your organization plan for the programming department, calculate a weekly budget for your projected programming costs. Before calculations can be done you must determine the quality level of your local and syndicated hosts in each time slot. You are adopting the role of Katie Pierce, program director, so do not forget to include her $65,000 salary in your calculation.
2. If there is a discrepancy between your budget and the $11,000 allocation, do one of two things:
   a. adjust your programming strategy and organization plan to create a balanced budget;

EXHIBIT 10.8. MAJOR BUDGET CATEGORIES FOR PROGRAMMING DEPARTMENT

Program director: Katie Pierce	$ 65,000
Local on-air host	
Syndicated host fees	
Producer/technicians	
News director and personnel	
Miscellaneous	
Total Program Budget	$575,000

b. develop a rationale as to *why* the discrepancy is acceptable.
(Note: The discrepancy may work both ways; you may have budgeted either too much or too little for programming.)

3. Convert the weekly budget to a programming department budget for 1987. Use the format shown in Exhibit 10.8.

When you have completed this problem, move on to Problem 4.

PROBLEM 4. STAFFING TO IMPLEMENT THE STRATEGY *DO THIS IN CONJUNCTION WITH CHAPTER 8*

Up to this point you have (or should have) done the following:

1. Developed a specific programming strategy and plan for KZZZ-FM's new talk/news format.
2. Outlined the organization of the programming department to implement your programming plan and identified the different kinds and numbers of on-air and off-air people you will need.
3. Fit your programming and organizing plans to your budget.

Current Staff Members in the Programming Department

Now you need to take the most concrete step yet in moving toward implementing your programming strategy and plan: You have to select the people to carry it out. By way of further help with that, the following is information about you (as Katie Pierce) and the individuals on your staff. The staff information includes ages, backgrounds, and racial identification, for those are factors which you may take into account when making staffing decisions, particularly in light of the station's shift in audience.

Katie Pierce: As Katie Pierce, you are a 33-year-old radio whiz. You have been the programming director at KZZZ-FM for only a month.

After Linda Remy, the station manager, and her management team made the decision to switch to a talk/radio format, they wooed and won you with the promise of a $65,000 salary and, equally or more important, their support of your efforts to turn KZZZ-FM around. Your contact with the personnel of the station prior to the interview was limited to phone calls and correspondence. Prior to this you've been programming director at two other stations. The first was a small outlet in Billings, Montana, where you grew up and started working right out of college as a producer; then you moved to program director. From there you went to a station in a market slightly smaller than KZZZ-FM's, but in the same geographic region of the country. During five years in that market, your station showed a 50 percent ratings' increase and it underwent a format change much like KZZZ-FM's, switching from a music format to a talk/news format with a fairly strong emphasis on its news operation. You view KZZZ-FM's situation as a challenge, but believe there is an excellent chance for success.

Reg Tremaine: A white 36-year-old, Reg is the leading figure among the programming staff. He has worked for the station for four years and has a consistent record of good ratings. He is now doing the morning drive-time slot, a show consisting primarily of Top 40 hits, and weather, news, and traffic updates. Before coming to KZZZ-FM, Reg was a disc jockey in a smaller market. He earns $50,000.

John Growe: John has been with the station for six years. Now 31, he started at KZZZ-FM as a producer after serving as a public affairs officer in the Army for three years and attending Grambling University. After graduating, he spent three years in production at KZZZ-FM and then started doing board shots (running the controls during a show) in addition to his production duties. His time slot is OK in the ratings, and he has managed to build a strong audience among blacks. His salary is $34,000, and John is black.

Chip Strong: Chip started at KZZZ-FM two years ago. Prior to that he worked for five years in television production and was the first black in this market to be executive producer of a news program. It was the sunrise program, however, and when the rumor started circulating that the early hours led to his disenchantment with TV, he was wooed by KZZZ-FM. His strong background, unfortunately, has not translated into high ratings; in fact, the reactions to his show are downright disappointing. Strong's show is characterized by lively talk and less music than on other programs, but so far that format hasn't taken off. He is currently earning $38,000 and is 30 years old.

Doug Jones: Doug joined KZZZ-FM after he graduated from Green Institute, the local broadcasting school. Now, two years out of school, Doug is 23 years old, and earns $20,000, and is a good disk jockey. Apart from a couple of classes at Green he has had no production experience. Doug is white.

Bob Freeman: Bob started at KZZZ-FM only six months ago. He had six months of production experience at another local station, where he was hired fresh out of a nearby state university. His college degree is in speech communications, with a concentration on intercultural communications. Bob was president of the Black Students' Association and hosted a short-lived talk show on the university radio station. He started at KZZZ-FM at $17,000, and is up for his six-month review and salary increase at the end of the month. Bob is 23 and black.

Joanne Hart: Joanne graduated from the University of Tennessee with a broadcast major and a journalism minor. After working for a year in news and production at a station in Knoxville, Tennessee, she moved to KZZZ-FM. The station hired her as news director with the understanding that she would also be responsible for a daily board shot. She did that for about six months, but for the past 18 months has concentrated on news. Joanne is 25, black, and earns $25,000. She is maturing into a strong professional.

Rick Johnson: After two years at the station, Rick's ratings are still a disappointment. At 34, he earns $45,000. That salary is the product of his huge success in a larger station in Minneapolis. A desire to escape the cold led him to interview with KZZZ-FM, who quickly hired him based on his track record. Rick has extensive on-air and production experience, but just hasn't found the right formula at KZZZ-FM. He got into radio through the sales department of a small station in North Dakota, but started moving quickly up the broadcasting ladder when he shifted to programming. He is white.

Joe Watten: A black student at the local university, Joe is paid about $9,000 a year for doing weekend production duties and board shots. He is a junior in broadcast journalism and, although he needed a lot of supervision when he started at KZZZ-FM 18 months ago, Joe has developed into a steady performer on the air. He has also proved to be a whiz at production.

Jim Sharpe: Jim is working part-time at KZZZ-FM while hunting for a full-time announcing job. Jim wouldn't mind staying at KZZZ-FM, but has not gotten much encouragement up to now about the possibility of a full-time position. He recently moved to the KZZZ-FM market area from a small town in the same state. There, he worked on a radio station that folded. He's had a good range of experience, everything from sales to trouble-shooting equipment. At his current $9,000 salary, however, he is looking hard for another job. Jim is 23 and Latino.

This problem has two separate parts. First, outline your staffing plan indicating:

- the present employees you will shift from one position to another;
- the type(s) of people you need to hire;
- staff members you may want to terminate.

For each of the internal changes you plan to make, indicate what incentives you may offer to facilitate those shifts. Will any retraining be necessary for those who are moving from one post to another? If you offer financial incentives, how much will those payments cost? Which of the incentives are one-time and which will become regular facets of the programming department's salary structure?

Also, why did you choose the incentives, both financial and nonfinancial, you've listed? What are their costs in terms of money, time, or other resources?

Next, how are you going to handle terminations, both psychologically and financially? Also, will your payment plans for both terminations and retraining stay within your department's budget? If they don't, can you provide a strong argument for the extra money you will need? What is your rationale?

The second part of your staffing plan should indicate how you will introduce the changes you propose. How will you communicate with your staff—by memo, by individual discussions, or by a large staff meeting? What kind of approaches might you take in introducing the staff changes with the group as a whole and with different individuals? Keeping in mind the individual differences of your staff, the key question here is, how do you best communicate with them.

Your format and staffing changes are likely to cause some adverse reaction within the station and also within the community, particularly among blacks. How do you plan to deal with these two possibilities?

When your changes are complete, and six months to a year has passed, what measurements will reflect the success or failure of the changes you've instituted? In other words, what benchmarks should Linda Remy, your station manager, use to judge your performance? Why do you choose the standards you just proposed?

Please answer each of these questions and then turn to a final section in the KZZZ-FM case.

Again, we suggest that you do not move ahead with the next section of this case until you complete this one. What appears on the next page will not help you here. Moreover, if you put a short-term restraint on your eagerness to see what comes next, you will learn far more from it.

LEGAL AND ETHICAL ISSUES IN THE KZZZ-FM CASE

If you were really program director Katie Pierce or station manager Linda Remy, you might not change KZZZ-FM to a talk/news format. In fact, you might try to maintain the station's present audience and add to it. In that case, it is unlikely that you would take the race or ages of your staff into account.

Assuming that you did make the decision to go after a new target audience with a talk/news format, however, then those characteristics should be reviewed. When you answered the questions in Problem 4, did you decide that when KZZZ-FM changed to talk/news, then most of the black employees would be terminated? Further, given the maturity required for talk radio, did you also fire all or most of the younger employees?

If you took that tack, then you should carefully review your decisions. Not only are they illegal, but they are also very shortsighted. Why? They are illegal because job discrimination based on race, age, or sex is prohibited by a variety of federal, state, and in some cases, local employment laws and rules. (That issue is covered more fully in Chapter 16.)

They are shortsighted because they do not make personnel choices on the basis of merit. After all, who says that a black or young announcer or newscaster cannot adapt to the new format? They are just as likely to be able to make that move as a white or more mature person.

Moreover, going in that direction overlooks the high probability that when the station moves to talk/news, Remy and Pierce will want to appeal to the more than half a million blacks in KZZZ-FM's current target audience. Wouldn't it make sense to have some of the present station staff fill that bill, as they are local and know the black community?

Further, imagine the black community's reaction to purging all the black staffers at what many of them understandably feel is their station. What kind of impact might this have on KZZZ-FM's success in both the short-term and the long-term?

Considerations like these regularly confront media managers as they make decisions. A variety of serious legal and ethical issues come into play as information executives carry out their managerial functions. Effective media leadership requires media managers to broaden their vision to include legal and ethical considerations. Part Four of this book will help you understand how this can be done.

PART THREE

Areas of Media Management Activity

CHAPTER 11

A Marketing Perspective for the Media

In Part One we gave you a framework for studying the management of media organizations. You read about the "manufacturing" of messages and about features of media companies that differentiate them from other businesses or industries. You also followed the development of various media, their revenue patterns, ownership structures, and audiences. Three specific firms—Williams Advertising Agency, KZZZ-FM, and *The New Gazette*—were compared in terms of the functions they performed, their structure, and their finances. Finally, you learned about some of a media firm's responsibilities and how they are exercised through the firm's mission, goals, and strategies.

In Part Two you concentrated on what media managers do, looking at their involvement in planning, organizing, financial management, and personnel. We also discussed how they can perform these functions, as a person who either simply carries out an assigned task or as a leader.

MEDIA MANAGERS' ACTIVITIES

Now, in Part Three, our attention is on the other side of how information executives spend their time; that is, we look not at what media managers do, but at what they manage. Here we talk about their activities. We focus on how they utilize the skills and functions outlined in Part Two in specific departments or areas of their media organization.

There is another way to explain Part Three. Remember, when we talked about media companies as "manufacturers" we said there were five steps involved in manufacturing and selling a media product? That progression looks like the one in Exhibit 11.1.

The fifth step (promoting or selling a media product) also fits in the picture, but it comes in at different points in the progression for differ-

EXHIBIT 11.1. STEPS IN MANUFACTURING AND SELLING MEDIA PRODUCTS

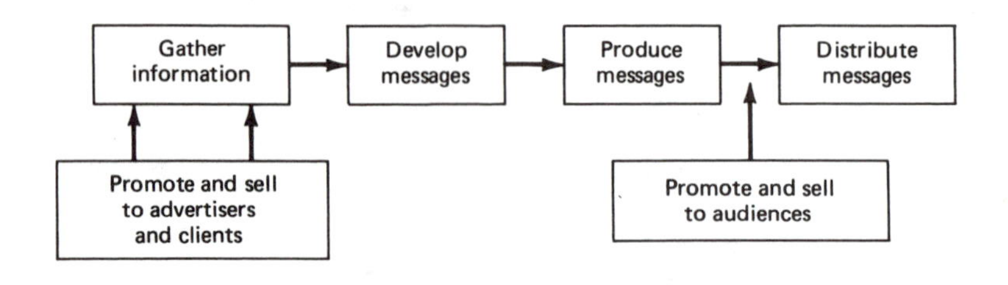

ent media. That is why we put it down below the other steps. There, depending on the specific medium, an arrow can be drawn from it to any point on the progression above.

Actually, a progression of that type can be applied to any media company. For a newspaper, it looks like Exhibit 11.2.

In a radio station the progression is quite similar, but the differences are found by studying Exhibit 11.3.

An advertising agency's progression follows in Exhibit 11.4.

In all media, similar activities occur as messages are developed, produced, promoted, and distributed. Consideration of these activities is the subject of Part Three of the text. Media managers carry out managerial functions as they direct their staffs in developing a product, then promoting, producing, and distributing it.

The basic approach we take in examining a media firm's activities is

EXHIBIT 11.2. MANUFACTURING AND SELLING NEWSPAPERS

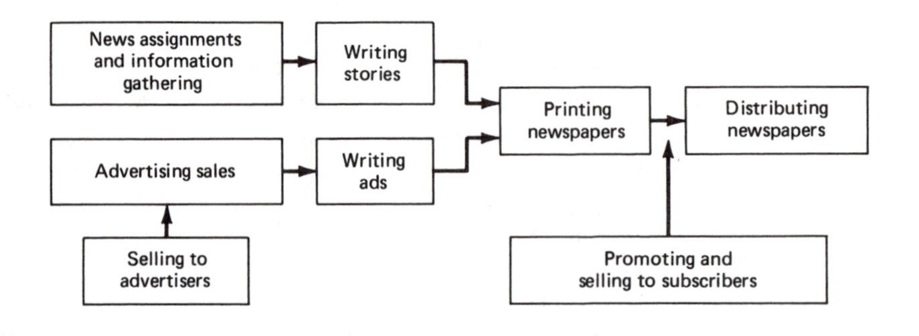

EXHIBIT 11.3. PACKAGING AND SELLING RADIO BROADCASTS

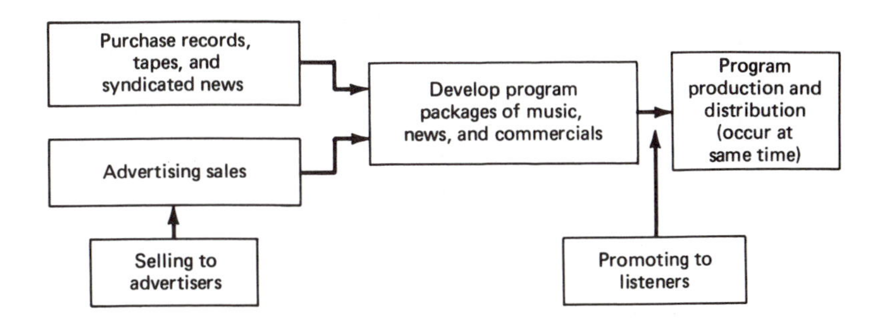

the marketing perspective. This approach, which was developed in the last 20 to 30 years, concentrates primary attention on consumers. Before the marketing perspective was adopted, companies took a product orientation; they focused primary attention on the features of the product itself.

Today, in an era of countless me-too media products, the chances of developing a breakthrough feature (a unique newspaper, TV show, movie, or advertising campaign) are minimal. Moreover, executives came to realize that what they felt the public should want did not necessarily correspond to people's interests. That led to a shift in emphasis. Media firms began to identify customers' needs and desires first; then they tailored news, entertainment, and advertising to match consumer interests. That proved to be a far more effective way of selling a company's information products or services.

The marketing perspective actually came to media companies later

EXHIBIT 11.4. DEVELOPING AND SELLING ADVERTISING CAMPAIGNS

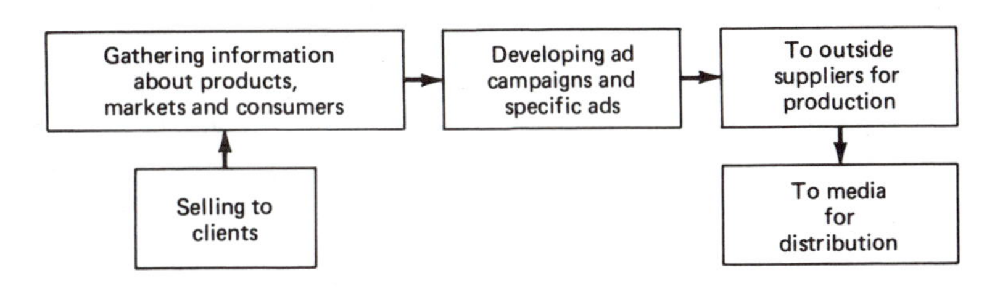

than it did to many industries. There are a number of reasons for this, but the most important is that it reflected an awareness of social responsibilities by editors, reporters, screen writers, and other message producers. They felt it was their job to decide what society should read or see. Judgments of that sort involved their expertise and integrity as professionals and they were loath to share that responsibility and power, even with the citizens for whom they were preparing a message.

In time that stance began to give way and the marketing perspective came to play a more important role in the media. As that happened, information companies' creative personnel learned that adopting the marketing perspective does not mean their responsibilities are replaced. In fact, it can improve their ability to develop more effective media products to serve their advertisers and consumers. For example, we saw how the marketing perspective, which was the guiding force behind the development of *Pediatric Neurology*, led to the publishing of the high-quality new medical journal described in Chapter 5.

Do not make the mistake of interpreting the marketing perspective too narrowly. As was the case for the medical journal, this perspective is not just finding out what customers want and, in a pandering manner, giving it to them. Rather, a sophisticated marketing perspective focuses just as much on the long-term responsibilities and credibility of the media as on the short-term desires of the audience and advertisers. It entails developing messages that balance audience members' preferences and advertisers' needs with the media's role in delivering information that citizens must have to be informed. Stated simply, a broad marketing perspective enables media firms to serve their market in the fullest sense.

MEDIA AS A BRIDGE BETWEEN ADVERTISERS AND AUDIENCES

Another reason for adopting the marketing perspective is the important role media companies play in this society as a bridge between those who primarily pay for time or space (advertisers), and the audiences those advertisers seek. Remember, too, in many instances the information from those advertisers is sought by consumers. In each medium where there is advertising, and that includes nearly all newspapers, magazines, and broadcasting outlets, the information concern's role in the economic system is quite clear. Moreover, advertiser-based media firms remain financially viable only when they develop media products that are read, heard, or seen by an audience attractive to their advertisers.

To create that audience, media companies must pay close attention to consumers' wants, needs, and preferences. Look at the similarities among different media as they do this: A television network develops programs to attract mass audiences in order to meet the needs of its large national advertisers. Magazines develop specialized information products attractive to smaller, select national advertisers. Newspapers report a package of stories, say on auto care, to attract mass local audiences for their advertisers who sell cars or auto-related goods and services. Radio stations, cable companies, and low-power television stations program to attract segmented local audiences that other advertisers want to reach.

This relationship between audiences and advertisers may seem obvious, but it is too often underplayed by people seeking to understand the media. They concentrate most of their efforts on the media's news or entertainment functions, paying little heed to either its vital advertising/information function or the role of advertising in making possible most media in this society.

Now, do not misunderstand our point. We are not arguing that news and editorial functions ought to be subservient to advertising. Absolutely not! What we are stressing is the importance of maintaining a "consumer" orientation for news, entertainment, and advertising messages. In this society, the overwhelming majority of print, broadcast, and visual media fulfill their social responsibilities only when they reach audiences which are themselves willing to pay for the media product or which are attractive enough to advertisers that they will pay the bills. In either case, the marketing perspective underscores the fact that audience members' preferences must be understood and taken into serious account as the media product is planned, developed, promoted, produced, and distributed.

THE MARKETING MIX

Marketing a media product involves identifying a target market, then creating a mix of marketing elements to both serve the target market and achieve the media firm's objectives. The ingredients included in the marketing mix are commonly known as the Four Ps: product, promotion, place, and price.

Product is the most fundamental of the Ps. It is the newspaper, newscast, broadcast program, P.R. release, advertising campaign, magazine, movie, or book produced by an information organization. Media products come in both tangible and intangible form. The tangible ones are media such as newspapers, books, magazines, records, videotapes. The transitory or intangible ones include broadcast messages, data-base services, P.R. ideas.

Promotion includes all the tools aimed at convincing customers (audience members and advertisers) to buy or use a media product. Major tools used in promotion include advertising, public relations, sales promotion, and direct sales.

Place refers to how a media firm distributes its product or service to an audience. For example, what combination of carrier delivery, U.S. mail, and newsstands will a newspaper use? Where will a TV station put its tower and how much transmission power will it emit? What pattern will a cable TV system follow in wiring a community? What type of theaters will a movie company select for showing its new film, and where will they be located? All of these are distribution questions. The way a media firm answers them determines how available and accessible to customers its product or service will be.

Price is the cost of a media product to the customer. Price is most commonly thought of in terms of dollars paid for subscriptions, tickets, advertising, or copies of the medium in a book store or at a newsstand. But there are other, nonmonetary costs involved in using the media. There is the precious commodity of time: how long does it take to read a newspaper, magazine, or book, or to watch a TV show or movie? There is also convenience: is a media product accessible in the home or is it necessary to go to some other place to access it? Yes, the old adage that "nothing is free" applies to all media, even those which claim they are free because no money is required for their use.

All the elements in the marketing mix must fit together to make a media product successful. Think back to the case of *Pediatric Neurology*, the new medical journal in Chapter 5. First it was necessary to determine whether a sizeable enough audience existed for the journal and whether some advertisers could be identified who would find that audience attractive. When the target audience and target advertiser groups were clearly identified, the elements of the marketing mix could be brought together to develop an overall marketing plan for the new magazine.

The *product* strategy for *Pediatric Neurology* had a number of features:

- a plan for securing articles, utilizing an editorial board consisting of highly respected pediatric neurologists who would review the submissions;
- setting a balance of 80 percent articles and 20 percent advertising;
- a system to receive articles electronically, thereby dramatically reducing the costs of typesetting;
- a plan to print the journal in a form that met the high-quality demands of the physician audience.

Promotion called for an early mailing to the target market of a carefully written letter asking researchers (and potential subscribers) to both submit articles for possible publication in the journal and to subscribe to it. That early promotional letter ensured that the target market response to the journal would be known long before the first issue was published. Further, subscriptions resulting from the letter provided working capital, which minimized borrowing.

It also necessitated finding advertising representatives who were experienced in selling to drug manufacturers and who were located in or near New York City, where most of the pharmaceutical agencies and offices are centered.

Distribution plans were straightforward. *Pediatric Neurology* would use the mailing facility of the publisher's newspaper; delivery would be through the U.S. mails.

Price was determined by setting a subscription cost target that was 55 to 60 percent of the price charged by the leading adult neurology journal. Careful analysis of probable revenues and expenses for the new journal followed. They confirmed that the target price was realistic. A similar process was used to set advertising rates.

As we noted in Chapter 5, all of these elements were blended together to achieve the goal of producing a quality information product with high-level service at a reasonable price. Balancing the triad of quality, service, and price served *Pediatric Neurology*'s audience, and it increased the journal's chances of success.

PRODUCT LIFE CYCLE

One further concept is significant when the marketing perspective is adopted. That is to recognize that all media products go through a series of phases called a product life cycle. Two primary reasons for the cycle are:

1. Audience and advertiser wants, needs, and preferences shift constantly.
2. New ideas and technologies create constant change in the competitive media environment, requiring information products to adapt; otherwise they will decline or even disappear entirely.

Some media products have a very long life. Most daily newspapers in the U.S. are 75 to 150 years old, if you trace them back to the weeklies from which they evolved. Some are older than that. For example *The New York Times* was founded in 1851, *The New York Post* in 1801, *The Boston Globe* in 1872, *The Milwaukee Journal* in 1882, and *The Los Angeles Times* in 1882. A few mass magazines are far older than that. *The New Yorker* was founded in 1834, *Harpers* in 1850, and *The Nation* in 1865. Even some movies, which typically have a very short life cycle, exhibit great staying power. *The Wizard of Oz* and *Gone with the Wind* continue to attract sizeable audiences when they are shown on television, in theaters, or are made available in VCR rental stores.

But for every media product with a long life, we can name many more that had a very brief life span. For every Elvis Presley or Beatles hit that is remembered and still played on the radio, thousands of songs by singers long forgotten are removed from the stations' record libraries. Hundreds of "best-selling" books have faded from memory. Many major magazines, such as *Look*, the weekly versions of *Life* and *The Saturday Evening Post*, and hundreds of "small" magazines have disappeared. Similarly, every season some television series shoot to the top of the ratings while just as suddenly other previously top-rated shows evaporate. Of course, most series do not even last beyond one season.

The idea of the product life cycle is important because the competitive strategy a media firm uses for its product is dependent on where the product is in its life cycle. Derek Abell (1975) at Harvard identifies five stages of that cycle and then outlines the major marketing strategy decisions that must be made because of a product's position in the life cycle, shown in Exhibit 11.5. Note how most of these relate to specific elements of the marketing mix:

1. Infancy. This is when the information product makes an innovative entry into the market. Here the breadth of the market segment must be determined: a big audience or a small one, one audience or more than one. Then a decision must be made about how strongly the market will be entered. What level of resources for promotion, production, and distribution are media managers willing to expend?

   A good example of this is the first personal computer magazine that reached the market in the latter 1970s and early 1980s. That was before IBM introduced its first personal computer and no one knew if the so-called pc market was for technological experts, who might be the only ones interested in learning how to use the new gadgets, or if they had broader appeal, as suggested by the pioneering Apple computer.

EXHIBIT 11.5. THE PRODUCT LIFE CYCLE

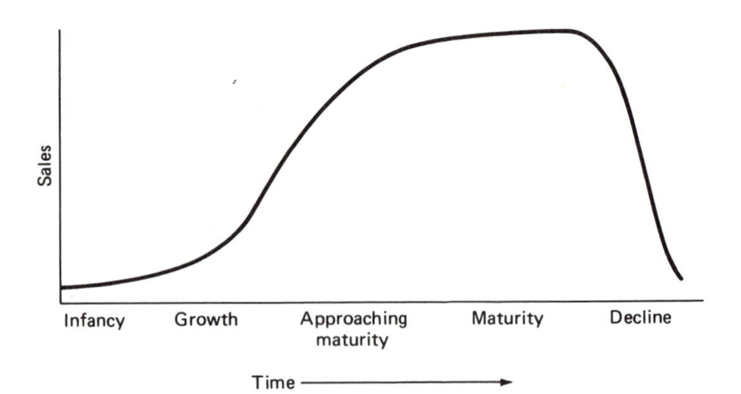

2. Growth. The product or service consolidates its position and it develops new ones. Here choices are made about what territory to cover, what strata of audience to reach, what product changes to make, what new products to offer, and how many resources will be used in promotion, production, and distribution.

   After the IBM personal computer was announced, it joined forces with the Apple II to prove there was a huge mass audience as well as numerous specialized segments within that larger group. At that time personal computer magazines boomed and various publishers quickly carved out separate niches by brand, application, level of complexity, etc.
3. Approaching maturity. The product or service jostles for relative advantage against other competitors. This stage of the life cycle may require taking on competitors directly, for instance, by increasing penetration of an audience through product promotion or distribution changes or by improving the quality of the product to attract a select segment of the audience.

   After the explosion of personal computer magazine titles, the war of one magazine against another began in earnest. As the market neared maturity, so did the competitors who battled fiercely for dominance over their segment of the market.
4. Maturity. Finally, the product or service slugs it out with its competitors. At this stage, price competition and promotional competition are key factors.

   The pc magazine battle continues, but now discounting and gift giving as part of magazine promotions are the watchwords of the day.
5. Decline. This final stage exists for almost all media products. Although it is far too simplistic to say that every media firm or service declines, a large percentage of them go into this stage. And of those that remain, there is a substantial adaptation to stay current and meet the continually changing needs of readers, viewers, listeners, or advertisers.

   After a hail storm of personal computer magazine failures, consolidations, and shifts in focus, a much leaner group of surviving periodicals remain. Even among those victors, there is a constant sensitivity by the magazines' editors to shifting reader and advertiser wants and needs in this dynamic, fluctuating market.

Media firms try to prolong their product's life cycle in various ways. Newspapers, magazines, and even books change their layout and design. TV series spin off separate shows or close down one series and start up another with the same lead character. Increasingly, movie makers try to prolong a movie concept's life cycle by offering sequels, e.g., *Rocky*, *Rocky II*, *Rocky III*, *Rocky IV*; the *Star Wars* and *Star Trek* series. At some point, however, even with these box office gold mines, decline sets in. They begin to attract smaller audiences or lose ratings and, inevitably, lose money.

Unfortunately, too many media managers fail to recognize that fact, although the signs are usually clear well in advance of the end. Nonetheless, the executives stay with the old because that format of newspaper, magazine, TV series, or radio format is "their baby," and they will do "everything they possibly can" to save it. It is extremely difficult, however, for any company, especially an information firm which is dependent on the public's or advertiser's instant acceptance or rejection, to prolong a media product that is in steep decline. To do so after a certain point is only to invite the loss of even more money.

That is the bad news. The good news is that not every medium or information product follows the life cycle pattern through to decline. In some cases such a course is not inevitable. To understand why decline does not happen, think of an analogy that you understand. The human species has evolved over time; it does so as long as it adapts to its changing environment. The media that survive follow the same pattern. How well media products adapt is dependent on the quality of the media executives who lead them as well as on the circumstances that surround them.

That is true of other industries as well. Think how "dead" everyone thought Chrysler Motors was in the late 1970s. Then Lee Iaccoca and his team took the helm and the auto maker rose like the phoenix back to a vigorous life. Even *The New York Times* was near the financial edge in the early 1970s, but as this text is written, the *Times* is stronger than it has ever been.

An essential part of the strength of both Chrysler and the *Times* was a realization by their executives that they could no longer be the kind of company they once were. They had to adapt. In the *Times*'s case that meant a willingness to modernize the "gray old lady of Manhattan" into an up-scale newspaper, which covered the suburbs and added sections on life styles, neighborhoods, etc. Later, it also meant going into business elsewhere by the purchase of other newspapers across the U.S.

APPLYING THE MARKETING PERSPECTIVE TO MEDIA MANAGERS' ACTIVITIES

The balance of Part Three uses the marketing perspective to explore the activities involved in creating, producing, and promoting media products.

Chapter 12 focuses on market analysis and product planning. It presents a framework for identifying target markets among both audiences and advertisers. Then it details how product strategies are developed to serve the needs of both audience members and advertisers.

Chapter 13 discusses one of the four Ps: promotion. It describes the strategies and tools media firms use in promoting their products, such things as advertising, public relations, sales promotion, and direct selling. It includes vignettes about promotional strategies conducted by a variety of media firms; they illustrate how creative information companies can be in using promotional tools.

Chapter 14 focuses on activities related to the other three Ps: place (distribution), product (production), and price. It discusses product objectives (a balance of quality, service, and price) that guide media managers as they organize and utilize their firm's resources to produce and distribute a product or service for a target market.

Chapter 15 presents a case study for a newspaper, *The New Gazette*, which was first introduced in Chapter 2. In the case study you will have an opportunity to use the concepts discussed in Part Three and to practice the management functions from Part Two.

We close this chapter with a summary that goes back to the chapter's opening. Media firms can be financially successful and still fulfill their social responsibilities when they use the marketing perspective in the broad sense in which we defined it here. The first step is to carefully identify a target market and develop a solid, quality product strategy based upon what the audience in the market really wants and needs. Next, the manager must effectively organize and utilize the firm's resources, people, money, information, service, time, and technology, to produce, promote, and distribute the information product or service. Although these tasks are difficult, media managers and their staffs can accomplish them skillfully and imaginatively. When they do so, the media firm succeeds in truly serving its market and society.

CHAPTER 12

Market Analysis and Product Planning

In this chapter we explore two crucial aspects of a media company. The first is market analysis: how can media managers clearly identify and learn about the consumer audience and advertiser market they want to attract? Second, how can they best utilize what they learn from their market analysis to plan their information product? Both of these activities begin with a medium's market.

MARKET ANALYSIS

The marketing concept focuses primarily on consumers. It emphasizes identifying customers' needs and desires and then creating media products to meet them. If it can be done effectively, this is one of the better ways to sell a media firm's products or services. You have already seen an application of this approach in the story of the start-up of a medical journal, *Pediatric Neurology*, which we detailed in Chapter 5. In the case of the journal, the market analysis began by identifying target groups of audiences and advertisers.

Target Markets

Of course, common sense suggests that the media can't please everyone. Business people face the same situation; they don't expect to sell to every person who walks by their stores, or even each shopper who comes in to browse. If they tried to reach that goal, they would fail. The opposite side of such an expectation is that no business needs to sell to all its potential customers. Success can come from only a fraction of the market choosing the product. The goal, then, is to attract and keep those customers who are the most desirable segments in the total market. Once those people (who we will call the target market) have been identified, a media company can mobilize its marketing mix (product, promotion, distribution, and price) to reach them.

The concept of market segmentation is central in this approach. Market segments are defined in many different ways, as shown below, but the principle is that information products are directed at only certain people (a market segment). In the case of radio stations and specialized magazines, that group is obvious. Each radio format, ranging from top 40 to country to talk/news to hard rock to religion, appeals to a specific market segment that is defined by such factors as age, income, and interests. Indeed, those formats were developed to attract sizeable target segments of people with similar program preferences.

Specialized magazines typically segment on the basis of interest. As a result, there are literally dozens of magazines about fishing, sailing, running, golf, and tennis; and those are just some of the publications devoted to sports and recreational interests. Think of the myriad specialized publications that focus on the endless list of topics that fascinate one consumer or another.

Don't assume that the idea of target markets applies only to specialized media. Mass media, such as newspapers and television, also appeal to market segments. Almost no one reads an entire daily newspaper. What readers do is look at their favorite sections or individual items. Thus, the newspaper audience should be viewed as a series of market segments, and individuals in each of them use the newspaper differently.

Television programming tries to reach a large segment of the U.S. audience, but even the networks develop prime-time programs that are directed at groups who are attractive to certain large advertisers. As a consequence, you can now guess why there is little prime-time programming designed to appeal to the youngest and oldest segments of society. The reason is simply that these segments are not attractive to enough advertisers. If programming is aired for them, then that narrower segmentation occurs at fringe times when large-income audiences are not available.

For example, Saturday mornings are devoted to children. Daytime programming historically has appealed to women at home and, more recently, to college students. Saturday and Sunday afternoons were programmed to attract men. Within any time period, however, the focus on relatively narrow segments works against programming diversity because the networks choose to compete for the same market segments during these time periods. That phenomena is likely to change in the future, however, as cable and VCR penetration create substantial changes in people's program selection patterns. The fragmentation of

TV that is on the rise from cable, low-power TV stations, and VCR rentals is sure to trigger major shifts in network programming strategies. The only thing that is not certain is when the network executives are going to accept the change that is being forced on them.

Identifying target markets has several advantages for media companies. It puts them in a better position to spot emerging market opportunities and helps to fine-tune their information products and promotional appeals. Most important, a sensitivity to the wants and needs of the audience forces marketing approaches and budgets to be based on informed assumptions as to the likely response of specific market segments. In turn that means that a media firm's resources can be directed to different target markets in line with each segment's probable purchase or usage patterns.

Considerations in Defining Target Markets

Few decisions are as important as the targeting decision an information executive makes. What should that decision be based upon? A number of market features might be considered, but four are particularly important:

1. Segment size. Are the segments large and profitable enough to justify the development of an entire marketing plan, i.e., product development, production, promotion, and distribution?
2. Segment activation. Can the entire marketing plan be designed so it will attract and serve the segments of interest to the media company? Suppose, for example, a magazine identified four potentially profitable market segments, but had only the resources to serve two or three. It would then need to choose those it could serve most effectively and profitably.
3. Segment access. To what extent can the media product reach the targeted segments through promotion and distribution? For example, the publishers of *The Minneapolis Star and Tribune* might desire home delivery to a young, professional, up-scale audience in a ring of cities about 100 miles from the Twin Cities. But if members of that audience do not subscribe in sufficient numbers, distribution costs would be too great to justify continued service to that market segment in these cities.
4. Segment measurability. Is appropriate information available on a characteristic the media manager might want to use for defining a target market? In the example above, let's assume that the reason *The Minneapolis Star and Tribune* had for expanding its distribution market was an opportunity to satisfy the needs of major advertisers. Suppose Northwest Airlines and Dayton's Department Stores, two major Twin Cities advertisers, both said they would increase their advertising substantially if the paper could reach a significant proportion of the up-scale audience in those cities. Is information available through census data, local and state government, and business and employment statistics, to estimate the size of the target audience. Further, is the information useful for guiding the development of promotion and distribution stratagies, and for monitoring progress?

Basic Targeting Strategies

The three different types of targeting strategies are:

Concentration. The media company focuses on a single market segment, developing a product and marketing plan directed specifically to that segment. Instead of attempting to capture a small share of a large market, the company tries to capture a large share of that narrow target market. Radio stations and specialized magazines usually use this type of strategy.

Differentiation. This strategy identifies two or more market segments and separate marketing programs are then developed for each. They often involve substantially different products for each segment. Thus, both *Time* magazine and *Newsweek* publish at least five different versions each week for different target audiences in the U.S. and abroad. When differentiation is used as the primary strategy, dissimilar products and promotion campaigns are created for each of the different magazine segments. That is, the cover stories of *Time* in the U.S. and in South America differ to appeal to the differing interests of readers in the northern or southern hemisphere. Moreover, the promotion for each of them would be hemisphere specific.

Undifferentiation. This strategy ignores market segment distinctions and develops a single product and marketing plan for all groups. This strategy is used by media companies that see people as a mass audience. Examples of this are the American television networks and local TV stations. Their undifferentiated approach can achieve substantial cost efficiencies, but unless a given medium's share of the total market is substantial, that strategy will not work. For many newspapers and television stations which penetrate (serve) a high number of households in a region, however, such a strategy works very well.

Segmenting Audiences

Target market definitions should reflect group differences that will affect the actions of media companies when they devise their product strategies. A number of different classifications have been used as a basis for identifying target audiences. Some of the more prominent are geographic, demographic, product usage, psychological, and lifestyle. Another important classification is based on benefits sought by consumers. Exhibit 12.2 will summarize these classifications.

Geographic. The oldest basis for defining target markets for the media is geographic. Historically, geography was used because of production and distribution limitations of print and broadcast media. Over the decades, improvements first in the transportation system and later in the means of distribution changed the conception of the markets of some media. Nevertheless, geographic segmentation is still important for newspapers and broadcast stations, not only because of the physical limits on their carrier-delivery systems or signals, but also because their advertisers, who pay most of the cost, want to reach only limited markets.

Actually, in newspapers, increased geographic considerations come into play in designing zoned editions, which typically correspond to the neighborhoods or regions of the area the newspaper serves. A special section reaches only a specific zone, and it contains news and advertising that is tailored to that zone. Moreover, a different product is designed for each of the other zones. Broadcast outlets are less likely to use a geographic basis for segmentation, except for those stations with very low transmission power; they must program with the needs of a geographically restricted audience in mind.

Demographic. Demographic divisions are the most frequently used basis for segmenting audiences. Primary demographic factors that differentiate target markets include:

age	family size
sex	family life cycle
income	race
education	religion
occupation	hobby, avocation

Radio, movies, and records target their products to younger audiences. In fact, because most films and songs are focused on the same segment, there are more and more product tie-ins to promote cross-media products. For example, movies in which music is a crucial factor link up with records and compact disks to play on radio and sell in stores; the movie makers also make videocassettes of the film's more popular songs. The cassettes are available for rent and purchase, as well as for airing on TV music channels.

To a great extent, network television focuses on a particular age group (the affluent 30- to 54-year-olds). That contrasts with television's targeting of 10 years ago, when more network programming was directed at teenagers and, to a lesser degree, young adults; then that younger age group seemed to control the operation of the TV receiver in homes, and it represented the "bulge" in the population. Now, the strategy and the largest group in the population has changed, but the idea of focusing on a particular age group remains constant.

Newspapers use age as a primary segmentation variable in thinking about a major potential problem. General survey data throughout the 1950s and 1960s showed that on an average day, 8 out of 10 adult

Americans read a newspaper. Newspaper circulation continued to grow until 1980, benefiting from the large numbers of people born in the baby boom of the post–World War II period, but readership trends in the 1980s are disturbing. They show a decrease in everyday readers from 73 percent in 1967 to 56 percent in 1983.* The major explanations for this trend are the wide acceptance of television and, perhaps, the development of a television-oriented generation or a generation that does not read to get its news. Continuation of such behavior among the adult audience could be devastating for newspapers.

Enter age as a possible market segmentation variable. Analysis of readership data by age group led Meyer (1985) to propose a "negative diffusion hypothesis," suggesting that people born after World War II have reduced their newspaper reading compared to people born before World War II. He found that habitual readers in the 18 to 30 age group went from 61 percent in 1967 to only 35 percent in 1983, a 26 percent decrease.

Everyday readers in the 31 to 43 age group decreased from 77 percent in 1967 to 52 percent in 1983, a decline of 25 percent. Other age groups showed only a slight decline over this same 16-year period, an average of 5 percent for each of the other segments, but they started at a much higher general readership level.

On the plus side, these data support the popular belief that habitual newspaper readership begins around age 30, when people's lives become fairly settled. Thus, over the same period of years, readership of the 30 to 43 age group was from 15 percent to 25 percent higher than habitual readership in the 18 to 30 age group.

Another form of analysis using age as a segmentation variable provides limited solace to newspaper publishers. Meyer performed a cohort analysis; that is, he traced the readership pattern over time for the same groups of people. In it the baby-boomers (born between 1945 and 1954) showed a remarkable stability from 1972, when they were 18 to 27 years old, through 1982, when they were 28 to 37 years old. During that period, the percent of habitual readers hovered around 48 percent. Meyer interprets these data as indicating that the newspaper industry may already have weathered the storm in terms of declining readership.

At the same time, it is clear from extrapolations of Meyer's data that the next age cohort (born in the 1955 to 1964 period) shows much lower levels of readership than the baby-boomers. Only about 35 percent of this group are habitual newspaper readers during their early adulthood. Whether a substantial number of them will become habitual readers as they reach 30 years old is a major unanswered question. What is known

* Figures about readership patterns are taken from *The Newspaper Survival Book* by Phillip Meyer (1985), Chapters 1 and 2.

is that this younger age group as well as the baby-boomers are very important market segments for newspapers. Whether newspaper editors can tailor their products to induce them to become habitual rather than sporadic readers is not yet known. Nevertheless, we can see that age, here viewed as a generational phenomenon, is a crucial variable for analyzing an information industry's market.

Other demographic variables are also used to identify target markets. Socioeconomic variables, such as income, occupation, and education, have been used by newspapers and television to identify audiences that are desirable to advertisers. As we indicated earlier, prime-time television's basic programming strategy is to attract the affluent viewer. Newspapers have expanded their coverage of suburban areas to capitalize on the flight of the affluent to the suburbs. In some cities it almost appears as though newspapers have abandoned the low-income (often black and other minority) audience that lives in the central city. If this continues to spread, as we noted earlier, newspapers will become a "class" rather than a "mass" medium, a point we will come back to in Chapter 17.

Magazines aggressively use socioeconomic variables to develop products catering to the interests of the well-to-do. Magazines also segment audiences on the basis of family life-cycle categories, such as young and single, young and married with no children, families with young children, and empty-nest families.

Product Usage Patterns. Product usage patterns are often combined with demographics to identify target markets. The market is usually divided into four categories of users: high, moderate, low, and nonusers. Usage patterns are then combined with other demographic indicators to identify important target markets.

In the newspaper readership data discussed earlier, high newspaper usage (habitual, everyday readers) was combined with age to identify some target markets that represent problems and opportunities for the newspaper industry. Such an analysis could be extended to include other trends among newspaper readers. For instance, data show that nonreaders (defined as reading a newspaper less than once a week) have been stable at about 10 to 12 percent throughout the 1967 to 1983 period. Thus, even among young adults, low or moderate reading (one to three times a week) is the norm as opposed to being complete nonreaders.

These data suggest newspapers may have a good opportunity with young readers. A product strategy that increases young readers' usage frequency is much easier to develop than a strategy to attract people who never read the paper. The former, after all, are already getting something out of the newspaper. If media managers give them more of what they want and need, usage is likely to increase. Nonreaders do not even pick up the product. It is far more difficult to get nonusers to take that first step to look at a medium they have been ignoring than it is to figure out what will make a consumer increase usage of a medium.

Psychographics/Lifestyles. Personality and lifestyle characteristics are bases for segmentation that have come into use recently. A number of methods that look at these data are used by the media as well as other companies. Perhaps the best known approach is the values and life styles (VALS) system, developed by Arnold Mitchell (1982). It identifies nine types of people, based on a combination of psychological and lifestyle characteristics. Types are described with such terms as:

- Survivors: the aged, poor, depressed, and far removed from the cultural mainstream; those who are struggling for survival.
- Sustainers: young, angry adults struggling on the edge of poverty, but who maintain hope for improvement over time.
- Belongers: traditional, conservative, conventional, sentimental; the large, stabilizing force of the nation. They are the people who would rather fit in than stand out.
- Emulators: ambitious, upwardly mobile, status conscious, competitive, distrustful of the establishment. They are trying to burst into the system, make it big, and emulate the rich and successful.

The nine lifestyle types included in the VALS™ typology are shown in Exhibit 12.1.

The power of these psychographic and lifestyle descriptions is that they provide an excellent picture of the motives, drives, and personality characteristics of consumers. For product planning they also give a much richer sense of the individuals in the target market—their interests, desires, needs, and values. This represents a major step forward in helping develop information products sensitive to the market.

A major problem with these typologies, however, is that they tend to be unstable. Psychological variables, which are helpful in providing a sensitive segmentation in one geographic region, may be unhelpful or even counterproductive in another. Profiles that are useful at one time may not work a few years later, as consumers respond to changes around them. Because of the instability of the psychographic and lifestyle systems over time and across geographic regions, a number of media companies that eagerly adopted them in the early 1980s have since abandoned them.

Benefit Segmentation. Benefit segmentation identifies specific wants or benefits that consumers are seeking to fulfill when they use a product. In newspapers, readers are interested in various kinds of content, for example, world events, national politics, local issues in politics, professional sports, college sports, and so forth. This information can then be used to plan coverage patterns for topics corresponding to

EXHIBIT 12.1. THE VALS TYPOLOGY

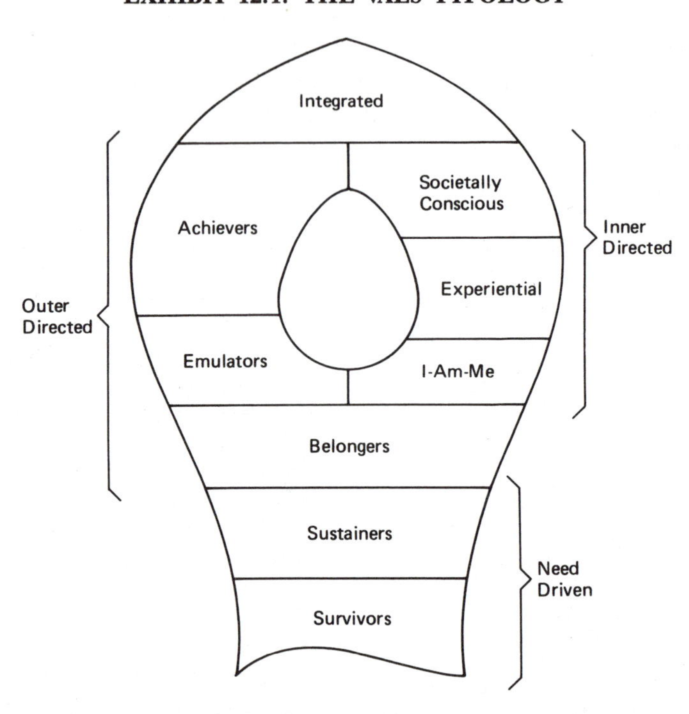

Source: Courtesy SRI International (Stanford Research Institute), Menlo Park, CA, USA 94025

reader interests. We will have more to say about how this kind of measurement is used in product planning later in this chapter.

Magazines and radio frequently use the "benefit segmentation" approach, which means identifying clusters of people with common inter-

EXHIBIT 12.2. BASES FOR SEGMENTING AUDIENCES

Geographic: region, county size, locality

Demographic: age, sex, income, education, occupation, family size, family life cycle, race, religion

Product usage: high, moderate, low, nonuse

Psychographics/lifestyles: social class, buying style, self-concept, VALS typology

Benefits: typically classified by product-specific benefits

ests and developing products to satisfy them (special interest magazines, for instance, or radio formats of religious or country music). Each of these and any other approach that uses benefit segmentation are all trying to identify a group of people with a similar interest who comprise a target market for media products. A specific example would be a magazine for runners attempting to reach people whom a variety of advertisers—running shoes and clothing manufacturers, marathon promoters, publishers of jogging and fitness books, and owners of health clubs—want to reach.

A limitation of this approach is that general information sources, which gather information about product consumption, demographic characteristics, and media use patterns, do not collect information about benefits sought for specific products. Thus, benefit segmentation can be used only when the media company conducts its own market research and gathers the appropriate information.

Segmenting Advertisers

Up to now we have been talking about ways of segmenting the audience. That is crucial for specifically defining the kind of audience a media company wants to attract. But remember that one of the primary reasons for attracting a particular audience is to be able to deliver it to advertisers who want to reach that group of potential consumers. Thus, market analysis must also examine the advertiser market. Here again, market segmentation is crucial, and the same kinds of major segmentation categories apply to the advertiser market as were used in analyzing audiences (see Exhibit 12.3).

Geographic. For many media companies, advertisers interested in reaching their audience are bound by geography. For instance, the great majority of advertising in newspapers is local or regional, individuals or firms trying to sell things in the newspaper's home community or within a reasonable distance of the advertiser's business. Radio stations also have a strong local orientation. On the other hand, a large proportion of

---

EXHIBIT 12.3. BASES FOR SEGMENTING ADVERTISERS

Geographic: local, regional, national

Demographic: manufacturer, service, or retailer—specific industry, revenue, advertising budget

Usage patterns: sporadic, or regular advertisers

Benefits: specific advertising objectives

---

television advertising is for products and services sold on a national basis because the advertisements run on stations across the land. That is true although, as we saw in Chapter 2, local TV stations have begun competing more aggressively for local advertising.

Demographics. The demographic categories of advertisers are not things such as age, sex, or income. Rather, they are segmentations of businesses which fall into three broad categories: manufacturers, service organizations, and retailers. For planning purposes, however, advertiser demographics are usually broken down more finely into specific industries, e.g., stores that sell furniture, electronics, groceries, jewelry, or clothing. The size of a business in terms of revenue is also a major segmentation category; used this way, revenue size of a store parallels the income of audience members.

Segmenting advertisers demographically becomes particularly important for newspapers when they develop special weekly or seasonal sections. Thus, midweek or Sunday food sections are crowded with grocery store ads. Entertainment pages, often published on Friday or Saturday, are full of movie, play, and restaurant advertisements. Then there are back-to-school, spring remodeling, and auto-care seasonal sections; each attracts advertisers who want to reach consumers interested in those subjects.

Of course, specialized magazines focus on a small number of industries and products in their efforts to sell advertising. This enables them to conduct highly focused promotion and sales efforts aimed at a relatively small set of advertisers, as well as readers.

Usage Patterns. In any media company, advertisers are segmented into low- , medium- , and high-usage categories. Regular high-volume advertisers are the lifeblood for any medium, for they provide financial stability. Rate cards from print and broadcast outlets detail the kinds of volume discounts that advertisers can obtain for higher volumes of advertising. The discount is based on the advertiser's agreeing to purchase a significant amount of advertising during the year; that commitment not only provides stability to the information firm, but also the opportunity to plan more aggressively during the year, as the information firm knows that a portion of its income is guaranteed by the advertiser's contract.

Benefit Segmentation. Advertisers can also be segmented based on the benefits they seek from their advertising. Although most advertising is designed to sell products, ad messages perform a variety of functions besides simply selling. They include:

- telling the market about a new product;

- suggesting new uses for a product;
- informing the market of a price change;
- explaining how a product works;
- building brand preference;
- changing consumers' perceptions of product attributes;
- reminding consumers that the product may be needed in the near future;
- reminding consumers where to buy the product.

Those are just a few of advertising's many functions. In fact, the DAGMAR (Defining Advertising Goals for Measured Advertising Results) model specifies 52 different communication objectives that advertising performs; only a few of them are designed to effect an immediate sale (Colley, 1961).

Benefit segmentation, based on specific advertising objectives, identifies advertisers who could best utilize the features a medium has to offer to achieve their objectives. We will have more to say about the strengths and weaknesses of different media as advertising vehicles in the product planning section which follows. Suffice it to say here that matching strengths of a medium with the benefits (advertising objectives) sought by individuals or firms with something to sell is crucial in planning a media product.

Sources of Information for Segmentation Analysis

The U.S. is a society with tons of data available; it is found everywhere, from government to data services to market research firms to a company's own records. Because a major part of a media manager's task is to understand and utilize the market perspective and data is an essential ingredient of that perspective let's take a brief look at some of those information sources.

The government, particularly at the federal level, gathers reams of data ranging from the census to industry profiles. Census data is useful for describing basic demographic characteristics of markets. Moreover, now that the census and zip code systems have been integrated, it is possible to analyze a variety of specific characteristics of zip code districts, thus enhancing the potential for combining demographic and geographic considerations in target marketing. Applications for direct marketers are obvious. Possibilities for newspaper publishers are also substantial, particularly as small, local retailers ask for narrower and narrower market segmentation.

Publications of the U.S. Departments of Commerce and Labor are useful, particularly in identifying purchasing trends and patterns. And the federal government is only one source of that sort of information. City and state governments produce similar data; what's more, these smaller units of government often update the U.S. census information on an annual basis rather than on the 5-year or 10-year basis that is done nationally.

Simmons Market Research Bureau (SMRB) and its new competitor, Mediamark Research, Inc. (MRI), collect information on a number of demographic, geographic, psychographic, product usage, and media factors. These are published in book form and on computer tape. They identify target markets for a wide variety of products. The data they provide is useful when looking at product usage information, but since they are based only on national samples, they are not helpful for locally distributed media. They are more useful to media that carry a high quantity of national advertising: national or specialized magazines, network television, and direct mail.

For analyzing the advertiser market, national spending figures are available from two sources: *Advertising Age* compiles a yearly summary of spending by major national advertisers; *Leading National Advertisers* publishes quarterly and yearly reports on spending in six media for literally thousands of nationally advertised brands. Again, because these are national data they may not be useful for locally based information firms; however, this information is helpful to television networks, national magazines, and major metropolitan newspapers.

The Newspaper Advertising Bureau and the Television Bureau of Advertising also provide information about advertiser markets. They regularly publish analyses of local sales patterns for a variety of industries, trends in retail sales, and other information about advertising in these two media.

In a related vein, Arbitron ratings of local TV and radio stations report audience usage patterns of those two media. These ratings include breakdowns by age and sex as well as usage patterns at different times of the day. Studying the trends reported in the rating books, which come out three times each year, is a rich source of information on the activities of audiences in a local market. There is no comparable general service for newspapers, though SMRB is beginning to develop one. Starch Reports, published by INRA Hooper, monitors readership patterns of many magazines on a regular basis.

Market research firms can be hired to do specific studies locally, regionally, or nationally. These firms are especially helpful for benefit segmentation studies to collect more precise information on the interests of a potential audience. Many large newspapers and television stations have their own market research departments that collect this kind of data or regularly update the work of others. The costs involved preclude smaller media outlets from engaging in such efforts.

Yet no media company is without data resources. Many have useful information, but don't realize it. Even the smallest media organization, if it maintains good records on its own sales to advertisers, can identify trends within the local market; those trends may represent major opportunities for the media organization. Regular analysis can identify where problems are cropping up before the difficulties become serious. Finally, the firm's sales staff is a rich resource for monitoring trends in the local advertiser market.

USING CONSUMER RESEARCH IN DEVELOPING PRODUCT STRATEGIES

A careful analysis of consumers in a target market is the focus of the backgrounding phase in the product planning process. Of course, a media firm should look at other information, such as the strengths and weaknesses of its product and service ideas and its organization, people, and financial resources. All of these are relevant to developing a product strategy, but from the marketing perspective, the most important data is generated by consumer analysis.

After finishing a market analysis, the next step in product planning is to develop a product strategy. How should media managers shape their information product to fit the needs and desires of the target market? Additional audience research can be very important here, too, but media executives face many key decisions as they think through product strategies before conducting further audience research. The following covers a number of examples of product strategy formulation.

Developing News/Editorial Strategy

In the 1970s, newspapers confronted a dynamic market. As we noted earlier, a few of the notable changes were in the age and structure of the audience, the continuing and growing impact of television and other forms of electronic media, and the segmentation of consumers' interests. Although circulation was increasing, its growth was not keeping pace with population increases. Further, evidence began to accumulate that readership was decreasing. The problem, from the marketing point of view, was to reshape the newspaper product to meet the needs and desires of the audience. Actually, the problem was twofold:

1. How to better serve existing readers' interests in order to motivate more regular readership;
2. How to attract new readers to increase circulation and increase the frequency of readership.

Phillip Meyer (1985) introduced the idea of using models to develop product strategies to deal with these kinds of marketing problems and opportunities. Models are explicit representations of an editor's strategies. By making implicit strategies explicit, they allow information to be collected to determine how well a given approach works. Meyer describes three possible models for developing a news/editorial product strategy:

The Referendum Model. To utilize the referendum model, readers are asked to indicate their interest in a variety of topics covered by the newspaper. Typically, high-interest topics elicit responses of "very interested" from 50 percent or more of the audience. Low-interest topics are those where less than 25 percent of the readers say they are "very interested." Measures of interest indicate consumer benefits; thus, this approach applies benefit segmentation to news/editorial planning.

The editorial strategy called for by the referendum model is to provide more space to those topics that are more popular and less space to less popular topics. Editors use the information to check how well their intuitive judgments match readers' interests. If there is a close match between the space devoted to a topic and its interest level, editors' judgments are confirmed. If topics given limited space are popular, editors may need to reexamine their judgments.

Meyer, who had a distinguished career with Knight–Ridder before becoming a professor, describes several ways in which this model can be formalized. Whether formalized or left relatively implicit, however, the referendum model has several major weaknesses:

1. The model is not very sensitive to the intensity of interest.
2. The model does not differentiate among people identified as members of a target group whom editors may be trying to attract for longer-term readership and other audience members whose readership is already assured.
3. Duplication of reader interest is not considered. Circulation can often be built by appealing to many specialized reader groups who have separate interests. The referendum model, however, guides the editor to broader interests, which often are shared by the same readers.

The Target Group Model. The underlying theory of the target group model is that if members of a target group have greater interest in a topic than nonmembers of the group, the newspaper can win new readers by shifting its emphasis toward a topic in which nonmembers show an interest. Current readers can be retained if the shift is not too extreme. As noted earlier, one group that editors identified in the 1970s as being important were younger readers, especially those from 25 to 29. This group was targeted because of evidence that regular newspaper readership begins at about age 30. Therefore, the most promising target would be those people closest to that age threshold.

In the target group model, interests of younger and older readers in various topics are compared. On many topics they are similar, but on some topics younger readers demonstrate higher interest. An information product strategy based on the target group model suggests increased coverage of topics of high interest to target group members. This is precisely what happened in the 1970s when more attention was paid to consumer advice, coverage of leisure-time activities, child rearing, and other topics of interest to young adults.

The Prioritization Model. Despite their strengths, the two previous models fail in that they don't explicitly recognize the editor's basic problem: how to choose among competing elements for space when there is a finite amount of news that will be presented (the news hole). While the referendum and target group models indicate those topics needing additional coverage to attract new readers, they do not provide guidance as to which topics should have coverage reduced to make way for the additions. (This assumes that economic realities dictate that the news hole cannot be expanded.) The prioritization model, on the other hand, explicitly recognizes that constraint.

Using a priority model entails the same information used in the other two models, but adds information about whether interest in a topic is related to frequency of newspaper readership. That is, some high-interest topics are strongly associated with reading a newspaper. For example, in Meyer's data (1985, p. 44), he found that interest in national politics is high and is strongly associated with newspaper readership. On the other hand, interest in consumer information, which is also high, is not related to newspaper readership.

By sorting topics into four categories, as shown in Exhibit 12.4, editors can see for each topic whether it is of high or low interest and whether it is associated with frequency of readership.

Each cell suggests a strategy for planning coverage:

(A) *Maintain.* People are deeply interested in these topics and their interest is strongly associated with readership. Editors are doing something right in their coverage of these topics; maintaining of this policy is warranted.

(B) *Observe.* Topics with low interest, but high linkage with readership may be important. When interest in the topics has low duplication with other interests, the topics should be considered for increased coverage. Cumulative effects of these topics can be important in producing circulation and readership gains.

(C) *Push.* Interest is high, but is not associated with readership and therefore opportunities for gaining new readers are great. Topics can be covered with target groups in mind to attract more readership or increased coverage can be directed at readers generally. If coverage of these topics is already adequate, promotional efforts should inform readers that the newspaper covers them.

(D) *Pass.* When interest in subjects is low and is not related to newspaper reading, editors may pass over those topics. They can shift resources to subjects that will provide a better chance of circulation and readership gain.

During the 1970s, many editors thought that readership among younger age groups could be increased by improving coverage of service and self-improvement topics. That led those media managers to add "soft" and service features to the extent of sacrificing traditional hard news stories. Yet, continuing low circulation and readership among younger age groups, coupled with declines among older readers, showed that this product strategy was not successful.

Had these editors relied on better research and had they used the prioritization model, they might have avoided this error. Exhibit 12.4 shows that traditional, hard news subjects are a newspaper's strengths (Cell A). If editors had not cut hard news in favor of soft stories, readership patterns might well have stabilized instead of declining in the 1970s, especially among older readers.

The audience research just described represents information that can help direct a media product. It does not replace the news executive's judgment; that is always primary. The research is supplemental, but monitoring it provides editors with a means of keeping abreast of readership changes. Other forms of consumer research are called for when a media organization is contemplating a major product change or is developing a new product.

Creating a New Radio Station Format

Radio stations in major markets face tough competition. The changes in rankings from ratebook to ratebook show substantial fluctuations in nearly every market. One radio station was confronted with the following situation (what follows is true; the identities of the station and individuals have been masked):

KOSY saw its ratings erode regularly over a three-year period. The

EXHIBIT 12.4. PRIORITIZATION MODEL CLASSIFICATION OF TOPICS FOR 25 TO 29 YEAR OLDS IN FOUR MARKETS

	High Interest	Low Interest
Associated with Readership	Cell A World events National politics Local issues State government Professional sports	Cell B Travel Gardening School board
Not Associated with Readership	Cell C Consumer advice Crime Budget structuring Food Child-rearing Leisure College sports	Cell D Coping Household repairs Home decorating High school sports

Source: The Newspaper Survival Book by Philip Meyer (Indiana University Press, Bloomington, IN, 1985), p. 45. Used with permission.

most recent ratings book showed the station falling to 10th place overall in a market of 22 radio outlets. KOSY management knew it needed to make a change. Top executives did a market analysis, focusing not so much on the current audience as on audience patterns in the market as a whole. Census data indicated that the 18 to 44 age group was a very promising segment; over half the adults in the metro area fell into that group. Looking more carefully, they saw disproportionate numbers of women in the group; more than 30 percent of the total population of the area were women 18 to 44 years old.

In light of the formats that the top stations in the market used, KOSY executives suspected that this group was not well served by their competitors. Over the last few sets of ratings they noticed many changes in the age group, especially in station preferences of women from 25 to 34 years old. KOSY managers thought a new format could be developed to target that narrow market segment directly, with spillover into the 35 to 44 age group. They decided to do some more audience research to check out their intuition.

Their first step was to conduct several focus group interviews with a carefully designed sample of women in the target age category. (A focus group, which includes in-depth interviews with both specific and open-ended questions, is an excellent technique for trying to get at underlying interests, desires, and wishes of members of a certain audience.) In this instance, researchers were looking for descriptions of the kinds of music women age 25 to 34 prefer. They paid close attention to the kinds of descriptive terms that the women used in the interviews: "easy listening," "lighter than one station that was operational, but not so syrupy as another station that already had a market share," "soft and light," and so forth. From those descriptors, KOSY managers settled on a station format described as "cosy listening." (This is not the term they used, but it conveys the sense of their format.)

The next step was to pick out music that represented what the target audience was seeking. Researchers selected 600 songs, then conducted a mass music test to help hone future selections. Over 100 members of the target audience were tested in the following manner:

Each person listened to 10-second excerpts from the 600 songs. Each subject in the test rated every song on a five-point scale ranging from "not very enjoyable" to "very enjoyable." When the testing was finished, the managers were able to construct a profile of listening preferences. Ratings were programmed into a computer which used them in selecting specific songs to play on the station after KOSY launched its new sound.

The new format was truly distinctive and very successful. Supported by a major promotion effort (described in Chapter 13), KOSY significantly improved its ratings. During the next Arbitron period the station moved from sixth to second place among women age 25 to 34, and from seventh to third place among women age 35 to 44. Clearly, the research was helpful in guiding the development of the general format and even in making specific song selections.

(As a follow-up to this story, KOSY subsequently encountered serious problems. In the next period, ratings slipped back as competitors responded to the challenge of KOSY's new sound. Even more serious, the station's executives undercut much of their research and work by forgetting the station's focus and trying to enlarge the target group. As this is being written, KOSY's ratings are still down, and it is struggling to regain its target market.)

Readership and listenership studies like those described are representative of audience research that moderately sized media companies can do themselves or can contract to have done. Larger companies, or those for whom specific messages involve enormous investments, e.g., multimillion dollar advertising campaigns and TV series, will utilize many more types of audience research.

Research Used in Developing a Major Advertising Campaign

In developing a major advertising campaign, an agency conducts a number of focus group interviews to determine the brand image of the product they are advertising. That is, it looks for the kinds of language and themes that consumers use in talking about a general product category and about specific brands. This research is often combined with survey data to create "perceptual maps" of the brand in relation to its competitors. From these analyses, the first step is to develop alternative campaign strategies to "position" the product. Four other research steps follow this first one.

The second step occurs after the alternative campaign strategies are translated into storyboards, i.e., mock-ups of ads. Focus groups test consumer reactions to various advertising concepts. Again, researchers look for language and themes as the various concepts are evaluated.

The third form of testing takes place after the strategies are executed as specific commercials or advertisements. Audiences composed of consumers in the target market view the commercials in theater tests. Researchers measure consumer responses in several ways:

- consumers manipulate dials as the commercial is shown to indicate favorability or unfavorability;
- they take a recall test to see if they can remember major points in the commercials;
- they respond to questions about their attitudinal reactions and about their intention to buy the product.

A fourth form of research utilizes a test market; that is, a community is specifically selected for testing the advertising campaign. Besides judging the campaign, a test market garners reactions to the packaging and promotional strategy of the product and to the effectiveness of the dealer distribution plan. Response to the commercials are measured and sales figures assess the impact of the overall marketing strategy.

A final type of research commonly used in advertising is a tracking study. It measures whether an advertising campaign continues to increase or maintain brand awareness and message recall. If not, then "commercial wear-out" may have set in, resulting in a decrease in effectiveness.

This series of studies is typically conducted only by very large companies when they face decisions about committing millions of dollars to a product and its advertising and promotion. In a more typical advertising campaign, only one or two of these studies are used. In many small campaigns no research is commissioned; that is typical for retail advertising. (It should be noted, however, that retail ads are more often designed to create direct purchase responses; the impact of the advertising in terms of sales is more easily measured. Retailers often know immediately how successful their advertising has been by the number of calls they receive and the number of customers they attract.)

When a new TV series is developed, network executives utilize many of these same kinds of research. When millions of dollars are at risk, TV executives want as much consumer information as possible. Such efforts are not always met with universal acceptance; creative personnel, both in advertising agencies and in TV production companies, often argue that research reduces their creative freedom. However, the enormous amount of money involved usually leads top media managers to reduce risks as much as possible by measuring audience reactions to advertising or programming proposals and to specific executions (test commercials or pilot programs).

In local TV programming, research is less sophisticated. However, even in local broadcasting, some research is regularly undertaken to assess the image of news anchors, as well as viewers' reactions to cover-

---

EXHIBIT 12.5. RESEARCH STRATEGIES USED IN DEVELOPING MAJOR ADVERTISING CAMPAIGNS

Brand image and positioning studies

Concept testing studies

Commercial reaction studies

Test market studies

Tracking studies

---

age patterns and production features. Frank Magid and Associates, of Cedar Rapids, Iowa, is the major supplier of this kind of research for broadcast news operations, among an increasing number of other market research firms.

OTHER CONSIDERATIONS IN DEVELOPING PRODUCT STRATEGIES

Many media companies face a tight profit squeeze, which is driven by two forces: the staggering increase in costs for developing messages and increased competition.

The cost of producing major movies, TV series, books, and records has escalated dramatically. A similar, though less dramatic, cost increase confronts newspapers and local broadcast stations. Only part of these costs can be passed on to consumers and advertisers because of the second factor: increased competition. With the spread of cable TV and VCRs, both theater attendance and prime-time TV viewing are facing powerful competition for audiences. Equally powerful competition for advertising dollars results from increased utilization of direct marketing (both direct mail and telemarketing), and heightened competition for local advertisers among broadcast stations, newspapers, and shoppers. (Remember that in Chapter 3, you saw that in the 1970s daily newspapers held increases in subscription and ad rates below inflation because of increased competition.)

Creating Multiple Income Streams as a Product Strategy

One product strategy developed to cope with a profit squeeze is to design new media products with several distribution systems in mind. For example, movies are distributed via theaters, cable networks (HBO, Cinemax, The Movie Channel, etc.), and videocassettes for use on VCRs at home. Top-selling songs result in multiple products (records, audio cassettes, compact discs, and videocassettes) for distribution and promotion via radio, TV music channels, record stores, video stores, and discos. Movies with blockbuster soundtracks are produced to provide multiple vehicles for reaching their primary target market: teenagers and young adults. (While a number of films over the years have accomplished this goal, few were directly and expressly created for that purpose until *Saturday Night Fever*, *Flashdance*, and *Footloose*. Now such packages are commonplace.) Even best-selling books are written with movies or TV miniseries in mind. Supported by large promotional campaigns, a movie or TV show based on a book and the book itself are sometimes released at the same time.

Moreover, creating multiple income streams is not restricted to entertainment media. An increasing number of local television stations sell their news shows for late-night replay on local cable systems. Newspapers sell sports information to local companies that distribute the information through a fee-for-service call-in telephone number. Broadcast stations and newspapers supply weather information to a number of information outlets in order to increase revenue. And some newspapers are bringing out real estate supplements drawn from the newspaper's classified advertisements.

In each of these examples, the basic strategy was to design products that create a number of income streams for the same information messages within a single target market. The media company develops a single product idea and packages it in a variety of ways, thereby creating multiple selling opportunities. As cost pressures and competition continue to intensify, more media managers will develop multiple-packaging and multiple-distribution product strategies, which often result in major cost efficiencies in both product development and promotion.

Product Features in Print Media

Any product, including those from the media, has a large number of features that must be considered when developing a product strategy. From the consumer's point of view (either the individual or the advertiser), three general product features are important: quality, service, and price. Let's look at each of these features as they apply to what audience members seek from the print media.

Quality. Quality is captured in many attributes of an information product. For a newspaper, both the breadth and depth of coverage are aspects of quality. So are the writing and writing style; very high-quality publications are written with more sophisticated language than lower-quality ones. Other production features bearing on quality include layout, the use of color and pictures, and special design features.

In magazines, quality is indicated by the type of paper stock on which the magazine is printed, cover design, and so forth. The amount or type of advertising may also be seen as an indicator of quality. Prestige magazines, such as *The New Yorker* have more editorial content than advertising, even though the magazine's audience is very attractive to advertisers. Maintaining a reasonable editorial-to-advertising ratio is important in communicating a sense of high quality. In up-scale magazines, the audience also responds to the perceived quality of the firms that advertise in them. Hence, if Tiffany & Company, the famous New York jeweler, or Rolls Royce advertises in *The New Yorker*, that adds to the magazine's image of quality.

(As an aside it is interesting to note that, despite its prestige, even *The New Yorker* faced a decline in advertising pages when the ad market softened in the mid-1980s. That led to its sale to the Newhouse brothers, who did not touch the editorial side of the magazine, but moved swiftly to increase the number of advertising pages and the promotion of *The New Yorker*.)

Service. Service usually means the effectiveness of the distribution system. The belief that even excellent newspapers lose customers because of poor carrier service is right on target. The fact that service complaints result in more discontinued subscriptions than do price increases has led many circulation managers to switch their carriers from youngsters to adults in order to improve the reliability of service.

Most magazines are delivered by the U.S. Postal Service, which has a record for reliable service. Recent increases in postal rates, however, are creating considerable pressure on magazines to raise their subscription prices.

Price. It is commonly believed that prices of information products are relatively elastic. That is, if a media manager increases the price, some consumers will discontinue their subscriptions. Many print companies believe that for every price increase, there is a predictable decrease in circulation.

This sensitivity to price is particularly true for newspaper readers who do not read the paper regularly. Sporadic readers subscribe for short periods of time and then drop their subscriptions. This so-called churning pattern is hidden by total circulation figures; overall circulation may remain constant even though a large number of readers drop in and drop out. This results in substantial turnover of subscribers in any given period. Price changes are one of the reasons for this phenomenon.

Magazine subscribers are also sensitive to price. That is why magazines use discounted prices in their promotional subscription efforts. Few subscribers will pay the regular newsstand price for a magazine because they know that discounts are offered. Magazine publishers, therefore, must offer discounts to insure an audience large enough to attract advertisers. (Note that good service and price are not independent. If a media firm decreases the price of its publication, service may suffer. Of course, the relationship between price and quality is even more obvious.)

Product Features in Broadcast Media

In the traditional broadcast media, price is not a relevant product attribute, for once a consumer purchases a radio or televi- broadcasts are free. Other features are important, however.

sion set, broadcasts are free. Other features are important, however.

Quality. In television, quality becomes a key factor in viewers' program choices. Program content is very important here. The quality of a network or station's schedule can be assessed by how well it fits with audience members' interests. Other aspects of quality are also important.

The high production quality built into network entertainment programming attracts viewers. It also creates clear contrasts with local programming and news, although many local stations are now heavily into improving the quality of their programs. This has led to concern that emphasis on production quality in broadcast news is replacing emphasis on the substance of the information offered as news.

Another aspect of quality in broadcasting is the station's or program's image. Image and style are important determinants of quality; that is why broadcast news operations do extensive screening of potential anchors and reporters, as well as constant monitoring of audience reaction to this personnel.

Service. Service is largely controlled by the wattage that the station is allowed to use in transmitting its messages. Location of transmission towers is important and in almost every metropolitan area, some areas receive a stronger signal than others. One place where service effectiveness led to dramatic changes in the radio industry is the shift in listeners from AM to FM stations, largely because of improved sound quality on FM broadcasts.

A Key Decision in Formulating Product Strategies: Balancing Quality, Service, and Price

One of the most important product strategy decisions media managers make is setting the level of quality, service, and price for their firm's product. As noted in the preceding, trade-offs among these factors make it difficult to achieve high quality and high service at a low price.

EXHIBIT 12.6. BALANCING KEY FEATURES IN A MEDIA PRODUCT STRATEGY

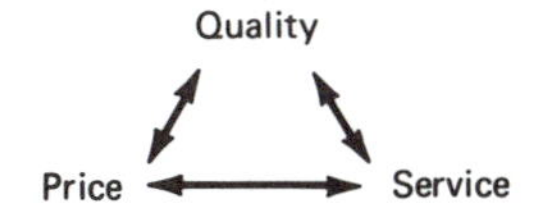

Setting performance levels for the three factors guides the development of an overall product strategy.

As media managers flesh out their product strategy, they often discover that they cannot simultaneously attain their quality, service, and price objectives. What is required is a careful rethinking of the plans for achieving these objectives. For example, a different option for producing the product or a different way of distributing it may be called for. In more extreme instances the objectives may have to be changed. Whichever approach is taken, it is crucial for media executives to set their objectives early in the process and to base their decisions on careful analysis of the audience's needs and willingness to pay. That will keep their product planning efforts on track.

(For a quick review of this issue, reread the discussion of the new medical journal in Chapter 5. That provides an example of product planning that balanced quality, service, and price, though the balance was easier and less tilted toward one factor than is usually the case.) The relationship among quality, service, and price is especially important in developing new media, such as the medical journal or fee-for-service media like pay television or data base services. Keep in mind that every media product has a certain utility value for audience members. If the information provided is extremely important, consumers will pay a substantial price for it. If it has only marginal utility, they will either pay little or skip the purchase entirely.

In any target market, however, the importance of information differs for each audience member. This makes pricing decisions extremely difficult and, at the same time, extremely important in determining the size of the audience and the profitability of a media company. As was just pointed out, price is only one factor; equally important is the quality of the information offered and the effectiveness of its distribution. High-quality, reliably distributed products that fill the market's needs command a good price; products that do not meet these criteria are far more likely to fail.

As if the equation is not complicated enough, remember that the U.S. public is used to very low-priced media: seemingly free television and radio, cheap newspapers and magazines. (And they are not just inexpensive; they are extremely so. The amount paid by subscribers for most U.S. daily newspapers equals the cost of the raw newsprint and ink in the warehouse. It does not cover costs incurred in gathering, writing, editing, producing, printing, or delivering the paper.) This history of low price puts fierce pressure on media managers to continue to keep prices low. On the other side, newspaper executives have only a few choices besides trying to reeducate the public about the value of their information product. The best of those choices are: create other revenue streams by broadening the advertiser market or repackage the paper's messages and sell them to additional audiences.

PRODUCT PLANNING FOR THE ADVERTISER MARKET

Media managers go through a process in developing their product strategy to attract advertisers similar to that employed to learn about and attract consumers. That is to be expected because the information executives are attempting to deliver a set of benefits that advertisers desire. The media company's task is to develop a product and capture an audience that will meet the needs of the advertiser target market.

Previously in this chapter we noted the wide variety of objectives an advertiser may have, e.g., the 52 communication objectives listed in the DAGMAR model (Colley, 1961). Some media address those objectives better than do others. In addition to communication objectives, advertisers have two types of objectives that are typically thought of as media objectives or audience-contact objectives. The first is high reach, that is, exposing a large proportion of the target audience to a single advertising message. (Cumulative reach is the total number of different consumers exposed to the advertisement during the entire campaign.) The second is high frequency, that is, reaching any single person a number of times during an advertising campaign.

Ideally, advertisers would have both high reach and high frequency. Contacting many people and doing so repeatedly are important for achieving communication objectives. Just as there are trade-offs among quality, service, and price, however, there are trade-offs between reach and frequency.

For instance, the higher the cumulative reach an advertiser seeks, the lower the frequency of exposure. The opposite is also true. Both reach and frequency can be raised by increasing the budget; however, all advertisers have budget limitations so they usually have to stress one objective over the other.

Different media have different strengths and weaknesses. In Exhibit 12.7, we list the primary strengths and limitations of the principal media (newspapers, magazines, television, and radio) so as to give you a better idea of specific advertising features that each medium brings to a marketing effort.

In planning a product strategy for the advertiser market, media managers try to maximize their medium's strengths and minimize its limitations. At the same time, modern technology is helping reduce at least some of the limitations for a number of media. For example, use of color and improvements in printing made it possible for newspapers to offer more attractive options to national and local advertisers. In the same way, in-house advertising production by broadcast stations made it possible for local advertisers—auto dealers, financial institutions, grocers, and department stores—to develop low-priced, yet effective, TV commercials.

EXHIBIT 12.7. STRENGTHS AND LIMITATIONS OF DIFFERENT MEDIA FOR ADVERTISERS

	Strengths	*Limitations*
Newspapers	Intense coverage Flexibility Prestige (sometimes) Dealer/national advertiser coordination	Short life Hasty reading Moderate to poor reproduction
Magazines	Market selectivity Long life High reproduction quality Prestige (sometimes) Extra services	Inflexible in area coverage and time Inflexible to copy changes Penetration of overall market may be low Wide distribution results in low geographic penetration
Television	Mass coverage Impact Repetition Prestige Flexibility	Fleeting message Commercial wear-out Lack of selectivity High costs (especially network)
Radio	Audience selectivity Immediacy Flexibility Mobility	Fragmentation Transient quality of listenership Limited sensory input

The inherent limitations of each medium can be reduced only so far, however. Smart advertisers recognize that fact. As a consequence, the best strategy for media managers is to clearly identify advertisers who seek the benefits their medium offers and to develop a strong promotional and sales effort to sell those strengths.

The three broad product features that are important to attract an audience—quality, service, and price—are equally useful in reaching and keeping advertisers, but experience suggests that service is especially important. For advertisers, service is how effectively a media manager works with the advertiser in coordinating advertising development, budgeting, and placement.

For example, in a study of the relationship between advertising agencies and their clients, the most important feature of the agency's work with their accounts was neither the quality of creative effort nor the fees charged by the agency (Wackman, Salmon, & Salmon, 1986). Overall satisfaction with agencies and with their creative work was most closely related to the personal relationships and effectiveness of the coordination patterns between the agency and the client. Both of these factors indicate that an agency's level of service to their clients is crucial in determining agency effectiveness and client retention.

Marketing expert Theodore Levitt (1983), a professor at the Harvard Business School, makes the same point about the crucial role of relationship factors in industrial marketing and selling. Because selling to advertisers is an industrial sales process, the same principle applies here as well. That principle is that a key factor in the effectiveness of a media company's advertising sales efforts will be the sales person's ability to develop a strong, positive working relationship with those who purchase advertising, e.g., the advertising manager or owner in a retail store or the media director in an advertising agency.

Now, let's summarize what we have said in this chapter about how media managers develop a strategy for their media product. It begins with a careful analysis of the target audience market and the target advertiser market. That analysis includes carefully defining those markets in terms of a variety of characteristics and identifying the benefits that members of the market want and need.

Next, media managers tailor their products to offer features corresponding to those benefits, recognizing the need to balance quality, service, and price. They must also keep in mind that the product strategy has significant implications for how the media product is produced, distributed, and promoted.

Finally, and in line with an overall emphasis on the marketing perspective, media managers put extraordinary effort into developing a promotion and sales effort for their product. Unless they have a solid strategy for informing target markets about their information product or service and for persuading consumers to buy it, all the effort and money spent on planning, producing, and distributing that product or service will be wasted.

CHAPTER 13

Promotion and Sales of Media Products

This chapter is about promoting and selling information products. It begins by presenting a broad framework for thinking about promotion, then it covers the major steps a media manager employs when planning a promotion strategy to attract an audience. Next, it discusses the most important tools available for implementing a promotion strategy and presents several media vignettes to show promotion in action. Finally, it explains how promotion and sales efforts can be directed at advertisers.

A FRAMEWORK FOR THINKING ABOUT PROMOTION

The essential idea of media promotion is to develop strategies that establish the firmest possible linkage with a firm's target markets, both consumer and advertiser. "Selling" to the audience market may mean individuals purchasing a single copy of a newspaper or magazine, subscribing for a year, or simply using a free printed or broadcast medium. "Selling" to advertisers means sales of space or time in order to reach target audiences.

Models of the Purchase Process

Of the various models of the buying/selling process, a typical sequence is the AIDA principle, shown in Exhibit 13.1.

That may sound simple, but it is very difficult. What's more, the AIDA principle is just one of a series of complex models for how the buying/selling process works. All of those models view the process as involving changes in consumers' cognition, motivation, and behavior.

Cognitive changes include becoming aware of the existence of an information product and learning about its features or benefits. A sub-

EXHIBIT 13.1. THE AIDA MODEL OF PROMOTION AND SALES

Create **Awareness** about the media product.

Stimulate **Interest** in the media product.

Turn interest into **Desire** for the media product.

Push up the level of desire so that **Action** is taken to purchase or use the media product.

---

stantial amount of media advertising is geared toward making the target audience aware of, for example, a TV special or a new book. Other ad campaigns call attention to specific features of possible interest to the audience, such as the major stories that will be covered in an upcoming TV news show.

Motivational or attitude-related changes include trying to generate interest in an information product and linking that interest with desire for the product. What we are talking about here is creating a brand preference that will strengthen the audiences' positive feelings toward the media product. When stars of TV series or movies appear in public or on talk shows, such as "The Tonight Show" or "Good Morning America," the public has the opportunity to see these people as likable individuals, perhaps strengthening the bond they feel with the TV series or movie. Author appearances at bookstores serve the same purpose; they establish a link between audience members and the author as a person. Newspapers' sponsorship of community events is an attempt to build a similar bond.

Action changes include increased conviction about a product's usefulness; they are best if accompanied by trial use of the product or by actual purchase. Discount pricing is used by many print media firms to give readers an extra reason for taking the action of purchasing their magazine, book, or newspaper; trial subscriptions are another example. Direct mail advertising done by magazines has the primary objective of selling subscriptions. Public television station fund drives involving special programming and strong appeals from prominent citizens are also designed to elicit a specific action from the audience: making a pledge.

The Learning Hierarchy. Most models of the buying process use this approach, which was developed many years ago. This model assumes that purchases occur by first creating awareness and comprehension of the product. That leads to increased interest and desire, which finally results in action. This is called the learning hierarchy of purchase behavior. It is valid, but when subjected to testing it was found to occur only some of the time, specifically, when the purchase is important (usually involving a substantial outlay of money) and when real differences exist between products.

The Low-Involvement Hierarchy. Another purchase sequence was identified in the 1960s. Herbert Krugman (1965) suggested that a low-involvement hierarchy occurs when a purchase is relatively unimportant (usually involving a low-cost item) and when there are few differences between alternative brands or products. In those instances, a different sequence occurs. Cognitive changes happen first, but the amount of cognitive change is relatively small; it may involve only awareness of the product and one or two of its attributes. This minor cognitive activity leads to behavioral action when the person purchases or uses the product. Afterwards, stronger attitudinal bonds may begin to develop between the person and the product, but only if there has been a positive experience.

Most media products are relatively low in cost and, in the minds of the public, many information packages do not differ greatly from available alternatives. For example, there is little difference among the three network's situation comedies, which typically air at the same time, or among the six rock stations that all carry the same music. Given that situation, the low-involvement model best characterizes audience members' usage or purchase of many media products. In turn, it has important implications for a media manager's decisions about promotions to attract audience members.

First, the low-involvement hierarchy implies that consumers do not spend a great deal of time or mental energy in making most media selections. That means that when people decide to watch television, they quickly flip through the TV schedule and decide which program they wish to watch. In many instances, they just turn on the set and push channel selection buttons, stopping when they see something that pleases them. The decision happens quickly and without much thought.

Second, because little thinking and effort is involved, the basis upon which consumers make a media choice is relatively simple. People watch a given channel's news because they like the anchor; they listen to KZZZ-FM because they like talk shows; they read their local paper because it has good sports coverage; they buy John McPhee's new book because he is one of the finest nonfiction writers in the English language.

Positioning. Al Ries and Jack Trout (1981) developed the concept of positioning to deal with the reality of the low-involvement buying process. Sometimes the idea is referred to as product positioning because the starting point is a product. Yet, positioning is not what is done to a product, but what a marketer does to the mind of the consumer.

The basic approach of positioning is not to create something new or different in the consumer's mind. It is to manipulate what is there, to rearrange connections that already exist.

Positioning of their products is necessary for media executives because of the three explosions that occurred in the 1970s and 1980s: the media explosion, product explosion, and advertising explosion. You should, by this time, be aware of the explosion of new forms of media. The explosion of all sorts of products in the U.S. is also obvious; indeed, the media explosion was part of that deluge. The advent of cable television alone has resulted in over 20 new networks since 1970. Radio stations proliferated as FM audiences increased; there are thousands of magazine titles today, and each year over 30,000 new books are published by U.S. book publishers.

Corresponding to the media explosion was another in advertising. With more media outlets, one should expect more advertising. But new forms of advertising have also been developed: (1) increased direct mail marketing including marriage mail where advertisements of more than one retailer are "married" together in one direct mail package, (2) telephone marketing, (3) more point-of-purchase displays in retail outlets, and the list goes on and on.

The result of these explosions is that Americans are living in an overcommunicated—or, at least, a very heavily communicated—society, besieged each day with torrents of communication. The only defense a person has against that onslaught is to develop what Ries and Trout call an "oversimplified mind." For companies confronted with the oversimplified mind-set, the best approach is to develop an oversimplified message, that is, a message based on positioning.

In the Minneapolis-St. Paul media market, for instance, radio stations sell their format: "K102 Country," "KQRS Rock," "WCCO's Real Radio." Television news touts the "EyeWitness News Team," "The Professionals," and "The People Who Care." Newspaper advertising promotes columnists, special sections, important series, and variety sections.

Note that in most of these examples, the message focuses on a benefit sought by members of a target audience. Advertising in the past also stressed consumer benefits. What positioning has done, however, is to concentrate attention on a single benefit. Proponents of positioning preach "simplification, simplification, simplification," because the essence of positioning is sacrificing a litany of product attributes and product benefits to single-mindedly present one powerful idea.

DEVELOPING PROMOTION STRATEGIES

Developing a promotion strategy for a media product includes four steps. The first is to identify the target market and devise a product strategy. The second is to set promotional objectives. The third is to determine audience-contact objectives. The fourth includes developing the tools to achieve promotional and audience-contact objectives within the target market identified in the first step.

Identifying Target Markets and Devising Product Strategy

This step was outlined in the process of developing a product strategy described in Chapter 12. It is particularly important when devising promotional strategy to keep in mind who the target market really is and what benefits that audience seeks. Benefits sought are especially important because they often provide the take-off point for positioning.

Setting Promotional Objectives

In Chapter 12 we indicated that advertising and promotion can be used to accomplish more than 50 different objectives. At one time or another most media companies try to achieve many of them. Of the 50-plus goals, three promotional ones are primary when media companies communicate with their target audience:

Increasing Product Usage. Since broadcast programming is free, consumers do not really purchase it. As a result, broadcast stations try to sell their audience on using their station more frequently. Radio stations do this with ads on billboards, in newspapers, or on television. These messages remind listeners about the station's basic format. Television stations use newspaper advertising, program excerpts, reviews by TV critics, and billboards with pictures of their news personnel to remind their viewers about the station and specific programs it offers.

Daily newspapers aim some of their advertising at nonsubscribers, trying to get them to appreciate the usefulness of the paper. They do that with radio and TV spots, billboards, and community promotions. At the same time, they use in-paper advertisements to motivate sporadic readers to become habitual, every-day readers. This is important because habitual readers are the core of a newspaper's circulation base.

Product and Company Image Building. The media engage in a great deal of institutional, image-oriented advertising. At each commercial break, TV stations air their call letters, either visually or in audio form. Newspapers hammer away with their name on the masthead on page one and with variations of that masthead inside the paper. Those papers that are committed to modern graphics have also developed an emblem or logo (i.e., a graphic symbol embedded in their masthead). It is used on their newsracks, trucks, stationery, bills, and billboards. The symbol is used even when the paper's name is absent. After a time, that logo becomes so accepted that it can be used without the name, and the audiences who look at the logo will mentally fill in the name.

Media companies also sponsor all kinds of local enterprises, ranging from Little League teams to concerts to shows in museums and schools. All of these are institutional, often charitable, image-building efforts designed to reinforce in the audience members' minds the fact that the media company is an active participant in the community.

One of the more skillful efforts of this sort that we've seen was done by the Gannett-owned affiliate in the Twin Cities. When Gannett purchased Channel 11, its ratings put it in a very weak number-three position in the market. Gannett spent millions building up the station, including buying the call letters W*USA. The station's leader also saw to it that his executives and news personnel became active in the community. To reinforce the theme of community involvement, W*USA utilized a variety of devices on its news programs to highlight community groups, e.g., showing children from schools around the Twin Cities while credits were running, having a separate five-minute "Prep Sports Report" on the 10 P.M. weekend shows, and so forth.

Then, it seemed as if the station was about to face a substantial setback. That happened when Gannett decided to shift Channel 11's call letters, W*USA-TV, to its newly purchased station in Washington, D.C. Many people thought the Minneapolis affiliate would lose ground when it lost such identifiable call letters. Not so. The Twin Cities' station quickly purchased the call letters KARE from another station to clearly position itself as the "People Who Care."

Product Sales. Having a specific sales objective is clearly more important for those media whose revenue base depends on subscriptions or purchases. This includes magazines, books, movies, cable television, and other fee-for-service companies, such as data bases. Advertising must accomplish the entire selling task for those organizations. Consequently, the promotional forms employed by firms of that sort are those that can perform an effective sales job. They include direct mail, telemarketing, and even door-to-door sales. Newspapers utilize similar strategies to win new subscribers.

Setting Audience-Contact Objectives

What we call audience-contact objectives are usually referred to as media objectives in discussions of advertising campaigns. We use a different term to avoid confusion. As noted in Chapter 12, advertisers have two audience-contact objectives: reach and frequency.

Reach is defined as the unduplicated percent of the target market exposed to a promotional message at least once during a specific time period, usually a month. When a promotional campaign is designed to create sales and the advertising vehicle chosen can perform the entire selling function, a media company will have a high-reach objective. For example, magazine publishers try to reach as many members of their target market as possible with their direct mail solicitations. Thus, *Pediatric Neurology,* the medical journal you read about in Chapter 5, buys or constructs mailing lists so its direct mail pieces go to every known pediatric neurologist in the country as well as to related specialists who are potential subscribers. Some name duplication occurs, of course, but that is of small concern to the publisher; even if two mailings go to some people, what counts is reaching as many members of the target market as possible.

Frequency is defined as the average number of instances that a member of the target market is exposed to an advertising message during a time period; again, usually a month. Achieving high frequency is especially significant for broadcasters whose major promotional objective is more frequent usage. In that respect, broadcasters are similar to advertisers of such high usage products as soft drinks, beer, fast foods, breakfast cereals, and deodorants. All of them want to enhance usage frequency.

High frequency is also a major objective where company image is important, a primary reason for much of the advertising by banks, insurance companies, telephone utilities, and even industrial firms, such as IBM and UNISYS. Maintaining a positive company image is also significant for media organizations. That is why many broadcasters and newspapers strive for high frequency in their advertising; they do so with institutional advertising, even when they are not touting a particular product.

As important as both objectives are, reach and frequency often require trade-offs. Given the same budget, moves made to maximize audience reach often result in a reduction in frequency of exposure to ads or commercials; the opposite is also true. Which objective a media executive chooses to stress depends largely on the medium's specific promotional objective, as the examples we provide later in this chapter illustrate.

Selecting Tools for Carrying Out the Promotional Strategy

The fourth and final step in planning a promotional strategy is to select specific promotional tools to achieve the communication and audience-contact objectives in the target market. There are literally hundreds of ways that media products and services can be promoted. The amount of creativity and diversity a media firm uses in promoting a new or modified media package is limited only by the imagination of those doing the promotion and, in some instances, timing and budget.

PROMOTIONAL TOOLS FOR ATTRACTING AUDIENCES

There are four major categories of promotional tools: advertising, publicity, sales promotion, and direct selling. Which one or combination media managers select to attract audiences depends on the firm's promotional objectives and resources. Although financial resources are significant in determining the choices media executives make, other resources, such as staff availability and time or space available in their own medium, also play a significant role. Exhibit 13.2 lists specific examples of promotional tools.

Advertising

In the U.S., everyone but a recluse is bombarded with hundreds of advertisements every day. If you turn on the radio or television when you wake up to hear the weather or news, a commercial comes at you unless you listen to public broadcasting. As you read the newspaper while eating breakfast or traveling to work or school you may glance at dozens of ads, and countless more flash by on billboards. Standing on the street corner waiting for a light to change as you cross the street, buses, taxis, and trucks rush through the intersection; many have commercial messages on their sides. Walking across campus or to work or to shop you see posters advertising concerts, lectures, places to rent, and

EXHIBIT 13.2. PROMOTIONAL TOOLS FOR REACHING AUDIENCES—READERS, LISTENERS, AND VIEWERS

Category	*Example*
Advertising	Print ads: newspapers, magazines Broadcast commercials: radio, television, cable Direct mail Other methods: billboards, transit
Publicity	Through media: news releases, interviews, press conferences Direct to public: staged events, meetings, newsletter to subscribers
Sales promotion	Price incentive: discounts, trial subscriptions Premiums Contests, games, sweepstakes
Selling	Point-of-purchase displays Telephone sales Door-to-door sales

things to buy. It is still early in the day, but you have already encountered several hundred advertising messages, some of which you've paid attention to. Throughout the rest of every American's day, the onslaught continues.

Advertisements come in many forms. You see print ads in newspapers, magazines, and in direct mail flyers. Broadcast commercials come from radio, television, and cable. Outdoor advertising is on billboards, sides of buildings, signs and posters, as well as on many buses, trucks, and cars. Advertisements are placed in a variety of specific programs, publications, and locations so as to reach specific and differing target markets. In those settings, careful coverage patterns can be established because the advertiser pays for the medium; the purchase of time, space, and location enables information organizations to control audience exposure.

Media companies use a variety of vehicles in their advertising, but many use their own medium for the bulk of it. Firms who self-promote do so with the objective of maintaining or creating high audience usage. For example, television stations run program previews to alert, or perhaps tease, the current audience about upcoming programs. Radio stations regularly indicate what's coming next on the air. Newspapers carry ads highlighting columnists, features, and upcoming special coverage. Magazines have subscription cards stuffed between the pages.

Broadcasters and newspapers also trade time with other media or purchase it from them. When companies in one medium use other media to promote them, that complements what they do in their own columns or broadcasts. Smart media managers understand that in-house advertising is useful for those who are already watching, listening, or reading; it enhances the chances for further attachment, but it does nothing for those who are not already using those media products. That is why many media executives use billboards and media vehicles other than their own to reach their target audience.

Public Relations

Public relations is another major promotional tool. This term is sometimes confused with publicity. Even though it includes publicity, public relations is a far broader effort. When we write "public relations" we mean it in the expansive sense. It involves the many practices companies, including media firms, use to build rapport with their target audience and other publics: advertisers, shareholders, and interested community groups. All these and more are used by public relations experts to reach an audience, just as advertising is used by ad agencies.

Publicity, one major form of public relations, uses the media to reach an audience just as advertising does. Publicity differs from advertising, however, in three important respects: (1) it is not paid for; (2) the sponsor of the message is usually not identified; (3) the sponsor does not have ultimate control.

When a media firm, for example, sends out a news release about an award it has won or holds a press conference to announce its plans to build a new station, people from other media decide if they wish to use the information. The broadcast station or newspaper generating the publicity does not control whether it will be used at all or, if it is, in what manner or form.

With the rise of newspaper sections devoted to entertainment and variety, more publicity channels have become available to broadcasters. Stations are anxious for reviews and criticisms of their programming, almost without respect to whether the reviews are good or bad. That is true because the reviews represent an additional way to reach present and new audiences. Television stations are also eager to have their programming listed in a TV guide format in other media. Networks and movie companies strive mightily to get their stars and directors on the cover of major news magazines or other popular magazines.

Publicity isn't aimed only at the print media. Increasingly the stars of broadcasting, both entertainment and news, make public appearances that earn media coverage. They act as grand marshals in parades, perform at state or county fairs, appear at conventions, or give speeches at political or charitable fund-raisers.

Another form of public relations tries to reach the target audience directly. Public tours of broadcast or newspaper facilities provide an opportunity for media concerns to create favorable impressions on the groups that tour the facility. Staging events, often as a co-sponsor, is another means. This enables media firms to be connected in the audience's mind with a variety of worthy causes. Public broadcasting outlets often publish newsletters or magazines to keep financial supporters abreast of upcoming programming. Newspapers and magazines insert letters into their bills to alert subscribers to changes in the medium or upcoming events of interest, such as a significant series of articles.

Sales Promotion

Sales promotion refers to activities that supplement advertising, publicity, and personal selling. It encompasses such activities as exhibitions, displays, demonstrations, contests, premium offers, coupons, and discounts. These promotional activities are utilized heavily by media companies.

The purpose of most sales promotion is to give audience members a special reason to buy or use an information product. Newspapers, for example, give 13-week trial subscriptions, with the first two weeks or month free. Magazines offer discount subscriptions, with offer premiums (clocks, watches, calendars, calculators) to first-time subscribers.

Usually, these kinds of offers are made on a limited-time basis. Public TV stations offer premiums for large donations to their fund drives. Cable systems or cable networks, such as HBO or The Movie Channel, offer free installation or free service for a trial period. These sales promotion devices are most effective when audience members pay for using the medium.

Many radio stations use contests and gimmicks to increase their listening audience. Call-ins to win prizes by identifying songs or answering questions are common. Reading the names of people on the air, then requiring them to call within a certain time period to win a prize, is another ploy to ensure listenership. Giveaways include cash, tickets to events, trips, merchandise, and, in some instances, big-ticket items like stereos or automobiles.

Another common broadcast gimmick is to have a jackpot that grows day by day. The station will call someone and ask how much money is in the jackpot. If the answer is correct the caller wins the money; if incorrect, more dollars are added to the jackpot and the new total is announced. This kind of contest is designed to achieve almost continuous listening among audience members.

Print media also use contests for promoting circulation. Rupert Murdoch is famous for spending huge sums in his newspapers to run variations of the Wingo game. In it, readers play a game that builds cash prizes from day to day. This promotion method brings significant short-term circulation gains and introduces people to the newspaper, but it has not been shown to be an effective method for creating sustained circulation gains.

Direct Selling

Direct selling takes a number of forms, of course, but the most common is via the telephone. Initially, telemarketing was introduced to sell new subscriptions to magazines and newspapers. More recently, it became important in getting subscription renewals. Many companies now regularly contact current subscribers by telephone shortly before their subscription expires. Previously, such reminders were almost entirely carried through direct mail marketing. Newspapers also call former subscribers to see if they might resubscribe, offering them a price discount, free trial period, or premium. With the rise of various sorts of shoppers owned by newspapers and the use of computers, daily newspapers actually keep track of every household in their circulation area, whether the household has ever subscribed or not. This allows expansion of the paper's contact to those who have never subscribed or who drop their subscription for one reason or another.

Public broadcasting stations utilize telephone selling in two ways. One is by having a bank of operators ready to receive calls from viewers during a fund-raising drive. More recently, the stations have begun to call subscribers before the fund-raising effort starts and ask for a subscription renewal.

As telemarketing increases, door-to-door sales become much less common. However, newspapers still use house-to-house circulation sweeps in designated areas to try to win new subscribers. And magazine marketing companies still employ platoons of high school and college students in the summer to go door to door, selling any of a hundred or so periodicals.

Packaging and point-of-purchase displays are powerful selling devices. Racks near check-out counters in supermarkets and other stores enable print companies to display their magazines and books at a time when consumers are particularly likely to purchase, e.g., when they are standing in line waiting to spend money on other products. The covers of such magazines and papers are crowded with headlines designed to pique the readers' interest. Similarly, cover illustrations of paperback books are carefully designed to lure readers. For many books and magazines, cover design and packaging is the most important promotional effort.

PROMOTIONAL STRATEGIES IN ACTION

The promotional tools described in the previous section provide just a hint of the ideas that can be used in creating promotional strategies. How media products and media companies are promoted depends on the creativity and imagination of the promotion personnel in the media firms or in their advertising agencies or public relations firms. The possibilities are truly limitless. In the following section we will look at some promotional strategies in action.

Radio Station KOSY

We begin with the radio station we discussed in Chapter 12, KOSY. Recall that the target market for KOSY's new format was 25- to 44-year-old women with special emphasis on those in the 25 to 34 age group. The promotional objectives were twofold: first, and most important, to introduce the new format to the target market in a very strong fashion; and second, to establish a linkage of the station with the activities and interests of women in the target age group (see Exhibit 13.3).

Initially, audience contact objectives were to have both high reach and high frequency within the very narrow target audience of 25- to 34-year-old women. The station knew there would be spillover into a somewhat older group of females and to males of the same and older ages, but by establishing a very narrow targeting both high reach and high frequency objectives could be sought within a reasonable budget.

The strategy followed this course: The promotional campaign began one month before the next ratings sweep (each sweep typically lasts 10 weeks). The promotional campaign continued through the sixth week of the sweep. Media scheduling during the first month was heavier than during the last 6 weeks of the 10-week campaign.

The advertising approach utilized many television spots on shows with high ratings in the narrow target market. The commercials themselves made heavy use of the very distinctive station logo that had been developed, and it played examples of music from the station's format. (The logo showed KOSY's call letters, which also expressed the theme for the format, a unique combination for a radio station.) The spots demonstrated the station's new approach by having only one 4-second announcement during the 30-second spot; this roughly corresponded to the ratio of music to commercial and announcer talk on the station.

KOSY also purchased numerous billboards located along freeways and major bus routes in the city. The billboards were simple, showing the station's logo. Little newspaper advertising was purchased because of low readership among the group the station wished to reach. A weekly newspaper distributed free downtown did, however, offer a good opportunity to deliver a message to some of the target audience who worked or shopped there, so some ads were purchased in it.

The overall weight of the media effort was substantial. In the first month of the campaign, 300 gross rating points (GRPs) were purchased in relation to the target market, and in the following six weeks of the campaign another 250 GRPs were added. (Gross rating points represent a combination of reach and frequency; more specifically, reach multiplied by average frequency. During the first month of the campaign, the

---

EXHIBIT 13.3. PROMOTING KOSY'S NEW FORMAT

Objectives

1. High reach and frequency for the target market of 25- to 34-year-old women
2. Establish station linkage with interests and activities of target market.

Strategy and tactics

1. Develop distinctive logo and commercials which demonstrate station format:
   - heavy TV schedule
   - many billboards
   - some newspaper advertisements in free distribution downtown newspaper
2. Promotional effort to establish linkage with target market interests:
   - sponsor bridal fair
   - broadcast and promote new sports team

---

station expected to achieve 80% reach within the target market at an average frequency of 3.75, for a total of 300 GRPs.)

Other elements of the promotional strategy implemented the second promotional objective, establish a linkage of the station with interests of the target group. KOSY became a major sponsor of the bridal fair for the metropolitan area, a fancy affair held at a concert hall. It also became the broadcast outlet and major promotional vehicle for a new sports team started in the city and known to appeal to the target market of 25- to 34-year-old women.

As was noted in Chapter 12, the immediate impact of a promotional strategy and format change can be impressive. And for a time it was. Then, the competition fought back; they began to cut into KOSY's ratings, and when the promotional effort returned to more normal levels, listenership declined.

A Metropolitan Daily: The Philadelphia Inquirer

The following example illustrates how research is used in developing promotional strategies. This example is discussed more fully in Phillip Meyer's (1985) *The Newspaper Survival Book.*

In the early 1970s, when the *Philadelphia Inquirer* was involved in a tough competitive situation, the paper wanted to evaluate its circulation performance in small geographic areas in the Philadelphia metropolitan area. Previously, the typical approach was to simply color a map a variety of colors, each to indicate a penetration rate. Management, however, knew that this could be misleading because of very different demographic characteristics of each area. That resulted in, for instance, media executives expecting a high-income, high-education area to have high penetration rates because of the kinds of people who typically subscribe to and read newspapers. On the other hand, areas with large numbers of minority or young people would be expected to have lower penetration rates. Filling in these areas with one color as an indicator of what was going on did not adequately represent actual circulation performance within the region.

To improve its decision making, the newspaper's managers combined Census Bureau data on a variety of demographic characteristics with the newspaper's penetration rates. It then developed a sophisticated statistical model to estimate readership of all the small areas of the city based on the demographic composition of each area. Next, actual household penetration was compared to the projections and those areas in which penetration fell substantially short of projected penetration were identified. In effect, the research was used to target a number of specific areas in the city for special circulation drives. Depending on where those target areas were, individual circulation strategies could be de-

---

EXHIBIT 13.4. CREATING A TARGETED CIRCULATION DRIVE FOR A METROPOLITAN NEWSPAPER

Objective
Create finer targeting for a circulation drive

Strategy and tactics
By using advanced statistical techniques, identify neighborhoods that subscribe at lower levels than predicted by demographic characteristics; then use appropriate circulation approaches:
- telephone selling
- door-to-door canvases
- discounts
- trial offers

---

vised; they might involve a combination of telephone selling, door-to-door sales, discounts, or trial offers.

Flashdance

Flashdance was a movie featuring a beautiful new actress, Jennifer Beal, and a thunderous musical score. The target market for this combined movie and recording product was teenagers and people in their early 20s. These two groups constituted the great bulk of both the movie-going and record-buying audiences of the early 1980s.

The promotion objective was to familiarize the target market with the music from the movie as a way of attracting movie attendance. A second objective was to highlight Jennifer Beal, who was thought to be very attractive to both women and men in the target audience. No specific audience-contact objectives were established because the strategy that was developed did not make this possible; however, it was hoped the promotion would reach many audience members in the target group.

The strategy that was utilized is interesting both for what it did and did not do. Three months in advance of the release of *Flashdance*, radio station DJs received copies of the top song from the movie, *Make It Happen*, along with an extensive promotion kit describing other music from the film, the movie itself, and Jennifer Beal. At the same time, a music video was released to 200 discos in the country. The video contained excepts from the movie, featuring Beal in a wild dance to *Make It Happen*. When DJs in the major markets began hearing about the success of the video in the discos, they gave the hit song regular play. Shortly thereafter the video was also released to MTV and it received a lot of attention on that cable network.

EXHIBIT 13.5. PROMOTING A NEW MOVIE, *FLASHDANCE*

Objectives

1. Promote music from the movie to attract attendance.
2. Promote the star of the movie, Jennifer Beal.

Strategy and tactics

1. Release the top record from the movie for play on radio stations three months before the movie's premiere.
2. Release a video of the music and the star three months before the movie's premiere. Also give it to the top discos and MTV.
3. Simultaneously release the movie and full record album, supported by a small amount of the newspaper advertising.

The full album and movie were released simultaneously at the close of the three-month promotional campaign. Of interest to those who study promotion is the fact that the project had only a small newspaper advertising budget at the time the movie actually reached theaters, less than one-fifth of the budget typically used when major movies are released. The reason: the momentum built through the extensive promotional campaign made it possible to have a minimal advertising budget.

The promotional strategy worked so well that *Flashdance* became an enormously successful film. Its success resulted in early release of a VCR-tape for home viewing because of the demand for the movie, and even led to merchandising of some new *Flashdance*-style clothing.

Now, we are not suggesting that the promotional campaign is the sole reason for the success of *Flashdance*. Not at all; but the promotional effort played a substantial part in the final outcome.

Alive and Aware

A publishing firm in which one of this text's authors was involved developed a program to help married couples learn to communicate better. The company published a workbook to support couples' learning and the training of 300 instructors throughout the United States to conduct couples' groups. Although this established the publisher's own distribution system, because the number of instructors was limited, the number of books the company could sell was severely restricted.

The owners of the firm decided to redo the workbook in the form of a book and named it *Alive and Aware*. They believed it could serve three markets:

- couples' groups, as text and resource material;
- college classes in interpersonal communication, marriage and family, and, perhaps, counselor education;
- stand-alone reading for persons interested in self-help materials.

Because of the expense involved, the publisher, with limited resources, could not afford a major national advertising campaign to the public. When small publishers face that situation they try to secure reviews in newspapers or magazines, but competition to be reviewed is fierce. An alternative strategy is to sell to and involve the people who control distribution to the consumer. In this case, instructors were the distributors for the couples market, college professors for the college text market, and wholesalers and retail book stores for the self-help reader market.

(As an aside it should be noted that in media businesses, where the message developer does not control final sale (books, movies, records, and, to some extent, magazines), much of the promotional effort is aimed at getting wholesalers and retailers to purchase products for direct sale to the audience. In this system, large publishers hold a substantial advantage over small ones because they can offer larger discounts for volume purchases, as they have more titles. Also, large publishers have consumer advertising budgets which they can share with retailers through cooperative advertising. Small publishers have great difficulty getting into retail stores because they have little to offer the wholesaler or retailer in price breaks or in marketing strength.)

In this situation, three different strategies were adopted to promote *Alive and Aware*. For the couples' market, promotion was aimed at instructors. A newsletter was sent to them describing the book and offering a free copy to instructors who had conducted a couples' group within the last six months. At the same time, a major effort was geared toward expanding the number of instructors by offering instructor workshops in major cities throughout the country. This workshop effort, supported by direct mail advertising campaigns, continued for three years. Quarterly newsletters were sent to all instructors so they would feel part of a large instructor network.

For the college market, a direct mail advertising campaign was developed to reach 15,000 college teachers. Different brochures were developed for instructors of the different types of courses, i.e., interpersonal communication, marriage and family, counselor education. A free examination copy of *Alive and Aware* was offered, as is commonly done in textbook promotion. Fifteen percent (2,200 teachers) requested copies of the book, a high percentage for this kind of text. The 350 teachers who adopted the book for the next school year was also a high percentage.

For the self-help market, it was necessary to promote to retail book store owners. The partners used some personal contacts to have the book introduced to a buyer in one of the major bookstore chains. When this person recommended *Alive and Aware* on a "promising new releases" list, 30 percent of the chain's stores ordered copies, an average of 10 copies per store. A review in the local paper resulted in the purchase of several hundred copies by a local wholesaler who, in turn, sold them to local independent bookstores. The review also created some requests from consumers, and many local bookstores responded with orders. Attempts to sell to wholesalers and retailers in other nearby metro areas were not as successful because of lack of contacts who could help get into those markets.

With continuing active recruitment of instructors, a second direct mail campaign to college instructors and continued sales through the bookstore chain, the local wholesaler, and independent bookstores, *Alive and Aware* was a success. In the next five years the company went through seven printings of the book and sold 110,000 copies. By that time, *Alive and Aware* was in the declining stage of its product life cycle and a new, revised version was published, spurring further sales.

*Promoting a Television Station's Image: W*USA-TV*

Up to now we have used examples involving sale of a specific product: a new station format, newspaper subscription, a movie, or a book. Media companies not only sell specific products, they also promote their company's image. When that is their goal they are like other major American companies that include much image-building effort in their overall promotion.

As you read earlier in this chapter, the target market for W*USA-TV's image-promotion campaign was twofold: major citizen groups and the broader mass audience. Both of these target markets were seen as important in the station's overall positioning of itself as "the community-conscious station" in the area.

The basic promotional objective was to demonstrate that W*USA-TV is deeply involved with the community and contributes to its region. No specific audience contact objective was set, but it was hoped that a wide reach in both target audiences would be achieved. The community issue selected for this promotional effort was a campaign to publicize the dangers of driving while drinking. A number of elements went into the strategy (see Exhibit 13.6).

1. Representatives of 300 relevant citizen groups were invited to the station for a prescreening of a TV show to be aired in mid-December. The show was hard-hitting; it detailed in graphic and often painful ways the impact of drunken driving on innocent people. The representatives of the citizen groups were told about the station's promotion plans and were offered suggestions as to how they might involve their organizations in promoting the same issue.

EXHIBIT 13.6. PROMOTING A TELEVISION STATION'S IMAGE: W*USA-TV

Objective

Demonstrate that the station is community conscious.

Strategy and tactics

Link the station with a broader community effort to publicize the problem of driving while under the influence of alcohol. Tools to do this include:

prescreening of hard-hitting TV show to representatives of 300 citizen groups.

airing of prime-time show as December holiday kick-off.

heavy airing of public service announcements on the topic during holiday period.

promoting a "designated nondrinker" program with local bars.

2. The station aired the show in prime time, preempting a popular network program to do so. During the previous week a number of previews were run about the special, and newspaper ads were purchased to alert the audience to the fact that it would be aired.
3. The station dedicated half of all its public service announcements (PSAs) to this cause during the following 30-day period, which spanned the holidays.
4. W*USA-TV promoted a "designated nondrinker" program. Many of the PSAs the station ran mentioned the importance of naming one person in every car as a designated nondrinker for the evening. Further, the station gained the cooperation of several soft drink companies and many bars to provide free soft drinks for designated nondrinkers during this time period. When the 30-day period ended, many bars continued that policy.

The five examples you've just read should give you a glimpse into the wide variety of strategies and approaches that media managers use to promote their information products and images. All these examples illustrate the kinds of strategies that can be used to win audiences and create a favorable company image.

PROMOTION AND SALES TO ADVERTISERS

Media companies sell to a second market beyond their viewers, listeners, and readers; they sell to advertisers. Promoting and selling in this market is quite different than selling to consumers. Because the dollars involved are usually large and advertisers have clear alternatives for spending them, the learning hierarchy described early in this chapter best characterizes the process involved in selling advertising. That means that potential advertisers gather solid information about the audience they are buying, and they think a lot about how best to reach that audience before they take action.

It is wisest to think of the purchase of audiences by advertisers in terms of the industrial buying process. In describing this process, additional stages in promotion are added:

- Prospecting: identifying members of the advertiser market particularly interested in the audience a medium offers;
- Qualifying: separating out those prospects who have the financial resources and promotional objectives to effectively use the medium;
- Selling: completing the actual transaction with the potential advertiser;
- Follow-up servicing: carrying out all the steps to actually run the advertisement or commercial in the medium.

This last step is particularly important in selling advertising where, for example, a newspaper works closely with the advertiser at several different times: writing and designing the advertisement, running proof to the advertiser to make sure that the design is correct, then delivering copies when the ad actually appears. Because of the high levels of service involved in advertising sales, relationship building is crucial for developing long-term, sustained bonds between the media and the advertiser.

Tools for Promoting and Selling to Advertisers

The prime tool that media use to reach retailers, the principal source of local advertising revenue, is direct sales calls. However, prior to sales calls, media companies have promotional objectives and strategies for reaching advertisers similar to those employed in consumer promotion (Exhibit 13.7). For instance, advertising in professional publications and in trade journals creates awareness of the media company or reminds advertisers of the station's position in its market. Direct mail advertising, involving letters and brochures, makes advertisers aware of special situations that are developing. For example, brochures are sent to selected advertisers to announce special sections, such as prep sports in the fall, bridal clothing in the winter, and gardening in the spring. Mailings also present price comparisons to alternative media, showing what a "good deal" a given medium provides.

Much specialty advertising goes to advertisers. Coffee mugs, key chains, and planning calendars contain the logo or masthead of a media company and serve as a regular reminder to advertising personnel of the media's presence.

Publicity is also utilized by media companies in their promotion to advertisers. Regular news releases to the trade press and business sections of newspapers describe personnel changes and developments in the media. Feature articles discuss new strategies for using media to reach audiences. Media firms try very hard to get pieces like these into the paper or trade press. These firms also let advertisers know about

EXHIBIT 13.7. PROMOTIONAL TOOLS FOR REACHING ADVERTISERS

Category	*Example*
Advertising	Print ads: trade journals Direct mail Specialty advertising: coffee mugs, key chains, calendars
Publicity	Through media: news releases, feature articles, participation in media competitions Direct to advertisers: gala events to open new facilities or celebrate major anniversaries
Sales promotion	Exhibits at conferences and trade associations Promotional tours and meetings with key contacts
Direct selling	Personal selling Telephone selling Sales-support materials and presentations

their awards and successes. Advertising agencies, in particular, publicize their successful ad campaigns and creative advertising awards they win.

Increasingly, media companies are using "premieres" to attract the attention of the business community. For example, most newspapers, which are older than other media, hold gala events when they have a major birthday (100 or 150 years). And all media celebrate their move into a new facility. These "happenings" are among the classic tools of public relations, and represent an attempt to attach some of the movie world glitter to the other media. With the celebrity quality of some local TV anchors and TV personalities, as well as important disc jockeys and radio personalities, events like these are ready-made for broadcasters.

Sales promotion efforts include appearances at trade association meetings and at national and regional conferences. They are particularly important for media interested in selling national advertising. Meetings with key contacts are another significant sales promotion device. For example, after Simmons (SMMR) completed a national study of newspaper usage for the American Newspaper Publishers Association, the firm conducted a promotional tour making presentations to top ad agencies in a dozen cities. They were alerting agencies to the powerful national audience their clients could reach by purchasing space in a network of newspapers and to a new tool, which compared newspaper and broadcast impact.

Direct selling is still the major promotional and sales tool for reaching advertisers, usually through in-person sales calls. More and more advertisers include telephone selling in the process, however, particularly to qualify prospects identified through direct mail or other means. Much effort is also put into preparing sales support materials, such as rate cards, coverage profiles, and data highlighting the media organization's strengths (i.e., primary features of its audience and important features of the media itself).

Additionally, media companies have become more adept at developing special target selling materials for certain types of potential customers (grocers, financial institutions, automobile dealers, and advertisers who utilize prices in their ads) or for specific major clients. Client-specific presentations may include slides, audio tapes, handouts, and sometimes even videotapes designed specifically for a major client. Major presentations by ad agencies to clients to demonstrate their capability often take the form of dazzling multimedia shows.

Nevertheless, the essence of selling advertising is the direct sales call. Much effort is spent on training, coaching, and working with the sales staff to help them to better understand the product and the people they work with. Sensitivity on both of these subject is crucial in effective selling.

To show how media companies use promotional tools to reach their business customers we offer three vignettes, beginning with a creative strategy adopted by an ad agency.

Increasing Awareness of an Advertising Agency

A medium-sized ad agency experienced moderate growth over the last three years, but it wanted to do better. As a result of a strategic planning effort, the agency set a goal of doubling its business within five years. Background information gathered in the planning process indicated that a major barrier to reaching this goal was lack of awareness of even the existence of the agency in the regional business community. So the first step in the agency's plan was to increase awareness of the firm.

A major part of that effort was its use of extremely innovative billboards rotated around the metropolitan area. The billboards touted the agency to prospective clients with pithy, eye-catching messages. One showed two bicyclists facing in opposite directions. The wheels of the bicycles were not flat pictures on the board; they were real, giant wheels that actually turned. The caption read, "Are you and your agency heading in opposite directions?" Then, in big letters, the name of the agency was shown. Only two boards were purchased, but their location was rotated monthly on major roadways leading into the downtown area. In the next advertising cycle, the agency had two boards constructed with a huge hole ripped out of the center and the broken shards of the hole left in place exposing the inner structure of the board. The message read "Break Through Stuff" and the name of the agency.

The obvious promotional objective was to increase the awareness of the agency, and it was successful. During the first year, 20 specific inquiries resulted from the ads, and the follow-up sales calls and presentations converted eight of those prospects into new clients. In the next two years, new billboards were developed resulting in further inquiries and new clients. By the end of the third year, agency billings had doubled.

Introducing a New Section in a Metropolitan Newspaper

For several years, a major metropolitan U.S. daily contemplated developing a new newspaper section devoted to covering business. After much discussion, management decided to go ahead and to focus the section on regional business matters, but with some information about national and international business trends. The paper's publisher saw an excellent opportunity for attracting more business-to-business advertising with the new section as the vehicle.

The target advertiser market was defined as major national and regional business-to-business accounts: banks, computer supply houses, lawyers, CPAs. The promotional objective was to create awareness of a much stronger advertising vehicle for reaching business leaders in one of the major markets in the country. The promotional strategy involved several phases:

1. A major launch was held in the metropolitan area itself. Business leaders throughout the region were invited to the event, which was accompanied by much fanfare.
2. A "road" show was conducted in New York and Chicago. Major presentations were made to large national and regional companies and ad agencies in these two cities.
3. Ads touting the new section were purchased in a number of major business publications including the *Wall Street Journal*, *Fortune*, and *Business Week*.
4. A consumer ad campaign was developed to attract readership among the business community. A series of TV commercials, emphasizing how "winners" in business and industry would become dependent on this new business section, were aired for six weeks. The consumer ad campaign was seen as an integral part of the strategy so as to attract increased readership for advertisers. In the business/industrial presentations, the TV commercials were shown and the importance of the consumer ad campaign was stressed.

The result of this multifaceted promotional campaign was that advertising revenues exceeded projections by 15 percent for the first year. In addition, the paper signed first-time contracts with 25 large businesses. There is no doubt that the newspaper succeeded in its objective of creating a significant new advertising vehicle to reach the business community.

A Strategy for Selling Yearly Advertising Contracts

A group of fourth-tier suburban weekly newspapers had a problem with their advertisers. Only a few of the local accounts purchased year-long contracts, so the papers were unable to make the long-term financial commitments necessary to increase efficiencies. The lack of annual contracts also made the advertising sales effort much more intensive and difficult; to some degree each merchant advertiser had to be sold anew each week because there was no agreement to advertise regularly.

To turn this tide, the paper established an objective to sell more year-long contracts to its advertisers. The target market was small- and medium-sized retailers. The promotional objective of the strategy was to strengthen the idea of developing a yearly advertising campaign for advertisers with an emphasis on the cost effectiveness of year-long contracts.

The key element in the promotional strategy was that a series of workshops was held on developing more effective advertising. Day-long workshops were conducted in each of the communities served by the chain, featuring a well-known advertising consultant. Businesses were charged a nominal fee for seminar participants. Each business could send as many people as it wished for the same price.

The thrust of the workshop was the key role of year-long planning to create more effective advertising. Through an introduction of a campaign-planning process, spiced with many examples of successful retail advertising campaigns, the concept of advertising as a campaign instead of just a selection of unrelated ads was illustrated. During the workshop, time was set aside for individual consultation with retailers. The consultant showed the merchants how to translate their advertising problems into campaign thinking. A major part of the consultant's message was the cost savings available by planned advertising with year-long contracts.

At the next sales contact after the workshop, advertising representatives gave a yearly planning calendar to the retailers and talked with them about the idea of developing ad campaigns for their stores. The sales manager for the newspaper group went with the sales rep when a retailer expressed interest in the idea of talking about ways to schedule advertising to fulfill campaign objectives. (The newspapers added another "carrot" for advertisers by offering a discount on each inch of advertising for those accounts who signed year-long contracts.) The results of this integrated promotional and selling effort were substantial. Each of the papers increased their contracts by over 50 percent in the next quarter, and one of the papers increased its total by over 150 percent.

These examples illustrate that in promoting a media firm's product (i.e., its audience or service) to the advertiser market, the wide variety of promotional tools available make it possible to develop extremely creative promotional strategies. Moreover, the innovativeness of promotional campaigns aimed at advertisers is bound only by the limits of a company's thinking.

CHAPTER 14
Distribution, Production, and Pricing of Media Products

Media firms differ considerably in the resources they devote to distribution and production. Some, such as daily newspapers, produce and deliver their own products. All firms that handle both of those activities commit major resources to that effort. That is why in *The New Gazette*, described in Chapter 2, 40 percent of the newspaper's expenses were devoted to production and 13 percent to distribution. Additionally, 23 percent of the newspaper's employees worked in production and another 21 percent in distribution.

Broadcast stations, such as KZZZ-FM, do little original production or distribution; most of their effort is devoted to packaging and/or distributing the messages of others. They put together messages, songs, news, and commercials that they receive from outside sources and transmit them to their audience via the air waves. At KZZZ-FM, 20 percent of the station's expenses go for distribution. (That figure includes depreciation of the equipment involved in packaging programs and transmission.) Thirteen percent of the station's employees work in positions involved with distribution.

Advertising agencies, like Williams Advertising described in Chapter 2, create information for other media to distribute. Agency personnel develop the messages, but they usually do very little, if any, final production. Instead, the agency's managers hire outside production houses and printers for those tasks. That is why at Williams, production accounts for only 4 percent of total expenses and only 6 percent of the employees work in production-related jobs. Even they are principally employed as coordinators who work with the outside suppliers.

(While the number of people involved in the coordination function is small, do not minimize the importance of production for advertising agencies. Skillful management of this interface is extremely important, since all of Williams' work on an ad campaign can be destroyed if production of the finished advertisements created by the agency's staff is not effective.)

Once production and distribution decisions have been made, then media managers face one of their most important and difficult decisions: What should be the price of their product? While that decision has many concrete parts, such as the costs of production and distribution, many of its components are illusive, dynamic, and very difficult to discern.

This chapter discusses production, distribution, and pricing. It focuses on key factors media managers take into account as they make decisions about these areas.

PERSPECTIVES FOR VIEWING DISTRIBUTION, PRODUCTION, AND PRICING

Two perspectives are vital to consider when a media manager looks at distribution, production, and pricing of an information firm's product. The first is that the marketing perspective outlined in Chapters 11 and 12 undergirds distribution, production, and pricing. Audience and advertiser wants and needs are crucial in defining both the distribution and production systems a medium develops. In turn, the distribution system shapes the way an information message is finally produced. That is why media managers view both distribution and production as arising out of the marketing perspective.

Second, as we discussed in Chapters 5 and 12, audiences and advertisers seek a balance between quality, price, and service when they purchase or use media products. These three elements provide the standards media executives use for making decisions about distribution, production, and pricing.

The Marketing Perspective Reviewed

Even though distribution follows production in media organizations, we discuss it first before looking at how a media product is produced. Why? Because the marketing perspective defines distribution. Then, distribution sets many of the parameters for production.

The marketing perspective emphasizes that media managers must design their information products with special sensitivity toward what the market wants and needs. That means more than simply assessing the audience's content desires (wants) or judging the views of media executives' about what should be in the information product (needs). To be most effective, the marketing perspective also includes consideration of how and when audience members want to receive messages (distribution), what specific forms the messages should take when they arrive (production), and how much the audience is willing to pay for the information (pricing).

For example, in most two-newspaper markets, afternoon dailies in the U.S. lost circulation during the past decade. As a result many went out of business or were combined with stronger morning newspapers. That happened in large measure because subscribers' preferences changed to morning papers. Similarly, radio audiences shifted from AM to FM stations because FM gave them far better sound reception. Both of these are examples of the impact on distribution of changes in audience wants.

Audience preferences concerning form and quality of production also have major impact. Widespread use of color in television and magazines created a new standard against which consumers now evaluate all visual media. Recently, newspapers responded to that standard with more and higher-quality color in photographs, graphics, and advertisements. In the same manner, high production quality in network television programming set new audience standards for local stations, resulting in increased production costs for local news and program efforts.

Audience and advertiser price sensitivity is important too. Daily newspapers see this graphically when they receive cancellations or a sharp drop-off in renewals after announcing a subscription price increase. They also see it when advertisers down-size their advertisements or shift to the use of preprints after increases in run-of-paper advertising rates are announced. Other media recognize price sensitivity of their products when they raise prices and then encounter unsold commercial time (broadcasting), nonrenewal of subscriptions (magazines and newsletters), and reductions of service contracts (advertising and public relations agencies).

All of this makes the point that to respond to the market, media executives have to look for ways to improve current distribution and production practices or develop new opportunities in both of these areas. They should also understand that the basis for many of their most fundamental decisions is the marketing perspective: it undergirds their decision making about products, promotion, distribution, production, pricing, and change.

Balancing Quality, Service, and Price

If they were asked, audiences and advertisers would prefer that media firms provide high-quality products with timely and effective service at a very low price. Indeed, some media companies do deliver this combination to consumers. Whether it is *The New York Times* or one of the nation's better local or regional newspapers, those information packages are high quality, they are usually delivered on schedule, and the cost to the reader is only for the ink and newsprint in their raw material form. Some television programming is also very high quality, e.g., "Masterpiece Theater," and it is aired on time and for no cost beyond the initial investment in a TV set, electricity, and viewer time. Yet in most instances all three elements—quality, price, and service—cannot be simultaneously maximized. Instead, media executives must establish an imperfect balance among them. The emphasis of one over the others is based on how important each element is to the firm's target audience or its advertisers.

The balance of quality, price, and service is tentatively determined when a media product strategy is developed. Subsequently, that preliminary balance may be changed when the details of distribution and production are finalized. That is because choices about the methods of distribution and production have implications for quality and service. Also, as soon as quality and service objectives are finalized, pricing may change. For example, providing timely service might be far more expensive than anticipated. If that happens, price will rise to offset the cost increases. But a price increase may well reduce the attractiveness of the media product to the audience. In that situation, media managers will launch a thorough review of their goals, objectives, strategies, and action plan.

The key point is that a balance of quality, price, and service must be established, and it should correspond to the target audience's wants and the media managers' best judgments.

The basic role of production and distribution managers is to effectively and efficiently utilize a media firm's resources to meet the quality, price, and service standards set for its information product. In the process, all the firm's resources, people, money, information, service, time, and technology, come into play, but people, technology, and money are the primary ones to consider.

One additional thought: Because distribution and production are so closely connected, decisions about one often impact strongly on the other. For the sake of clarity we discuss them separately in this chapter. As you read the following, however, you should keep their close linkage in mind.

EXHIBIT 14.1. BALANCING QUALITY, PRICE, AND SERVICE

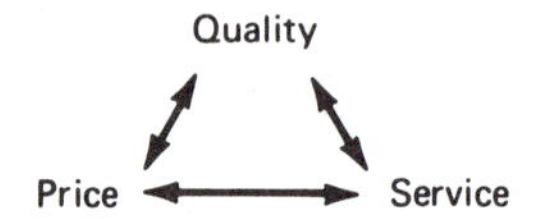

DISTRIBUTION

The Balance of Objectives

The distribution objectives for a media product seldom result in an equal balance between quality, service, and price. Usually one of them is primary.

Quality of Distribution. The idea of high-quality distribution can be confusing because it is sometimes taken to mean "timely and reliable" delivery, i.e., a high level of service. We mean quality in another sense, as the following example illustrates.

A movie theater offers high-quality distribution when it has a large screen, Dolby stereo sound, reclining seats, and an adequate staff to quickly sell popcorn, soft drinks, and candy. Similarly, an electronic data firm offers high-quality distribution when it provides 24-hour-a-day access and is compatible with many different kinds of computer systems. A radio station's distribution is high quality when it broadcasts in stereo and plays compact disks. In each of those examples, audience members are receiving extra "quality" benefits.

By contrast, you can see a classic example of distribution problems if you look at National Public Radio. NPR serves a special niche with comparative class and substance, but its distribution is uneven across the U.S. In some regions it is clear and easily received; in others the listener must put up a high antenna or buy a more powerful receiver because the signal is marginal. Although there is no initial price to receive the NPR signal, the cost to boost the quality of distribution to even a minimal level can be considerable in fringe areas where the listener must purchase extra equipment to hear the broadcasts. Thus, even when the content is fine, if the distribution quality is poor, the benefits for those who want to listen to NPR are reduced.

For advertisers, high-quality distribution occurs when a medium reaches a high proportion of a specialized audience. For example, firms that sell a highly specialized product (a prescription drug that is used only for a children's malady or Rolls Royce automobiles for the rich and famous) want their advertising to reach only a very narrow segment of customers in the marketplace. It is wasteful for Rolls dealers to send an advertisement to anyone who cannot afford a car that sells for more than $100,000. It is equally useless for that drug manufacturer to reach physicians who treat adults. The Rolls or pharmaceutical executives in charge of marketing these products will go to extremes to find a medium with high-quality, finely targeted distribution, e.g., a targeted pediatric medical journal or a mailing list of the wealthiest families in the region.

In both these examples, reaching an audience quickly (good service) or at a low price is meaningless. The drug company does not care if its message arrives quickly; it hopes the drug will be around for years. What the firm wants is for its message to reach the specific group of pediatricians who will use their product. In the same vein, the Rolls dealer would be happy to pay dearly to have its message reach the wealthiest families in its territory. For both the drug company and Rolls, within the triad of quality, service, and price, the quality of distribution is paramount.

Service. Daily news media, both print and electronic, pay primary attention to the service aspect of their distribution efforts. For them, timeliness of delivery is absolutely vital. That is not to say that price and distribution quality do not matter; they do. But if timeliness is not paramount, the news will be out of date, and then price and quality won't matter.

Reliability is another aspect of high-level service. Making sure customers actually receive their product is an ongoing problem for newspapers. The low reliability of carrier-delivery forced some papers to shift entirely to adults for delivery. The lowering of delivery standards by the U.S. Postal Department also reduced the reliability of magazine and newspaper distribution though the mails. Some cable systems have continual problems in delivering signals reliably to customers; that also results in service cancellations.

Price. In other instances, price is a primary concern for members of a media audience. Indeed, the high price of equipment needed to receive Knight-Ridder's Viewtron videotex service was a major factor in the failure of the project. Low-priced theaters thrive by offering slightly older movies (low service) at cut-rate prices. The theaters are not fancy; they often have small screens (low distribution quality), and many are located in inconvenient places requiring considerable driving (low service). Nonetheless, their favorable price attracts a sizeable audience. The advent of inexpensive, mass market paperbacks created a similar new segment of the book industry. Their success is based heavily on their attractive pricing, although ease of purchase in groceries, drug stores, and other outlets (high service) contributes.

Sometimes price is also a dominant consideration for advertisers. Businesses that have a small cash flow, operate on a very slim margin, or are in financial trouble, all fit in this category. Thus, a farm implement dealer who is in financial trouble wants to get a message out, but whether it goes out in the Monday or Thursday edition of a newspaper (timeliness of service), or to just the farmers who may need new or used tractors (quality of distribution) is not paramount. The difference of a few days does not matter. Moreover, there is no way to know which farmers in a region might see the ad and decide to buy a tractor, even if

EXHIBIT 14.2. KEY FEATURES FOR EVALUATING DISTRIBUTION STRATEGIES

Quality
- signal strength and level of "noise"
- accessibility for audience members
- comfort of setting for audience members

Service
- timeliness of information
- reliability of delivery

Price
- capital-equipment costs required for use
- costs for individual messages

they do not perceive a need for such a machine at the moment. What interests the dealer most is getting his message out at the lowest possible cost. Price in the quality, price, and service trio is overriding.

Managing Resources in Distribution

Keeping a media firm's distribution objectives in mind, media managers should organize their firm's resources to accomplish their objectives. In the following we discuss some trends and issues information executives confront as they organize and oversee the distribution of their firm's information product. In it we pay special attention to the resources that are most important when it comes to distribution and production: technology, people, and money.

Technology. Technology can be a crucial factor in distribution. In the "good old days," distribution technology was comparatively simple. Radio and television broadcasters used towers, newspapers used trucks and carriers, and magazines used the U.S. mail and newsstands. Books and films were delivered by distributors to stores, stands, and theaters.

Today all of that is just the beginning. Technology is far more expensive and complex. Moreover, its impact on distribution, for both new opportunities and problems, is extraordinary.

Broadcasters now use not only towers, but microwave relay stations, satellite uplinks and downlinks, cables, and lasers on fiber optics. The print media augment their trucks and young carriers with adult carriers, private mail systems, public mail systems, computers and telecommunications. Even book publishers' channels of distribution have changed. Not only are there far larger distributors, such as huge book chains like B. Dalton and Waldenbooks, but books are found everywhere, from the traditional musty shops to supermarkets and mail order clubs. And, if that weren't enough, new channels for book distribution are bursting on the scene with the advent of books on cassette tape as well as on compact disks where they can be read by a laser on a computer. A few years ago those were unheard of technologies and distribution channels; now they are near commonplace.

A classic example of how the technology of distribution is becoming more complex and expensive can also be seen with records. In the past, music recorded for the general public appeared on records sold in a few exclusive stores. Then came reel-to-reel and, subsequently, cassette tapes. Recently there has been a new explosion of distribution means with the advent of compact disks. It is also not at all unusual to find the same song distributed by an artist live at a concert; then, at virtually the same time, it appears on records, cassette tape, compact disk, videotape, and in a movie. Think of that; six separate ways to achieve distribution of a single song!

Records are not the only medium where technology has provided new avenues of distribution. With the advent of videocassettes, movies are no longer restricted to theaters. Now they can be viewed at home with a VCR or on commercial-free cable channels. Because movie distribution has broadened, the movie-viewing audience has also boomed. Meanwhile, even TV has moved from the early days, when it was VHF-delivered from one station and one tower, to the present where it is delivered in low power or high power, through the air, through cables, or on tape. Similar changes hit text-based news and advertising media; they come carrier delivered, through the mails, and, increasingly, by computer and over phone lines or by satellite.

The preceding examples illustrate the explosion of new distribution technologies. In planning a distribution system, media managers must consider quality, service, and price implications of alternative technologies. However, depending on the nature of their market and product, one of the three dominates here, just as it did in our earlier examples.

Thus, satellite and computer technology now makes it possible to deliver the electronic configuration of pages in *The Wall Street Journal* from New York City to one of Dow Jones's printing plants on the West Coast. The timeliness that the technology of satellites and computers provides is vital to facilitating the newspaper's national distribution. By contrast, *Smithsonian* magazine is not as interested in the speed of the technology's delivery as it is in the quality of picture reproduction from a remote site to the museum's Washington office and then to the reader of the magazine itself. For magazines of the *Smithsonian*'s or *National Geographic*'s caliber, only extraordinary picture content and reproduction are acceptable.

Finally, suppose you produced and distributed fliers for a single neighborhood pizza shop. You would want to blanket the nearby neighborhood with them, but the difference in cost between a motorized adult delivering them and the old-fashioned "technology" of a responsible youngster on a bicycle would quickly rule out the adult. Cost would be the key factor in your decision, and the price of paying an adult for three hours' time and gas cannot be compared to the youngster who will do it for a free pizza.

In each of these examples, some distribution technology is employed. The technology that media managers choose usually depends on whether quality, service, or price dominates.

People. Distribution has a significant impact on human resources. Think how challenging it is to organize and direct the many people involved in a far-flung distribution chain. The people along the chain's links cannot be directly supervised, and many are only part-time employees. When you add to that challenge the fact that much of the chain may be formed by 12-year-old news carriers who are often more difficult to manage than adults, you begin to understand the complexity of the problem.

And the problem does not end there. New organizational structures are required as the distribution system changes; for instance, shifts may necessitate different kinds of employees, such as moving from youngsters to adults to third-party distribution companies. Those changes are likely to be disruptive to a media firm's ability to deliver its product and to employee morale, management training, recruitment, and company plans and policies.

Today, information companies' distribution systems must become more sophisticated. That is true because U.S. consumers increasingly seek higher quality information; that makes the movement toward complexity inexorable. It also necessitates a substantial increase in the technical skills of distribution personnel. Some must now be computer programmers or experts on the mails or telecommunications technicians who run everything from broadcast facilities to satellite delivery equipment. This trend pushes distribution toward higher quality and better service, but at an increased price in salaries and staff education.

That's fine in some instances, but in others, price is more important than quality or service; for example, when the media product cannot bear high distribution costs. That is why many newspapers use young carriers and why small book publishers share the cost of centralized book distributors; both are means to keep the employee costs of distribution low.

In other situations the value and perishability of the organization's information makes timeliness of service the key consideration. Think of Federal Express or any of the costly delivery services. They provide the one thing that short-lived information messages require: extremely rapid delivery. Media firms accomplish a similar goal when they use telecommunications or satellites to deliver information almost instantaneously. In whatever form, rapid delivery requires skilled personnel, which drives up employee costs.

Money. Distribution costs have grown rapidly, putting great pressure on many media products. In fact, their rise killed off some legendary media ventures. *Life* magazine died as a weekly news publication when the mail (distribution) costs rose to a point where other revenues could not keep pace. The same thing is true of Knight-Ridder's and the Times Mirror's initial ventures into videotex and to Rupert Murdoch's withdrawal from the race to establish a direct broadcast satellite (DBS) system across the United States. All those wealthy media giants found that the cost of delivering their messages in a country as large and diverse as America was simply too great for the number of people who were willing to receive that information.

At the same time, distribution advances provided the opportunity to create some new, nationwide, information businesses. The advance of *The Wall Street Journal*, *USA Today*, and *The New York Times* as national newspapers came about because they could be satellite distributed from their home offices to regional printing plants across the country. The same thing is true of the regional editions of *Business Week*, *Time*, or other major magazines. The huge costs to set up and run their distribution systems is paid for by the new markets these national print products reach.

At the same time, some regional newspapers now use their carrier distribution systems to add the "plus business" of delivering magazines. Newspapers also carry preprinted inserts (sections produced outside and stuffed in the newspaper). Retailers such as K-Mart and Sears choose the newspaper as their distributor instead of the post office or direct mail companies like *Advo*. In making that choice, those retailers buy access to the paper's distribution system and then receive a secondary benefit: association with the newspaper.

The same phenomenon is true of motion picture companies, which developed distribution arms to handle their own films as well as movies of other producers. Similarly, several book publishers followed the same course and developed distribution operations. Some of these companies now dwarf the primary publishing (or in the case of cinema, film-making enterprise) that they were formed to assist. In Europe, information distribution flourishes in some ways that are more advanced than in the United States. Rupert Murdoch's Sky Channel and France's videotex are viable operations, which demonstrate that someday these may also be profitable ventures in America.

In all of these instances, the media companies used their costly, increasingly sophisticated distribution systems to generate new income streams. And when they did they were able to finance the increased cost of their distribution and add profit in the process.

The preceding also demonstrates how challenging it is to manage a distribution operation. That is why John Henry, publisher of the *St. Paul Pioneer Press Dispatch*, told journalism students that one of the best ways to get started in a newspaper management career was to begin in circulation. Henry said, "There is no more challenging area of a newspaper. The best circulation managers understand marketing, selling, pricing, managing people, cold calling, delegating, and team building of the most difficult sort of staff: 12-year-olds. They also learn to both appreciate what the newspaper contains and to really listen to the public. All of these are wonderful tools for an eventual publisher to know."

PRODUCTION

The Balance of Standards

Once the market perspective is used to decide who needs what media message (product) and how that message will be delivered, then media executives shift to producing the information. There too, quality, price, and service are the standards, and, again, a balance among them must be developed.

Quality. There are times when the quality of the media's product is paramount to its audience. Remember that in the development of *Pediatric Neurology* the first attempt to produce the journal was on high-grade newsprint. That was a relatively less expensive production method because the journal's publisher owned presses which could do the work.

In fact, however, the idea was quickly discarded because the "look" (the production quality) of the magazine on white newsprint was below the standard of any other publication. In that form, even if the journal had superlative content the marketplace would believe it was inferior. To the audience (physicians and other health professionals), the quality of production and content are far more important than price or timeliness.

For many advertisers, quality production is also a primary consideration. The Rolls Royce advertisements discussed earlier must be exquisitely produced to reinforce the company's overall image. Many national advertisers spend literally millions of dollars on production to guarantee that their TV commercials achieve the highest possible standards. In recent years daily newspapers also spent millions of dollars enhancing their use of color and improving their overall reproduction in order to provide finer production quality for their advertisers and readers.

Service. There are many examples where the timeliness of production (the speed of producing the media product) is the all-important criteria.

One that we vividly recall is the 1986 trek to the North Pole undertaken by a U.S. team led by Will Steger. They were the first group in modern times to reach the North Pole by dogsled, using a route similar to the one Perry followed when the top of the world was first reached. During their two-month odyssey, television crews periodically flew into the Arctic to meet and cover the expedition. The production quality of that TV coverage was, at best, fair. And the price of those "remote" stories was exorbitant because the TV crews had to be flown in and out of a distant place that always had terrible weather resulting in numerous TV equipment problems. The fact is, however, that as long as the pictures made it back to U.S. viewers, their quality meant very little. What counted was that the story of the adventure entered the living rooms of the home TV audience on a real-time basis.

Service is also crucial for many advertisers. The advertisements of grocery, retail, and auto dealers must reach consumers in a timely fashion. Otherwise the merchants' "specials" and "sales" will not attract the customers the businesses need. That is why newspapers, and increasingly local broadcast stations, have adopted late deadlines and have such short production timetables. They want to respond to those advertisers who need timely service.

Price. While timeliness was paramount for the polar trek, in other instances production service and quality count for little. As we said earlier, paperback books built the modern book publishing industry. Before their advent, only a small segment of the population could afford hardcover editions. With the rise of those inexpensive volumes, the number of books produced and sold increased dramatically; so did the number of outlets that carried them. The simple fact is that if a production

---

EXHIBIT 14.3. KEY FEATURES FOR EVALUATING PRODUCTION STRATEGIES

Quality
- reproductive quality
- production features, e.g., color, paper, music, design, technical excellence
- look of the media product

Service
- timeliness of information
- (for advertisers) convenience and reliability in preparing and producing advertisements

Price
- price costs for individual messages
- (for advertisers) pricing options to reach target markets effectively

---

process to manufacture a less expensive book had not been found, the mass book market could not have been tapped. In that instance, "price," not quality or service, would have remained the overriding factor.

Many advertisers are also price conscious. That is what prompted newspapers to offer zoned rates, enabling newspaper advertisers to pay a smaller amount to reach only their primary customers and not readers throughout the paper's entire region. Shortening commercials from 60 to 30 seconds, and now even to 15 seconds, is also in partial response to advertisers' demands to reduce costs. Some advertisers have even shifted out of newspapers, magazines, and broadcast media entirely; they use such media,—direct mail, marriage mail, and telemarketing—to reduce their promotional expenses.

Managing a Media Firm's Production

Just as with distribution, production managers in media companies must organize resources to achieve the company's objectives for quality, service, and price. The same three resources are of principal concern here as they are when media executives consider trends and issues in distribution: technology, people, and money.

Technology. New production technology is a seductive temptation that many managers cannot resist. These executives see "new gadgets" or "wonderful new ways to produce a message" and buy expensive equipment that makes such claims. In fact, production equipment (technology) should be purchased only when it matches the media firm's quality, service, and price objectives and when it links up well with the distribution system used to deliver the company's product to the audience. That latter consideration is particularly important, for when timeliness of delivery counts, media managers face a situation that is different from most other industries. That is, all production processes, systems, and equipment must be designed and built for peak demand, not average usage, if delivery schedules are to be met.

Newspapers and television news operations both face this situation because of the short time between gathering, producing, and delivering the news. The newspaper's presses have to be able to print and collate the peak number of pages required for the largest edition. In the same vein, the television station must have equipment which can cover a natural disaster and deliver that information back to the viewer, even if capacity at that level is seldom used. (Note: These are instances when media companies create the "slack resources," discussed in Chapter 6, to reduce the pressure to coordinate activities across departmental lines. Similarly, excess capacity makes it possible for a pressroom to routinely print editions with extra pages or for the better TV stations to do frequent "live remotes" of stories that otherwise would not necessitate such coverage.)

The investment required to handle peak demand is substantial and making it drives up production costs resulting in increased subscription and/or advertising rates. That is the bad news. The good news is that media managers can often find uses for their excess production capacity to generate new revenue for their firms. Do you remember the example we noted earlier of TV stations that use their studio facilities during slack times to produce commercials or documentaries for private use by other business and industries? Many newspapers also do printing for other companies when their presses are not printing their newspaper.

When media managers make production or technology decisions, they not only create new opportunities but they also set limits for their firms and information products. Each technology presents opportunities, such as increased speed, improved quality, reductions in staffing, or more sophisticated distribution. The very act of adopting a particular technology, however, establishes absolute limits for a variety of factors ranging from the number, type, and configurations of products to their cost and speed of delivery.

Examples of these points come easily to mind. Think of the skilled blue-collar hot-metal printers previously employed at publishing companies. When computers first came out the machines could replace those workers, but they were too expensive and too slow to meet production demands. Then, along came small, fast, dedicated computers and, eventually microcomputers. They were comparatively inexpensive and could be operated by the news staff in place of their typewriters. The micro- and minicomputers enabled reporters to do a better job editing their work. They used sophisticated software to check stories for spelling errors and even grammatical mistakes, thereby reducing the errors discovered during proofreading.

The computer met a need. Newspapers could produce a better product (quality), faster (service), and at a lower cost (price). In the process, production technology came near to achieving a rare balance among the triad, but the cost savings had to come first in order to provide the money to pay off the investment in new technology.

In radio, technological advances enable stations in small communities to buy very sophisticated "packaged" sound, e.g., to import "big city" disc jockeys and more up-to-date music. In many instances, these automated systems replace most of the local radio staff and announcers. The same is true even in talk radio, where national personalities or experts use computers, satellites, and phone lines to give the appearance that they are working at the local station.

Sometimes the new production systems increase the radio station's costs, but that is worthwhile if the station is to maintain high enough quality production to compete successfully with others using a similar format. Saving money or reaching the market in a timely fashion are less important considerations in that situation than quality.

People. Each of the preceding examples signal many changes vis-à-vis media production employees. Where sophisticated computers or satellite-delivered messages are concerned, employees' knowledge and skill must increase. They also must increase when publishers produce complex color printing.

It is ironic, however, that the use of computers by writers has dramatically reduced the skills required in other parts of print media production. In fact, computers for typesetting and automated broadcast systems have eliminated many skilled workers and replaced them, if they are replaced at all, with people who possess only minimal skills. The new print-production employees have to know only how to handle a scissors and stick pieces of paper on a page as if one were doing it in a scrapbook or, in broadcast, push a button when an electronic cue says to. That change in the type of employees required by the media resulted in a significant reduction in production payrolls.

The changes in production personnel also require managers to have more sophisticated people-management skills. Modern production executives must know a great deal about electronics and, often, chemistry, photography, and the more advanced forms of information processing. But more than ever before, they must be skilled in employee training and motivation, for it is no longer the case that employees trained to do one job will spend their careers doing it. The rapid changes in media technology dictate that they will not do the same job for long. In fact, even the structure of production is likely to change in concert with shifts in the functions that production workers perform and in the way these tasks are accomplished. This means that production managers need to adopt a long-term horizon with their employees; they should focus part of their attention on helping their staffs to prepare for the changes that will inevitably occur.

Production changes also have had a visible impact on media unions. In the print industry the user friendliness of new technology eroded the craft unions' power, because media managers could replace skilled printers with comparatively unskilled workers who require little or no training and work for lower pay. At the same time, technological changes gave rise to a new set of unions, many of which deal with the more sophisticated ends of production. Recently, for example, after lengthy negotiations and a number of unsuccessful attempts at merger, the International Typographic Union (the printers of newspapers) merged with the Communication Workers of America, one of the powerful production unions of broadcasting and telecommunications.

Money. Production also has a major impact on the financial resources of many media organizations. As we saw in *The New Gazette*, media companies that produce their own product devote a large proportion of their operating expenses to production. Capital investment for production facilities and equipment is a formidable item for many of these firms.

The advances in technology drive up the cost of most production equipment. Usually, that rise is so rapid and reaches such a high level that media companies cannot accumulate sufficient cash to pay for the equipment. As a result, borrowing to buy new technology gives rise to major interest expense, and it usually encumbers a substantial percentage of the information organization's credit and borrowing capacity.

All of these considerations mean that media managers must allocate money for production not only in terms of increases in productivity and reductions in costs (price), but also with an eye toward opportunities for improved quality, better service, and new income streams. The use of satellites to send the *Wall Street Journal* across the country is an example of spending money for improved service. A magazine publisher's investment in the newest generation of high-quality color separation cameras creates a new business: doing color separations for firms that cannot do work of that caliber, providing an example of spending money for higher-quality production tied to new income potential.

Even when personnel savings are not possible, new production capabilities can pay for themselves by opening new markets. Today many U.S. newspapers employ approximately the same number of staff they did 20 years ago. The difference is that then those workers produced a single newspaper each day; now they daily produce their own paper as well as scores of other products in the same number of hours.

Some production advances do not increase productivity or create additional market opportunities. In these instances money is spent merely to keep the media organization competitive. That phenomenon is commonplace for television stations which buy more advanced color equipment or satellite and remote transmission facilities just to keep up with the competition. Another reason to spend money on production is to improve employee morale. Such an investment may bring no immediate, tangible return, but it can be very important in the overall operation of an information organization.

PRICING

Pricing is very complex. For media firms, it includes setting subscription prices, advertising rates, and fees for extra services (e.g., featured channels on a cable system, such as HBO, the Disney Channel, and Cinemax). In setting a price for a new media product or in changing the price of an existing one, many considerations come into play, some of which require extensive financial analysis.

Pricing is subtle, complex, and dynamic. The pricing decision is crucial, but it is difficult to make because so many of the questions that

EXHIBIT 14.4. MAJOR QUESTIONS TO ANSWER IN PRICING A MEDIA PRODUCT

What are the costs involved in creating, producing, and distributing this product?

What will be the cost of promoting and selling to the audience and to advertisers?

What is the perceived value of the information, now and in the future?

What is the audience willing to pay for the information/entertainment product?

What will competitors do in their pricing?

What technological changes are coming and how will they affect costs and value?

How will suppliers shift their prices?

What interest rates will be charged for borrowing in years to come?

---

must be answered are illusive, as can be seen in Exhibit 14.4. In this section we will touch only on some of the key elements and considerations to take into account as price levels are established.

In two senses price is a dynamic element in the marketing mix. First, the price of a media product must shift in response to changes in competitors' and market's actions and demands. Indeed, in broadcasting, advertising rates can change on a daily basis, because many of them are established through negotiations with specific advertisers and agencies. That is more volatile than in most situations, but advertising rates change regularly in every medium.

The second sense in which price is dynamic is that it is set in a tentative fashion early in a planning process, then it is revised as the process unfolds. A tentative price is established during the strategy stage and then reviewed after the action plan is in concrete form. This iterative process in price setting may involve a number of repeating loops.

The Pricing Process

The description of the process that follows is based on establishing a price for a new medium, but media firms use this same approach when setting and changing their prices for any of their information products.

The first step is to establish a tentative price. Several considerations enter into that:

1. Profit targets for the firm: In considering a new information product, media executives will typically have a profit target in mind. It will be expressed either in a percentage of sales or in absolute numbers. For many new

information products, top management will expect a loss in the first year or two. Even if that is the case, the firm's leaders will set acceptable loss figures and project them out to a point where profits should prevail.

2. Competitors' prices: As media executives develop background information they carefully monitor the pricing levels established by competitors, both for the competitor's product and for the advertising that supports that product. Those prices are usually easy to discover because they often exist in printed form, but true prices may differ substantially from published ones. This is especially likely for broadcast advertising rates and rates for free distribution shoppers. The wise media manager devotes a great deal of effort to determine the true prices that competitors are offering and receiving.
3. Price objectives for the product: A third important element is the price objective set by media managers in the product strategy. As examples earlier in this chapter made clear, the price objective is based on judgments about the price sensitivity of the marketplace. For many media products, product quality and level of service are more important than price in determining consumers' purchase or usage. Thus, media executives should estimate the level of price acceptable to the bulk of their readers, viewers, or listeners. It may or may not be low.

After taking these three considerations into account, media managers establish a tentative price. Recall that for *Pediatric Neurology*, the medical journal, the first, tentative subscription level was set at between 55 and 60 percent of the rate for the larger, adult neurology journals. Based on a rough analysis of the competitors' numbers, that price appeared to be adequate to achieve the firm's major goals of market penetration and profit within a reasonable period.

As action plans are developed, more specific ideas about producing, promoting, and distributing the product come into play. During that phase of the process much more specific financial analysis is done and revenue and expense estimates are calculated. Here is one area where the financial management skills of media managers really count.

1. Revenue estimates: Sales projections grow out of an analysis of relevant target markets, both audience and advertiser. In making these projections, media managers usually set several price levels and then estimate sales volume based on those prices. Often three levels of sales are projected; one is conservative, the second moderate, and the final one optimistic. Wise media leaders seldom rely on optimistic estimates in doing their product planning. Instead, they use the more conservative figures to avoid being carried along in the excitement of launching a new product.

   Sales depend heavily on the success of the firm's promotional strategy. Consequently, sales estimates must take into account the level of promotion the firm will mount and the expected response rates of audience members and advertisers to those promotional efforts. Media firms that regularly develop new products can usually make quite accurate estimates of likely responses to various forms of advertising and promotion. But if an information organization is entering a new market, it is often necessary to check with others in the industry who have experience in a similar venture or with outside experts who can more thoughtfully predict likely response rates.

2. Expense estimates: These grow from analysis of the promotion, production, and distribution plans that media executives establish. Cost estimates are made for each of those activities; again, several sets of numbers are developed to reflect different possibilities for promoting, producing, or distributing the product. The cost estimates that are typically used in further analyses are the high ones, not the low. That tack is followed to avoid being carried along too much by the momentum of an exciting new product.
3. Finally, after media managers have "run the numbers," they compare their projected price level, which is based on their financial analysis, to the tentative price they established when the initial plan was worked out. Sometimes the figures correspond and a real price is easily finalized. More often, however, there is a discrepancy between the two numbers. That's when financial reality sets in and a thorough examination of all goals, objectives, strategies, and action plans may be required. If, after such a review, a substantial discrepancy still exists, it may be necessary to radically modify or scrap the plans for a new information product. When that happens, executives and staff typically feel great sadness and, sometimes, anger because they have all worked so hard on planning the new product. However, prudent information professionals realize that when a product cannot succeed financially it is better to simply drop the idea than to invest further, precious company resources in it.

In closing, let us return to where we began this chapter. Media distribution, production, and pricing are driven by the marketing perspective. They implement a media company's product strategy by turning messages into finished products and delivering them to the audience. The goal in production, distribution, and pricing is to create a product featuring high quality, fine service, and low price. But since it is seldom possible to reach balance among that triad, the wise media manager strives to clearly discern which of the three should be first in priority and why. Whatever priority ordering results, the final balance is best achieved by effectively and efficiently utilizing all the resources of the media firm, especially its technology, people, and money.

CHAPTER 15

The New Gazette: A Case Study for Part Three

The purpose of this case is to provide you with additional depth, understanding, and a hands-on feel about the material you covered in Part Three. Read this case and then work through the assignments at the end of it. That should substantially increase your appreciation of the prime activities of media managers.

THE SITUATION

After working as assistant advertising director of a strong daily newspaper in the West, you've just taken a job as advertising director of *The New Gazette*, a daily newspaper in the fictional town of Garrison, Minnesota. (You may recall that you first encountered *The New Gazette* in Chapter 2. Don't bother rereading that chapter. We provide all the information you need as the case unfolds.)

To begin, read the following background memo which you just received from the *Gazette's* copublishers. The purpose of the memo is to provide you with more depth about your department, the newspaper as a whole, and some of the problems that you will face when you report for your first days at work next week. It is also given to you so you can "hit the deck running" on the problem of a competitor that is challenging the *Gazette*. Finally, it gives you a list of the problems and issues that your new employers want solved as your first order of business when you arrive at the newspaper.

MEMO

TO: You, advertising director of *The New Gazette*
FROM: Copublishers Lavine and Wackman
SUBJECT: Combating the *Zippy Shopper*

BACKGROUND

For many years we and others in the newspaper industry railed against shoppers, claiming that no one asked for them, no one reads them, and no one wants them. Now, this uninvited guest is at the *Gazette's* doorstep as well as the doorsteps of 50,000 households in the Garrison metropolitan area. Our new competitor is not just a minor irritant. It is a foe with ability and strength, and it must be taken seriously.

Profile of The New Gazette

Here are some facts about the paper and the region it serves.

The New Gazette is a daily newspaper published in central Minnesota. We serve the city of Garrison, the city's metropolitan area, and all of Marc and Willow counties as well as parts of seven other counties around Marc and Willow. The *Gazette* has an average daily circulation of 27,500 and is published six days a week, Monday through Friday evening and Saturday morning. A typical issue of the paper is 32 to 44 pages with approximately 45 percent news/editorial content and 55 percent advertising. That translates into about 17 pages of news/editorial content and 21 pages of advertising on a typical day. *The New Gazette* is a broadsheet (full size, not tabloid) publication.

In 1975, when the newspaper was purchased by our present owners, a major newspaper chain, circulation was 23,000. It grew to its present level five years ago and, despite our consistent campaigns, has been stationary ever since. *The New Gazette* is profitable. As can be seen in Exhibit 15.1, pretax profits for the year that ended six months ago were nearly 18 percent on sales of $7 million.

As we face *Zippy Shopper*'s challenge the *Gazette's* strengths include:

1. An advertising department with a well-trained display advertising staff. They are knowledgeable and in a position to expand existing accounts and solicit new business;
2. Resources, though not unlimited, sufficient to expand the newspaper if such expansion makes sense;
3. A solid editorial capacity enabling our news/editorial staff to produce quality content for any new product(s) that it might be prudent to develop;
4. A generally positive image and a reputation for integrity with both readers and advertisers.

EXHIBIT 15.1. INCOME STATEMENT OF *THE NEW GAZETTE*

Income		
Circulation	$1,560,000	
Advertising	4,890,000	
Preprint	620,000	
Total income		$7,070,000
Raw materials expenses (newsprint and ink)	$1,234,000	
Gross margin		$5,836,000
Operating expenses:		
News/editorial	$ 804,000	
Advertising	488,000	
Production	905,000	
Circulation	746,000	
Business and general administrative	$1,410,000	
Total operating expenses	$4,353,000	
Total operating profit		$1,483,000
Nonoperating expenses		
Building depreciation	$ 38,000	
Equipment depreciation	184,000	
Total nonoperating expenses	$ 222,000	
Profit before tax (17.9 percent)		$1,261,000
Taxes	$ 517,000	
Profit after tax		$ 744,000

The Garrison Market

Garrison is located about 75 miles northwest of the Twin Cities of Minneapolis and St. Paul. *The New Gazette*'s coverage area is large and extends mainly to the west of Garrison.

Currently, *Gazette* advertising is divided into two very different-size zones. Zone 1 is the Garrison metro area; it covers a circular region with a 12-mile radius including the city. Circulation in that zone is 24,100 out of about 35,000 households the newspaper covers. That provides a penetration rate of 70 percent.

Population is approximately 115,000 in the Garrison metro area and the Garrison work force includes approximately 56,000 people. The primary industries are manufacturing of heavy machinery and scientific equipment, education (Garrison State University is located in the city), and agriculture on the outer fringe of the metro area. Characteristics of the Garrison metropolitan market (Zone 1) are shown in Exhibit 15.2.

Zone 2 is an area from 12 to 38 miles west of Garrison; circulation in

EXHIBIT 15.2. CHARACTERISTICS OF GARRISON METRO MARKET: ZONE 1

Retailers	
Banks	4
Savings and loans	8
Shopping centers	5
Restaurants	10
Variety stores	4
Chain drug stores	4
Chain supermarkets	8
Other grocers	6
Other branch stores	67
Auto dealers	12
Real estate outlets	8
Other large retailers	14
Total large merchants	150
Total small merchants	750
Metro Area Spending	
Total food sales	$ 115,493,000
Total drug sales	14,526,000
Total retail sales	936,355,000
Total consumer spending	$1,370,000,000

zone 2 is 3,400 out of 12,000 households for a 30 percent penetration rate. Data are not available to show depth or detail for zone 2 villages and townships. We do know that the predominant industry in that region is similar to the outlying sectors of the metro area: crop farming and animal raising. Villages and cities in zone 2 are spread out and sparsely populated in comparison to Garrison; total population is 42,000. The hub of this region appears to be the city of Willow Center, which has 6,000 plus residents and the highest *Gazette* circulation in the zone. Our advertising representatives in the area report that there are a number of mom-and-pop grocery stores, small restaurants, and retail outlets in zone 2, though *Gazette* advertising lineage from them is minimal at present.

Profile of the Zippy Shopper

The *Zippy Shopper* began 11 months ago and claims a circulation of about 48,000, covering the city of Garrison and south toward Minneapolis. That means that the shopper's total circulation is 20,000 more than ours. The *Zippy Shopper* reaches its audience by mail except in the city of Garrison, where it is delivered in the morning by carrier. Our competitor is printed in a plant 30 miles from here.

The *Zippy Shopper* is tabloid in format with lots of spot and process color; it comes out on Tuesdays, the day before Garrison's major grocery advertising day. Our competitor gives away spot color and charges half our process color rate. The *Shopper*'s rates are provided on a rate card, but our account representatives say that *Zippy*'s sales people will discount their rates, depending on the size or importance of the account. On average we estimate that *Shopper* advertisers pay approximately 75 percent of what it would cost them to run the same space with us.

Zippy's total advertising is about 50 percent of the *Gazette*'s on our largest advertising day. The shopper has also taken 50 percent of our preprints by undercutting price. We still have K-Mart and several grocery stores, but the *Zippy Shopper* has Sears plus two major groceries.

Many of the big and small advertisers we've lost appear to be only too happy to leave, despite the business we've helped them develop. Reasons for this include:

- price—the *Shopper* costs less than we do;
- supposed total market coverage by *Zippy* and not by the *Gazette*;
- anger over *The New Gazette*'s "power" and reporting of "bad" news (as an example, the owner of the Ford dealership was livid when we printed the story of his drunk driving conviction on page one);
- desire to cut *The New Gazette* and our big, absentee owners "down to size";
- an honest commitment by some advertisers to foster print media competition in hopes of reducing advertising rates.

Advertising Sales

Further analysis of advertising revenues is found in Exhibit 15.3. Note that 93 percent of the local ad sales were in zone 1, almost entirely in the city of Garrison. By contrast, only 7 percent were in zone 2 that runs to the west of the city, and 70 percent of that 7 percent came from five merchants trying to attract traffic from Garrison. (That means that of the $230,000 of local sales revenue that we receive from zone 2, $161,000 came from five advertisers.)

EXHIBIT 15.3. ADVERTISING REVENUES FOR *THE NEW GAZETTE:* LAST YEAR

	Zone 1	*Zone 2*	*Total*
Local	$3,085,000	$230,000	$3,315,000
Classified and Legal	1,035,000	140,000	1,175,000
National			400,000
Preprints			620,000
Total advertising and preprint sales			$5,510,000

Classified revenue showed slightly less concentration, with about $140,000 (12 percent) coming from zone 2 and an estimated $150,000 from parts of zone 1 that are out beyond the limits of the Garrison metro area.

We have mixed reports on advertiser reaction to the *Zippy Shopper*'s large circulation, its coverage pattern, and its total market coverage. A number of advertisers are not at all interested in reaching as far south of Garrison as the *Zippy* goes. They feel that people from that region bypass area merchants and, once in their cars, go to shopping centers on the northern periphery of the Twin Cities, as reaching them is only a few more minutes driving time. However, there is another large group of advertisers who are very high on the *Zippy Shopper*'s "100 percent market coverage." They do not critically assess where that coverage goes as long as its says 100 percent.

We do not have complete data on the impact of the *Shopper* on our advertising sales, but we know that it has hurt us. We've lost several of our preprint customers, and our local display advertising sales for last quarter were up only 2 percent from the same period one year ago. At the beginning of the year—prior to the advent of *Zippy*—we projected a 13 percent increase for the past quarter, not 2 percent. Maybe business is not as strong as we projected, but a fair assessment would be that the *Shopper* caused between a 7 and 10 percent loss in our local sales. If there is a bright spot in all of this, it is that our classified sales fell only 4 percent short of projections. That would appear to mean that the *Zippy Shopper* has not had major impact in classified so far, which is usually a strength of shoppers. (We do not understand the reason for that trend, but it is certainly something to be explored and, perhaps, exploited, in the positive sense of that term.)

Organization of Advertising Department

You will find the organization of our advertising department in Exhibit 15.4. It has 17 full-time sales personnel; 1 national and 10 local representatives sell display and preprint advertising while six full-time representatives sell classified. Two part-time staff members also work in classified. Besides their managerial duties, each of your subdepartment managers either sells, creates advertising designs, or functions as a working manager in dispatch. Your sales force generates about $5.5 million in sales of display, preprint, and classified advertising.

The geographic dispersal, demographics, and background of your staff may contribute to the heavy concentration of sales in zone 1. All but one of the display advertising staff live in the city of Garrison; four of the six full-time classified sales representatives also reside here. The average age of display sales personnel is 28, and three-quarters of them have been with the newspaper for three years or less. Two-thirds of your employees are college educated, and only two of them were raised in this region. By contrast, the average age of the classified staff is 38;

EXHIBIT 15.4. ORGANIZATION CHART OF THE ADVERTISING DEPARTMENT

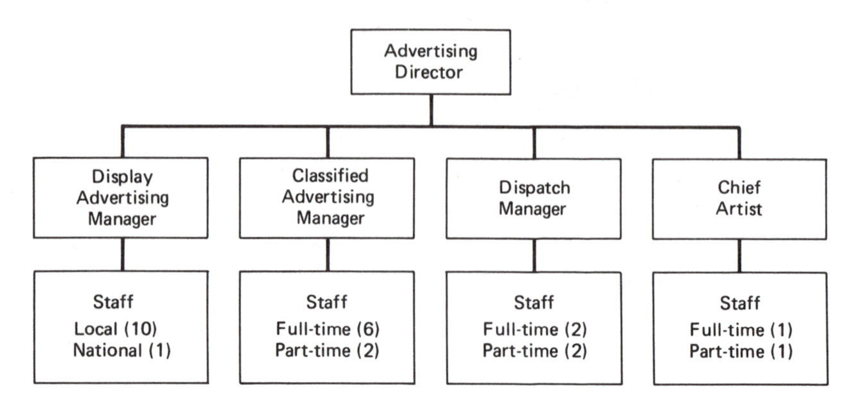

most are high school educated and female, on average they joined us within the last four years, and all but one of them were raised here.

Thus, the display sales reps have more formal education, but they do not really know the merchants in zone 2 communities. They also have comparatively short tenure at *The New Gazette*, they are new to the region, and they do not live in zone 2. Classified ad reps are reasonably well trained; they have little formal education, but they do know about the towns and people in zones 1 and 2.

Expenses of the advertising department are shown in Exhibit 15.5. Subdepartment managers' salaries range from $20,000 to $30,000, averaging about $25,000. Display advertising representatives earn salaries ranging from $10,000 to $15,000 per year (average = $12,500) and a 1

EXHIBIT 15.5. ADVERTISING DEPARTMENT EXPENSES

Salary: advertising director	$ 43,000
Salary: subdepartment managers	101,000
Salary: staff	214,000
Commissions	40,000
Printing and art services	58,000
Auto expenses	12,000
Entertainment	10,000
Sales support materials	8,000
Miscellaneous	2,000
Total	$488,000

percent commission on sales. Classified sales personnel are on straight salary, averaging $11,000. Promotional expenses include entertainment and sales support materials, but no money was spent last year in other promotional efforts such as advertising in other media, direct mail, and how-to clinics for accounts.

TENTATIVE CONCLUSIONS AND GOALS

1. The *Zippy Shopper* poses a very real and immediate threat to our advertising and circulation base. It also bodes ill for the long-term health of our franchise unless we are willing to acknowledge it, face it, and do something about it.
2. Zippy is not going to fold tomorrow and, in fact, will probably grow, as it appears to have adequate financial backing and, from its inception, established a presence for readers and advertisers. The *Shopper*'s readers are already accustomed to receiving it on Tuesday mornings, and its advertisers are used to its lower rates.
3. A realistic appraisal of *The New Gazette*'s position in the market relative to the *Zippy Shopper* suggests that our short-term goals should be to protect our franchise and sustain current profitability. The previous advertising director's delay in responding to the *Shopper*—a grievous error—cost us dearly in both revenue and market share; it also makes regaining that lost ground far more difficult because we are so late.
4. In the long term, our goal should be to expand the *Gazette* franchise and improve profitability, but for the immediate future our posture should be as much defensive as it is offensive.

BASIC STRATEGY

As the *Gazette*'s publishers, we have decided to develop a nonduplicating coverage (NDC) shopper to be published on Tuesday, competing head-to-head with the *Zippy Shopper*. For our subscribers the NDC section will be inserted into home-delivered copies of the newspaper. It will be sent to nonsubscribers by mail on Tuesdays. We made that decision because we believe launching a shopper of our own provides a solid opportunity to substantially increase advertising revenues in the outlying areas. We have three reasons for that conclusion:

1. Penetration rates in areas outside of Garrison range from 25 to 42 percent, compared to 80 percent in the Garrison city zone. Our NDC shopper will provide 100 percent coverage of that territory.
2. Competition other than from the *Shopper* is minimal, except in southern Marc County, where we face not only *Zippy*, but also the Twin Cities' newspapers. In the other outlying areas, however, there are no major competing publications. (And, as you will see below, we will minimize the

problems of competition from the Twin Cities by not extending our shopper's coverage as far south as does *Zippy* because we believe that circulation in that area does not serve our present or potential advertisers.)

3. One significant reason for the lack of *Gazette* advertising in areas outside of Garrison is because our sales personnel do not live there. Because the staff is so concentrated in Garrison itself they have put minimal effort into outlying areas, particularly in zone 2, to the west.

To capitalize on our new opportunity in the outlying western areas we have decided to establish five zones instead of our present two. The present zone 1 will be broken up into three areas: a city zone with a population of 23,000 households and two outlying zones. The current zone 2 will be divided into two smaller zones. All four outlying zones will contain about 6,000 households. Advertisers will be able to purchase a single zone, combinations of any two or three zones, or all of the zones. Moreover, as noted above, our zones will not extend as far south toward Minneapolis and St. Paul as does our competition's. We will have the same total circulation as *Zippy*, but it will be more to the west, which is a market that can really serve our present advertisers and those we hope to develop in that region. At the same time this should give us a major selling point against our competition.

YOUR TASK

As you come on-board as our new advertising director, we would like you to create a promotion and selling strategy aimed at *advertisers*, especially those in outlying areas. The point of that campaign should be to sell the new 100-percent-coverage NDC shopper we are launching. Then, develop and put into operation an action plan to implement your strategy.

Promotion and Sales Strategy

So that we may understand how you are proceeding, please answer the following questions. That is, outline your strategy, and be sure that with each response you provide a rationale for your answer. Also, at the end, tell us the overall rationale for your promotion and sales strategy.

1. How should *The New Gazette* segment our advertiser market in planning our promotion and sales strategy? Should we do it only by geographic considerations or by size and/or type of advertiser, such as grocery, auto, bank, etc., or in some other way(s)? (Review Chapter 12 if you need more background information for this question.)
2. What kind of promotional vehicles will you use to reach the different segments you have identified: direct mail, announcements and ads in the *Gazette*, publicity events, telemarketing, personal sales call, other? (Review Chapter 13 for more information on this question.)

3. What types of promotional and sales support materials do you need to develop: ads, brochures, mock-ups of the new sections, rate cards, maps of coverage areas, other?
4. What needs to be done to minimize the negative impact on your current advertising sales and to increase your sales potential with your current advertisers?
5. Last year classified advertising sales were almost $1.2 million; slightly more than 20 percent of total advertising revenues. What special promotional efforts need to be developed to make classified advertisers aware of our new NDC shopper?
6. Preprint revenues were over $600,000 last year; about 12 percent of total advertising revenue. What special promotional efforts need to be developed for current and potentially new preprint customers? Also, should *The New Gazette* include preprints in the new NDC shopper?

Action Plan

Develop an organizational plan for the advertising department to implement your promotion and sales strategies. When you do that, please respond to the following questions:

1. How should we organize the selling effort in areas beyond the Garrison city zone?
   a. Should we use full-time or part-time staff members?
   b. How many people will we need?
   c. Should some of the current sales reps be encouraged to move from Garrison into outlying communities? How can this be done: by assignment, by monetary incentives, by hiring new sales reps when others leave? Are there any legal concerns with making policies of this sort?
   d. Should we consider shifting our classified sales reps who live in the western area over to display sales? What training and what kinds of incentives will they need to agree to this change?
   e. If we decide to hire some new sales reps, what should their educational background and experience be? Where should we go to recruit them?
2. Should we open sales offices in each of the four outlying zones? What are the advantages and disadvantages of making such a move? (Consider such issues as costs, coordination, and control.)
3. Should we make a dramatic move and reorganize the advertising department entirely? For example, should we switch to zone structure rather than the functional one we now use? That is, should we replace the subdepartments of display, classified, art, and dispatch with a structure that clusters sales people by zones, not by the types of advertising they sell? In that configuration, all sales people could handle both display and classified, or we could assign separate personnel to each type of advertising. What are the advantages and disadvantages of each form of organization? What management positions would be needed in the new structure?
4. Does someone need to be assigned to a full-time job of developing and carrying out a promotional plan for our new shopper? What would a job description be for this position?
5. Develop a rough budget for the promotional efforts you outlined earlier.

(Call local advertising agencies, printers, and other vendors for cost estimates of direct mail expenses, brochure costs, rate cards, specialty advertising options.) Where you cannot get specific figures tell us at least what the cost factors will be.

6. How should we change the salary structure to provide greater and more meaningful incentives for your department's personnel? Should those changes apply only to sales staff or to all staff? If you do extend them to people who are not involved in sales, what sort of incentives do you propose for nonsales personnel? How will your staff be involved in developing a new salary structure, if at all? Finally, what impact would the salary plan you propose have on the overall budget of your department?

Optional

Some instructors may wish to create a more complete case study for the NDC shopper. We have provided the following financial and employment data for your use.

EXHIBIT 15.6. TOTAL REVENUE AND EXPENSE FIGURES

Revenue	$3,333,333	$3,333,333
Local advertising revenue	$3,273,700	
National advertising revenue	386,000	
Classified advertising revenue	1,044,300	
Legal advertising revenue	104,500	
Color comic revenue	4,100	
Total ROP advertising revenue		$4,812,600
Preprint revenue		596,700
Circulation revenue		1,560,200
Miscellaneous revenue		39,300
Total revenue		$7,009,300
Expenses		
News/editorial	$ 804,100	
Advertising	487,600	
Production	905,100	
Circulation	746,300	
Newsprint, ink, and handling	1,233,600	
General and administrative	1,407,200	
Total operating expenses		$5,583,900
Building depreciation	38,000	
Equipment depreciation	$ 187,500	
Total nonoperating expenses		$225,700
Total expenses		$5,809,600
Profit		$1,199,700

EXHIBIT 15.7. NEWS/EDITORIAL DEPARTMENT

News/editorial expense	$804,100
News/editorial expense as % of total revenue	11.5%
News/editorial salaries	$579,300
Number of news/editorial employees (The / divides full- and part-time)	32/5
Typical salary of news/editorial employee (Divide number of employees into payroll with two part-time equaling one full-time)	$16,791
Other news/editorial expenses (less payroll)	$224,800
News/editorial cost/subscriber	$23.65
News/editorial salaries/subscriber (Salaries divided by circulation)	$17.04
Other news/editorial expenses/subscriber (Other expenses divided by circulation)	$6.61
Pages of news/editorial content	5,848
News/editorial cost/page (Total news/editorial cost divided by number of news/editorial pages)	$137.50

EXHIBIT 15.8. ADVERTISING DEPARTMENT

Total ROP advertising revenue	$4,812,600
Total advertising revenue/subscriber (Homeprint revenue divided by circulation)	$141.46
Total advertising inches sold	1,168,800
Total ad revenue/inch	$4.11
Local advertising revenue	$3,273,700
Local as % of ROP	68.1%
Local inches sold	818,100
Local advertising revenue/inches	$4.00
National advertising revenue	$386,000
National as % of ROP	8.1%
National inches sold	70,000
National advertising revenue/inches	$5.51
Classified revenue	$1,044,300
Classified as % of ROP	21.7%
Classified inches sold	252,400
Classified revenue/inches	$4.14
Legal advertising revenue	$104,500
Legal as % of ROP	2.2%
Legal advertising inches sold	28,000
Legal advertising revenue/inches	$3.73

Exhibit 15.8 continued on page 346

EXHIBIT 15.8. ADVERTISING DEPARTMENT (*cont.*)

Color comic revenue	$4,100
Color comic inches	758
Color comic revenue/inches	$5.41
Total preprint revenue	$596,700
Advertising department expense	$487,600
Advertising department expense as % of total revenue	7.0%
Advertising department salaries	$390,600
Advertising department employees	25/4
Typical advertising department salary	$14,466
Advertising department other expenses (Advertising expenses less salaries)	$97,000
Advertising as % of total space	53.6%
Pages of unpaid advertising	257

EXHIBIT 15.9. PRODUCTION DEPARTMENT

Mechanical expense	$905,100
Mechanical expense as % of total revenue	12.9%
Mechanical payroll	$636,300
Other mechanical expenses (Expense less payroll)	$268,800
Mechanical supply cost/page	$10.89
Mechanical cost/page	$69.70
Mechanical hours/page	5.1
Mechanical cost/subscribers	$26.62
Newsprint, ink, and handling cost/subscriber	$36.28
Mechanical, newsprint, and ink cost/subscribers	$62.90
Newsprint, ink, and handling as % of total revenue	17.6%
Tons of newsprint used	2,762
Approximate price per ton	$446.60
Lbs. of newsprint used	5,524,000
Number of homeprint pages	12,985
Number of printed pages (Pages x circulation)	441,490,000
Pages/lb.	79.9
% of newsprint waste	3.0%
Composing room expense	$540,200
Composing room expense as % total revenue	7.7%
Composing room payroll	$425,900
Composing room employees	22/2
Approximate salary	$18,517

EXHIBIT 15.9. PRODUCTION DEPARTMENT *(cont.)*

Other composing room expenses (Expense less payroll)	$114,300
Composing room supply cost/page	$4.94
Composing room payroll	$425,900
Composing room employees	22/2
Approximate salary	$18,517
Composing journeyman's scale/hour	$8.56
Approximate salary	$17,805
Composing pay/page	$32.80
Composing room productive hours	42,700
Composing pay/productive hours	$9.97
Composing room productive hours/page	3.3
Other mechanical expense	$364,900
Other mechanical expense as % of total revenue	5.2%
Other mechanical payroll	$210,400
Other mechanical employees	12/0
Approximate salary	$17,534
Other mechanical expense (Expense less payroll)	$154,500
Other mechanical supply costs/page	$5.97
Other mechanical pay/page	$16.20
Other mechanical productive hours/page	1.9

EXHIBIT 15.10. CIRCULATION DEPARTMENT

Circulation revenue	$1,560,200
% of total revenue	22.3%
Circulation and distribution expense	$746,300
% of total revenue	10.6%
% of circulation revenue	47.8%
Net circulation revenue	$813,900
Circulation revenue/subscriber	$45.89
Circulation and distribution expense/subscriber	$21.95
Net revenue/subscriber	$23.94
Average weekly net revenue/subscriber	$0.46
Circulation and distribution salaries	$318,000
Circulation and distribution employees (The / divides full- and part-time)	17/26
Circulation and distribution expenses other than salaries (Total expense less salaries)	$428,300
Newsprint, ink and handling expense	$1,233,600
Newsprint, ink and handling expense/subscriber	$36.28
Net circulation revenue less newsprint expense/subscriber	$60.46

EXHIBIT 15.11. GENERAL AND ADMINISTRATIVE

Circulation	34,000
Total revenue	$7,009,300
Total expense	$5,809,600
Apparent gross profit	$1,119,700
Apparent gross profit as % of total revenue	17.1%
Newspaper payroll as % of total revenue	33.4%
Newsprint, ink, and handling expense	$1,233,600
Newsprint, ink, and handling expense as % of total revenue	17.6%
Total revenue/subscriber (Total revenue divided by circulation)	$206.16
Total expense/subscriber (Total expense divided by circulation)	$170.74
Apparent profit/subscriber (Profit divided by circulation)	$35.42
General and administrative expense	$1,632,900
General and administrative expense as % of total revenue	23.3%
Building depreciation	$38,200
Building depreciation as % of total revenue	0.5%
Other depreciation	$183,500
Other depreciation as % of total revenue	2.6%
General and administrative payroll	$417,600
Other general and administrative expense (Expense less payroll and depreciation)	$993,600
Pages of news content	5,848
Pages of ad content	6,957
Advertising as % of total homeprint space	53.6%
Pages of unpaid advertising	257
Total revenue	$7,009,300
Total operating expense (Total expense less depreciation)	$5,583,900
Operating profit (Subcription operating expense from total revenue)	$1,425,400
% Operating profit	20.3%

EXHIBIT 15.12. NONOPERATING ITEMS

Building depreciation	$38,200
Building depreciation as % of total revenue	0.5%
Other depreciation	$183,500
Other depreciation as % of total revenue	2.6%

PART FOUR

A Management Perspective on Legal and Social Responsibility Issues

CHAPTER 16

Media Managers and the Legal Issues that Confront Media Companies

Similar legal and regulatory issues face executives in every medium. Despite recent deregulation trends, including the loosening of some limits on television, radio, and cable by the Federal Communications Commission (FCC), the United States is a litigious society. All business executives confront increasing local, state, and federal statutes and rules. Added to those general constraints are the special ones directed only at those who gather, produce, and distribute information. Media-specific statues arise from the Constitutional protection afforded the press and from the media's visibility and unique role in American society and culture.

The challenge for information executives is to recognize that when they respond to laws and regulations, they should base their reactions on a high level of lay knowledge of the law, and on a well-developed managerial perspective towards legal matters. The principles undergirding such an approach are listed in Exhibit 16.1.

Examples of a managerial perspective toward legal matters abound. Suppose a major advertiser, say an auto dealer, wants the local newspaper to keep his ugly divorce out of the paper. At the same time the editor is told by the courthouse reporter that the divorce settlement was larger than any in recent memory and that the court hearing lasted a full week, not the typical day or two. Further, the advertiser's liaisons with several prominent married local citizens were documented in open court during the trial.

The expedient route would be to cave in to the advertiser's demand.

EXHIBIT 16.1. MANAGERIAL PRINCIPLES FOR LEGAL MATTERS

Prevention. Most problems related to legal and regulatory matters can be avoided.

The importance of a reasonable, swift response. When difficulties with statutes or regulations do arise, handling them rapidly and reasonably is the best way for information executives to protect the health and viability of their firms.

A tough, unyielding attitude towards negotiating basic values. When important values are at risk, toughness and an unyielding attitude should be the executive's stance. Allowing key values to erode for the sake of expediency or short-term monetary gain will undermine the executive's own company in the long run, and also the medium in which it exists.

The wise route would be for the editor, advertising manager, or publisher to patiently explain to the auto dealer that the newspaper makes no exceptions; it runs all major cases where the court reaches a verdict.

The newspaper executive should also note that if this story was not run, everyone in the region would wonder what else was being kept from the public, since rumors about the trial were "all over town." That would undermine the newspaper's credibility and, in the long run, fewer people would subscribe, which would diminish the effectiveness of the advertisements the auto dealer put in the paper.

Therefore, the paper should run the story about the divorce. Not publishing it might protect the auto dealer's billings in the short run, but the newspaper would risk losing far more money over time because word would quickly spread that an advertiser had strong-armed the newspaper's management. That sort of information is a cancer that eats away the strength of any media firm. Furthermore, when the auto dealer's anger cools, he will probably resume advertising. After all, his competition will continue to use the newspaper. Can he afford to be absent from its columns for a long time?

Although protecting a basic value demands toughness, that strength should be mixed with healthy doses of reasonableness, for example, when media managers must balance societal values against those of their medium. Recently the leaders of a number of media outlets decided not to report kidnappings in process if doing so would jeopardize the victims. The media have—and must preserve—the right to report such crimes, but just because they *can* broadcast or print a kidnap story does not mean that news directors or editors will exercise that prerogative. They may decide not to do so as a matter of choice and moral imperative.

Other situations do not involve values, but matters of fact, interpretation, or style. For instance, when a citizen comes to complain about how a story is covered or about a fact in a story, editors and reporters have a choice. They can be contentious, curt, or even rude. Or they can be sympathetic, responsive, and interested. The advantage of the latter position is that news executives may learn something.

That was how a smart news director we know responded when a citizen complained about the station's handling of the citizen's testimony at a rate hearing. The news director listened carefully, then told the man who was upset that she would follow up on the points raised. Next, she talked to the reporter who had covered the hearing, and discovered that the staff member missed some subtle but important aspects of the story. The reporter agreed to listen to tapes of the testimony and to call the complainant. The next day the reporter submitted a story that elaborated on the complainant's testimony and included further comments from several other expert witnesses. The second story added an important new dimension to the station's coverage of the rate-setting process.

Another common situation involves violations of open meeting statutes. In every state, information companies have access to government's actions via open meetings and open records laws. Violation of those statutes by governmental authorities provides grounds for prosecution. Instead of rushing to prosecute officials who make an innocent error, however, many media executives first consider the legal cost and time involved. Then, unless the news value of the story is very high, they talk with the governmental officials and warn them that if access is denied again, the media executives will prosecute.

Another approach is to publish stories about apparent violations of the open meeting or record laws, so the public will know that their officials are preventing the media from telling citizens what their government is doing. Oftentimes, public exposure is enough to cause officials to back down and let reporters do their job. We know of numerous instances where meetings were rescheduled or otherwise changed to open them to the public in response to a story or broadcast.

Similarly, we recall the time when Carol Rydsack, a *Shawano* (Wisconsin) *Evening Leader* reporter/photographer, reported the trial of some tough political extremists. During the course of the hearing a few supporters of the defendants threatened the award-winning photojournalist with bodily harm if she continued to cover the trial. Rydsack's editor put an account of the threat on the front page next to the story and photo about that day's trial proceedings. Thereafter the defendants and their supporters went out of their way to treat Rydsack with particular courtesy and concern, for they correctly feared that if anything happened to the journalist they and their cause would lose favor with the public and the rest of the press corps.

PREVENTING LEGAL PROBLEMS

How do media managers carry out the first facet of the managerial perspective: prevention? A fundamental is for media executives to possess a fine working knowledge of the thrust of the laws and regulations that govern their personnel and operations. One does not have to go to law school to learn a great deal about the comparatively narrow section of the law that deals with the press. That alone is not adequate, however; other elements are involved.

To begin with, information organization managers should assess whether their attitude toward the law is defensive or reactive. For example, does a leader of an investigative team say that the team should "get the story at all costs and worry about being sued later?" Or does she say, "Look, we have a job to do and I want you to get the story. But remember, the individuals we cover have the same rights that are important to each of us. I expect you to know what those rights are and to talk with me if you have any questions about them. I also expect each of us to do our job and still not breach those protections. If you trample on people's rights, I will not only scrub the story, but you will, for sure, be off this team, and I will recommend that you lose your job at the station. That's how seriously I take the dual goal of doing our job but doing it within the law, and I am sure that I reflect the feelings of our senior management when I tell you this."

Such an admonition highlights how media executives can often act preventively, well in advance of the time when problems could arise. That is why the investigative team leader, and every media manager, should always ask new employees what they know about such things as false claims about products, antitrust, invasion of privacy, libel, and slander. It is also the manager's responsibility to observe whether older staffers remember what they have been taught about these things or whether senior staff may have developed some bad habits that need straightening out.

There are many ways to develop a preventive orientation toward matters of media law. Some of the better ones include holding regular in-service training to increase staffers' awareness of legal issues and company policies; bringing in experts to talk about those issues; having senior management congratulate staffers who avoided a difficult situation by being aware of legal or individual rights.

It is true that any individual or business can sue an information firm, even if there isn't a justifiable claim. Yet it is also a fact that effective executives can reduce the likelihood of suits by sensitizing their staffs to the limits and issues involved in carrying out their work. Another effective method of instilling the importance of prevention is for the staff and managers to set up hypothetical situations and solve them so that everyone will learn what is appropriate and what is inappropriate before they encounter legal trouble in their work.

On a related front, prevention is the reason a Boston attorney we know spends full time verifying advertising claims made by a huge corporation. If the claims in its ads are false or deceptive, the company and its advertising agency want to face that fact before the ads reach the public, not afterwards. At that point, lawsuits and the cost of defending those suits can far outstrip the comparatively modest salary of the in-house watchdog attorney.

In summary, although few legal problems reach a media manager before the fact, almost every legal action arises because of what an employee of an information company did or failed to do. Ongoing training about corporate, employee, news/editorial, and advertising law can, therefore, reduce or eliminate the likelihood of a firm having to face legal claims. Moreover, since employees and laws that affect the media both change regularly, knowledge must be constantly updated and taught to everyone on the staff.

DEALING WITH LEGAL PROBLEMS THAT ARISE

Even after adopting such a philosophy, a legal matter may erupt. If it does, media managers have guidelines they can follow.

When the firm is contacted, a high-ranking executive should respond immediately. Most threats of legal action diminish or evaporate if the reader, viewer, subscriber, or client feel the organization is responsive. Even if the media firm's answer is negative, the importance of a rapid response is crucial. People's anger increases if no one considers their complaint. Also, when the media make a mistake, the pain of that error doubles for each time period that it is not corrected.

For any media firm to be responsive, employees at every level must know that immediately telling top management about potential legal threats is mandatory and that the top priority for everyone, beginning with the person in charge, is to develop a rapid response.

Media executives should identify competent counsel in each of the subject areas where their firm may run into problems. It is one thing to have a general practice lawyer handle routine business matters. But becoming an expert in libel, antitrust, or affirmative action law requires just what that term implies: expertise. That means that the attorney should have special, in-depth knowledge, and extensive, ongoing experience with those sorts of issues.

Even though specialists charge more per hour, they do not necessarily cost more. Why is that seeming contradiction true? Here is a simple example: An attorney we know who is a libel expert was called by a client about a potential problem. In that 20-minute phone call the lawyer came up with a suggestion that minimized the chances of a lawsuit. The expert knew all that was necessary to work things out. The cost for the expert at $200 per hour: $65. By contrast, a lawyer who seldom deals with such matters would have to spend at least half a day doing research in the law library. Although the generalist charges only $75 per hour, the fee for the generalist's four hours of research and a one-hour phone call is $375.

Perhaps more significantly, the quality of the general practice attorney's work is likely to be far below the expert's; the less experienced lawyer might miss an important subtlety, even after hours of study. Moreover, the chance of winning if a suit is actually filed and the matter goes to court is far better if the expert is in charge.

Having praised experts, it is also prudent for information executives to understand that sometimes they must make business decisions that ignore their lawyer's advice. Such decisions should not take precedence casually or frequently, but at times they should prevail.

To highlight that point, we know a lawyer who negotiated a purchase contract with a paper supplier for a magazine. The contract was legal, sound, and contained very low prices. Nonetheless, the magazine publisher rejected it because the executive's staff had encountered increasing quality problems with the paper supplier. As a way of handling the mounting quality difficulties, the lawyer negotiated severe penalties if there were further problems with the paper. Yet in the end the publisher rejected the pact because the morale of the magazine's editorial and production staffs was at an all-time low from dealing with defective paper. No contract provisions, even very tough ones, were worth the continuing morale concerns. The wise business decision was to buy paper from another vendor, even though it had to be purchased at a higher price.

Note also that lawyers usually do a much better job if they have interested, involved clients. This does not mean that media executives should take on the role of legal counsel. Absolutely not. What it does mean, however, is that the knowledge of an informed manager complements the lawyer's expertise, but does not supplant it.

Because media managers have expertise in running a department or a whole media firm, they can often provide valuable knowledge to add to the attorney's thinking. For instance, they may raise questions or suggest nuances or point out connections from an operating viewpoint that the lawyer might miss or could not know. It is from that experience, not knowledge of the law, that the sensitive client can sometimes propose scenarios that the lawyer might otherwise miss or provide information that the attorney cannot obtain.

Take the situation facing the son of a newspaper publisher who had recently died. Shortly after his father's death the young man received a walloping estimated valuation from the Internal Revenue Service (IRS) on the worth of the two small newspapers he inherited. The valuation was three or four times greater than the fair market value for the properties. It was justified by the IRS, however, on the basis of a "list of comparables," that is, newspapers in seven states of the same size that were sold in the past three years for similarly high amounts.

The tax lawyers handling the estate for the young man were stymied; they knew that the IRS would produce sales records of similar newspapers if the matter went to court. (The Internal Revenue Service had to have real transactions because there was the possibility that their valuation could be contested and end up in federal court, where the federal tax agency would have to provide the basis of its claim.)

The young publisher's attorneys proposed that their client try to negotiate a settlement which would lower the value to a point somewhere between what the IRS wanted and the real market value. The young man said that was not fair; such a payment would still be excessive. Moreover, given the lack of cash in the estate, he would have to sell one of the newspapers just to generate the cash to pay the tax.

The lawyers said that the only other way out was to show the Internal Revenue Service that its "comparables" were not comparable to the young man's newspapers. That gave the young publisher an idea. Over the next few weeks he telephoned friends of his father in each of the states where the IRS said it had similar sales. Those publishers were able to tell their young caller who had sold those papers and who purchased them. The young man then called either the selling or purchasing party and asked if there was anything involved in the sale that made it out of the ordinary.

In each case the answer was affirmative. In one, the sale included the newspaper and a large section of downtown real estate. In another it included the paper and a significant ownership interest in a highly profitable television station. When the young man finished, the IRS list of comparables was changed into a list of noncomparables.

Developing a counterargument could not have been done by the lawyers. The client was the only one who could get the information because only he could use long-time family friendships and professional associations to collect the needed information. When the young man's lawyers presented the results of their client's calls to the IRS agent in change of the case, the agent capitulated; he agreed on a lower, fair market value for the newspapers.

Let us again stress that even in this situation, the young publisher was not his own lawyer nor did his actions alone carry the day, though they certainly were helpful. As is true of most estates that contain an ongoing business, determining the value of the enterprise was only one of the important issues involved in the estate's settlement. The young man helped with that matter, but he did not replace his lawyers. Moreover, he had no knowledge of the other tax law that was necessary for settling the overall estate case. What he did was help his attorney; that was his only role.

Building on the principles we suggested earlier, there are some other lessons in this situation. First is that the young man's general counsel brought in lawyers who specialized in handling tax matters. That saved time and money. It also ensured that the young man would be well represented. Second, everyone remained reasonable and levelheaded even though the emotions of the moment, both from the father's death and the disagreements with the IRS, were high.

There is one other lesson. It falls outside the perspective with which we began this chapter, but it is important for all people in business to bear in mind when dealing with the Internal Revenue Service and with some other regulatory agencies. That lesson is that in many situations the burden of proof is on the citizen, not the government; to a significant degree, the legal standard of "innocent until proven guilty" is reversed. Just as happened in this case, the young man had to prove the IRS was wrong, not the other way around. Thinking that a citizen has to disprove an unfair government contention is a shift in attitude that may may not come easily for media managers, as it conflicts with all of the lessons learned in school about how the law works. Yet that is what executives should expect in dealing with many government agencies.

MAJOR AREAS OF THE LAW

With the preceding as the foundation of a managerial perspective toward laws and regulations, we next focus on five major areas of the law which media managers should know. They are corporate, employee, news/editorial, advertising, and regulatory/new technologies.

For each area, we will discuss only the topics that are most relevant to media managers. If you are interested in other topics under those categories, you might consult the excellent work, *Mass Communication Law*, fourth edition, by Donald Gillmor and Jerome A. Barron. We also recommend *Law of Mass Communication*, fifth edition, by Harold L. Nelson and Dwight L. Teeter, Jr.; *The First Amendment and the Fourth Estate: The Law of Mass Media*, third edition, by T. Barton Carter, Marc Franklin, and Jay B. Wright. If you want the latest information on developments in the field at an expert's level, read the two volumes entitled *Communications Law* that are published by The Practicing Law Institute.

Corporate Law

Antitrust is the prime corporate legal matter for the media. In simplest terms, violating antitrust means that a media firm acts in a way that unfairly forces competitors out of the market or stops them from entering or competing in the market. Antitrust violations happen in a variety of ways. The most common is to offer advertising space or time at a price below what it costs the print or broadcast firm to produce and/ or distribute the advertisement. To avoid violating antitrust laws, a television station cannot charge less for commercials than they cost to produce and air, nor can a magazine charge less for its advertising space than the costs of producing and distributing it.

Antitrust is not limited to any one medium nor to large media firms. There are many ways to thwart fair competition: teaming up with other media to set artificially low or high prices (price fixing); colluding to control distribution of services such as network affiliation, syndicated services, newsprint or other supplies; influencing local laws and rules so that, for example, cable competitors cannot enter a market.

Antitrust laws, as they apply to media, are based on two principles. The first, which holds for all businesses, is that in a free, competitive economy no firm should be allowed to unfairly thwart another. The second, which is special to the media, is based on the importance of having a multiplicity of information voices in the society.

Over the years many efforts have been made to prevent the concentration of voices in only a few hands. For example, the Federal Communications Commission (FCC) limited the number of broadcast stations one person or company could own. In the middle 1980s, when that number increased, a limit was set on the percentage of listeners in the country that any one broadcaster's stations could reach. American Telephone and Telegraph (AT&T) was also broken up because of the belief that this private, highly regulated company, the largest corporation in the world at the time, had too much dominance over the delivery of information.

As the size of newspaper groups increased, Congressman Morris Udall (D-Arizona) jumped into the fray. He introduced a bill that attempted to give special advantages to small newspaper groups and to family-owned newspapers so that the present owners would be more likely to pass the newspaper on to their next of kin instead of selling to large groups.

The Udall bill did not move though the House of Representatives, in part because more owners of one or only a few individual newspapers opposed the act than supported it. The opponents did not like preferential tax legislation for just their industry. They believed a bill should be passed to help all small business people pass on their enterprises, rather than one which just helped newspapers.

However, there is an exclusion in antitrust laws just for newspapers. It is called a Joint Operating Agreement (JOA), which comes from enabling legislation called the Newspaper Preservation Act. JOAs permit two newspapers in a market to share all functions except news if indications are that one of the papers would fail if the antitrust laws were not waived. Although today some believe JOAs are primarily to make money for the newspapers involved, the intent of Congress in passing the legislation was to enhance the multiplicity of newspaper voices in a community.

Antitrust exceptions like JOAs are comparatively rare, however; media executives should not concentrate on them, but rather on day-to-day activities with antitrust implications, e.g., setting prices (price cutting or fixing), and unfair forms of competition (monopolizing sources of supply, territories or markets). That is especially true for controlling distribution channels by such means as cutting off other media's use of third-party distribution channels. Some media companies have done that by contracting to keep other magazines, books, or records off of a store's shelf, or by purchasing exclusive rights to the sole source of distribution.

According to the *Wall Street Journal* on July 18, 1986, antitrust can even invade something so small and seemingly simple as greeting cards. After ignoring the off-beat, so-called alternative greeting cards for years, giant Hallmark introduced alternative cards of its own. Then the legal war began. Said the newspaper, "Hallmark . . . the industry leader with annual sales of about $1.5 billion . . . finds itself beset with antitrust and trade infringement lawsuits totaling more than $80 million. Raising issues of free choice and free speech, the suits . . . as well as some of Hallmark's own dealers, contend the giant is copying its smaller competitors' designs and illegally using its financial muscle to push their (competitors') offerings off card racks around the country."

Even historic business practices may turn out to be illegal if pursued today. For instance, many newspapers buy syndicated services, such as columnists and comics. For decades these were purchased on an exclusive basis; only one media outlet in each market or region would be given the service. At first that seemed like a reasonable practice. After all, why would a media outlet take the risk on a new service if the same comic strip or columnist could soon appear in their competitor's pages? Recently, in case after case across the country, editors and publishers have threatened legal actions that resulted in a breakdown of the monopolistic control of syndicated columnists and comics.

Other areas where antitrust law pertains include vertical and horizontal mergers and acquisitions which thwart competition. They should always be checked by antitrust experts before the deal is consummated. So should "agreements" between media companies to compete against a third firm; that could be conspiracy to restrain trade, fix prices, or monopolize a market.

Antitrust problems are sure to increase as media conglomerates grow larger. In this time of large companies with lots of resources it is important for managers to think about antitrust concerns not only when setting rates, but in relation to routine managerial acts. Thus, a basic

EXHIBIT 16.2. CORPORATE LAW

Antitrust
- Advertising and circulation: pricing
- News/editorial: purchases of services

Contract
- Customers
- Suppliers

Environment
- Clean air
- Clean water

Property
- Real estate
- Signs

Liability
- Personal injury
- Auto

rule for media managers is to not allow their firms to lose money to lure people to a new product; to do so could be a restraint of trade. Moreover, every information organization leader should regularly check with experts in their industry to find out the latest on antitrust issues that affect their medium, and those findings should be regularly communicated to everyone in the organization.

The management perspective vis-à-vis antitrust includes knowing both the letter and spirit of the law and teaching employees about them. Matters such as carefully defining new markets and paying detailed attention to cost accounting must be considered in advance of any action that might have antitrust implications. And as in all legal areas, getting prompt, sound, expert legal advice is crucial if a problem arises. No information company, no matter what its size, is exempt from potential antitrust problems, but actual problems can be prevented if media managers are well schooled, vigilant, and careful to fully document everything.

Other topics in corporate law are listed in Exhibit 16.2.

Employee Laws and Rules

Because information executives are responsible for the work of others, supervisors must be conversant with a broad range of employee laws and regulations. The importance of such rules is heightened if managers work in a union environment where there are special state and federal regulations. Whether a media firm has unions or not, however, employee laws apply in such day-to-day matters as workmen's compensation, wage and hour guidelines, pension and profit sharing rules, and employee theft. Because legal, personnel, and professional journals cover those matters in depth we will not deal with them here. Instead, we will concentrate on one employee area that has special meaning for the media. It is called by various names: equal employment opportunity (EEO), affirmative action, or the hiring of women and minorities.

In light of the EEO laws and the 1986 Supreme Court decision upholding affirmative action, every business should be sensitive to this issue. But because of their special role in society, the media must mirror that society if they are to maintain insight and credibility. Put another way, how can information companies represent the problems of society's citizens unless they are staffed and led by representatives of all facets of society? How can the press be sensitive to the unique role of women and minorities if their employees are only white males? In our experience the answer to both of those questions is, at best, "poorly."

That fact has not escaped the media's advertisers, audiences, or leadership. If the media are to be believable, its executives must follow both the letter and spirit of the Equal Employment Opportunity laws. Their actions must lead to meaningful integration of their firms and a better balance of information for the public.

At least preliminarily, media industries have recognized this responsibility. They have mounted aggressive programs of scholarships for school-age minority students as well as special programs to recruit, train, and hire minorities at entry and managerial levels. (If you are interested in some of these efforts, contact groups like the National Association of Broadcasters, the American Newspaper Publishers Association Foundation, the American Society of Newspaper Editors, the Public Relations Society of America, the American Association of Advertising Agencies, and numerous other groups in advertising, public relations, film, and video).

What we just cited are efforts on an industry level. Media managers can take many actions to carry out similar efforts within their firms. The front runner in this regard is Gannett which, in the 1970s, began what is now a growing corporate commitment to promote women and minorities. Christy Bulkeley and Gloria Biggs were the media firm's first female publishers. Today one of the formal objectives of Gannett managers is to develop and promote underrepresented people. That objective is part of the manager's MBO plan and is rewarded not just by praise from top management for advancing minorities, but by money added to the manager's salary.

Gannett's efforts have produced results. As reported in *Business Week* on June 23, 1986, "Gannett's policy translates into impressive numbers; 19 women newspaper publishers out of 74. Among them is Cathleen P. Black, publisher of the national daily *USA Today*." That puts Black in charge of the largest daily newspaper ever headed by a woman.

Writing in the May-June *Bulletin* of the American Society of Newspaper Editors (ASNE), Robert P. Clark, the outgoing ASNE president and the vice president of news of Harte-Hanks, summed up the importance of this subject:

" . . . I see this as a moral issue, yes. But I also see it as an economic one. Every time we gain a few percentage points in the minority representation in our newsrooms, the general population is surging ahead that much faster. By 1990, minorities will be 25 percent of this country's population. By the year 2000, 29 percent. And here we stand in our newsrooms at 6.3 percent.

"What this means is that more and more of our readers—or our potential readers—are minorities. Did you know that in 25 percent of this country's large cities, the minority population is now the majority? . . . But, you may say, I'm from a small paper, or I'm from an area where there are few minorities. Why do I need any minorities in my newsroom? That is a bit tougher to answer, but I thought Rolfe Neill, one of our directors, put it well in the February issue of the *ASNE Bulletin*. He said: 'A pluralistic country such as ours cheats itself when one of the principal organs responsible for preserving democracy

EXHIBIT 16.3. EMPLOYEE LAW

Equal employment opportunity
- Affirmative action
- Fair hiring

Honesty/theft
- Company rules
- Safeguards
- Insurance bond coverage

Labor
- Collective bargaining: good faith, organizing, elections
- National Labor Relations Board rules
- State Labor Department rules

Pension and profit sharing
- Voluntary profit sharing
- Fixed pension
- IRAs
- KEOGHs

Workmen's compensation
- State and federal rules
- Insurance coverage

Wage and hour
- Federal and state statutes/rules
- Child age/hours/wages
- Minimum wage

is itself a ghetto. When the only glasses through which society is observed are worn by a white middle-class reporter or editor, the view is bound to be incomplete.'

"In other words, we have a responsibility to inform all Americans about all of America: about race relations as well as business triumphs, about poverty as well as wealth. The problems of race affect us all. And I am convinced that we cannot report, even in the hinterland, what is happening in this country without the help and input of a cross section of Americans in our newsrooms."

The key to a media firm's success in implementing EEO laws is the attitudes its leaders hold. Are they truly supportive of these laws? Do they see them in legal, moral, and economic terms or do they simply pay lip service to them? As a potential media manager, what are your own attitudes?

Other topics in employee law are listed in Exhibit 16.3.

News/Editorial

At their core, media firms have an extraordinary level of potential for harm as well as good. In response to that power, the United States developed laws of libel, slander, privacy, copyright, and plagiarism. Our discussion focuses on the laws that are most important for the visibility, credibility, and responsibility of the media. They are the category of laws and rules that deal with disseminating information that can injure the public.

What is especially important for media managers is their perspective toward such matters. What attitudes do they telegraph to their staff? Are those attitudes uncaring, ill-advised, defensive, and reactive or are they proactive and constructive? Are they the attitudes of the television station investigative team leader who said, "Get the story at all costs and worry about being sued later." Or are they those of the executive we noted earlier who told her team, "We want to get the story, but, remember, the individuals we cover have rights and you are expected to respect them."

A guiding principle for media leaders thinking about information that intrudes on citizens should be:

- What is fair?
- What would the manager wish done if he or she were the subject of the story?
- What will the public accept, not just as legal, but as responsible?

Do not be confused by what we just said. We are not advocating timid journalism. Quite the contrary. It is vitally important that journalists dig and report in depth, but they can do that and also take into account fairness. Information executives should demonstrate to their staffs that just as the media have broad rights protected by the Constitution, they also have responsibilities, which must be carried out if the rights of the press are to continue. Media people must do their part to make fairness a reality.

We have seldom seen an instance when a reporter operating near the line of libel, slander, or invasion of privacy cannot come up with a way to get the full story without violating the subject's rights or the yardstick of fairness. It might take more work to do the job in a fair and responsible way, but that extra effort is a sound investment in the information industries' credibility.

In this area as in every legal and regulatory matter, there are times when the best intended media manager or staff member makes mistakes. They violate the letter or spirit of the law or they do not give adequate heed to the management philosophy about the law, with which we began this chapter.

For instance, a TV station general manager on the East Coast (who for obvious reasons would rather remain anonymous) saw a story on his evening news broadcast about a private school headmaster. The story was clearly libelous. Despite ongoing efforts to educate the station's executives and staff on these matters, a reporter put together a story saying that the headmaster was bilking the parents of his students. The reporter cited no proof of that charge; indeed, the school's headmaster was not even interviewed. The reporter simply heard the allegation from an unnamed parent and reported it. Worse yet, before it aired the story was reviewed by the station's news director, who never asked about the reporter's sources or validation of the charge. The news director just slotted it in the evening news, saying later that he was in a hurry and it "seemed all right to me."

Shortly thereafter an attorney for the headmaster contacted the station. Because of a well-known policy that the station manager be told about any pending legal action, the general manager was immediately notified. After reviewing the story, talking to everyone involved, and consulting with the station's lawyer, the general manager took the only reasonable action under the circumstances. He told the attorney that the story should not have gone on the air and that in the next prime-time news program a sizeable correction would be aired in a more prominent spot than the original story's.

Not wanting to further jeopardize the broadcast facility's legal position the general manager did not admit to libel, but simply said that upon reflection everyone realized that the story had not been validated and should not have been aired without substantiation. He also said that the station always promptly responded when matters were inappropriately reported.

The attorney for the headmaster and his client were so startled and pleased by the prompt reaction that much of their anger vanished. When they subsequently raised the issue of a settlement for the situation, the station manager, on advice of an attorney who was an expert on libel, took a line which was both conciliatory and tough. He noted that under the state's law his station's retraction protected the television company against a finding of punitive damages: damages for malice. He also said that given the station's prompt reaction and the prominent positioning of the retraction it was unlikely that there was much actual damage. He said that the station would therefore pay a small settlement: all of the school attorney's fees and, to show good will, a contribution of $1,000 to the school's scholarship fund.

The station manager acted preventively, promptly, and reasonably. As a result the matter was settled amicably at comparatively modest cost. As another matter of executive responsibility it should be noted that after the affair was over, the news director was quietly discharged. Management found it wholly unacceptable that an executive in the news director's position would know so little of the law or fairness that he could allow that story to run and later defend his decision.

Not every potentially harmful situation ends up so well, however. For instance, Carol Burnett won a huge settlement against the *National Enquirer*. That was a situation where the editors of the newspaper did not act to correct a libelous story and did not back down when confronted with it.

Other topics in news editorial law are:

- Libel
- Slander
- Invasion of privacy
- Copyright
- First amendment
- Journalist's Privilege (Shield Laws)

Advertising Law

News or opinions are not the only information products where laws and statutes are important. Many media put out advertising messages which are subject to all of the legal limits of news as well as other regulations. As a starting point, media managers have a right to refuse advertisements. Magazines and newspapers do not have to take political ads (or allow politicians access to their news columns). Broadcasters, however, under a Federal Communication Commission rule known as the Equal Time provision, are required to make an opportunity for equal air time available to one candidate for federal office if they provide similar time to another candidate for the same office. Similarly, broadcasters are faced with the Fairness Doctrine, which says that if a station makes time available to people supporting one side of a controversial issue it must provide an opportunity for reply to those who support the other side of the issue. (Both of these provisions apply to advertising and news programming.)

Beyond those rules are governmental regulations which affect advertising on both state and federal levels. For example, federal law requires that cigarette companies print a health warning in each of their ads. Most states also strictly control the pricing of legal notices.

Whether media executives are in broadcasting or print firms and whether they are required to take advertisements or are allowed to reject them, they should develop a value-based policy for dealing with objectionable advertisements. Considering such problems in advance is smart; that way the pressure to make quick choices is avoided and media managers can take a longer-term view that considers their medium's credibility. That is far wiser than trying to react to a ticking clock. Like all legal matters, those that affect advertising are often not as simple as one might assume. We are reminded, for instance, of a newspaper publisher who faced the following situation.

A home owned by a member of a political extremist group was confiscated by the IRS for nonpayment of taxes. The IRS put the house up for auction and placed a legal notice in the publisher's newspaper indicating when the auction would take place. The response of the man who owned the house was to come to the newspaper with an advertisement of his own. In the ad the evicted owner threatened to involve the winner of the auction in a court battle and that the purchaser would incur extraordinary legal fees.

The advertisement put the newspaper's management in a quandary. If they turned down the advertisement the extremist might claim that he was denied access to the newspaper, that the newspaper was discriminating against him, restraining trade, etc. On the other hand, if the advertisement was accepted, the newspaper would be running a notice the purpose of which was to threaten the paper's readers (who may bid on the house because they saw the auction advertisement placed by the IRS in the newspaper). Moreover, the paper's lawyers said that the basis of the political extremist's advertisement was not embodied in the law; that is, the extremist had no grounds to claim that the IRS could not sell his house, which was the basis of his advertisement.

After a great deal of thought the newspaper rejected the advertisement and refunded the money collected for it, and explained why the advertisement was unacceptable. The paper also offered to run a different advertisement if an acceptable one was submitted.

When weighing the pro's and con's of that situation, the newspaper executives and their lawyers realized that there was no "safe" solution. If the advertisement was run, readers could be intimidated by it. If the advertisement was withheld, the newspaper would open itself to a lawsuit and the paper's philosophic commitment to giving people who wish to purchase advertising space the widest possible latitude to express their opinions would be thwarted.

On balance the executives felt that this was an instance where protecting their readers was more important than the possible monetary drain on the paper by having to defend itself against litigation. It also was more important than the paper's philosophy not to limit people's right to express themselves in advertisements. (In fact a substitute advertisement was never submitted nor was there any litigation against the newspaper or the winner of the auction.)

Despite the case just noted, in many instances problems with advertisements can be avoided. That is why many agencies routinely run ads or commercials past their lawyers to check for potential legal difficulties before the advertisements are shown to a client or the public. Although some lawyers adopt a legalistic "yes/no" posture on such questions, many try to work closely with the agency and client to modify the advertisements in ways that will retain their creative strategy, but avoid legal problems. That legal approach is more compatible with the managerial perspective with which we began this chapter than is the highly legalistic, absolutist manner that some attorneys adopt.

Other topics in advertising law are:

- Regulation of commercial speech
- The right to refuse advertising
- Regulation of advertising
- Libel
- Slander
- Invasion of privacy
- Copyright
- First amendment

Regulation of New Media and Technologies

Legal and regulatory issues connected with new technology are exploding, just as is the technology itself. It is impossible for legislatures to adequately protect citizens in the area of invasion of privacy by high-speed computers because advances in the technology can almost always circumvent the letter of the law. Similarly, they cannot provide across-the-board free access to public information because that data can be moved at the speed of light from one location to another. As a result, this is an area of the law that is growing in complexity from both the media and societal perspective. It is also a subject with which media managers must become more familiar as new technology rushes onto their stage.

Despite the reluctance of many media executives to engage in legislative lobbying, most have found that they must work with legislators if such basics as open record laws are to be maintained. Further, if those firms which offer the new information technologies are going to have any constructive input into shaping the laws that govern them, they must work closely with legislators and regulators. Media executives also spend a great deal of time watching for political attempts to craft legislation that protects individual citizens' right to privacy at the expense of

EXHIBIT 16.4. NEW MEDIA AND TECHNOLOGY REGULATION

- Federal Regulation
  - FCC
    - Electronic mass media
      - Broadcasting
      - Cable television
      - New uses of electronic media
    - Regulation of market access
    - Regulation of rates
    - Regulation of content
    - Regulation of competition
  - Computers, information services, and data processing
    - Computer I, II, III
    - Satellite services
    - Spectrum management
- Private corporations with governmental charters
  - Communications Satellite Corporation ("COMSAT")
  - Corporation for Public Broadcasting ("CPB")
- Governmental protection of information property rights
  - Eavesdropping
  - Copyright law
- State/local regulation
  - Common carriers
  - Cable television
- International issues
  - Spectrum management and negotiations
  - Copyright
  - "New World Information Order"

another fundamental value; the freedom to report what is happening in society.

Exhibit 16.4 lists a few specifics of what is coming in the area of new media and technology law.

Insurance-Related Legal Matters

Insurance and the law are inseparable for most U.S. media. Insurance can be purchased to cover libel, slander, copyright, privacy, and plagiarism. There are also policies that cover corporate liability, employee theft, and many other corporate matters. Again, specific industry trade journals, training seminars, and professional organizations provide media executives with much information on various types of professional insurance.

In this section we note a few management points related to insurance. The United States is a highly litigious society. Furthermore, legal actions are very costly, not just because of large settlements but also because of the enormous legal costs to mount an effective defense. Both make it essential that media managers know what items can and cannot be insured.

Insurance protection should be purchased with an eye toward the policies' restrictions, limits, and guidelines, as well as its price. For instance, can the insurance company decide when a settlement should be made or does the head of the media firm retain that power? Does the insurance company have the right to pick the defense lawyer, or does the media leader, or is that power shared? These factors should be carefully reviewed; many times the cheapest insurance carries with it limits on managerial authority that are far more expensive than the dollar differential between two policies of different prices.

Again, a real-life incident explains why this is so important. A radio news director we know is being sued by some militant, tough political reactionaries, who claim they were libeled when they were identified as members of a reactionary political group. Ironically, they object to that label even though their membership was affirmed by one of the group's leaders, the U.S. marshal, and the local sheriff. The station's insurance company and its top executives believe the claim is true, that it was fairly researched, and that the station will prevail when the case reaches court. Months have been spent in legal wrangling with the defendants and considerable expense incurred working with libel lawyers to prepare a defense. At this point, however, the insurance company has decided that it wants to give the defendants a sizeable settlement because the company fears that it will cost a lot more to try the case than to settle it.

The radio executives agree with the insurance company's conclusion about the cost. Although the media managers expect their station to prevail they realize it will take a lengthy trial to win and legal expenses will far outstrip a settlement. The radio executives point out, however, that if the case is settled, every reporter who encounters the reactionaries will shy away from really reporting what the extremists are doing for fear of being sued for even a simple, factual report about members of the organization. In short, the media managers argue that to settle will unleash the subtle but dangerous disease of self-censorship and intimidation of the press.

What is especially ironic is that in the long run a settlement could also cost the insurance company more money than if the insurer toughs it out. The reason is that if the political militants think they can get a quick settlement by suing every time they don't like a story, they will resort to suits as frequently as possible. Each time that occurs the insurance company will have to defend its many clients against the militants or pay another settlement.

There is a second management point in these matters: media managers should not allow the presence of insurance to lull them into forgetting their responsibility to teach their employees sensitivity to laws, regulations, and a well-developed management perspective about these matters. The presence of insurance should not cause media employees or employers to deal with these issues in a casual manner or by default. Effective media leaders know that they must remain constantly aware of legal and regulatory issues and confront them with a clear eye toward both the long-term legal good of their organization and with an equal commitment to preserving the values of their medium.

Executive Philosophy about Legal and Regulatory Responsibility

We close this chapter where we began, with an admonition. Although laws and rules are important for executives in all businesses, they are particularly important for those who deal with information. When media people violate such standards, the results are more visible. They also undercut the media's credibility and their place in society.

That is not the case in many industries. If a local manufacturing firm hurts one of its 300 industrial customers by a product it delivers, the results are seldom known beyond the two businesses involved. Yet if the media hurts someone, the results are headline news and the credibility of all media is undermined. Maintaining that credibility is essential if the special protections afforded the media by the Constitution and law are to continue and the media's role in American society is not to be diminished.

Because of the media's importance, information managers must become intimately familiar with the kind of laws and rules we've noted in this chapter and with the many others that are part of running their organizations. The responsibility for regular updating of their knowledge and for training employees in the spirit and letter of the law should not be forgotten or delegated away. It is central, and effective media managers recognize it, nurture it, and make it a fundamental part of their organization's day-to-day consciousness.

CHAPTER 17
The Media's Social Responsibilities

Throughout this book we emphasize the crucial role media leaders have in determining the mission, goals, plans, activities, and staffs of their firms. They also are central when it comes to deciding:

- the degree of emphasis their organizations place on profit and other business goals;
- the level of their firms' commitment to the media's social responsibilities;
- the balance between business goals and social responsibilities (that balancing role is most evident in the decisions that leaders make when they respond to the problems and opportunities presented by major U.S. business trends).

In this chapter we examine a managerial perspective that creates an even balance between business considerations and social responsibilities, as media executives position their firms for the future.

MAJOR TRENDS INFLUENCING THE MEDIA

While many trends affect the future of U.S. information companies, we focus on four essential trends. They have a significant impact on the media now and in the future. And despite our discussing them sepa-

EXHIBIT 17.1. FOUR MAJOR TRENDS INFLUENCING MEDIA ORGANIZATIONS

Many-faceted movement toward bigness
Dramatic advances in technology
Increased emphasis on markets and the market perspective
Heightened profit consciousness

rately so that you can see them with greater clarity, these trends are interrelated. They are listed in Exhibit 17.1.

Trend 1. The Movement toward Bigness

The move toward bigness has many facets including: ownership concentration, financial (such as sales, expenses, and investments), and employment.

Ownership Concentration. As was noted in Chapter 2, there is a clear trend toward ownership concentration within most media industries. Additionally, acquisitions across industry lines have resulted in the development of huge multimedia conglomerates such as CBS, Inc.; Gannett Co.; Time, Incorporated; Capital Cities Communications; Knight-Ridder, Inc.; The Times-Mirror Co.; The Tribune Company; and The Hearst Corporation.

Typically, persons interested in ownership concentration focus on the takeover by groups of family-owned media. Most often that translates into acquisition of family-owned daily newspapers by chains. However, such definitions are far too simplistic, for concentration takes many forms.

Analysis of ownership concentration should include the more sophisticated, broad horizon of factors listed below:

- The fiscal size of the information company
- Whether it is publicly or privately owned
- The number and types of media properties it owns
- The degree to which it controls a market or an audience
- The numbers and types of people in its audience and, in some cases, the audience's spending power
- What if any is the monopoly or oligopoly status of the media outlets it owns

Big Money. Today media industries generate a lot of money. In the mid-1980s advertising revenues for the major media exceeded $50 billion. Combined with revenues from other income streams, total media sales amounted to more than $100 billion in 1985. *Business Week* reported that publishing, radio, and TV broadcasting alone had combined sales of $62.333 billion and that does not take into account film, advertising, public relations, etc.

In each media industry, sales are heavily concentrated. If you look at the print and film media, the 20 largest companies generate more than 50 percent of those industries' total sales. In broadcast the three largest companies: CBS, ABC (now owned by Capital Cities Communications), and NBC (owned by RCA which is owned by General Electric), generate over one-third of total broadcast revenues. The biggest firms in newspapers and broadcast have sales in the billions and are the prime information outlets for a majority of the audiences.

Whatever the size of a media firm, its earnings are used to fund new products, enter new markets, or pay for acquisitions or new technology. Even for small firms, the required investments mean large expenditures and, as a result, sizeable profits to fund them.

Exhibit 17.2 shows the level of investment needed for various kinds of new products, acquisitions, and technology. Note that for local media to do something as straightforward and necessary as upgrading facilities takes several million dollars.

As you can imagine, generating and accumulating profits that are adequate to finance these kinds of expenditures is a formidable task. Gathering such resources is often easier for publicly held corporations because of the policies of the Internal Revenue Service and because public firms can more easily raise funds through the sale of additional shares of stock. For example, if a privately held media firm accumulates a substantial amount of cash, it risks being taxed for what the IRS calls excess earnings or undeclared dividends. But publicly held corporations can accumulate far more money without risking such pressure, though at some point the IRS will force those firms to declare a dividend if they do not spend the money they are putting aside.

EXHIBIT 17.2. INVESTMENTS IN PRODUCTS, ACQUISITIONS, AND TECHNOLOGY

Size of Investment ($)	*Product*	*Acquisition*	*Technology*
100s of millions	National newspaper or magazine	TV network Major metropolitan daily Motion picture studios	Direct broadcast satellite system Large printing facilities
10s of millions	TV series Major movie Large consumer magazine	Medium-size newspaper Medium-size magazine company Top 100 TV stations	Wiring a city for cable TV Printing/distribution facility for major daily Motion picture facilities
Millions	Mass-market books Major records	Small newspapers Broadcast stations Magazines	Local production and transmission facility for TV Printing plants

Employees. Media industries employ large numbers of people. In 1980, magazines, newspapers, books, films, broadcasts, cable, records, and advertising agencies employed more than 1 million (Compaine, et al., 1982). By 1990 that number is expected to be closer to 1.5 million. Depending on the definition of employment one adopts, newspapers may be the largest manufacturing industry in the United States in terms of the number of employees.

Media firms are highly variable in scope, both in terms of the markets they serve and the size of their organizations. As a result, a multitiered employment structure has emerged in each medium. In many respects it is similar to professional baseball, with its various levels of minor leagues leading up to the major leagues. In the media, the majors would include New York, Chicago, and Los Angeles advertising agencies, the television networks and TV stations in major markets, major metropolitan newspapers, Hollywood film studios, and the national magazines. The result is a highly stratified salary structure within each industry. For example, see the survey data in Exhibit 17.3 (Miller, 1986).

As employees seek major salary increments, a pay structure of this sort provides substantial incentive for media workers to move from organization to organization and from market to market. Also, because

EXHIBIT 17.3. AVERAGE NEWSROOM SALARIES BY CIRCULATION SIZE

	Under 5,000	*5,000-10,000*	*10,000-18,000*	*18,000 25,000*
Beginning reporter	$10,816	$11,076	$12,116	$13,312
Beginning copy editor	—	12,272	13,208	14,196
5-yr. reporter	13,278	15,262	17,212	19,996
5-yr. copy editor	—	17,472	18,512	20,176
Department head	13,500	16,314	18,726	21,462
Editor	22,366	24,642	32,672	38,323

	25,000-50,000	*50,000-100,000*	*100,000-250,000*	*Over 250,000*
Beginning reporter	$14,664	$16,224	$18,304	$22,984
Beginning copy editor	15,860	16,588	19,292	23,972
5-yr. reporter	21,996	24,648	29,120	35,412
5-yr. copy editor	22,932	24,960	29,744	35,828
Department head	26,805	32,392	41,071	55,044
Editor	51,229	61,971	93,222	165,539

of the star system that has emerged in a number of media industries, salaries from more than $100,000 to more than $1 million are possible.

Trend 2. Advances in Technology

The most exciting and challenging media trend is the dramatic advance in each medium's technology. Such developments as videotex make it possible for two-way information to be instantly delivered across the U.S. and the globe via satellite. Businesses are now connected worldwide with the touch of a computer key. Despite various fits and false starts, some combination of computers, satellites, and/or lasers will change the way that information is received by everyone in the developed nations and eventually in many of the developing and underdeveloped countries.

Even people who know little about the media are aware of the onslaught of advances in information delivery by the new and not so new words that have entered the vocabulary: computers, videotex, VCRs, compact disks, and satellite delivery of all sorts of signals. Those advances are enhanced by modems and telecommunications that allow a home computer access to faraway giant data bases, such as Dow Jones News Retrieval which carries not only the *Wall Street Journal*, but repackages other newspapers and wire services. Other data bases contain thousands of scholarly and specialized research articles, publications, and data.

For more than a decade the computer used by most daily newspapers, as well as many home data base users, has employed software that can rapidly search electronic files for any given name or subject. That made it easy for newspaper editors to create sections or sets of stories that focus on a specialized list of interests.

In the early 1980s United Press International took that advance one step further. Despite its beleaguered financial condition, it developed a 4,000-item menu which allowed a broadcast or print editor to designate subjects that the editor wanted to regularly highlight because of special reader, listener, or viewer interest. That gave significant additional tools to local newspapers to customize international, national, and state news for local readers.

Computer and satellite technologies have also changed television news programming in conjunction with other technological developments in cameras and editing equipment. Computer graphics altered the display of information in print, television, and movies. New photographic technology improved production quality in both print and video presentations of visual images. Digitalization of recording and production has transformed the sound media: records, tapes, compact disks, and radio.

For the media manager all of this is a portent of extraordinary and exciting change. The print media were technologically almost static from Gutenberg's first movable type until computers and phototypesetting, a phenomenon that began in the 1930s, but didn't extensively spread in the U.S. until the 1960s. Changes in technology have been equally rapid and profound in each of the other media.

Technological developments create new possibilities for the kind and amount of information that can be presented and for the best methods to present it. At the same time, these leaps cost media firms a great deal. They involve enormous outlays for new broadcast or print equipment; amounts that are well beyond the capability of many small media firms (see Exhibit 17.2). That has forced many media organizations to consider selling out to bigger companies.

Trend 3. Increased Emphasis on the Marketing Perspective

Increased competition for audiences and advertisers has placed greater emphasis on the marketing perspective, which we explained and utilized in Part Three. Media managers are using more thorough information about audience preferences to tailor their products to match research results. This often results in successful products, but sometimes the research is accompanied by faulty analysis and/or findings that do more harm than good.

For example, in the 1970s much of the newspaper industry concentrated on soft (feature) news in response to research indicating that readers were more interested in human-interest stories than hard (events-based) news. Yet during that period regular readership of newspapers by younger adults declined dramatically; readership by older people also fell, though at a slower rate. Subsequently, more sophisticated and accurate research showed that what readers really want in their newspapers is "hard news" about the day's major events; only when those stories are covered does the public want "soft news" features.

The failure rate of new television series is also as high as ever, despite the extensive audience research that is undertaken before new ones are launched. At the same time, smaller media do narrower and narrower audience targeting to reach affluent audiences willing to pay for certain types of information, and such efforts are carried to even more finely targeted extremes when such audiences are also attractive to a group of advertisers.

Meanwhile, in other settings, information conglomerates capitalize on audience synergism to create multimedia products that generate many income streams from one creative effort, such as a film that spawns records, compact disks, music videos, books, and, on occasion, television spin-offs.

On the negative side, some of these strategies could possibly shut out audience segments that lack sales potential or that are not, for some other reason, attractive to advertisers. Senior citizens and minorities are examples of audiences that have been largely ignored or treated as secondary targets by many media.

In the face of this increased competition for audiences, media firms promote their products much more aggressively than ever before. Some of those efforts focus on product improvement or new product features, but much of it is predicated only on surface qualities. Thus, TV stations and networks spend millions of dollars promoting the image of their "star" news anchors; so do publishers of newspapers and books for their most popular columnists and authors.

Trend 4. Heightened Profit Consciousness

America is an antihistorical society. One consequence of this is that in many aspects of their lives Americans search for quick fixes and short-term solutions. Examples abound in attempts to deal with political, economic, educational, and social problems. The stock market also fosters a short-term orientation, and the media play a significant role in reinforcing that view by emphasizing weekly, monthly, and quarterly financial results.

Americans' negative attitude toward the importance of history and their short-term view of the economic system combine to create an enormous pressure for immediate profits. That often results in a reluctance by media managers to commit large sums for long-term product development or advances that could position their companies more securely in the future. Instead, decisions are made to heighten current profits, often at the expense of the future, so that in the next financial report the bottom line looks good.

When these patterns are combined with the three trends we noted above: movement toward bigness, advances in technology, and increased reliance on the marketing perspective, they collectively concentrate many media managers' attention on profit consciousness. In turn, that causes two reactions that have far-reaching implications.

Implications of the Four Trends

One reaction is to search for new income streams to maintain profitability in the face of more competition. For example, in response to a decline in their share of national advertising, magazines raised their prices to gain a greater proportion of their revenues from circulation. Increases in preprint sections of newspapers resulted in a decline in the more profitable run-of-press advertising. That trend caused many newspapers to increase their subscription rates in order to make up for the lost revenue. Indeed, in a speech at the 100th anniversary of the Inland Daily Press Association in October 1985, Gannett chairman Allen Neuharth advised daily newspaper publishers to double their subscription rates.

If the newspaper industry followed Neuharth's suggestion, the subscription increases might cost the publishers their lower- and middle-class readers. That would turn newspapers from a mass medium into a class medium at just the time that the television market is being fragmented by increases in the number of cable systems, VCRs, satellite delivered programs, and low-power television stations.

That mass-to-class phenomenon is already present in much of the Third World, where people regularly make the decision between such necessities of life as food and housing and the purchase of a newspaper. It is also true in part of the U.S., where newspapers have abandoned low-income or distant subscribers in their traditional markets.

Further, no one is quite sure what it would mean to the fundamental operation of the U.S. society if it had neither a print nor an electronic mass medium to deliver information to the broadest cross section of its people. Similarly, the narrower targeting of specialized information media may also contribute to a division of Americans into media-rich and media-poor audience segments. In combination, these two changes will have a profound impact on the governmental, cultural, informational, and social systems of the country.

The second consequence of the media's heightened profit consciousness is the attempt to find ways to reduce investment risks. The offering of "copy cat" information products is a prime example of this phenomena. Thus, nearly every hit TV series spawns imitators, and in the movies the pattern is so commonplace that the public almost expects sequels to successful films, especially those that center on action, adventure, or an interesting character.

A variation on this theme is to invest major resources to create blockbuster books* that sell hundreds of thousands of copies and movies that make tens of millions of dollars. Production and marketing resources are marshaled and huge sums are invested in production and promotion to create the "big winner." When it succeeds, that strategy produces enormous profits, but the ratio of hits to failures makes the odds at Las Vegas seem favorable.

Both of those risk reduction strategies—copy-cat products and creation of blockbusters—have other serious consequences for the media. They concentrate an enormous share of an information organization's human, fiscal, and intellectual resources, as well as its energy and drive, on a limited set of products. As a result, new ideas, authors, and

* Thomas Whiteside's (1981) *The Blockbuster Complex* presents a thorough and penetrating analysis of the impact of these four trends on one medium, trade-book publishing. Whiteside shows how the emergence of these trends in the 1960s and their acceleration in the 1970s have combined to change the very nature of book publishing in the United States in the 1980s. Many of the changes he details illustrate the serious negative consequences when profitability becomes the dominant concern.

product improvements do not receive the attention they need. That causes both the audience and the media companies to lose because variety and innovation are stifled.

When profit consciousness dominates or combines with the other three trends it causes many media managers to concentrate on making their products respond to the market in the narrowest, most pandering sense of the term.

That is, they "inform," but only in surface ways, not in depth. If they "interpret," it is from a shallow, narrow point of view. Even when they "transmit culture or entertain," too often it is for the lowest common denominator of the audience. When they "act as a bridge of information in the economic system," small businesses are excluded by the escalating cost of meaningful entry. And minority and dissident voices are seldom provided adequate means to make real and alive "the entry of a multiplicity of voices about information and ideas" in the media system.

On the other hand, when a longer-term view dominates, the positive possibilities created by bigness, technology, and the marketing perspective are substantial. Let's look at some of them.

A LONG-TERM MANAGERIAL PERSPECTIVE

Throughout this book we have argued that information companies are better served by a long-term business perspective than one that is short term. Recall the mission and goals we proposed for an information company in Chapter 3, which are shown in Exhibit 17.4. They place customers ahead of stockholders or employees; that requires a longer-term view.

Note that our listing includes making a profit, which is essential if an information firm is to meet its other goals. Yet, on the list profits are not the top priority. Instead we've argued that effectively serving the me-

---

EXHIBIT 17.4. MISSION AND GOALS OF AN INFORMATION COMPANY

The mission of a media/information organization is to constructively serve the company's customers, employees and stockholders. Its goals are to:

1. Know and serve its market.
2. Produce a quality product and/or service.
3. Attract, train, challenge, promote, and keep the best possible employees.
4. Increase and/or maintain profits.
5. Position the organization to prosper in the future.
6. Protect the company's franchise.

---

dia's markets and the needs of their employees are the primary goals, for if both are taken care of, adequate profits will be realized. The company will be effectively positioned for a healthy financial future.

In summary, the long-term business perspective demands that profits be put in their proper place: not as the principal goal of the media firm, but as a vital, key item on the list. Note, however, that the priority position of profits for a company increases when the economic strength of the media enterprise declines.

Now let's look more closely at the notion of media effectively serving their market. From the point of view of the people and organizations who constitute information firm's markets (audiences and/or advertisers), there are a variety of needs:

- delivery of timely and useful information about events and issues from the U.S. and around the world;
- interpretation of those news reports;
- development of ways to socialize individuals and to pass on values and culture to succeeding generations;
- enhancement of opportunities for the hearing of a diversity of political, social, and cultural voices;
- opportunity to receive both news and advertising about the business and economic systems.

These are some of the media's major social responsibilities. To varying degrees the decisions that information company managers and employees make have implications for how well the media fulfill their social responsibilities.

Further, the support that society provides the media, in terms of economic advantages, protective laws, and, of course, its constitutional privileges, depends on the media's effectiveness in carrying out those social responsibilities. Farsighted media executives know that short-term actions which ignore these social obligations undermine the media's public support, and it is that support that is the basis of the special place the media hold. Indeed, the news media's repeated inquiries on what the public feels about them—and the credibility crises that result from polls on this question—show how seriously many news leaders feel about the public's opinion of them. Trust of the media has slipped, and media managers are wise to view that fact as a reason to reassess their own firm's long-term actions. To shunt it aside as something that should be rectified by the whole industry but not by the specific firm, department, or employee is dangerous.

It is important for the media manager to understand that a long-term perspective towards social responsibilities does not conflict with an aggressive business perspective; in fact, they complement each other. That is, a mature managerial philosophy emphasizes that information organizations should fulfill their societal responsibilities, not just because they have a social obligation to do so, but because doing so is good for business. One of the more cogent and thoughtful statements we have heard on this point was a speech given by James H. Ottaway, Jr., chairman of Ottaway Newspapers Inc., a subsidary of Dow Jones & Company, Inc. Speaking to a gathering of media professionals and educators at the Johnson Foundation in Racine, Wisconsin, in March 1987, this officer of Dow Jones argued for the importance of quality in newspapers, for a long-term view by managers, and for a managerial philosophy that would support newspapers being high-quality, responsible institutions in their communities.

Put another way, those information companies that protect their franchise by effectively carrying out their social responsibilities over a longer period of time will have healthier bottom lines and a brighter economic future.

How well a media firm fulfills its social responsibilities is largely determined by its executives' decisions and by the major trends we noted above. In turn, those trends are also influenced by media leaders' decisions about the products (news reports, editorials, advertisements, movies, books, and even music) their companies create, produce, and distribute, which is another reason why information leaders must take their social responsibilities seriously.

BUSINESS OBJECTIVES AND SOCIAL RESPONSIBILITIES

How can media executives capitalize on opportunities to enhance both business objectives and the performance of their firm's social responsibilities? What plans and actions can they take to do both successfully? As the following examples show, some information organizations are already constructively addressing that question. Others, perhaps the majority, are not.

Using the Market Perspective Effectively

Daily newspapers increasingly use market research and the market perspective to identify promising target markets, and tailor their news/editorial product to respond to market interests. Earlier we saw how this perspective was misapplied in the 1970s to emphasize soft news.

An example of this was the targeting by many metropolitan papers of market segments of particular interest to advertisers. As a result, a number of newspapers came to the conclusion that "yuppies" were the most promising market segment. They based that conclusion on several reasons. The first was that yuppies had high incomes and spent their money in ways that appealed to retailers. They also had interests that were relatively distinct, so that information products could be tailored specifically to them. Finally, yuppies had relatively low readership rates;

hence newspapers had the potential to show major increases in readership if they could build a product that was effective in attracting yuppie readers. In response to these considerations a number of newspapers allocated major resources to such an effort.

As a result of this decision other audience segments, such as minority groups and whites with lower levels of education and readership, were ignored. In particular, a number of papers virtually abandoned coverage of the central city and the minorities who lived there. Needless to say, that led to further declines in readership among those audience segments.

What is the long-term consequence of this? Researchers have identified a phenomenon called the knowledge gap (Tichenor, Donohue, & Olien, 1970, 1980; Gaziano, 1983, 1984). The knowledge gap suggests that as information increases about a topic, particularly one that is complex or technical, the knowledge of different audience segments increases at different rates. More specifically, as information about public affairs or scientific topics increases over time, the knowledge of groups with little education also increases, but the better-educated segment's amount of knowledge about those topics increases at a much more rapid rate. That pattern is illustrated in Exhibit 17.5.

One of the main reasons this phenomenon occurs is because of differential access to information among audience segments. Newspapers and other print media typically carry much more in-depth information about these topics than broadcast media, and the print media are used more heavily by the better-educated audience segments.

Thus, if a newspaper applies a limited marketing perspective and moves toward being a class instead of a mass medium, focusing most of its efforts on the better-educated groups in the society, the knowledge gap is likely to increase. As a consequence American society may become even more divided into information haves and have nots. And in a time when the power and importance of information is greater than ever

EXHIBIT 17.5. THE KNOWLEDGE GAP

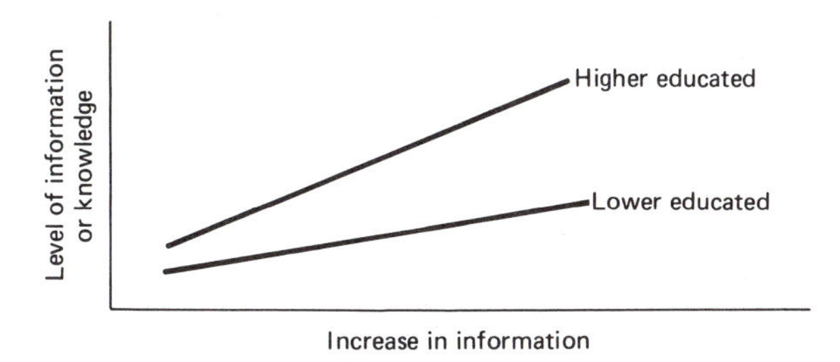

before, that would have enormous long-run implications for the country as a whole.

Of course the future of the country should be important to media executives because as citizens, their lives are directly affected by patterns occurring in society. But if that societal connection is not direct enough, media managers can consider their own business self-interest, for it turns out that making a decision to disregard major segments of the community is also a poor business choice: it is dangerous for any mass medium to ignore a sizeable market segment.

Such danger comes on a number of fronts. First, once a market segment stops using a medium, it is very hard to regain their allegiance. Witness the difficulty that movie theaters have had attracting older patrons.

Second, advertisers' interests are famous for their mercurial nature. The audience segment of low interest for advertisers today may become a hot, high-profile target segment tomorrow. Witness the sudden interest among advertisers in marketing to senior citizens when it was discovered how large a proportion of discretionary income that segment of the population controlled. In turn, abandoning the minority and less-educated segments of the population may, beyond its societal damage, hurt the newspapers ability to deliver retailers' messages to new target market segments. As that happens the profits of the papers will suffer and the newspapers' franchise will be eroded.

An alternative approach is exemplified by the reaction of Knight-Ridder executives at the *Miami Herald* to the large Spanish-speaking populations in their home county; it grew from approximately 300,000 in 1970 to 750,000 in 1975. The county's Planning Department reported that Hispanics account for about 90 percent of the net increase of 490,000 county residents, and 85 percent of them have Cuban background with 42 percent of the county's total population being Hispanic in 1985.

The *Herald*'s management recognized that their newspaper was not serving those groups. Instead of abandoning the Spanish-speaking population, the newspaper's heads decided to risk major resources by starting a Spanish-language supplement, *El Miami Herald*, to come free with the main newspaper for those readers who want it. The main newspaper has also extensively expanded its English language coverage of Hispanics. All of those efforts—including the elevation of Angel Castillo, Jr., a leading Hispanic, to assistant managing editor/news, and the bringing back to Miami of Janet Chusmir, one of Knight-Ridder's more able executives as executive editor—point to the commitment by the newspaper to inform, interpret, and allow a multiplicity of voices for all segments of society.

Such decisions were not easy. They entailed building a new staff with Spanish fluency. Even more complex, they required establishing or tremendously improving coverage of the Spanish and Cuban communities, not only in Miami but throughout the Caribbean and Central and South America. Coverage from each of those areas was the top priority of most of the new readers that the *Herald* wanted.

The decision also required finding, recruiting, hiring, and training bilingual advertising and circulation staffs and setting up sales and delivery networks across whole new regions of the metro area. And all of that had to take place at the same time as the *Herald* faced new, devastating competition from the Tribune Company's powerfully improved newspaper at Ft. Lauderdale, which cut into a large percentage of the *Herald's* circulation in the northern, wealthy counties.

Still, the Miami efforts to reach the Hispanic population made sense. For the Ft. Lauderdale competition would have come whether Miami reached out to its changing home-county readership or not. By making ties with the Hispanic community, the *Herald* and *El Herald* were, at least, positioned to bring new revenues from advertisers who wanted to reach the Hispanic population of the Miami area. Further, the extensive marketing and community contact activities associated with the Spanish-language edition also gave the English-language *Miami Herald* additional credibility with its traditional advertisers. As savvy media executives, Knight-Ridder understood the growing importance of their new customers, and despite difficulties in doing it, those customers felt reassured by the newspaper's connection with them.

Capitalizing on Bigness

The trend toward bigness in the media, especially the concentration of ownership through mergers and acquisitions, creates enormous financial and people resources for media companies. Effective utilization of these resources allows information firms to more effectively perform their social responsibilities.

For example, we saw in Chapter 3 how some newspaper companies use the dollars freed up by technological innovations to expand both news coverage and advertising, thereby better serving both their audience and advertiser markets. And some newspaper groups, such as Knight-Ridder, have done just that; they have invested major resources to improve the news/editorial product of their newspapers. That is certainly part of the basis that resulted in their winning an unprecedented seven Pulitzer prizes in 1986.

Unfortunately, using the resources offered by group ownership to strengthen the news product does not appear to be a general pattern in the newspaper industry. For example, a recent study by Barry Litman and Janet Bridges (1986) of a sample of 100 newspapers in 78 communities concluded that "chain size is associated with both a smaller amount of actual news space and a smaller staff to fill it. . . ." (p. 22).

Let's look at how bigness is affecting two other media industries, trade book publishing and records, and the fulfillment of their responsibility to provide the public with access to a multiplicity of artistic voices.

Earlier we mentioned that one aspect of bigness is the increasing emphasis on producing big sellers: "blockbuster" books and "gorilla" records. Book publishing firms and record companies that are purchased by multimedia conglomerates receive increasing pressure to produce large profits. Marketing books and records with enormous sales are a quick way to respond to that demand. The emphasis on multimedia tie-ins is another important part of this trend.

One result of this increased emphasis on marketing products to create huge sales is a change in the balance of power in both book publishing and record companies. The influence of marketing, promotion, and sales departments increases, and the importance of creative people—artists, editors, writers, and directors—is reduced.

For example, the emphasis on creating blockbuster books has had a major impact on book publishing (Powell, 1982). An important part of the blockbuster publishing strategy is to create the appearance of a best seller by paying huge advances and creating star authors. That results in less acquisition dollars available to be spent on authors who are not so well known, even though they may represent the next generation of talent in the literary world. Further, agents and lawyers, not the authors and editors, take on important roles in the decision-making process. That shifts the emphasis from what should be tried as a new literary form to what will sell.

In the record business, the emphasis on marketing resulted in development of what is called a product-image orientation toward songs (Ryan & Peterson, 1982). Songs are referred to by words indicating the stage in the decision process through which the song passes: "property," "copyright," "demo," "tape," "cut," "master," "release," and, finally, a "hit" or a "dud." That sort of product-image language focuses the attention of the creative people on the commercial rather than the artistic values of the work; it also increases the power of the marketing/promotion departments. Indeed, in a typical record company, five of the seven major departments have marketing, promotion, or sales responsibilities.

The marketing/promotion emphasis has also changed the work of creative employees. For example, book editors have less time to spend working with authors and their manuscripts (Powell, 1982). Providing less help to authors to develop removes the craftlike atmosphere that used to prevail in the author-editor process. Editors now spend more time acquiring manuscripts and making deals with the result that many publishing executives prefer to sign books that require less editing.

The big-hit emphasis has had a similar impact on song writers (Ryan & Peterson, 1982). Frequently, composers must take into account the product image that a recording company is attempting to portray for its recordings. Indeed, some successful song writers have developed what is termed a commercial professional strategy based on an image of what will be accepted by music publishers and others down the decision chain in the production and marketing processes.

The emphasis on producing big-selling books and records may result in a reduction in the number and diversity of artistic voices in the media, with long-term negative consequences for the media firms that produce such works. For example, having less resources to develop new authors reduces the long-term financial strength of many trade book publishers. Over time, many of their blockbusters are bound to fail, and they will have few other offerings to provide profits to the firm. Further, focusing on only a few star writers or performers reduces the pool of talent that the media companies need to position themselves successfully for the future.

The executives who lead book publishing and record firms can make decisions that will redress the imbalance that has developed in their organizations. They can adopt strategies that will take into account both long-term business and social consequences. For example, they can consciously develop decision-making structures to increase the authority of editors and other creative executives. In trade publishing this does not mean a return to an earlier era when scant attention was paid to marketing considerations, but it would tilt the balance back toward the time when literary considerations were significant.

With the substantial resources available to book publishers and record companies resulting from their purchase by media conglomerates, media leaders at those firms can now develop conscious strategies to invest some of their resources in finding and nurturing new talent. From a strictly business viewpoint, a broadened talent pool is the most likely source from which to broaden the potential audience for these products. And society benefits too, for such a strategy will increase the diversity of artistic voices that reach the populace.

How can this be done in practice? By its personnel policies a publisher could free enough financial and personnel resources to give the best editors time to work closely with a few promising authors. It could also tie editors' bonuses to such work. Instead of straight salary as a basis of pay, incentives could also be provided to middle- and lower-level editors to seek and sign up new talent; this is already working in a few publishing houses.

In short, a turn to the big-seller mentality is not the only possibility offered by the concentration of ownership and, as a result, financial resources. That approach is an unimaginative response to a short-sighted demand for quick profits; it is also a route to long-term profit decline. Wouldn't it be better to adopt a strategy that takes into account the long-term financial health of the organization and focuses on developing a pool of creative talent? That may cut into the bottom line now, but which approach will protect the firm's financial health in the future? At the same time, an added benefit of a long-term strategy is that the media will be far more effective in carrying out their responsibility to provide outlets for diverse artistic voices.

Capitalizing on Technological Improvements

All media are confronted with an onslaught of major technological advances. This is especially true of television where a combination of higher quality video, miniaturization of cameras, utilization of satellites, and stereo sound has created scores of new possibilities.

For instance, satellite technology has afforded tremendous new opportunities for remote coverage of both events and issues. It makes possible shows such as "Nightline," which gather together panelists from diverse locations in the United States and the world for discussion and debate on timely issues, on a daily basis. It also allows instant news coverage from virtually any spot a reporter and equipment can reach on the globe.

Too often, however, this technology is used not to push news coverage to its limit. Instead, it is primarily employed to promote a station's image. Even if the event is trivial, many news directors seek out events which can demonstrate their station's remote transmission capabilities, accompanied by graphics to remind viewers how technologically up to date they are. This kind of coverage does little to strengthen the station's news operation and, in fact, often diverts financial resources, weakening the news gathering process.

New technology also provides an opportunity to serve a segment of advertisers more effectively than television could in the past. Historically, making TV commercials was very costly and the professionals involved in ad agencies and production companies were the only people who could produce high-quality work, and commercials done by the local TV station were quite amateurish. They were limited to either "talking heads" (simply a camera pointing at a merchant speaking) or they had poor sound, bad video, and thin copy, partly because of the station's reliance less on sophisticated equipment than was being used by the networks and the production houses.

New technology has dramatically improved the possible quality of video productions and reduced the price of many pieces of television equipment. Today local stations can produce electronic images that are indistinguishable from those that used to come only on film. Because of the possibilities of retaping and ease of editing, production costs have also been reduced.

This availability of low-cost, high-quality equipment occurred at the same time that there was an increased demand for TV advertising by local retailers, even relatively small ones. As we saw in Chapter 2, TV stations have begun to more aggressively sell in local markets. Of course, the stations use the new technology to produce commercials for their own customers. Because the cost is so reasonable the stations are also in a position to open the door to advertising accounts who might previously never have put their message on television. As those accounts air their messages, the station's financial performance is strengthened, and its service to its market improved.

Some stations have taken technology advances a step further. Seizing upon the broader opportunity to do better work at less cost, they have set up separate units or divisions to use the station's production capabilities to serve as an alternative to advertising agencies. The stations produce commercials for placement wherever the advertiser wishes: a competing station in the market, a cable system, anywhere. Because of heavy utilization of their production equipment, the stations can offer lower pricing to attract small advertisers. Special advertising sales personnel work with small retailers to create high-quality, low-cost commercials, which can be targeted to specific zones via careful placement on cable systems and on low-power TV stations.

Such a strategy strengthens the station as a business in several ways. It increases the station's income by providing a new income stream. It enhances the station's overall revenue base by expanding the number of advertisers with whom the station is working. It also allows for faster amortization of the equipment and, in turn, more rapid purchase of the next generation of technology.

At the same time, the strategy helps TV stations to serve more effectively as a bridge of information in the economic system. It opens a powerful advertising channel to a set of advertisers previously excluded because of cost considerations. And it effectively fulfills both business and social responsibility objectives. Moreover, similar results can often be obtained if media leaders learn to view technology not just from a cost effectiveness and efficiency point of view but also from the perspective of better serving the market. High performance of a medium's social responsibility flows from effectively serving its market.

SOME LESSONS FOR MEDIA MANAGERS

What lessons can managers of various media extrapolate from the foregoing discussion? There are many, but several are particularly important:

1. The effective media manager should be aware of the danger of taking a short-term view, focusing too heavily on quick profits at the expense of long-term financial gains. The wise executive balances short-term and long-term implications. A start toward achieving such a balance is for media leaders to ask and answer the question: "What will this decision, action, or plan mean to this department or this firm 5 years and 10 years from now?" Confronting

those answers in a thoughtful way will greatly improve every media executive's long-term record.

2. Managers should also be aware of the implications of the trends outlined in this chapter and of the importance to their firm of fulfilling its social responsibilities to protect both their company's franchise and its bottom line. The examples we presented illustrate that a long-range managerial philosophy can and should include elements of both a sound business perspective and a deep, ongoing commitment to being socially responsible.
3. Information executives should realize that there is little that anyone except the top executives in their firm can do to change the direction of the trends we cited. Yet every manager, even down at the departmental level, can influence how these trends are viewed in the company and how they "play out" on the local scene.
4. To make real the awareness of the trends we have just outlined as well as a commitment to the media's social responsibility, individual managers should set their own agenda of how they are going to deal with these forces. What are they going to do in their own firm or department to ensure there is balance between profit and social responsibility? How are they going to teach others that striking such a balance is important for business?
5. Recognize the importance of not raising questions about budgets, plans, and objectives in isolation, but, rather, link those questions to the impact of the trends and social responsibilities we've just discussed. These linkages must be made continually as a way to divert excessive focus on the bottom line. That is a pattern on the rise as media organizations grow, as people with business rather than journalistic orientations fill prominent positions, and as the investing public, spurred on by the media's reporting of quarterly profits and losses, demands quick, high, continually rising returns.
6. Linking profit and social responsibility considerations together isn't just a nice thing to do; it is good business. Thus, instead of simply asking, "Is it wise to buy a new piece of technology?" the department head or the local radio or television station manager might ask the boss whether the purchase will help protect the franchise of their organization five years hence. That combines business and social responsibility in a realistic, fused package.
7. A similar approach should be applied when the inevitable cutbacks are proposed. The executive should ask what the proposed reduction will do to the franchise of the medium 5 or 10 years down the road. Do the short-term savings really turn out to be savings if the media firm loses market share as well as the ability to deliver market segments to its advertisers or readers? Sometime the answer is yes, but there are many other instances where it makes long-term financial sense not to make cuts or, at least, to moderate the cuts proposed and reduce the length of time they are allowed to remain in place.

By maintaining a focus on long-term business goals, media managers at every level will be able to keep in mind sound business objectives, profits, and their company's social responsibilities. Adopting the long-term perspective also allows the individual, no matter what the orientation of the firm, to take some small actions to protect the media franchise and to respond constructively to the one group who will always expect the media to uphold a special place in society: the public.

A CLOSING NOTE

We hope this journey through the world of media management has given you a sense of the excitement that is possible in exercising leadership in an information organization. Because of the trends we noted throughout this text, the U.S. media are among the most dynamic, fast-changing industries in the world. The rapid change that confronts them also creates enormous responsibilities and challenges for those who direct them. In addition, as we hope you now recognize, the unique character and role of the media in America creates special social responsibilities for the executives who lead them.

As long as you are a part of the media world we hope that your career will see you creating, implementing, or supporting plans that will enable your media firm to be a sound, well-managed, profitable enterprise, but one that also actively acknowledges and fulfills its social responsibilities. In the long run, good business demands that the media take their social responsibilities seriously.

At the same time, neither media executives nor staffs should take themselves too seriously. Hence, our last rule for media management is straightforward:

Make quality things happen and have fun.

References

Abell, Derek F. "Competitive Market Strategies: Some Generalizations and Hypotheses," (Marketing Science Institute Working Paper, Report no. 75-107). Cambridge, MA: Marketing Science Institute, 1975.

Adler, Renata. *Reckless Disregard: Westmoreland v. CBS, Sharon v. Time, Inc.* New York: Knopf, 1986.

Bales, Robert F. *Interaction Process Analysis*. Reading, MA: Addison-Wesley, 1951.

Barro, Robert J. *Macroeconomics*. New York: Wiley, 1984.

Barnard, Chester I. *The Functions of the Executive*. Cambridge, MA: Harvard University Press, 1938.

Baumal, William J., and Blinder, Alan S. *Economics: Principles and Policy: Macroeconomics* (3rd ed.). New York: Harcourt Brace Jovanovich, 1986.

Bennis, Warren. "The 4 Competencies of Leadership." *Training & Development Journal*, August 1984, 15-19.

Blake, Robert R., and Mouton, Jane S. *The Managerial Grid III: The Key to Leadership Excellence*. Houston: Gulf Publishing, 1985.

Blanchard, Kenneth, and Johnson, Spencer. *The One Minute Manager*. New York: Morrow, 1982.

Bogart, Leo. "The Public's Use and Perception of Newspapers," *Public Opinion Quarterly* (Winter 1984) *48*:709-719.

Carter, T. Barton, Franklin, Marc, and Wright, Jay B. *The First Amendment and the Fourth Estate: The Law of Mass Media* (3rd ed.). Mineola, NY: Foundation Press, 1985.

Chandler, Alfred D. Jr. *Strategy and Structure: Chapters in the History of the American Industrial Enterprise*. Cambridge, MA: MIT Press, 1962.

Colley, Russell H. *Defining Advertising Goals for Measured Advertising Results*. New York: Association of National Advertisers, 1961.

Compaine, Benjamin, Sterling, Christopher H., Guback, Thomas, and Noble, J. Kendrick Jr. *Anatomy of the Communications Industry: Who Owns the Media?* White Plains, NY: Knowledge Industry Publications, 1982.

Dominick, Joseph R. *The Dynamics of Mass Communication*. Reading, MA: Addison-Wesley, 1983.

Donnelly, James H. Jr., Gibson, James L., and Ivanevich, John M. *Fundamentals of Management* (5th ed.). Plano, TX: Business Publications, 1984.

Drucker, Peter F. *The Practice of Management*. New York: Harper & Row, 1954.

Evans, Martin G. "Leadership and Motivation: A Core Concept," *Academy of Management Journal* (March 1970) *13*:91-102.

Fayol, Henri. *General and Industrial Management*. Constance Storrs (trans). London: Sir Isaac Pitman & Sons, 1949.

Fiedler, Fred E. "The Contingency Model," In Harold Proshansky and Bernard Seidenberg, Eds. *Basic Studies in Social Psychology*. (pp. 538-551), New York: Holt, Rinehart & Winston, 1965.

Fiedler, Fred E. "Validation and Extension of the Contingency Model of Leadership Effectiveness," *Psychology Bulletin* (August 1971) *76*:128-148.

Freeman, Richard B., and Medoff, James L. *What do Unions do?* New York: Basic Books, 1984.

Follett, Mary P. *The New State*. Glocester, MA: Peter Smith, 1918.

Galbraith, J. R. "Designing the Innovating Organization," *Organizational Dynamics* (Winter 1982) 3-24.

Gaziano, Cecilie. "Neighborhood Newspapers, Citizen Groups and Public Affairs Knowledge Gaps," *Journalism Quarterly* (Autumn 1984) *61*(3):556-566, 599.

Gaziano, Cecilie. "The Knowledge Gap: An Analytical Review of Media Effects." *Communication Research* (October 1983) *10*(4):447-486.

Ghiselli, Edwin E. *Explorations in Managerial Talent*. Pacific Palisades, CA: Goodyear, 1971.

Gillmor, Donald M., and Barron, Jerome A. *Mass Communication Law Cases and Comment*. St. Paul, MN: West Publishing, 1984.

Gollin, Albert E., and Bloom, Nicolas A. *Newspapers in American News Habits: A Comparative Assessment*. New York: Newspaper Advertising Bureau, 1983.

Griffin, Ricky W. *Management*. Boston: Houghton Mifflin, 1983.

Hackman, J. Richard. "Work Design" in J. Richard Hackman and J. Lloyd Suttle, Eds. *Improving Life at Work*. (pp. 128-130), Santa Monica, CA: Goodyear, 1977.

Hersey, Paul. *The Situational Leader*. New York: Warner Books, 1985.

Herzberg, Frederick. *Work and the Nature of Man*. New York: World Publishing, 1966.

Hofstede, G. W. "The Colors of Collars," *Columbia Journal of World Business* (1972) 7(5):72-79.

House, Robert J. "A Path-Goal Theory of Leader Effectiveness." *Administrative Science Quarterly* (September 1971) *16*(5):321-328.

House, Robert J., and Baetz, Mary L. "Leadership: Some Empirical Generalizations and New Research Directions," In Barry M. Shaw, Ed. *Research in Organization Behavior* (vol 1). (pp. 348-354), Greenwich, CT: JAI Press, 1979.

Jeffres, Leo W. *Mass Media Processes and Effects*. Prospect Heights, IL: Waveland Press, 1986.

Kanter, Rosabeth Moss. *The Change Masters*. New York: Simon & Schuster, 1983.

Katz, Robert L. "Skills of an Effective Administrator," *Harvard Business Review* (September-October 1974) 52(5):90-102.

Kenichi, Ohmae. *The Mind of the Strategist*. New York: Penguin Books, 1983.

Kipnis, David, and Schmidt, Stuart. "The Language of Persuasion," *Psychology Today* (April 1985) 40-46.

Krugman, Herbert. "The Impact of Television Advertising: Learning without Involvement," *Public Opinion Quarterly* (1965) 29:349-356.

Levitt, Theodore. *The Marketing Imagination*. New York: The Free Press, 1983.

Likert, Renis. *New Patterns of Management*. New York: McGraw-Hill, 1961.

Likert, Renis. *The Human Organization*. New York: McGraw-Hill, 1967.

Litman, Barry, and Bridges, Janet. "An Economic Analysis of Daily Newspaper Performance." *Newspaper Research Journal* (Spring 1986) 7(3):9-26.

Mahoney, Thomas A., Jerdee, Thomas H., and Carroll, Stephen J. "The Jobs of Management." *Industrial Relations* (February 1965) *4*(2):97-110.
Mansfield, Edwin. *Microeconomics: Theory/Applications* (5th ed.). New York: Norton, 1985.
March, James G. "Decisions in Organizations and Theories of Choice." In A. Van de Ven and W. F. Joyce, Eds. *Perspectives on Design and Behavior*. New York: Wiley, 1981.
Maslow, Abraham H. *Motivation and Personality* (2nd ed.). New York: Harper & Row, 1970.
Mayo, Elton. *The Human Problems of an Industrial Civilization*. New York: Macmillan, 1953.
McGregor, Douglas. *The Human Side of Enterprise*. New York: McGraw-Hill, 1960.
Meyer, Herbert H., Kay, Emanual, and French, John R. P. "Split Roles in Performance Appraisal," *Harvard Business Review* (January-February 1965) *43*(1):123-139.
Meyer, Phillip. *The Newspaper Survival Book*. Bloomington, IN: Indiana University Press, 1985.
Miller, S. "Measuring Newsroom Salaries: Is the Glass Half Full or Half Empty?" *The Bulletin of the American Society of Newspaper Editors* (May-June 1986) 4-7.
Miller, Sherod, Wackman, Daniel B., Demmitt, Dallas R., and Demmitt, Nancy J. *Working Together: Productive Communication on the Job*. Littleton, CO: Interpersonal Communication Programs, 1985.
Mitchell, Arnold. *Nine American Life Styles*. New York: Macmillan, 1983.
Mockler, Robert J. *The Management Control Process*. Englewood Cliffs, NJ: Prentice-Hall, 1972.
Munsterberg, Hugo. *Psychology and Industrial Efficiency* (reprint of 1913 ed.). New York: Arno Press, 1930.
Nelson, Harold L., and Teeter, Dwight L. Jr. *Law of Mass Communication: Freedom and Control of Print and Broadcast Media* (5th ed.). Mineola, NY: Foundation Press, 1986.
Ohmae, Kenichi. *The Mind of the Strategist: The Art of Japanese Business*. New York: McGraw-Hill, 1982.
Ouchi, William G. *Theory Z: How American Business Can Meet the Japanese Challenge*. Reading, MA: Addison-Wesley, 1981.
Powell, Walter W. "From Craft to Corporation: The Impact of Outside Ownership on Book Publishing" in Ettema and Whitney, eds. *Individuals in Mass Media Organizations: Creativity and Constraint*. Beverly Hills: Sage Publications, 1982.
Ries, Al, and Trout, Jack. *Positioning: The Battle for Your Mind*. New York: McGraw-Hill, 1981.
Robinson, John P. *Changes in Americans' Use of Time: 1965-1975*. Cleveland: Communication Research Center, Cleveland State University, August 1977.
Roper Organization, The. *Public Perceptions of Television and Other Mass Media: A Twenty-five Year Review, 1959-1980*. New York: Television Information Office, 1981.
Rothschild, William. *Putting It All Together: A Guide to Strategic Thinking*. New York: Amacom Books, 1976.
Ryan, John, and Peterson, Richard A. "The Product Image: The Fate of Creativity in Country Music Songwriting," In James Ettema and D. Charles Whitney, Eds. *Individuals in Mass Media Organizations: Creativity and Constraint*, Beverly Hills: Sage Publications, 1982.

Samuelson, P. A. *Economics* (11th ed.). New York: McGraw-Hill, 1980.
Schon, D. *Beyond the Stable State*. New York: Norton, 1971.
Southwick, Lawrence Jr. *Managerial Economics*. Plano, TX: Business Publications, 1985.
Steil, Lyman K., et al. *Effective Listening: Key to Your Success*, New York: Random House, 1983.
Sterling, Christopher H., and Haight, Timothy R. *The Mass Media: Aspen Institute Guide to Communications Industry Trends*. New York: Praeger Special Studies, 1978.
Stogdill, Ralph M. "Personal Factors Associated with Leadership: A Survey of the Literature," *Journal of Psychology* (January 1948) *25*(1):35-71.
Stokes, Paul M. *A Total Systems Approach to Management Control*. New York: American Management Associations, 1968.
Stoner, James A. F. *Management* (2nd ed.). Englewood Cliffs, NJ: Prentice-Hall, 1982.
Taylor, Frederick W. *The Principles of Scientific Management*. New York: Harper & Row, 1911.
Taylor, Frederick W. *Scientific Management*. New York: Harper & Row, 1947.
Tichenor, Phillip J., Donohue, George A., and Olien, Clarice N. *Community Conflict and the Press*. Beverly Hills: Sage Publications, 1980.
Tichenor, Phillip J., Donohue, George A., and Olien, Clarice N. "Mass Media Flow and Differential Growth of Knowledge." *Public Opinion Quarterly* (1970) *34*(2):159-170.
Times Mirror Company. *The People and the Press*. Los Angeles: Times Mirror Company, 1986.
Van de Ven, Andrew. "Problem Solving, Planning, and Innovation: Part 1, Test of the Program Planning Model." *Human Relations* (1980) *33*:711-740.
Van de Ven, Andrew. "Problem Solving, Planning, and Innovation: Part 2, Speculations for Theory and Practice." *Human Relations* (1980) *33*:757-779.
Veronis, Suhler & Associates. *Communications Industry Report*. New York: Veronis, Suhler & Associates, 1986.
Vroom, Victor H. "Leadership," In Marvin D. Dunnette, Ed. *Handbook of Industrial and Organizational Psychology* (pp. 1527-1551), Chicago: Rand McNally, 1976.
Wackman, Daniel B., Salmon, Charles T., and Salmon, Caryn C. "Key Factors in Developing an Advertising Agency-Client Relationship." *Journal of Advertising Research 26*: no. 6, 21-28, 1986.
Wagner, Harvey M. *Principles of Management Science*. Englewood Cliffs, NJ: Prentice-Hall, 1970.
Weick, Karl. *The Social-Psychology of Organizing*. Reading, MA: Addison-Wesley, 1979.
Whiteside, T. *The Blockbuster Complex*. Middletown, CT: Wesleyan University Press, 1981.
Whitney, D. Charles. *The Media and the People: Soundings From Two Communities*. Working Paper Series of the Gannett Center for Media Studies of Columbia University, November, 1985.
Wright, B.E., and Lavine, John M. *The Constant Dollar Newspaper: An Economic Analysis Covering the Last Two Decades*. Chicago: Inland Daily Press Association, 1982.
Zenger, John H. "Leadership: Management's Better Half." *Training* (December 1985) 44-53.

Bibliography of Media Management and Economics

Prepared by
Rita Du Charme and John M. Lavine

ADVERTISING

Aaker, David A., and Myers, John G. *Advertising Management.* Englewood Cliffs, NJ: Prentice-Hall, 1982.

Albion, Mark S., and Farris, Paul W. *The Advertising Controversy: Evidence on the Economic Effects of Advertising.* Boston: Auburn, 1981.

Anderson, Robert L., and Barry, Thomas E. *Advertising Management: Text and Cases.* Columbus, OH: Charles E. Merrill, 1979.

Bergendorff, Fred L., Smith, Charles H., and Webster, Lance. *Broadcast Advertising and Promotion.* New York: Hastings House, 1983.

Bogart, Leo. *Strategy in Advertising: Matching Media and Messages to Markets and Motivation* (2nd ed). Chicago: Crain Books, 1984.

Colley, Russell H. *Defining Advertising Goals for Measured Advertising Results.* New York: Association of National Advertisers, 1961.

Cross, Donna Wolfolk. *Mediaspeak: How Television Makes Up Your Mind.* New York: Putnam, 1983.

Ferguson, James M. *The Advertising Rate Structure in the Daily Newspaper Industry.* Englewood Cliffs, NJ: Prentice-Hall, 1963.

Heighton, Elizabeth J., and Cunningham, Don R. *Advertising in the Broadcast and Cable Media.* Belmont, CA: Wadsworth, 1984.

International Advertising Association. *Controversy Advertising: How Advertisers Present Points of View in Public Affairs.* New York: Hastings House, 1977.

Jamieson, Kathleen Hall, and Campbell, Karolyn Kohn. *The Interplay of Influence: Mass Media and Their Publics in News, Advertising, Politics.* Belmont, CA: Wadsworth, 1983.

Maroney, Denman. *The Cable Television Advertising Market, 1986–90.* White Plains, NY: Knowledge Industry Publications, 1986.

McGann, Anthony, and Russell, J. Thomas. *Advertising Media: A Management Approach.* Homewood, IL: Irwin Publishing, 1983.

McIver, Colin. *Case Studies in Marketing, Advertising and Public Relations.* North Pomfret, VT: David & Charles, 1984.

Meyers, William. *The Image-Makers: Power and Persuasion on Madison Avenue.* New York: Times Books, 1984.

Patti, Charles H., ed. *Cases in Advertising and Promotion Management.* New York: Wiley, 1983.

Preston, Ivan. *The Great American Blow-Up: Puffery in Advertising and Selling.* Madison, WI: University of Wisconsin Press, 1975.

Ray, Michael L. *Advertising and Communication Management.* Englewood Cliffs, NJ: Prentice-Hall, 1982.

Rohrer, Daniel Morgan, ed. *Mass Media, Freedom of Speech, and Advertising.* Dubuque, IO: Kendall/Hunt, 1979.

Schudson, Michael. *Advertising, the Uneasy Persuasion: Its Dubious Impact on American Society.* New York: Basic Books, 1984.

Weilbacher, William M. *Advertising.* New York: Macmillan, 1984.

Wilmshurst, John. *The Fundamentals of Advertising.* London: Heineman, 1985.

Young, Judy, ed. *Videotex and Teletext in the US and UK.* London: Financial Times Media Intelligence Unit, 1984.

BOOK PUBLISHING

Armstrong, Donald. *Book Publishing: A Working Guide.* Houston: D. Armstrong Co., 1979.

Association of American University Presses. *One Book—Five Ways: The Publishing Procedures of Five University Presses.* Los Altos, CA: William Kaufman, 1978.

Cadman, Eileen, et al. *Rolling Our Own: Women as Printers, Publishers and Distributors.* Minority Press Group Series No. 4. London: Minority Press Group, 1981.

Compaine, Benjamin M. *The Book Industry in Transition: An Economic Analysis of Book Distribution and Marketing.* White Plains, NY: Knowledge Industry Publications, 1978.

Coser, Lewis, et al. *Books: The Culture and Commerce of Publishing.* New York: Basic Books, 1982.

Dessauer, John. *Book Publishing: What It Is, What It Does* (2nd ed). Ann Arbor, MI: R.R. Bowker, 1981.

DuBoff, Leonard D. *Book Publishers' Legal Guide.* Newton Upper Falls, MA: Butterworth Legal Publications, 1983.

Duke, Judith S. *The Technical, Scientific and Medical Publishing Market.* White Plains, NY: Knowledge Industry Publications, 1985.

Geiser, Elizabeth, and Dolin, Arnold, eds. *The Business of Book Publishing.* Boulder, CO: Westview Press, 1984.

Greenberger, Martin, ed. *Electronic Publishing Plus: Media for a Technological Future.* White Plains, NY: Knowledge Industry Publications, 1985.

Hacker, Jeffrey H. *Publishing Books for Consumers: Market Trends and Forecasts, 1985–88.* White Plains, NY: Knowledge Industry Publications, 1985.

Joyce, Donald Franklin. *Gatekeepers of Black Culture: Black-Owned Book Publishing in the United States, 1817–1981.* Contributions in Afro-American and African Studies, No. 70. Westport, CT: Greenwood Press, 1983.

BROADCASTING

Alten, Stanley R. *Audio in Media* (2nd ed). Belmont, CA: Wadsworth Publishing, 1986.

Baehr, Helen, and Ryan, Michelle. *Shut Up and Listen! Women and Local Radio: A View from the Inside.* London: Comedia, 1984.

Bergendorff, Fred L., Smith, Charles H., and Webster, Lance. *Broadcast Advertising and Promotion.* New York: Hastings House, 1983.

Beville, Hugh Malcolm, Jr. *Audience Ratings: Radio, Television and Cable.*

Hillsdale, NJ: Lawrence Erlbaum Associates, 1985.
Bittner, John R. *Broadcast Laws and Regulations*. Englewood Cliffs, NJ: Prentice-Hall, 1982.
Bittner, John R. *Broadcasting and Telecommunication: An Introduction* (2nd ed). Englewood Cliffs, NJ: Prentice-Hall, 1985.
Coleman, Howard W. *Case Studies in Broadcast Management* (2nd ed). New York: Hastings House, 1978.
Eastman, Susan Tyler. *Broadcast/Cable Programming: Strategies and Practices*. Belmont, CA: Wadsworth Publishing, 1985.
Gross, Lynne S. *Telecommunications: An Introduction to Radio, Television and the Developing Media*. Dubuque, IO: William C. Brown, 1983.
Heighton, Elizabeth J., and Cunningham, Don R. *Advertising in the Broadcast and Cable Media*. Belmont, CA: Wadsworth, 1984.
Hilliard, Robert L. *Radio Broadcasting: An Introduction to the Sound Medium* (3rd ed). White Plains, NY: Longman, 1985.
Howard, Herbert H. *Group and Cross-media Ownership of Television Stations: 1986*. Washington, DC: National Association of Broadcasters, 1986.
Lewis, John F. *Who Are Those Guys? A Monograph for Business on the News Media Today*. Washington, DC: The Media Institute, 1982.
Marcus, Norman. *Broadcast and Cable Management*. Englewood Cliffs, NJ: Prentice-Hall, 1986.
Medoff, Norman J., and Tanquary, Tom. *Portable Video: ENG and EFP*. White Plains, NY: Knowledge Industry Publications, 1986.
Mueller, Milton. *Property Rights in Radio Communications: The Key to the Reform of Telecommunications Regulation*. Policy Analysis Study (No. 11). Washington, DC: The Cato Institute, 1983.
Nadel, Mark, and Noam, Eli, eds. *The Economics of Traditional Broadcasting (VHF/UHF): An Anthology*. New York: Columbia University Graduate School of Business, 1983.
Quaal, Ward L., and Brown, James A. *Broadcast Management* (2nd ed). New York: Hastings House, 1976.
Roper Organization, The. *Public Perceptions of Television and Other Mass Media: A Twenty-Five Year Review, 1959–1980*. New York: Television Information Office, 1981.
Rowan, Ford. *Broadcast Fairness: Doctrine, Practice, Prospects*. White Plains, NY: Longman, 1984.
Smith, F. Leslie. *Perspectives on Radio and Television: Telecommunications in the United States* (2nd ed). New York: Harper & Row, 1986.
Straus, Lawrence. *Electronic Marketing: Emerging TV and Computer Channels for Interactive Home Shopping*. White Plains, NY: Knowledge Industry Publications, 1983.
U.S. House of Representatives. Committee on Energy and Commerce. Subcommittee on Telecommunications, Consumer Protection, and Finance. *Broadcast Regulation and Station Ownership*. Washington, DC: Government Printing Office, 1985.
Warner, Charles. *Broadcast and Cable Selling*. Belmont, CA: Wadsworth, 1986.

CABLE

Baldwin, Thomas F. *Cable Communication*. Englewood Cliffs, NJ: Prentice-Hall, 1983.

Beville, Hugh Malcolm, Jr. *Audience Ratings: Radio, Television and Cable.* Hillsdale, NJ: Lawrence Erlbaum Associates, 1985.
Dixie, David, ed. *Cable Television in the USA.* London: Financial Times Business Information, 1984.
Eastman, Susan Tyler. *Broadcast/Cable Programming: Strategies and Practices.* Belmont, CA: Wadsworth Publishing, 1985.
Harrell, Bobby. *The Cable Television Technical Handbook.* Dedham, MA: Artech House, 1985.
Heighton, Elizabeth J., and Cunningham, Don R. *Advertising in the Broadcast and Cable Media.* Belmont, CA: Wadsworth, 1984.
Hollowell, Mary Louise, ed. *The Cable/Broadband Communications Book.* White Plains, NY: Knowledge Industry Publications, 1983.
Joint Communications Corporation. *The Causes of Pay-TV Disconnects.* Toronto: Ministry of Transportation and Communications, 1984.
Kaatz, Ronald B. *Cable: An Advertiser's Guide to the New Electronic Media.* Chicago, IL: Crain Books, 1982.
Marcus, Norman. *Broadcast and Cable Management.* Englewood Cliffs, NJ: Prentice-Hall, 1986.
Maroney, Denman. *The Cable Television Advertising Market, 1986–90.* White Plains, NY: Knowledge Industry Publications, 1986.
Marshall, Christine, ed. *Programming in the UK and USA.* London: Financial Times Media Intelligence Unit, 1984.
Maynard, Jeff. *Cable Television.* London: Collins, 1985.
Medoff, Norman J., and Tanquary, Tom. *Portable Video: ENG and EFP.* White Plains, NY: Knowledge Industry Publications, 1986.
Neustadt, Richard M. *The Birth of Electronic Publishing: Legal and Economic Issues in Telephone, Cable and Over-the-Air Teletext and Videotext.* White Plains, NY: Knowledge Industry Publications, 1982.
Smith, R.L. *The Wired Nation.* New York: Harper & Row, 1972.
Warner, Charles. *Broadcast and Cable Selling.* Belmont, CA: Wadsworth, 1986.

CASE STUDIES

Anderson, Robert L., and Barry, Thomas E. *Advertising Management: Text and Cases.* Columbus, OH: Charles E. Merrill, 1979.
Armstrong, Michael. *Case Studies in Personnel Management.* New York: Nichols, 1979.
Bamberger, Nancy. *Videotex Production: A Case Study.* San Diego: Electronic Text Consortium, 1984.
Christians, Clifford G., Rotzoll, Kim B., and Fackler, Mark. *Media Ethics: Cases and Moral Reasoning.* White Plains, NY: Longman, 1983.
Coleman, Howard W. *Case Studies in Broadcast Management* (2nd ed). New York: Hastings House, 1978.
Harvard Business School. *Directory of Harvard Business School Cases and Related Course Materials: 1985–86.* Boston: Harvard Business School, annual.
Hurly, Paul, Laucht, Matthias, and Hlynka, Denis. *The Videotex and Teletext Handbook: Home and Office Communications Using Microcomputers and Terminals.* New York: Harper & Row, 1985.
Joint Communications Corporation. *The Causes of Pay-TV Disconnects.* Toronto: Ministry of Transportation and Communications, 1984.

Luck, David J., Ferrell, O. C. *Marketing Strategy and Plans* (2nd ed). Englewood Cliffs, NJ: Prentice-Hall, 1985.

Mallette, Malcolm F. *How Newspapers Communicate Internally: Case Studies and Samplings from a Changing Workplace.* Reston, VA: American Press Institute, 1981.

McIver, Colin. *Case Studies in Marketing, Advertising and Public Relations.* North Pomfret, VT: David & Charles, 1984.

Patti, Charles H., ed. *Cases in Advertising and Promotion Management.* New York: Wiley, 1983.

Sachsman, David, and Sloat, Warren. *The Press and the Suburbs: The Daily Newspapers of New Jersey.* New Brunswick, NJ: Rutgers, 1985.

Wilcox, Dennis L., Ault, Phillip H., and Agee, Warren K. *Public Relations: Strategies and Tactics.* New York: Harper & Row, 1986.

CIRCULATION

American Newspaper Markets, Inc. *Circulation.* Northfield, IL: American Newspaper Markets, annual.

Institute of Newspaper Controllers and Finance Officers. *Circulation Accounting Methods and Procedures.* Moorestown, NJ: INCFO, 1970.

Macklin, Robert A. *Newspaper Circulation Management Training.* Washington, DC: International Circulation Managers Association, 1979.

Standard Rate and Data Service, Inc. *SRDS Newspaper Circulation Analysis.* Skokie, IL: Standard Rate and Data Service, Inc., annual.

Thorn, William J. and Pfeil, Mary Pat. *Newspaper Circulation: Marketing the News.* White Plains, NY: Longman, 1987.

CORPORATIONS

Deal, Terrence E., and Kennedy, Allan A. *Corporate Cultures: The Rites and Rituals of Corporate Life.* Reading, MA: Addison-Wesley, 1982.

Millstein, Ira M. *The Limits of Corporate Power.* New York: Macmillan, 1981.

Naisbitt, John, and Aburdene, Patricia. *Re-Inventing the Corporation: Transforming Your Job and Your Company for the New Information Society.* New York: Warner Books, 1985.

Rubin, Bernard. *Big Business and the Mass Media.* Lexington, MA: Lexington Books, 1977.

Schiller, Herbert I. *Who Knows: Information in the Age of the Fortune 500.* Norwood, NJ: Ablex, 1982.

DESKTOP PUBLISHING

Bove, Tony, Rhodes, Cheryl, and Thomas, Wes. *The Art of Desktop Publishing.* New York: Bantam Books, 1986.

Collier, Harry, et al., eds. *Electronic Publishing Review: The International*

Journal of the Transfer of Published Information via Videotex and Online Media (1984 ed). Medford, NJ: Learned Information, 1984.

Davis, Frederic E., Wiesenberg, Michael, Barry, John A., and Langfeldt, Eva. *Desktop Publishing*. Homewood, IL: Dow Jones-Irwin, 1986.

Greenberger, Martin, ed. *Electronic Publishing Plus: Media for a Technological Future*. White Plains, NY: Knowledge Industry Publications, 1985.

Ritvo, Ken, and Kearsley, Greg. *Desktop Publishing*. La Jolla, CA: Park Row Press, 1986.

ECONOMICS

Albion, Mark S., and Farris, Paul W. *The Advertising Controversy: Evidence on the Economic Effects of Advertising*. Boston: Auburn, 1981.

Austin, Bruce A., ed. *Current Research in Film: Audiences, Economics and Law: Volume I*. Norwood, NJ: Ablex, 1985.

Baer, Walter S., et al. *Concentration of Mass Media Ownership*. Santa Monica, CA: Rand Corp., 1974.

Bagdikian, Ben H. *The Information Machines: Their Impact on Men and the Media*. New York: Harper & Row, 1971.

Bagdikian, Ben H. *The Media Monopoly*. Boston: Beacon Press, 1983.

Benjaminson, Peter. *Death in the Afternoon: America's Newspaper Giants Struggle for Survival*. Kansas City: Andrews, McMeel, Partker, Fairway, 1985.

Bensen, Stanley M. *Regulation of Media Ownership by the Federal Communications Commission: An Assessment*. Santa Monica, CA: Rand Corp., 1984.

Biel, Jacquelyn. *Low Power Television: Development and Current Status of the LPTV Industry*. Washington, DC: National Association of Broadcasters, 1985.

Braddon, Russell. *Roy Thomson of Fleet Street*. Huntington, NY: Fontana, 1968.

Chisholm, Roger K. *Principles of Economics*. Glenview, IL: Scott, Foresman, 1978.

Clarkson, Kenneth W., and Muris, Timothy J., eds. *The Federal Trade Commission Since 1970: Economic Regulation and Bureaucratic Behavior*. New York: Cambridge University Press, 1981.

Compaine, Benjamin M. *Anatomy of the Communications Industry: Who Owns the Media?* White Plains, NY: Knowledge Industry Publications, 1983.

Compaine, Benjamin M. *The Book Industry in Transition: An Economic Analysis of Book Distribution and Marketing*. White Plains, NY: Knowledge Industry Publications, 1978.

Compaine, Benjamin M. *The Newspaper Industry in the 1980s: An Assessment of Economics and Technology*. White Plains, NY: Knowledge Industry Publications, 1980.

Compaine, Benjamin M., Sterling, Christopher, Guback, Thomas, and Noble, J. Kendrick, Jr. *Who Owns the Media? Concentration of Ownership in the Communications Industry* (2nd ed). White Plains, NY: Knowledge Industry Publications, 1982.

Coser, Lewis, et al. *Books: The Culture and Commerce of Publishing*. New York: Basic Books, 1982.

Dertouzos, James, and Thorpe, Kenneth. *Newspaper Groups: Economies of Scale, Tax Laws and Merger Incentives*. Santa Monica, CA: Rand Corp., 1982.

Dixie, David, ed. *Cable Television in the USA*. London: Financial Times Business Information, 1984.

Ferguson, James M. *The Advertising Rate Structure in the Daily Newspaper Industry.* Englewood Cliffs, NJ: Prentice-Hall, 1963.

Ghiglione, Loren. *The Buying and Selling of America's Newspapers*. Indianapolis, IN: R.J. Berg, 1984.

Glatzer, Hal. *The Telecommunications Revolution: Who Controls the Airwaves?* Indianapolis, IN: Howard Sams, 1984.

Gormley, William T., Jr. *The Effects of Newspaper-Television Cross-Ownership on News Homogeneity.* Chapel Hill, NC: Institute for Research in Social Science, University of North Carolina, 1976.

Herring, James M., and Gross, Gerald C. *Telecommunications: Economics and Regulations*. Salem, NH: Ayer, 1974.

Heskett, James L. *Managing in the Service of Economy.* Boston: Harvard Business School Press, 1986.

Hirsch, Fred, and Gordon, David. *Newspaper Money.* London: Hutchinson, 1978.

Horsfield, Peter G. *Religious Television: The American Experience*. White Plains, NY: Longman, 1984.

Hoyer, Svennik, Hadenius, Stig, and Weibull, Lennart. *The Politics and Economics of the Press: A Developmental Perspective*. Beverly Hills: Sage, 1975.

Kohlmeier, Louis M., Jr., Udell, Jon G., and Anderson, Laird B., eds. *Reporting on Business and the Economy.* Englewood Cliffs, NJ: Prentice-Hall, 1981.

Lazer, Ellen A., ed. *Guide to Videotape Publishing*. White Plains, NY: Knowledge Industry Publications, 1985.

Lipsey, Richard G. *Economics*. New York: Harper & Row, 1984.

Marshall, Christine, ed. *Programming in the UK and USA*. London: Financial Times Media Intelligence Unit, 1984.

Martin, L. John, and Chaudhary, Anju Grover. *Comparative Mass Media Systems*. White Plains, NY: Longman, 1983.

Medoff, Norman J., and Tanquary, Tom. *Portable Video: ENG and EFP.* White Plains, NY: Knowledge Industry Publications, 1986.

Nadel, Mark, and Noam, Eli, eds. *The Economics of Traditional Broadcasting (VHF/UHF): An Anthology.* New York: Columbia University Graduate School of Business, 1983.

Neustadt, Richard M. *The Birth of Electronic Publishing: Legal and Economic Issues in Telephone, Cable and Over-the-Air Teletext and Videotext*. White Plains, NY: Knowledge Industry Publications, 1982.

Newsom, D. Earl. *The Newspaper: Everything You Need to Know to Make It in the Newspaper Business*. Englewood Cliffs, NJ: Prentice-Hall, 1981.

Noam, Eli M., ed. *Video Media Competition Regulation, Economics, and Technology.* New York: Columbia University Press, 1985.

Noll, Roger G., Peck, Merton J., and McGowan, John J. *Economic Aspects of Television Regulation*. Washington, DC: The Brookings Institution, 1973.

Owen, Bruce M. *Economics and Freedom of Expression: Media Structure and the First Amendment*. Cambridge, MA: Ballinger, 1975.

Owen, Bruce M., Beebe, Jack, and Manning, Willard. *Television Economics*. Lexington, MA: Lexington Books, 1974.

Pappas, James L. *Managerial Economics* (3rd ed). Hinsdale, IL: Dryden Press, 1979.

Rhoads, Steven. *The Economist's View of the World*. Cambridge, England: Cambridge University Press, 1985.

Rubin, Bernard. *When Information Counts: Grading the Media.* Lexington, MA: Lexington Books, 1985.

Scherer, Frederic M. *Industrial Market Structure and Economic Performance.* Boston: Houghton Mifflin, 1980.

Schiller, Herbert I. *Who Knows: Information in the Age of the Fortune 500.* Norwood, NJ: Ablex, 1982.

Simons, Howard, and Califano, Joseph A., eds. *The Media and Business.* New York: Vintage Books, 1979.

Snow, Marcellus. *Marketplace for Telecommunications: Regulation and Deregulation in Industrialized Democracies.* White Plains, NY: Longman, 1986.

Southwick, Larence, Jr. *Managerial Economics.* Plano, TX: Business Publications, 1985.

Sterling, Christopher H., and Haight, Timothy R. *The Mass Media: Aspen Institute Guide to Communication Industry Trends.* New York: Praeger (in cooperation with the Aspen Institute for Humanistic Studies), 1978.

U.S. House of Representatives. Committee on Energy and Commerce. Subcommittee on Telecommunications, Consumer Protection, and Finance. *Broadcast Regulation and Station Ownership.* Washington, DC: Government Printing Office, 1985.

Udell, Jon G. *The Economics of the American Newspaper.* New York: Hastings House, Communication Arts Books, 1978.

Ungurait, Donald F., Bohn, Thomas W., and Hiebert, Ray Eldon. *Media Now.* White Plains, NY: Longman, 1985.

Veronis, Suhler and Associates. *Communications Industry Report: 1980–1984 Financial Performance by Segment* (February 1986). New York: Veronis, Suhler and Associates, 1986.

Wiese, Michael. *Film and Video Budgets.* Westport, CT: Michael Wiese Film Productions, 1984.

Wolpert, Samuel A., and Wolpert, Joyce F. *Economics of Information.* New York: Van Nostrand Reinhold, 1986.

Wright, B.E., and Lavine, John. *The Constant Dollar Newspaper: An Economic Analysis Covering the Last Two Decades.* Chicago: Inland Daily Press Association, 1982.

Young, Judy, ed. *Videotex and Teletext in the US and UK.* London: Financial Times Media Intelligence Unit, 1984.

ELECTRONIC MEDIA

Bamberger, Nancy. *Video Production: A Case Study.* San Diego: Electronic Text Consortium, 1984.

Bove, Tony, Rhodes, Cheryl, and Thomas, Wes. *The Art of Desktop Publishing.* New York: Bantam Books, 1986.

Burkhardt, Friedrick W. *Newspapers and Electronic Media.* Darmsstadt, Federal Republic of Germany: International Association for Newspaper and Media Technology, 1983.

Collier, Harry, et al., eds. *Electronic Publishing Review: The International Journal of the Transfer of Published Information via Videotex and Online Media* (1984 ed). Medford, NJ: Learned Information, 1984.

Compaine, Benjamin M., ed. *Understanding New Media.* Cambridge, MA: Ballinger, 1984.

Davis, Frederic E., Wiesenberg, Michael, Barry, John A., and Langfeldt, Eva. *Desktop Publishing*. Homewood, IL: Dow Jones-Irwin, 1986.

Dordick, Herbert S., Bradley, Helen G., and Nanus, Burt. *The Emerging Network Marketplace*. Norwood, NJ: Ablex, 1981.

Garvey, Daniel E., and Rivers, William L. *Newswriting for the Electronic Media: Principles, Examples, Applications*. Belmont, CA: Wadsworth, 1982.

Greenberger, Martin, ed. *Electronic Publishing Plus: Media for a Technological Future*. White Plains, NY: Knowledge Industry Publications, 1985.

Hurly, Paul, Laucht, Matthias, and Hlynka, Denis. *The Videotex and Teletext Handbook: Home and Office Communications Using Microcomputers and Terminals*. New York: Harper & Row, 1985.

Information Gatekeepers, Inc. *The Second Viewtext Exposition VT'82*. Boston: Information Gatekeepers, 1981.

Information Management Associates. *Document III: Trends in Electronic Publishing in Europe and the U.S.* Medford, NJ: Learned Information, 1983.

International Resource Development. *Electronic Newspapers* (Reports Ser. No. 179). Norwalk, CT: International Resource Development, 1981.

Kaatz, Ronald B. *Cable: An Advertiser's Guide to the New Electronic Media*. Chicago: Crain Books, 1982.

Knowledge Industry Publications. *Data Base/Electronic Publishing: Review and Forecast 1985*. White Plains, NY: Knowledge Industry Publications, 1985.

Lazer, Ellen A., ed. *Guide to Videotape Publishing*. White Plains, NY: Knowledge Industry Publications, 1985.

Mascioni, Michael. *Electronic Retailing*. White Plains, NY: Knowledge Industry Publications, 1986.

McCavitt, William E., and Pringle, Peter K. *Electronic Media Management*. Boston: Focal Press, 1986.

McCormick-Prichett, Nancy, ed. *Women on the Job: Careers in Electronic Media*. Washington, DC: American Women in Radio and Television; Women's Bureau, U.S. Dept. of Labor, 1984.

Medoff, Norman J., and Tanquary, Tom. *Portable Video: ENG and EFP.* White Plains, NY: Knowledge Industry Publications, 1986.

Neustadt, Richard M. *The Birth of Electronic Publishing: Legal and Economic Issues in Telephone, Cable and Over-the-Air Teletext and Videotext*. White Plains, NY: Knowledge Industry Publications, 1982.

Noam, Eli M., ed. *Video Media Competition Regulation, Economics, and Technology.* New York: Columbia University Press, 1985.

Online International Ltd. *Electronic Publishing: Corporate and Commercial Publishing*. (Proceedings of the International Conference Held in London, November 1985). White Plains, NY: Knowledge Industry Publications, 1985.

Online Publications Ltd. *Videotex Key to the Information Revolution*. Middlesex, U.K.: Online Publications Ltd., 1982.

Osborne, G. Scott. *Electronic Direct Marketing: Your Marketing Tool for the 80s*. Englewood Cliffs, NJ: Prentice-Hall, 1984.

Patten, David A. *Newspapers and New Media*. White Plains, NY: Knowledge Industry Publications, 1986.

Presentation Consultants. *Home Video Publishing: The Distribution of Videocassettes, 1986–90*. White Plains, NY: Knowledge Industry Publications, 1986.

Rice, Ronald E., and Associates. *The New Media: Communication, Research and Technology.* Beverly Hills: Sage, 1984.

Ritvo, Ken, and Kearsley, Greg. *Desktop Publishing.* La Jolla, CA: Park Row Press, 1986.
Salvaggio, Jerry L. *Telecommunications: Issues and Choices for Society.* White Plains, NY: Longman, 1983.
Saunier, Fredric. *Online Marketing Strategies.* White Plains, NY: Knowledge Industry Publications, 1986.
Sigel, Efrem, et al. *The Future of Videotext: Worldwide Prospects for Home/Office Electronic Information Services.* White Plains, NY: Knowledge Industry Publications, 1983.
Smith, Anthony. *Goodbye Gutenberg: The Newspaper Revolution of the 1980s.* New York: Oxford University Press, 1980.
Smith, R. L. *The Wired Nation.* New York: Harper & Row, 1972.
Straus, Lawrence. *Electronic Marketing: Emerging TV and Computer Channels for Interactive Home Shopping.* White Plains, NY: Knowledge Industry Publications, 1983.
Tydeman, John, and Lipinski, Hurbert. *Teletext and Videotex in the United States.* New York: McGraw-Hill, 1982.
Vietor, Richard, and Dyer, Davis, eds. *Telecommunications in Transition: Business and Regulatory Change.* Harvard Business School, Boston: Course Module Series, 1986.
Weaver, David H. *Videotex Journalism: Teletext, Viewdata, and the News.* Hillsdale, NJ: Lawrence Erlbaum Associates, 1983.
Young, Judy, ed. *Videotex and Teletext in the US and UK.* London: Financial Times Media Intelligence Unit, 1984.

ENTREPRENEURSHIP

Braddon, Russell. *Roy Thomson of Fleet Street.* Huntington, NY: Fontana, 1968.
Drucker, Peter F. *Innovation and Entrepreneurship: Practice and Principles.* New York: Harper & Row, 1985.
Elson, Robert T. *The World of Time, Inc.* New York: Atheneum, 1973.
Henderson, Carter F. *Winners: The Successful Strategies Entrepreneurs Use to Build New Businesses.* New York: Simon and Schuster, 1985.
Joyce, Donald Franklin. *Gatekeepers of Black Culture: Black-Owned Book Publishing in the United States, 1817–1981.* Contributions in Afro-American and African Studies, No. 70. Westport, CT: Greenwood Press, 1983.
Keely, Tom. *The Imperial Post: The Meyers, The Grahams and The Paper That Rules Washington.* New York: 1983.
Leapman, Michael. *Arrogant Aussie: The Rupert Murdoch Story.* Secaucus, NJ: Lyle Stuart, 1985.
Meeker, Richard H. *Newspaperman: S.I. Newhouse and the Business of News.* New Haven, CT: Ticknor & Fields, 1983.
Peabody, Richard, ed. *Mavericks: Nine Independent Publishers.* Washington, DC: Paycock Press, 1983.
Swanberg, W.A. *Luce and His Empire.* New York: Dell, 1972.

ETHICS/SOCIAL RESPONSIBILITY

Christians, Clifford G., and Rotzoll, Kim B. *Media Ethics: Cases and Moral Reasoning.* White Plains, NY: Longman, 1983.

Cohen, Bernard C. *The Press, The Public and Foreign Policy.* Princeton, NJ: Princeton University Press, 1963.

Crawford, Nelson A. *The Ethics of Journalism.* New York: Knopf, 1924.

Emerson, Thomas. *The System of Freedom of Expression.* New York: Random House, 1970.

Fry, Don, ed. *Believing the News* (Poynter Institute Ethics Center Report). St. Petersburg, FL: Poynter Institute for Media Studies, 1985.

Gandy, Oscar H., Jr. *Beyond Agenda-Setting: Information Subsidies and Public Policy.* Norwood, NJ: Ablex, 1982.

Gillmor, Donald M., and Barron, Jerome A. *Mass Communication Law: Cases and Comment* (4th ed). St. Paul, MN: West Publishing Company, 1984.

Goldstein, Tom. *The News at Any Cost: How Journalists Compromise Their Ethics to Shape the News.* New York: Simon & Schuster, 1985.

Hachten, William A., and Giffard, C. Anthony. *The Press and Apartheid: Repression and Propaganda in South Africa.* Madison, WI: University of Wisconsin Press, 1984.

Hiebert, Ray E., and Reuss, Carol, eds. *Impact of Mass Media: Current Issues.* White Plains, NY: Longman, 1985.

Horsfield, Peter G. *Religious Television: The American Experience.* White Plains, NY: Longman, 1984.

Howard, Carole, and Mathews, Wilma. *On Deadline: Managing Media Relations.* White Plains, NY: Longman, 1985.

Leape, Jonathon, Baskin, Bo, and Underhill, Stefan. *Business in the Shadow of Apartheid.* Lexington, MA: Lexington Books, 1985.

MacDougall, Curtis Daniel. *The Press and Its Problems.* Dubuque, IO: W.C. Brown, 1964.

Martin, L. John, and Chaudhary, Anju Grover. *Comparative Mass Media Systems.* White Plains, NY: Longman, 1983.

Meyer, Philip. *Editors, Publishers, and Newspaper Ethics.* Washington, DC: American Society of Newspaper Editors Foundation, 1983.

Nelson, Harold L., and Teeter, Dwight L., Jr. *Law of Mass Communication: Freedom and Control of Print and Broadcast Media* (5th ed). Mineola, NY: Foundation Press, 1986.

Pascarella, Perry. *The New Achievers: Creating a Modern Work Ethic.* New York: Free Press, 1984.

Rowan, Ford. *Broadcast Fairness: Doctrine, Practice, Prospects.* White Plains, NY: Longman, 1984.

Salvaggio, Jerry L. *Telecommunications: Issues and Choices for Society.* White Plains, NY: Longman, 1983.

Schmidt, Benno C., Jr. *Freedom of the Press vs. Public Access.* New York: Praeger, 1976.

Schudson, Michael. *Advertising, the Uneasy Persuasion: Its Dubious Impact on American Society.* New York: Basic Books, 1984.

Schwoebel, Jean. *Newsroom Democracy: The Case for Independence of the Press.* Iowa City, IO: University of Iowa School of Journalism and Mass Communication, 1976.

Sigal, Leon V. *Reporters and Officials: The Organization and Politics of Newsmaking.* Lexington, MA: D.C. Heath, 1973.

Smith, Anthony. *The Politics of Information: Problems of Policy in Modern Media.* London: Macmillan, 1979.

Twentieth Century Fund Task Force on the International Flow of News. *A Free and Balanced Flow.* Lexington, MA: Lexington Books, 1978.

Ungurait, Donald F., Bohn, Thomas W., and Hiebert, Ray Eldon. *Media Now.* White Plains, NY: Longman, 1985.

FILM

Alten, Stanley R. *Audio in Media* (2nd ed). Belmont, CA: Wadsworth Publishing, 1986.

Austin, Bruce A., ed. *Current Research in Film: Audiences, Economics and Law: Volume I.* Norwood, NJ: Ablex, 1985.

Balio, Tino, ed. *The American Film Industry.* Madison, WI: The University of Wisconsin Press, 1985.

Burger, Richard, ed. *The Producers: A Descriptive Directory of Film and Television Producers in the Los Angeles Area* (3rd ed). Venice, CA: Richard Burger, 1984.

Goodell, Gregory. *Independent Feature Film Production.* New York: St. Martin's Press, 1982.

Hissong, Deborah, and Miller, Marian, eds. *The Professional Reference for Commercial Film and Tape Production.* Los Angeles, CA: LA 411 Publishing, 1985.

Lidwell, Wendy, and Guzzy, Mary, eds. *The AIVF Guide to Film and Video Distributors.* New York: Association of Independent Video and Filmmakers, 1984.

Marshall, Christine, ed. *Programming in the UK and USA.* London: Financial Times Media Intelligence Unit, 1984.

Wiese, Michael. *Film and Video Budgets.* Westport, CT: Michael Wiese Film Productions, 1984.

GENERAL/REFERENCE

American Newspaper Publishers Association. *It's For You: A Newspaper's Guide to Telecommunications Equipment, Management and Consultants.* Washington, DC: ANPA, 1986.

American Newspaper Publishers Association. *It's For You: Opportunities and Obstacles: A Survey of Newspaper Telecommunication Systems.* Washington, DC: ANPA, 1986.

Ashley, Perry J., ed. *Dictionary of Literary Biography, Volume 29: American Newspaper Journalists, 1926–1950.* Detroit, MI: Gale Research, 1984.

Block, Peter. *Flawless Consulting: A Guide to Getting Your Expertise Used.* San Diego: Learning Concepts, 1981.

Brownstone, David M., and Franck, Irene M. *Dictionary of Publishing.* New York: Van Nostrand Reinhold, 1982.

Bureau of the Census. *Statistical Abstract of the United States: National Data Book and Guide to Sources: 1986.* (106th ed). Washington, DC: U.S. Department of Commerce, 1986.

Burger, Richard, ed. *The Producers: A Descriptive Directory of Film and Television Producers in the Los Angeles Area* (3rd ed). Venice, CA: Richard Burger, 1984.

Cassata, Mary, and Skill, Thomas. *Television: A Guide to the Literature.* Phoenix, AZ: Oryx Press, 1985.

Clarkson, Kenneth W., and Muris, Timothy J., eds. *The Federal Trade Commission Since 1970: Economic Regulation and Bureaucratic Behavior.* New York: Cambridge University Press, 1981.

Connors, Tracy Daniel. *Longman Dictionary of Mass Media and Communication.* White Plains, NY: Longman, 1982.

Dizard, Wilson P., Jr. *The Coming Information Age: An Overview of Technology, Economics, and Politics.* White Plains, NY: Longman, 1982.
Editor and Publisher. *Editor and Publisher International Yearbook.* New York: Editor and Publisher, annual.
Editor and Publisher. *Editor and Publisher Market Guide.* New York: Editor and Publisher, annual.
Elson, Robert T. *The World of Time, Inc.* New York: Atheneum, 1973.
Ensign, Lynne Naylor, and Knapton, Robyn Eileen. *The Complete Dictionary of Television and Film.* Briarcliff Manor, NY: Stein and Day, 1985.
Finch, Frank. *The Facts on File Encyclopedia of Management Techniques.* New York: Facts on File, 1985.
Gardner, John W. *Excellence: Can We Be Equal and Excellent Too?* (rev. ed). New York: Norton, 1984.
Garvey, Daniel E., and Rivers, William L. *Newswriting for the Electronic Media: Principles, Examples, Applications.* Belmont, CA: Wadsworth, 1982.
Gavin, Kathy. *Media Law: A Legal Handbook for the Working Journalist.* Berkeley, CA: Nolo Press, 1984.
Gilmore, Gene. *Modern Newspaper Editing* (3rd ed). San Francisco, CA: Boyd & Fraser, 1982.
Green, Jonathan. *Newspeak: A Dictionary of Jargon.* New York: Routledge & Kegan Paul, 1984.
Hauer, Mary, et al. *Books, Librarians, and Research.* Dubuque, IO: Kendall-Hunt, 1983.
Hill, George H. *Black Media in America: A Resource Guide.* Boston: G.K. Hall, 1984.
Hill, George H., and Hill, Sylvia Saverson. *Blacks and Television: A Selectively Annotated Bibliography.* Metuchen, NJ: The Scarecrow Press, 1985.
Hissong, Deborah, and Miller, Marian, eds. *The Professional Reference for Commercial Film and Tape Production.* Los Angeles, CA: LA 411 Publishing, 1985.
Horowitz, Lois. *Knowing Where To Look: The Ultimate Guide to Research.* Cincinnati, OH: Writers Digest Books, 1984.
Information Management Associates. *Document III: Trends in Electronic Publishing in Europe and the U.S.* Medford, NJ: Learned Information, 1983.
Karolevitz, Robert F. *From Quill to Computer: The Story of America's Community Newspapers.* Freeman, SD: Pine Hill Press for the National Newspaper Foundation, 1985.
Lidwell, Wendy, and Guzzy, Mary, eds. *The AIVF Guide to Film and Video Distributors.* New York: Association of Independent Video and Filmmakers, 1984.
McCormack, Mark H. *What They Don't Teach You at Harvard Business School.* New York: Bantam Books, 1984.
McKerns, Joseph P. *News Media and Public Policy: An Annotated Bibliography.* New York: Garland, Inc., 1985.
Meyer, Philip. *Precision Journalism: A Reporter's Introduction to Social Science Methods* (2nd ed). Bloomington, IN: Indiana University Press, 1979.
Murray, John. *Media Law Dictionary.* Lanhan, MD: University Press of America, 1978.
Pascarella, Perry. *The New Achievers: Creating a Modern Work Ethic.* New York: Free Press, 1984.
Penney, Edmund. *A Dictionary of Media Terms.* New York: G.P. Putnam's Sons, 1984.
Pool, Ithiel de Sola. *Technologies of Freedom.* Boston: Harvard University Press, 1983.

Rosenberg, Jerry M. *Dictionary of Business and Management.* New York: Wiley, 1978.

Rothschild, William E. *Putting It All Together: A Guide to Strategic Thinking.* New York: AMACOM (a division of American Management Associations), 1976.

Schiller, Herbert I. *Who Knows: Information in the Age of the Fortune 500.* Norwood, NJ: Ablex, 1982.

Sims, Norman. *The Literary Journalists.* New York: Ballantine Books, 1984.

Snorgrass, J. William, and Woody, Gloria T., comps. *Blacks and Media: A Selected, Annotated Bibliography, 1962–1982.* Tallahassee, FL: A&M University Press, 1985.

Sterling, Christopher, and Haight, Timothy R. *The Mass Media: Aspen Institute Guide to Communication Industry Trends.* New York: Praeger (in cooperation with the Aspen Institute for Humanistic Studies), 1978.

Stewart, David W. *Secondary Research: Information Sources and Methods.* Beverly Hills: Sage, 1984.

Veronis, Suhler and Associates. *Communications Industry Report: 1980–1984 Financial Performance by Segment* (February 1986). New York: Veronis, Suhler and Associates, 1986.

Ward, Jean, and Hansen, Kathleen A. *Search Strategies in Mass Communication.* White Plains, NY: Longman, 1987.

Weaver, David H., and Wilhoit, Cleveland. *The American Journalist: A Portrait of U.S. News People and Their Work.* Bloomington, IN: Indiana University Press, 1986.

Weisberger, Bernard A. *The American Newspaperman.* Chicago: University of Chicago Press, 1961.

Whiteside, T. *The Blockbuster Complex.* Middletown, CT: Wesleyan University Press, 1981.

Wolseley, Roland E. *The Journalist's Bookshelf* (8th ed). Indianapolis, IN: R.J. Berg, 1986.

INFORMATION

Bennett, James. *Control of Information in the United States.* Westport, CT: Meckler Publishing, 1986.

Machlup, Fritz, and Leeson, Kenneth W. *Information Through the Printed Word: The Dissemination of Scholarly, Scientific, and Intellectual Knowledge: Book Publishing* (Vol. 1). Westport, CT: Greenwood Press, 1978.

Machlup, Fritz, and Leeson, Kenneth W. *Information Through the Printed Word: The Dissemination of Scholarly, Scientific, and Intellectual Knowledge: Journals* (Vol. 2). Westport, CT: Greenwood Press, 1978.

Machlup, Fritz, and Leeson, Kenneth W. *Information Through the Printed Word: The Dissemination of Scholarly, Scientific, and Intellectual Knowledge: Libraries* (Vol. 3). Westport, CT: Greenwood Press, 1978.

Machlup, Fritz, and Leeson, Kenneth W. *Information Through the Printed Word: The Dissemination of Scholarly, Scientific, and Intellectual Knowledge: Books, Journals, and Bibliographic Services* (Vol. 4). Westport, CT: Greenwood Press, 1980.

Stewart, David W. *Secondary Research: Information Sources and Methods.* Beverly Hills: Sage, 1984.

Ward, Jean, and Hansen, Kathleen A. *Search Strategies in Mass Communication.* White Plains, NY: Longman, 1987.

JOURNALISTS

Ashley, Perry J., ed. *Dictionary of Literary Biography, Volume 29: American Newspaper Journalists, 1926–1950*. Detroit, MI: Gale Research, 1984.

Ghiglione, Loren, ed. *Gentlemen of the Press*. Indianapolis, IN: R.J. Berg, 1984.

Hess, Stephen. *The Washington Reporters*. Washington, DC: The Brookings Institution, 1981.

Johnston, John W.C. *The News People: A Sociological Portrait of American Journalists*. Chicago: University of Illinois Press, 1976.

MacDougall, Curtis Daniel. *The Press and Its Problems*. Dubuque, IO: W.C. Brown, 1964.

Meyer, Philip. *Precision Journalism: A Reporter's Introduction to Social Science Methods* (2nd ed). Bloomington, IN: Indiana University Press, 1979.

Sigal, Leon V. *Reporters and Officials: The Organization and Politics of News-making*. Lexington, MA: D.C. Heath, 1973.

Sims, Norman. *The Literary Journalists*. New York: Ballantine Books, 1984.

LEADERSHIP AND MANAGEMENT

Aaker, David A., and Myers, John G. *Advertising Management*. Englewood Cliffs, NJ: Prentice-Hall, 1982.

American Newspaper Publishers Association. *Three to Zero: The Story of the Birth and Death of the World-Tribune in New York City.* Reston, VA: ANPA, 1967.

Anderson, Robert L., and Barry, Thomas E. *Advertising Management: Text and Cases*. Columbus, OH: Charles E. Merrill, 1979.

Argyris, Chris. *Behind the Front Page*. San Francisco: Jossey-Bass, 1974.

Argyris, Chris, and Schon, Donald P. *Theory in Practice: Increasing Professional Effectiveness*. San Francisco: Jossey-Bass, 1974.

Armstrong, Michael. *Case Studies in Personnel Management*. New York: Nichols, 1979.

Beach, Dale S., ed. *Managing People at Work: Readings in Personnel* (3rd ed). New York: Macmillan, 1980.

Bennis, Warren G., and Nanus, Burt. *Leaders: The Strategies of Taking Charge*. New York: Harper & Row, 1985.

Bennis, Warren G., ed. *Leadership and Motivation: Essays of Douglas McGregor.* Cambridge, MA: The MIT Press, 1966.

Blanchard, Kenneth H., Zigarmi, Patricia, and Zigarmi, Drea. *Leadership and the One Minute Manager.* New York: Morrow, 1985.

Blanchard, Kenneth H., and Lorber, Robert. *Putting the One-Minute Manager to Work*. New York: Morrow, 1984.

Blanchard, Kenneth H., and Johnson, Spencer. *The One-Minute Manager.* New York: Morrow, 1982.

Braddon, Russell. *Roy Thomson of Fleet Street*. Huntington, NY: Fontana, 1968.

Burnett, John J. *Promotion Management: A Strategic Approach*. St. Paul, MN: West Publishing, 1984.

Burns, James MacGregor. *Leadership*. New York: Harper & Row, 1978.

Burns, Tom, and Stalker, O.M. *The Management of Innovation*. London: Tavistock Publications, 1961.

Cantor, Bill. *Experts in Action: Inside Public Relations.* White Plains, NY: Longman, 1984.

Christopher, William F. *Management for the Nineteen Eighties.* Englewood Cliffs, NJ: Prentice-Hall, 1979.

Clabes, Judith G., ed. *New Guardians of the Press: Selected Profiles of America's Women Newspaper Editors.* Indianapolis, IN: R.J. Berg, 1983.

Cole, Robert S. *The Practical Handbook of Public Relations.* Englewood Cliffs, NJ: Prentice-Hall, 1981.

Coleman, Howard W. *Case Studies in Broadcast Management* (2nd ed). New York: Hastings House, 1978.

Coventry, W.F., and Burstiner, Irving. *Management, a Basic Handbook.* Englewood Cliffs, NJ: Prentice-Hall, 1977.

Culligan, Matthew J., Deakins, Suzanne, and Young, Arthur H. *Back to Basics Management: The Lost Craft of Leadership.* New York: Facts on File, 1983.

Deal, Terrence E., and Kennedy, Allan A. *Corporate Cultures: The Rites and Rituals of Corporate Life.* Reading, MA: Addison-Wesley, 1982.

Donnelly, James H., Jr. *Fundamentals of Management* (5th ed). Plano, TX: Business Publications, 1984.

Dreyfack, Raymond. *Making It in Management—The Japanese Way.* New York: Farnsworth, 1982.

Drucker, Peter F. *Innovation and Entrepreneurship: Practice and Principles.* New York: Harper & Row, 1985.

Drucker, Peter F. *Management: Tasks, Responsibilities, Practices.* New York: Harper & Row, 1974.

Drucker, Peter F. *Managing for Results.* New York: Harper & Row, 1967.

Drucker, Peter F. *Managing in Turbulent Times.* New York: Harper & Row, 1980.

Drucker, Peter F. *The Practice of Management.* New York: Harper & Row, 1954.

Ettema, James S., and Whitney, D. Charles, eds. *Individuals in Mass Media Organizations: Creativity and Constraint* (Sage Annual Reviews of Communication Research, Vol. 10). Beverly Hills: Sage, 1982.

Finch, Frank. *The Facts on File Encyclopedia of Management Techniques.* New York: Facts on File, 1985.

Gardner, John W. *Excellence: Can We Be Equal and Excellent Too?* (rev. ed). New York: Norton, 1984.

Ghiglione, Loren, ed. *Gentlemen of the Press.* Indianapolis, IN: R.J. Berg, 1984.

Ghiselli, Edwin E. *Explorations in Managerial Talent.* Pacific Palisades, CA: Goodyear, 1971.

Gibson, James L. *Organizations: Behavior, Structure, Processes.* Dallas: Business Publications, 1979.

Gibson, John E. *Managing Research and Development.* New York: Wiley, 1981.

Giles, Robert H. *Newsroom Management.* Indianapolis, IN: R.J. Berg, 1986.

Glasser, Alan. *Research and Development Management.* Englewood Cliffs, NJ: Prentice-Hall, 1982.

Glassman, Alan M., ed. *The Challenge of Management.* New York: Wiley, 1978.

Griffin, Ricky W. *Management.* Boston: Houghton Mifflin Company, 1984.

Grove, Andrew S. *High Output Management.* New York: Random House, 1983.

Gudykunst, William B., Stewart, Lea P., and Ting-Toomey, Stella, eds. *Communication, Culture, and Organizational Processes.* Beverly Hills: Sage, 1985.

Hackman, Richard J., ed. *Perspectives on Behavior in Organizations.* New York: McGraw-Hill, 1977.

Halberstam, David. *The Powers That Be.* New York: Knopf, 1979.

Harvard Business School. *Directory of Harvard Business School Cases and Related Course Materials: 1985–86.* Boston: Harvard Business School, annual.

Hennig, Margaret, and Jardim, Anne. *The Managerial Woman.* Garden City, NY: Anchor Press/Doubleday, 1977.

Hersey, Paul, and Blanchard, Kenneth H. *Management of Organizational Behavior: Utilizing Human Resources* (4th ed). Englewood Cliffs, NJ: Prentice-Hall, 1982.

Hersey, Paul. *The Situational Leader.* New York: Warner Books, 1985.

Heskett, James L. *Managing in the Service of Economy.* Boston: Harvard Business School, 1986.

Hilliard, Robert L. *Radio Broadcasting: An Introduction to the Sound Medium* (3rd ed). White Plains, NY: Longman, 1985.

Horngren, Charles T. *Introduction to Management Accounting* (4th ed). Englewood Cliffs, NJ: Prentice-Hall, 1978.

Jacobson, Aileen. *Women in Charge: Dilemmas of Women in Authority.* New York: Van Nostrand Reinhold, 1985.

Kanter, Rosabeth Moss. *The Change Masters: Innovations for Productivity in the American Corporation.* New York: Simon & Schuster, 1983.

Lawler, Edward E., III, Nadler, David A., and Cammann, Cortlandt. *Organizational Assessment: Perspectives on the Measurement of Organizational Behavior and the Quality of Work Life.* New York: Wiley, 1980.

Leapman, Michael. *Arrogant Aussie: The Rupert Murdoch Story.* Secaucus, NJ: Lyle Stuart, 1985.

Litterer, Joseph A. *Management: Concepts and Controversies.* New York: Wiley, 1978.

Marlow, Eugene. *Managing the Corporate Media Center.* White Plains, NY: Knowledge Industry Publications, 1981.

McCormack, Mark H. *What They Don't Teach You at Harvard Business School.* New York: Bantam Books, 1984.

McGann, Anthony, and Russell, J. Thomas. *Advertising Media: A Management Approach.* Homewood, IL: Irwin Publishing, 1983.

Meeker, Richard H. *Newspaperman: S.I. Newhouse and the Business of News.* New Haven, CT: Ticknor & Fields, 1983.

Mikovich, George T., and Glueck, William F. *Personnel: A Diagnostic Approach* (4th ed). Plano, TX: Business Publications, 1985.

Miller, Sherod, Wackman, Daniel B., Demmitt, Dallas R., and Demmitt, Nancy J. *Working Together: Productive Communication on the Job.* Littleton, CO: Interpersonal Communication Programs, 1985.

Mills, D. Quinn. *The New Competitors: A Report on American Managers from D. Quinn Mills of the Harvard Business School.* New York: Wiley, 1985.

Mintzberg, Henry. *Structuring of Organizations.* Englewood Cliffs, NJ: Prentice-Hall, 1979.

Mintzberg, Henry. *The Nature of Managerial Work.* Englewood Cliffs, NJ: Prentice-Hall, 1980.

Nager, Norman R., and Harrell, Thomas. *Public Relations: Management by Objectives.* White Plains, NY: Longman, 1984.

Naisbitt, John. *Megatrends.* New York: Warner, 1982.

Naisbitt, John, and Aburdene, Patricia. *Re-Inventing the Corporation: Transforming Your Job and Your Company for the New Information Society.* New York: Warner Books, 1985.

Odiorne, George S. *Executive Skills: A Management-By-Objective Approach.* Dubuque, IO: W.C. Brown, 1980.

Odiorne, George S. *How Managers Make Things Happen* (2nd ed). Englewood

Cliffs, NJ: Prentice-Hall, 1982.

Odiorne, George S. *Management and the Activity Trap.* New York: Harper & Row, 1974.

Odiorne, George S. *Management Decisions by Objectives.* Englewood Cliffs, NJ: Prentice-Hall, 1969.

Odiorne, George S. *MBO II: A System of Managerial Leadership for the 80s.* Belmont, CA: Fearon Pitman, 1979.

Odiorne, George S. *The Change Registers: How They Prevent Progress and What Managers Can Do About It.* Englewood Cliffs, NJ: Prentice-Hall, 1981.

Ouchi, William. *Theory Z: How American Business Can Meet the Japanese Challenge.* Reading, MA: Addison-Wesley, 1981.

Pascarella, Perry. *Industry Week's Guide to Tomorrow's Executive: Human Management in the Future Corporation.* New York: Van Nostrand Reinhold, 1980.

Perlson, Michael R. *How to Understand and Influence People and Organizations: Practical Psychology for Goal Achievement.* New York: AMACOM (a division of American Management Associations), 1982.

Peters, Thomas J. *A Passion for Excellence: The Leadership Difference.* New York: Random House, 1985.

Peters, Thomas J., and Waterman, Robert H. *In Search of Excellence: Lessons From America's Best-Run Companies.* New York: Harper & Row, 1982.

Porter, Michael E. *Competitive Advantage: Creating and Sustaining Superior Performance.* New York: The Free Press, 1985.

Rankin, William Parkman. *The Practice of Newspaper Management.* New York: Praeger, 1986.

Rankin, William Parkman, and Waggaman, Eugene S., Jr. *Business Management of General Consumer Magazines.* New York: Praeger, 1984.

Ray, Michael L. *Advertising and Communication Management.* Englewood Cliffs, NJ: Prentice-Hall, 1982.

Reuss, Carol, and Silvis, Donn, eds. *Inside Organizational Communication* (2nd ed). White Plains, NY: Longman, 1985.

Rewoldt, Stewart Henry, Scott, James Dacon, and Warshaw, Martin R. *Introduction to Marketing Management* (4th ed). Homewood, IL: R.D. Irwin, 1981.

Rosenberg, Jerry M. *Dictionary of Business and Management.* New York: Wiley, 1978.

Rothschild, William E. *Putting It All Together: A Guide to Strategic Thinking.* New York: AMACOM (a division of American Management Associations), 1976.

Scott, William G., and Hart, David K. *Organizational America.* Boston: Houghton Mifflin, 1980.

Selznick, Philip. *Leadership in Administration: A Sociological Approach.* Berkeley: University of California Press, 1957.

Shea, Gordon F. *Creative Negotiating.* New York: Van Nostrand Reinhold, 1983.

Sigal, Leon V. *Reporters and Officials: The Organization and Politics of Newsmaking.* Lexington, MA: D.C. Heath, 1973.

Sohn, Ardyth, Ogan, Chris, and Polich, John. *Newspaper Leadership.* Englewood Cliffs, NJ: Prentice-Hall, 1986.

Stoner, James A. *Management.* Englewood Cliffs, NJ: Prentice-Hall, 1982.

Townsend, Robert. *Further Up the Organization.* New York: Knopf, 1984.

Uris, Auren. *Techniques of Leadership.* New York: McGraw-Hill, 1964.

Van Deusen, Richard E. *Practical AV/Video Budgeting.* White Plains, NY: Knowledge Industry Publications, 1984.

Wallace, Marc J. *Managing Behavior in Organizations.* Glenview, IL: Scott, Foresman, 1982.

Westin, Alan F., Schweder, Heather A., Baker, Michael A., and Lehman, Shelia. *The Changing Workplace: A Guide to Managing the People, Organizational and Regulatory Aspects of Office Technology.* White Plains, NY: Knowledge Industry Publications, 1985.

Wiegand, Ingrid. *Professional Video Production.* White Plains, NY: Knowledge Industry Publications, 1985.

Williams, Herbert L., and Rucker, Frank W. *Newspaper Organization and Management* (5th ed). Ames, IO: Iowa State University Press, 1978.

Zettl, Herbert. *Television Production Handbook* (4th ed). Belmont, CA: Wadsworth Publishing, 1984.

MAGAZINES/JOURNALS

Byron, Christopher. *The Fanciest Dive: What Happened When the Giant Empire of Time/Life Leaped Without Looking Into the Age of High Tech.* New York: Norton, 1986.

Compaine, Benjamin M. *The Business of Consumer Magazines.* White Plains, NY: Knowledge Industry Publications, 1982.

Duke, Judith S. *The Technical, Scientific and Medical Publishing Market.* White Plains, NY: Knowledge Industry Publications, 1985.

Elson, Robert T. *The World of Time, Inc.* New York: Atheneum, 1973.

Friedrich, Otto. *Decline and Fall.* New York: Harper & Row, 1970.

Gans, Herbert W. *Deciding What's News: A Study of CBS Evening News, NBC Nightly News, and Time.* New York: Pantheon Books, 1979.

Hacker, Jeffrey H. *Consumer Magazines: Industry and Market Trends, 1985–88.* White Plains, NY: Knowledge Industry Publications, 1985.

Mogel, Leonard. *The Magazine.* Englewood Cliffs, NJ: Prentice-Hall, 1979.

Paine, Fred K., and Paine, Nancy E. *Magazines: A Bibliography for Their Analysis with Annotations and Study Guide.* Metuchen, NJ: Scarecrow Press, 1987.

Rankin, William Parkman, and Waggaman, Eugene S., Jr. *Business Management of General Consumer Magazines.* New York: Praeger, 1984.

Swanberg, W.A. *Luce and His Empire.* New York: Dell, 1972.

MARKETING

Bogart, Leo. *Strategy in Advertising: Matching Media and Messages to Markets and Motivation* (2nd ed). Chicago: Crain Books, 1984.

Compaine, Benjamin M. *The Book Industry in Transition: An Economic Analysis of Book Distribution and Marketing.* White Plains, NY: Knowledge Industry Publications, 1978.

Crimp, Margaret. *The Marketing Research Process* (2nd ed). Englewood Cliffs, NJ: Prentice-Hall, 1985.

Hise, Richard T., Gillett, Peter L., and Ryan, John K., Jr. *Basic Marketing: Concepts and Decisions.* Cambridge, MA: Winthrop Publishers, Inc., 1979.

Irwin, Manley R. *Telecommunications America: Market Without Boundaries.* Westport, CT: Greenwood Press, 1984.
Levitt, Theodore. *Marketing Imagination.* New York: Free Press, 1983.
Luck, David J., and Ferrell, O.C. *Marketing Strategy and Plans* (2nd ed). Englewood Cliffs, NJ: Prentice-Hall, 1985.
Mascioni, Michael. *Electronic Retailing.* White Plains, NY: Knowledge Industry Publications, 1986.
McIver, Colin. *Case Studies in Marketing, Advertising and Public Relations.* North Pomfret, VT: David & Charles, 1984.
Meyer, Philip. *The Newspaper Survival Book: An Editor's Guide to Marketing Research.* Bloomington, IN: Indiana University Press, 1985.
Meyers, William. *The Image-Makers: Power and Persuasion on Madison Avenue.* New York: Times Books, 1984.
Nickels, William G. *Marketing and Promotion.* Columbus, OH: Grid Publishing Co., 1980.
Osborne, G. Scott. *Electronic Direct Marketing: Your Marketing Tool for the 80s.* Englewood Cliffs, NJ: Prentice-Hall, 1984.
Poltrack, David F. *Television Marketing.* New York: McGraw-Hill, 1983.
Rice, Ronald E., and Associates. *The New Media: Communication, Research and Technology.* Beverly Hills: Sage, 1984.
Ries, Al, and Trout, Jack. *Positioning: The Battle for Your Mind.* New York: McGraw-Hill, 1981.
Saunier, Fredric. *Online Marketing Strategies.* White Plains, NY: Knowledge Industry Publications, 1986.
Straus, Lawrence. *Electronic Marketing: Emerging TV and Computer Channels for Interactive Home Shopping.* White Plains, NY: Knowledge Industry Publications, 1983.
Warner, Charles. *Broadcast and Cable Selling.* Belmont, CA: Wadsworth, 1986.
Young, Judy, ed. *Videotex and Teletext in the US and UK.* London: Financial Times Media Intelligence Unit, 1984.

MASS MEDIA

Agee, Warren K., Ault, Phillip H., and Emery, Edwin. *Introduction to Mass Communications.* New York: Harper & Row, 1982.
Agee, Warren K. *Maincurrents in Mass Communications.* New York: Harper & Row, 1986.
Altschull, J. Herbert. *Agents of Power: The Role of the News Media in Human Affairs.* White Plains, NY: Longman, 1984.
Baer, Walter S., et al. *Concentration of Mass Media Ownership.* Santa Monica, CA: Rand Corp., 1974.
Bagdikian, Ben H. *The Information Machines: Their Impact on Men and the Media.* New York: Harper & Row, 1971.
Bagdikian, Ben H. *The Media Monopoly.* Boston: Beacon Press, 1983.
Chafee, Zechariah. *Government and Mass Communications.* Chicago: University of Chicago Press, 1947.
Cohen, Bernard C. *The Press, The Public and Foreign Policy.* Princeton, NJ: Princeton University Press, 1963.
Compaine, Benjamin M. *Anatomy of the Communications Industry: Who Owns the Media?* White Plains, NY: Knowledge Industry Publications, 1983.
Compaine, Benjamin M., ed. *Understanding New Media.* Cambridge, MA: Ballinger, 1984.

Compaine, Benjamin M., Sterling, Christopher, Guback, Thomas, and Noble, J. Kendrick, Jr. *Who Owns the Media? Concentration of Ownership in the Communications Industry* (2nd ed). White Plains, NY: Knowledge Industry Publications, 1982.

Connors, Tracy Daniel. *Longman Dictionary of Mass Media and Communication.* White Plains, NY: Longman, 1982.

Cross, Donna Wolfolk. *Mediaspeak: How Television Makes Up Your Mind.* New York: Putnam, 1983.

Czitrom, Daniel J. *Media and the American Mind.* Chapel Hill, NC: University of North Carolina Press, 1982.

Dertouzos, James N., and Quinn, Timothy H. *Bargaining Responses to the Technology Revolution: The Case of the Newspaper Industry.* Santa Monica, CA: Rand Corp., 1982.

Devol, Kenneth S., ed. *Mass Media and the Supreme Court.* New York: Hastings House, 1971.

Dizard, Wilson P., Jr. *The Coming Information Age: An Overview of Technology, Economics, and Politics.* White Plains, NY: Longman, 1982.

Dominick, Joseph R. *The Dynamics of Mass Communication.* Reading, MA: Addison-Wesley, 1983.

Emery, Edwin, and Emery, Michael. *The Press and America: An Interpretative History of Journalism* (5th ed). Englewood Cliffs, NJ: Prentice-Hall, 1984.

Emery, Michael, and Smythe, Ted Curtis. *Readings in Mass Communication: Concepts and Issues in the Mass Media* (5th ed). Dubuque, IO: W.C. Brown, 1983.

Ettema, James S., and Whitney, D. Charles, eds. *Individuals in Mass Media Organizations: Creativity and Constraint* (Sage Annual Reviews of Communication Research, Vol. 10). Beverly Hills: Sage, 1982.

Hiebert, Ray E., and Reuss, Carol, eds. *Impact of Mass Media: Current Issues.* White Plains, NY: Longman, 1985.

Hill, George H. *Black Media in America: A Resource Guide.* Boston: G.K. Hall, 1984.

Hoyer, Svennik, Hadenius, Stig, and Weibull, Lennart. *The Politics and Economics of the Press: A Developmental Perspective.* Beverly Hills: Sage, 1975.

Jamieson, Kathleen Hall, and Campbell, Karolyn Kohn. *The Interplay of Influence: Mass Media and Their Publics in News, Advertising, Politics.* Belmont, CA: Wadsworth, 1983.

Jeffres, Leo W. *Mass Media Processes and Effects.* Prospect Heights, IL: Waveland Press, 1986.

MacDougall, Curtis Daniel. *The Press and Its Problems.* Dubuque IO: W.C. Brown, 1964.

Martin, L. John, and Chaudhary, Anju Grover. *Comparative Mass Media Systems.* White Plains, NY: Longman, 1983.

McCormick-Prichett, Nancy, ed. *Women on the Job: Careers in Electronic Media.* Washington, DC: American Women in Radio and Television; Women's Bureau, U.S. Dept. of Labor, 1984.

McKerns, Joseph P. *News Media and Public Policy: An Annotated Bibliography.* New York: Garland, 1985.

Mitchell, Craig. *Media Promotion.* Chicago: Crain Books, 1985.

Owen, Bruce M. *Economics and Freedom of Expression: Media Structure and the First Amendment.* Cambridge, MA: Ballinger, 1975.

Peabody, Richard, ed. *Mavericks: Nine Independent Publishers.* Washington, DC: Paycock Press, 1983.

Pool, Ithiel de Sola. *Technologies of Freedom.* Boston: Harvard University Press, 1983.

Rice, Ronald E., and Associates. *The New Media: Communication, Research and Technology.* Beverly Hills: Sage, 1984.
Ries, Al, and Trout, Jack. *Positioning: The Battle for Your Mind.* New York: McGraw-Hill, 1981.
Rohrer, Daniel Morgan, ed. *Mass Media, Freedom of Speech, and Advertising.* Dubuque, IO: Kendall/Hunt, 1979.
Roper Organization, The. *Public Perceptions of Television and Other Mass Media: A Twenty-Five Year Review, 1959–1980.* New York: Television Information Office, 1981.
Rubin, Bernard. *Big Business and the Mass Media.* Lexington, MA: Lexington Books, 1977.
Rubin, Bernard. *When Information Counts: Grading the Media.* Lexington, MA: Lexington Books, 1985.
Simons, Howard, and Califano, Joseph A., eds. *Media and the Law.* New York: Praeger, 1976.
Simons, Howard, and Califano, Joseph A., eds. *The Media and Business.* New York: Vintage Books, 1979.
Smith, Anthony. *The Politics of Information: Problems of Policy in Modern Media.* London: Macmillan, 1979.
Snorgrass, J. William, and Woody, Gloria T., comps. *Blacks and Media: A Selected, Annotated Bibliography, 1962–1982.* Tallahassee, FL: A&M University Press, 1985.
Sterling, Christopher H., and Haight, Timothy R. *The Mass Media: Aspen Institute Guide to Communication Industry Trends.* New York: Praeger (in cooperation with the Aspen Institute for Humanistic Studies), 1978.
Tichenor, Phillip J., Donohue, George A., and Olien, Clarice N. *Community Conflict and the Press.* Beverly Hills: Sage, 1980.
Turow, Joseph. *Media Industries: The Production of News and Entertainment.* White Plains, NY: Longman, 1984.
UNESCO. *Mass Media in Society: The Need of Research* (Reports and Papers on Mass Communication: No. 59). New York: Unipub, 1970.
Ungurait, Donald F., Bohn, Thomas W., and Hiebert, Ray Eldon. *Media Now.* White Plains, NY: Longman, 1985.
Veronis, Suhler and Associates. *Communications Industry Report: 1980–1984 Financial Performance by Segment* (February 1986). New York: Veronis, Suhler and Associates, 1986.
Wimmer, Roger, and Dominick, Joseph R. *Mass Media Research.* Belmont, CA: Wadsworth, 1983.

MEDIA LAW

Austin, Bruce A., ed. *Current Research in Film: Audiences, Economics and Law: Volume I.* Norwood, NJ: Ablex, 1985.
Bittner, John R. *Broadcast Laws and Regulation.* Englewood Cliffs, NJ: Prentice-Hall, 1982.
Blanchard, Margaret A. *Exporting the First Amendment: The Press-Government Crusade of 1945–1953.* White Plains, NY: Longman, 1986.
Carter, T. Barton, Franklin, Marc, and Wright, Jay B. *The First Amendment and The Fifth Estate: Regulation of Electronic Mass Media.* Mineola, NY: Foundation Press, 1986.

Carter, T. Barton, Franklin, Marc, and Wright, Jay B. *The First Amendment and The Fourth Estate: The Law of Mass Media* (3rd ed). Mineola, NY: Foundation Press, 1985.

Chamberlin, Bill F., and Brown, Charlene J., eds. *The First Amendment Reconsidered: New Perspectives on the Meaning of Freedom of Speech and the Press*. White Plains, NY: Longman, 1982.

Degen, Clara, ed. *Understanding and Using Video: A Guide for the Organizational Communicator.* White Plains, NY: Longman, 1985.

Devol, Kenneth S., ed. *Mass Media and the Supreme Court*. New York: Hastings House, 1971.

Diamond, Edwin, et al. *Telecommunications in Crisis: The First Amendment, Technology, and Deregulation*. Washington, DC: Cato Institute, 1983.

DuBoff, Leonard D. *Book Publishers' Legal Guide*. Newton Upper Falls, MA: Butterworth Legal Publications, 1983.

Emerson, Thomas. *The System of Freedom of Expression*. New York: Random House, 1970.

Finnegan, John R., Sr., and Hirl, Patricia A. *Law and the Media in the Midwest: A Seven-State Handbook Covering Illinois, Iowa, Minnesota, Nebraska, North Dakota, South Dakota, and Wisconsin*. St. Paul, MN: Butterworth Legal Publishers, 1984.

Francois, William E. *Mass Media Law and Regulation* (2nd ed). Columbus, OH: Grid Publishing, 1978.

Gandy, Oscar H., Jr. *Beyond Agenda-Setting: Information Subsidies and Public Policy.* Norwood, NJ: Ablex, 1982.

Gavin, Kathy. *Media Law: A Legal Handbook for the Working Journalist*. Berkeley, CA: Nolo Press, 1984.

Gillmor, Donald M., and Barron, Jerome A. *Mass Communication Law: Cases and Comment* (4th ed). St. Paul, MN: West Publishing, 1984.

Haiman, Franklyn S. *Speech and Law in a Free Society.* Chicago: University of Chicago Press, 1981.

Lahav, Pnina, ed. *Press Law in Modern Democracies: A Comparative Study.* White Plains, NY: Longman, 1985.

Martin, L. John, and Chaudhary, Anju Grover. *Comparative Mass Media Systems*. White Plains, NY: Longman, 1983.

Mueller, Milton. *Property Rights in Radio Communications: The Key to the Reform of Telecommunications Regulation* (Policy Analysis Study No. 11). Washington, DC: Cato Institute, 1983.

Murray, John. *Media Law Dictionary.* Lanhan, MD: University Press of America, 1978.

Nelson, Harold L., and Teeter, Dwight L., Jr. *Law of Mass Communication: Freedom and Control of Print and Broadcast Media* (5th ed). Mineola, NY: Foundation Press, 1986.

Neustadt, Richard M. *The Birth of Electronic Publishing: Legal and Economic Issues in Telephone, Cable and Over-the-Air Teletext and Videotext*. White Plains, NY: Knowledge Industry Publications, 1982.

Nimmo, Dan, and Mansfield, Michael W., eds. *Government and the News Media: Comparative Dimensions*. Waco, TX: Baylor University Press, 1982.

Noam, Eli M., ed. *Telecommunications Regulation Today and Tomorrow.* New York: Harcourt Brace Jovanovich, 1984.

Noam, Eli M., ed. *Video Media Competition Regulation, Economics, and Technology.* New York: Columbia University Press, 1985.

Noll, Roger G., Peck, Merton J., and McGowan, John. *Economic Aspects of Television Regulation*. Washington, DC: The Brookings Institution, 1973.

Oppenheim, S. Chesterfield, and Shields, Carrington. *Newspapers and the Antitrust Laws*. Charlottesville, VA: The Michie Co., 1982.

Overbeck, Wayne, and Pullen, Rick D. *Major Principles of Media Law* (2nd ed). New York: Holt, Rinehart and Winston, 1985.

Owen, Bruce M. *Economics and Freedom of Expression: Media Structure and the First Amendment*. Cambridge, MA: Ballinger, 1975.

Pember, Don R. *Mass Media Law* (3rd ed). Dubuque, IO: William C. Brown, 1984.

Pool, Ithiel de Sola. *Technologies of Freedom*. Cambridge, MA: Harvard University Press, 1983.

Rohrer, Daniel Morgan, ed. *Mass Media, Freedom of Speech, and Advertising*. Dubuque, IO: Kendall/Hunt, 1979.

Rowan, Ford. *Broadcast Fairness: Doctrine, Practice, Prospects*. White Plains, NY: Longman, 1984.

Sack, Robert D. *Libel, Slander, and Related Problems*. New York: Practising Law Institute, 1980.

Schmidt, Benno C., Jr. *Freedom of the Press vs. Public Access*. New York: Praeger, 1976.

Schwoebel, Jean. *Newsroom Democracy: The Case for Independence of the Press*. Iowa City, IO: University of Iowa School of Journalism and Mass Communication, 1976.

Simons, Howard, and Califano, Joseph A., eds. *Media and the Law*. New York: Praeger, 1976.

Smith, Anthony. *Newspapers and Democracy*. Cambridge, MA: The MIT Press, 1980.

Snow, Marcellus. *Marketplace for Telecommunications: Regulation and Deregulation in Industrialized Democracies*. White Plains, NY: Longman, 1986.

Surette, Ray, ed. *Justice and the Media: Issues and Research*. Springfield, IL: Thomas, 1984.

U.S. House of Representatives. Committee on Energy and Commerce. Subcommittee on Telecommunications, Consumer Protection, and Finance. *Broadcast Regulation and Station Ownership*. Washington, DC: Government Printing Office, 1985.

Van Alstyne, William W. *Interpretations of the First Amendment*. Durham, NC: Duke University Press, 1984.

MEDIA MANAGEMENT

American Society of Newspaper Editors (ASNE). *Newsroom Management Handbook*. Washington, DC: American Society of Newspaper Editors, 1985.

Cadman, Eileen, et al. *Rolling Our Own: Women as Printers, Publishers and Distributors*. (Minority Press Group Series No. 4). London: Minority Press Group, 1981.

Evans, Harold. *Good Times, Bad Times*. New York: Atheneum Books, 1984.

Friedrich, Otto. *Decline and Fall*. New York: Harper & Row, 1970.

Gandy, Oscar H., Jr. *Beyond Agenda-Setting: Information Subsidies and Public Policy*. Norwood, NJ: Ablex, 1982.

Marlow, Eugene. *Managing the Corporate Media Center*. White Plains, NY: Knowledge Industry Publications, 1981.

McCavitt, William E., and Pringle, Peter K. *Electronic Media Management.* Boston: Focal Press, 1986.

National Association of Broadcasters (NAB). *Great Expectations: A Television Manager's Guide to the Future.* Washington, DC: NAB, 1986.

Rankin, William Parkman, and Waggaman, Eugene S., Jr. *Business Management of General Consumer Magazines.* New York: Praeger, 1984.

Rucker, Frank W., and Williams, Herbert L. *Newspaper Organization and Management.* Ames, IO: Iowa State University Press, 1955.

Vietor, Richard, and Dyer, Davis, eds. *Telecommunications in Transition: Managing Business and Regulatory Change* (Course Module Series). Boston: Harvard Business School, 1986.

MINORITIES

Agee, Warren K., Ault, Phillip H., and Emery, Edwin. *Maincurrents in Mass Communications.* New York: Harper & Row, 1986.

Hiebert, Ray E., and Reuss, Carol, eds. *Impact of Mass Media: Current Issues.* White Plains, NY: Longman, 1985.

Hill, George H. *Black Media in America: A Resource Guide.* Boston: G.K. Hall, 1984.

Hill, George H., and Hill, Sylvia Saverson. *Blacks and Television: A Selectively Annotated Bibliography.* Metuchen, NJ: The Scarecrow Press, 1985.

Hutmacher, Barbara. *In Black and White: Voices of Apartheid.* Frederick, MD: University Publications of America, Inc., 1982.

Joyce, Donald Franklin. *Gatekeepers of Black Culture: Black-Owned Book Publishing in the United States, 1817–1981.* (Contributions in Afro-American and African Studies, No. 70.) Westport, CT: Greenwood Press, 1983.

Littlefield, Daniel F., Jr., and Parins, James W., eds. *American Indian and Alaska Native Newspapers and Periodicals, 1826–1924.* Westport, CT: Greenwood Press, 1984.

Littlefield, Daniel F., Jr., and Parins, James W., eds. *American Indian and Alaska Native Newspapers and Periodicals, 1971–1985.* Westport, CT: Greenwood Press, 1986.

Rubin, Bernard, ed. *Small Voices and Great Trumpets: Minorities and the Media.* New York: Praeger, 1980.

Snorgrass, J. William, and Woody, Gloria T., comps. *Blacks and Media: A Selected, Annotated Bibliography, 1962–1982.* Tallahassee, FL: A&M University Press, 1985.

Ungurait, Donald F., Bohn, Thomas W., and Hiebert, Ray Eldon. *Media Now.* White Plains, NY: Longman, 1985.

Wilson, Clint, II, and Gutierrez, Felix. *Minorities and the Media.* Beverly Hills: Sage, 1985.

NEWS

Altschull, J. Herbert. *Agents of Power: The Role of the News Media in Human Affairs.* White Plains, NY: Longman, 1984.

Blanchard, Margaret A. *Exporting the First Amendment: The Press-Government*

Crusade of 1945–1953. White Plains, NY: Longman, 1986.
Bogart, Leo. *Press and Public: Who Reads What, Where and Why in American Newspapers.* Hillsdale, NJ: Erlbaum Associates, 1981.
Crawford, Nelson A. *The Ethics of Journalism.* New York: Knopf, 1924.
Epstein, Edward Jay. *Between Fact and Fiction: The Problem of Journalism.* New York: Random House, 1975.
Epstein, Edward Jay. *News from Nowhere: Television and the News.* New York: Random House, 1974.
Fenby, Jonathan. *The International News Services: A Twentieth Century Fund Report.* New York: Schocken, 1986.
Fishman, Mark. *Manufacturing the News.* Austin, TX: University of Texas Press, 1980.
Fry, Don, ed. *Believing the News* (Poynter Institute Ethics Center Report). St. Petersburg, FL: Poynter Institute for Media Studies, 1985.
Gans, Herbert W. *Deciding What's News: A Study of CBS Evening News, NBC Nightly News, and Time.* New York: Pantheon Books, 1979.
Garvey, Daniel E., and Rivers, William L. *Newswriting for the Electronic Media: Principles, Examples, Applications.* Belmont, CA: Wadsworth, 1982.
Gitlin, Todd. *Inside Prime Time.* New York: Pantheon Books, 1983.
Goldstein, Tom. *The News at Any Cost: How Journalists Compromise Their Ethics to Shape the News.* New York: Simon & Schuster, 1985.
Gollin, Albert E., and Bloom, Nicolas A. *Newspapers in American News Habits: A Comparative Assessment.* New York: Newspaper Advertising Bureau, 1985.
Graber, Doris A. *Processing the News: How People Tame the Information Tide.* White Plains, NY: Longman, 1984.
Green, Jonathan. *Newspeak: A Dictionary of Jargon.* New York: Routledge & Kegan Paul, 1984.
Gussow, Donald. *The New Business Journalism: An Insider's Look at the Workings of America's Business.* New York: Harcourt Brace Jovanovich, 1984.
Hartley, John. *Understanding News.* London: Methuen, 1982.
Hess, Stephen. *The Washington Reporters.* Washington, DC: The Brookings Institution, 1981.
Hulteng, John L. *Playing It Straight.* Chester, NY: American Society of Newspaper Editors, 1981.
Hutmacher, Barbara. *In Black and White: Voices of Apartheid.* Frederick, MD: University Publications of America, Inc., 1982.
Jamieson, Kathleen Hall, and Campbell, Carolyn Kohn. *The Interplay of Influence: Mass Media and Their Publics in News, Advertising, Politics.* Belmont, CA: Wadsworth, 1983.
Kohlmeier, Louis M., Jr., Udell, Jon G., and Anderson, Laird B., eds. *Reporting on Business and the Economy.* Englewood Cliffs, NJ: Prentice-Hall, 1981.
Lewis, John F. *Who Are Those Guys? A Monograph for Business on the News Media Today.* Washington, DC: The Media Institute, 1982.
MacDougall, Curtis Daniel. *The Press and Its Problems.* Dubuque, IO: W.C. Brown, 1964.
McKerns, Joseph P. *News Media and Public Policy: An Annotated Bibliography.* New York: Garland, 1985.
Melvin, Marvin. *News Reporting and Writing* (2nd ed). Dubuque, IO: W.C. Brown, 1981.
Meyer, Philip. *Editors, Publishers, and Newspaper Ethics.* Washington, DC:

American Society of Newspaper Editors Foundation, 1983.
Meyer, Philip. *Precision Journalism: A Reporter's Introduction to Social Science Methods* (2nd ed). Bloomington, IN: Indiana University Press, 1979.
Modern Media Institute. *Making Sense of the News*. St. Petersburg, FL: Modern Media Institute (changed to Poynter Institute for Media Studies), 1983.
Modern Media Institute. *The Adversary Press*. St. Petersburg, FL: Modern Media Institute (changed to Poynter Institute for Media Studies), 1983.
Neilson, Winthrop. *What's News—Dow Jones*. Radnor, PA: Chilton 1973.
Nimmo, Dan, and Mansfield, Michael W., eds. *Government and the News Media: Comparative Dimensions*. Waco, TX: Baylor University Press, 1982.
Roshco, Bernard. *Newsmaking*. Chicago, IL: University of Chicago Press, 1975.
Schudson, Michael. *Discovering the News: A Social History of American Newspapers*. New York: Basic Books, 1978.
Schwoebel, Jean. *Newsroom Democracy: The Case for Independence of the Press*. Iowa City, IO: University of Iowa School of Journalism and Mass Communication, 1976.
Sigal, Leon V. *Reporters and Officials: The Organization and Politics of Newsmaking*. Lexington, MA: D.C. Heath, 1973.
Thompson, Tom. *Organizational TV News*. Philadelphia, PA: Media Concepts Press, 1980.
Tuchman, Gaye. *Making News: A Study in the Construction of Reality*. New York: The Free Press, 1978.
Turow, Joseph. *Media Industries: The Production of News and Entertainment*. White Plains, NY: Longman, 1984.
Twentieth Century Fund Taskforce on the International Flow of News. *A Free and Balanced Flow*. Lexington, MA: Lexington Books, 1978.
Weaver, David H., and Wilhoit, G. Cleveland. *The American Journalist: A Portrait of U.S. News People and Their Work*. Bloomington, IN: Indiana University Press, 1986.
Weaver, David H. *Videotex Journalism: Teletext, Viewdata, and the News*. Hillsdale, NJ: Lawrence Erlbaum Associates, 1983.
Weisberger, Bernard A. *The American Newspaperman*. Chicago, IL: University of Chicago Press, 1961.
White, Theodore H. *In Search of History*. New York: Harper & Row, 1978.
Wicker, Tom. *On Press*. New York: Viking Press, 1978.

NEWSPAPER MANAGEMENT

American Newspaper Publishers Association (ANPA). *Three to Zero: The Story of the Birth and Death of the World-Tribune in New York City*. Reston, VA: ANPA, 1967.
American Society of Newspaper Editors (ASNE). *Newsroom Management Handbook*. Washington, DC: ASNE, 1985.
Giles, Robert H. *Newsroom Management*. Indianapolis, IN: R.J. Berg, 1986.
Macklin, Robert A. *Newspaper Circulation Management Training*. Washington, DC: International Circulation Managers Association, 1979.
Mallette, Malcolm F. *How Newspapers Communicate Internally: Case Studies and Samplings from a Changing Workplace*. Reston, VA: American Press Institute, 1981.

Meeker, Richard H. *Newspaperman: S.I. Newhouse and the Business of News.* New Haven, CT: Ticknor & Fields, 1983.
Newsom, D. Earl. *The Newspaper: Everything You Need to Know to Make It in the Newspaper Business.* Englewood Cliffs, NJ: Prentice-Hall, 1981.
Rankin, William Parkman. *The Practice of Newspaper Management.* New York: Praeger, 1986.
Rucker, Frank W., and Williams, Herbert L. *Newspaper Organization and Management* (5th ed). Ames, IO: Iowa State University Press, 1978.
Scharff, Edward E. *Worldly Power: The Making of the Wall Street Journal.* New York: Beaufort Books, 1986.
Sohn, Ardyth, Ogan, Chris, and Polich, John. *Newspaper Leadership.* Englewood Cliffs, NJ: Prentice-Hall, 1986.
Tillinghast, Diana S. *Inside the Los Angeles Times.* New York: Praeger, 1983.

NEWSPAPERS

American Newspaper Markets, Inc. *Circulation.* Northfield, IL: American Newspaper Markets, annual.
American Newspaper Publishers Association (ANPA). *Three to Zero: The Story of the Birth and Death of the World-Tribune in New York City.* Reston, VA: ANPA, 1967.
American Society of Newspaper Editors (ASNE). *Newsroom Management Handbook.* Washington, DC: ASNE, 1985.
Argyris, Chris. *Behind the Front Page.* San Francisco: Jossey-Bass Publishers, 1974.
Ashley, Perry J., ed. *Dictionary of Literary Biography, Volume 29: American Newspaper Journalists, 1926–1950.* Detroit, MI: Gale Research, 1984.
Benjaminson, Peter. *Death in the Afternoon: America's Newspaper Giants Struggle for Survival.* Fairway, KA: Andrews, McMeel, Partker, 1985.
Bogart, Leo. *Press and Public: Who Reads What, Where and Why in American Newspapers.* Hillsdale, NJ: Erlbaum Associates, 1981.
Braddon, Russell. *Roy Thomson of Fleet Street.* Huntington, NY: Fontana, 1968.
Burkhardt, Friedrick W. *Newspapers and Electronic Media.* Darmsstadt, Federal Republic of Germany: International Association for Newspaper and Media Technology, 1983.
Carter, Nancy M., and Cullen, John B. *The Computerization of Newspaper Organizations: The Impact of Technology on Organizational Structuring.* Lanham, MD: University Press of America, Inc., 1983.
Clabes, Judith G., ed. *New Guardians of the Press: Selected Profiles of America's Women Newspaper Editors.* Indianapolis, IN: R.J. Berg, 1983.
Compaine, Benjamin M. *The Newspaper Industry in the 1980s: An Assessment of Economics and Technology.* White Plains, NY: Knowledge Industry Publications, 1980.
Dertouzos, James N., and Quinn, Timothy H. *Bargaining Responses to the Technology Revolution: The Case of the Newspaper Industry.* Santa Monica, CA: Rand Corp., 1982.
Dertouzos, James N., and Thorpe, Kenneth. *Newspaper Groups: Economies of Scale, Tax Laws and Merger Incentives.* Santa Monica, CA: Rand Corp.,

1982.
Emery, Michael. *America's Leading Daily Newspapers*. Indianapolis, IN: R.J. Berg, 1983.
Engwall, Lars. *Newspapers as Organizations*. Brookfield, VT: Gower, 1979.
Ferguson, James M. *The Advertising Rate Structure in the Daily Newspaper Industry*. Englewood Cliffs, NJ: Prentice-Hall, 1963.
Garcia, Mario R. *Contemporary Newspaper Design*. Englewood Cliffs, NJ: Prentice-Hall, 1981.
Garcia, Mario R., et al., eds. *Color in American Newspapers*. St. Petersburg, FL: Poynter Institute for Media Studies, 1986.
Ghiglione, Loren, ed. *Evaluating the Press: The New England Newspaper Survey*. Southbridge, MA: Loren Ghiglione, 1973.
Ghiglione, Loren. *Gentlemen of the Press*. Indianapolis, IN: R.J. Berg, 1984.
Ghiglione, Loren. *The Buying and Selling of America's Newspapers*. Indianapolis, IN: R.J. Berg, 1984.
Giles, Robert H. *Editors and Stress*. New York: Associated Press Managing Editors Association, 1983.
Giles, Robert H. *Newsroom Management*. Indianapolis, IN: R.J. Berg, 1986.
Gilmore, Gene. *Modern Newspaper Editing* (3rd ed). San Francisco: Boyd & Fraser, 1982.
Gollin, Albert E., and Bloom, Nicolas A. *Newspapers in American News Habits: A Comparative Assessment*. New York: Newspaper Advertising Bureau, 1985.
Gormley, William T., Jr. *The Effects of Newspaper-Television Cross-Ownership on News Homogeneity*. Chapel Hill, NC: Institute for Research in Social Science, University of North Carolina, 1976.
Hachten, William A., and Giffard, C. Anthony. *The Press and Apartheid: Repression and Propaganda in South Africa*. Madison, WI: University of Wisconsin Press, 1984.
Halberstam, David. *The Powers That Be*. New York: Knopf, 1979.
Hirsch, Fred, and Gordon, David. *Newspaper Money*. London: Hutchinson, 1978.
Hodgson, F. W. *Modern Newspaper Practice*. North Pomfret, VT: David & Charles, 1984.
Hulteng, John L. *Playing It Straight*. Chester, NY: American Society of Newspaper Editors, 1981.
Hynds, Ernest C. *American Newspapers in the 1980s*. New York: Hastings House, 1980.
International Resource Development. *Electronic Newspapers* (Reports Ser.: No. 179). Norwalk, CT: International Resource Development, 1981.
Jackson, Charles L., and Shooshan, Harry M. *Newspapers and Videotex: How Free a Press?* St. Petersburg, FL: Poynter Institute for Media Studies (formerly Modern Media Institute), 1981.
Keely, Tom. *The Imperial Post: The Meyers, The Grahams and The Paper That Rules Washington*. New York: Morrow, 1983.
Limprecht, Hollis J. *A Century of Service, 1885–1985: The World-Herald Story*. Omaha: Omaha World-Herald Co., 1985.
Littlefield, Daniel F., Jr., and Parins, James W., eds. *American Indian and Alaska Native Newspapers and Periodicals, 1826–1924*. Westport, CT: Greenwood Press, 1984.
Lutz, William W. *The News of Detroit*. Boston: Little, Brown, 1973.
Mallette, Malcolm F. *How Newspapers Communicate Internally: Case Studies*

and Samplings from a Changing Workplace. Reston, VA: American Press Institute, 1981.
Melvin, Marvin. *News Reporting and Writing* (2nd ed). Dubuque, IO: W.C. Brown, 1981.
Meyer, Philip. *Editors, Publishers, and Newpaper Ethics*. Washington, DC: American Society of Newspaper Editors Foundation, 1983.
Meyer, Philip. *The Newspaper Survival Book: An Editor's Guide to Marketing Research*. Bloomington, IN: Indiana University Press, 1985.
Neilson, Winthrop. *What's News—Dow Jones*. Radnor, PA: Chilton, 1973.
Newsom, D. Earl. *The Newspaper: Everything You Need to Know to Make It in the Newspaper Business*. Englewood Cliffs, NJ: Prentice-Hall, 1981.
Oppenheim, S. Chesterfield, and Shields, Carrington. *Newspapers and the Antitrust Laws*. Charlottesville, VA: The Michie Co., 1982.
Patten, David A. *Newspapers and New Media*. White Plains, NY: Knowledge Industry Publications, 1986.
Rankin, William Parkman. *The Practice of Newspaper Management*. New York: Praeger, 1986.
Roper Organization, The. *Public Perceptions of Television and Other Mass Media: A Twenty-Five Year Review, 1959–1980*. New York: Television Information Office, 1981.
Rucker, Frank W., and Williams, Herbert L. *Newspaper Organization and Management* (5th ed). Ames, IO: Iowa State University Press, 1978.
Sachsman, David, and Sloat, Warren. *The Press and the Suburbs: The Daily Newspapers of New Jersey*. New Brunswick, NJ: Rutgers, 1985.
Salisbury, Harrison. *Without Fear or Favor*. New York: Times Books, 1980.
Scharff, Edward E. *Worldly Power: The Making of the Wall Street Journal*. New York: Beaufort Books, 1986.
Schudson, Michael. *Discovering the News: A Social History of American Newspapers*. New York: Basic Books, 1978.
Schweitzer, John C. *Conference on Problems of Declining Newspaper Circulation Among Young Adults*. Bloomington, IN: Center for New Communications, School of Journalism, Indiana University, 1976.
Sims, Norman. *The Literary Journalists*. New York: Ballantine Books, 1984.
Smith, Anthony. *Goodbye Gutenberg: The Newspaper Revolution of the 1980s*. New York: Oxford University Press, 1980.
Smith, Anthony. *Newspapers and Democracy*. Cambridge, MA: The MIT Press, 1980.
Smith, Anthony. *The Newspaper: An International History*. London: Thames and Hudson, 1979.
Sohn, Ardyth, Ogan, Chris, and Polich, John. *Newspaper Leadership*. Englewood Cliffs, NJ: Prentice-Hall, 1986.
Stamm, Keith R. *Newspaper Use and Community Ties: Toward a Dynamic Theory*. Norwood, NJ: Ablex, 1985.
Standard Rate and Data Service, Inc. *SRDS Newspaper Circulation Analysis*. Skokie, IL: Standard Rate and Data Service, (annual).
Stewart, Walter, ed. *Canadian Newspapers: The Inside Story*. Edmonton: Hurtig, 1980.
Tillinghast, Diana S. *Inside the Los Angeles Times*. New York: Praeger, 1983.
Udell, Jon G. *The Economics of the American Newspaper*. New York: Communication Arts Books, Hastings House, 1978.
Wright, B.E., and Lavine, John M. *The Constant Dollar Newspaper: An Economic Analysis Covering the Last Two Decades*. Chicago: Inland Daily Press Association, 1982.

ORGANIZATION

Carter, Nancy M., and Cullen, John B. *The Computerization of Newspaper Organizations: The Impact of Technology on Organizational Structuring.* Lanham, MD: University Press of America, Inc., 1983.

Domhoff, G. William, Dye, Thomas R., eds. *Power Elites and Organizations.* Newbury Park, CA: Sage, 1986.

Gibson, James L. *Organizations: Behavior, Structure, Processes.* Dallas: Business Publications, 1979.

Gudykunst, William B., Stewart, Lea P., and Ting-Toomey, Stella, eds. *Communication, Culture, and Organizational Processes.* Beverly Hills: Sage, 1985.

Hackman, Richard J., ed. *Perspectives on Behavior in Organizations.* New York: McGraw-Hill, 1977.

Lawler, Edward E., III, Nadler, David A., Cammann, Cortlandt. *Organizational Assessment: Perspectives on the Measurement of Organizational Behavior and the Quality of Work Life.* New York: Wiley, 1980.

Lawler, Edward E., III. *Pay and Organization Development.* Reading, MA: Addison-Wesley, 1981.

Mintzberg, Henry. *Structuring of Organizations.* Englewood Cliffs, NJ: Prentice-Hall, 1979.

Morgan, Gareth. *Images of Organization* (2nd printing). Newbury Park, CA: Sage, 1986.

Naisbitt, John, and Aburdene, Patricia. *Re-Inventing the Corporation: Transforming Your Job and Your Company for the New Information Society.* New York: Warner Books, 1985.

Reuss, Carol, and Silvis, Donn, eds. *Inside Organizational Communication* (2nd ed). White Plains, NY: Longman, 1985.

Rucker, Frank W., and Williams, Herbert L. *Newspaper Organization and Management.* Ames, IO: Iowa State University Press, 1955.

Scott, William G., and Hart, David K. *Organizational America.* Boston: Houghton Mifflin, 1980.

Sigal, Leon V. *Reporters and Officials: The Organization and Politics of Newsmaking.* Lexington, MA: D.C. Heath, 1973.

Wallace, Marc J. *Managing Behavior in Organizations.* Glenview, IL: Scott, Foresman, 1982.

PERSONNEL

Armstrong, Michael. *Case Studies in Personnel Management.* New York: Nichols, 1979.

Beach, Dale S., ed. *Managing People at Work: Readings in Personnel* (3rd ed). New York: Macmillan, 1980.

Ettema, James S., and Whitney, D. Charles, eds. *Individuals in Mass Media Organizations: Creativity and Constraint* (Sage Annual Reviews of Communication Research, Vol 10). Beverly Hills: Sage, 1982.

Giles, Robert. *Editors and Stress.* New York: Associated Press Managing Editors Association, 1983.

Hackman, Richard J., ed. *Perspectives on Behavior in Organizations.* New York: McGraw-Hill, 1977.

Johnston, John W. C. *The News People: A Sociological Portrait of American Journalists.* Chicago: University of Illinois Press, 1976.

Latham, Gary P., and Wexley, Kenneth W. *Increasing Productivity Through Performance Appraisal.* Reading, MA: Addison-Wesley, 1981.

Lawler, Edward E., III. *Pay and Organization Development.* Reading, MA: Addison-Wesley, 1981.

Mikovich, George T., and Glueck, William F. *Personnel: A Diagnostic Approach* (4th ed). Plano, TX: Business Publications, 1985.

Miller, Sherod, Wackman, Daniel B., Demmitt, Dallas R., and Demmitt, Nancy J. *Working Together: Productive Communication on the Job.* Littleton, CO: Interpersonal Communication Programs, Inc., 1985.

Pascarella, Perry. *Industry Week's Guide to Tomorrow's Executive: Human Management in the Future Corporation.* New York: Van Nostrand Reinhold, 1980.

Pascarella, Perry. *The New Achievers: Creating a Modern Work Ethic.* New York: Free Press, 1984.

Wallace, Marc J. *Managing Behavior in Organizations.* Glenview, IL: Scott, Foresman, 1982.

Weaver, David H., and Wilhoit, G. Cleveland. *The American Journalist: A Portrait of U.S. News People and Their Work.* Bloomington, IN: Indiana University Press, 1986.

Weisberger, Bernard A. *The American Newspaperman.* Chicago: University of Chicago Press, 1961.

PROMOTION

Bergendorff, Fred L., Smith, Charles, H., and Webster, Lance. *Broadcast Advertising and Promotion.* New York: Hastings House, 1983.

Meyers, William. *The Image-Makers: Power and Persuasion on Madison Avenue.* New York: Times Books, 1984.

Mitchell, Craig. *Media Promotion.* Chicago: Crain Books, 1985.

Nickels, William G. *Marketing and Promotion.* Columbus, OH: Grid Publishing, Co., 1980.

Patti, Charles H., ed. *Cases in Advertising and Promotion Management.* New York: Wiley, 1983.

Ries, Al, and Trout, Jack. *Positioning: The Battle for Your Mind.* New York: McGraw-Hill, 1981.

PUBLIC RELATIONS

Cantor, Bill. *Experts in Action: Inside Public Relations.* White Plains, NY: Longman, 1984.

Cole, Robert S. *The Practical Handbook of Public Relations.* Englewood Cliffs, NJ: Prentice-Hall, 1981.

Grunig, James E. *Managing Public Relations.* New York: Holt, Rinehart & Winston, 1984.

Howard, Carole, and Mathews, Wilma. *On Deadline: Managing Media Relations*. White Plains, NY: Longman, 1985.

International Advertising Association. *Controversy Advertising: How Advertisers Present Points of View in Public Affairs*. New York: Hastings House, 1977.

McIver, Colin. *Case Studies in Marketing, Advertising and Public Relations*. North Pomfret, VT: David & Charles, 1984.

Nager, Norman R., and Harrell, Thomas. *Public Relations: Management by Objectives*. White Plains, NY: Longman, 1984.

Reuss, Carol, and Silvis, Donn, eds. *Inside Organizational Communication* (2nd ed). White Plains, NY: Longman, 1985.

Seital, Fraser P. *The Practice of Public Relations*. Columbus, OH: Charles E. Merrill, 1983.

Wilcox, Dennis L., Ault, Phillip H., and Agee, Warren K. *Public Relations: Strategies and Tactics*. New York: Harper & Row, 1986.

RESEARCH METHODOLOGIES

Anderson, James A. *Communication Research: Issues and Methods*. New York: McGraw-Hill, 1987.

Austin, Bruce A., ed. *Current Research in Film: Audiences, Economics and Law: Volume I*. Norwood, NJ: Ablex, 1985.

Crimp, Margaret. *The Marketing Research Process* (2nd ed). Englewood Cliffs, NJ: Prentice-Hall, 1985.

Dexter, Lewis A., and White, David M., eds. *People, Society and Mass Communications*. New York: Free Press, 1964.

Epton, S. R., et al., eds. *Managing Interdisciplinary Research*. New York: Wiley, 1984.

Ettema, James S., and Whitney, D. Charles, eds. *Individuals in Mass Media Organizations: Creativity and Constraint* (Sage Annual Reviews of Communication Research, Vol. 10). Beverly Hills: Sage, 1982.

Fielding, Nigel G., and Fielding, Jane L. *Linking Data*. Newbury Park, CA: Sage, 1985.

Fowler, Floyd J., Jr. *Survey Research Methods*. Beverly Hills: Sage, 1984.

Gibson, John E. *Managing Research and Development*. New York: Wiley, 1981.

Glasser, Alan. *Research and Development Management*. Englewood Cliffs, NJ: Prentice-Hall, 1982.

Graber, Doris A. *Processing the News: How People Tame the Information Tide*. White Plains, NY: Longman, 1984.

Hauer, Mary, et al. *Books, Librarians, and Research*. Dubuque, IO: Kendall/Hunt, 1983.

Horowitz, Lois. *Knowing Where To Look: The Ultimate Guide to Research*. Cincinnati, OH: Writers Digest Books, 1984.

Kline, F. Gerald, and Tichenor, Phillip J., eds. *Current Perspectives in Mass Communications Research* (Sage Annual Reviews of Communication Research Ser.: Vol. 1). Beverly Hills: Sage, 1974.

Lowery, Shearon, and DeFleur, and Melvin L. *Milestones in Mass Communication Research*. White Plains, NY: Longman, 1988.

Meyer, Philip. *The Newspaper Survival Book: An Editor's Guide to Marketing Research*. Bloomington, IN: Indiana University Press, 1985.

Morgan, Gareth, ed. *Beyond Method: Strategies for Social Research*. Beverly Hills: Sage, 1983.

Stempel, Guido H., III, and Westley, Bruce H. *Research Methods in Mass Communications*. Englewood Cliffs, NJ: Prentice-Hall, 1981.

Stewart, David W. *Secondary Research: Information Sources and Methods.* Beverly Hills: Sage, 1984.

Surette, Ray, ed. *Justice and the Media: Issues and Research.* Springfield, IL: Thomas, 1984.

UNESCO. *Mass Media in Society: The Need of Research* (Reports and Papers on Mass Communication: No. 59). New York: Unipub, 1970.

Ward, Jean, and Hansen, Kathleen A. *Search Strategies in Mass Communication.* White Plains, NY: Longman, 1987.

Wimmer, Roger, and Dominick, Joseph R. *Mass Media Research.* Belmont, CA: Wadsworth, 1983.

TECHNOLOGY AND TELECOMMUNICATIONS

American Newspaper Publishers Association. *It's For You: A Newspaper's Guide to Telecommunications Equipment, Management and Consultants.* Washington, DC: ANPA, 1986.

American Newspaper Publishers Association. *It's For You: Opportunities and Obstacles: A Survey of Newspaper Telecommunication Systems.* Washington, DC: ANPA, 1986.

Baughcum, Allan, Faulhaber, Gerald, and Voigt, Melvin J., eds. *Telecommunications Access and Public Policy.* Norwood, NJ: Ablex, 1984.

Belitsos, Byron, and Misra, Jay. *Business Telematics: Corporate Networks for the Information Age.* Homewood, IL: Dow, Jones-Irwin, 1986.

Bernstein, Jeremy. *Three Degrees Above Zero: The Bell Labs in the Information Age.* New York: Scribner, 1984.

Bittner, John R. *Broadcasting and Telecommunication: An Introduction* (2nd ed). Englewood Cliffs, NJ: Prentice-Hall, 1985.

Carey, John. *Telecommunications Technologies and Public Broadcasting 1986.* Washington, DC: Corporation for Public Broadcasting, 1986.

Carter, Nancy M., and Cullen, John B. *The Computerization of Newspaper Organizations: The Impact of Technology on Organizational Structuring.* Lanham, MD: University Press of America, Inc., 1983.

Diamond, Edwin, et al. *Telecommunications in Crisis: The First Amendment, Technology, and Deregulation.* Washington, DC: Cato Institute, 1983.

Glatzer, Hal. *The Telecommunications Revolution: Who Controls the Airwaves?* Indianapolis, IN: Howard Sams, 1984.

Gross, Lynne S. *Telecommunications: An Introduction to Radio, Television and the Developing Media.* Dubuque, IO: William C. Brown, 1983.

Herring, James M., and Gross, Gerald C. *Telecommunications: Economics and Regulations.* Salem, NH: Ayer, 1974.

Irwin, Manley R. *Telecommunications America: Market Without Boundaries.* Westport, CT: Greenwood Press, 1984.

Lewin, Leonard, ed. *Telecommunications in the U.S. Trends and Policies.* Dedham, MA: Artech House, Inc., 1981.

Maynard, Jeff. *Cable Television.* London: Collins, 1985.

Mueller, Milton. *Property Rights in Radio Communications: The Key to the Reform of Telecommunications Regulation* (Policy Analysis Study No. 11). Washington, DC: The Cato Institute, 1983.

Noam, Eli M., ed. *Telecommunications Regulation Today and Tomorrow.* New York: Harcourt Brace Jovanovich, 1984.

Pool, Ithiel de Sola. *Technologies of Freedom.* Boston: Harvard University Press, 1983.

Salvaggio, Jerry L. *Telecommunications: Issues and Choices for Society.* White Plains, NY: Longman, 1983.

Smith, F. Leslie. *Perspectives on Radio and Television: Telecommunications in the United States* (2nd ed). New York: Harper & Row, 1986.

Snow, Marcellus. *Marketplace for Telecommunications: Regulation and Deregulation in Industrialized Democracies.* White Plains, NY: Longman, 1986.

U.S. House of Representatives. Committee on Energy and Commerce. Subcommittee on Telecommunications, Consumer Protection, and Finance. *Broadcast Regulation and Station Ownership.* Washington, DC: Government Printing Office, 1985.

Vietor, Richard, and Dyer, Davis, eds. *Telecommunications in Transition: Managing Business and Regulatory Change* (Course Module Series). Boston: Harvard Business School, 1986.

Williams, Frederick. *Technology and Communication Behavior.* Belmont, CA: Wadsworth, 1987.

TELEVISION

Alten, Stanley R. *Audio in Media* (2nd ed). White Plains, NY: Knowledge Industry Publications, 1986.

Beville, Hugh Malcolm, Jr. *Audience Ratings: Radio, Television and Cable.* Hillsdale, NJ: Lawrence Erlbaum Associates, 1985.

Biel, Jacquelyn. *Low Power Television: Development and Current Status of the LPTV Industry.* Washington, DC: National Association of Broadcasters, 1985.

Brown, Bortz, and Coddington, Consulting Firm. *Great Expectations: A Television Manager's Guide to the Future.* Washington, DC: National Association of Broadcasters, 1986.

Cassata, Mary, and Skill, Thomas. *Television: A Guide to the Literature.* Phoenix, AZ: Oryx Press, 1985.

Cross, Donna Wolfolk. *Mediaspeak: How Television Makes Up Your Mind.* New York: Putnam, 1983.

D'Agostino, Peter, ed. *Transmission.* New York: Tanam Press, 1985.

Dessart, George. *Television in the Real World.* New York: Hastings House, 1978.

Dordick, Herbert S., Bradley, Helen G., and Nanus, Burt. *The Emerging Network Marketplace.* Norwood, NJ: Ablex, 1981.

Ensign, Lynne Naylor, and Knapton, Robyn Eileen. *The Complete Dictionary of Television and Film.* Briarcliff Manor, NY: Stein and Day, 1985.

Epstein, Edward Jay. *News From Nowhere: Television and the News.* New York: Random House, 1974.

Feel, A. Frank. *The Networks.* New York: Scribner, 1979.

Gans, Herbert W. *Deciding What's News: A Study of CBS Evening News, NBC Nightly News, and Time.* New York: Pantheon News, 1979.

Gitlin, Todd. *Inside Prime Time.* New York: Pantheon Books, 1983.

Gormley, William T., Jr. *The Effects of Newspaper-Television Cross-Ownership on News Homogeneity.* Chapel Hill, NC: Institute for Research in Social Science, University of North Carolina, 1976.

Gross, Lynne S. *Telecommunications: An Introduction to Radio, Television and the Developing Media.* Dubuque, IO: William C. Brown, 1983.

Hill, George H., and Hill, Sylvia Saverson. *Blacks and Television: A Selectively Annotated Bibliography.* Metuchen, NJ: The Scarecrow Press, 1985.
Howard, Herbert H. *Group and Cross-Media Ownership of Television Stations: 1986.* Washington, DC: National Association of Broadcasters, 1986.
Horsfield, Peter G. *Religious Television: The American Experience.* White Plains, NY: Longman, 1984.
Marshall, Christine, ed. *Programming in the UK and USA.* London: Financial Times Media Intelligence Unit, 1984.
McCormick-Prichett, Nancy, ed. *Women on the Job: Careers in Electronic Media.* Washington, DC: American Women in Radio and Television; Women's Bureau, U.S. Dept. of Labor, 1984.
Nadel, Mark, and Noam, Eli, eds. *The Economics of Traditional Broadcasting (VHF/UHF): An Anthology.* New York: Columbia University Graduate School of Business, 1983.
Noll, Roger G., Peck, Merton J., and McGowan, John. *Economic Aspects of Television Regulation.* Washington, DC: The Brookings Institution, 1973.
Owen, Bruce, Beebe, Jack, and Manning, Willard. *Television Economics.* Lexington, MA: Lexington Books, 1974.
Poltrack, David F. *Television Marketing.* New York: McGraw-Hill, 1983.
Roper Organization, The. *Public Perceptions of Television and Other Mass Media: A Twenty-Five Year Review, 1959–1980.* New York: Television Information Office, 1981.
Smith, F. Leslie. *Perspectives on Radio and Television: Telecommunications in the United States* (2nd ed). New York: Harper & Row, 1986.
Smith, R.L. *The Wired Nation.* New York: Harper & Row, 1972.
Thompson, Tom. *Organizational TV News.* Philadelphia, PA: Media Concepts Press, 1980.
Zettl, Herbert. *Television Production Handbook* (4th ed). White Plains, NY: Knowledge Industry Publications, 1984.

UNIONS

Bakke, E. Wright, Kerr, Clark, and Anrod, Charles W. (Eds.). *Unions, Management, and the Public* (3rd ed.). New York: Harcourt, Brace Jovanovich, 1976.
Barbash, Jack. *American Unions: Structure, Government, and Politics.* New York: Random House, 1967.
Beharrell, Peter and Philo, Greg (Eds.). *Trade Unions and the Media.* London: Macmillan, 1977.
Daniels, Gene, Till-Retz, Roberta, Casey, Larry, and DeAngelis, Anthony. *Labor Guide to Local Union Leadership.* Englewood Cliffs, NJ: Prentice-Hall, 1986.
Douglas, Sara U. *Labor's New Voice: Unions and the Mass Media.* Norwood, NJ: Ablex, 1986.
Flack, Richard (Ed.). *Conformity, Resistance, and Self-Determinism: The Individual and Authority.* Boston: Little, Brown, 1973.
Freeman, Richard B. *What Do Unions Do?* New York: Basic Books, 1984.
Gorman, Robert A. *Basic Text on Labor Law: Unionization and Collective Bargaining.* St. Paul, MN: West Publishing, 1976.
Herbert, Gerard. *Labor Relations in the Newspaper Industry* (Research Publications, Vol. 5). Ottawa: Royal Commission on Newspapers, 1981.

Lester, Richard A. *As Unions Mature: An Analysis of the Evolution of American Unionism*. Princeton, NJ: Princeton University Press, 1958.

Livernash, E. Robert. *Note on Collective Bargaining in the United States*. Boston: Harvard University, 1976.

Tyler, Gus. *The Political Imperative: The Corporate Character of Unions*. New York: Macmillan, 1968.

VIDEO AND VIDEOTEX

Alten, Stanley R. *Audio in Media* (2nd ed). White Plains, NY: Knowledge Industry Publications, 1986.

Bamberger, Nancy. *Videotex Production: A Case Study*. San Diego: Electronic Text Consortium, 1984.

Harry Collier, et al., eds. *Electronic Publishing Review: The International Journal of the Transfer of Published Information via Videotex and Online Media* (1984 ed). Medford, NJ: Learned Information, 1984.

Compaine, Benjamin M., ed. *Understanding New Media*. Cambridge, MA: Ballinger, 1984.

Degen, Clara, ed. *Understanding and Using Video: A Guide for the Organizational Communicator*. White Plains, NY: Longman, 1985.

Hurly, Paul, Laucht, Matthias, and Hlynka, Denis. *The Videotex and Teletext Handbook: Home and Office Communications Using Microcomputers and Terminals*. New York: Harper & Row, 1985.

Iuppa, Nicholas V. *A Practical Guide to Interactive Video Design*. White Plains, NY: Knowledge Industry Publications, 1984.

Jackson, Charles L., and Shooshan, Harry M. *Newspapers and Videotex: How Free a Press?* St. Petersburg, FL: Poynter Institute for Media Studies (formerly Modern Media Institute), 1981.

Lidwell, Wendy, and Guzzy, Mary, eds. *The AIVF Guide to Film and Video Distributors*. New York: Association of Independent Video and Filmmakers, 1984.

Marshall, Christine, ed. *Programming in the UK and USA*. London: Financial Times Media Intelligence Unit, 1984.

Murphy, Brian. *International Politics of News Information Technology*. New York: St. Martin's Press, 1986.

Nadel, Mark, and Noam, Eli, eds. *The Economics of Traditional Broadcasting (VHF/UHF): An Anthology*. New York: Columbia University Graduate School of Business, 1983.

Noam, Eli M., ed. *Video Media Competition Regulation, Economics, and Technology*. New York: Columbia University Press, 1985.

Online Publications Ltd. *Videotex Key to the Information Revolution*. Middlesex, U.K.: Online Publications Ltd., 1982.

Patten, David A. *Newspapers and New Media*. White Plains, NY: Knowledge Industry Publications, 1986.

Salvaggio, Jerry L. *Telecommunications: Issues and Choices for Society*. White Plains, NY: Longman, 1983.

Sigel, Efrem, et al. *The Future of Videotext: Worldwide Prospects for Home/Office Electronic Information Services*. White Plains, NY: Knowledge Industry Publications, 1983.

Straus, Lawrence. *Electronic Marketing: Emerging TV and Computer Channels for Interactive Home Shopping*. White Plains, NY: Knowledge Industry Publications, 1983.

Tydeman, John, and Lipinski, Hurbert. *Teletext and Videotex in the United States*. New York: McGraw-Hill, 1982.

Van Deusen, Richard E. *Practical AV/Video Budgeting*. White Plains, NY: Knowledge Industry Publications, 1984.

Vietor, Richard, and Dyer, Davis, eds. *Telecommunications in Transition: Managing Business and Regulatory Change* (Course Module Series). Boston: Harvard Business School, 1986.

Weaver, David H. *Videotex Journalism: Teletext, Viewdata, and the News*. Hillsdale, NJ: Lawrence Erlbaum Associates, 1983.

Wiegand, Ingrid. *Professional Video Production*. White Plains, NY: Knowledge Industry Publications, 1985.

Wiese, Michael. *Film and Video Budgets*. Westport, CT: Michael Wiese Film Productions, 1984.

Young, Judy, ed. *Videotex and Teletext in the US and UK*. London: Financial Times Media Intelligence Unit, 1984.

WOMEN

Agee, Warren K., Ault, Phillip H., and Emery, Edwin. *Maincurrents in Mass Communications*. New York: Harper & Row, 1986.

Baehr, Helen, and Ryan, Michelle. *Shut Up and Listen! Women and Local Radio: A View from the Inside*. London: Comedia, 1984.

Beasley, Maurine and Gibbons, Sheila. *Women in Media: A Documentary Source Book*. Washington, DC: Women's Institute for Freedom of the Press, 1979.

Blaxall, Martha, and Reagan, Barbara B., eds. *Women and the Workplace: The Implications of Occupational Segregation*. Chicago: University of Chicago Press, 1976.

Cadman, Eileen, et al. *Rolling Our Own: Women as Printers, Publishers and Distributors* (Minority Press Group Series No. 4). London: Minority Press Group, 1981.

Clabes, Judith G., ed. *New Guardians of the Press: Selected Profiles of America's Women Newspaper Editors*. Indianapolis, IN: R.J. Berg, 1983.

Gutek, Barbara A., and Larwood, Laurie, eds. *Women's Career Development*. Newbury Park, CA: Sage, 1986.

Hennig, Margaret, and Jardim, Anne. *The Managerial Woman*. Garden City, NY: Anchor Press/Doubleday, 1977.

Hiebert, Ray E., and Reuss, Carol, eds. *Impact of Mass Media: Current Issues*. White Plains, NY: Longman, 1985.

Jacobson, Aileen. *Women in Charge: Dilemmas of Women in Authority*. New York: Van Nostrand Reinhold, 1985.

McCormick-Prichett, Nancy, ed. *Women on the Job: Careers in Electronic Media*. Washington, DC: American Women in Radio and Television; Women's Bureau, U.S. Dept. of Labor, 1984.

Stromberg, Ann H., Larwood, Laurie, and Gutek, Barbara S., eds. *Women and Work 2: An Annual Review*. Newbury Park, CA: Sage, 1986.

Ungurait, Donald F., Bohn, Thomas W., and Hiebert, Ray Eldon. *Media Now*. White Plains, NY: Longman, 1985.

Walters, Patricia, et al. *Women in Top Jobs: Four Studies in Achievement* (Political and Economic Planning Series). Winchester, MA: Allen Unwin, 1971.

Wilcox, Dennis L., Ault, Phillip H., and Agee, Warren K. *Public Relations: Strategies and Tactics*. New York: Harper & Row, 1986.

Index

AAAA, (Four-A's), 210. *See* American Association of Advertising Agencies
ABC, 373
Abell, Derek, 258
Access to media
  advertising policies, 367–369
  computer technology, 376
  open meeting statutes, 353
  target market, 264
Accounting, 159, 179–181
Account planner, role of, 154
Account services and personnel, 45–48
Accounts receivable turnover, 179
Accrued expenses, 177
Accumulated retained earnings, 178
Adler, Renata, 18
Advertisement(s)
  as promotional tools, 297–298, 308–312
  laws regarding acceptance of, 367–368
Advertiser market, 14, 111
  product planning, 287–290
  segmentation of, 271–275
Advertiser(s), 24, 325–327, 384–385
  audience segments, 236
  expenditures of and revenues from, 26–31
  KZZZ-FM, 49–51
  market, 160
  planning, 100–101, 106
  The New Gazette, 52, 55
Advertising, 251–257, 297–298
  agencies, 10–11
    as large employers, 375
  backgrounding, 100–103, 111–112
  benefit segmentation of, 272
  blurring of media lines, 18–20
  business/farm publications, 27
  campaigns, 280–283
  Charles Advertising Agency, 150–158
  Constant Dollar Study, 30
  contracts, 313
  DAGMAR model, 273
  demographics, 266, 272
  expenditures, national totals, 26–28
  implications of shifts, 29
  KZZZ-FM, 49–50
  law and legal aspects of, 366–368
  message development, 11
  The New Gazette, 51–55, 334–348
  new sources, 30
  product planning, 287–289
  promotion and sales of, 308–312
  research, 280
  revenues, total national and local, 26–32
  ROP, 29
  segmentation, 271–274
  strategies, 14, 45, 106–107, 110, 283–284, 293–294
  trends, 25
  usage patterns, 272
  Williams Advertising Agency, 44–48
Advertising Age, 274
Affirmative action, 362. *See also* Equal Employment Opportunity (EEO)
Agenda, hidden, 202
Agreements, Joint Operating (JOA), 17, 359–360
Ahneman, Edward, 159
AIDA, 290–329
Alive and Aware, 300
Ambition, 187–188
Amendment, First. *See* First Amendment
American Association of Advertising Agencies, (AAAA), 362
American Newspaper Publishers Association, (ANPA), 213, 310
  and training, 210
American Press Institute, 210
American Society of Newspaper Editors, (ASNE), 362
  Bulletin of, 363
American Telephone and Telegraph, (AT&T) and antitrust law, 359
ANPA, 213, 310

Antitrust, 17, 107, 354–355, 358–361
Arbitron ratings, 103, 274
Artistic. *See* Creativity; *See also* Employees
Ashton, David, 159
ASNE Bulletin, 363
Associated Press, (AP), 239
Assets
  employees as, 35, 59
  financial, 3, 160, 173, 176–181
Associations, 76,
Attorneys, 357, 368. *See also* Lawyers
Audience, 242, 331–333, 337
  characteristics of, 38–42
  competition for, 377–380
  -contact objectives, reach, 295
    frequency, 296
  fragmentation, 42
  KZZZ-FM 48, 49, 100, 101, 114, 233, 244–248
  market, 14, 160
  market perspective, 254–264
  The New Gazette, 57–61
  Pediatric Neurology, 118–121
  promotional strategies for attracting an, 290–314
  psychographics/lifestyles, 269
  segmentation, 233, 236, 265–275
  social responsibility to serve, 383–385
  strategies, 105–106
  synergism, 42
  target, 233
Audiocassettes, 315–322
Audiovisual, 10
Authority, 139–140
  as a management principle, 78–80
Autonomy, 136, 142, 191–192, 212, 214

Babbage, Charles, 77–79
Backgrounding, 91–94
  Charles Advertising Agency, 151
  KZZZ-FM, 100–105, 111–112
  Pediatric Neurology, 119–122
Balance of power
  as a communication strategy, 197
Balance sheet, 176
Bales, Robert, 221
Banking, 165, 337
  advertising, 296, 312
Bargaining
  collective, 363
  strategy, 198
Barnard, Chester I., 79–80
Barro, Robert J., 4
Batten, James, 219
Baumal, William J., 4
Behaviorists, 80–83
Behavior, management theories of, 82–83, 185, 190
Benchmarks, 111, 114, 207
Benefit segmentation, 269
Bennis, Warren, 86, 217, 223–225, 229, 231
Bigness, 372, 385–386
  acquisitions, 385
  book publishers, 386
  larger firms, 373
  mergers, 36–37, 385
  multimedia conglomerates, 386
  ownership concentration, 373–376
  record companies, 386
Billboards, 49, 98, 100, 294, 297–298, 302, 311–312
Blacks, 234–235
  KZZZ-FM, 245–248
Biggs, Gloria, 362
Blake, Robert R., 183–185, 222
Blanchard, Kenneth, 197
Blinder, Alan S., 4
Blockbuster(s), 86–87
Book(s)
  as a media product, 14–15, 42, 255–256, 267, 282
  promotion and distribution of, 291–293, 305–307, 320–327
  trends in publishing, 377–379, 386–387
Bookkeeping, 123, 144
Bosses. *See* Leader(s)
Boston Globe, The, 257
Bottom-up budget, 168–169. *See also* Budget
Bradley, Benjamin, 218
Bridges, Janet, 385
Broadcasting, 11–20, 133–137. *See also* Networks
  advertising changes in, 29–32
  audience, characteristics of, 38–42
  credibility of, 43–44
  development of, 22–29, 372–383
  FCC, 36, 358–359, 368–371
  industry, structure of, 32–37
  KZZZ-FM (case study), 48–52, 100–105, 232–248
  legal matters, 352–353, 365–368
  product strategies, 282–287
  promotion and sales of, 291–314
Brumback, Charles, 196
Budgeting, 99, 109, 209. *See also* Financial Management
  bottom-up, 168
  components of, 166
  KZZZ-FM (case study), 166–181, 241–244
  The New Gazette, (case study), 343–348
  process of, 115–116, 144, 170

top-down, 168
zero-based, 171
Bulkeley, Christy, 362
Businessweek, 362
Byer, Carly, 218

CBS, 18, 135, 218, 373
Cable TV, 10–11, 320–322
blurring of media lines, 19–20
industry, 30–31, 38–40
legal issues, 351, 359, 369
marketing, 263–264, 282–283, 293–300
trends, 60, 379, 389
Cable News Network, (CNN), 133, 218, 228
Capital, 35, 60, 330
equipment, 321
investment, 175
working, 173–178
Capitol Cities Communications, 373
Capitol Times, code of ethics of, 18
Case studies
Charles Advertising Agency, 150–158
KZZZ-FM, 232–248
The New Gazette, 334–348
Cash flow, 126. *See also* Finance(s), Financial Management
Castillo, Angel, Jr. *See El Miami Herald*, 384
Carter, Jimmy, 33
Cassettes, video, 31, 266, 282, 322
Catalogues, 10
Chief executive officer (CEO), 96–97, 210
Chain of command, 137
Challenges, 71, 391
of working with creative staff, 212–214
Change(s), 1, 24–25, 60, 135, 140–141, 150–151, 329, 344, 390–391
in behavior, 197–199
in Charles Advertising Agency, 151–158
in KZZZ-FM, 102–112, 164–170, 245–247
in manufacturing/distribution of media messages, 12, 376, 379
of company ownership, 35
Chapman, Alvah, 220
Charles Advertising Agency, 150–158
Chicago Sun Times, 16
Chicago Tribune, 196
Chrysler, Inc., 16, 260
Chusmir, Janet, 384
Cinema, 324
Cinemax, 31, 282, 330
Class, media, 31, 42, 379, 383
Client(s), 36–37, 195, 288–289, 311–312, 355–357
Mischa Advertising, 112–123
Williams Advertising Agency, 45–46, 48, 150–158
Child Neurological Society (CNS), 119
Codes of ethics, 18
Coen, Robert, 25
Columnists, 360, 378
Commercials, 11, 18–19, 280–281, 297–298, 312, 327–328, 388–389
KOSY, 302
Williams Advertising Agency, 45–46
Communication, 293, 296. *See also* Listening
attentive listening, 199–204
coordination, 137
DAGMAR model of, 287–289
Equal Time provision, 366
in organizations, 145–149
lateral, 157
listening, 199
strategies, 197
Winsor Communications, 144
Communication Workers of America, 329
Compact discs, 10
Compaine, Benjamin, 35, 37, 39, 375
Company, family-owned, 35–36, 359, 373
Compensation, 77, 168, 170, 192, 214, 362–363
Competition, 24, 26, 59, 65–66, 93–94, 108, 214, 259. *See also* Antitrust
implications of, 29–30, 42, 60–61
in newspaper industry, 68–70, 303, 341–342, 352
KZZZ-FM, 57, 101, 104–105, 233–236
Pediatric Neurology, 121–124
pricing for, 331–332
product strategies for, 278–279, 282–283, 306
regulation of, 358–361
Competitors, 331–332, 358–360
KZZZ-FM, 100–108, 114
Computers, 12–13, 24, 18–19, 24, 31, 60–61, 68, 76, 118, 124–125, 134, 300, 321–323, 328–329, 368–369, 376–377
graphics, 376
Pediatric Neurology, 118, 124–125
product cycle, 258–259
COMSAT, 369
Concentration, 33–37, 60–61, 135, 338–339, 359, 373
as a targeting strategy, 265
of ownership, 385–387
Conglomerates, 1, 37, 61, 147, 167, 360, 373, 377, 386–387
Congress, 360
Consumers, 14, 30, 44–46, 152–156, 253–254, 307–308, 323
low-income, 30, 268, 379
market analysis, 262–265, 269–275

Consumers (*cont.*)
  models of purchasing, 290–294
  product strategy, 282–289, 294–296, 301
  research, 275, 280–282
Constant Dollar Study, 30
Coordination, as an element of organizing, 136–142
Copyright, 17, 364, 366–369, 386
Copywriters, 11, 16, 46, 152, 155, 188, 191, 206
Corporation for Public Broadcasting (CPB), 369
Cost Of Living Index, 66
Cousins, Norman, 218
CPAs, 179, 312. *See also* Accounting
Creative staff, working with, 212
Creativity, 10–11, 15, 46–47, 112–113, 116, 281. *See also* Innovation
  in Charles Advertising Agency, 150–158
  in employees, 20, 59, 83–84, 134, 199, 210
  methods to enhance, 213–214
Credibility, 367, 371, 381, 385
  in media, 43, 364–365
  in newspapers, 352
  public expectation of media, 18
Current assets, 176
Cycle, 15–16, 223
  people development, 204–215
  planning, 112
  product life, 257–260, 307
  production, 59–61, 148
  profit, 160–162
  supervision, 194–197
  work, 136, 182

DAGMAR, 273, 287
Damages, 198, 366
Databanks, 10
Database(s) 10–11, 30–31, 38, 190, 376. *See also* Dow Jones News Retrevial
  as information sources, 101–103, 149, 156, 273–274, 303
  electronic, 24–25
  regulation of, 368–369
Deadlines, 17, 132, 183, 197, 326
Debt-to-worth ratio, 181
Decision(s), 30–31, 95, 115, 137–138, 159, 221–222, 248, 264, 275, 292, 372, 381–382,
  human factors in, 116
  intuitive, 116–117
  making, 134–135, 90–91
  management, 65–71, 85, 88
  product strategy, 285–286, 292, 384
  rational, 116–117
  translating goals to, 66–68
Decisiveness, 217, 221
Defamation, 17
Delegation, 137–138
Deregulation, 102, 351
Demographics, 235, 268, 272, 339
Departments, separation of, 3
Depreciation, 176
Dialogue, as a media type, 10
Differentiation, as a targeting strategy, 265
Direct Broadcast Satellite (DBS), 324
Direct mail. *See also* Mail
  advertising, 309
  as a media type, 10
Direct selling, 300
Directories, 10
Discounting, 259
Discrimination, 248
Discs, 282, 322, 376
Disk(s), 13, 49, 239, 245, 266, 319, 322, 376–377
Disney, Walt, 31, 134, 330
Distribution of media products, 315, 319–325
Documentaries, 107, 328
Dominick, Joseph R., 39
Donnelly, James H., Jr., 4
Donohue, George A., 383
Dow Jones News Retrieval, 10, 13, 20, 135, 190, 220, 322, 376
Downlinks, 321
Drive-time, 245
Drucker, Peter F., 144, 207, 208

Earnings, 177–178, 191, 374
Economics, 4
Economics, 134
Economics: Principles and Policy: Macroeconomics, 4
Economy, 38, 62, 70, 102, 359
Editor(s), 11–13, 38, 53, 68, 87, 98, 128–129, 184–185, 195–197, 201–203, 210–211, 276, 384–386
  as leaders, 217–221, 228
  legal issues confronting, 251–253, 364–371
  salaries of, 375–376
Editorial(s), 52–53, 98–99, 123–126, 283–284. *See also* News/Editorial
  style, 221
Editorial-to-advertising ratio, 283
Education, 9, 40, 134, 150, 306
  demographic classification, 266–270, 303, 336, 340, 383
Effectiveness, 15, 75, 102, 132–133, 211, 286, 313
  in leadership, 218–219, 226, 228
  in management, 182–184, 211, 289
Efficiency, 60, 75, 77, 122–123, 132–133, 174,

184, 191, 389
Electronic media. *See also* Media
as an industry, 23–25
as message manufacturers, 10–13
audiovisual, 10
blurring of lines between, 19–20
El Miami Herald, 384–385
Employees, 15, 59–60, 133–139, 329–330. *See also* Law
affirmative action laws, 362
as creative people, 212
as professionals, 16, 323–324
at Charles Advertising Agency, 152–157
at *The New Gazette*, 53–56, 339–344
at Williams Advertising Agency, 45–46, 49–50
at KZZZ-FM, 102–103, 168–170, 240–248
equal opportunity laws, 212
evaluation of, 207–210
finding good ones, 205, 285
hiring, 206–207
incentives for and motivation of, 143–144, 190–192, 199
interviewing, 206
law, 354, 361–364
liason, 139
managerial, 75–89
needs of, 191
personnel development cycle, 182–183
readiness, 185
rewards, 192–194, 210
terminating, 211
training, 210–211, 230–231, 329
Employers, 2, 16–17, 142, 210–211, 334
employee/employer communication, 200–204
people development cycle, 205–215
Employment, 189–190, 207, 212, 248, 344, 375
Empowerment, 150, 225
Equal Employment Opportunity Laws, (EEO), 362, 364
Ethics, 18, 63, 117
issues in KZZZ-FM case, 247
Excellence, 218, 326
Executive(s). *See* Managers
Expenses, 66, 125, 174, 176–177. *See also* Budgets
general and administrative, 164–165
KZZZ-FM, 49–52, 162–169, 175–177, 233–242
operating, definition of, 162, 173
Pediatric Neurology, 125
NDC Shopper, 344–347
nonoperating, definition of, 162
The New Gazette, 57–58, 315, 335, 340–341
Williams Advertising, 47–48.
Expertise, 122, 134, 149, 355–356
Experts, 97, 103
management, 80–81, 114
use in legal matters, 354–356, 360–361

Failure, 100, 114, 142, 189, 224, 377
of businesses, 31–32, 377
Fairness Doctrine, 366
Family-owned business, 35–36, 359, 373
Fanning, Kay, 218
Fayol, Henri, 78–79
Principles of Management, 78
Federal Communications Commission (FCC), 18, 33, 36, 176–177, 351, 359, 366, 369
Feedback, 83
and creativity, 214
as a characteristic of media jobs, 136
communication, 200
controlling mechanism, 143
management tool, 196–197, 207–208
motivation control, 189
Fiedler, Fred E., 222
Film, as a medium, 11, 256, 373–375, 377
Flashdance, 304–305
Finances, 60, 86, 138, 329–333, 376, 378, 381, 387–390
accounting, 179
cash flow, 126
concepts, definitions of, 173–181
financial management, 99–101, 103
financial methods, 144
financial rewards, 192–194
income statement, 162
KZZZ-FM, 50–52
Pediatric Neurology, 125–156
terms, 160
The New Gazette, 56–59
Williams Advertising Agency, 47–48
Financial management, 159–181
Firing, 56, 86, 170, 211, 212
First Amendment, 17, 366, 368
Fiscal planning, 166–171
Fixed assets, 176
Follett, Mary Parker, 79, 80
Format, 48, 263, 293–294, 307, 337
KZZZ-FM, 48, 100–105, 111–114, 167, 233–239, 247–248
KOSY, 278–280, 301–303
Fragmentation, 288
audience, 40–42, 60–61
of media, 30–31
Franchise, 17, 44, 59, 384. *See also* Federal Communications Commission
protection of, 64–67, 160, 341, 380, 390
Frankel, Max, 220–222

Franklin, Marc, 358
Freedom, 17, 142–143, 214
of the press, 369
Freeman, Richard F., 215
Frequency, 268, 277, 287, 295–296, 301–303
Fulfillment, 190–191
Functions, 52, 182, 216, 221–222
of leaders, 226–229
of managers, 5, 44–46, 73–89, 94, 225–226, 232, 248
of organizing, 136
Fundamentals of Management, 4
Future, 215, 231, 331, 341
long-term, 380–384, 387–388
planning for the, 75, 92

Galbraith, J.R., 148
Gallup poll, 43
Gannett Company, 34, 106–107, 135, 141, 148, 210, 218–219, 295, 373, 378
employment policies, 362
Gannett Center for Media Studies, 43
Gannett, Frank, 228
Gantt, Henry, 77, 79
Gaziano, Cecilie, 383
General Motors, 62
Genius, 218
Ghiselli, Edwin E., 220
Giago, Tim, 228
Gibson, James L., 4
Gilbreth, Lillian, 77, 79
Gillmor, Donald M., 358
Goal-directed, 190
Goal(s), 38, 66–68, 96–100, 110–112, 136–138, 190, 207–209, 230, 372, 390. *See also* Decisions, Strategies
Charles Advertising, 151–153
DAGMAR, 273
of media companies, 5, 17, 63–67, 71, 86, 91–94, 380–381
of organizing, 132–133
organizational, 188
path/goal leadership, 223–224
profit, 38
setting, 118–119
Zippy Shopper, 341–342
Goldwyn, Samuel, 218
Gollin, Albert E., 41–42
Gottlieb, Robert, 221
Government, 22, 98, 103, 128–129, 163, 264, 273, 278, 353, 358
Graham, Katherine, 218, 228
Griffin, Ricky W., 4
Gross National Product (GNP), 25
Gross Rating Points, 302–303

Hackman, J. Richard, 137, 192
Haight, Timothy R., 32
Harte-Hanks, 363
Harvard University, 258
Harvard Business School, 289
Hawthorne effect, 80–81. *See also* Mayo, Elton
Hearst Corporation, The, 373
Hefner, Christy, 228
Henry, John, newspaper management, 325
Hersey, Paul, 184–185, 23
Herzberg, Frederick, 190–192
Two Factor Theory, 190
Hierarchy
as business structure, 3, 17
Low involvement, 182
Maslow's, of needs, 78, 190–192, 292, 308
of learning, 291–292, 308
Hispanic, 233, 384–385
Hofstede, G.W., on needs of employees, 191
Home Box Office, 31, 282, 300, 330
Home movies (VCR), 10
Hooper, INRA, 274
Horizontal, 145. *See also* Organization
coordination, 138–39
organization structure, 17, 37, 56, 145–147, 212

IBM, 124, 258–259, 296
Iaccoca, Lee, 260
Idealism, 171
Idea(s), 91–92
IDPA, 378
Image(s), 307–308, 325
building, 294–295
Imagination, 214, 296, 301
Incentives, 79, 81, 143–144, 169, 192–194, 214, 247, 344
non-financial, 143
Income statement, 162
Individual Retirement Accounts, (IRAs), 363
Ineffectiveness, 142, 212
Inflation, 66, 69, 70, 282
Information, 3, 5–6, 202–203, 254, 260–261, 380–381. *See also* Database(s), Demographics, Marketing, Media Organizations, Media Products, Financial Information
as a perishable commodity, 14–15, 325–329
background, 111–112, 119–221, 238–239
distribution of, 11–13, 315–325

gathering, 9–11, 49, 52, 59–60, 101–105, 264
regulation of, 368–369
sources, 273–274
Infringement, 360
Ingersoll Publications Co., 34
Inland Daily Press Association (IDPA), 378
Innovation(s), 15, 22, 132, 210, 226, 311, 314, 385
organizing for, 148–150
The Change Masters, 148, 150
INRA, 274
Insert(s). *See* Preprint(s)
Insurance, 47, 363
and the law, 369–371
costs for William Advertising Agency
Integration, 158, 362
Integrity, 16, 254, 336
Intelligence, 217–218, 221
Interdependence, 137, 146, 184
Interest, 44, 78–79, 82, 276–277, 291, 330–331
on borrowings, 47–48, 51–52, 58, 162–167, 173, 178, 236–237, 242, 331
on investments, 175
Internal Revenue Service, (IRS), 357–358, 367, 374
International Typographic Union, 329
Invasion of privacy. *See* Legal Matters
Investing, 164
in new technology, 67–68, 149
Investment(s), 62–64, 68, 105, 126, 166, 328, 379
capital, 330, 374
return on 174–175
Ivancevich, John M., 4

Japanese management, 189
Jeffres, Leo W, 39
Jerdee, Thomas H., 87
Jews, 217
Job(s). *See also* Work
analysis, 136
characteristics in media, 136
definition, 136
depth, 136
enlargement, 137, 192
enrichment, 137, 192
scope, 136
Johnson, Spencer, 197. *See also* Blanchard, Ken
Joint operating agreement, (JOA), 17, 359–360
Jones, Dow News Retrieval, 13, 20, 135, 190, 220, 376
Jones, Dow & Company, 382
Journal(s), 286, 309–310
Pediatric Neurology, 118–126, 254, 256, 262, 296
Journalism, 5, 9, 16, 221, 246, 325, 364
Journalist(s), 18, 19, 76, 353, 364, 366
Judgment(s), 94–96, 103–104, 114, 116, 173–174, 276, 278, 318

KARE, 295
KEOGHS, 363
KOSY, 278–280, 301–303
KQRS, 293
KZZZ-FM, (Case Study), 100–114, 243–248
K-Mart, 324, 338
Kanter, Rosabeth Moss, 148–150, 158, 223–224, 229
Katz, Robert L., 88
Kenichi, Ohmae, 105
King, Larry, 240
Kipnis, David, 197
Knight-Ridder, Inc. 31, 135, 193, 207, 210, 219–220, 276, 320, 324, 373, 384–385
Knopf, Alfred A., Inc., 221
Knowledge gap, 383
Krause Publications, 147
Krugman, Herbert, 292

Labor, division of, 77
Lakota Times, 228
Lasers, 321, 376
Lateral communication, 157
Lavine, John M., 30, 65, 117–126, 159, 334
Law, 351–371
advertising, 366–368
corporate, 358–361
employee, 361–364
equal opportunity laws, 212
Fairness Doctrine, 366
legal issues, KZZZ-FM case, 247
major areas of, 358–371
media, texts on, 358
news/editorial, 364–366
open meetings, 353
Law Institute, The Practicing, 358
Law of Mass Communication, 5th ed., 358
Law of Mass Media, The, 3rd ed., 358
Lawsuits, 355, 360
Lawyers, 6, 103, 312, 356–358, 367–370, 386
Leader(s), 1, 3, 65, 71, 149, 157–158, 205, 223–225, 364, 387. *See also* Media Managers
as individuals, 216–220
development of, 229–231
functions of, 5–6, 43, 65, 86, 96, 226–229, 370–371
Leadership, 182–231. *See also* Management

Leadership (*cont.*)
Bennis' conceptions of, 224
characteristics, 217–219
competencies of, 223–225
contingency approaches, 222
functions of, 226
managerial grid, 183–184
path/goal model, 223
qualities of, 225–226
research about, 219, 221
situational, 184, 227
styles, 220
training, 230
Leading national advertisers, 274
Learning, 197, 223, 232, 258, 290–291, 305, 308
Legal matters, 20, 175, 206, 349
advertising, 366–369
copyright, 364
issues in media, 247–248, 343–344, 351–371
libel, 364
news/editorial, 364–366
plagiarism, 364
principles for managers, 352–353, 371
privacy, 364
problems, 355–358, (IRS case)
prevention of, 354–355
slander, 364
Legislation, 212, 359–360, 368
Legislators, 368
Leisure time, 276
Lenders, 177
Levitt, Theodore, 289
Lexis, 10
Liability, 48, 177–178, 361, 369
Liabilities, as on a balance sheet, 177
Libel, 16–17, 354–356, 364–370. *See also* Legal matters
Licensing, 33–34
Life
family life cycle, 266
of product, 257–260
psychographics, lifestyles, 269–270
Life, 324
Lifestyle, 265, 269
Likert, Rensis, 222
Limits, 221, 314, 328, 370
of behavioral theory, 82
of management science theory, 85
Liquidity, 180–181
Liquid assets, 179
Listener(s). *See* Audience(s)
Listenership, 280, 288, 300, 303
Listening, a key communication skill, 199–204
Literacy, 31
Litigation, 368
Litman, Barry, 385
Lobbying, 368
Louisville Journal-Courier, 34
Low-involvement hierarchy, 292
Low-power television, 13, 19, 30, 255, 264, 379, 389
Lukas film, 134

MTV, 304, 305
MacGregor, Douglas, 187
Machiavelli, 217
Macroeconomics, 4
Madison, WI, 18. *See also Capitol Times*, work rules
Magazine(s), 4, 10–12, 265, 287–288, 360, 366, 374–375
advertising revenues, 27
distribution, 321–324
media industry, 23–29, 32–33
ownership concentration, 33–37
personal computer, 258–259
product features, 283–284, 286
publishers, 147–148, 219, 265
sales and promotion of, 290–291, 295, 297–301
trends, 29–31, 59–60, 378
usage patterns, 39, 41–42, 268–272, 274
Magid, Frank, and Associates, 282
Mahoney, Thomas A., 87
Mail
direct, 10, 25–29, 274, 327
direct, Advo, 324
direct, and advertising, 309, 310
direct, and unions, 213
marriage, 327
private systems, 321
room, automation in, 12–13
second class, 18
Management, 4
Management. *See also* Leadership
activities, 251–252
and creative staff, 212
and outside circumstances, 227
as leaders, 184, 216–231
behavioral theories, 80–83
behaviors as leaders, 185
Bennis' competencies of, 224
brand, 141
classical theory, 78
controls by, 143
coordination, 138
decision making 116
empowerment, 150
functions of, 5

information systems, (MIS), 138
Japanese and American, 189
lessons for, 390
liason, roles of, 139
marketing perspective, 260
motivation, 187
of projects, role of, 140
people development cycle, 204–214
scientific, 77–78, 83, 85
social responsibilities of, 254
subordinate, 144
supervision cycle, 194–204
task forces, 139
Theories X, Y, Z, 187–189
training of, 230
unions and, 213
Management by objectives, (MBO), 97, 208, 143–144, 208–210, 362
Managerial accounting, 178–179
Managerial decisions, 138
Managerial functions, 75–89
Managerial Grid, 183–184
Managerial perspective, long-term, 380–382
Managerial vs. leadership functions, 229
Managerial economics, 4
Managers. *See also* Management
as leaders, 184–185, 216–231
balance between profit and social values, 390
functions of, 5–6
Mansfield Edwin, 4
Manufacturing
media messages, 10–14, 251–252, 325–330
steps in, 252
March, James G., 148
Market(s), 64–66, 360, 369, 374, 380, 390
acceptance, 162
advertiser, 14, 287–289, 308, 312–314
analysis, 5, 262–289
audience, 14
-based, 147
data, 120
Garrison metro, 336–344
Pediatric Neurology, 118–126
penetration, 52, 66, 70, 98–99, 124, 259, 288, 303, 332, 336, 341
perspective, 63–64, 251–261, 316, 325, 333, 372, 382–383
segmentation, 238, 263, 265–271, 382
variable, 267
serving a, 380–381, 389–390
target, 238, 263–275, 290–296, 301–302, 382
targeting strategies, 265
total market coverage, (TMC), 66–68
Marketing, 47, 128, 147, 152. *See also* Promotion
concept, 262
department goal, 99
Four Ps, 255
mix, 255, 263
perspective, 154, 251–261, 333, 377–378
product life cycle, 257
Marketplace, 108, 121, 155, 176, 223, 319
Maslow, Abraham H., 82, 190–192, 212
hierarchy of needs, 190
Mass audiences, 28–29, 255, 307
Mass media, 23, 76, 369
Mass medium, 30–31, 40, 379, 383
Mass Communication Law, 4th ed., 358
Mayo, Elton, 80, 82, 188
MBO. *See* Management by objectives
McCann-Erickson Advertising, Inc., 25
McGregor, Douglas, 82, 188
McPhee, John, 219, 292
Mechanical, 65, 68, 346, 347
NDC Shopper, expenses, 344–347
Media. *See also* Organizations, Media
access. *See* Access to media
alternative, 24
as manufacturers, 9
audiences, 38
blurring of lines between, 19
as a bridge, 254
broadcast, 33
characteristics of, 14–19
concentration of ownership, 33–37
conglomerates, 34
class, 31
credibility of, 43
development patterns, 60
diffusion of, 22–24
functions of managers in, 73–248
limitations of, for advertisers, 288
managers' time, 86
mass-to-class, 379
mission and goals of, 63–71
organization of, 17
products
distribution of, 315, 319–325
pricing of, 315, 326, 330–333
production of, 315, 325–330
professional organizations, 76
revenue, patterns of, 24
trends in, 25
societal role of, 17
statutes covering, 17
strategies, plans, 106
strengths of, for advertisers, 288
structure of, 32
usage patterns, 39

Media Management and Economics Resource Center (MMERC), 213
Media Organization(s)
as distributors, 11–16
as manufacturers, 9–11
assets of, 59
development patterns in, 60–61
external factors influencing, 69–71
financial management of, 159–181
income streams for, 32, 378
leading, 216–231
legal issues confronting, 351–371
management functions in, 22–24
market analysis and product planning for, 262–289
marketing, 251–261
missions and goals of, 63–65
modes of operation, 147
organization of, 127–158
as political systems, 149–150
planning and decision making in, 90–126
promotion of sales and products of, 290–314
responsibilities of, 62–63
social, 372–391
societal role of, 17–19
structural determinants of, 133
unique characteristics of, 14–17, 19–21
Media-specific, 351
Mediamark, 103, 274
Medical journal. *See Pediatric Neurology*
Medoff, James L., 215
Mega-agencies, 36
Megamergers, 36
Merchandising, 305
Merger(s), 36–37, 107, 171, 329, 360, 385
Merit. *See* Pay, Rewards
Message(s), 160–161, 251–252, 254–255, 315, 327
advertising, 297–298, 310–311
content, 2
development, 59–60, 282–286
distribution of, 10, 106–108, 120, 147, 319–325
electronic distribution of, 13
frequency, 287, 296, 302
manufacturing of, 11–13, 75–76
perishability of, 14–16, 204, 326
production, 327–328
reach, 287, 295, 302
Methods, 269
of controlling employees, 143–144
of manufacturing messages, 12–13
of promoting and selling, 13–14, 297
to enhance creativity, 214
Metro markets, 234, 279, 307, 336–337, 385
Meyer, Herbert H., 208–209
Meyer, Phillip, 39, 267, 275–276, 278
Miami Herald, 384–385
Microcomputer(s), 68, 118–119, 123–124, 227–228, 328
Microeconomics: Theory and Application, 4
Microwave transmission, 11, 13, 321
Middle class, the, 364, 379
Miller, Paul, 228
Miller, Sherod, 194, 375
Milwaukee Journal, The, 257
Mini-series, 42
Miniaturization, 388
Minicomputers, 328
Miniseries, 282
Minneapolis, 141, 213, 246, 264
W*USA-TV, 295
Minneapolis Star and Tribune, 264
Minneapolis-St. Paul, 293
Minnesota, 141, 213, 228, 334-335
Minorities, 117, 362, 363, 378, 383
Mirror, Times, 34, 43, 239, 362
Mischa Advertising, 112–113
Mission,
and goal setting, 91–94, 96–100, 380
statement, of a media company, 63–65, 95
Misunderstandings, 204
Mitchell, Arnold, 269
Mix, 331
client, 153
marketing, 255–258, 263, 331
Mockler, Robert J., 142
Model(s),
AIDA, 291
consumer research, 276–278
learning hierarchy, 291–292
low-involvement hierarchy, 292
mathematical, 83–84
of purchase process, 290–291
Modem, 31, 124
Mode(s),
operational, 145, 147–148
structures, 145
Momentum, 305, 333
Money. *See also* Pricing
as a resource, 3, 60, 327–330
as a reward, 188–193
big, 373–374
budgeting of, 168–173
use of, 66–69, 126, 173–181, 247, 300-301
Monopoly. *See* Antitrust
Moore, Henry, 219
Moral issues, 363–364. *See* Social responsibilities
Morale, 102, 147, 151, 170, 184, 221, 323, 330, 356

Mortgages, 177
Motivation(s), 156–157, 275, 290, 294
  as a leadership skill, 225–226
  in contingency approaches to leadership, 222–223
  of employees, 75, 78, 81, 86, 102, 109, 137, 168, 172, 182, 187–215, 329
Mouton, Jane S., 183, 185, 222
Movies, 3, 11, 14, 15, 17, 20, 40, 83, 107–108, 116, 133, 197, 209, 253–256, 259, 272, 282, 291, 299, 300, 304–305, 307, 310, 319, 322, 374, 384
Moviemakers, 266
Market Research Inc., (MRI), 274
Multimedia, 1, 37, 106, 144, 311, 373, 377, 386
Multinational, 36
Multiple-distribution, 283
Multiple-packaging, 283
Munsterberg, Hugo, 80, 82
Murdoch, Rupert, 16, 34, 107, 300
Music, 266, 271, 279, 282, 292, 322, 377
  Flashdance, 304–305
  KZZZ-FM, 233–248
  station, 48, 328
Music-licensing, 218
Musicians, 218

NDC, 66–67, 341–344
Nation(s), 62, 219, 257, 269, 376
National,
  advertisers, 271, 274, 287–288, 325
  advertising revenues, 26–29, 51, 164–167, 344–345
  distribution, 324
  information products, 106–108, 113, 135
National Association of Broadcasters, (NAB), 362
National Broadcasting Corporation, (NBC), 224, 373
National Enquirer, 363
National Geographic, 322
National Labor Relations Board, 363
National Public Radio (NPR), 16, 319
Needs, 269, 316, 343
  clients, 157, 262, 381
  employees, 30, 184, 191–192, 204–205
  for coordination, 138–142
  Maslow's Hierarchy of, 190
Negotiation(s), 46, 87–88, 227, 331, 352, 357
  union, 214, 329
Neill, Rolfe, 363
Nelson, Harold L., 358
Network(s), 149, 205
  regulation of, 359–361
  television, 10–11, 27, 40, 43, 106–107, 113, 133, 138, 218, 228, 255, 266, 274, 285, 304, 308, 374
Neuharth, Allen, 106, 218–219, 228, 378–379
Neurology. *See Pediatric Neurology*
Neurosurgeon(s), 119, 121
Newhouse brothers. *See The New Yorker*, 284
New Haven Register, 34
New(s), 3. *See also* Media
  audience for, 41–42
  consumption by U.S. adults, 41, 268
  distribution, 12–14, 315–325
  gathering, 59
  manufacturing, 11–15
  news/editorial, 53, 98, 361, 345, 364–366
    staff, 66–67, 130–132
    stories, 103, 128–129
    strategies, 275–278
  print, 19
Newscast, 15, 255
Newscaster, 248
Newsletter, 297, 299, 306, 317
Newsmagazine, 133, 228
Newspaper(s), 11–13, 39, 66–67, 81–82, 95, 106–108, 286, 324–325, 376, 378, 382–385. *See also* Media, Distribution, Pricing and production, Legal matters; Media organizations
  and advertising, 28–29, 297–301, 312–314, 366–368
  chain ownership of, 35, 373–374, 385
  Constant Dollar Study of, 30, 65–66
  corporate law, 358–361
  decisions of in 1970s, 68–71
  goals for a daily, 98–100
  Joint Operating Agreement, 359–360
  leaders, 218–222
  news department, 128–132
  numbers of, 32
  ownership of, 33–37
  Philadelphia Inquirer, 303–307
  print, 19
  product life cycle of, 257–261
  revenues, 30
  target markets, 264, 266–269, 273–278
  The New Gazette, 52–59, 87, 334–348
  trade unions in, 76
  USA Today, 106–107, 141
Newspaper Preservation Act, 359
Newsroom, 87, 130, 193, 221, 363, 375
Newsstand, 11, 30, 53, 107, 256, 284, 321
Newsweek, 43, 195–196, 228, 265
Nexis, 10
Niche, 108, 119, 121, 126, 319
Nielson, A.C, 103

Nonreaders, 268

O'Keeffe, Georgia, 219
Objective(s). *See* Goal(s)
Observations, 189, 196
Observers, 217
Occupation, 5, 266–270
Offensive, 341
Offers. *See* Premiums
Ogilvy, David, 218
Ohmae, Kenichi, 105
Olien, Clarice N., 383
Oligopoly, 373
Open-ended, 112, 202, 279
Open meeting law, 353. *See also* Law, Statutes
Openness, 171
Operating expenses,
KZZZ-FM, 51, 162–167, 173–176, 237
The New Gazette, 57–58, 330, 335, 348
Joint Operating Agreement, 17, 359–360
revenue or income, 173
units, 37–38, 60, 135, 141
Operation(s), 156, 136, 139, 157
manager, 50
research, 83–84
Operational mode, 279
product-based, 147
Operators, 179, 300
Opinion(s), 53, 62, 195, 199
Opponent(s), 104–105, 224, 359
Opportunities, 4, 61, 108, 264, 366–367, 381, 372, 381–382, 388
for advancement, 37, 60, 328–330
for training, 214
Optics, 321
Options. *See* Decisions
Organization(s), Media. *See* Media Organization(s)
Organizing
functions of, 136
goals of, 132–133
horizontal structure, 145
major elements of, 136–137
sequence of, 127–130
vertical structure, 145
workflow, 127–130
Ottoway, James H., 382
Ottoway Newspapers, Inc., 382
Ouchi, William G., 189
Outdoor advertising, 9–10, 25–26, 28, 106, 298
Outlets, media, 32, 293
Outline, 5, 90, 92, 110–111, 246, 342. *See* Planning
Outsider(s), 91, 147, 206, 211
Ownership. *See* Media, Media Organizations

Ps, Four, 255
Pace, 24–25, 60, 101, 138, 190, 200, 275, 324
Packaging, 15, 20, 59, 281, 301, 315
Paging Service, 166, 173, 174
Paley, William, 218
Paper(s). *See* Newspaper(s)
Paperbacks, 320
Parents, 365
Participant(s), 155, 295, 313
Pattern(s),
demographic, 42, 267, 274
of development, 60–61, 68, 135, 378–379, 390
of media revenue, 24, 26–28, 251
of media spending, 24, 28
of ownership, 34–36
product usage, 268, 272–273, 278–280, 284
staffing, 239–240
Pay. *See also* Salaries, 147, 191–192, 208
differential scale, 77
incentive, 77–79
Payback, 166, 175
Payroll, 56, 58, 65, 68, 329, 345–348
Peer(s), 115, 123, 191, 197
Penalties, 356
Penetration. *See* Market(s)
Pension, 362–363
People. *See also* Employees, Leaders, Managers
and automation, 13
and growth of media industries, 22–24
empowerment, 150
working with, 109, 182–215
People-intensive, 60
People-management, 81, 88, 329
in distribution of media products, 323
people development cycle, 204–215
supervision cycle, 194–204
Perceptions of media by the public, 43
Performance quotas, 77
Perishability of media messages, 14, 15, 323
Personalities, 105, 224–225, 240, 269, 310, 328
Personnel. *See* Employees
Perspective. *See* Market(s), Behaviorists, Goal(s)
Peterson, Richard A., 386
Philadelphia Inquirer, The, 219, 303
Picasso, 219
Picture Week, 113
Pierce, Katie, (KZZZ-FM case), 239–248
Pillsbury, 141
Place, (Four Ps), 256
Plagiarism, 364, 369
Planning. *See* Goal(s) and Organizing
and decision making 90–126
as a media leader function, 226–227
backgrounding, 92–93, 100–105

benchmarks, 114
budgets, 170–173
creating strategies, 93
cycle, 112
employee involvement, 114
in action, 93, 100–105, 117–126, 150, 155–158
long-range, 80, 158, 390
mission plans, statements, 91–93, 95
principles and tips for, 110–117
product, 262–228
strategic, 93, 105–108, 296
the process of, 91–92, 155, 170–171
Platemaking, 11, 55
Politics, 53, 269, 277–278
Position, 280–281. *See also* Market(s)
Positioning, 292–295. *See also* Market(s)
Poverty, 269, 364
Powell, Walter W., 386
Power, 80, 110, 135, 157–158, 228, 364
balance of, 197–199, 223,
tools, 149–150,
Poynter Institute, The, 210. *See also* Training
Practising Law Institute, The, 358
Praise, 159, 197, 220, 362
Predictability, 132–133. *See also* Goal(s)
Premiums, 297–299, 300
Preprint, 52, 56–57, 317, 324, 335–339, 343–334, 346, 378
Prescreening, 307–308
Presentation(s), 49, 310–312, 376
Presley, Elvis, 257
Press. *See* Freedom of the Press, Magazine(s), Newspaper(s)
Pressmen, 56, 76
Pressroom, 327
Pressure. *See* Competition
Preston, Frances, 218
Prevention of legal problems, 352–355. *See also* Legal matters
Price(s), 285–289, 320–321, 326–327
competition, 259
increases, 69–70
product, promotion, place, price, (Four Ps), 255–257, 261
purchase, 35, 66
subscription, 30–31, 66, 107
churning, 284
Pricing
media products, 315, 330–333
perspectives, 316–318
strategy, 107, 117, 119, 123–125
Prime-time, 40, 263, 268, 282, 308, 365
Principles. *See* Management, Planning
Print, 19. *See also* Magazine(s), Media, Newspaper(s), Organization(s)
Printers, 12, 46, 60, 68, 76, 119, 122, 315, 328–329, 344
Printing, 117–118, 122–125
technology, 24, 82, 322, 324, 328–329, 374
unions, 76, 329
Priorities, 65, 76, 100, 105, 172
establishing, 195
setting of, 195
Prioritization
model in consumer research, 277–278
of goals, 67
Privacy, 17, 43–44, 354, 364–366, 368–369
Problem(s), 83–85, 139, 208–209, 368
economic, 38
legal, 354–358
solving, 150–156, 236–239
Procedures
operation research, 83–84
rules and, 137–138, 156
Processes. *See* Budgeting, Communication, Management, Decision(s), Manufacturing, Personnel, Planning, Pricing, and Production
Product(s), Media, 66–67, 98–99, 160, 209–210, 291–333, 374, 379. *See also* Distribution, Manufacturing, Marketing, Planning, Pricing, Production, Promotion, and Sales
-based organizations, 147
features, 283–285
and consumer research, 276–278
(Four Ps), 255–260
life cycle, 257–260
nature of the, 14–15, 57-60, 119
percentage of GNP, 25
quality of, 325, 383–388
-specific, 279
strategies, 121–124, 155, 275–278, 282–283, 285–286
usage patterns, 268–269
Production, 5, 17–19, 59, 99, 325–333, 388–389
balance of standards for, 325
cost of, 282, 326, 330
department, 46, 55–56, 346–347
employees, 329
impact on resources, 329
managing of, 327–330
of finished copies of messages, 11–13
of *Pediatric Neurology*
of *The New Gazette*, 52–57
quality of, 325
technology, 327
unions and, 329
Productivity, 77–83, 136–137,

Profit(s), 47, 161–170, 378–380. *See also* Finances
and loss, 174
and money, 161
net, 162–163
pretax, 34, 165, 242, 336
Profitability
and KZZZ-FM, 233
and *The New Gazette*, 56–59
and Williams Advertising, 47–48
Profit-sharing, 192
Programming, 263
and technology, 376
computer, 134
KZZZ, case study of, 49, 238–247
organizing, 240
strategy for, 240
Projections, 125, 178, 233, 235, 242, 303, 312, 332, 339. *See also* Budgeting, Planning
demographic, 303
pricing, 330–333
Promotion
(Four Ps), 255–257
image building, 294–295
objectives, 294
of media products, 9, 13–14, 290–314
of *The New Gazette*, 342–343
strategies, 293–295
Protection, 1, 44, 160, 351, 369–370
Psychographics, 269–270
Publicity, 3, 159, 297–299, 309–310, 342
Public relations firms, 10
Publishers. *See* Managers, Organizations
Pulitzer Prizes, 219, 221, 385

Qualities, of leaders, 183–187, 217–229
Quality
of distribution, 319
of legal advisors, 355–358
of media products, 15, 283, 285, 317–318
of production, 325
Quantity, 76, 106, 274
Quick ratio, 179
Quotas, 77, 143

Radio. *See also* Media
advertising revenues, 26–28
as a media type, 10
audience characteristics, 40–42
blurring of lines, 19–20
concentration of ownership, 36–37
KOSY, 278–280, 301–303
KZZZ-FM, 48–59, 232–248
major developments in, 60
usage patterns, 39–40
Ratebook, 278
Ratings, Arbitron, 103, 274
Ratio analysis, 179–181
RCA, 373
Readership. *See* Audience, Media
and consumer research models, 276–278
demographic segmentation of, 266–268
Reagan, Ronald, 16, 33
Receivables, 179
Record laws, 353
Records, 304, 386–387
as a media type, 10, 255
multiple income streams, 282
Recruiting, 385
employees, *See* Equal Employment Opportunity Laws
Referendum, model in product strategies, 276
Regression analysis, 179
Regulation, 98, 368, 369
of new media, 369
technology, media, 369
Regulation(s), 351–371
Regulators, 368. *See also* Federal Communications Commission
Relationships, 189–191, 204, 289
client, 154
human relations approach, 188
Theory Z, 189–190
Religion, 263, 266, 270
Remy, Linda, 100–104, 109, 111, 114, 168–169, 170, 172, 174, 236–148. *See also* Case study, KZZZ-FM, 232–246
Reporters. *See* Employees
Reporting, 43–44
Reprint sales, 121, 125
Reproduction
color, 99, 106, 322
quality, 288, 325
Research. *See also* Backgrounding
advertising, 280–282
audience, 42, 46, 60, 238, 303
for Charles Advertising, 150–153
leadership, 221–224
management, 76, 80, 82–83, 184, 191
market, 14, 38
Reservations American Indian, newspaper, 228
Resistance, 198. *See also* Motivation(s), of employees
Resources. *See also* Finances, Employees, Money
definition of, 3
scarcity of, 34
Responsibility
as a motivational factor, 191

of media companies, 62–71
to society, 253–254, 372–391
Restaurants, as accounts, 44, 337
Restraint, 171, 247, 361
Restructuring
at Charles Advertising, 153–158
growth, 135
Retirement, 221
Retraining, 247
Return on net worth, 180–181, 203
Revenue. *See also* Income statement
and action plans, 332
financial management, 159–181
KZZZ–FM, 51, 237
local advertising, 28
multiple income streams, 282–283
national advertising, 26
The New Gazette, 57, 335, 338, 344–348
trends in advertising, 25–32
Williams Advertising Agency, 47
Reward(s), 192–194, 197. *See also* Motivation
Classical and Behavior Management Theories, 76–83.
to enhance creativity, 214
to leaders, 230
Ries, Al, 292, 293
Risk(s)
as innovation, 150–158
in training, 211
reduction of, 42, 379
strategies, 105–108
to enhance creativity, 214
Roberts, Eugene, 219
Robinson, John P., 38
Return On Investment(ROI), 62, 64, 175, 178
Rolls Royce, 283, 319, 325
Roper Organization, 41, 42
Rosenthal, Abe, 218, 220, 221
Rothschild, William E., 105
Royko, Mike, 16
Run-of-paper advertising(ROP), 29, 56, 317, 344–345
Run-of-press, 56, 378
Ruth, Dr. *See* Westheimer, Dr. Ruth
Ryan, John, 386
Rydsack, Carol, 353

S-curve, 22
Saatchi, 218
Safeguards, 363
Safety, 180, 181, 190
Salaries. *See* Pay, Rewards
Sales. *See* Finances, Revenue
Salmon, Caryn C., 289
Salmon, Charles T., 289
Samuelson, Paul A., 4
Satellites. *See* Technology
Schmidt, Stuart, 197
Schon, D.,148
Securities, 175–176
Segmentation. *See also* Advertiser(s), Audience, Market(s)
advertisers, 271
analysis, sources for, 273
audience, 265–270
benefit, 269
market, 263
research companies, 274
Selectivity,
audience, 288
market, 288
Self-actualization, 190–192. *See also* Motivation
Selling. *See also* Marketing
direct, 300–301
media businesses, 34–37
media products, 13, 251–261, 377–378
examples of, 304–308
to advertisers, 308–311
examples of, 311–314, 325, 342–343
promotion, 290–291, 295, 297, 299
Seminars, 83, 210–211, 369
Seniority, 82
Service(s). *See also* Advertising, Market(s)
as a product feature, 284–285
as a product objective, 261
as a resource, 3
balancing with quality and price, 317–321, 324–327
beeper, 165–166
creative, 10
data. *See* Backgrounding
in product planning, 286, 288
mission and goals, 380
of accounts, 45–46, 59, 152
in distribution of media products, 320
Shareholders, 21, 67, 298
Sharpe, Jim, (KZZZ-FM case), 246
Shawano Evening Leader, 353
Shawn, William, 219, 221
Shield laws, 17. *See also* Law
Shopper, Zippy. See Zippy Shopper
Short-term
employment, 189
goals, 96
solutions, 378
supervision cycle, 194
vs. long-term views, 389–390
Simmons Market Research Bureau, 103, 274, 310

Simons, Howard, 218
Simplification, 137, 293
Single-medium, 5
Size. *See also* Bigness
  as a determinant of structure, 133–135
  concentration of ownership, 33–38, 373–374, 385–388
Skill. *See also* Communication, Employees, Leadership
  as a determinant of structure, 133, 148
  training, 210
  people, 217
Sky Channel, 324
Slander, 16–17, 354, 364–369. *See also* Law
Smithsonian, 322
Social responsibilities
  historic patterns in, 22–44
  of media, 253–254, 372–391
Society, and the media, 372–391
Software, 31, 124, 328, 376
Solvency, 179
Sound recording companies, 10
Southwick, Lawrence Jr., 4
Special publications, 10. *See also* Magazine(s)
Specialists, 83, 120, 134, 141, 230, 296, 355
Specialty magazines. *See* Magazine(s)
Spectrum management, 88, 369
Spin-offs, 377
Sponsors, 49
Sponsorship, 291
Stability, and media leadership, 216, 225
Staff. *See* Employees
Standards
  as methods to enhance creativity, 214
  balance of, in production, 325–327
Starch Reports, 274
Start-up. *See Pediatric Neurology*, 117–126
Statement, income. *See* Finances
Station. *See* Radio, Television
Statistics. *See also* Constant Dollar Study, 65–66, KZZZ-FM, 233–236
  on managers, 87–88
  on media industries and firms, 22–42
  on newspapers, 65–71
  on segmenting advertisers, 271–275
  on segmenting audiences, 265–271
Statutes. *See also* Laws, EEO, FCC, FTC
  covering the media, 17–18
  of records, 353
  open meeting, 353
St. Cloud Daily Times, 141. *See also* Management coordination
Steger, Will, 326
Steil, Lyman K., 204
Stereotypers, 12, 13
Sterling, Christopher, 32
Stogdill, Ralph M., 220, 231
Stokes, Paul M., 144
Stoner, James A. F., 4, 105
Storyboards, 280
Straight-line depreciation, 166
Strategies
  action plans, 108–117
  advertising, 13–14
  creating, 93–95, 105
  evaluating, 107–108
  in communication, 197–204
  levels of, 106
  of KZZZ-FM, 236–247
  of KOSY, 301–303
  of *The New Gazette*, 341–344
  product, 275, 282–283, 285–286
  promotion, 293–296
  targeting, 265
Structure
  horizontal and vertical, 145–147
  matrix, 148
Sub-editors, 53
Subordinates, 80, 145, 148, 184, 191, 222–223
Substrategies, 106
Sulzberger, Punch, 221, 228
Supermarkets, 301, 322, 337
Supervision cycle, 194–204
Supervisor, 80, 87, 203
Swaiman, Dr. Kenneth, 118–126
Syndication, 32, 242, 243
Synergism, 41, 42, 377

Table-top publishing, 13, 118–119, 122, 124
Tabloid, 336–337
Tactics, 106, 198, 302, 304–305, 308
Take-over, 373
Talent, 136, 152–153, 206, 212, 231, 386, 387
Talk-radio, 245
Talk-show, 238
Target. *See also* Audience, Goals, Markets
  markets, defining, 264
  markets, identifying, 294
  group, model in product strategies, 276
Taxes, 35, 47, 51–52, 57, 162–167, 175, 177, 180–181, 237, 335, 367
Taylor, Fredrick, 77, 79, 188
Team-orientation, 157
Teamsters, 76
Teamwork, 153, 155, 157, 184
Technology
  in distributing media products, 321–322
  in media, regulation of, 369

regulation of, 368
Telecommunications, 134, 376. *See also* Technology
Telemarketing
as a media type, 10
direct selling, 300–301
Television. *See* Technology
Television Bureau of Advertising, (TBA), 274
Terminations, 247
Testing, 279–281, 291
a market. *See* Backgrounding, KOSY
Thompson Newspapers, 190
Tichenor, Phillip J., 383
Time, Incorporated, 113, 135
Times-Mirror, 135, 373
Total Market Coverage (TMC), 66, 67
Top-down budget, 168
Trade-offs, 31, 285, 287, 296
Training, 56, 134, 329, 385
leadership, 230–231
on-the-job, 83, 148, 208, 210–211, 354–355, 371
out-of-house, 214
sales, 109–110, 343
Transportation, 129, 266
Travel, 47, 90, 192, 278
Trends, 372–391
in advertising revenues, 25
influencing the media, 372–380
in marketing, 377–378
readership, 267–268, 273–274
technological advances, 321, 376–377
toward bigness, 373–376
toward concentration, 37–38
Tribune Company, The, 373
Trout, Jack, 292–293
Turnover, of staff, 211
Turner, Ted, 218, 220, 228
Turnover, accounts receivable, 179, 181. *See also* Finances
Types of media, 10
Typesetting, 12
Typesetters, 46, 60, 81
Typographical Union, The International, 76

UHF, 33
Udall, Morris, 359
Underled, 217
Underutilized, 188
Undifferentiation as a targeting strategy, 265
Unions, 76, 213–215, 329, 361
Unique characteristics of media, 14–21, 351, 391
UNISYS, 296
United Press International (UPI),
and technology, 376
Unity of command, 78
University of Minnesota Conference on Productivity, 213
Uplinks, 321. *See also* Satellite
USA Today, 324
User-friendly, 31, 76

VALS, 269–270
Valuation of a private company, 357
Value-based policies and advertisements, 367
Values, 62, 205, 381, 386
and decisions, 116
and legal issues, 371
and psychographics, 269
societal, protection of, 352
use of in strategy evaluation, 107
Van de Ven, Andrew, 148
Video Cassette Recorders (VCR), 40, 60, 263–264, 282, 322, 376, 379
Veronis, Suhler, and Associates, 34
Vertical, 145. *See also* Organizations, media
coordination, 138
organization structure, 17, 145–148
Very High Frequency (VHF), 322
Videos, 3, 377. *See also* Video Cassette Recorder
Videotape, 13, 160, 255, 311, 322
Videotex, 1, 13, 19, 24, 31, 135, 190, 220, 320, 324, 376
as a media type, 10
Viewpoint, 96, 224, 356, 387
Viewtron, 220, 320
failure of, 31
Vroom, Victor, 222

Wackman, Daniel B., 195, 289, 334. *See also* *Alive and Aware*
Wages, 23, 47. *See also* Pay, Income Statement
and incentives, 81
rewards, 192
Waldenbooks, 321
Wall Street Journal, 322
Waste, 115, 143, 196, 200, 346
Watchdog(s),17, 62, 355
Watergate, 43, 218
WCCO-TV, 293
Wealth, 112, 152, 196, 201, 364
Weeklies, 19, 29, 257
Weick, Karl, 148
Westheimer, Dr. Ruth
Whiteside, T., 379
Whitney, D. Charles, 43
Williams Advertising Agency, 44–48, 51, 56, 58, 201–203, 251, 315, 316

Winsor, James Jr., 144, 210
Winsor, James Sr., 144, 210
Wipfli, Ullrich and Co., CPAs, 159
Wire service, 49
Wisconsin, 18, 159, 228, 353, 382
Wisdom, 104, 106, 115, 126, 193
WordStar, 124
Work cycle, supervision of, 182
Workflow,
  control of, 129
  in management theory, 78
  organizing, 127–130
Workgroup, 80
Wright, B.E., 30, 65, 368
WUSA-TV, 295, 307–308

X, Theory, 187–188

Y, Theory, 187, 188, 194, 208
Yellow pages, 25

Z, Theory, 189
Zenger, John H., 224, 226, 229
Zero-based Budgeting, 170, 171
Zippy Shopper, 336
  action plan for, 343
  basic strategy, 341
  financial statements, 344–348
Zuckerman, Morton, 179